United States Past and Future

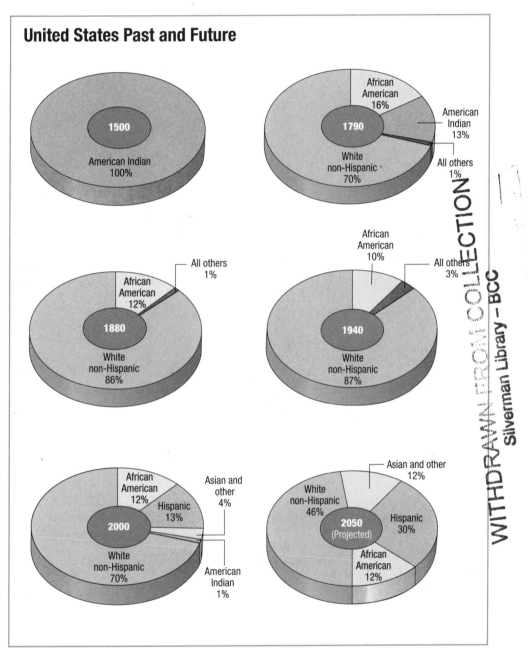

Sources: Author's estimates based Bittingham and de la Cruz (2004), U.S. Bureau of the Census (1975, 2008d), and Thornton (1987).

Racial and Ethnic Groups

Twelfth Edition

Richard T. Schaefer

DePaul University

Prentice Hall
Upper Saddle River London Singapore
Toronto Tokyo Sydney Hong Kong Mexico City

Editorial Director: Leah Jewell
Editor-in-Chief: Dickson Musslewhite
Publisher: Nancy Roberts
Project Manager: Vanessa Gennarelli
Director of Marketing: Brandy Dawson
Marketing Manager: Kelly May
Senior Operations Supervisor: Sherry Lewis
Operations Specialist: Christina Amato
Full-Service Project Management: Laura Lawrie, Macmillan
  Publishing Solutions
Production Liaison: Barbara Reilly
Editorial Assistant: Nart Varoqua
Senior Art Director: Nancy Wells
Media Director: Karen Scott

Media Editor: Melanie McFarlane
Lead Media Project Manager: Diane Lombardo
Supplements Editor: Mayda Bosco
Manager, Rights and Permissions: Zina Arabia
Manager, Visual Research: Beth Brenzel
Manager, Cover Visual Research and Permissions: Karen Sanatar
Photo Researcher: Rachel Lucas
Image Permissions Coordinator: Joanne Dippel
Cover Art: Thinkstock Images / Jupiter Images; Creatas Images /
  Jupiter Images; Goodhoot / Jupiter Images; Radius Images /
  Jupiter Images; Stockbyte / Getty Images, Inc.; UpperCut
  Images / Getty Images, Inc.
Printer/Binder: Webcrafters, Inc.
Cover Printer: Coral Graphics

This book was set in 10/12 New Baskerville.

Credits and acknowledgments borrowed from other sources and reproduced, with permission, in this textbook appear on page 446.

Library of Congress Cataloging-in-Publication Data

Schaefer, Richard T.
  Racial and ethnic groups / Richard T. Schaefer. — 12th ed.
    p. cm.
  Includes bibliographical references and index.
  ISBN-13: 978-0-205-68366-6 (alk. paper)
  ISBN-10: 0-205-68366-5
    1. Minorities—United States. 2. United States—Ethnic relations. 3. United States—Race relations.
  4. Prejudices—United States. I. Title.
  E184.A1.S3 2010
  305.800973—dc22

                                                    2008043264

10 9 8 7 6 5 4 3 2 1

Prentice Hall
is an imprint of

www.pearsonhighered.com

Student Copy ISBN 13: 978-0-205-68366-6
           ISBN 10:   0-205-68366-5

Exam Copy ISBN 13: 978-0-205-68755-8
         ISBN 10:   0-205-68755-5

To the students in my classes who assist me in understanding our multicultural society

Brief Contents

7 The Making of African Americans in a White America   172

8 African Americans Today   196

9 Hispanic Americans   218

10 Mexican Americans and Puerto Ricans   236

11 Muslim and Arab Americans: Diverse Minorities   260

12 Asian Americans: Growth and Diversity   282

13 Chinese Americans and Japanese Americans 306

14 Jewish Americans: Quest to Maintain Identity 328

PART IV
OTHER PATTERNS OF DOMINANCE

15 | Women: The Oppressed Majority 354

16 | Beyond the United States: The Comparative Perspective 376

17 Overcoming Exclusion   400

Features

Research Focus

Listen to Our Voices

A Global View

Preface

"A Generation Away, Minorities May Become the Majority in U.S." read front-page newspaper headlines in 2008 when the U.S. Bureau of the Census released its annual population estimates. By 2042, ethnic and racial minorities will collectively constitute the majority of the population. Already in more than 300 counties, Latinos, African Americans, Asian Americans, Native American tribal members, and others outnumber Whites who are not Hispanic. But do these groups wield the power in all of these counties? In any of these counties? Does the growing diversity of the United States signify a significant advancement in the quality of life of people of color relative to gains made by White Americans?

These are the real questions, and rarely are they asked, and almost never are they answered. Some people who have not followed these trends seemed stunned that back in 2003, Orange County, surf and sun capital of southern California and home of Disneyland, now has a minority majority. Yet we should not have been surprised that in the wake of Hurricane Katrina in 2005, New Orleans's poor were overwhelmingly African American. Although these changes may not signify a major shift in social inequality among groups, they do underscore the importance of being familiar with the nature of race and ethnicity in the United States.

Race and ethnicity are an important part of the national agenda. Thirty years ago, when the first edition of this book was being written, it was noted that race is not a static phenomenon and that, although it is always a part of the social reality, specific aspects change. At that time, the presence of a new immigrant group, the Vietnamese, was duly noted, and the efforts to define affirmative action were described. Today we seek to describe the growing presence of El Salvadorans, Haitians, Tongans, and Arab Americans all overseen by in African American President in the White House.

Specific issues may change over time, but they continue to play out against a backdrop of discrimination that is rooted in the social structure and changing population composition as influenced by immigration patterns and reproduction patterns. One unanticipated change is that the breakup of the Soviet Union and further disinterest of the major industrial powers in the political and social events in Africa, Latin America, and much of Asia have made ethnic, language, and religious divisions even more significant sources of antagonism between and within nations. The old ideological debates about communism and capitalism have been replaced by emotional divisions over religious dogma and cultural traditions.

We continue to be reminded about the importance of the social construction of many aspects of racial and ethnic relations. What constitutes a race in terms of identity? What meaning do race and ethnicity have amid the growing number of interracial marriages and marriages across cultural boundaries? Beyond the spectrum of race and ethnicity, we see the socially constructed meaning attached to all religions as members debate who is the "true" keeper of the faith. As we consider matters of gender, we see again that differences are largely the result of social constructions. And, finally, as we consider all groups that have been subjected to discrimination—such as people with disabilities, the elderly, and gays and lesbians—we see, in a similar manner, the power of labeling. The very issue of national identity is also a part of the agenda. The public and politicians alike ask, "How many immigrants can we accept?" and "How much should be done to make up for past discrimination?" We are also witnessing the emergence of race, ethnicity, and national identity as global issues.

Changes in the Twelfth Edition

As with all previous editions, every line, every source, and every number has been rechecked for its currency. We pride ourselves on providing the most current information possible to document the patterns in intergroup relations both in the United States and abroad.

Relevant scholarly findings in a variety of disciplines, including economics, anthropology, and communication sciences, have been incorporated. The Listen to Our Voices feature appears in every chapter. These selections include excerpts from the writings or speeches of noted members of racial and ethnic groups, such as Martin Luther King, Jr., Elie Wiesel, W. E. B. DuBois, and Nelson Mandela. Their writings will help students appreciate the emotional and the intellectual energies felt by subordinate groups.

The twelfth edition includes entirely new sections on color-blind racism, mixed-status households with respect to immigration, German Americans, African immigrants to the United States, and the presence of a pan-Asian identity.

We also introduce a new feature called A Global View that consists of boxes in seven chapters that profile racial and ethnic issues in other nations. These discussions are intended to create a dialogue between the student reader and the material in this book concerning the similarities in racial and ethnic issues globally.

Another new feature is a Summary located at the end of every chapter to provide the reader a numbered second look at the chapter contents.

Added to the inside cover of this book is a summary table titled "Top Ten" that outlines in what states various groups are most populous as of the latest data from the American Community Survey.

In addition to all these revisions and new material, the twelfth edition includes the following additions and changes (with chapter numbers indicated in parentheses):

- New key terms such as *color-blind racism* (Chapter 2), *cultural capital* (Chapter 13), *mestizo* (Chapter 16), *mixed status* (Chapter 4), *occupational segregation by gender* (Chapter 15), *Québécois* (Chapter 16), and *social capital* (Chapter 13)
- New table and figure "World Colonial Empires" and "Typical Metropolitan Neighborhoods: Continued Segregation from Each Other" (Chapter 1)
- New representation of the Spectrum of Intergroup Relations (Chapters 1, 5, 6, 7, 8, 11, 13, 14, and 16)
- New section titled "Color-Blind Racism" (Chapter 2)
- New Research Focus in Chapter 2 on interracial friendships titled "Few of My Best Friends Are . . ." and a new Listen to Our Voices box titled "National Media Should Stop Using Obscene Words," by Tim Giago, on mascots for sports teams that use American Indian names (Chapter 2)
- New table "Stereotyping in the Twenty-First Century" (Chapter 2)
- New political cartoons (Chapters 2, 3, 4, 5, 7, 11, 12)
- A new A Global View box called "The Roma: A Thousand Years of Discrimination" (Chapter 3)
- A new Listen to Our Voices box titled "The Next Americans" by Tomás Jiménez and a new A Global View box called "Immigration and South Africa" (Chapter 4)
- New figures "Foreign-Born Population for States, 2006" and "Ten Languages Most Frequently Spoken at Home, Other Than English and Spanish" (Chapter 4)
- A new section "The German Americans" (Chapter 5)
- New Research Focus in Chapter 5 titled "Immigrants: Yesterday and Today"
- New figures "Immigration from Germany, Ireland, Italy, and Poland" and "Racial and Ethnic Makeup of Selected Religions in the United States" (Chapter 5)
- A new Listen to Our Voices box titled "Iyeska: Notes from Mixed-Blood Country," by Charles A. Trimble, and a new A Global View box called "Australia's Aboriginal People" (Chapter 6)
- New table "Urban Native Americans, 2006" (Chapter 6)
- Section on "The New Immigration," profiling the growing immigration of Blacks from Africa to the United States (Chapter 7)
- New figures "Slave Concentration 1860" and "Religious Profile of African Americans" (Chapter 7)
- A new Listen to Our Voices box titled "Divided," by Mary Pattillo, and a new Research Focus titled "Medical Apartheid" (Chapter 8)

- New Research Focus in Chapter 9 titled "English-Language Acquisition"
- New figure "Proportion of Immigrant Group Members Speaking Mother Tongue by Generation" (Chapter 9)
- A new A Global View box called "The Salvadoran Connection" (Chapter 9)
- New Research Focus in Chapter 10 titled "The Latino Family Circle: Familism"
- New figure "Religious Profile of Latinos" and table "Metropolitan Areas with the Largest Latino Concentration" (Chapter 10)
- A new Listen to Our Voices box titled "Hate Crime Punished," by James Zogby, on how Arab Americans are viewed and a new A Global View box called "Muslims in France" (Chapter 11)
- A new Listen to Our Voices box titled "Asian America Still Discovering Elusive Identity," by Jean Han (Chapter 12)
- Table "Selected Social and Economic Characteristics of Asian Americans" (Chapter 12)
- A new Research Focus "Social Capital and Chinatowns Today," which introduces the sociological use of cultural and social capital (Chapter 13)
- A new A Global View box called "Argentina's Jewish Community" (Chapter 14)
- New table "Metropolitan Areas with the Largest Asian Pacific Islander Concentrations, 2000" (Chapter 13)
- Added material on pan-Asian identity and expansion of material on Hawaiian sovereignty movement (Chapter 12)
- A new Listen to Our Voices box titled "What Do Women and Men Want?" by Kathleen Gerson, and a new A Global View box titled "Women Elected Officials: Rwanda and Beyond" (Chapter 15)
- New table and figures "Women in National Legislatures (Selected Countries)," "Hours Spent Providing Child Care," and "Matrix of Domination" (Chapter 15)
- New Research Focus in Chapter 15 titled "Child Care and the Gender Divide"
- New table and figures "Can you match the famous person with the disability?" "Actual and Projected Growth of the Elderly Population of the United States, 1980–2050," and "Minority Population Aged 65 and Older Actual and Projected" (Chapter 17)
- Research Focus "Passing on the Old Job Applicant" (Chapter 17)
- Updated tables, figures, maps, political cartoons, and Internet sources in the appendix.

Complete Coverage in Four Parts

Any constructive discussion of racial and ethnic minorities must do more than merely describe events. Part I, "Perspectives on Racial and Ethnic Groups," includes the relevant theories and operational definitions that ground the study of race and ethnic relations in the social sciences. We specifically present the functionalist, conflict, and labeling theories of sociology in relation to the study of race and ethnicity. We show the relationship between subordinate groups and the study of stratification. We also introduce the dual labor market theory and the irregular economy theory from economics and the reference group theory from psychology. The extensive treatment of prejudice and discrimination covers anti-White prejudice as well as the more familiar topic of bigotry aimed at subordinate groups. Discrimination is analyzed from an economic perspective, including the latest efforts to document discrimination in environmental issues such as location of toxic waste facilities and the move to dismantle affirmative action.

In Part II, "Ethnic and Religious Sources of Conflict," we examine some often-ignored sources of intergroup conflict in the United States: White ethnic groups and religious minorities. Diversity in the United States is readily apparent when we look at the ethnic and religious groups that have resulted from waves of immigration. Refugees, now primarily from Haiti and Central America, also continue to raise major issues.

Any student needs to be familiar with the past to understand present forms of discrimination and subordination. Part III, "Major Racial and Ethnic Minority Groups in the United States," brings into sharper focus the history and contemporary status of Native Americans, African Americans, Latinos, Arab and Muslim Americans, Asian Americans, and Jews in the United States. Social institutions such as education, economy, family, housing, the criminal justice system, health care, and politics receive special attention for the subordinate groups. The author contends that institutional discrimination, rather than individual action, is the source of conflict between the subordinate and dominant elements in the United States.

Part IV, "Other Patterns of Dominance," includes topics related to American racial and ethnic relations. The author recognizes, as have Gunnar Myrdal and Helen Mayer Hacker before, that relations between women and men resemble those between Blacks and Whites. Therefore, in this book, we consider the position of women as a subordinate group. Since the first edition of *Racial and Ethnic Groups*, published more than 25 years ago, debates over equal rights and abortion have shown no sign of resolution. For women of color, we document the matrix of domination suffered because of their subordinate status of race and gender.

Perhaps we can best comprehend intergroup conflict in the United States by comparing it with the ethnic hostilities in other nations. The similarities and differences between the United States and other societies treated in this book are striking. We examine the tensions in Canada, Israel, Mexico, Brazil, and South Africa to document further the diversity of intergroup conflict.

The final chapter highlights other groups that have been the subject of exclusion: the aged, people with disabilities, and gay men and lesbians. This chapter also includes a concluding section that ties together thematically the forces of dominance and subordination and the persistence of inequality that have been the subject of this book.

Features to Aid Students

Several features are included in the text to facilitate student learning. A Chapter Outline appears at the beginning of each chapter and a short introductory section alerts students to important issues and topics to be addressed. To help students review, each chapter ends with a Conclusion and the new feature of a numbered Summary list. The Key Terms are highlighted in bold when they are first introduced in the text and are listed with page numbers at the end of each chapter. Periodically throughout the book, the Spectrum of Intergroup Relations first presented in Chapter 1 is repeated to reinforce major concepts while addressing the unique social circumstances of individual racial and ethnic groups.

In addition, there is an end-of-book Glossary with full definitions referenced to page numbers. This edition includes both Review Questions and Critical Thinking Questions. The Review Questions are intended to remind the reader of major points, whereas the Critical Thinking Questions encourage students to think more deeply about some of the major issues raised in the chapter. An Internet Resource Directory has been greatly expanded to allow access to the latest electronic sources. An extensive illustration program, which includes maps and political cartoons, expands the text discussion and provokes thought.

Ancillary Materials

This book is accompanied by an extensive learning package to enhance the experience of both instructors and students.

Print and Media Supplements for Instructors

Instructor's Resource Manual with Tests (0-205-68754-7)   For each chapter in the text, this valuable resource provides a chapter overview, list of objectives, lecture suggestions, discussion questions, student assignments and projects, and multimedia resources. In addition, test questions in multiple-choice, short answer, and essay formats are available for each chapter; the answers to all questions are page-referenced to the text. For easy access, this manual is available within the instructor section of MySocKit for *Racial and Ethnic Groups, Twelfth Edition,* or at www.pearsonhighered.com.

MyTest (0-205-68919-1) This computerized software allows instructors to create their own personalized exams, to edit any or all of the existing test questions and to add new questions. Other special features of this program include random generation of test questions, creation of alternate versions of the same test, scrambling question sequence, and test preview before printing. For easy access, this software is available within the instructor section of MySocKit for *Racial and Ethnic Groups, Twelfth Edition,* or at www.pearsonhighered.com.

ABCNEWS **ABC News/Prentice Hall Video Library for Sociology, Race and Ethnic Relations, Series 1 DVD (0-13-179107-9)** Prentice Hall and *ABC News* are working together to bring to you the best and most comprehensive video material available in the college market. Through its wide variety of award-winning programs—*Nightline, This Week, World News Tonight,* and *20/20*—ABC News offers a resource for feature and documentary-style videos related to the chapters in *Racial and Ethnic Groups, Twelfth Edition.* An excellent instructor's guide carefully and completely integrates the videos into your lecture. The guide has a synopsis of each video showing its relation to the chapter and discussion questions to help students focus on how concepts and theories apply to real-life situations. Please see your local Pearson representative for more information.

PowerPoint Presentation (0-205-68756-3) These PowerPoint slides combine graphics and text for each chapter in a colorful format to help you convey sociological principles in a new and exciting way. For easy access, they are available within the instructor section of MySocKit for *Racial and Ethnic Groups, Twelfth Edition,* or at www.pearsonhighered.com.

Print and Media Supplements for Students

MySocKit (0-205-68927-2) This Web-based application contains book-specific resources to aid student learning and comprehension. MySocKit includes a rich array of interactive tools enhanced with audio and video to engage students in their study of sociology. Features include

- Practice tests to aid in comprehension of key textbook objectives
- A wealth of book-specific activities for students, including flashcards, Web links, maps, images, and additional multimedia resources
- Book-specific learning objectives and chapter summaries to help students focus as they work through the text.

CourseSmart (0-205-68513-7) This Pearson Choice offers students an online subscription to *Racial and Ethnic Groups, Twelfth Edition.* With CourseSmart, students can search the text, make notes online, print out reading assignments, and bookmark important passages. Ask your Pearson representative for details or visit www.coursesmart.com.

10 Ways to Fight Hate Brochure (0-13-028146-8) Produced by the Southern Poverty Law Center, the leading hate-crime and crime-watch organization in the United States, this supplement walks students through 10 steps that they can take on their own campus or in their own neighborhood to fight hate every day. See your local Pearson sales representative for more information.

Acknowledgments

The twelfth edition benefited from the thoughtful reaction of my students in classes. My faculty colleague Kiljoong Kim of DePaul University provided data analysis of the General Social Survey and U.S. Bureau of the Census data sets. Department assistant

Valerie Paulson and Susan Hammond, a student at DePaul, assisted with special tasks related to the preparation of the manuscript.

The twelfth edition was improved by the suggestions of:

Sharon M.Allen	University of South Dakota
Krystal Beamon	University of Oklahoma
Jac Bulk	University of Wisconsin, La Crosse
Kebba Darboe	Minnesota State University
Judith Gomez	Pima Community College
Karen Hardin	Mesa Community College
Sangeeta Jha	St. Cloud State University
Dale Lanigan	Lourdes College
Ryan Jerome LeCount	Purdue University
Jim Taylor	Ohio University

I would also like to thank my editors at Prentice Hall, Nancy Roberts and Vanessa Gennarelli, for developing this twelfth edition. They make a great team in the production of academic books.

The truly exciting challenge of writing and researching has always been for me an enriching experience, mostly because of the supportive home I share with my wife, Sandy. She knows so well my appreciation and gratitude, now as in the past and in the future.

Richard T. Schaefer
schaeferrt@aol.com
www.schaefersociology.net

About the Author

Richard T. Schaefer grew up in Chicago at a time when neighborhoods were going through transitions in ethnic and racial composition. He found himself increasingly intrigued by what was happening, how people were reacting, and how these changes were affecting neighborhoods and people's jobs. In high school, he took a course in sociology. His interest in social issues caused him to gravitate to more sociology courses at Northwestern University, where he eventually received a B.A. in sociology.

"Originally as an undergraduate I thought I would go on to law school and become a lawyer. But after taking a few sociology courses, I found myself wanting to learn more about what sociologists studied and was fascinated by the kinds of questions they raised," Dr. Schaefer says. "Perhaps most fascinating and, to me, relevant to the 1960s was the intersection of race, gender, and social class." This interest led him to obtain his M.A. and Ph.D. in sociology from the University of Chicago. Dr. Schaefer's continuing interest in race relations led him to write his master's thesis on the membership of the Ku Klux Klan and his doctoral thesis on racial prejudice and race relations in Great Britain.

Dr. Schaefer went on to become a professor of sociology. He has taught sociology and courses on multiculturalism for 30 years. He has been invited to give special presentations to students and faculty on racial and ethnic diversity in Illinois, Indiana, Missouri, North Carolina, Ohio, and Texas.

Dr. Schaefer is the author of *Racial and Ethnicity in the United States*, fifth edition (Pearson Prentice Hall, 2009). Dr. Schaefer is the general editor of the three-volume *Encyclopedia of Race, Ethnicity, and Society* (2008). He is also the author of the eleventh edition of *Sociology* (2007), the eighth edition of *Sociology: A Brief Introduction* (2009), and the fourth edition of *Sociology Matters* (2009). Schaefer coauthored with William Zellner the eighth edition of *Extraordinary Groups* (2008). His articles and book reviews have appeared in many journals, including *American Journal of Sociology, Phylon: A Review of Race and Culture, Contemporary Sociology, Sociology and Social Research, Sociological Quarterly,* and *Teaching Sociology*. He served as president of the Midwest Sociological Society from 1994 to 1995. In recognition of his achievements in undergraduate teaching, he was named Vincent de Paul Professor of Sociology in 2004.

Exploring Race and Ethnicity

MINORITY GROUPS ARE SUBORDINATED IN TERMS OF POWER and privilege to the majority, or dominant, group. A minority is defined not by being outnumbered but by five characteristics: unequal treatment, distinguishing physical or cultural traits, involuntary membership, awareness of subordination, and in-group marriage. Subordinate groups are classified in terms of race, ethnicity, religion, and gender. The social importance of race is derived from a process of racial formation; any biological significance is relatively unimportant to society. The theoretical perspectives of functionalism, conflict theory, and labeling offer insights into the sociology of intergroup relations.

Immigration, annexation, and colonialism are processes that may create subordinate groups. Other processes such as extermination and expulsion may remove the presence of a subordinate group. Significant for racial and ethnic oppression in the United States today is the distinction between assimilation and pluralism. Assimilation demands subordinate-group conformity to the dominant group, and pluralism implies mutual respect among diverse groups.

Walking into the room together are the Texas son of a German immigrant, a Mormon, an African American, a Baptist preacher, a White woman, a Latino, a Roman Catholic, and the White son of a North Carolina textile mill worker. Sounds like the beginning of a joke, but actually, it was the gathering, for a televised debate in New Hampshire, of all the contenders for the 2008 Democrat and Republican presidential nominations. Dramatically, it was Barack Obama, the African American, who was elected president with 53 percent of the popular vote, receiving substantial support from all segments of the nation.

Much of the world joined people in the United States in celebrating Obama's victory, hailing it as a transforming moment for the world. Was it also perhaps a well-overdue event for a diverse country? Let's consider that as Obama vacated his seat in the United States Senate, there once again was no African American elected to this assembly. While the issue of race was not explicitly a campaign issue, Senator Obama was the only presidential candidate who felt the public pressure to make a major address outlining his position on race in the United States. And on a much lighter but significant note, the nation had been entertained by political skits on *Saturday Night Live* for months during the campaign. Yet this prestigious venue for comedy relied on a White man to play Barack Obama.

Race and ethnicity is exceedingly complex in the United States. Consider the racial stereotypes that are shamelessly exhibited on Halloween, when many young adults view the festivities as a "safe" way to defy social norms. College students report seeing Whites dressed in baggy jeans wearing gold chains and drinking malt liquor to represent "gangstas." Some add blackface makeup to complete the appearance. Such escapades are not limited to misguided youth. National retailers stock a "Kung Fool" ensemble complete with Japanese kimono and a buck-toothed slant-eyed mask. Also available is "Vato Loco," a stereotyped caricature of a bandana-clad tattooed Latino gang thug (Mueller, Dirks, and Pica 2007; Obama 2008).

Barack Obama's historic campaign and his elevation to becoming the 44th president of the United States in January of 2009 marks a significant moment in U.S. history. The fact that he is the first African American (and also the first person who is not White) to serve as president demonstrates how much progress has been achieved in race relations in this country. It also serves to underscore both how long it has taken and how much more needs to accomplished for the United States to truly be "a more perfect union" as stated in the Constitution.

Who would have expected the hangman's noose, symbolic of at least 4,700 U.S. lynchings from the 1880s through the 1960s, to reemerge in the twenty-first century? In 2006, an uproar began when Black students at a high school in Jena, Louisiana, said they should be allowed to sit under what was traditionally known as the "White tree" in the courtyard. School officials agreed, but three nooses hung from the tree the next day. The White boys responsible for hanging them were suspended, but no hate crime charges were filed. In the stormy aftermath, fights broke out, including one in which Black students beat up a White schoolmate, who was treated at a hospital, released, and attended a school event the same evening. The Black juveniles were charged as adults for attempted murder. Was this justice? In response to massive demonstrations drawing protesters from across the nation, the charges were reduced. But the use of the noose was not limited to youth. The next fall, an African American college professor found a noose on the doorknob of her office door.

In 2008, during a period when Tiger Woods dominated professional golf tournaments, a commentator on the Golf Channel jokingly suggested that young players who were faced with the challenge of playing Woods should "lynch him in a back alley." Woods, who personally knew the commentator, said he took no offense, but many people did when *Golfweek* magazine displayed a noose on its cover to discuss the event. In response, the publisher fired the editor; the Golf Channel had already suspended its commentator. Action was taken in both cases, but how is it that such events still unfold in the first place (Kupper Jr. 2008; Potok et al. 2007)?

What is the welcome mat like for immigrants in the United States? There is no single response to the complexity of immigration in either days past or today.

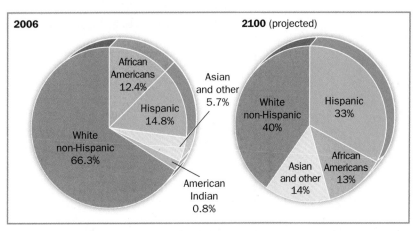

Hazelton, Pennsylvania, for example, impatient over federal inaction in addressing immigration problems, adopted ordinances in 2006 to bar illegal immigrants from working or renting homes. Shortly after, 100 other communities adopted similar measures, but in 2007 a federal judge struck down the actions as interfering with federal jurisdiction in such matters. At the very same time, Fort Wayne, Indiana, was welcoming another 300 people from the Darfur region of Sudan. The first Darfur families arrived in the late 1990s, attracted by jobs, an extensive web of charities, and volunteer church groups. They occasionally encounter stares when the women wear Muslim headdress while at their factory jobs and when they eat using only their hands, as is their tradition, at buffet restaurants, but mostly they have found peace and a welcoming spirit (Saulny 2007; Preston 2007a).

Racial and ethnic tensions are not limited to the real world; they are also alive and well in the virtual world. Hate groups, anti-Jewish organizations, and even the Ku Klux Klan thrive on Web sites. Such fringe groups, enjoying their First Amendment rights in the United States, spread their messages in many languages globally via the Internet, whereas the creation of such hate sites is banned in Canada, Europe, and elsewhere.

Facebook has emerged as a significant way in which people interact, but it also is a means to learn about others by their online profile. By 2007, colleges and universities cited Facebook as the major source of prospective students (or their parents) requesting roommate changes even before arriving on campus, because of the intended roommate's race, religion, or sexual orientation (Collura 2007; Working 2007).

The United States is a very diverse nation and is becoming even more so, as shown in Table 1.1. In 2006, approximately 19 percent of the population were members of racial minorities, and another 15 percent or so were Hispanic. These percentages represent one out of three people in the United States, without counting White ethnic groups. As shown in Figure 1.1, between 2006 and 2100 the Black, Hispanic, Asian, and Native American portion of the population in the United States is expected to increase from 34 percent to 60 percent. Although the composition of the population is changing, problems of prejudice, discrimination, and mistrust remain.

FIGURE 1.1
Population of the United States by Race and Ethnicity, 2006 and 2100 (Projected)

According to projections by the census bureau, the proportion of residents of the United States who are White and non-Hispanic will decrease significantly by the year 2100. By contrast, there will be a striking rise in the proportion of both Hispanic Americans and Asian Americans.

Source: Author's analysis based on American Community Survey 2006 in Bureau of the Census 2007b and data for 2100 from Bureau of the Census 2004.

What Is a Subordinate Group?

Identifying a subordinate group or a minority in a society seems to be a simple task. In the United States, the groups readily identified as minorities—Blacks and Native Americans, for example—are outnumbered by non-Blacks and non–Native Americans. However, minority status is not necessarily the result of being outnumbered. A social minority need not be a mathematical one. A **minority group** is a subordinate group whose members have significantly less control or power over their own lives than do the members of a dominant or

minority group
A subordinate group whose members have significantly less control or power over their own lives than do the members of a dominant or majority group.

TABLE 1.1
Racial and Ethnic Groups in the United States, 2006

Classification	Number in Thousands	Percentage of Total Population
RACIAL GROUPS		
Whites (non-Hispanic)	198,744	66.3
Blacks/African Americans	37,051	12.4
Native Americans, Alaskan Natives	2,369	0.8
Asian Americans	13,100	4.4
Chinese	3,090	1.0
Filipinos	2,328	0.8
Asian Indians	2,482	0.8
Vietnamese	1,476	0.5
Koreans	1,335	0.4
Japanese	830	0.3
Pacific Islanders and other Asian Americans	1,559	0.5
ETHNIC GROUPS		
White ancestry (single or mixed, non-Hispanic)		
Germans	50,764	17.0
Irish	35,976	12.0
English	28,339	9.4
Italians	17,829	6.0
Scottish and Scotch-Irish	11,400	3.8
Poles	10,025	3.3
French	9,651	3.2
Jews	6,452	2.2
Hispanics (or Latinos)	44,252	14.8
Mexican Americans	28,339	9.5
Puerto Ricans	3,988	1.3
Cubans	1,520	0.5
Salvadorans	1,300	0.4
Dominicans	1,100	0.4
Other Hispanics	8,005	2.7
TOTAL (ALL GROUPS)	299,398	

Note: Percentages do not total 100 percent, and subheads do not add up to figures in major heads because of overlap between groups (e.g., Polish American Jews or people of mixed ancestry such as Irish and Italian). White ancestry is for 2000 and percentages based on 2000's total population.

Source: Author estimates based on Bureau of the Census 2006 American Community Survey, Table DP-1, and Sheskin and Dashefsky 2006.

majority group. In sociology, *minority* means the same as *subordinate,* and *dominant* is used interchangeably with *majority*.

Confronted with evidence that a particular minority in the United States is subordinate to the majority, some people respond, "Why not? After all, this is a democracy, so the majority rules." However, the subordination of a minority involves more than its inability to rule over society. A member of a subordinate or minority group experiences a narrowing of life's opportunities—for success, education, wealth, the pursuit of happiness—that goes beyond any personal shortcoming he or she may have. A minority group does not share in proportion to its numbers what a given society, such as the United States, defines as valuable.

Being superior in numbers does not guarantee a group control over its destiny and ensure majority status. In 1920, the majority of people in Mississippi and South Carolina were African Americans. Yet African Americans did not have as much control over their lives as did Whites, let alone control of the states of Mississippi and South Carolina.

Throughout the United States today are counties or neighborhoods in which the majority of people are African American, Native American, or Hispanic, but where White Americans are the dominant force. Nationally, 50.7 percent of the population is female, but males still dominate positions of authority and wealth well beyond their numbers.

A minority or subordinate group has five characteristics: unequal treatment, distinguishing physical or cultural traits, involuntary membership, awareness of subordination, and in-group marriage (Wagley and Harris 1958):

1. Members of a minority experience unequal treatment and have less power over their lives than members of a dominant group have over theirs. Prejudice, discrimination, segregation, and even extermination create this social inequality.

2. Members of a minority group share physical or cultural characteristics such as skin color or language that distinguish them from the dominant group. Each society has its own arbitrary standard for determining which characteristics are most important in defining dominant and minority groups.

3. Membership in a dominant or minority group is not voluntary: people are born into the group. A person does not choose to be African American or White.

4. Minority-group members have a strong sense of group solidarity. William Graham Sumner, writing in 1906, noted that people make distinctions between members of their own group (the in-group) and everyone else (the out-group). When a group is the object of long-term prejudice and discrimination, the feeling of "us versus them" often becomes intense.

5. Members of a minority generally marry others from the same group. A member of a dominant group often is unwilling to join a supposedly inferior minority by marrying one of its members. In addition, the minority group's sense of solidarity encourages marriage within the group and discourages marriage to outsiders.

Although "minority" status is not about numbers, there is no denying that the White American majority is diminishing in size relative to the growing diversity of racial and ethnic groups, as illustrated in Figure 1.2.

Types of Subordinate Groups

There are four types of minority or subordinate groups. All four, except where noted, have the five properties previously outlined. The four criteria for classifying minority groups are race, ethnicity, religion, and gender.

Racial Groups

The term **racial group** is reserved for minorities and the corresponding majorities that are socially set apart because of obvious physical differences. Notice the two crucial words in the definition: *obvious* and *physical*. What is obvious? Hair color? Shape of an earlobe? Presence of body hair? To whom are these differences obvious, and why? Each society defines what it finds obvious.

In the United States, skin color is one obvious difference. On a cold winter day when one has clothing covering all but one's head, however, skin color may be less obvious than hair color. Yet people in the United States have learned informally that skin color is important and hair color is unimportant. We need to say more than that. In the United States, people have traditionally classified and classify themselves as either Black or White. There is no in-between state except for people readily identified as Native Americans or Asian Americans. Later in this chapter, we will explore this issue more deeply and see how such assumptions have very complex implications.

Other societies use skin color as a standard but may have a more elaborate system of classification. In Brazil, where hostility between races is less than in the United States, numerous categories identify people on the basis of skin color. In the United States, a person is Black or White. In Brazil, a variety of terms such as *cafuso, mazombo, preto,* and *escuro* are applied to describe various combinations of skin color, facial features, and hair texture.

racial group
A group that is socially set apart because of obvious physical differences.

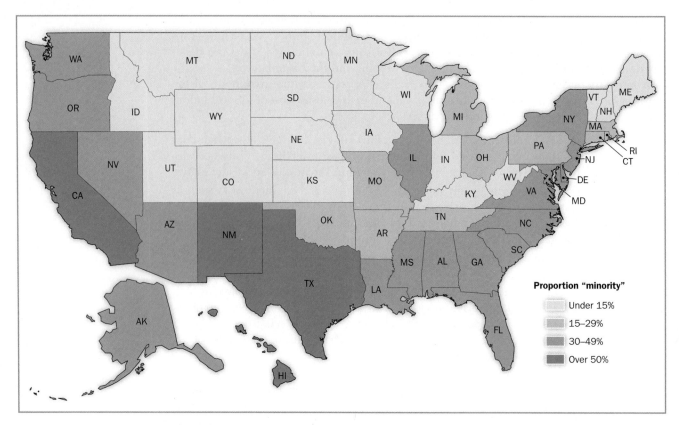

FIGURE 1.2

Minority Population by State

By the year 2004, non-Whites and Latinos represented a majority of 4 states. Several more states are close to reaching a "minority majority."

Source: 2004 data released by the Bureau of the Census 2005b.

The designation of a racial group emphasizes physical differences as opposed to cultural distinctions. In the United States, minority races include Blacks, Native Americans (or American Indians), Japanese Americans, Chinese Americans, Arab Americans, Filipinos, Hawaiians, and other Asian peoples. The issue of race and racial differences has been an important one, not only in the United States but also throughout the entire sphere of European influence. Later in this chapter, we will examine race and its significance more closely. We should not forget that Whites are a race too. As we will consider in Chapter 5, who is White has been subject to change over time as certain European groups historically were felt not to deserve being considered White, but over time, partly to compete against a growing Black population, the "Whiting" of some European Americans has occurred.

Some racial groups may also have unique cultural traditions, as we can readily see in the many Chinatowns throughout the United States. For racial groups, however, the physical distinctiveness and not the cultural differences generally proves to be the barrier to acceptance by the host society. For example, Chinese Americans who are faithful Protestants and know the names of all the members of the Baseball Hall of Fame may be bearers of American culture. Yet these Chinese Americans are still part of a minority because they are seen as physically different.

Ethnic Groups

ethnic group
A group set apart from others because of its national origin or distinctive cultural patterns.

Ethnic minority groups are differentiated from the dominant group on the basis of cultural differences such as language, attitudes toward marriage and parenting, and food habits. **Ethnic groups** are groups set apart from others because of their national origin or distinctive cultural patterns.

Ethnic groups in the United States include a grouping that we call *Hispanics* or *Latinos* and includes Mexican Americans, Puerto Ricans, Cubans, and other Latin Americans in the United States. Hispanics can be either Black or White, as in the case of a dark-skinned Puerto Rican who may be taken as Black in central Texas but be viewed as a Puerto Rican in New York City. The ethnic group category also includes White ethnics such as Irish Americans, Polish Americans, and Norwegian Americans.

The cultural traits that make groups distinctive usually originate from their homelands or, for Jews, from a long history of being segregated and prohibited from becoming a part of the host society. Once in the United States, an immigrant group may maintain distinctive cultural practices through associations, clubs, and worship. Ethnic enclaves such as a Little Haiti or a Greektown in urban areas also perpetuate cultural distinctiveness.

Ethnicity continues to be important, as recent events in Bosnia and other parts of Eastern Europe have demonstrated. More than a century ago, African American sociologist W. E. B. Du Bois, addressing in 1900 an audience at a world antislavery convention in London, called attention to the overwhelming importance of the color line throughout the world. In "Listen to Our Voices," we read the remarks of Du Bois, the first Black person to receive a doctorate from Harvard, who later helped to organize the National Association for the Advancement of Colored People (NAACP). Du Bois's observations give us a historic perspective on the struggle for equality. We can look ahead, knowing how far we have come and speculating on how much further we have to go.

Religious Groups

Association with a religion other than the dominant faith is the third basis for minority-group status. In the United States, Protestants, as a group, outnumber members of all other religions. Roman Catholics form the largest minority religion. Chapter 5 focuses on the increasing Judeo-Christian-Islamic diversity of the United States. For people who are not a part of the Christian tradition, such as followers of Islam, allegiance to the faith often is misunderstood and stigmatizes people. This stigmatization became especially widespread and legitimated by government action in the aftermath of the attacks of September 11, 2001.

Religious minorities include groups such as the Church of Jesus Christ of Latter-day Saints (the Mormons), Jehovah's Witnesses, Amish, Muslims, and Buddhists. Cults or sects associated with practices such as animal sacrifice, doomsday prophecy, demon worship, or the use of snakes in a ritualistic fashion would also constitute minorities. Jews are excluded from this category and placed among ethnic groups. Culture is a more important defining trait for Jewish people worldwide than is religious dogma. Jewish Americans share a cultural tradition that goes beyond theology. In this sense, it is appropriate to view them as an ethnic group rather than as members of a religious faith.

Gender Groups

Gender is another attribute that creates dominant and subordinate groups. Males are the social majority; females, although numerous, are relegated to the position of the social minority, a subordinate status that is explored in detail in Chapter 15. Women are considered a minority even though they do not exhibit all the characteristics outlined earlier (e.g., there is little in-group marriage). Women encounter prejudice and discrimination and are physically distinguishable. Group membership is involuntary, and many women have developed a sense of sisterhood. Women who are members of racial and ethnic minorities face a special challenge to achieving equality. They suffer from greater inequality because they belong to two separate minority groups: a racial or ethnic group plus a subordinate gender group.

Other Subordinate Groups

This book focuses on groups that meet a set of criteria for subordinate status. People encounter prejudice or are excluded from full participation in society for many reasons.

Listen to Our Voices

PROBLEM OF THE COLOR LINE

In the metropolis of the modern world, in this the closing year of the nineteenth century, there has been assembled a congress of men and women of African blood, to deliberate solemnly upon the present situation and outlook of the darker races of mankind. The problem of the twentieth century is the problem of the color line, the question as to how far differences of race—which show themselves chiefly in the color of the skin and the texture of the hair—will hereafter be made the basis of denying to over half the world the right of sharing to their utmost ability the opportunities and privileges of modern civilization. . . .

W. E. B. Du Bois

To be sure, the darker races are today the least advanced in culture according to European standards. This has not, however, always been the case in the past, and certainly the world's history, both ancient and modern, has given many instances of no despicable ability and capacity among the blackest races of men.

In any case, the modern world must remember that in this age when the ends of the world are being brought so near together, the millions of black men in Africa, America, and Islands of the Sea, not to speak of the brown and yellow myriads elsewhere, are bound to have a great influence upon the world in the future, by reason of sheer numbers and physical contact. If now the world of culture bends itself towards giving Negroes and other dark men the largest and broadest opportunity for education and self-development, then this contact and influence is bound to have a beneficial effect upon the world and hasten human progress. But if, by reason of carelessness, prejudice, greed and injustice, the black world is to be exploited and ravished and degraded, the results must be deplorable, if not fatal—not simply to them, but to the high ideals of justice, freedom and culture which a thousand years of Christian civilization have held before Europe. . . .

Let the world take no backward step in that slow but sure progress which has successively refused to let the spirit of class, of caste, of privilege, or of birth, debar from life, liberty, and the pursuit of happiness a striving human soul.

Let not color or race be a feature of distinction between white and black men, regardless of worth or ability. . . .

Thus we appeal with boldness and confidence to the Great Powers of the civilized world, trusting in the wide spirit of humanity, and the deep sense of justice of our age, for a generous recognition of the righteousness of our cause.

Source: From W. E. B. Du Bois 1900 [1969a], *ABC of Color*, pp. 20–21, 23. Copyright 1969 by International Publishers.

Racial, ethnic, religious, and gender barriers are the main ones, but there are others. Age, disability status, physical appearance, and sexual orientation are among some other factors that are used to subordinate groups of people. Halloween may signal the appearance of ghosts or space creatures, but it also reaffirms existing stereotypes as we noted earlier.

Does Race Matter?

We see people around us—some of whom may look quite different from us. Do these differences matter? The simple answer is no, but because so many people have for so long acted as if difference in physical characteristics as well as geographic origin and shared

SECRET ASIAN MAN by Tak Toyoshima

FREE SCREENING DAY AT THE BUREAU FOR THE ETHNICALLY CONFUSED.

Given the diversity in the nation, it is not always self-evident how people view themselves in terms of ethnic and racial background, as the cartoonist Tak Toyoshima humorously points out.

culture do matter, distinct groups have been created in people's minds. Race has many meanings for many people. Often these meanings are inaccurate and based on theories discarded by scientists generations ago. As we will see, race is a socially constructed concept (Young 2003).

Biological Meaning

The way the term *race* has been used by some people to apply to human beings lacks any scientific meaning. We cannot identify distinctive physical characteristics for groups of human beings the same way that scientists distinguish one animal species from another. The idea of **biological race** is based on the mistaken notion of a genetically isolated human group.

Absence of Pure Races Even among past proponents who believed that sharp, scientific divisions exist among humans, there were endless debates over what the races of the world were. Given people's frequent migration, exploration, and invasions, pure genetic types have not existed for some time, if they ever did. There are no mutually exclusive races. Skin color among African Americans varies tremendously, as it does among White Americans. There is even an overlapping of dark-skinned Whites and light-skinned African Americans. If we grouped people by genetic resistance to malaria and by fingerprint patterns, then Norwegians and many African groups would be of the same race. If we grouped people by some digestive capacities, some Africans, Asians, and southern Europeans would be of one group and West Africans and northern Europeans of another (Leehotz 1995; Shanklin 1994).

Biologically there are no pure, distinct races. For example, blood type cannot distinguish racial groups with any accuracy. Furthermore, applying pure racial types to humans is problematic because of interbreeding. Contemporary studies of DNA on a global basis have determined that 85 percent of human genetic variation is within "local populations," such as within the French or within the Afghan people. Another 5 to 9 percent is between local populations thought to be similar in public opinion, such as the Koreans and Chinese. The remaining 6 to 9 percent of total human variation is what we think of today as constituting races and accounts for skin color, hair form, nose shape, and so forth (Lewontin 2005).

Research as a part of the Human Genome Project mapping human DNA has only served to confirm genetic diversity with differences within traditionally regarded racial groups (e.g., Black Africans) much greater than that between groups (e.g., between Black Africans and Europeans). Research has also been conducted to determine whether personality characteristics such as temperament and nervous habits are inherited among minority groups. It is no surprise that the question of whether races have different innate levels of intelligence has led to the most explosive controversies (Bamshad and Olson 2003).

biological race
The mistaken notion of a genetically isolated human group.

intelligence quotient (IQ)
The ratio of a person's mental age (as computed by an IQ test) to his or her chronological age, multiplied by 100.

Intelligence Tests Typically, intelligence is measured as an **intelligence quotient (IQ)**, which is the ratio of a person's mental age to his or her chronological age, multiplied by 100, with 100 representing average intelligence and higher scores representing greater intelligence. It should be noted that there is little consensus over just what intelligence is, other than as defined by such IQ tests. Intelligence tests are adjusted for a person's age so that 10-year-olds take a very different test from someone 20 years old. Although research shows that certain learning strategies can improve a person's IQ, generally IQ remains stable as one ages.

A great deal of debate continues over the accuracy of these tests. Are they biased toward people who come to the tests with knowledge similar to that of the test writers? Skeptics argue that such test questions do not truly measure intellectual potential. The issue of cultural bias in tests remains an unresolved concern. The most recent research shows that differences in intelligence scores between Blacks and Whites are almost eliminated when adjustments are made for social and economic characteristics (Brooks-Gunn, Klebanov, and Duncan 1996; Herrnstein and Murray 1994, 30; Kagan 1971; Young 2003).

The second issue, trying to associate these results with certain subpopulations such as races, also has a long history. In the past, a few people have contended that Whites have more intelligence on average than Blacks. All researchers agree that within-group differences are greater than any speculated differences between groups. The range of intelligence among, for example, Korean Americans is much greater than any average difference between them as a group and Japanese Americans.

The third issue relates to the subpopulations themselves. If Blacks or Whites are not mutually exclusive biologically, then how can there be measurable differences? Many Whites and most Blacks have mixed ancestry that complicates any supposed inheritance-of-intelligence issue. Both groups reflect a rich heritage of very dissimilar populations, from Swedes to Slovaks and Zulus to Tutus.

In 1994, an 845-page book unleashed a new national debate on the issue of IQ. This research effort of psychologist Richard J. Herrnstein and social scientist Charles Murray (1994), published in *The Bell Curve*, concluded that 60 percent of IQ is inheritable and that racial groups offer a convenient means to generalize about any differences in intelligence. Unlike most other proponents of the race–IQ link, the authors offered policy suggestions that included ending welfare to discourage births among low-IQ poor women and changing immigration laws so that the IQ pool in the United States is not diminished. Herrnstein and Murray even made generalizations about IQ levels among Asians and Hispanics in the United States, groups subject to even more intermarriage. It is not possible to generalize about absolute differences between groups, such as Latinos versus Whites, when almost half of Latinos in the United States marry non-Hispanics.

More than a decade later, the mere mention of "the bell curve" still signals to many people a belief in a racial hierarchy with Whites toward the top and Blacks near the bottom. The research present then and repeated today points to the difficulty in definitions: what is intelligence, and what constitutes a racial group, given generations (if not centuries) of intermarriage? How can we speak of definitive inherited racial differences if there has been intermarriage between people of every color? Furthermore, as people on both sides of the debate have noted, regardless of the findings, we would still want to strive to maximize the talents of each individual. All research shows that the differences within a group are much greater than any alleged differences between group averages.

Why does such IQ research reemerge if the data are subject to different interpretations? The argument that "we" are superior to "them" is very appealing to the dominant group. It justifies receiving opportunities that are denied to others. We can anticipate that the debate over IQ and the allegations of significant group differences will continue. Policy makers need to acknowledge the difficulty in treating race as a biologically significant characteristic.

Who are we in terms of race or ethnicity? Do you ever ask someone "What are you?" or "Where are you from?" because you are uncomfortable not knowing? Concepts of race and ethnicity in the United States are socially constructed and, although most of the time we think we correctly identify people around us, sometimes we cannot.

Social Construction of Race

If race does not distinguish humans from one another biologically, then why does it seem to be so important? It is important because of the social meaning people have attached to it.

The 1950 (UNESCO) Statement on Race maintains that "for all practical social purposes 'race' is not so much a biological phenomenon as a social myth" (Montagu 1972, 118). Adolf Hitler expressed concern over the "Jewish race" and translated this concern into Nazi death camps. Winston Churchill spoke proudly of the "British race" and used that pride to spur a nation to fight. Evidently, race was a useful political tool for two very different leaders in the 1930s and 1940s.

Race is a social construction, and this process benefits the oppressor, who defines who is privileged and who is not. The acceptance of race in a society as a legitimate category allows racial hierarchies to emerge to the benefit of the dominant "races." For example, inner-city drive-by shootings have come to be seen as a race-specific problem worthy of local officials cleaning up troubled neighborhoods. Yet, schoolyard shoot-outs are viewed as a societal concern and placed on the national agenda.

From the conflict perspective, the emphasis should not be primarily on the attributes of the individual (that is, "blaming the victim") but on structural factors such as the labor market, affordable housing, and availability of programs to assist people with addiction or mental health issues.

People could speculate that if human groups have obvious physical differences, then they could have corresponding mental or personality differences. No one disagrees that people differ in temperament, potential to learn, and sense of humor. In its social sense, race implies that groups that differ physically also bear distinctive emotional and mental abilities or disabilities. These beliefs are based on the notion that humankind can be divided into distinct groups. We have already seen the difficulties associated with pigeonholing people into racial categories. Despite these difficulties, belief in the inheritance of behavior patterns and in an association between physical and cultural traits is widespread. It is called **racism** when this belief is coupled with the feeling that certain groups or races are inherently superior to others. Racism is a doctrine of racial supremacy that states one race is superior to another (Bash 2001; Bonilla-Silva 1996).

We questioned the biological significance of race in the previous section. In modern complex industrial societies, we find little adaptive utility in the presence or absence of prominent chins, epicanthic folds of the eyelids, or the comparative amount of melanin in the skin. What is important is not that people are genetically different but that they approach one another with dissimilar perspectives. It is in the social setting that race is decisive. Race is significant because people have given it significance.

Race definitions are crystallized through what Michael Omi and Howard Winant (1994) called **racial formation**, a sociohistorical process by which racial categories are created, inhibited, transformed, and destroyed. Those in power define groups of people in a certain way that depends on a racist social structure. The Native Americans and the creation of the reservation system for Native Americans in the late 1800s is an example of this racial formation. The federal American Indian policy combined previously distinctive tribes into a single group. No one escapes the extent and frequency to which we are subjected to racial formation.

In the southern United States, the social construction of race was known as the "one-drop rule." This tradition stipulated that if a person had even a single drop of "Black blood," that person was defined and viewed as Black. Today children of biracial or multiracial marriages try to build their own identities in a country that seems intent on placing them in some single, traditional category—a topic we will return to later in this chapter.

With rising immigration from Latin America in the latter part of the twentieth century, the fluid nature of racial formation is evident. As if it happened in one day, people in the United States have spoken about the Latin Americanization of the United States or that the

racism
A doctrine that one race is superior.

racial formation
A sociohistorical process by which racial categories are created, inhibited, transformed, and destroyed.

biracial order of Black and White was now replaced with a triracial order. It is this social context of the changing nature of diversity that we examine to understand how scholars have sought to generalize about intergroup relations in the United States and elsewhere.

Sociology and the Study of Race and Ethnicity

Before proceeding further with our study of racial and ethnic groups, let us consider several sociological perspectives that provide insight into dominant–subordinate relationships. **Sociology** is the systematic study of social behavior and human groups, so it is aptly suited to enlarge our understanding of intergroup relations. There is a long, valuable history of the study of race relations in sociology. Admittedly, it has not always been progressive; indeed, at times it has reflected the prejudices of society. In some instances, scholars who are members of racial, ethnic, and religious minorities, as well as women, have not been permitted to make the kind of contributions they are capable of making to the field.

Stratification by Class and Gender

All societies are characterized by members having unequal amounts of wealth, prestige, or power. Sociologists observe that entire groups may be assigned less or more of what a society values. The hierarchy that emerges is called **stratification**. Stratification is the structured ranking of entire groups of people that perpetuates unequal rewards and power in a society.

Much discussion of stratification identifies the **class**, or social ranking, of people who share similar wealth, according to sociologist Max Weber's classic definition. Mobility from one class to another is not easy. Movement into classes of greater wealth may be particularly difficult for subordinate-group members faced with lifelong prejudice and discrimination (Banton 2007; Gerth and Mills 1958).

Recall that the first property of subordinate-group standing is unequal treatment by the dominant group in the form of prejudice, discrimination, and segregation. Stratification is intertwined with the subordination of racial, ethnic, religious, and gender groups. Race has implications for the way people are treated; so does class. One also has to add the effects of race and class together. For example, being poor and Black is not the same as being either one by itself. A wealthy Mexican American is not the same as an affluent Anglo American or as Mexican Americans as a group.

Public discussion of issues such as housing or public assistance often is disguised as discussion of class issues, when in fact the issues are based primarily on race. Similarly, some topics such as the poorest of poor or the working poor are addressed in terms of race when the class component should be explicit. Nonetheless, the link between race and class in society is abundantly clear (Winant 2004).

sociology
The systematic study of social behavior and human groups.

stratification
A structured ranking of entire groups of people that perpetuates unequal rewards and power in a society.

class
As defined by Max Weber, people who share similar levels of wealth.

Another stratification factor that we need to consider is gender. How different is the situation for women as contrasted with men? Returning again to the first property of minority groups—unequal treatment and less control—treatment of women is not equal to that received by men. Whether the issue is jobs or poverty, education or crime, the experience of women typically is more difficult. In addition, the situation faced by women in areas such as health care and welfare raises different concerns than it does for men. Just as we need to consider the role of social class to understand race and ethnicity better, we also need to consider the role of gender. Later in this chapter we will consider how these different social dimensions intersect.

Theoretical Perspectives

Sociologists view society in different ways. Some see the world basically as a stable and ongoing entity. The endurance of a Chinatown, the general sameness of male–female roles over time, and other aspects of intergroup relations impress them. Some sociologists see society as composed of many groups in conflict, competing for scarce resources. Within this conflict, some people or even entire groups may be labeled or stigmatized in a way that blocks their access to what a society values. We will examine three theoretical perspectives that are widely used by sociologists today: the functionalist, conflict, and labeling perspectives.

Functionalist Perspective In the view of a functionalist, a society is like a living organism in which each part contributes to the survival of the whole. The **functionalist perspective** emphasizes how the parts of society are structured to maintain its stability. According to this approach, if an aspect of social life does not contribute to a society's stability or survival, then it will not be passed on from one generation to the next.

It seems reasonable to assume that bigotry between races offers no such positive function, and so we ask, why does it persist? Although agreeing that racial hostility is hardly to be admired, the functionalist would point out that it serves some positive functions from the perspective of the racists. We can identify five functions that racial beliefs have for the dominant group:

1. Racist ideologies provide a moral justification for maintaining a society that routinely deprives a group of its rights and privileges.

2. Racist beliefs discourage subordinate people from attempting to question their lowly status; to do so is to question the very foundation of the society.

3. Racial ideologies not only justify existing practices but also serve as a rallying point for social movements, as seen in the rise of the Nazi party.

4. Racist myths encourage support for the existing order. Some argue that if there were any major societal change, the subordinate group would suffer even greater poverty, and the dominant group would suffer lower living standards (Nash 1962).

5. Racist beliefs relieve the dominant group of the responsibility to address the economic and educational problems faced by subordinate groups.

As a result, racial ideology grows when a value system (e.g., that underlying a colonial empire or slavery) is being threatened.

There are also definite dysfunctions caused by prejudice and discrimination. **Dysfunctions** are elements of society that may disrupt a social system or decrease its stability. There are six ways in which racism is dysfunctional to a society, including to its dominant group:

1. A society that practices discrimination fails to use the resources of all individuals. Discrimination limits the search for talent and leadership to the dominant group.

2. Discrimination aggravates social problems such as poverty, delinquency, and crime and places the financial burden of alleviating these problems on the dominant group.

3. Society must invest a good deal of time and money to defend the barriers that prevent the full participation of all members.

4. Racial prejudice and discrimination undercut goodwill and friendly diplomatic relations between nations. They also negatively affect efforts to increase global trade.

5. Social change is inhibited because change may assist a subordinate group.

6. Discrimination promotes disrespect for law enforcement and for the peaceful settlement of disputes.

That racism has costs for the dominant group as well as for the subordinate group reminds us that intergroup conflict is exceedingly complex (Bowser and Hunt 1996; Feagin, Vera, and Batur 2000; Rose 1951).

functionalist perspective
A sociological approach emphasizing how parts of a society are structured to maintain its stability.

dysfunction
An element of society that may disrupt a social system or decrease its stability.

Faced with new laws restricting rights of noncitizens, 6,000 people representing countries from around the world participate in naturalization ceremonies in Pomona, California, in 2007.

Conflict Perspective In contrast to the functionalists' emphasis on stability, conflict sociologists see the social world as being in continual struggle. The **conflict perspective** assumes that the social structure is best understood in terms of conflict or tension between competing groups. The result of this conflict is significant economic disparity and structural inequality in education, the labor market, housing, and health care delivery. Specifically, society is a struggle between the privileged (the dominant group) and the exploited (the subordinate groups). Such conflicts need not be physically violent and may take the form of immigration restrictions, real estate practices, or disputes over cuts in the federal budget.

The conflict model often is selected today when one is examining race and ethnicity because it readily accounts for the presence of tension between competing groups. According to the conflict perspective, competition takes place between groups with unequal amounts of economic and political power. The minorities are exploited or, at best, ignored by the dominant group. The conflict perspective is viewed as more radical and activist than functionalism because conflict theorists emphasize social change and the redistribution of resources. Functionalists are not necessarily in favor of inequality; rather, their approach helps us understand why such systems persist.

Those who follow the conflict approach to race and ethnicity have remarked repeatedly that the subordinate group is criticized for its low status. That the dominant group is responsible for subordination is often ignored. William Ryan (1976) calls this an instance of **blaming the victim**: portraying the problems of racial and ethnic minorities as their fault rather than recognizing society's responsibility.

Conflict theorists consider the costs that come with residential segregation. Besides the more obvious cost of reducing housing options, racial and social class isolation reduces for people (including Whites) all available options in schools, retail shopping, and medical care. People can travel to access services and businesses, and it is more likely that racial and ethnic minorities will have to make that sometimes costly and time-consuming trip (Carr and Kutty 2008).

Labeling Approach Related to the conflict perspective and its concern over blaming the victim is **labeling theory**, a concept introduced by sociologist Howard Becker to explain why certain people are viewed as deviant and others engaging in the same behavior are not. Students of crime and deviance have relied heavily on labeling theory.

conflict perspective
A sociological approach that assumes that the social structure is best understood in terms of conflict or tension between competing groups.

blaming the victim
Portraying the problems of racial and ethnic minorities as their fault rather than recognizing society's responsibilities.

labeling theory
A sociological approach introduced by Howard Becker that attempts to explain why certain people are viewed as deviants and others engaging in the same behavior are not.

According to labeling theory, a youth who misbehaves may be considered and treated as a delinquent if she or he comes from the "wrong kind of family." Another youth from a middle-class family who commits the same sort of misbehavior might be given another chance before being punished.

The labeling perspective directs our attention to the role that negative stereotypes play in race and ethnicity. The image that prejudiced people maintain of a group toward which they hold ill feelings is called a **stereotype**. Stereotypes are unreliable generalizations about all members of a group that do not take individual differences into account. The warrior image of Native American (American Indian) people is perpetuated by the frequent use of tribal names or even names such as "Indians" and "Redskins" for sports teams. In Chapter 2, we will review some of the research on the stereotyping of minorities. This labeling is not limited to racial and ethnic groups, however. For instance, age can be used to exclude a person from an activity in which he or she is qualified to engage. Groups are subjected to stereotypes and discrimination in such a way that their treatment resembles that of social minorities. Social prejudice exists toward ex-convicts, gamblers, alcoholics, lesbians, gays, prostitutes, people with AIDS, and people with disabilities, to name a few.

The labeling approach points out that stereotypes, when applied by people in power, can have very negative consequences for people or groups identified falsely. A crucial aspect of the relationship between dominant and subordinate groups is the prerogative of the dominant group to define society's values. U.S. sociologist William I. Thomas (1923), an early critic of racial and gender discrimination, saw that the "definition of the situation" could mold the personality of the individual. In other words, Thomas observed that people respond not only to the objective features of a situation (or person) but also to the meaning these features have for them. So, for example, a lone walker seeing a young Black man walking toward him may perceive the situation differently than if the oncoming person is an older woman. In this manner, we can create false images or stereotypes that become real in their social consequences.

In certain situations, we may respond to negative stereotypes and act on them, with the result that false definitions become accurate. This is known as a **self-fulfilling prophecy**. A person or group described as having particular characteristics begins to display the very traits attributed to him or her. Thus, a child who is praised for being a natural comic may focus on learning to become funny to gain approval and attention.

Self-fulfilling prophecies can be devastating for minority groups (Figure 1.3). Such groups often find that they are allowed to hold only low-paying jobs with little prestige

stereotypes
Unreliable, exaggerated generalizations about all members of a group that do not take individual differences into account.

self-fulfilling prophecy
The tendency to respond to and act on the basis of stereotypes, a predisposition that can lead one to validate false definitions.

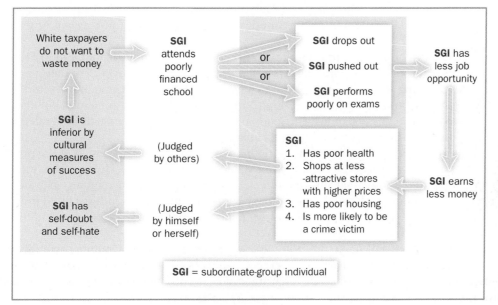

FIGURE 1.3
Self-Fulfilling Prophecy

The self-validating effects of dominant-group definitions are shown in this figure. The SGI attends a poorly financed school and is left unequipped to perform jobs that offer high status and pay. He or she then gets a low-paying job and must settle for a standard of living far short of society's standards. Because the person shares these societal standards, he or she may begin to feel self-doubt and self-hatred.

or opportunity for advancement. The rationale of the dominant society is that these minority people lack the ability to perform in more important and lucrative positions. Training to become scientists, executives, or physicians is denied to many subordinate-group individuals (SGIs), who are then locked into society's inferior jobs. As a result, the false definition becomes real. The subordinate group has become inferior because it was defined at the start as inferior and was, therefore, prevented from achieving the levels attained by the majority.

Because of this vicious circle, a talented subordinate-group person may come to see the worlds of entertainment and professional sports as his or her only hope for achieving wealth and fame. Thus, it is no accident that successive waves of Irish, Jewish, Italian, African American, and Hispanic performers and athletes have made their mark on culture in the United States. Unfortunately, these very successes may convince the dominant group that its original stereotypes were valid—that these are the only areas of society in which subordinate-group members can excel. Furthermore, athletics and the arts are highly competitive areas. For every LeBron James and Jennifer Lopez who makes it, many, many more SGIs will end up disappointed.

The Creation of Subordinate-Group Status

Three situations are likely to lead to the formation of a relationship between a subordinate group and the dominant group. A subordinate group emerges through migration, annexation, and colonialism.

Migration

People who emigrate to a new country often find themselves a minority in that new country. Cultural or physical traits or religious affiliation may set the immigrant apart from the dominant group. Immigration from Europe, Asia, and Latin America has been a powerful force in shaping the fabric of life in the United States. **Migration** is the general term used to describe any transfer of population. **Emigration** (by emigrants) describes leaving a country to settle in another; **immigration** (by immigrants) denotes coming into the new country. From Vietnam's perspective, the "boat people" were emigrants from Vietnam to the United States, but in the United States they were counted among this nation's immigrants.

Although people may migrate because they want to, leaving the home country is not always voluntary. Conflict or war has displaced people throughout human history. In the twentieth century, we saw huge population movements caused by two world wars; revolutions in Spain, Hungary, and Cuba; the partition of British India; conflicts in Southeast Asia, Korea, and Central America; and the confrontation between Arabs and Israelis.

In all types of movement, even the movement of a U.S. family from Ohio to Florida, two sets of forces operate: push factors and pull factors. Push factors discourage a person from remaining where he or she lives. Religious persecution and economic factors such as dissatisfaction with employment opportunities are possible push factors. Pull factors, such as a better standard of living, friends and relatives who have already emigrated, and a promised job, attract an immigrant to a particular country.

Although generally we think of migration as a voluntary process, much of the population transfer that has occurred in the world has been involuntary. The forced movement of people into another society guarantees a subordinate role. Involuntary migration is no longer common; although enslavement has a long history, all industrialized societies today prohibit such practices. Of course, many contemporary societies, including the United States, bear the legacy of slavery.

Migration has taken on new significance in the twenty-first century partly because of **globalization**, or the worldwide integration of government policies, cultures, social movements, and financial markets through trade and the exchange of ideas. The increased

migration
A general term that describes any transfer of population.

emigration
Leaving a country to settle in another.

immigration
Coming into a new country as a permanent resident.

globalization
Worldwide integration of government policies, cultures, social movements, and financial markets through trade, movements of people, and the exchange of ideas.

movement of people and money across borders has made the distinction between temporary and permanent migration less meaningful. Although migration has always been fluid, people in today's global economy are connected across societies culturally and economically as never before. Even after they have relocated, people maintain global linkages to their former country and with a global economy (Richmond 2002).

Annexation

Nations, particularly during wars or as a result of war, incorporate or attach land. This new land is contiguous to the nation, as in the German annexation of Austria and Czechoslovakia in 1938 and 1939 and in the U.S. Louisiana Purchase of 1803. The Treaty of Guadalupe Hidalgo that ended the Mexican–American War in 1848 gave the United States California, Utah, Nevada, most of New Mexico, and parts of Arizona, Wyoming, and Colorado. The indigenous peoples in some of this huge territory were dominant in their society one day, only to become minority-group members the next.

When annexation occurs, the dominant power generally suppresses the language and culture of the minority. Such was the practice of Russia with the Ukrainians and Poles and of Prussia with the Poles. Minorities try to maintain their cultural integrity despite annexation. Poles inhabited an area divided into territories ruled by three countries but maintained their own culture across political boundaries.

Colonialism

Colonialism has been the most common way for one group of people to dominate another. **Colonialism** is the maintenance of political, social, economic, and cultural dominance over people by a foreign power for an extended period (Bell 1991). Colonialism is rule by outsiders but, unlike annexation, does not involve actual incorporation into the dominant people's nation. The long-standing control that was exercised by the British Empire over much of North America, parts of Africa, and India is an example of colonial domination (see Figure 1.4).

Societies gain power over a foreign land through military strength, sophisticated political organization, and investment capital. The extent of power may also vary according to the dominant group's scope of settlement in the colonial land. Relations between the colonial nation and the colonized people are similar to those between a dominant group and exploited subordinate groups. The colonial subjects generally are limited to menial jobs and the wages from their labor. The natural resources of their land benefit the members of the ruling class.

By the 1980s, colonialism, in the sense of political rule, had become largely a phenomenon of the past, yet industrial countries of North America and Europe still dominated the world economically and politically. Drawing on the conflict perspective, sociologist Immanuel Wallerstein (1974) views the global economic system of today as much like the height of colonial days. Wallerstein has advanced the **world systems theory**, which views the global economic system as divided between nations that control wealth and those that provide natural resources and labor. The limited economic resources available in developing nations exacerbate many of the ethnic, racial, and religious conflicts noted at the beginning of this chapter. In addition, the presence of massive inequality between nations only serves to encourage immigration generally and, more specifically, the movement of many of the most skilled from developing nations to the industrial nations.

A significant exception to the end of foreign political rule is Puerto Rico; its territorial or commonwealth status with the United States is basically that of a colony. The nearly 4 million people on the island are U.S. citizens but are unable to vote in presidential elections unless they migrate to the mainland. In 1998, 50 percent of Puerto Ricans on the island voted to continue commonwealth status, 47 percent favored statehood, and less than 3 percent voted for independence. Despite their poor showing, proindependence forces are very vocal and enjoy the sympathies of others who are concerned about the cultural and economic dominance of the U.S. mainland (Navarro 1998; Saad 1998).

colonialism
A foreign power's maintenance of political, social, economic, and cultural dominance over people for an extended period.

world systems theory
A view of the global economic system as divided between nations that control wealth and those that provide natural resources and labor.

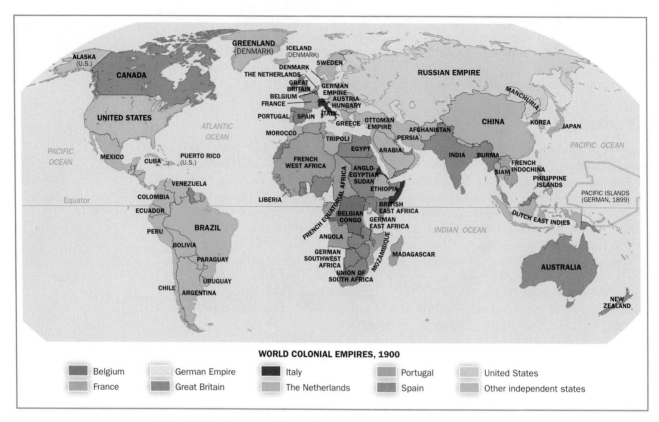

FIGURE 1.4

World Colonial Empires (1900)

Events of the nineteenth century increased European dominance over the world. By 1900, most independent African nations had disappeared, and the major European powers and Japan took advantage of China's internal weakness to gain both trading ports and economic concessions.

Source: H. W. Brands et al. 2009, 582.

Colonialism is domination by outsiders. Relations between the colonizer and the colony are similar to those between the dominant and subordinate peoples within the same country. This distinctive pattern of oppression is called **internal colonialism**. Among other cases, it has been applied to the plight of Blacks in the United States and Mexican Indians in Mexico, who are colonial peoples in their own country. Internal colonialism covers more than simple economic oppression. Nationalist movements in African colonies struggled to achieve political and economic independence from Europeans. Similarly, some African Americans also call themselves nationalists in trying to gain more autonomy over their lives (Blauner 1969, 1972).

The Consequences of Subordinate-Group Status

There are several consequences for a group with subordinate status. These differ in their degree of harshness, ranging from physical annihilation to absorption into the dominant group. In this section, we will examine six consequences of subordinate-group status: extermination, expulsion, secession, segregation, fusion, and assimilation. The figure on the next page illustrates how these consequences can be defined using the spectrum of intergroup relations.

internal colonialism
The treatment of subordinate peoples as colonial subjects by those in power.

Extermination

genocide
The deliberate, systematic killing of an entire people or nation.

The most extreme way of dealing with a subordinate group is to eliminate it. Today, the term **genocide** is used to describe the deliberate, systematic killing of an entire people

SPECTRUM OF INTERGROUP RELATIONS

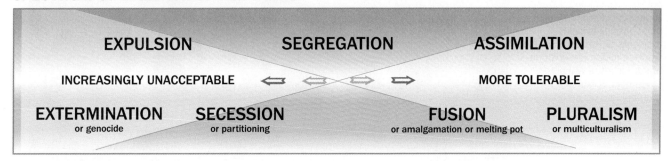

or nation. This term is often used in reference to the Holocaust, Nazi Germany's extermination of 12 million European Jews and other ethnic minorities during World War II. The term **ethnic cleansing** refers to the forced deportation of people, accompanied by systematic violence. The term was introduced in 1992 to the world's vocabulary as ethnic Serbs instituted a policy intended to "cleanse"—eliminate—Muslims from parts of Bosnia. More recently, a genocidal war between the Hutu and Tutsi people in Rwanda left 300,000 school-aged children orphaned (Chirot and Edwards 2003; Naimark 2004).

However, genocide also appropriately describes White policies toward Native Americans in the nineteenth century. In 1800, the American Indian population in the United States was approximately 600,000; by 1850, it had been reduced to 250,000 through warfare with the U.S. Army, disease, and forced relocation to inhospitable environments.

In 2008, the Australian government officially apologized for past treatment to its native people, the Aboriginal population. Not only did this involve brutality and neglect, but also a quarter of their children, the so-called lost generation, were taken from their families until the policy was finally abandoned in 1969 (Johnston 2008).

Expulsion

Dominant groups may choose to force a specific subordinate group to leave certain areas or even vacate a country. Expulsion, therefore, is another extreme consequence of minority-group status. European colonial powers in North America and eventually the U.S. government itself drove almost all Native Americans out of their tribal lands and into unfamiliar territory.

More recently, in 1979, Vietnam expelled nearly 1 million ethnic Chinese from the country, partly as a result of centuries of hostility between the two Asian neighbors. These "boat people" were abruptly eliminated as a minority within Vietnamese society. This expulsion meant that they were uprooted and became a new minority group in many nations, including Australia, France, the United States, and Canada. Thus, expulsion may remove a minority group from one society; however, the expelled people merely go to another nation, where they are again a minority group.

Secession

A group ceases to be a subordinate group when it secedes to form a new nation or moves to an already established nation, where it becomes dominant. After Great Britain withdrew from Palestine, Jewish people achieved a dominant position in 1948, attracting Jews from throughout the world to the new state of Israel. Similarly, Pakistan was created in 1947 when India was partitioned. The predominantly Muslim areas in the north became Pakistan, making India predominantly Hindu. Throughout this century, minorities have repudiated dominant customs. In this spirit, the Estonian, Latvian, Lithuanian, and Armenian peoples, not content to be merely tolerated by the majority, all seceded to form independent states after

ethnic cleansing
Policy of ethnic Serbs to eliminate Muslims from parts of Bosnia.

Let's play Scrabble! This is not your typical board game. To preserve their language among young people, residents of the Lake Traverse Indian Reservation of the Sisseton Wahpeton Oyate hold Scrabble tournaments where only Dakotah language words are permitted.

the demise of the Soviet Union in 1991. In 1999, ethnic Albanians fought bitterly for their cultural and political recognition in the Kosovo region of Yugoslavia.

Some African Americans have called for secession. Suggestions dating back to the early 1700s supported the return of Blacks to Africa as a solution to racial problems. The settlement target of the American Colonization Society was Liberia, but proposals were also advanced to establish settlements in other areas. Territorial separatism and the emigrationist ideology were recurrent and interrelated themes among African Americans from the late nineteenth century well into the 1980s. The Black Muslims, or Nation of Islam, once expressed the desire for complete separation in their own state or territory within the modern borders of the United States. Although a secession of Blacks from the United States has not taken place, it has been proposed.

Segregation

Segregation is the physical separation of two groups in residence, workplace, and social functions. Generally, the dominant group imposes segregation on a subordinate group. Segregation is rarely complete, however; intergroup contact inevitably occurs even in the most segregated societies.

Sociologists Douglas Massey and Nancy Denton (1993) wrote *American Apartheid*, which described segregation in U.S. cities on the basis of 1990 data. The title of their book was meant to indicate that neighborhoods in the United States resembled the segregation of the rigid government-imposed racial segregation that prevailed for so long in the Republic of South Africa.

Analysis of census data from the last 50 years shows continuing segregation despite racial and ethnic diversity in the nation. White people live isolated from non-Whites. African Americans typically live in largely Black neighborhoods, as we can see in Figure 1.5. Latinos and Asian Americans are somewhat less segregated.

Although there has been very modest decline in residential segregation since 1980, the racial isolation remains dramatic. The typical White lives in a neighborhood 80 percent White; the typical African American resides in an area 51 percent Black. The corresponding figures for Latinos and Asian Americans are 46 percent and 18 percent, respectively. Even when we consider social class, the patterns of minority segregation persist (Lewis Mumford Center 2001; Logan et al. 2004; Wilkes and Iceland 2004).

segregation
The physical separation of two groups, often imposed on a subordinate group by the dominant group.

This focus on metropolitan areas should not cause us to ignore the continuing legally sanctioned segregation of Native Americans on reservations. Although the majority of our nation's first inhabitants live outside these tribal areas, the reservations play a prominent role in the identity of Native Americans. Although it is easier to maintain tribal identity on the reservation, economic and educational opportunities are more limited in these areas, which are segregated from the rest of society.

The social consequences of residential segregation are significant. Given the elevated rates of poverty experienced by racial and ethnic minorities, their patterns of segregation mean that the consequences of poverty (dismal job opportunities, poor health care facilities, delinquency, and crime) are much more likely to be experienced by even middle-class Blacks, Latinos, and tribal people than by middle-class Whites. Race, rather than class, explains the persistence of segregation (Adelman and Gocker 2007; Massey 2004).

A particularly troubling pattern has been the emergence of **resegregation**, or the physical separation of racial and ethnic groups

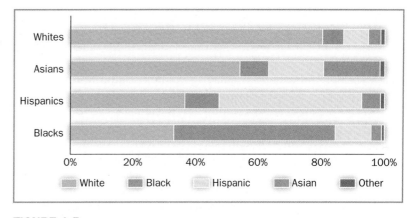

FIGURE 1.5

Typical Metropolitan Neighborhoods: Continued Segregation from Each Other

The basic message is that Whites live in neighborhoods with low minority representation whereas minorities live in neighborhoods with high minoriity representation and limited White representation.

Source: Analysis of the 2000 census by the Lewis Mumford Center (2001, www.albany.edu/mumford/census).

reappearing after a period of relative integration. Resegregation has occurred in both neighborhoods and schools after a transitional period of desegregation. For example, in 1954, only one in 100,000 Black students attended a majority White school in the South. Thanks to the civil rights movement and a series of civil rights measures, by 1968, this was up to 23 percent and then 47 percent by 1988. But after White households relocated or alternatives reemerged through private schools and homeschooling, the proportion had dropped back to 27 percent in 2004. The latest analysis shows continuing if not increasing racial isolation (Orfield 2007; Orfield and Lee 2007; Rich 2008).

Given segregation patterns, many Whites in the United States have limited contact with people of other racial and ethnic backgrounds. In one study of 100 affluent powerful White men that looked at their experiences past and present, it was clear they had lived in a "White bubble"—neighborhoods, schools, elite colleges, and workplaces were overwhelmingly White. The continuing pattern of segregation in the United States means our diverse population grows up in very different nations (Bonilla-Silva and Embrick 2007; Feagin and O'Brien 2003).

Fusion

Fusion occurs when a minority and a majority group combine to form a new group. This combining can be expressed as A + B + C → D, where A, B, and C represent the groups present in a society and D signifies the result, an ethnocultural-racial group sharing some of the characteristics of each initial group. Mexican people are an example of fusion, originating as they do out of the mixing of the Spanish and indigenous Indian cultures. Theoretically, fusion does not entail intermarriage, but it is very similar to **amalgamation**, or the process by which a dominant group and a subordinate group combine through intermarriage into a new people. In everyday speech, the words *fusion* and *amalgamation* are rarely used, but the concept is expressed in the notion of a human **melting pot** in which diverse racial or ethnic groups form a new creation, a new cultural entity (Newman 1973).

The analogy of the cauldron, the "melting pot," was first used to describe the United States by the French observer Crèvecoeur in 1782. The phrase dates back to the Middle Ages, when alchemists attempted to change less-valuable metals into gold and silver. Similarly, the idea of the human melting pot implied that the new group would represent only the best qualities and attributes of the different cultures contributing to it. The belief in the United States as a melting pot became widespread in the early twentieth century. This belief suggested that the United States had an almost divine mission to destroy artificial divisions and create a single kind of human. However, the dominant group had indicated its unwillingness to welcome such groups as Native Americans, Blacks, Hispanics,

resegregation
The physical separation of racial and ethnic groups reappearing after a period of relative integration.

fusion
A minority and a majority group combining to form a new group.

amalgamation
The process by which a dominant group and a subordinate group combine through intermarriage to form a new group.

melting pot
Diverse racial or ethnic groups or both, forming a new creation, a new cultural entity.

Jews, Asians, and Irish Roman Catholics into the melting pot. It is a mistake to think of the United States as an ethnic mixing bowl. Although there are superficial signs of fusion, as in a cuisine that includes sauerkraut and spaghetti, most contributions of subordinate groups are ignored (Gleason 1980).

Marriage patterns indicate the resistance to fusion. People are unwilling, in varying degrees, to marry outside their own ethnic, religious, and racial groups. Until relatively recently interracial marriage was outlawed in much of the Unied States. At the time that President Barack Obama's parents married in Hawaii, their union would have been illegal and unable to have occurred in 22 other states. Surveys show that 20 percent to 50 percent of various White ethnic groups report single ancestry. When White ethnics do cross boundaries, they tend to marry within their religion and social class. For example, Italians are more likely to marry Irish, who are also Catholic, than they are to marry Protestant Swedes.

Although it may seem that interracial matches are everywhere, there is only modest evidence of a fusion of races in the United States. Racial intermarriage has been increasing, and the number of interracial couples immigrating to the United States has also grown. In 1980, there were 167,000 Black–White couples, but by 2006, there were 403,000. That is still less than one out of every 100 marriages involving a White and Black person.

Among couples in which at least one member is Hispanic, marriages with a non-Hispanic partner account for 37 percent. Taken together, all interracial and Hispanic–non-Hispanic couples account for 7.5 percent of married couples today (Bureau of the Census 2007a, Table 59).

Assimilation

Assimilation is the process by which a subordinate individual or group takes on the characteristics of the dominant group and is eventually accepted as part of that group. Assimilation is a majority ideology in which A + B + C → A. The majority (A) dominates in such a way that the minorities (B and C) become indistinguishable from the dominant group. Assimilation dictates conformity to the dominant group, regardless of how many racial, ethnic, or religious groups are involved (Newman 1973, 53).

To be complete, assimilation must entail an active effort by the minority-group individual to shed all distinguishing actions and beliefs and the unqualified acceptance of that individual by the dominant society. In the United States, dominant White society encourages assimilation. The assimilation perspective tends to devalue alien culture and to treasure the dominant. For example, assimilation assumes that whatever is admirable among Blacks was adapted from Whites and that whatever is bad is inherently Black. The assimilation solution to Black–White conflict has been typically defined as the development of a consensus around White American values.

Assimilation is very difficult. The person must forsake his or her cultural tradition to become part of a different, often antagonistic culture. Members of the subordinate group who choose not to assimilate view those who do as deserters.

Assimilation does not occur at the same pace for all groups or for all individuals in the same group. Typically, assimilation is not a process completed by the first generation. Assimilation tends to take longer under the following conditions:

- The differences between the minority and the majority are large.
- The majority is not receptive, or the minority retains its own culture.
- The minority group arrives over a short period of time.
- The minority-group residents are concentrated rather than dispersed.
- The arrival is recent, and the homeland is accessible.

Assimilation is not a smooth process (Warner and Srole 1945).

Assimilation is viewed by many as unfair or even dictatorial. However, members of the dominant group see it as reasonable that people shed their distinctive cultural traditions. In public discussions today, assimilation is the ideology of the dominant group in forcing people how to act. Consequently, the social institutions in the United States—the educational system, economy, government, religion, and medicine—all push toward assimilation, with occasional references to the pluralist approach.

assimilation
The process by which a subordinate individual or group takes on the characteristics of the dominant group.

The Pluralist Perspective

Thus far, we have concentrated on how subordinate groups cease to exist (removal) or take on the characteristics of the dominant group (assimilation). The alternative to these relationships between the majority and the minority is pluralism. **Pluralism** implies that various groups in a society have mutual respect for one another's culture, a respect that allows minorities to express their own culture without suffering prejudice or discrimination. Whereas the assimilationist or integrationist seeks the elimination of ethnic boundaries, the pluralist believes in maintaining many of them.

There are limits to cultural freedom. A Romanian immigrant to the United States cannot expect to avoid learning English and still move up the occupational ladder. To survive, a society must have a consensus among its members on basic ideals, values, and beliefs. Nevertheless, there is still plenty of room for variety. Earlier, fusion was described as A + B + C → D and assimilation as A + B + C → A. Using this same scheme, we can think of pluralism as A + B + C → A + B + C, with groups coexisting in one society (Manning 1995; Newman 1973; Simpson 1995).

In the United States, cultural pluralism is more an ideal than a reality. Although there are vestiges of cultural pluralism—in the various ethnic neighborhoods in major cities, for instance—the rule has been for subordinate groups to assimilate. Yet as the minority becomes the numerical majority, the ability to live out one's identity becomes a bit easier. African Americans, Hispanics, and Asian Americans already outnumber Whites in 10 of the 11 largest cities, with San Diego having a slight majority of White non-Hispanics (Figure 1.6). The trend is toward even greater diversity. Nonetheless, the cost of cultural integrity throughout the nation's history has been high. The various Native American tribes have succeeded to a large extent in maintaining their heritage, but the price has been bare subsistence on federal reservations.

In the United States, there is a reemergence of ethnic identification by groups that had previously expressed little interest in their heritage. Groups that make up the dominant majority are also reasserting their ethnic heritages. Various nationality groups are rekindling interest in almost forgotten languages, customs, festivals, and traditions. In some instances, this expression of the past has taken the form of a protest against exclusion from the dominant society. For example, Chinese youths chastise their elders for forgetting the old ways and accepting White American influence and control.

The most visible expression of pluralism is language use. As of 2006, nearly one of every five people (19.1 percent) over age five speaks a native language other than English at home. Later, in Chapters 4 and 5, we will consider how language use figures into issues relating to immigration and education (Bureau of the Census 2007c, Table R1601).

Facilitating a diverse and changing society emerges in just about every aspect of society. Yet another nod to pluralism, although not nearly so obvious as language to the general population, has been the changes within the funeral industry. Where Christian and Jewish funeral practices have dominated, funeral homes are now retraining to accommodate a variety

pluralism
Mutual respect between the various groups in a society for one another's cultures, allowing minorities to express their own culture without experiencing prejudice or hostility.

FIGURE 1.6
Race and Ethnicity, 15 Largest Cities, 2005
Source: Author analysis based on date from the American Community Survey 2006 in Bureau Census 2007b.

Racial and ethnic groups do not merely accept the definitions and ideology proposed by the dominant group. Here we see a protest outside the Supreme Court in 2006. Concerns focused around cases that school districts were potentially violating the U.S. Constitution in their efforts to integrate their classrooms by imposing ranges for racial composition.

of practices. Latinos often expect 24-hour viewing of their deceased, whereas Muslims may wish to participate in washing the deceased before burial in a grave pointing toward Mecca. Hindu and Buddhist requests to participate in cremation are now being respected (Brulliard 2006).

Biracial and Multiracial Identity—Who Am I?

People are now more willing to accept and advance identities that do not neatly fit into mutually exclusive categories. Hence, increasing numbers of people are identifying themselves as biracial or multiracial or, at the very least, explicitly viewing themselves as reflecting a diverse racial and ethnic identity. This is especially true among younger people, which is not too surprising given that 94 percent of the people born since 1977 approve of interracial dating, compared to 84 percent for baby boomers (those born between 1946 and 1964) and only 65 percent born before 1946 (Brunsma 2006; Lewis 2007).

When Tiger Woods first appeared on *The Oprah Winfrey Show*, he was asked whether it bothered him, the only child of a Black American father and a Thai mother, to be called an African American. He replied, "It does. Growing up, I came up with this name: I'm a Cabalinasian" (White 1997, 34). This is a self-crafted acronym to reflect that Tiger Woods is one-eighth Caucasian, one-fourth Black, one-eighth American Indian, one-fourth Thai, and one-fourth Chinese. Soon after he achieved professional stardom, another golfer was strongly criticized for making racist remarks based on seeing Woods only as African American. If Tiger Woods was not so famous, would most people on meeting him see him as anything but an African American? Probably not. Tiger Woods's problem is really the challenge to a diverse society that continues to try to place people in a few socially constructed racial and ethnic boxes.

The diversity of the United States today has made it more difficult for many people to place themselves on the racial and ethnic landscape. It reminds us that racial formation continues to take place. Obviously, the racial and ethnic landscape, as we have seen, is constructed not naturally but socially and, therefore, is subject to change and different interpretations. Although our focus is on the United States, almost every nation faces the same problems.

The United States tracks people by race and ethnicity for myriad reasons, ranging from attempting to improve the status of oppressed groups to diversifying classrooms. But how can we measure the growing number of people whose ancestry is mixed by anyone's definition? In "Research Focus" we consider how the U.S. Bureau of the Census dealt with this issue.

Besides the increasing respect for biracial identity and multiracial identity, group names undergo change as well. Within little more than a generation during the twentieth century, labels that were applied to subordinate groups changed from *Negroes* to *Blacks* to *African Americans*, from *American Indians* to *Native Americans* or *Native Peoples*. However, more Native Americans prefer the use of their tribal name, such as *Seminole*, instead of a collective label. The old 1950s statistical term of "people with a Spanish surname" has long been discarded, yet there is disagreement over a new term: *Latino* or *Hispanic*. Like Native Americans, Hispanic Americans avoid such global terms and prefer their native names, such as *Puerto Ricans* or *Cubans*. People of Mexican ancestry indicate preferences for a variety of names, such as *Mexican American*, *Chicano*, or simply *Mexican*.

In the United States and other multiracial, multiethnic societies, **panethnicity**, the development of solidarity between ethnic subgroups, has emerged. The coalition of tribal groups as Native Americans or American Indians to confront outside forces, notably the federal government, is one example of panethnicity. Hispanics or Latinos and Asian Americans are other examples of panethnicity. Although it is rarely recognized by dominant society, the very term *Black* or *African American* represents the descendants of many different ethnic or tribal groups, such as Akamba, Fulani, Hausa, Malinke, and Yoruba (Lopez and Espiritu 1990).

Is panethnicity a convenient label for "outsiders" or a term that reflects a mutual identity? Certainly, many people outside the group are unable or unwilling to recognize ethnic differences and prefer umbrella terms such as *Asian Americans*. For some small groups, combining with others is emerging as a useful way to make them heard, but there is always a fear that their own distinctive culture will become submerged. Although many Hispanics share the Spanish language and many are united by Roman Catholicism, only one in four native-born people of Mexican, Puerto Rican, or Cuban descent prefers a panethnic label to nationality or ethnic identity. Yet the growth of a variety of panethnic associations among many groups, including Hispanics, continued through the 1990s (de la Garza et al. 1992; Espiritu 1992).

Add to this cultural mix the many peoples with clear social identities that are not yet generally recognized in the United States. Arabs are a rapidly growing segment whose identity is heavily subject to stereotypes or, at best, is still ambiguous. Haitians and Jamaicans affirm that they are Black but rarely accept the identity of African American. Brazilians, who speak Portuguese, often object to being called Hispanic because of that term's association with Spain. Similarly, there are White Hispanics and non–White Hispanics, some of the latter being Black and others Asian (Bennett 1993; Omi and Winant 1994, 162).

Another challenge to identity is **marginality**, the status of being between two cultures, as in the case of a person whose mother is a Jew and father a Christian. Du Bois (1903) spoke eloquently of the "double consciousness" that Black Americans feel—caught between the concept of being a citizen of the United States but viewed as something quite apart from the dominant social forces of society. Incomplete assimilation by immigrants also results in marginality. Although a Filipino woman migrating to the United States may take on the characteristics of her new host society, she may not be fully accepted and may, therefore, feel neither Filipino nor American. The marginalized person finds himself or herself being perceived differently in different environments, with varying expectations (Billson 1988; Park 1928; Stonequist 1937).

As we seek to understand diversity in the United States, we must be mindful that ethnic and racial labels are just that: labels that have been socially constructed. Yet these social constructs can have a powerful impact, whether self-applied or applied by others.

panethnicity
The development of solidarity between ethnic subgroups, as reflected in the terms Hispanic or Asian American.

marginality
The status of being between two cultures at the same time, such as the status of Jewish immigrants in the United States.

MEASURING MULTICULTURALISM

Approaching Census 2000, a movement was spawned by people who were frustrated by government questionnaires that forced them to indicate only one race. Take the case of Stacey Davis in New Orleans. The young woman's mother is Thai and her father is Creole, a blend of Black, French, and German. People seeing Stacey confuse her for a Latina, Filipina, or Hawaiian. Officially, she has been "White" all her life because she looked White. Congress was lobbied by groups such as Project RACE (Reclassify All Children Equally) for a category "biracial" or "multiracial" that one could select on census forms instead of a specific race. Race is only one of six questions asked of every person in the United States on census day every 10 years. After various trial runs with different wordings on the race question, Census 2000 for the first time gave people the option to check off one or more racial groups. "Biracial" or "multiracial" was not an option because pretests showed very few people would use it. This meant that the government recognized in Census 2000 different social constructions of racial identity—that is, a person could be Asian American and White.

Most people did select one racial category in Census 2000. Overall, approximately 7 million people, or 2.4 percent of the total population, selected two or more racial groups. This was a smaller proportion than many observers had anticipated. In fact, not even the majority of mixed-race couples identified their children with more than one racial classification. As shown in Figure 1.7, White and American Indian were the most common multiple identity, with 1 million people or so selecting that response. As a group, American Indians were most likely to select a second category and Whites least likely. Race is socially defined.

Complicating the situation is that people are asked separately whether they are Hispanic or non-Hispanic. So a Hispanic person can be any race. In the 2000 census, 94 percent indicated they were one race, but 6 percent indicated two or more races; this proportion was three times higher than among non-Hispanics. Therefore, Latinos are more likely than non-Hispanics to indicate a multiracial ancestry.

The census bureau's decision does not necessarily resolve the frustration of hundreds of thousands of people such as Stacey Davis, who daily face people trying to place them in some racial or ethnic category that is convenient for them. However, it does underscore the complexity of social

Resistance and Change

By virtue of wielding power and influence, the dominant group may define the terms by which all members of society operate. This is particularly evident in a slave society, but even in contemporary industrialized nations, the dominant group has a disproportionate role in shaping immigration policy, the curriculum of the schools, and the content of the media.

Subordinate groups do not merely accept the definitions and ideology proposed by the dominant group. A continuing theme in dominant–subordinate relations is the minority group's challenge to its subordination. Resistance by subordinate groups is well documented as they seek to promote change that will bring them more rights and privileges, if not true equality. Often traditional notions of racial formation are overcome not only through panethnicity but also because Black people with Latinos and sympathetic Whites join in (Moulder 1996; Winant 2004).

Resistance can be seen in efforts by racial and ethnic groups to maintain their identity through newspapers and organizations and in today's technological age through cable television stations, blogs, and Internet sites. Resistance manifests itself in social movements

Research Focus

construction and trying to apply arbitrary definitions to the diversity of the human population. Symbolic of this social construction of race can be seen in President Barack Obama, born of a White woman and a Black immigrant from Kenya. Although he has always identified himself as a Black man, it is worthy to note he was born in Hawaii, a state in which 21.4 percent of people see themselves as more than one race, compared to the national average of 2.4 percent.

Sources: El Nasser 1997; Grieco and Cassidy 2001; Jones and Smith 2001; Tafoya, Johnson, and Hill 2004; Williams 2005.

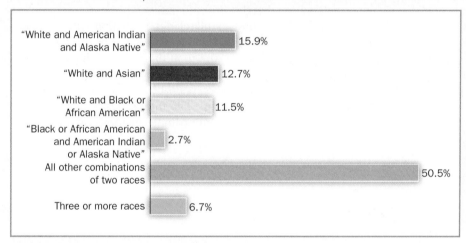

FIGURE 1.7

Multiple-Race Choices in Census 2000

This figure shows the percentage distribution of the 6.8 million people who chose two or more races (out of the total population of 281.4 million).

Source: Grieco and Cassidy 2001.

such as the civil rights movement, the feminist movement, and gay rights efforts. The passage of such legislation as the Age Discrimination Act or the Americans with Disabilities Act marks the success of oppressed groups in lobbying on their own behalf.

Resistance efforts may begin through small actions. For example, residents of a reservation question why a toxic waste dump is to be located on their land. Although it may bring in money, they question the wisdom of such a move. Their concerns lead to further investigations of the extent to which American Indian lands are used disproportionately to house dangerous materials. This action in turn leads to a broader investigation of the way in which minority-group people often find themselves "hosting" dumps and incinerators. As we will discuss later, these local efforts eventually led the Environmental Protection Agency to monitor the disproportionate placement of toxic facilities in or near racial and ethnic minority communities. There is little reason to expect that such reforms would have occurred if we had relied on traditional decision-making processes alone.

Change has occurred. At the beginning of the twentieth century, lynching was practiced in many parts of the country. At the beginning of the twenty-first century, laws

Afrocentric perspective
An emphasis on the customs of African cultures and how they have pervaded the history, culture, and behavior of Blacks in the United States and around the world.

punishing hate crimes were increasingly common and embraced a variety of stigmatized groups. Although this social progress should not be ignored, the nation needs to focus concern ahead on the significant social inequalities that remain. It is too easy to look at the accomplishments of Barack Obama and Hillary Clinton and conclude "mission accomplished" in terms of racial and gender injustices (Best 2001).

An even more basic form of resistance is to question societal values. In this book, we avoid using the term *American* to describe people of the United States because geographically Brazilians, Canadians, and El Salvadorans are Americans as well. It is very easy to overlook how our understanding of today has been shaped by the way institutions and even the very telling of history have been presented by members of the dominant group. African American studies scholar Molefi Kete Asante (2007, 2008) has called for an **Afrocentric perspective** that emphasizes the customs of African cultures and how they have pervaded the history, culture, and behavior of Blacks in the United States and around the world. Afrocentrism counters Eurocentrism and works toward a multiculturalist or pluralist orientation in which no viewpoint is suppressed. The Afrocentric approach could become part of our school curriculum, which has not adequately acknowledged the importance of this heritage.

The Afrocentric perspective has attracted much attention in education. Opponents view it as a separatist view of history and culture that distorts both past and present. Its supporters counter that African peoples everywhere can come to full self-determination only when they are able to overthrow White or Eurocentric intellectual interpretations (Conyers 2004).

In considering the inequalities present today, as we will in the chapters that follow, it is easy to forget how much change has taken place. Much of the resistance to prejudice and discrimination in the past, either to slavery or to women's prohibition from voting, took the active support of members of the dominant group. The indignities still experienced by subordinate groups continue to be resisted as subordinate groups and their allies among the dominant group seek further change.

Conclusion

One hundred years ago, sociologist and activist W. E. B. Du Bois took another famed Black activist, Booker T. Washington, to task for saying that the races could best work together apart, like fingers on a hand. Du Bois felt that Black people had to be a part of all social institutions and not create their own. Now with an African American elected to the presidency, Whites, African Americans, and other groups continue to debate what form society should take. Should we seek to bring everyone together into an integrated whole? Or do we strive to maintain as much of our group identities as possible while working cooperatively as necessary?

In this chapter, we have attempted to organize our approach to subordinate–dominant relations in the United States. We observed that subordinate groups do not necessarily contain fewer members than the dominant group. Subordinate groups are classified into racial, ethnic, religious, and gender groups. Racial classification has been of interest, but scientific findings do not explain contemporary race relations. Biological differences of race are not supported by scientific data. Yet as the continuing debate over standardized tests demonstrates, attempts to establish a biological meaning of race have not been swept entirely into the dustbin of history. However, the social meaning given to physical differences is very significant.

People have defined racial differences in such a way as to encourage or discourage the progress of certain groups.

Subordinate-group members' reactions include the seeking of an alternative avenue to acceptance and success: "Why should we forsake what we are, to be accepted by them?" In response to this question, there has been a resurgence of ethnic identification. Pluralism describes a society in which several different groups coexist, with no dominant or subordinate groups. The hope for such a society remains unfulfilled, except perhaps for isolated exceptions.

Subordinate groups have not and do not always accept their second-class status passively. They may protest, organize, revolt, and resist society as defined by the dominant group. Patterns of race and ethnic relations are changing, not stagnant. Indicative of the changing landscape, biracial and multiracial children present us with new definitions of identity emerging through a process of racial formation, reminding us that race is socially constructed.

The two significant forces that are absent in a truly pluralistic society are prejudice and discrimination. In an assimilation society, prejudice disparages out-group differences, and discrimination financially rewards those who shed their past. In the next two chapters, we will explore the nature of prejudice and discrimination in the United States.

Summary

1. When sociologists define a minority group, they are concerned primarily with the economic and political power, or powerlessness, of the group.
2. A racial group is set apart from others primarily by physical characteristics; an ethnic group is set apart primarily by national origin or cultural patterns.
3. People cannot be sorted into distinct racial groups; so race is best viewed as a social construct subject to different interpretations over time.
4. Functionalists point out that discrimination is both functional and dysfunctional for a society. Conflict theorists see racial subordination through the presence of tension between competing groups. Labeling theory directs our attention to the role that negative stereotypes play in race and ethnicity.
5. Subordinate-group status has emerged through migration, annexation, and colonialism.
6. The social consequences of subordinate-group status include extermination, expulsion, secession, segregation, fusion, assimilation, and pluralism.
7. A small but still significant number of people in the United States—more than 7 million—readily see themselves as having a biracial or multiracial identity.
8. Racial, ethnic, and other minorities maintain a long history of resisting efforts to restrict their rights.

Key Terms

Afrocentric perspective 30	functionalist perspective 15	panethnicity 27
amalgamation 23	fusion 23	pluralism 25
assimilation 24	genocide 20	racial formation 13
biological race 11	globalization 18	racial group 7
blaming the victim 16	immigration 18	racism 13
class 14	intelligence quotient (IQ) 12	resegregation 23
colonialism 19	internal colonialism 20	segregation 22
conflict perspective 16	labeling theory 16	self-fulfilling prophecy 17
dysfunction 15	marginality 27	sociology 14
emigration 18	melting pot 23	stereotypes 17
ethnic cleansing 21	migration 18	stratification 14
ethnic group 8	minority group 5	world systems theory 19

Review Questions

1. In what ways have you seen issues of race and ethnicity emerge? Identify groups that have been subordinated for reasons other than race, ethnicity, or gender.
2. How can a significant political or social issue (such as bilingual education) be viewed in assimilationist and pluralistic terms?
3. How do the concepts of "biracial" and "multiracial" relate to W. E. B. Du Bois's notion of a "color line"?

Critical Thinking

1. How diverse is your city? Can you see evidence that some group is being subordinated? What social construction of categories do you see that may be different in your community as compared to elsewhere?
2. In 2006, "Nuestro Himno" ("Our Anthem") hit the airwaves as a Spanish-language version of Francis Scott Key's original words. Do you think this represents a positive development or a step backward? How does it relate to the spectrum of intergroup relations pictured on page 21?
3. Identify some protest and resistance efforts by subordinated groups in your area. Have they been successful? Why are some people who say they favor equality uncomfortable with such efforts? How can people unconnected with such efforts either help or hinder such protests?

2

Prejudice

PREJUDICE IS A NEGATIVE ATTITUDE THAT REJECTS AN ENTIRE group; discrimination is behavior that deprives a group of certain rights or opportunities. Prejudice does not necessarily coincide with discrimination, as is made apparent by a typology developed by sociologist Robert Merton. Several theories have been advanced to explain prejudice: scapegoating, authoritarian personality, exploitation, and the normative approach. Although widespread expression of prejudice has declined, color-blind racism allows the status quo of racial and ethnic inequality to persist. Prejudice is not limited to the dominant group; members of subordinate groups often dislike one another. The mass media seem to be of limited value in reducing prejudice and may even intensify ill feeling. Equal-status contact and the shared-coping approach may reduce hostility between groups, but data show few friendships cross racial lines. In response to increasing diversity in the workplace, corporations and organizations have mounted diversity-training programs to increase organizational effectiveness and combat prejudice. There are also 10 identifiable steps that we as individuals can take to stop prejudice and hatred.

33

Imagine one is a "shooter" who is faced with making a decision whether to shoot a threatening, potentially dangerous person. Social psychologists have created such a constructed situation for police, everyday community residents, and even volunteer college students, using a video simulation. As one might expect, the police as shooters were faster in responding and were more accurate in determining whether the "criminal" was armed with a gun. But what if the situation sometimes shows the target to be Black and sometimes as White? Reflecting general stereotypes, response time is fastest to decide whether to shoot or hold fire if the White target is unarmed and the Black target is armed. Yet when the image does not follow the notion that Black people are less trustworthy, response time falls. People hesitate to shoot armed White targets and take longer to decide whether to shoot unarmed Black targets. This measured bias seems to hold across race and ethnicity in that there were no significant differences based on whether the shooters themselves were White or Black or Hispanic. Particularly troubling was the finding that police assigned to predominantly Black neighborhoods rather than White communities are even quicker to shoot armed Black targets and more hesitant to fire at armed White targets.

These results were not unusual. In a similar study at the University of Washington, psychologists asked college students to distinguish virtual citizens and police officers from armed criminals. They found that subjects were more likely to misperceive and shoot images of Black men than of White men in the video game they created. For the last three decades, in fact, research has suggested that people in the United States are likely to see Black men as being more violent than White men, which translated in this study into the Black men being more likely to be shot at (Correll et al. 2007).

The immigration debate has persisted for years with little action on a complex issue. Some people have advocated measures to allow long-term illegal residents a way to become permanent residents, but loud cries have been made, taking a "What part of *illegal* don't they get?" argument. It is not too surprising that hate crimes against Latinos have increased by 35 percent over the last three years. The rhetoric over immigration has often stigmatized, or dehumanized, immigrants (even legal arrivals at times) as "invaders," "criminal aliens," and "cockroaches."

Prejudice is so prevalent that it is tempting to consider it inevitable or, even more broadly, just part of human nature. Such a view ignores its variability from individual to individual and from society to society. People must learn prejudice as children before they exhibit it as adults. Therefore, prejudice is a social phenomenon, an acquired characteristic. A truly pluralistic society would lack unfavorable distinctions made through prejudicial attitudes among racial and ethnic groups.

Ill feeling between groups may result from **ethnocentrism**, or the tendency to assume that one's culture and way of life are superior to all others'. The ethnocentric person judges other groups and other cultures by the standards of his or her own group. This attitude leads people quite easily to view other cultures as inferior. We see a woman with a veil and may regard it as strange and backward yet find it baffling when other societies see U.S. women in short skirts and view the dress as

Imagine seeing this billboard. What is it for? It is an expression of prejudice. One would easily find that it is making a case for an organization that argues White Americans have an unconditional right to territorial and political self-determination.

inappropriate. Ethnocentrism and other expressions of prejudice are voiced very often, but unfortunately they also become the motivation for criminal acts.

Hate Crimes

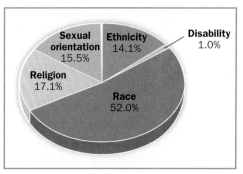

FIGURE 2.1
Distribution of Reported Hate Crimes in 2007
Source: Department of Justice 2008.

Although prejudice certainly is not new in the United States, it is receiving increased attention as it manifests itself in neighborhoods, at meetings, and on college campuses. The Hate Crime Statistics Act, which became law in 1990, directs the Department of Justice to gather data on hate or bias crimes. The government defines an ordinary crime as a **hate crime** when offenders are motivated to choose a victim because of some characteristic—for example, race, ethnicity, religion, sexual orientation, or disability—and provide evidence that hatred prompted them to commit the crime. Hate crimes are also sometimes referred to as *bias crimes* (Department of Justice 2008).

This law created a national mandate to identify such crimes, whereas previously only 12 states had monitored hate crimes. In 1994, the act was amended to include disabilities, both physical and mental, as factors that could be considered as a basis for hate crimes.

In 2008, law enforcement agencies released hate crime data submitted by police agencies covering 85 percent of the United States. Even though many, many hate crimes are not reported (less than one in seven participating agencies reported an incident), a staggering number of offenses that come to law agencies' attention were motivated by hate. There were official reports of more than 7,600 hate crimes and bias-motivated incidents. As indicated in Figure 2.1, race was the apparent motivation for the bias in approximately 52 percent of the reports, and religion, sexual orientation, and ethnicity accounted for 14 percent to 17 percent each. Vandalism and intimidation were the most common crimes, but 58 percent of the incidents against people involved assault, rape, or murder.

The vast majority of hate crimes are directed by members of the dominant group toward those who are, relatively speaking, powerless, but that does not account for every hate crime. One in five bias incidents based on race are anti-White. Hate crimes, except for those that are most horrific, receive little media attention, and anti-White incidents probably receive even less. Hostility based on race knows no boundaries (Department of Justice 2008; Witt 2007).

The official reports of hate or bias crimes appear to be only the tip of the iceberg. Government-commissioned surveys conducted over a national cross section indicate that 192,000 people annually report they have been victims of hate crimes, but only half of these are reported to police. Of these, only 1 out of 10, according to the victims, are confirmed as hate crimes. Although definitions vary, considerable racial hostility in the country becomes violent (Harlow 2005; Perry 2003).

National legislation and publicity have made hate crime a meaningful term, and we are beginning to recognize the victimization associated with such incidents. A current proposal would make a violent crime a federal crime if it were motivated by racial or religious bias. Although passage is uncertain, the serious consideration of the proposal indicates a willingness to consider a major expansion of federal jurisdiction. Currently, federal law prohibits crimes motivated by race, color, religion, or national origin only if they involve violation of a federally guaranteed right such as voting.

Victimized groups are not merely observing hate crimes and other acts of prejudice. Watchdog organizations play an important role in documenting bias-motivated violence; among such groups are the Anti-Defamation League, the National Institute Against Prejudice and Violence, the Southern Poverty Law Center, and the National Gay and Lesbian Task Force.

Established hate groups have even set up propaganda sites on the World Wide Web. This also creates opportunities for previously unknown haters and hate groups to promote

ethnocentrism
The tendency to assume that one's culture and way of life are superior to all others.

hate crime
Criminal offense committed because of the offender's bias against a race, religion, ethnic/national origin group, or sexual orientation group.

prejudice
A negative attitude toward an entire category of people, such as a racial or ethnic minority.

ethnophaulisms
Ethnic or racial slurs, including derisive nicknames.

discrimination
The denial of opportunities and equal rights to individuals and groups because of prejudice or for other arbitrary reasons.

themselves. However, hate crime legislation does not affect such outlets, because of legal questions involving freedom of speech. An even more recent technique has been to use instant messaging software, which enables Internet users to create a private chat room with another individual. Enterprising bigots use directories to target their attacks through instant messaging, much as harassing telephone calls were placed in the past. Even more creative and subtle are people who have constructed Web sites to attract people who are surfing for information on Martin Luther King, Jr., only to find a site that looks educational but savagely discredits the civil rights activist. A close inspection will reveal that the site is hosted by a White-supremacist organization (M. Davis 2008; Simon Wiesenthal Center 2008; Working 2007).

What causes people to dislike entire groups of other people? Is it possible to change attitudes? This chapter tries to answer these questions about prejudice. Chapter 3 focuses on discrimination.

Prejudice and Discrimination

Prejudice and discrimination are related concepts but are not the same. **Prejudice** is a negative attitude toward an entire category of people. The two important components in this definition are *attitude* and *entire category*. Prejudice involves attitudes, thoughts, and beliefs, not actions. Prejudice often is expressed through the use of **ethnophaulisms**, or ethnic slurs, which include derisive nicknames such as *honky, gook,* and *wetback*. Ethnophaulisms also include speaking to or about members of a particular group in a condescending way, such as saying "José does well in school for a Mexican American" or referring to a middle-aged woman as "one of the girls."

A prejudiced belief leads to categorical rejection. Prejudice is not disliking someone you meet because you find his or her behavior objectionable. It is disliking an entire racial or ethnic group, even if you have had little or no contact with that group. A college student who requests a room change after three weeks of enduring his roommate's sleeping all day, playing loud music all night, and piling garbage on his desk is not prejudiced. However, he is displaying prejudice if he requests a change on arriving at school and learning that his new roommate is of a different nationality.

Prejudice is a belief or attitude; discrimination is action. **Discrimination** is the denial of opportunities and equal rights to individuals and groups because of prejudice or for other arbitrary reasons. Unlike prejudice, discrimination involves *behavior* that excludes members of a group from certain rights, opportunities, or privileges. Like prejudice, it is categorical, perhaps making for a few rare exceptions. If an employer refuses to hire as a computer analyst an Italian American who is illiterate, it is not discrimination. If an employer refuses to hire any Italian American because he or she thinks they are incompetent and does not make the effort to see whether an applicant is qualified, it is discrimination.

Merton's Typology

Prejudice does not necessarily coincide with discriminatory behavior. In exploring the relationship between negative attitudes and negative behavior, sociologist Robert Merton (1949, 1976) identified four major categories (Figure 2.2). The label added to each of Merton's categories may more readily identify the type of person being described. These are

1. the unprejudiced nondiscriminator—or all-weather liberal;
2. the unprejudiced discriminator—or reluctant liberal;
3. the prejudiced nondiscriminator—or timid bigot; and
4. the prejudiced discriminator—or all-weather bigot.

As the term is used in types 1 and 2, liberals are committed to equality among people. The all-weather liberal believes in equality and practices it. Merton was quick to observe that all-weather liberals may be far removed from any real competition with subordinate

Suppose you encounter a person whose prejudice is obvious? Will you say or do anything? What if it is a friend who speaks disparagingly of all members of some ethnic or religious group? Will you speak out? When do you speak out?

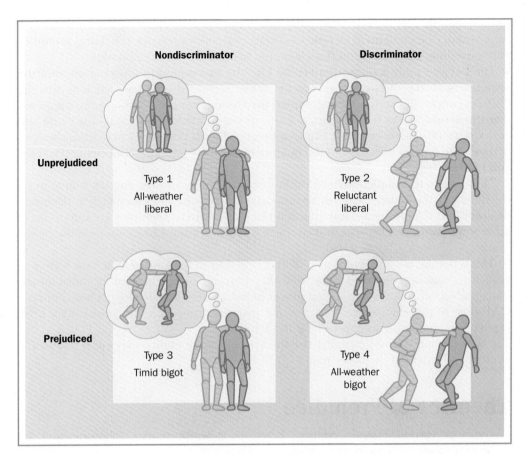

FIGURE 2.2
Prejudice and Discrimination
As sociologist Robert Merton's formulation shows, prejudice and discrimination are related to each other but are not the same.

groups such as African Americans or women. Furthermore, such people may be content with their own behavior and may do little to change themselves. The reluctant liberal is not that committed to equality between groups. Social pressure may cause such a person to discriminate. Fear of losing employees may lead a manager to avoid promoting women to supervisory capacities. Equal-opportunity legislation may be the best way to influence the reluctant liberals.

Types 3 and 4 do not believe in equal treatment for racial and ethnic groups, but they vary in their willingness to act. The timid bigot, type 3, will not discriminate if discrimination costs money or reduces profits or if he or she is pressured not to by peers or the government. The all-weather bigot unhesitatingly acts on the prejudiced beliefs he or she holds.

LaPiere's Study

Merton's typology points out that attitudes should not be confused with behavior. People do not always act as they believe. More than a half century ago, Richard LaPiere (1934, 1969) exposed the relationship between racial attitudes and social conduct. From 1930 to 1932, LaPiere traveled throughout the United States with a Chinese couple. Despite an alleged climate of intolerance of Asians, LaPiere observed that the couple was treated courteously at hotels, motels, and restaurants. He was puzzled by the good reception they received; all the conventional attitude surveys showed extreme prejudice by Whites toward the Chinese.

Was it possible that LaPiere had been fortunate during his travels and consistently stopped at places operated by the tolerant members of the dominant group? To test this possibility, he sent questionnaires asking the very establishments at which they had been served whether the owner would "accept members of the Chinese race as guests in your establishment." More than 90 percent responded no, even though LaPiere's

Chinese couple had been treated politely at all of these establishments. How can this inconsistency be explained? People who returned questionnaires reflecting prejudice were unwilling to act based on those asserted beliefs; they were timid bigots.

The LaPiere study is not without flaws. First, he had no way of knowing whether the respondent to the questionnaire was the same person who had served him and the Chinese couple. Second, he accompanied the couple, but the questionnaire suggested that the arrival would be unescorted (and, in the minds of some, uncontrolled) and perhaps would consist of many Chinese people. Third, personnel may have changed between the time of the visit and the mailing of the questionnaire (Deutscher, Pestello, and Pestello 1993).

The LaPiere technique has been replicated with similar results. This technique raises the question of whether attitudes are important if they are not completely reflected in behavior. But if attitudes are not important in small matters, then they are important in other ways: lawmakers legislate and courts may reach decisions based on what the public thinks.

This is not just a hypothetical possibility. Legislators in the United States often are persuaded to vote in a certain way by what they perceive to be changed attitudes toward immigration, affirmative action, and prayer in public schools. Sociologists have enumerated some of prejudice's functions. For the majority group, it serves to maintain privileged occupations and more power for its members.

The following sections examine the theories of why prejudice exists and discuss the content and extent of prejudice today.

Theories of Prejudice

Prejudice is learned. Friends, relatives, newspapers, books, movies, television, and the Internet all teach it. Awareness begins at an early age that there are differences between people that society judges to be important. Several theories have been advanced to explain the rejection of certain groups in a society. We will examine four theoretical explanations. The first two (scapegoating and authoritarian personality) tend to be psychological, emphasizing why a particular person harbors ill feelings. The second two are more sociological (exploitation and normative), viewing prejudice in the context of our interaction in a larger society.

Scapegoating Theory

Some expressions of prejudice are so that people can blame others and refuse to accept responsibility. **Scapegoating theory** says that prejudiced people believe they are society's victims.

The term *scapegoat* comes from a biblical injunction telling the Hebrews to send a goat into the wilderness to symbolically carry away the people's sins. Similarly, the theory of scapegoating suggests that, rather than accepting guilt for some failure, a person transfers the responsibility for failure to some vulnerable group. In the major tragic twentieth-century example, Adolf Hitler used the Jews as the scapegoat for all German social and economic ills in the 1930s. This premise led to the passage of laws restricting Jewish life in pre–World War II Germany and eventually escalated into the mass extermination of Europe's Jews.

Today in the United States, both legal and illegal immigrants often are blamed by "real Americans" for their failure to secure jobs or desirable housing. The immigrant becomes the scapegoat for one's own lack of skills, planning, or motivation. It is so much easier to blame someone else.

Public figures who should know better express their ill feelings. Longtime civil rights leader Andrew Young, in 2006, applauded the expansion of Wal-Mart, noting that the big-box stores were merely replacing small stores run by Jews, Koreans, and Arabs that ripped off customers. In the same year, a drunk Mel Gibson was pulled over by a police officer who was Jewish and told him that "Jews are responsible for all the wars in the world." Both Young

scapegoating theory
A person or group blamed irrationally for another person's or group's problems or difficulties.

and Gibson quickly apologized for their inflammatory remarks, but finding scapegoats among racial and ethnic groups occurs all the time (McGhee 2006; McNamara 2006).

Authoritarian Personality Theory

Prejudice may be influenced by one's upbringing and the lessons taught early in life. Several efforts have been made to detail the prejudiced personality, but the most comprehensive effort culminated in a volume titled *The Authoritarian Personality* (Adorno et al. 1950). Using a variety of tests and relying on more than 2,000 respondents, ranging from middle-class Whites to inmates of San Quentin (California) State Prison, the authors claimed they had isolated the characteristics of the authoritarian personality.

In these authors' view, the basic characteristics of the **authoritarian personality** construct a personality type that is likely to be prejudiced. It encompasses adherence to conventional values, uncritical acceptance of authority, and concern with power and toughness. With obvious relevance to the development of intolerance, the authoritarian personality was also characterized by aggressiveness toward people who did not conform to conventional norms or obey authority. According to the researchers, this personality type developed from an early childhood of harsh discipline. A child with an authoritarian upbringing obeyed and then later treated others as he or she had been raised.

This study has been widely criticized, but the very existence of such wide criticism indicates the influence of the study. Critics have attacked the study's equation of authoritarianism with right-wing politics (although liberals can also be rigid); its failure to see that prejudice is more closely related to other individual traits, such as social class, than to authoritarianism as it was defined; the research methods used; and the emphasis on extreme racial prejudice rather than on more-common expressions of hostility.

Despite these concerns about specifics in the study completed 60 years ago, annual conferences continue to draw attention to how authoritarian attitudes contribute to racism, sexism, and even torture (Kinloch 1974; O'Neill 2008).

Exploitation Theory

Racial prejudice is often used to justify keeping a group in a subordinate economic position. Conflict theorists, in particular, stress the role of racial and ethnic hostility as a way for the dominant group to keep its position of status and power intact. Indeed, this approach maintains that even the less-affluent White working class uses prejudice to minimize competition from upwardly mobile minorities.

This **exploitation theory** is clearly part of the Marxist tradition in sociological thought. Karl Marx emphasized exploitation of the lower class as an integral part of capitalism. Similarly, the exploitation or conflict approach explains how racism can stigmatize a group as inferior so that the exploitation of that group can be justified. As developed by Oliver Cox (1942), exploitation theory saw prejudice against Blacks as an extension of the inequality faced by the entire lower class.

The exploitation theory of prejudice is persuasive. Japanese Americans were the object of little prejudice until they began to enter occupations that brought them into competition with Whites. The movement to keep Chinese out of the country became strongest during the late nineteenth century, when Chinese immigrants and Whites fought over dwindling numbers of jobs. Both the enslavement of African Americans and the removal westward of Native Americans were to a significant degree economically motivated.

Normative Approach

Although personality factors are important contributors to prejudice, normative or situational factors must also be given serious consideration. The **normative approach** takes the view that prejudice is influenced by societal norms and situations that encourage or discourage the tolerance of minorities.

authoritarian personality
A psychological construct of a personality type likely to be prejudiced and to use others as scapegoats.

exploitation theory
A Marxist theory that views racial subordination in the United States as a manifestation of the class system inherent in capitalism.

normative approach
The view that prejudice is influenced by societal norms and situations that encourage or discourage the tolerance of minorities.

TABLE 2.1
Theories of Prejudice

There is no one satisfactory explanation of why prejudice exists, but several approaches taken together offer insight.

Theory	Explanation	Example
Scapegoating	People blame others for their own failures.	An unsuccessful applicant assumes that a minority member or a woman got "his" job.
Authoritarian	Child rearing leads one to develop intolerance as an adult.	The rigid personality type dislikes people who are different.
Exploitation	People use others unfairly for economic advantage.	A minority member is hired at a lower wage level.
Normative	Peer and social influences encourage tolerance or intolerance.	A person from an intolerant household is more likely to be openly prejudiced.

Analysis reveals how societal influences shape a climate for tolerance or intolerance. Societies develop social norms that dictate not only what foods are desirable (or forbidden) but also what racial and ethnic groups are to be favored (or despised). Social forces operate in a society to encourage or discourage tolerance. The force may be widespread, such as the pressure on White Southerners to oppose racial equality even though there was slavery or segregation. The influence of social norms may be limited, as when one man finds himself becoming more sexist as he competes with three women for a position in a prestigious law firm.

We should not view the four approaches to prejudice summarized in Table 2.1 as mutually exclusive. Social circumstances provide cues for a person's attitudes; personality determines the extent to which people follow social cues and the likelihood that they will encourage others to do the same. Societal norms may promote or deter tolerance; personality traits suggest the degree to which a person will conform to norms of intolerance. To understand prejudice, we need to use all four approaches together.

Stereotypes

On Christmas Day 2001, Arab American Walied Shater boarded an American Airlines flight from Baltimore to Dallas carrying a gun. Immediately, the cockpit crew refused to let him fly, fearing that Shater would take over the plane and use it as a weapon of mass destruction. Yet Walied Shater carried documentation that he was a Secret Service agent, and calls to Washington, D.C., confirmed that he was flying to join a presidential protection force at President George W. Bush's ranch in Texas. Nevertheless, the crew could not get past the stereotype of Arab American men posing a lethal threat (Leavitt 2002).

What Are Stereotypes?

stereotypes
Unreliable, exaggerated generalizations about all members of a group that do not take individual differences into account.

In Chapter 1, we saw that stereotypes play a powerful role in how people come to view dominant and subordinate groups. **Stereotypes** are unreliable generalizations about all members of a group that do not take individual differences into account. Numerous scientific studies have been made of these exaggerated images. This research has shown the willingness of people to assign positive and negative traits to entire groups of people, which are then applied to particular individuals. Stereotyping causes people to view Blacks as superstitious, Whites as uncaring, and Jews as shrewd. Over the last 80 years of such research, social scientists have found that people have become less willing to express such views openly, but prejudice persists, as we will see later (Quillian 2006).

Listen to Our Voices

NATIONAL MEDIA SHOULD STOP USING OBSCENE WORDS

I am just sick and tired of hearing students and faculty from schools using Indians as mascots say they are doing it to "honor us. . . ."

Who or what is a redskin? It is a derogatory name for a race of people. It's as simple as that. It is akin to the racist names "nigger" or "gook" or "kike" or "wop." It is not, I repeat NOT, an honor to be called a racist name nor is it an honor to see football fans dressed in supposed Indian attire nor to hear them trumpeting some ludicrous war chant nor to see them mimic or ape our dress, culture, or person.

When I saw the Florida State fans doing the ridiculous "tomahawk chop" and heard their Johnny-one-note band play that asinine version of an Indian song over and over, I was heartsick. I was also highly embarrassed for the people of the Seminole Nation of Florida for allowing their good name to be taken in vain.

I am also sick and tired of fanatical sports fans telling Indians who object to this kind of treatment to "lighten up." You know, I didn't hear those same White folks saying this to African Americans in the 1960s when they were objecting to the hideous Black caricature at Sambo's Restaurants or to the Step-in-Fetch-It character used so often in the early movie days to portray Blacks as dimwitted, shiftless people. I didn't hear anybody tell them to "lighten up."

Tim Giago

However, 2000 did give us (Indians) a little reprieve. The Cleveland Indians and their hideous mascot were clobbered and didn't make the playoffs. The Washington Redskins turned into the Washington "Deadskins." The Kansas City Chiefs were real losers. And almost best of all, the Florida State Seminoles were steamrolled by an Oklahoma team with real Indians serving as bodyguards to the Oklahoma coach Bob Stoops. My thrill at watching the Seminoles lose was topped only by watching Ted Turner's Atlanta Braves get "tomahawked" this year. Now that was truly an "honor. . . ."

Webster's Ninth New Collegiate Dictionary, note the word "collegiate" here, reads the word *redskin* quite simply as "American Indian usually taken to be offensive."

"Usually taken to be offensive." Now what is so hard to understand about this literal translation of the word "redskin"?

Attention major newspapers, CNN, Fox, ABC, CBS and NBC: the word "redskin" is an obscenity to Indians and to people who are sensitive to racism. It is translated by *Webster's* to be offensive. Now what other proof do you need to discontinue its usage?

Source: "National Media Should Stop Using Obscene Words" by Tim Giago, as reprinted in *The Denver Post,* January 21, 2001. Copyright © 2001 by Tim Giago. Reprinted by permission of Tim Giago.

If stereotypes are exaggerated generalizations, then why are they so widely held, and why are some traits more often assigned than others? Evidence for traits may arise out of real conditions. For example, more Puerto Ricans live in poverty than Whites, and so the prejudiced mind associates Puerto Ricans with laziness. According to the New Testament, some Jews were responsible for the crucifixion of Jesus, and so, to the prejudiced mind, all Jews are Christ killers. Some activists in the women's movement are lesbians, and so all feminists are seen as lesbians. From a kernel of fact, faulty generalization creates a stereotype.

In "Listen to Our Voices," journalist Tim Giago, born a member of the Oglala Sioux tribe on the Pine Ridge Reservation, comments on the use by college and professional teams of mascots patterned after American Indians. He finds the use neither harmless nor providing honor to the tribal people of the United States.

Power of Stereotypes

The labeling of individuals through negative stereotypes has strong implications for the self-fulfilling prophecy. Studies show that people are all too aware of the negative images other people have of them. When asked to estimate the prevalence of hard-core racism among Whites, one in four Blacks agrees that more than half "personally share the attitudes of groups like the Ku Klux Klan toward Blacks"; only one Black in 10 says "only a few" share such views. Stereotypes not only influence how people feel about themselves but also, and perhaps equally important, affect how people interact with others. If people feel that others hold incorrect, disparaging attitudes toward them, then it undoubtedly makes it difficult to have harmonious relations (Sigelman and Tuch 1997).

Do only dominant groups hold stereotypes about subordinate groups? The answer is clearly no. White Americans even believe generalizations about themselves, although admittedly these are usually positive. Subordinate groups also hold exaggerated images of themselves. Studies before World War II showed a tendency for Blacks to assign to themselves many of the same negative traits assigned by Whites. Today, African Americans, Jews, Asians, and other minority groups largely reject stereotypes of themselves.

Although explicit expressions of stereotypes are less common, it is much too soon to write the obituary of racial and ethnic stereotypes. In Chapter 6, we will consider the persistence of two stereotypes: the model minority and acting White. Here we will next consider the use of stereotypes in the contemporary practice of racial profiling.

Stereotyping in Action: Racial Profiling

A Black dentist, Elmo Randolph, testified before a state commission that he was stopped dozens of times in the 1980s and 1990s while traveling the New Jersey Turnpike to work. Invariably state troopers asked, "Do you have guns or drugs?" "My parents always told me, be careful when you're driving on the turnpike," said Dr. Randolph, 44. "White people don't have that conversation" (Purdy 2001, 37; also see Fernandez and Fahim 2006).

Little wonder that Dr. Randolph was pulled over. Although African Americans accounted for only 17 percent of the motorists on that turnpike, they were 80 percent of the motorists pulled over. Such occurrences gave rise to the charge that a new traffic offense was added to the books: DWB, or "driving while Black" (Bowles 2000).

In recent years, government attention has been given to a social phenomenon with a long history: racial profiling. According to the Department of Justice, **racial profiling** is any police-initiated action based on race, ethnicity, or national origin rather than the person's behavior. Generally, profiling occurs when law enforcement officers, including customs officials, airport security, and police, assume that people fitting certain descriptions are likely to be engaged in something illegal. Beginning in the 1980s with the emergence of the crack cocaine market, skin color became a key characteristic. This profiling can be a very explicit use of stereotypes. For example, the federal antidrug initiative, Operation Pipeline, specifically encouraged officers to look for people with dreadlocks and for Latino men traveling together.

racial profiling
Any arbitrary police-initiated action based on race, ethnicity, or natural origin rather than a person's behavior.

The reliance on racial profiling persists despite overwhelming evidence that it is misleading. Whites are more likely to be found with drugs in the areas in which minority group members are disproportionately targeted. A federal study made public in 2005 found little difference nationwide in the likelihood of being stopped by officers, but African Americans were twice as likely to have their vehicles searched, and Latinos were

Ask yourself, how do the images we see affect how we view people? On the left is a scene from the familiar motion picture *The King and I*. On the right is the real monarch, King Chulalongkorn, and his son. The king in real life bore limited similarity to the portrayal made famous by the Russian-born actor Yul Brynner. Is what we know about many ethnic and religious groups more likely the result of portrayals in the popular media than any actual study of their history and customs?

five times more likely. A similar pattern emerged in the likelihood of force being used against drivers: it was three times more likely with Latinos and Blacks than with White drivers. A 2007 study of New York City police officers found that Whites and racial minorities are equally likely to be stopped, but the officers were more likely to frisk, search, arrest, or give summonses to Black and Latino people (Lichtblau 2005; Ridgeway 2007).

Back in the 1990s, increased attention to racial profiling led not only to special reports and commissions but also to talk of legislating against it. This proved difficult. The U.S. Supreme Court in *Whren v. United States* (1996) upheld the constitutionality of using a minor traffic infraction as an excuse to stop and search a vehicle and its passengers. Nonetheless, states and other government units are discussing policies and training that would discourage racial profiling. At the same time, most law enforcement agencies reject the idea of compiling racial data on traffic stops, arguing that it would be a waste of money and staff time.

The effort to stop racial profiling came to an abrupt end after the September 11, 2001, terrorist attacks on the United States. Suspicions about Muslims and Arabs in the United States became widespread. Foreign students from Arab countries were summoned for special questioning. Legal immigrants identified as Arab or Muslim were scrutinized for any illegal activity and were prosecuted for routine immigration violations that were ignored for people of other ethnic backgrounds and religious faiths (Withrow 2006).

National surveys have found little change since 2001 in support for profiling Arab Americans at airports. In 2006, 53 percent of Americans favored requiring Arabs, including those who are U.S. citizens, to undergo special and more-intensive security checks before boarding planes in the United States (Saad 2006b).

Color-Blind Racism

Over the last three generations, nationwide surveys have consistently shown growing support by Whites for integration, interracial dating, and having members of minority groups attain political office, including even becoming president of the United States. Yet how can this be true and the type of hatred described at the beginning of the chapter persist and thousands of hate crimes occur annually?

Color-blind racism refers to the use of race-neutral principles to defend the racially unequal status quo. Yes, there should be "no discrimination for college admission," yet

color-blind racism
Use of race-neutral principles to defend the racially unequal status quo.

Color-blind racism can take many forms. Why should the United States not have an official language as most nations do? Typically, calls today for English as the official language reassert values superior to someone else's. Here we see a meeting at a Wisconsin county making English the official language—a move with little practical significance but one that speaks loudly in terms of symbolism in an area with a large presence of Hmong, a South Asian ethnic group from Laos.

the disparity in educational experiences means that the use of formal admissions criteria will privilege White high school graduates. "Health care is for all," but if you fail to have workplace insurance, you are unlikely to afford it.

Color-blind racism has also been referred to as "laissez-faire" or "postracialism" or "aversive racism," but the common theme is that notions of racial inferiority are rarely expressed and that proceeding color-blind into the future will serve to perpetuate inequality. In the post–civil rights era and with the election of President Barack Obama, people are more likely to assume discrimination is long past and express views that are more proper—that is, lacking the overt expressions of racism of the past.

An important aspect of color-blind racism is the recognition that race is rarely invoked in public debates on social issues. Instead, people emphasize lower social class or the lack of citizenship or illegal aliens; these descriptions serve, in effect, as proxies for race. Furthermore, the emphasis is on individuals failing rather than recognizing patterns of groups being disadvantaged. This leads many White people to declare they are not racist and that they really do not know anyone who is racist. It leads to the mistaken conclusion that more progress has been made toward racial and ethnic equality and even tolerance than has really taken place.

When we survey White attitudes toward African Americans, three conclusions are inescapable. First, attitudes are subject to change; during periods of dramatic social upheaval, dramatic shifts can occur within one generation. Second, less progress was made in the late twentieth and the beginning of the twentieth-first centuries than was made in the relatively brief period of the 1950s and 1960s. Third, the pursuit of a color-blind agenda has created lower levels of support for politics that could reduce racial inequality if implemented.

Economically less-successful groups such as African Americans and Latinos have been associated with negative traits to the point that issues such as urban decay, homelessness, welfare, and crime are now viewed as race issues even though race is rarely spoken of explicitly. Besides making the resolution of very difficult social issues even harder, this is another instance of blaming the victim. These perceptions come at a time when the willingness of the government to address domestic ills is limited by increasing opposition to new taxes and continuing commitments to fight terrorism here and abroad. The color line remains even if more and more people are unwilling to accept its divisive impact on everyone's lives (Ansell 2008; Bonilla-Silva 2006, 2008; Bonilla-Silva and Baiocchi 2001; Dovidio 2001; Ferber 2007; Krysan 1998; Mazzocco et al. 2006; Quillian 2006; Winant 2004, 106–108).

The Mood of the Oppressed

Sociologist W. E. B. Du Bois relates an experience from his youth in a largely White community in Massachusetts. He tells how, on one occasion, the boys and girls were exchanging cards, and everyone was having a lot of fun. One girl, a newcomer, refused his card as soon as she saw that Du Bois was Black. He wrote,

Then it dawned upon me with a certain suddenness that I was different from others . . . shut out from their world by a vast veil. I had therefore no desire to tear down that veil, to creep through; I held all beyond it in common contempt and lived above it in a region of blue sky and great wandering shadows. (Du Bois 1903, 2)

In using the image of a veil, Du Bois describes how members of subordinate groups learn that they are being treated differently. In his case and that of many others, this leads to feelings of contempt toward all Whites that continue for a lifetime.

Opinion pollsters have been interested in White attitudes on racial issues longer than they have measured the views of subordinate groups. This neglect of minority attitudes reflects, in part, the bias of the White researchers. It also stems from the contention that the dominant group is more important to study because it is in a better position to act on its beliefs. The results of a nationwide survey conducted in the United States in 2007 offer insight into sharply different views on the state of race relations today (Figure 2.3). Latinos, African Americans, and Asian Americans all have strong reservations about the state of race relations in the United States. They are skeptical about the level of equal opportunity and perceive a lot of discrimination. It is interesting to note that Hispanics and Asian Americans, overwhelmingly immigrants, are more likely to feel they will succeed if they work hard. Yet the majority of all three groups have a positive outlook for the next 10 years (New America Media 2007; Preston 2007b).

National surveys showed that the 2008 presidential bid of Senator Barack Obama led to a sense of optimism and national pride among African Americans even though political observers saw Obama running a race-neutral campaign and rarely addressing issues specifically of concern to African Americans. Unlike Whites or Hispanics, Black voters still saw his campaign as addressing issues important to the Black community. Survey researchers will be closely following these perceptions in the 2008 election aftermath (ISERP 2008).

We have focused so far on what usually comes to mind when we think about prejudice: one group hating another group. But there is another form of prejudice: a group may come to hate itself. Members of groups held in low esteem by society may, as a result, either hate themselves or have low self-esteem themselves, as many social scientists once believed. Similarly, these theorists argued that Whites had high self-esteem, meaning that an individual has fundamental respect for him- or herself, appreciates his or her own merits, and is aware of personal faults and will strive to overcome them. Indeed, the research literature of the 1940s through the 1960s emphasized the low self-esteem of minorities. Usually, the subject was African Americans, but the argument has also been generalized to include any subordinate racial, ethnic, or nationality group.

This view is no longer accepted. We should not assume that minority status influences personality traits in either a good or a bad way. First, such assumptions may create a stereotype. We cannot describe a Black personality any more accurately than we can a White personality. Second, characteristics of minority-group members are not entirely the result of subordinate racial status; they are also influenced by low incomes, poor neighborhoods, and so forth. Third, many studies of personality imply that certain values are normal or preferable, but the values chosen are those of dominant groups.

If assessments of a subordinate group's personality are so prone to misjudgments, then why has the belief in low self-esteem been so widely held? Much of the research rests on studies with preschool-aged Black children asked them to express their preferences for dolls with different facial colors. Indeed, one such study by psychologists Kenneth and Mamie Clark (1947) was cited in the arguments before the U.S. Supreme Court in the landmark 1954 case *Brown v. Board of Education*. The Clarks' study showed that Black children preferred White dolls, a finding suggesting that the children had developed a negative

How do children come to develop an image about themselves? Toys and playthings play an important role, and for many children of racial and ethnic minorities, it is unusual to find toys that look like them. In 2005, a new doll was released called Fulla—an Arab who reflects modesty, piety, and respect, yet underneath she wears chic clothes that might be typically worn by a Muslim woman in private.

FIGURE 2.3

What Is the State of Race Relations? Three Views

Note: Answers of "very important problem" or "strongly agree" with statements listed. Based on 1,105 interviews in August–September 2007, with bilingual questioners used as necessary.

Source: New America Media 2007, 6, 12, 14, 24, 26.

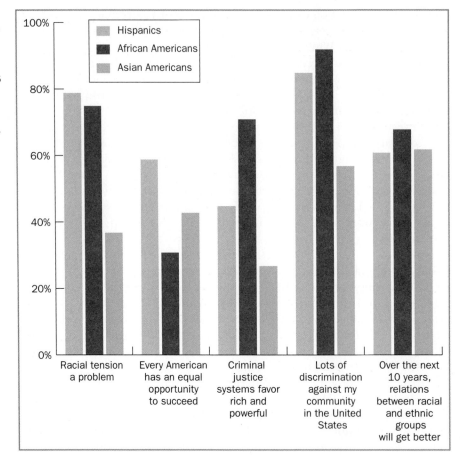

self-image. Although subsequent doll studies have sometimes shown Black children's preference for white-faced dolls, other social scientists contend that this shows a realization of what most commercially sold dolls look like rather than documenting low self-esteem (Bloom 1971; Powell-Hopson and Hopson 1988).

Because African American children, as well as other subordinate groups' children, can realistically see that Whites have more power and resources and, therefore, rate them higher does not mean that they personally feel inferior. Indeed, studies, even those with children, show that when the self-images of middle-class or affluent African Americans are measured, their feelings of self-esteem are more positive than those of comparable Whites (Gray-Little and Hafdahl 2000).

Intergroup Hostility

Prejudice is as diverse as the nation's population. It exists not only between dominant and subordinate peoples but also between specific subordinate groups. Unfortunately, until recently little research existed on this subject except for a few social distance scales administered to racial and ethnic minorities.

A national survey revealed that, like Whites, many African Americans, Hispanic Americans, and Asian Americans held prejudiced and stereotypical views of other racial and ethnic minority groups:

■ Majorities of Black, Hispanic, and Asian American respondents agreed that Whites are "bigoted, bossy, and unwilling to share power." Majorities of these non-White groups also believed that they had less opportunity than Whites to obtain a good education, a skilled job, or decent housing.

■ Forty-six percent of Hispanic Americans and 42 percent of African Americans agreed that Asian Americans are "unscrupulous, crafty, and devious in business."

- Sixty-eight percent of Asian Americans and 49 percent of African Americans believed that Hispanic Americans "tend to have bigger families than they are able to support."

- Thirty-one percent of Asian Americans and 26 percent of Hispanic Americans agreed that African Americans "want to live on welfare."

Members of oppressed groups obviously have adopted the widely held beliefs of the dominant culture concerning oppressed groups. At the same time, the survey also revealed positive views of major racial and ethnic minorities:

- More than 80 percent of respondents admired Asian Americans for "placing a high value on intellectual and professional achievement" and "having strong family ties."

- A majority of all groups surveyed agreed that Hispanic Americans "take deep pride in their culture and work hard to achieve a better life."

- Large majorities from all groups stated that African Americans "have made a valuable contribution to American society and will work hard when given a chance" (National Conference of Christians and Jews 1994).

Do we get along? Although this question often is framed in terms of the relationships between White Americans and other racial and ethnic groups, we should recognize the prejudice between groups. In a national survey conducted in 2000, people were asked whether they felt they could generally get along with members of other groups. In Figure 2.4, we can see that Whites felt they had the most difficulty getting along with Blacks. We also see the different views that Blacks, Latinos, Asian Americans, and American Indians hold toward other groups.

It is curious that we find that some groups feel they get along better with Whites than with other minority groups. Why would that be? Often, low-income people are competing daily with other low-income people and do not readily see the larger societal forces that contribute to their low status. As we can see from the survey results, many Hispanics are more likely to see Asian Americans as getting in their way than the White Americans, who are actually the real decision makers in their community.

Most troubling is when intergroup hostility becomes violent. Ethnic and racial tension among African Americans, Latinos, and immigrants may become manifest in hate crimes. Violence can surface in neighborhoods where there is competition for scarce resources such as jobs and housing. Gangs become organized along racial lines, much like private clubs "downtown." In recent years, Los Angeles has been particularly concerned about rival Black and Hispanic gangs. Conflict theorists see this violence as resulting from larger structural forces, but for the average person in such areas, life itself becomes more of a challenge (Archibold 2007).

Members of racial and ethnic minorities do not often appear on a regular basis in starring roles on television drama and comedy shows; when they do, it is often in roles that reflect negative stereotypes.

Reducing Prejudice

Focusing on how to eliminate prejudice involves an explicit value judgment: prejudice is wrong and causes problems for those who are prejudiced and for their victims. The obvious way to eliminate prejudice is to eliminate its causes: the desire to exploit, the fear of being threatened, and the need to blame others for one's own failure. These might be eliminated by personal therapy, but therapy, even if it works for every individual, is no solution for an entire society in which prejudice is a part of everyday life.

The answer appears to rest with programs directed at society as a whole. Prejudice is attacked indirectly when discrimination is attacked. Despite prevailing beliefs to the contrary, we *can* legislate against prejudice: statutes and decisions do affect attitudes. In the past, people firmly believed that laws could not overcome norms, especially racist ones. Recent history, especially after the

FIGURE 2.4

Do We Get Along?

Percentage saying groups get along with each other ("Don't Knows" excluded).

[1] Sample size for American Indians is very small and subject to large sample variance.

Note: The wording of the question was, "We hear a lot these days about how various groups in society get along with each other. I'm going to mention several groups and ask whether you think they generally get along with each other or generally do not get along with each other." So, in the "Asked of White Respondents" graph, Whites are asked how Whites get along with each ethnic group; in the "Asked of Black Respondents" graph, Blacks are asked how Blacks get along with each ethnic group, and so on.

Source: T. Smith 2006, 65. Reprinted by permission of the author.

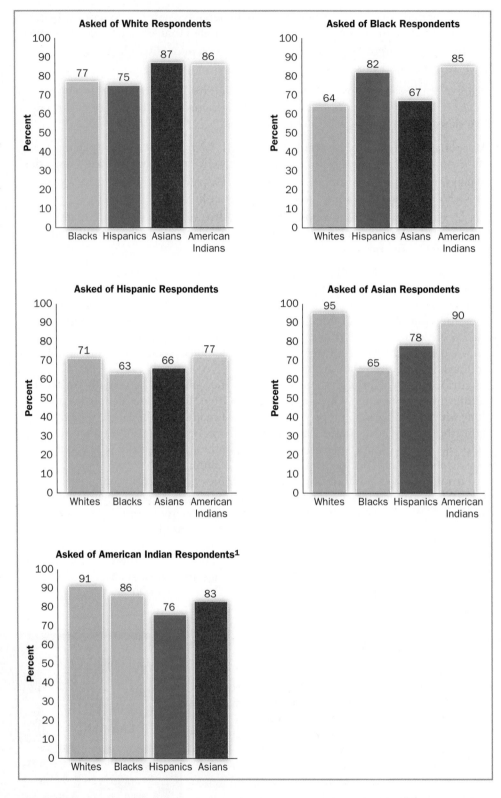

civil rights movement began in 1954, has challenged that common wisdom. Laws and court rulings that have equalized the treatment of Blacks and Whites have led people to reevaluate their beliefs about what is right and wrong. The increasing tolerance by Whites during the civil rights era from 1954 to 1965 seems to support this conclusion.

Much research has been done to determine how to change negative attitudes toward groups of people. The most encouraging findings point to education, mass media, intergroup contact, and workplace training programs.

Education

Research on education and prejudice considers special programs aimed at promoting mutual respect as well as what effect more formal schooling generally has on expressions of bigotry.

Most research studies show that well-constructed programs do have some positive effect in reducing prejudice, at least temporarily. The reduction is rarely as much as one might wish, however. The difficulty is that a single program is insufficient to change life-long habits, especially if little is done to reinforce the program's message once it ends. Persuasion to respect other groups does not operate in a clear field because, in their ordinary environments, people are still subjected to situations that promote prejudicial feelings. Children and adults are encouraged to laugh at Polish jokes and cheer for a team named "Redskins." Black adolescents may be discouraged by peers from befriending a White youth. All this undermines the effectiveness of prejudice-reduction programs (Allport 1979).

Studies document that increased formal education, regardless of content, is associated with racial tolerance. Research data show that highly educated people are more likely to indicate respect and liking for groups different from themselves. Why should more years of schooling have this effect? It could be that more education gives a broader outlook and makes a person less likely to endorse myths that sustain racial prejudice. Formal education teaches the importance of qualifying statements and the need to question rigid categorizations, if not reject them altogether. Colleges increasingly include a graduation requirement that students complete a course that explores diversity or multiculturalism. Another explanation is that education does not actually reduce intolerance but simply makes people more careful about revealing it. Formal education may simply instruct people in the appropriate responses, which in some settings could even be prejudiced views. Despite the lack of a clear-cut explanation, either theory suggests that the continued trend toward a better-educated population will contribute to a reduction in overt prejudice.

However, college education may not reduce prejudice uniformly. For example, some White students will come to believe that minority students did not earn their admission into college. Students may feel threatened to see large groups of people of different racial and cultural backgrounds congregating together and forming their own groups. Racist confrontations do occur outside the classroom and, even if they do involve only a few individuals, the events themselves will be followed by hundreds more. Therefore, some aspects of the college experience may only foster "we" and "they" attitudes (Schaefer 1986, 1996).

Mass Media

Mass media, like schools, may reduce prejudice without requiring specially designed programs. Television, radio, motion pictures, newspapers, magazines, and the Internet present only a portion of real life, but what effect do they have on prejudice if the content is racist or antiracist, sexist or antisexist? As with measuring the influence of programs designed to reduce prejudice, coming to strong conclusions on mass media's effect is hazardous, but the evidence points to a measurable effect.

Today, 40 percent of all youths in the nation are children of color, yet few of the faces they see on television reflect their race or cultural heritage. As of spring 2007, only five of the nearly 60 primetime series carried on the four major networks featured performers of color in leading roles, and only two—*Ugly Betty* and *George Lopez*—focused on minority performers. What is more, the programs that show earlier in the evening, when young people are most likely to watch television, are the least diverse of all.

Why the underrepresentation? Incredibly, network executives seemed surprised by the research demonstrating an all-White season. Producers, writers, executives, and advertisers blamed each other for the alleged oversight. In recent years, the rise of both cable television and the Internet has fragmented the broadcast entertainment market,

We often are unaware of all the social situations that allow us to meet people of different ethnic and racial backgrounds. Such opportunities may increase understanding.

siphoning viewers away from the general-audience sitcoms and dramas of the past. With the proliferation of cable channels such as Black Entertainment Television (BET) and the Spanish-language Univision and Web sites that cater to every imaginable taste, there no longer seems to be a need for broadly popular series such as *The Cosby Show*, whose tone and content appealed to Whites as well as Blacks in a way that newer series do not. The result of these sweeping technological changes has been a sharp divergence in viewer preferences.

It is not surprising that young people quickly develop expectations of the roles that various racial and ethnic group members are likely to play in television and motion pictures. A national survey of teens (people ages 12 to 18) asked what characters members of racial and ethnic groups would be likely to play. The respondents' perception of media, as shown in Table 2.2, shows a significant amount of stereotyping occurring in their minds, in the media, or both.

Television series are only part of the picture. News broadcasting is done predominantly by Whites, and local news emphasizes crime often featuring Black or Hispanic perpetrators; print journalism is nearly the same. This is especially troubling given another finding in the study discussed at the beginning of the chapter. Research showed that people were quicker to "shoot" an armed Black person than a White man in a video stimulation. In another variation of that same study, the researchers showed subjects fake newspaper articles describing a string of armed robberies that showed either Black or White suspects. The subjects were quicker to "shoot" the armed suspect if he was Black but had no impact on their willingness to "shoot" the armed White criminal. This is a troubling aspect of the potential impact that media content may have (Correll et al. 2007b).

Avoidance versus Friendship

Is prejudice reduced or intensified when people cross racial and ethnic boundaries? Two parallel paths have been taken to look at this social distance and equal-status contact.

social distance
Tendency to approach or withdraw from a racial group.

Bogardus scale
Technique to measure social distance toward different racial and ethnic groups.

The Social Distance Scale Robert Park and Ernest Burgess first defined **social distance** as the tendency to approach or withdraw from a racial group (1921, 440). Emory Bogardus (1968) conceptualized a scale that could measure social distance empirically. His social distance scale is so widely used that it is often called the **Bogardus scale**.

The scale asks people how willing they would be to interact with various racial and ethnic groups in specified social situations. The situations describe different degrees of social contact or social distance. The items used, with their corresponding distance scores, follow. People are asked whether they would be willing to work alongside someone

TABLE 2.2

Stereotyping in the Twenty-First Century

When asked to identify the role a person of a particular ethnic or racial background would be most likely to play in a movie or on television, teenagers cited familiar stereotypes.

Group	Media Roles Identified
African American	Athlete, gang member, police officer
Arab American	Terrorist, convenience store clerk
Asian American	Physician, lawyer, CEO, factory worker
Hispanic	Gang member, factory worker
Irish American	Drunkard, police officer, factory worker
Italian American	Crime boss, gang member, restaurant worker
Jewish American	Physician, lawyer, CEO, teacher
Polish American	Factory worker

Note: Based on national survey of 1,264 people between ages 13 and 18.
Source: Zogby 2001.

or be a neighbor with someone of a different group, and, showing the least amount of social distance, be related through marriage. Over the 70-year period in which the tests were administered, certain patterns emerged. In the top third of the hierarchy are White Americans and northern Europeans. Held at greater social distance are eastern and southern Europeans, and generally near the bottom are racial minorities (Bogardus 1968; Song 1991; Wark and Galliher 2007).

Generally, the researchers also found that among the respondents who had friends of different racial and ethnic origin, they were more likely to show greater social distance—that is, they were less likely to have been in each other's homes, shared in fewer activities, and were less likely to talk about their problems with each other. This is unlikely to promote mutual understanding.

Equal Status Contact An impressive number of research studies have confirmed the **contact hypothesis**, which states that intergroup contact between people of equal status in harmonious circumstances will cause them to become less prejudiced and to abandon previously held stereotypes. Most studies indicate that such contact also improves the attitude of subordinate-group members. The importance of equal status in the interaction cannot be stressed enough. If a Puerto Rican is abused by his employer, little interracial harmony is promoted. Similarly, the situation in which contact occurs must be pleasant, making a positive evaluation likely for both individuals. Contact between two nurses, one Black and the other White, who are competing for one vacancy as a supervisor may lead to greater racial hostility (Schaefer 1976).

The key factor in reducing hostility, in addition to equal-status contact, is the presence of a common goal. If people are in competition, as already noted, contact may heighten tension. However, bringing people together to share a common task has been shown to reduce ill feelings when these people belong to different racial, ethnic, or religious groups. A study released in 2004 traced the transformations that occurred over the generations in the composition of the Social Service Employees Union in New York City. Always a mixed membership, the union was founded by Jews and Italian Americans, only to experience an influx of Black Americans. More recently, it comprises Latin Americans, Africans, West Indians, and South Asians. At each point, the common goals of representing the workers effectively overcame the very real cultural differences among the rank and file of Mexican and El Salvadoran immigrants in Houston. The researchers found when the new arrivals had contact with African Americans, intergroup relations generally improved, and the absence of contact tended to foster ambivalent, even negative, attitudes (Fine 2008; Foerstrer 2004; Sherif and Sherif 1969).

contact hypothesis
An interactionist perspective stating that intergroup contact between people of equal status in noncompetitive circumstances will reduce prejudice.

FEW OF MY BEST FRIENDS ARE . . .

Do people really have close friends of different racial and ethnic backgrounds? Some sociologists have attempted to gauge the degree of White–Black interaction in the United States. They indicate that many people overestimate the degree of "racial togetherness" in our society.

Sociologist Tom Smith, who directs the respected General Social Survey, has noticed that a high proportion of both White and African American respondents claim to have close friends of another race. But is that really true? When Smith and fellow researchers analyzed the survey data, they found that response rates varied with the way the question was phrased. When asked whether any of the friends they felt close to was Black, 42.1 percent of Whites said yes. Yet when asked to give the names of friends they felt close to, only 6 percent of Whites listed a close friend of a different race or ethnicity (Figure 2.5).

When asked the race of their best same-sex friend, most Americans choose someone of the same race as themselves. In a national study of adolescents, more than 91 percent of non-Hispanic Whites claimed a White non-Hispanic as their best same-sex friend. The General Social Survey yielded almost the same result for all adults. Given the fact that more than one-third of the teens in the United States are either non-White or Hispanic, we might have expected to find more cross-race friendships. Members of minority groups seem more willing than Whites to cross racial and ethnic boundaries, however. A slightly lower 85 percent of Black adolescents selected a Black for a best friend, and a markedly lower 62 percent of Mexican Americans named another Mexican American.

In yet another study, in 2004, sociologists Grace Kao and Kara Joyner considered the responses of more than 90,000 adolescents nationwide in an in-school survey. Among many questions, students were asked to identify their best friend and later to identify that person's race and ethnicity. For their primary friendships, most people chose someone of the same race or ethnicity.

We can see that more than 81 percent of White youths had as their best friend someone who was also White. Other racial and ethnic groups are more likely to venture outside their group's boundaries, but friendships within racial and ethnic groups still dominate, especially when one considers the potential to befriend a member of the White majority.

Research of the last 10 years shows that regardless of one's racial or ethnic group, friendships that cross racial and ethnic boundaries are less likely than others to

Although such studies are encouraging, what remains troubling is how little significant intergroup contact exists. In "Research Focus," we consider recent efforts to measure how much contact occurs.

The limited amount of intergroup contact is of concern given the power of the contact hypothesis. If there is no positive contact, then how can we expect there to be less prejudice? National surveys show prejudice directed toward Muslim Americans, but social contact bridges that hatred. In a 2006 survey, 50 percent of people who were not acquainted with a Muslim favor special identification for Muslim Americans, but only 24 percent of those who know a Muslim embrace that same view. Similarly, people personally familiar with Muslims are more than one-third less likely to endorse special security checks just for Muslims and are nervous to see a Muslim man on the same flight with themselves. Although negative views are common toward Muslim Americans today, they are much less likely to be endorsed by people who have had intergroup contact (Saad 2006a).

Research Focus

involve visits to each other's homes. They are also less likely than others to feature a sharing of personal problems.

In sum, careful research shows that to a great degree, our society's growing diversity is not necessarily reflected in our choice of friends.

Source: Briggs 2007; Hamm, Brown, and Heck 2005; Kao and Joyner 2004; Kao and Vaquera 2006; Mouw and Entwisle 2006; Smith 1999.

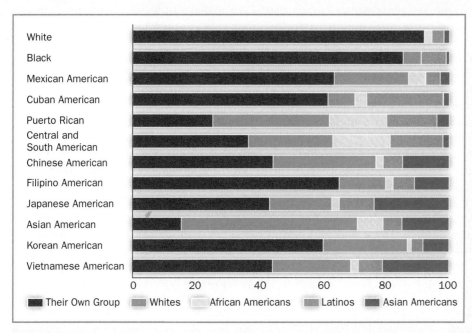

FIGURE 2.5
Who's Your Best Friend?
Source: Adapted from Table 1 in Kao and Joyner 2004, 564. Reprinted by permission of Wiley-Blackwell Publishing.

As African Americans and other subordinate groups slowly gain access to better-paying and more-responsible jobs, the contact hypothesis takes on greater significance. Usually, the availability of equal-status interaction is taken for granted, yet in everyday life intergroup contact does not conform to the equal-status idea of the contact hypothesis. Furthermore, as we have seen, in a highly segregated society such as the United States, contact tends to be brief and superficial, especially between Whites and minorities. The apartheid-like friendship patterns prevent us from learning firsthand not just how to get along but also how to revel in interracial experiences (Bonilla-Silva and Embrick 2007; Miller 2002).

Corporate Response: Diversity Training

Prejudice carries a cost. This cost is not only to the victim but also to any organization that allows prejudice to interfere with its functioning. Workplace hostility can lead to lost productivity and even staff attrition. Furthermore, if left unchecked, an organization—whether a corporation, government agency, or nonprofit enterprise—can develop a reputation for having a "chilly climate." This reputation of a business unfriendly to people of color or to women discourages both qualified people from applying for jobs and potential clients from seeking products or services.

In an effort to improve workplace relations, most organizations have initiated some form of diversity training. These programs are aimed at eliminating circumstances and relationships that cause groups to receive fewer rewards, resources, or opportunities. Typically, programs aim to reduce ill treatment based on race, gender, and ethnicity. In addition, diversity training may deal with (in descending order of frequency) age, disability, religion, and language, as well as other aspects, including citizenship status, marital status, and parental status (Society for Human Resource Management 2008).

It is difficult to make any broad generalization about the effectiveness of diversity-training programs because they vary so much in structure between organizations. At one extreme are short presentations that seem to have little support from management. People file into the room feeling that this is something they need to get through quickly. Such training is unlikely to be effective and may actually be counterproductive by heightening social tensions. At the other end of the continuum is a diversity training program that is integrated into initial job training, reinforced periodically, and presented as part of the overall mission of the organization, with full support from all levels of management. In these businesses, diversity is a core value, and management demands a high degree of commitment from all employees (Dobbin, Kalev, and Kelly 2007).

As shown in Figure 2.6, the workforce is becoming more diverse, and management is taking notice. An increasing proportion of the workforce is foreign-born, and the numbers of U.S.-born African Americans, Latinos, and Asian Americans are also growing. Growing research in business and the social sciences is documenting that diversity is an asset in bringing about creative changes. The benefits of workplace diversity is especially true at management levels where leadership teams can develop innovative solutions (DiTomaso, Post, and Parks-Yancy 2007; Page 2007)

It is not in an organization's best interests if employees start to create barriers based on, for example, racial lines. We saw in the previous section that equal-status contact can reduce hostility. However, in the workplace, people compete for promotions, desirable work assignments, and better office space, to name a few sources of friction. When done well, an organization undertakes diversity training to remove ill feelings among workers, which often reflect the prejudices present in larger society.

If it is to have a lasting impact on an organization, diversity training should not be separated from other aspects of the organization. For example, even the most inspired program will have little effect on prejudice if the organization promotes a sexist or ethnically offensive image in its advertising. The University of North Dakota launched an initiative in 2001 to become one of the top institutions for Native Americans in the nation. Yet at almost the same time, the administration reaffirmed its commitment, despite tribal objections, to having as its mascot for athletic teams the "Fighting Sioux." It does little to do diversity training if overt actions by an organization propel it in the opposite direction. In 2005, the National Collegiate Athletic Association began a review of logos and mascots that could be considered insulting to Native Americans. Some colleges have resisted suggestions to change or alter their publicity images, although others have abandoned the practice (University of North Dakota 2008).

Despite the problems inherent in confronting prejudice, an organization with a comprehensive, management-supported program of diversity training can go a long way toward reducing prejudice in the workplace. The one major qualifier is that the rest of the organization must also support mutual respect.

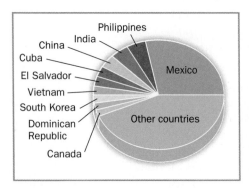

FIGURE 2.6

Foreign-Born Workers in the United States, by Country

About 15 percent of the civilian labor force is foreign-born, with Mexico the largest source.

Source: Data for 2004 from the Bureau of Labor Statistics, in Mosisa 2006, 48.

Ways to Fight Hate

What can schools do? Television and movie producers? Corporate big shots? It is easy to shift the responsibility for confronting prejudice to the movers and shakers, and certainly they do play a critical role. Yet there definitely are actions one can take in the course of everyday life to challenge intergroup hostility.

The Southern Poverty Law Center (SPLC), founded in 1971 and based in Montgomery, Alabama, organized committed activists all over the country to mount legal cases and challenges against hate groups such as the Ku Klux Klan. The center's courtroom challenges led to the end of many discriminatory practices. Its cases have now gone beyond conventional race-based cases, with the center winning equal benefits for women in the armed forces, helping to end involuntary sterilization of women on welfare, and working to reform prison and mental health conditions.

Recognizing that social change can also begin at the individual level, the SPLC has identified 10 ways to fight hate on the basis of its experience working at the community level:

1. *Act.* Do something. In the face of hatred, apathy will be taken as acceptance even by the victims of prejudice themselves. The SPLC tells of a time when a cross was burned in the yard of a single mother of Portuguese descent in Missouri; one person acted and set in motion a community uprising against hatred.

2. *Unite.* Call a friend or co-worker. Organize a group of like-thinking friends from school or your place of worship or club. Create a coalition that is diverse and includes the young, the old, law enforcement representatives, and the media. Frustrated when a neo-Nazi group got permission to march in Illinois, a Jewish couple formed Project Lemonade. Money raised helps to create education projects or monuments in communities that witness such decisive events.

3. *Support the victims.* Victims of hate crimes are especially vulnerable. Let them know you care by words, in person, or by e-mail. If you or your friend is a victim, report it. In the wake of an outbreak of anti–Native American and anti-Jewish activity in Montana, a manager of a local sports shop replaced all his usual outdoor advertising and print advertisements with "Not in Our Town," which soon became a community rallying point for a support network of hate victims.

4. *Do your homework.* If you suspect a hate crime has been committed, do your research to document it. An Indiana father spotted his son receiving a "pastor's license," did some research, and found that the source was a White supremacist group disguised as a church. It helped explain the boy's recent fascination with Nazi symbols. The father wrote to the "church," demanded that the contacts be stopped, and threatened suit.

5. *Create an alternative.* Never attend a rally where hate is a part of the agenda. Find another outlet for your frustration, whatever the cause. When the Ku Klux Klan held a rally in Wisconsin, a coalition of ministers organized citizens to spend the day in minority neighborhoods.

6. *Speak up.* You, too, have First Amendment rights. Denounce the hatred, the cruel jokes. If you see a news organization misrepresenting a group, speak up. When a newspaper exposed the 20-year-old national leader of the Aryan Nation, he resigned and closed his Web site.

7. *Lobby leaders.* Persuade policy makers, business heads, community leaders, and executives of media outlets to take a stand against hate. Levi Strauss contributed $5 million to an antiprejudice project and a program that helps people of color to get loans in communities where it has plants.

8. *Look long range.* Participate or organize events such as annual parades or cultural fairs to celebrate diversity and harmony. Supplement it with a Web site that can be a 24/7 resource. In Selma, Alabama, a major weekend street fair is held on the anniversary of Bloody Sunday, the day in 1965 when voting-rights activists

attempted to walk across a bridge to Montgomery but were attacked and beaten back by police.

9. *Teach tolerance.* Prejudice is learned, and parents and teachers can influence the content of curriculum. In Brooklyn, New York, an interracial basketball program called Flames was founded in the mid-1970s. Since then, it has brought together more than 10,000 youths of diverse backgrounds.

10. *Dig deeper.* Look into the issues that divide us—social inequality, immigration, and sexual orientation. Work against prejudice. Dig deep inside yourself for prejudices and stereotypes you may embrace. Find out what is happening and act!

Expressing prejudice and expressing tolerance are fundamentally personal decisions. These steps recognize that we have the ability to change our attitudes, resist ethnocentrism and prejudice, and avoid the use of ethnophaulisms and stereotypes (SPLC 2000; Willougby 2004).

Conclusion

This chapter has examined theories of prejudice and measurements of its extent. Several theories try to explain why prejudice exists. Some emphasize economic concerns (the exploitation and scapegoating theories) whereas other approaches stress personality or normative factors. No one explanation is sufficient. Surveys conducted in the United States over the past 60 years point to a reduction of prejudice as measured by the willingness to express stereotypes or maintain social distance. Survey data also show that African Americans, Latinos, Asian Americans, and American Indians do not necessarily feel comfortable with each other. They have adopted attitudes toward other oppressed groups similar to those held by many White Americans.

The absence of widespread public expression of prejudice does not mean prejudice itself is absent by any means. Recent prejudice aimed at Hispanics, Asian Americans, and large recent immigrant groups such as Arab Americans and Muslim Americans is well documented. Issues such as immigration and affirmative action reemerge and cause bitter resentment. Furthermore, ill feelings exist between subordinate groups in schools, in the streets, and in the workplace. Color-blind racism allows one to appear to be tolerant while allowing racial and ethnic inequality to persist.

Equal-status contact may reduce hostility between groups. However, in a highly segregated society defined by inequality, such opportunities are not typical. The mass media can be of value in reducing discrimination, but they have not done enough and may even intensify ill feeling by promoting stereotypical images.

Even though we can be encouraged by the techniques available to reduce intergroup hostility, there are still sizable segments of the population that do not want to live in integrated neighborhoods, do not want to work for or be led by someone of a different race, and certainly object to the idea of their relatives marrying outside their own group. People still harbor stereotypes toward one another, and this tendency includes racial and ethnic minorities having stereotypes about one another.

Reducing prejudice is important because it can lead to support for policy change. There are steps we can take as individuals to confront prejudice and overcome hatred. Another real challenge and the ultimate objective is to improve the social condition of oppressed groups in the United States. To consider this challenge, we turn to discrimination in Chapter 3. Discrimination's costs are high to both dominant and subordinate groups. With this fact in mind, we will examine some techniques for reducing discrimination.

Summary

1. Prejudice consists of negative attitudes, and discrimination consists of negative behavior toward a group.

2. Hate crimes highlight hostility that culminates in a criminal offense.

3. Robert Merton's formulation clarifies how individuals may be prejudiced and not necessarily discriminatory and find themselves acting in discriminatory ways while not harboring prejudices.

    Theories for prejudice include two that tend to be psychological (scapegoating and authoritarian personality) and emphasize why a particular person harbors ill feelings. Others are more sociological (exploitation and normative), viewing prejudice in the context of our interaction in a larger society.

4. Although evidence indicates that the public expression of prejudice has declined, there is ample evidence that people are expressing race-neutral principles or color-blind racism that still serves to perpetuate inequality in society.

5. Typically, members of minority groups have a significantly more negative view of social inequality and are more pessimistic about the future compared to Whites.

6. Not only is prejudice directed at racial and ethnic minorities by people in dominant positions but also intergroup hostility among the minorities themselves persists and may become violent.

7. Various techniques are utilized to reduce prejudice, including educational programs, mass media, friendly intergroup contact, and diversity-training programs by the corporate sector.

Key Terms

authoritarian personality 39	ethnocentrism 34	prejudice 36
Bogardus scale 50	ethnophaulisms 36	racial profiling 42
color-blind racism 43	exploitation theory 39	scapegoating theory 38
contact hypothesis 51	hate crime 35	social distance 50
discrimination 36	normative approach 39	stereotypes 40

Review Questions

1. How are prejudice and discrimination both related and unrelated to each other?

2. How do theories of prejudice relate to different expressions of prejudice?

3. How is color-blind racism expressed?

4. Are there steps that you can identify that have been taken against prejudice in your community?

Critical Thinking

1. Identify stereotypes associated with a group of people such as older adults or people with physical disabilities.

2. What social issues do you think are most likely to engender hostility along racial and ethnic lines?

3. Consider the television programs you watch the most. In terms of race and ethnicity, how well do the programs you watch tend to reflect the diversity of the population in the United States?

3

Discrimination

JUST AS SOCIAL SCIENTISTS HAVE ADVANCED THEORIES
to explain why prejudice exists, they have also presented
explanations of why discrimination occurs. Social scientists look more
and more at the manner in which institutions, not individuals, discriminate. Institutional discrimination is a pattern in social institutions that
produces or perpetuates inequalities, even if individuals in the society
do not intend to be racist or sexist. Income data document that gaps
exist between racial and ethnic groups. Historically, attempts have
been made to reduce discrimination, usually through strong lobbying
efforts by minorities themselves. Patterns of total discrimination make
solutions particularly difficult for people in the informal economy or the
underclass. Affirmative action was designed to equalize opportunity but
has encountered significant resentment by those who charge that it
constitutes reverse discrimination. Despite many efforts to end
discrimination, glass ceilings and glass walls remain in the workplace.

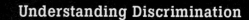
NOTICE

IT IS REQUIRED BY LAW. UNDER
PENALTY OF FINE OF $5.00 TO $25.00.
THAT <u>WHITE</u> AND <u>NEGRO</u> PASSENGERS MUST
OCCUPY THE RESPECTIVE SPACE OR SEATS
INDICATED BY SIGNS IN THIS VEHICLE.

TEXAS PENAL CODE. ARTICLE 1659 SEC 4
DALLAS CITY ORDINANCE. NO 2904

59

The human casualties from natural disasters are well documented. This has been especially true with the impact of Hurricane Katrina on the Gulf Coast in 2005. Also well known now are the ill-planned evacuation plan in New Orleans, the subsequent high death toll, the ineffectiveness of levee construction and maintenance, and the initial slow response and the subsequent prolonged recovery, especially for low-income residents.

The persistent role of discrimination in the aftermath has been less a part of the national consciousness. Although Hurricane Katrina made victims of everyone, poor minority people have been especially victimized. Rural tribal Native American groups and Vietnamese American Gulf residents fell through the cracks of recovery plans. Latino workers who came to the area in the aftermath have been disadvantaged.

The storms destroyed more than 200,000 homes and apartments in Louisiana. Therefore, housing for those who wish to remain or move back is at a premium. But if you are Black and especially of modest means, the ability to reestablish a homestead is much more difficult in metropolitan New Orleans. Courts have had to intervene to restrain St. Bernard Parish, a county just outside New Orleans that is 93 percent White, from limiting rentals to only blood relatives and limiting new residential construction to single-family homes.

On March 8, 2007, an African American responded to a housing advertisement in another area but was told that the owner was out of state and would send information when he or she was back in town and could show the property. Nothing ever happened. A White person responded to the same advertisement the next day and learned from the same person that he or she would be in town that weekend and could arrange to show the property. The absentee landlord told the person that he or she could apply immediately and stated, "We don't want any loud rap music," and "We are looking for people who are more settled."

This is just one example from a study that sent Black and White well-trained testers presenting similar financial circumstances and family types out to attempt to rent housing throughout metropolitan New Orleans. When discrimination appeared to be present, follow-up testing occurred. In the final analysis, in six of every 10 cases, African American testers faced differential treatment. Whites were granted appointments when Blacks were not. Whites were told about available apartments, Blacks were told nothing was available. Blacks were frequently quoted a higher monthly rental charge. White testers' voice mail requests for information were returned whereas many Black testers did not receive call-backs. Recovery is a much harder road if you are a person of color (Greater New Orleans Fair Housing Center 2007; Kao 2006; Simmons 2007; Trujillo-Pagan 2006).

Discrimination has a long history, right up to the present, of taking its toll on people. We will examine the many faces of discrimination, its many victims, and the many ways scholars have documented its presence today in the United States. We will not only return to more examples of discrimination in housing but also look at differential treatment in employment opportunities, wages, voting, vulnerability to environmental hazards, and even access to membership in private clubs.

Understanding Discrimination

discrimination
The denial of opportunities and equal rights to individuals and groups because of prejudice or for other arbitrary reasons.

Discrimination is the denial of opportunities and equal rights to individuals and groups because of prejudice or for other arbitrary reasons. People in the United States find it difficult to see discrimination as a widespread phenomenon. "After all," it is often said, "these minorities drive cars, hold jobs, own their homes, and even go to college." Many groups worldwide are victims of discrimination. In Global View, we consider how the Roma (or Gypsies) have been victimized.

A Global View

THE ROMA: A THOUSAND YEARS OF DISCRIMINATION

The Roma people (also referred to as Gypsies) are members of a minority group numbering 12 million to 15 million people who are dispersed over many countries. The people originated in India, but most Roma now live in Europe, with perhaps as many as 1 million in North America. They continue to be characterized by a nomadic lifestyle, often in response to prejudice and discrimination. Certain common activities such as fortune telling, traveling together in large caravans, and arranged marriages create hostile responses to their arrival in communities. Although the Roma speak their own distinctive language, they have usually adopted the religion of their home region, such as Roman Catholic, Orthodox Christian, or Muslim.

The Roma are the largest ethnic minority in the European Union and are the objects of that organization's efforts to address their poor housing levels, little formal schooling, and high levels of unemployment. Progress is evident in a decline in racially motivated murders of Roma since the early 1990s. Historically, they had been subjected to expulsion, but large numbers died in the Holocaust as a part of Hitler's racial purification efforts.

In addition to the efforts of the European Union, Gypsies themselves have begun to work through established channels to confront discrimination. Simply being Roma makes many authorities assume a child is ill prepared, as in the Czech Republic, where the majority of children in special schools for the learning disabled are Roma. The Roma brought legal action to stop this practice. In a case compared to the 1954 *Brown v. Board of Education* decision in the United States, the European Court of Human Rights ruled in 2007 that the Czech practice was discriminatory with Gypsy children receiving inappropriate placements and substandard education.

Sources: European Roma Rights Centre 2008; Hacek 2008; Schaefer and Zellner 2008.

An understanding of discrimination in modern industrialized societies such as the United States must begin by distinguishing between relative and absolute deprivation.

Relative versus Absolute Deprivation

Conflict theorists have said correctly that it is not absolute, unchanging standards that determine deprivation and oppression. Although minority groups may be viewed as having adequate or even good incomes, housing, health care, and educational opportunities, it is their position relative to some other group that offers evidence of discrimination.

Relative deprivation is defined as the conscious experience of a negative discrepancy between legitimate expectations and present actualities. After settling in the United States, immigrants often enjoy better material comforts and more political freedom than were possible in their old countries. If they compare themselves with most other people in the United States, however, they will feel deprived because, although their standards have improved, the immigrants still perceive relative deprivation.

Absolute deprivation, on the other hand, implies a fixed standard based on a minimum level of subsistence below which families should not be expected to exist. Discrimination

relative deprivation
The conscious experience of a negative discrepancy between legitimate expectations and present actualities.

absolute deprivation
The minimum level of subsistence below which families or individuals should not be expected to exist.

Studies document that African Americans seeking to find housing in New Orleans encounter differential treatment compared to Whites with the same income, financial history, and household size.

does not necessarily mean absolute deprivation. A Japanese American who is promoted to a management position may still be a victim of discrimination if he or she had been passed over for years because of corporate reluctance to place an Asian American in a highly visible position.

Dissatisfaction is also likely to arise from feelings of relative deprivation. The members of a society who feel most frustrated and disgruntled by the social and economic conditions of their lives are not necessarily worse off in an objective sense. Social scientists have long recognized that what is most significant is how people perceive their situations. Karl Marx pointed out that although the misery of the workers was important in reflecting their oppressed state, so was their position relative to the ruling class. In 1847, Marx wrote, "Although the enjoyment of the workers has risen, the social satisfaction that they have has fallen in comparison with the increased enjoyment of the capitalist" (Marx and Engels 1955, 94).

This statement explains why the groups or individuals who are most vocal and best organized against discrimination are not necessarily in the worst economic and social situation. However, they are likely to be those who most strongly perceive that, relative to others, they are not receiving their fair share. Resistance to perceived discrimination, rather than the actual amount of absolute discrimination, is the key.

Total Discrimination

Social scientists—and increasingly policy makers—have begun to use the concept of **total discrimination**, which, as shown in Figure 3.1, refers to current discrimination operating in the labor market, and past discrimination. Past discrimination experienced by an individual includes the poorer education and job experiences of racial and ethnic minorities compared with those of many White Americans. When considering discrimination, therefore, it is not enough to focus only on what is being done to people now. Discrimination is cumulative in its impact over what occurs in one's own lifetime. Sometimes a person may be dealt with fairly but may still be at a disadvantage because he or she suffered from poorer health care, inferior counseling in the school system, less access to books and other educational materials, or a poor job record resulting from absences to take care of brothers and sisters (Pager and Shepherd 2008).

Discrimination casts a wide net. Although the poor and less educated are most vulnerable and unable to access resources that might help them, discrimination also is faced by the affluent with professional degrees. In Listen to Our Voices on page 64, respected law professor Patricia J. Williams, an African American, describes her inability to secure a mortgage despite initial approval after an analysis of her financial status but before the bank realized she was Black. Her recent experience is not unusual and helps to explain the persistence of discrimination.

William's experience is not unusual. A study released by the National Fair Housing Alliance and the federal Department of Housing and Urban Development found that discriminatory housing practices were routine. Consider the sobering results of a two-year study conducted in 12 metropolitan areas with 73 real estate firms: White real estate shoppers are steered away from houses in mixed neighborhoods even when they express interest in integrated areas. Latinos and African Americans looking for housing are steered toward minority neighborhoods even when their incomes justify seeing more-affluent neighborhoods. The challenge to being a minority homebuyer does not stop there. Studies document that Black and Hispanic homebuyers tend to pay higher interest rates than Whites with similar credit ratings. All things are hardly equal in home buying (Bocian, Ernst, and Li 2006).

total discrimination
The combination of current discrimination with past discrimination created by poor schools and menial jobs.

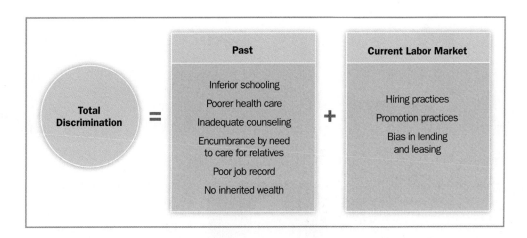

FIGURE 3.1
Total Discrimination

We find another variation of this past-in-present discrimination when apparently nondiscriminatory current practices have negative effects because of prior intentionally biased practices. Although unions that purposely discriminated against minority members in the past may no longer do so, some people are still prevented from achieving higher levels of seniority because of those past practices. Personnel records include a cumulative record that is vital in promotion and selection for desirable assignments. Blatantly discriminatory judgments and recommendations in the past remain part of a person's record.

Institutional Discrimination

Individuals practice discrimination in one-to-one encounters, and institutions practice discrimination through their daily operations. Indeed, a consensus is growing today that this institutional discrimination is more significant than acts committed by prejudiced individuals.

Social scientists are particularly concerned with the ways in which patterns of employment, education, criminal justice, housing, health care, and government operations maintain the social significance of race and ethnicity. **Institutional discrimination** is the denial of opportunities and equal rights to individuals and groups that results from the normal operations of a society.

Civil rights activist Stokely Carmichael and political scientist Charles Hamilton are credited with introducing the concept of institutional racism. *Individual discrimination* refers to overt acts of individual Whites against individual Blacks; Carmichael and Hamilton reserved the term *institutional racism* for covert acts committed collectively against an entire group. From this perspective, discrimination can take place without an individual intending to deprive others of privileges and even without the individual being aware that others are being deprived (Ture and Hamilton 1992).

How can discrimination be widespread and unconscious at the same time? The following are a few documented examples of institutional discrimination:

1. Standards for assessing credit risks work against African Americans and Hispanics who seek to establish businesses, because many lack conventional credit references. Businesses in low-income areas where these groups often reside also have much higher insurance costs.

2. IQ testing favors middle-class children, especially the White middle class, because of the types of questions included.

3. The entire criminal justice system, from the patrol officer to the judge and jury, is dominated by Whites who find it difficult to understand life in poverty areas.

4. Hiring practices often require several years' experience at jobs only recently opened to members of subordinate groups.

5. Many jobs automatically eliminate people with felony records or past drug offenses, which disproportionately reduces employment opportunities for people of color.

institutional discrimination
A denial of opportunities and equal rights to individuals or groups, resulting from the normal operations of a society.

OF RACE AND RISK

Patricia J. Williams

Several years ago, at a moment when I was particularly tired of the unstable lifestyle that academic careers sometimes require, I surprised myself and bought a real house. Because the house was in a state other than the one where I was living at the time, I obtained my mortgage by telephone. I am a prudent little squirrel when it comes to things financial, always tucking away stores of nuts for the winter, and so I meet the criteria of a quite good credit risk. My loan was approved almost immediately.

A little while later, the contract came in the mail. Among the papers the bank forwarded were forms documenting compliance with the Fair Housing Act, which outlaws racial discrimination in the housing market. The act monitors lending practices to prevent banks from redlining—redlining being the phenomenon whereby banks circle certain neighborhoods on the map and refuse to lend in those areas. It is a practice for which the bank with which I was dealing, unbeknownst to me, had been cited previously—as well as since. In any event, the act tracks the race of all banking customers to prevent such discrimination. Unfortunately, and with the creative variability of all illegality, some banks also use the racial information disclosed on the fair housing forms to engage in precisely the discrimination the law seeks to prevent.

I should repeat that to this point my entire mortgage transaction had been conducted by telephone. I should also note that I speak a Received Standard English, regionally marked as Northeastern perhaps, but not easily identifiable as black. With my credit history, my job as a law professor, and, no doubt, with my accent, I am not only middle class but apparently match the cultural stereotype of a good white person. It is thus, perhaps, that the loan officer of the bank, whom I had never met, had checked off the box on the fair housing form indicating that I was white.

Race shouldn't matter, I suppose, but it seemed to in this case, so I took a deep breath, crossed out "white" and sent the contract back. That will teach them to presume too much, I thought. A done deal, I assumed. But suddenly the transaction came to a screeching halt. The bank wanted more money, more points, and a higher rate of interest. Suddenly I found myself facing great resistance and much more debt. To make a long story short, I threatened to sue under the act in question, the bank quickly

Institutional discrimination is so systemic that it takes on the pattern of what has been termed "woodwork racism" in that racist outcomes become so widespread that African Americans, Latinos, Asian Americans, and others endure them as a part of everyday life (Feagin and McKinney 2003).

In some cases, even apparently neutral institutional standards can turn out to have discriminatory effects. African American students at a midwestern state university protested a policy under which fraternities and sororities that wanted to use campus facilities for a dance were required to post a $150 security deposit to cover possible damage. The Black students complained that this policy had a discriminatory impact on minority student organizations. Campus police countered that the university's policy applied to all student groups interested in using these facilities. However, because almost all White fraternities and sororities at the school had their own houses, which they used for dances, the policy affected only African American and other subordinate groups' organizations.

backed down, and I procured the loan on the original terms. What was interesting about all this was that the reason the bank gave for its newfound recalcitrance was not race, heaven forbid. No, it was all about economics and increased risk: The reason they gave was that property values in that neighborhood were suddenly falling. They wanted more money to buffer themselves against the snappy winds of projected misfortune.

Initially, I was surprised, confused. The house was in a neighborhood that was extremely stable. I am an extremely careful shopper; I had uncovered absolutely nothing to indicate that prices were falling. It took my realtor to make me see the light. "Don't you get it," he sighed. "This is what always happens." And even though I suppose it was a little thick of me, I really hadn't gotten it: For, of course, I was the reason the prices were in peril. . . .

In retrospect, what has remained so fascinating to me about this experience was the way it so exemplified the problems of the new rhetoric of racism. For starters, the new rhetoric of race never mentions race. It wasn't race but risk with which the bank was so concerned. . . .

By this measure of mortgage-worthiness, the ingredient of blackness is cast not just as a social toll but also as an actual tax. A fee, an extra contribution at the door, an admission charge for the high costs of handling my dangerous propensities, my inherently unsavory properties. I was not judged based on my independent attributes or financial worth; not even was I judged by statistical profiles of what my group actually does. (For, in fact, anxiety-stricken, middle-class black people make good cake-baking neighbors when not made to feel defensive by the unfortunate historical strategies of bombs, burnings, or abandonment.) Rather, I was being evaluated based on what an abstraction of White Society writ large thinks we—or I—do, and that imagined "doing" was treated and thus established as a self-fulfilling prophecy. It is a dispiriting message: that some in society apparently not only devalue black people but devalue themselves and their homes just for having us as part of their landscape.

"I bet you'll keep your mouth shut the next time they plug you into the computer as white," laughed a friend when he heard my story. It took me aback, this postmodern pressure to "pass," even as it highlighted the intolerable logic of it all. For by these "rational" economic measures, an investment in my property suggests the selling of myself.

Source: Williams. Reprinted with permission from the December 29, 1997, issue of *The Nation.*

Ten years later, the entire nation scrambled to make aviation safer in the wake of the September 11, 2001, terrorist attacks. The government saw airport security as a weak link and federalized airport screeners under the newly formed Transport Security Administration. Wages improved and training strengthened. The new screeners also had to be U.S. citizens. This latter provision eliminated the many legal immigrants from Asia, Africa, and Latin America who had previously worked as screeners. Airport screening went from overwhelmingly minority to 61 percent White. Clearly, this measure had the unintended consequences of discriminating against people of color (Alonso-Zaldivar and Oldhan 2002).

Even efforts to right injustices can be discriminatory in their outcome. Numerous instances are documented of low-income potential homeowners entering into very undesirable financial agreements when they go to buy that first home, that eventually lead to foreclosure. In an effort to protect people from being taken advantage of, beginning in 2006, the State of Illinois required buyers with poor credit records in certain areas of Chicago to go through mandatory financial counseling. As a result, more than 20 lenders

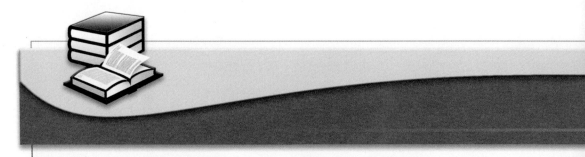

DISCRIMINATION IN JOB SEEKING

A dramatic confirmation of discrimination came with research begun by sociologist Devah Pager in 2003. She sent four men out as trained "testers" to look for entry-level jobs in Milwaukee, Wisconsin, that required no experience or special training. Each tester was a 23-year-old college student, but each one presented himself as having a high school diploma and similar job history.

The job-seeking experiences with 350 different employers were vastly different among the four men. Why was that? Two of the testers where Black and two were White. Furthermore, one tester of each pair indicated in the job application that he had served 18 months of jail time for a felony conviction (possession of cocaine with intent to distribute). As you can see in Figure 3.2, applicants with a prison record received significantly fewer callbacks. But as dramatic a difference as a criminal record made, race was clearly more important.

The differences were to the point that a White job applicant with a jail record actually received more callbacks for further consideration than a Black man with no criminal record. Whiteness has a privilege even when it comes to jail time; race, it seems, was more of a concern to potential employers than a criminal background.

"I expected there to be an effect of race, but I did not expect it to swamp the results as it did," Pager told an interviewer. Her finding was especially significant because the majority of convicts who are released from prison each year (52 percent) are, in fact, Black men. Pager's research, which was widely publicized, eventually contributed to a change in public policy. In his 2004 State of the Union address, and specifically referring to Pager's work, President George W. Bush announced a $300 million monitoring program for ex-convicts who are attempting to reintegrate into society.

have curtailed granting home loans in these areas, not wanting to deal with the further restrictions. More than 80 percent of the people in the affected area are Black or Latino. A well-intentioned attempt to help people is making it very difficult for people who want to live in an area that is overwhelmingly populated by racial and ethnic minorities (Umberger 2006).

The 2000 presidential election created headlines because it took weeks to resolve who won—Bush or Gore. Yet for 1.4 million African Americans who were denied the right to vote, this seemed like a national issue that had left them on the sidelines. The prohibition was not because they were Black, which would have been clearly racist and legally discriminatory, but because they were convicted felons. In 11 states, a felony conviction can result in a ban from voting for life, even after a prison sentence is served. Because many of these states are in the South and have large Black populations, the voting prohibition disproportionately covers African American men. Currently, 13 percent of the nation's Black male population is precluded from voting by such laws. Florida was the deciding state in the close 2000 elections, and more than 200,000 potential Black voters were excluded. This case of institutional discrimination may have changed the outcome of a presidential election (Cooper 2004; Sentencing Project 2008).

Institutional discrimination continuously imposes more hindrances on and awards fewer benefits to certain racial and ethnic groups than it does to others. This is the underlying and painful context of American intergroup relations.

Research Focus

These findings, however, are not isolated to this one study or to one city. Similar studies sending out job applicants have confirmed discrimination in action in Chicago, New York City, San Diego, and Washington, D.C.

Sources: Bordt 2005; Bureau of Justice Statistics 2004; Favreault 2008; Kroeger 2004; Pager 2003, 2007a, 2007b; Pager and Quillian 2005; Pager and Western 2006.

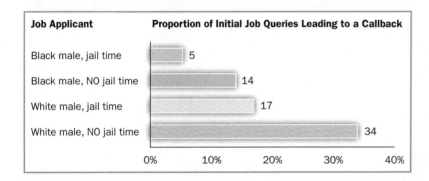

Job Applicant	Proportion of Initial Job Queries Leading to a Callback
Black male, jail time	5
Black male, NO jail time	14
White male, jail time	17
White male, NO jail time	34

FIGURE 3.2
Discrimination in Job Seeking
Source: Pager 2003, 958. Reprinted by permission of the University of Chicago.

Low-Wage Labor

Disproportionate shares of racial and ethnic minority members are either unemployed or employed in low-wage labor. Much of this low-wage labor is in a part of the labor market that provides little opportunities for improvement during one's working years and virtually no protection in terms of health insurance or retirement benefits.

The secondary labor market affecting many members of racial and ethnic minorities has come to be called the **informal economy** (or **irregular** or **underground economy**) and consists of transfers of money, goods, or services that are not reported to the government. This label describes much of the work in inner-city neighborhoods and poverty-stricken rural areas, which is in sharp contrast to the rest of the marketplace. Workers are employed in the informal economy seasonally or infrequently. The work they do may resemble the work of traditional occupations such as mechanic, cook, or electrician, but these workers lack the formal credentials to enter such employment. Indeed, workers in the informal economy may work sporadically or may moonlight in the regular economy. The informal economy also includes unregulated child care services, garage sales, and the unreported income of craftspeople and street vendors.

According to the dual labor market model, minorities have been relegated to the informal economy. Although the informal economy may offer employment to the jobless, it provides few safeguards against fraud or malpractice that victimizes the workers.

informal economy
Transfers of money, goods, or services that are not reported to the government. Common in inner-city neighborhoods and poverty-stricken rural areas.

irregular or **underground economy**
See informal economy.

It's never this clear.

Instead, you'll hear things like: "Sorry, we just rented the last apartment." "There are several applications ahead of you." "We seem to have misplaced your application." Learn the signs of discrimination and fight back.

If you suspect unfair housing practices, contact HUD or your local Fair Housing Center. Everyone deserves a fair chance.

EQUAL HOUSING OPPORTUNITY

FAIR HOUSING IS THE LAW!
U.S. Department of Housing and Urban Development • 1-800-669-9777 • TDD 1-800-927-9275

Despite numerous laws and steep penalties, discrimination continues in the housing market.

dual labor market
Division of the economy into two areas of employment, the secondary one of which is populated primarily by minorities working at menial jobs.

There are also few of the fringe benefits of health insurance and pensions that are much more likely to be present in the conventional marketplace. Therefore, informal economies are criticized for promoting highly unfair and dangerous working conditions. Being consigned to the informal economy is yet another example of social inequality.

Sociologist Edna Bonacich (1972, 1976) outlined the **dual** or **split labor market** that divides the economy into two realms of employment, the secondary one being populated primarily by minorities working at menial jobs. Even when not manual, labor is still rewarded less when performed by minorities. In keeping with the conflict model, this dual market model emphasizes that minorities fare unfavorably in the competition between dominant and subordinate groups.

The workers in the informal economy are ill prepared to enter the regular economy permanently or to take its better-paying jobs. Frequent changes in employment or lack of a specific supervisor leaves them without the kind of résumé that employers in the regular economy expect before they hire. Some of the sources of employment in the informal economy are illegal, such as fencing stolen goods, narcotics peddling, pimping, and prostitution. More likely, the work is legal but not transferable to a more traditional job. An example is an "information broker," who receives cash in exchange for such information as where to find good buys or how to receive maximum benefits from public assistance programs (Pedder 1991).

Workers in the informal economy have not necessarily experienced direct discrimination. Because of past discrimination, however, they are unable to secure traditional employment. Working in the informal economy provides income but does not lead them into the primary labor market. A self-fulfilling cycle continues that allows past discrimination to create a separate work environment.

Efforts to end discrimination continue to run up against discrimination of all sorts. As described in Research Focus, although we can document discrimination in research studies, it is often very difficult to prove, even if we had the time and money to bring the incident to the attention of the legal system.

Not all low-wage laborers are a part of the informal economy, but many workers are driven into such jobs as better-paying jobs either move far away from where African Americans and Latinos live or even abroad as globalization creates more and more of an international labor market.

The absence of jobs casts a wider shadow in poor neighborhoods, beyond the lousy employment opportunities. People in poor urban neighborhoods often live in what have been called "commercial deserts," where they have little access to major grocers, pharmacies, or other retailers but have plenty of liquor stores and fast-food restaurants nearby. This not only affects the quality of life but also exacerbates the exodus of good job opportunities (Gallagher 2005; Shaffer and Gottlieb 2007).

It is commonly believed that there are jobs available for the inner-city poor but that they just do not seek them. A study looked at jobs that were advertised in a help-wanted section of the *Washington Post*. The analysis showed that most of the jobs were beyond the reach of the underclass; perhaps 5 percent of all openings could even remotely be considered reasonable job prospects for people without skills or experience. During interviews with the employers, researchers found that an average of 21 people applied for each position, which typically was filled within three days of the time the advertisement appeared. The mean hourly wage was $6.12, 42 percent of the jobs offered no fringe benefits, and the remaining positions offered meager fringe benefits after six months or one year of employment. This study, like others before it, counters the folk wisdom that there are plenty of jobs around for the underclass (Pease and Martin 1997).

Discrimination Today

Discrimination is widespread in the United States. It sometimes results from prejudices held by individuals. More significantly, it is found in institutional discrimination and the presence of the informal economy. The presence of an underclass is symptomatic of many social forces, and total discrimination—past and present discrimination taken together—is one of them.

Measuring Discrimination

How much discrimination is there? As in measuring prejudice, problems arise in quantifying discrimination. Measuring prejudice is hampered by the difficulties in assessing attitudes and by the need to take many factors into account. It is further limited by the initial challenge of identifying different treatment. A second difficulty of measuring discrimination is assigning a cost to the discrimination.

Some tentative conclusions about discrimination can be made, however. Figure 3.3 uses income data to show vividly the disparity in income between African Americans and Whites and also between men and women. This encompasses all full-time workers. White men, with a median income of $51,509, earn one-third more than Black men and nearly twice what Hispanic women earn in wages.

Why do Asian American men earn so much if race serves as a barrier? The economic picture is not entirely positive. Some Asian American groups such as Laotians and Vietnamese have high levels of poverty. However, a significant number of Asian Americans with advanced educations have high-earning jobs, which brings up the median income. However, as we will see, given their high levels of schooling, their incomes should be even higher.

Clearly, regardless of race or ethnicity, men outpace women in annual income. This disparity between the incomes of Black women and White men has remained unchanged over the more than 50 years during which such data have been tabulated. It illustrates yet another instance of the greater inequality experienced by minority women. Also, Figure 3.3 includes only data for full-time, year-round workers; it excludes homemakers

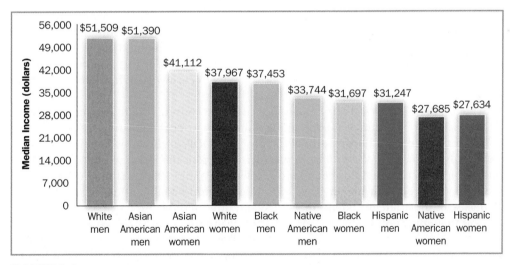

FIGURE 3.3

Median Income by Race, Ethnicity, and Gender

Even at the very highest levels of schooling, the income gap remains between Whites and Blacks. Education also has little apparent effect on the income gap between male and female workers. Even a brief analysis reveals striking differences in earning power between White men and other groups in the United States. Furthermore, the greater inequality is apparent for African American and Hispanic women.

Note: Data released in 2008 for income earned in 2007. Median income is from all sources and is limited to year-round, full-time workers at least 25 years old. Data for White men and women are for non-Hispanics.

Source: DeNavas-Walt, Proctor, and Smith, 2008. For Native Americans, author's estimate based on Bureau of the Census data in Ogunwole 2006.

Many people work in the informal economy with little prospect of moving into the primary, better-paying economy. Pictured is a street vendor selling jewelry in New York City.

and the unemployed. Even in this comparison, the deprivation of Blacks, Hispanics, and women is confirmed again.

Are these differences entirely the result of discrimination in employment? No, individuals within the four groups are not equally prepared to compete for high-paying jobs. Past discrimination is a significant factor in a person's current social position. As discussed previously and illustrated in Figure 3.3, past discrimination continues to take its toll on modern victims. Taxpayers, predominantly White, were unwilling to subsidize the public education of African Americans and Hispanics at the same levels as White pupils. Even as these actions have changed, today's schools show the continuing results of this uneven spending pattern from the past. Education clearly is an appropriate variable to control.

In Table 3.1, median income is compared, holding education constant, which means that we can compare Blacks and Whites and men and women with approximately the same amount of formal schooling. More education means more money, but the disparity remains. The gap between races does narrow somewhat as education increases. However, both African Americans and women lag behind their more affluent counterparts. The contrast remains dramatic: women with a master's degree typically receive $55,426, which means they earn almost $7,000 less than men who complete only a bachelor's degree.

Thinking over the long term, a woman with a bachelor's degree will work full-time four years to earn $180,000. The typical male can work just three years, take the fourth year off without pay, and match the woman's earnings. Women, regardless of race, pay at every point. They are often hired at lower starting salaries in jobs comparable to those held by women. Salary increases come slower. And by their 30s, they rarely recover from even short maternity leaves (Dey and Hill 2007; Gittell and McKinney 2007; Jacobs 2008).

Note what happens to Asian American households. Although highly educated Asian Americans earn a lot of money, they trail well behind their White counterparts. With a doctorate holder in the family, the typical Asian American household earns an estimated $116,000, compared to $138,000 in a White household. To put this another way, these highly educated Asian Americans will work six years to earn what Whites do in less than five years.

What do these individual differences look like if we consider them on a national level? Economist Andrew Brimmer (1995), citing numerous government studies, estimates that about 3 or 4 percent of the gross domestic product (GDP, or the value of goods and services) is lost annually by the failure to use African Americans' existing education. There had been little change in this economic cost from the mid-1960s to the mid-1990s. This estimate would be even higher if we took into account economic losses caused by the underuse of the academic talents of women and other minorities.

Now that education has been held constant, is the remaining gap caused by discrimination? No, not necessarily. Table 3.1 uses only the amount of schooling, not its quality. Racial minorities are more likely to attend inadequately financed schools. Some efforts have been made to eliminate disparities between school districts in the amount of wealth available to tax for school support, but they have met with little success.

The inequality of educational opportunity may seem less important in explaining sex discrimination. Although women usually are not segregated from men, educational institutions encourage talented women to enter fields that pay less (nursing or elementary education) than other occupations that require similar amounts of training. Even when they do enter the same occupation, the earnings disparity persists. Even controlling for age, a study of census data showed that female physicians and surgeons earned 69 percent of what their male counterparts did (Weinberg 2007).

TABLE 3.1
Median Income by Race and Sex, Holding Education Constant

Even at the very highest levels of schooling, the income gap remains between Whites and Blacks. Education also has little apparent effect on the income gap between male and female workers (income values in dollars).

	Race				Sex	
	White Families	**Black Families**	**Asian Families**	**Hispanic Families**	**Male**	**Female**
Total	70,999	41,859	78,747	41,590	47,004	36,086
HIGH SCHOOL						
Nongraduate	35,833	22,279	33,597	29,669	29,317	20,398
Graduate	54,147	35,004	47,728	41,695	37,855	27,240
COLLEGE						
Some college	65,750	43,980	70,481	54,308	44,899	32,887
Bachelor's degree	97,570	77,450	98,000	70,631	62,087	45,773
Master's degree	111,000	90,952	114,000	95,599	76,284	55,426
Doctorate degree	138,000	109,000	116,000	99,000	92,089	68,989

Notes: Data released in 2008 for income earned in 2007. Figures are median income from all sources except capital gains. Included are public assistance payments, dividends, pensions, unemployment compensation, and so on. Incomes are for all workers 25 years of age and older. High school graduates include those with GEDs. Data for Whites are for White non-Hispanics. "Some college" excludes associate degree holders. Family data above bachelor's degree are derived from median incomes, and data for doctorate-holders' families are author's estimate.

Source: DeNavas-Walt, Proctor, and Smith 2008 (detailed tables at www.census.gov).

Eliminating Discrimination

Two main agents of social change work to reduce discrimination: voluntary associations organized to solve racial and ethnic problems and the federal government, including the courts. The two are closely related: Most efforts initiated by the government were urged by associations or organizations that represent minority groups, following vigorous protests by African Americans against racism. Resistance to social inequality by subordinate groups has been the key to change. Rarely has any government of its own initiative sought to end discrimination based on such criteria as race, ethnicity, and gender.

All racial and ethnic groups of any size are represented by private organizations that are, to some degree, trying to end discrimination. Some groups originated in the first half of the twentieth century, but most have been founded since World War II or have become significant forces in bringing about change only since then. These include church organizations, fraternal social groups, minor political parties, and legal defense funds, as well as more militant organizations operating under the scrutiny of law enforcement agencies. The purposes, membership, successes, and failures of these resistance organizations dedicated to eliminating discrimination are discussed throughout this book.

Government action toward eliminating discrimination is also recent. Each branch of the government has taken antidiscrimination actions: the executive, the judicial, and the legislative.

The first antidiscrimination action at the executive level was President Franklin D. Roosevelt's 1943 creation of the Fair Employment Practices Commission (FEPC), which handled thousands of complaints of discrimination, mostly from African Americans, despite strong opposition by powerful economic and political leaders and many Southern Whites. The FEPC had little actual power. It had no authority to compel employers to stop discriminating but could only ask for voluntary compliance. Its jurisdiction was limited to federal government employees, federal contractors, and labor unions. State and local governments and any business without a federal contract were not covered. Furthermore, the FEPC never enjoyed vigorous support from the White House, was denied adequate funds, and was part of larger agencies that were hostile to the commission's existence. This weak antidiscrimination agency was finally dropped in 1946, only to be succeeded by an even weaker one in 1948.

The judiciary, charged with interpreting laws and the U.S. Constitution, has a much longer history of involvement in the rights of racial, ethnic, and religious minorities. However, its early decisions protected the rights of the dominant group, as in the 1857 U.S. Supreme Court's *Dred Scott* decision, which ruled that slaves remained slaves even when living or traveling in states where slavery was illegal. Not until the 1940s did the Supreme Court revise earlier decisions and begin to grant African Americans the same rights as those held by Whites. The 1954 *Brown v. Board of Education* decision, which stated that "separate but equal" facilities—including education—were unconstitutional, heralded a new series of rulings, arguing that distinguishing between races in order to segregate was inherently unconstitutional.

It was assumed incorrectly by many that *Brown* and other judicial actions would lead quickly to sweeping change. In fact, little change occurred initially, and resistance to ending racism continued.

The most important legislative effort to eradicate discrimination was the Civil Rights Act of 1964. This act led to the establishment of the Equal Employment Opportunity Commission (EEOC), which had the power to investigate complaints against employers and to recommend action to the Department of Justice. If the justice department sued and discrimination was found, then the court could order appropriate compensation. The act covered employment practices of all businesses with more than 25 employees and nearly all employment agencies and labor unions. A 1972 amendment broadened the coverage to employers with as few as 15 employees.

The Civil Rights Act of 1964 prohibited different voting registration standards for White and Black voting applicants. It also prohibited discrimination in public accommodations— that is, hotels, motels, restaurants, gasoline stations, and amusement parks. Publicly owned facilities such as parks, stadiums, and swimming pools were also prohibited from discriminating. Another important provision forbade discrimination in all federally supported programs and institutions such as hospitals, colleges, and road construction projects.

The Civil Rights Act of 1964 covered discrimination based on race, color, creed, national origin, and sex. Although the inclusion of gender in employment criteria had been prohibited in the federal civil service since 1949, most laws and most groups pushing for change showed little concern about sex discrimination. There was little precedent for attention to such discrimination even at the state level. Only Hawaii and Wisconsin had enacted laws against sex discrimination before 1964. As first proposed, the Civil Rights Act did not include mention of gender. One day before the final vote, opponents of the measure offered an amendment on gender bias in an effort to defeat the entire act. The act did pass with prohibition against sex bias included, an event that can only be regarded as a milestone for women seeking equal employment rights with men.

The Civil Rights Act of 1964 was not perfect. Since 1964, several acts and amendments to the original act have been added to cover the many areas of discrimination it left untouched, such as criminal justice and housing. Even in areas singled out for enforcement in the act, discrimination still occurs. Federal agencies charged with enforcement complain that they are underfunded or are denied wholehearted support by the White House. Also, regardless of how much the EEOC may want to act in a particular case, the person who alleges discrimination has to pursue the complaint over a long time that is marked by long periods of inaction. Despite these efforts, devastating forms of discrimination persist. African Americans, Latinos, and others fall victim to **redlining**, or the pattern of discrimination against people trying to buy homes in minority and racially changing neighborhoods. Research finds that in 25 metropolitan areas, housing agents showed fewer housing units to Blacks and Latinos, steered them to minority neighborhoods, and gave far less assistance in finding housing that met homebuyer needs. The concept of redlining is now being applied to areas other than home buying.

People living in predominantly minority neighborhoods have found that service deliverers refuse to go to their area. In one case that attracted national attention in 1997, Kansas City's Pizza Hut refused to deliver 40 pizzas to an honor program at a high school

redlining
The pattern of discrimination against people trying to buy homes in minority and racially changing neighborhoods.

in an all-Black neighborhood. A Pizza Hut spokesperson called the neighborhood unsafe and said that almost every city has "restricted areas" to which the company will not deliver. This admission was particularly embarrassing because the high school already had a $170,000-a-year contract with Pizza Hut to deliver pizzas as a part of its school lunch program. Service redlining covers everything from parcel deliveries to repair people as well as food deliveries. The red pencil appears not to have been set aside in cities throughout the United States (Fuller 1998; Rusk 2001; Schwartz 2001; Turner et al. 2002; Yinger 1995).

Although civil rights laws often have established rights for other minorities, the Supreme Court made them explicit in two 1987 decisions involving groups other than African Americans. In the first of the two cases, an Iraqi American professor asserted that he had been denied tenure because of his Arab origins; in the second, a Jewish congregation

Although more and more Latinos and African Americans are buying their own homes, the assets of accumulation run well behind those of White households—a legacy, in part, of past and current discrimination.

brought suit for damages in response to the defacement of its synagogue with derogatory symbols. The Supreme Court ruled unanimously that, in effect, any member of an ethnic minority may sue under federal prohibitions against discrimination. These decisions paved the way for almost all racial and ethnic groups to invoke the Civil Rights Act of 1964 (Taylor 1987).

A particularly insulting form of discrimination seemed finally to be on its way out in the late 1980s. Many social clubs had limitations that forbid membership to minorities, Jews, and women. For years, exclusive clubs argued that they were merely selecting friends, but, in fact, a principal function of these clubs is as a forum to transact business. Denial of membership meant more than the inability to attend a luncheon; it also seemed to exclude certain groups from part of the marketplace, as Lawrence Otis Graham observed at the beginning of this chapter. In 1988, the Supreme Court ruled unanimously in *New York State Clubs Association v. City of New York* that states and cities may ban sex discrimination by large private clubs where business lunches and similar activities take place. Although the ruling does not apply to all clubs and leaves the issue of racial and ethnic barriers unresolved, it did chip away at the arbitrary exclusiveness of private groups (Steinhauer 2006; Taylor 1988).

Memberships and restrictive organizations remain perfectly legal. The rise to national attention of professional golfer Tiger Woods, of mixed Native American, African, and Asian ancestry, made the public aware that there were at least 23 golf courses where he would be prohibited from playing by virtue of race. In 2002, women's groups tried unsuccessfully to have the golf champion speak out as the Master's and British Open were played on courses closed to women as members (Scott 2003).

Proving discrimination even as outlined for generations in legislation continues to be difficult. In the 2007 *Ledbetter v. Goodyear Tire and Rubber Co.* ruling, the Supreme Court affirmed that victims had to file a formal complaint within 180 days of the alleged discrimination. This set aside thousands of cases where employees learned their initial pay was lower to comparably employed White or male workers only after they had been in a job for years. Given the usual secrecy in workplaces around salaries, it is now all the more difficult for potential cases of pay disparity to be effectively advanced. Initial efforts by Congress to enact the Lilly Ledbetter Fair Pay Act that give victims more time to file a lawsuit have failed (Hulse 2008).

The inability of the Civil Rights Act, similar legislation, and court decisions to end discrimination does not result entirely from poor financial and political support, although it does play a role. The number of federal employees assigned to investigate and prosecute bias cases is insufficient. Many discriminatory practices, such as those described as institutional discrimination, are seldom subject to legal action.

Wealth Inequality: Discrimination's Legacy

Discrimination that has occurred in the past carries into the present and future. As noted in Figure 3.1, a lack of inherited wealth is one element of the past. African American and other minority groups have had less opportunity to accumulate assets such as homes, land, and savings that can insulate them and later their children from economic setbacks.

Income refers to salaries and wages, and **wealth** is a more inclusive term that encompasses all of a person's material assets, including land, stocks, and other types of property. Wealth allows one to live better; even modest assets provide insurance against the effects of job layoffs, natural disasters, and long-term illness, and they afford individuals much better interest rates when they need to borrow money. It allows children to graduate from college relatively debt free or perhaps without any college loans to pay back. This reminds us that for many people it is not a question of wealth in the sense of assets but wealth as measured by indebtedness.

Studies document that the kinds of disparities in income we have seen are even greater when wealth is considered. In 2004, only 4 percent of homebuyers were African Americans—at least one-third of what we would expect. This makes sense, however, because if individuals experience lower incomes throughout their lives, they are less likely to be able to put anything aside. They are more likely to have to pay interest rather than save for their future or their children's future.

Little wonder then that White children are more likely to surpass parents' income than Black children are. Furthermore, White children are more likely to move up the economic social class ladder than are Black children, who are also more likely to actually fall back in absolute terms.

A close analysis of wealth shows that typically African American families have $86,000 less in wealth than their White counterparts, even when comparing members of comparably educated and employed households. Evidence indicates that this inequality in wealth has been growing over the last 10 years rather than staying the same or declining (Bureau of the Census 2007a; Economic Mobility Project 2007a; Oliver and Shapiro 2006).

Environmental Justice

Discrimination takes many forms and is not necessarily apparent, even when its impact can be far reaching. Take the example of Kennedy Heights, a well-kept working-class neighborhood nestled in southeastern Houston. This community faces a real threat, and it is not from crime or drugs. The threat that community residents fear is right under their feet in the form of three oil pits abandoned by Gulf Oil in 1927. The residents, mostly African American, argue that they have suffered high rates of cancer, lupus, and other illnesses because the chemicals from the oil fields poison their water supply. The residents first sued Chevron USA in 1985, and the case is still making its way through the courtrooms of no fewer than six states and the federal judiciary.

Lawyers and other representatives for the residents say that the oil company is guilty of environmental racism because it knowingly allowed a predominantly Black housing development to be built on the contaminated land. They are able to support this charge with documents, including a 1954 memorandum from an appraiser who suggested that the oil pits be drained of any toxic substances and the land filled for "low-cost houses for White occupancy." When the land did not sell right away, an oil company official in a 1967 memorandum suggested a tax-free land exchange with a developer who intended to use the land for "Negro residents and commercial development." For this latter intended use by African Americans, there was no mention of any required environmental cleanup of the land. The oil company counters that it just assumed the developer would do the necessary cleanup of the pits (Maning 1997; Sze and London 2008).

The conflict perspective sees the case of the Houston suburb as one in which pollution harms minority groups disproportionately. **Environmental justice** refers to the

income
Salaries, wages, and other money received.

wealth
An inclusive term encompassing all of a person's material assets, including land and other types of property.

environmental justice
Efforts to ensure that hazardous substances are controlled so that all communities receive protection regardless of race or socioeconomic circumstances.

efforts to ensure that hazardous substances are controlled so that all communities receive protection regardless of race or socioeconomic circumstance. After the Environmental Protection Agency and other organizations documented discrimination in the locating of hazardous waste sites, an executive order was issued in 1994 that requires all federal agencies to ensure that low-income and minority communities have access to better information about their environment and have an opportunity to participate in shaping government policies that affect their communities' health. Initial efforts to implement the policy have met widespread opposition, including criticism from some proponents of economic development who argue that the guidelines unnecessarily delay or altogether block locating new industrial sites.

Low-income communities and areas with significant minority populations are more likely to be adjacent to waste sites than are affluent White communities. Studies in California show the higher probability that people of color live closer to sources of air pollution. Another study concluded that grade schools in Florida nearer to environmental hazards are disproportionately Black or Latino. People of color jeopardized by environmental problems also lack the resources and political muscle to do something about it (Pastor, Morello-Frosch, and Saad 2005; Pellow and Brulle 2007; Stretesky and Lynch 2002).

Issues of environmental justice are not limited to metropolitan areas. Another continuing problem is abuse of Native American reservation land. Many American Indian leaders are concerned that tribal lands are too often regarded as dumping grounds for toxic waste that go to the highest bidder. On the other hand, the economic devastation faced by some tribes in isolated areas has led one tribe in Utah to actually seek out becoming a depot for discarded nuclear waste (*New York Times* 2005a; Skull Valley Goshutes 2006).

As with other aspects of discrimination, experts disagree. There is controversy within the scientific community over the potential hazards of some of the problems, and there is even some opposition within the subordinate communities being affected. This complexity of the issues in terms of social class and race is apparent, as some observers question the wisdom of an executive order that slows economic development coming to areas in dire need of employment opportunities. On the other hand, some observers counter that such businesses typically employ few less-skilled workers and only make the environment less livable for those left behind. Despite such varying viewpoints, environmental justice is an excellent example of resistance and change in the 1990s that could not have been foreseen by the civil rights workers of the 1950s.

A setback in antidiscrimination lawsuits came when the Supreme Court told Lilly Ledbetter, in effect; she was "too late." Ledbetter had been a supervisor for many years at the Godsden, Alabama, Goodyear Tire Rubber plant when she realized that she was being paid $6,500 less per year than the lowest-paid male supervisor. The Court ruled that she must sue within 180 days of the initial discriminatory paycheck even though it had taken years before she even knew of the differential payment.

Affirmative Action

Affirmative action is the positive effort to recruit subordinate-group members, including women, for jobs, promotions, and educational opportunities. The phrase *affirmative action* first appeared in an executive order issued by President Kennedy in 1961. The order called for contractors to "take affirmative action to ensure that applicants are employed, and that employees are treated during employment, without regard to their race, creed, color, or national origin." However, at that time, no enforcement procedures were specified. Six years later, the order was amended to prohibit discrimination on the basis of sex, but affirmative action was still defined vaguely.

Today, affirmative action has become a catchall term for racial preference programs and goals. It has also become a lightning rod for opposition to any programs that suggest special consideration of women or racial minorities.

Affirmative Action Explained

Affirmative action has been viewed as an important tool for reducing institutional discrimination. Whereas previous efforts were aimed at eliminating individual acts of discrimination, federal measures under the heading of affirmative action have been aimed at procedures that deny equal opportunities, even if they are not intended to be overtly discriminatory. This policy has been implemented to deal with both current discrimination and past discrimination outlined earlier in this chapter.

affirmative action
Positive efforts to recruit subordinate group members, including women, for jobs, promotions, and educational opportunities.

So desperate are the economic conditions of isolated Indian tribes that they often seek out questionable forms of economic development. The Skull Valley Goshute Indian Reservation in Utah is trying to attract a nuclear waste dump, and local and state officials are trying to block this possibility.

Affirmative action has been aimed at institutional discrimination in such areas as the following:

- height and weight requirements that are unnecessarily geared to the physical proportions of White men without regard to the actual characteristics needed to perform the job and that therefore exclude women and some minorities;

- seniority rules, when applied to jobs historically held only by White men, that make more recently hired minorities and females more subject to layoff—the "last hired, first fired" employee—and less eligible for advancement;

- nepotism-based membership policies of some unions that exclude those who are not relatives of members who, because of past employment practices, are usually White;

- restrictive employment leave policies, coupled with prohibitions on part-time work or denials of fringe benefits to part-time workers, that make it difficult for the heads of single-parent families, most of whom are women, to get and keep jobs and also meet the needs of their families;

- rules requiring that only English be spoken at the workplace, even when not a business necessity, which result in discriminatory employment practices toward people whose primary language is not English;

- standardized academic tests or criteria geared to the cultural and educational norms of middle-class or White men when these are not relevant predictors of successful job performance;

- preferences shown by law and medical schools in admitting children of wealthy and influential alumni, nearly all of whom are White; and

- credit policies of banks and lending institutions that prevent the granting of mortgages and loans in minority neighborhoods or that prevent the granting of credit to married women and others who have previously been denied the opportunity to build good credit histories in their own names.

Employers have also been cautioned against asking leading questions in interviews such as "Did you know you would be the first Black to supervise all Whites in that factory?" or "Does your husband mind your working on weekends?" Furthermore, the lack of minority-group or female employees may in itself represent evidence for a case of unlawful exclusion (Commission on Civil Rights 1981; also see Bohmer and Oka 2007).

The Legal Debate

How far can an employer go in encouraging women and minorities to apply for a job before it becomes unlawful discrimination against White men? Since the late 1970s, a number of bitterly debated cases on this difficult aspect of affirmative action have reached the U.S. Supreme Court. The most significant cases are summarized in Table 3.2.

TABLE 3.2
Key Decisions on Affirmative Action

In a series of split and often very close decisions, the Supreme Court has expressed a variety of reservations in specific situations.

Year	Favorable (+) or Unfavorable (−) to Policy	Case	Vote	Ruling
1971	+	Griggs v. Duke Power Co.	9–0	Private employers must provide a remedy where minorities were denied opportunities, even if unintentional.
1978	−	Regents of the University of California v. Bakke	5–4	Prohibited holding specific number of places for minorities in college admissions.
1979	+	United Steelworkers of America v. Weber	5–2	Okay for union to favor minorities in special training programs.
1984	−	Firefighters Local Union No. 1784 (Memphis, TN) v. Stotts	6–1	Seniority means recently hired minorities may be laid off first in staff reductions.
1986	+	International Association of Firefighters v. City of Cleveland	6–3	May promote minorities over more-senior Whites.
1986	+	New York City v. Sheet Metal	5–4	Approved specific quota of minority workers for union.
1987	+	United States v. Paradise	5–4	Endorsed quotas for promotions of state troopers.
1987	+	Johnson v. Transportation Agency, Santa Clara, CA	6–3	Approved preference in hiring for minorities and women over better-qualified men and Whites.
1989	−	Richmond v. Croson Company	6–3	Ruled a 30 percent set-aside program for minority contractors unconstitutional.
1989	−	Martin v. Wilks	5–4	Ruled Whites may bring reverse discrimination claims against Court-approved affirmative action plans.
1990	+	Metro Broadcasting v. FCC	5–4	Supported federal programs aimed at increasing minority ownership of broadcast licenses.
1995	−	Adarand Constructors Inc. v. Peña	5–4	Benefits based on race are constitutional only if narrowly defined to accomplish a compelling interest.
1996	−	Texas v. Hopwood	*	Let stand a lower court decision covering Louisiana, Mississippi, and Texas that race could not be used in college admissions.
2003	+	Grutter v. Bollinger	5–4	Race can be a limited factor in admissions at the University of Michigan Law School.
2003	−	Gratz v. Bollinger	6–3	Cannot use a strict formula awarding advantage based on race for admissions to the University of Michigan.

*U.S. Court of Appeals Fifth Circuit decision.

In the 1978 *Bakke* case (*Regents of the University of California v. Bakke*), by a narrow 5–4 vote, the Court ordered the medical school of the University of California at Davis to admit Allan Bakke, a qualified White engineer who had originally been denied admission solely on the basis of his race. The justices ruled that the school had violated Bakke's constitutional rights by establishing a fixed quota system for minority students. However, the Court added that it was constitutional for universities to adopt flexible admission programs that use race as one factor in making decisions.

Colleges and universities responded with new policies designed to meet the Bakke ruling while broadening opportunities for traditionally underrepresented minority students. However, in 1996, the Supreme Court allowed a lower court decision to stand: that affirmative action programs for African American and Mexican American students at the University of Texas law school were unconstitutional. The ruling effectively prohibited schools in the lower court's jurisdiction of Louisiana, Mississippi, and Texas from taking race into account in admissions. In 2003, the Supreme Court made two rulings concerning the admissions policies at the University of Michigan. In one case involving the law school, the Court upheld the right of the school to use applicants' race as criteria for admission decisions but ruled against a strict admissions formula awarding points to minority applicants who applied to the university's undergraduate school. Given the various legal actions, further challenges to affirmative action can be expected (Colburn et al. 2008).

Has affirmative action actually helped alleviate employment inequality on the basis of race and gender? This is a difficult question to answer, given the complexity of the labor market and the fact that there are other antidiscrimination measures, but it does appear that affirmative action has had a significant impact in the sectors where it has been applied. Sociologist Barbara Reskin (1998) reviewed available studies looking at workforce composition in terms of race and gender in light of affirmative action policies. She found that gains in minority employment can be attributed to affirmative action policies. This includes both firms mandated to follow affirmative action guidelines and those that took them on voluntarily. There is also evidence that some earnings gains can be attributed to affirmative action. Economists M. V. Lee Badgett and Heidi Hartmann (1995), reviewing 26 other research studies, came to similar conclusions: affirmative action and other federal compliance programs have had a modest impact, but it is difficult to assess, given larger economic changes such as recessions or the rapid increase in women in the paid labor force.

Reverse Discrimination

Although researchers debated the merit of affirmative action, the public—particularly Whites but also some affluent African Americans and Hispanics—questioned the wisdom of the program. Particularly strident were the charges of reverse discrimination: that government actions cause better-qualified White men to be bypassed in favor of women and minority men. **Reverse discrimination** is an emotional term, because it conjures up the notion that somehow women and minorities will subject White men in the United States to the same treatment received by minorities during the last three centuries. Such cases are not unknown, but they are uncommon—fewer than 10 of the race-related complaints to the federal government were filed by Whites, and only 18 percent of gender-related complaints and 4 percent of the course cases were filed by men.

Increasingly, critics of affirmative action call for color-blind policies that would end affirmative action and, they argue, allow all people to be judged fairly. However, will that mean an end to the institutional practices that favored Whites? For example, according to the latest data, 40 percent of applicants who are children of Harvard's alumni, who are almost all White, are admitted to the university, compared to 11 percent of nonalumni children. Ironically, studies show that these children of alumni typically are far more likely than either minority students or athletes to run into academic trouble (*Economist* 2004b; Massey and Mooney 2007; Pincus 2003, 2008).

Is it possible to have color-blind policies prevail in the United States in the twenty-first century? Supporters of affirmative action contend that as long as businesses rely on informal social networks, personal recommendations, and family ties, White men will have a distinct advantage built on generations of being in positions of power. Furthermore, an end to affirmative action should also mean an end to the many programs that give advantages to certain businesses, homeowners, veterans, farmers, and others. Most of these preference holders are White (Kilson 1995; Mack 1996).

reverse discrimination
Actions that cause better-qualified White men to be passed over for women and minority men.

Consequently, by the 1990s and into the twenty-first century, affirmative action had emerged as an increasingly important issue in state and national political campaigns. As noted earlier, in 2003, the Supreme Court reviewed the admission policies at the University of Michigan, which may favor racial minorities (see Table 3.2). In 2006, Michigan citizens, by a 58 percent margin, voted to restrict all their state universities from using affirmative action in their admissions policies. Generally, discussions have focused on the use of quotas in hiring practices. Supporters of affirmative action argue that hiring goals establish "floors" for minority inclusion but do not exclude truly qualified candidates from any group. Opponents insist that these "targets" are, in fact, quotas that lead to reverse discrimination (Lewin 2006).

The State of California, in particular, was a battleground for this controversial issue. The California Civil Rights Initiative (Proposition 209) was placed on the ballot in 1996 as a referendum to amend the state constitution and prohibit any programs that give preference to women and minorities for college admission, employment, promotion, or government contracts. Overall, 54 percent of the voters backed the state proposition.

Legal challenges continue concerning Proposition 209, which is being implemented unevenly throughout the state. Much of the attention has focused on the impact that reducing racial preference programs will have in law and medical schools, in which competition for admission is very high. The courts have upheld the measures in California, Michigan, and Washington, and subsequently several other states were considering measures in statewide referenda that would prohibit affirmative action in public realms such as employment, education, and contracting (Dolan 2000; Khadaroo 2008; Schmidt 2007).

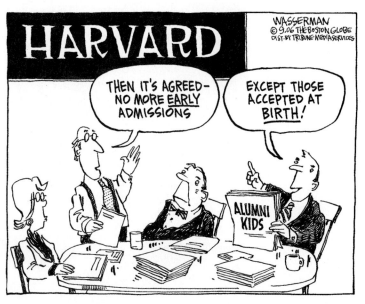

Affirmative action is criticized for giving preferential treatment, but colleges have a long history of giving admissions preferences to relatives of past graduates who are much more likely to be White rather than Black or Latino.

The Glass Ceiling

We have been talking primarily about racial and ethnic groups as if they have uniformly failed to keep pace with Whites. Although this notion is accurate, there are tens of thousands of people of color who have matched and even exceeded Whites in terms of income. For example, in 2007, more than 1.4 million Black households and another 1.3 million Hispanic families earned more than $100,000. What can we say about financially better-off members of subordinate groups in the United States (DeNavas-Walt, Proctor, and Lee 2008, HINC tables)?

Prejudice does not necessarily end with wealth. Black newspaper columnist De Wayne Wickham (1993) wrote of the subtle racism he had experienced. He heard a White clerk in a supermarket ask a White customer whether she knew the price of an item the computer would not scan; when the problem occurred while the clerk was ringing up Wickham's groceries, she called for a price check. Affluent subordinate-group members routinely report being blocked as they move toward the first-class section aboard airplanes or seek service in upscale stores. Another journalist, Ellis Cose (1993), has called these insults the soul-destroying slights to affluent minorities that lead to the "rage of a privileged class."

Discrimination persists for even educated and qualified people from the best family backgrounds. As subordinate-group members are able to compete successfully, they sometimes encounter attitudinal or organizational bias that prevents them from reaching their full potential. They have confronted what has come to be called the **glass ceiling**. This refers to the barrier that blocks the promotion of a qualified worker because of gender or minority membership (Figure 3.4). Often, people entering nontraditional areas of employment become marginalized and are made to feel uncomfortable, much like the situation of immigrants who feel a part of two cultures, as we discussed in Chapter 1.

glass ceiling
The barrier that blocks the promotion of a qualified worker because of gender or minority membership.

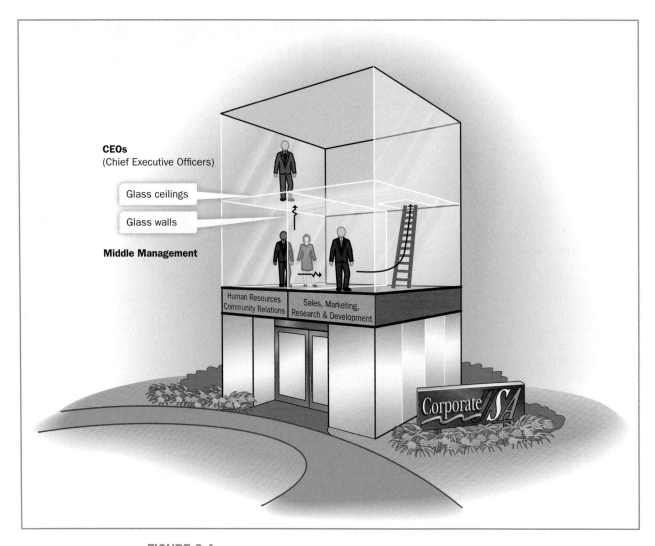

FIGURE 3.4
Glass Ceilings and Glass Walls
Women and minority men are moving up in corporations but encounter glass ceilings that block entry to top positions. In addition, they face glass walls that block lateral moves to areas from which executives are promoted. These barriers contribute to women and minority men not moving into the ultimate decision-making positions in the nation's corporate giants.

The reasons for glass ceilings are as many as the occurrences. It may be that one Black or one woman vice president is regarded as enough, so the second potential candidate faces a block to movement up through management. Decision makers may be concerned that their clientele will not trust them if they have too many people of color or may worry that a talented woman could become overwhelmed with her duties as a mother and wife and thus perform poorly in the workplace.

Concern about women and minorities climbing a broken ladder led to the formation in 1991 of the Glass Ceiling Commission, with the U.S. secretary of labor chairing the 21-member group. Initially, it regarded the following as some of the glass ceiling barriers:

- lack of management commitment to establishing systems, policies, and practices for achieving workplace diversity and upward mobility;
- pay inequities for work of equal or comparable value;
- sex-, race-, and ethnicity-based stereotyping and harassment;
- unfair recruitment practices;
- lack of family-friendly workplace policies;

- "parent-track" policies that discourage parental leave policies; and
- limited opportunities for advancement to decision-making positions.

This significant underrepresentation of women and minority males in managerial positions results in large part from the presence of glass ceilings. Sociologist Max Weber wrote more than 100 years ago that the privileged class monopolizes the purchase of high-priced consumer goods and wields the power to grant or withhold opportunity from others. To grasp just how White and male the membership of this elite group is, consider the following: eighty-two percent of the 11,500 people who serve on the boards of directors of *Fortune* 1,000 corporations are White non-Hispanic males. For every 82 White men on these boards, there are two Latinos, two Asian Americans, three African Americans, and 11 White women (Strauss 2002; Weber [1913–1922] 1947).

Glass ceilings are not the only barrier. There are also glass walls. Catalyst, a nonprofit research organization, conducted interviews in 1992 and, again, in 2001 with senior and middle managers from larger corporations. The study found that even before glass ceilings are encountered, women and racial and ethnic minorities face **glass walls** that keep them from moving laterally. Specifically, the study found that women tend to be placed in staff or support positions in areas such as public relations and human resources and are often directed away from jobs in core areas such as marketing, production, and sales. Women are assigned to and, therefore, trapped in jobs that reflect their stereotypical helping nature and encounter glass walls that cut off access to jobs that might lead to broader experience and advancement (Bjerk 2008; Catalyst 2001; Lopez 1992).

Researchers have documented a differential impact that the glass ceiling has on White males. It appears that men who enter traditionally female occupations are more likely to rise to the top. Male elementary teachers become principals, and male nurses become supervisors. The **glass escalator** refers to the male advantage experienced in occupations dominated by women. Whereas females may become tokens when they enter traditionally male occupations, men are more likely to be advantaged when they move out of sex-typical jobs. In summary, women and minority men confront a glass ceiling that limits upward mobility and glass walls that reduce their ability to move into fast-track jobs leading to the highest reaches of the corporate executive suite. Meanwhile, men who do choose to enter female-dominated occupations are often rewarded with promotions and positions of responsibility coveted by their fellow female workers (Budig 2002; Cognard-Black 2004).

glass wall
A barrier to moving laterally in a business to positions that are more likely to lead to upward mobility.

glass escalator
The male advantage experienced in occupations dominated by women.

Conclusion

The job advertisement read "African Americans and Arabians tend to clash with me so that won't work out." Sounds like it was from your grandfather's era? Actually, it appeared on the popular craigslist Web site in 2006 and is just one example of how explicit discrimination thrives even in the digital age (Hughlett 2006).

Discrimination takes its toll, whether or not a person who is discriminated against is part of the informal economy or looking for a job on the Internet. Even members of minority groups who are not today being overtly discriminated against continue to fall victim to past discrimination. We have also identified the costs of discrimination to members of the privileged group.

From the conflict perspective, it is not surprising to find the widespread presence of the informal economy proposed by the dual labor market model and even an underclass. Derrick Bell (1994), an African American law professor, has made the sobering assertion that "racism is permanent." He contends that the attitudes of dominant Whites prevail, and society is willing to advance programs on behalf of subordinate groups only when they coincide with needs as perceived by those Whites.

The surveys presented in Chapter 2 show gradual acceptance of the earliest efforts to eliminate discrimination, but that support is failing as color-blind racism takes hold, especially as it relates to affirmative action. Indeed, concerns about doing something about alleged reverse discrimination are as likely to be voiced as concerns about racial or gender discrimination or glass ceilings and glass walls.

Institutional discrimination remains a formidable challenge in the United States. Attempts to reduce discrimination by attacking institutional discrimination have met with staunch resistance. Partly as a result of this outcry from some of the public, especially White Americans, the federal government gradually deemphasized its affirmative action efforts, beginning in the 1980s and into the twenty-first century. Most of the material in this chapter has been about racial groups, especially Black and White Americans. It would be easy to see intergroup hostility as a racial phenomenon, but that would be incorrect. Throughout the history of the United States, relations between some White groups have been characterized by resentment and violence. The next two chapters examine the ongoing legacy of immigration and the nature and relations of White ethnic groups.

Summary

1. Discrimination has a cumulative effect so that people today are victims of post- and current differential practices.

2. Racial and ethnic minorities are more likely to be unemployed, engaged in low-wage labor, or relegated to the informal (or underground) economy.

3. Institutional discrimination results from the normal operations of a society.

4. Discrimination in hiring is documented through job-testing experiments.

5. Inequality continues to be apparent in the analysis of annual incomes, controlling for the amount of education attained and wealth, and even in the absence of environmental justice.

6. Presidential executive orders, legislative acts, and judicial decisions have all played a part in reducing discrimination.

7. For almost 50 years, affirmative action as a remedy to inequality has been a hotly contested issue, with its critics contending it amounts to reverse discrimination.

8. Upwardly mobile professional women and minority males may encounter a glass ceiling and be thwarted in their efforts by glass walls to become more-attractive candidates for advancement.

Key Terms

absolute deprivation 61
affirmative action 75
discrimination 60
dual or split labor
 market 68
environmental justice 74
glass ceiling 79

glass escalator 81
glass wall 81
income 74
informal economy 67
institutional
 discrimination 63

irregular or underground
 economy 67
redlining 72
relative deprivation 61
reverse discrimination 78
total discrimination 62
wealth 74

Review Questions

1. Why might people feel disadvantaged even though their incomes are rising and their housing circumstances have improved?
2. Why does institutional discrimination sometimes seem less objectionable than individual discrimination?
3. In what way does the economy of the United States operate on several economic levels?
4. Why are questions raised about affirmative action although inequality persists?
5. Distinguish among glass ceilings, glass walls, and glass escalators. How do they differ from more-obvious forms of discrimination in employment?

Critical Thinking

1. Discrimination can take many forms. Select a case of discrimination that you think just about everyone would agree is wrong. Then describe another incident in which the alleged discrimination was of a more subtle form. Who is likely to condemn and who is likely to overlook such situations?
2. Resistance is a continuing theme of intergroup race relations. Discrimination implies the oppression of a group, but how can discrimination also unify the oppressed group to resist such unequal treatment? How can acceptance, or integration, for example, weaken the sense of solidarity within a group?
3. Voluntary associations such as the National Association for the Advancement of Colored People (NAACP) and government units such as the courts have been important vehicles for bringing about a measure of social justice. In what ways can the private sector—corporations and businesses—also work to bring about an end to discrimination?

4

Immigration

THE DIVERSITY OF THE AMERICAN PEOPLE IS UNMISTAKABLE evidence of the variety of places from which immigrants have come. Yet each succeeding generation of immigrants found itself being reluctantly accepted, at best, by the descendants of earlier arrivals. The Chinese were the first immigrant group to be singled out for restriction, with the passage of the 1882 Exclusion Act. The initial Chinese immigrants became scapegoats for America's sagging economy in the last half of the nineteenth century. Growing fears that too many non-American types were immigrating motivated the creation of the national origin system and the quota acts of the 1920s. These acts gave preference to certain nationalities until the passage of the Immigration and Nationality Act in 1965 ended that practice. Many immigrants today in the United States are transnationals who still maintain close ties to their countries of origin, sending money back, keeping current with political events, and making frequent return trips. Concern about both illegal and legal immigration continues with renewed attention in the aftermath of the September 11, 2001, terrorist attacks. Restrictionist sentiment has grown, and debates rage over whether immigrants, even legal ones, should receive services such as education, government-subsidized health care, and welfare. The challenges to an immigrant household upon arrival are not evenly felt, as women play the central role in facilitating the transition. Controversy also continues to surround the policy of the United States toward refugees.

85

The small farming community of Mattawa, Washington, seems an unlikely location for seeing the social impact of immigration; but today the flow of immigrants is nationwide. Nearly everyone in Mattawa speaks Spanish, with more than 90 percent of residents using it at home. Adjustment by old-timers has been slow. City government and the police force lack bilingual employees and have only now begun to hire translators. Chain stores continue to bypass the community even though it has grown from 300 to more 3,200 in 20 years. Yet residents find authentic meals from their home countries locally at El Jato, El Caribe, and La Maravita.

Mohammed Reza Ghaffarpour is willing to adjust and is not against assimilating. The Iranian-born engineering professor aced his citizenship test in 2003 but had to wait until 2008 to gain citizenship. His trips from his Chicago home to Iran for academic meetings and tending to ailing parents led to scrutiny by the U.S. authorities. The 53-year-old man felt discriminated against but is not bitter; although he waited to become a citizen, he feels the "system is working."

Then there are the special legal permissions for supermodels and athletes that allow them to jump to the head of the immigration line. Marching into Beijing's Olympic stadium under the United States flag in 2008 were a kayaker from Poland, table tennis players from China, a triathlete from New Zealand, a distance runner from Kenya, and an equestrian from Australia—all newly minted U.S. citizens (Glascock 2008; Olicio 2008, and Wilson and Lehren 2008).

Faeza Jaber is a 48-year-old single mother in her first months in the United States with her 7-year-old son, Khatab. When she arrived in Phoenix, Arizona, it was 114 degrees, which is hotter than her home in Baghdad. She was granted her refugee status after her husband, who was an office manager and interpreter for *Time* magazine, was murdered in 2004 on his way to work at a time when Iraqi interpreters for foreign companies were being targeted. Previously a computer programmer at the Baghdad airport, Jaber has found the transition difficult as she works as a part-time teacher's assistant at Khatab's elementary school. She is striving to learn English and is encouraged by the knowledge that of the 600 Iraqi refugees who pass annually through Phoenix, 91 percent find a job and are able to support themselves without any state and federal subsidies within five months of their arrival (Bennett 2008).

The armed immigration agents arrived at the Petit Jean Poultry Plant in Arkadelphia, Arkansas, just before the 7:30 A.M. early morning shift break for breakfast. Half the shift, 119 workers, was taken away in plastic handcuffs to a detention center from which all but six were sent back to Mexico. In the weeks following, the 10,000 residents of Arkadelphia were upset that their community had been disrupted. People they had known as classmates at the local community college, neighbors, customers, fellow churchgoers, and clients had disappeared. Although the people of this Arkansas town usually embrace law enforcement, they did not like what had happened. Some even went so far as to reach the deported workers in Mexico and try to arrange to bring them back to town by crossing the border illegally (Chu and Mustafa 2006; Hennessy-Fiske 2006).

These dramas being played out in Chicago and Phoenix, Arkansas and Washington State illustrate the themes in immigration today. Immigrant labor is needed, but concerns over illegal immigration persist and, even for those who arrive legally, the transition can be difficult. For the next generation it gets a little easier and, for some, perhaps too easy as they begin to forget their family's heritage. Many come legally, applying for immigrant visas, but others enter illegally. In the United States, we may not like lawbreakers, but often we seek services and low-priced products made by people who come here illegally. How do we control this immigration without violating the principle of free movement within the nation? How do we decide who enters? And how do we treat those who come here either legally or illegally?

The world is now a global network, with the core and periphery countries, described in world systems theory (see p. 19 in Chapter 1) linking not only commercial goods but also families and workers across political borders. The social forces that cause people to emigrate are complex. The most important have been economic: financial failure in the old country and expectations of higher incomes and standards of living in the new land. Other factors include dislike of new political regimes in their native lands, the experience of being victims of racial or religious bigotry, and a desire to reunite families. All these factors push people from their homelands and pull them to other nations such as the United States. Immigration into the United States, in particular, has been facilitated by cheap ocean transportation and by other countries' removal of restrictions on emigration.

Refugee Faeza Jaber and her son, Khatab, pause outside a mall in Phoenix, Arizona, where they relocated after the killing of her husband, Omar, who was shot by an unknown assailant in Baghdad in March 2004.

Immigration: A Global Phenomenon

Immigration, as we noted in Chapter 1, is a worldwide phenomenon and contributes to globalization as more and more people see the world as their "home" rather than one specific country, as shown in Figure 4.1. People move across national borders throughout the world. Generally, immigration is from countries with lower standards of living to those that offer better wages. However, wars and famine may precipitate the movement of hundreds of thousands of people into neighboring countries and sometimes permanent resettlement.

Scholars of immigration often point to *push* and *pull factors*. For example, economic difficulties, religious or ethnic persecution, and political unrest may push individuals from their homelands. Immigration to a particular nation, the pull factors, may be a result of perceptions of a better life ahead or a desire to join a community of their fellow nationals already established abroad.

A potent factor contributing to immigration anywhere in the world is chain immigration. **Chain immigration** refers to an immigrant who sponsors several other immigrants who, on their arrival, may sponsor still more. Laws that favor people who desire to enter a given country who already have relatives there or someone who can vouch for them financially may facilitate this sponsorship. But probably the most important aspect of chain immigration is that immigrants anticipate knowing someone who can help them adjust to their new surroundings and find a new job, place to live, and even the kind of foods that are familiar to them. Later in this chapter, we will revisit the social impact that immigration has worldwide.

Patterns of Immigration to the United States

There have been three unmistakable patterns of immigration to the United States: the number of immigrants has fluctuated dramatically over time largely because of government policy changes, settlement has not been uniform across the country but centered in certain regions and cities, and the source of immigrants has changed over time. We will first look at the historical picture of immigrant numbers.

chain immigration
Immigrants sponsor several other immigrants who upon their arrival may sponsor still more.

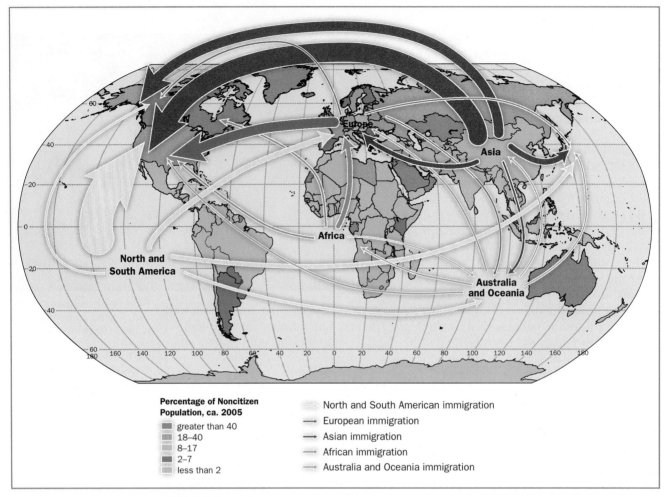

Percentage of Noncitizen
Population, ca. 2005

- greater than 40
- 18–40
- 8–17
- 2–7
- less than 2

⇒ North and South American immigration
→ European immigration
→ Asian immigration
→ African immigration
⇒ Australia and Oceania immigration

FIGURE 4.1
International Migration

Source: Fernandez-Armesto 2007, 1006.

Vast numbers of immigrants have come to the United States. Figure 4.2 indicates the high but fluctuating number of immigrants who arrived during every decade from the 1820s through the beginning of the twenty-first century. The United States received the largest number of legal immigrants during the first decade of the 1900s, which is likely to be surprised in the first decade of twenty-first century, but because the country was much smaller in the period from 1900 through 1910, the numerical impact was even greater then.

The reception given to immigrants in this country has not always been friendly. Open bloodshed, restrictive laws, and the eventual return of almost one-third of immigrants and their children to their home countries attest to some Americans' uneasy feelings toward strangers who want to settle here.

Opinion polls in the United States from 2000 through 2008 have never shown more than 10 percent of the public in favor of more immigration, and usually about 45 percent to 55 percent want less. Even a 2007 survey of Latinos found a sizable 30 percent advocated having immigration levels decreased. We want the door open until we get through, and then we want to close it (Gallup 2008).

Today's Foreign-Born Population

Before considering the sweep of past immigration policies, let us consider today's immigrant population. About 12 percent of the nation's people are foreign-born; this proportion is between the high figure of about 15 percent in 1890 and a low of 4.7 percent in 1970. By global comparisons, the foreign-born population in the United States is large but not unusual.

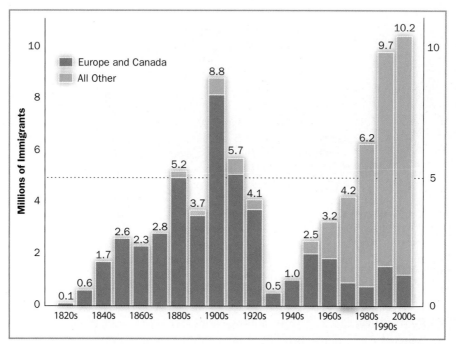

FIGURE 4.2
Legal Immigration to the United States, 1820–2010

Source: Office of Immigration Statistics 2007 and estimates by the author for the period 2000–2010.

Whereas most industrial countries have a foreign population of around 5 percent, Canada's foreign population is 19 percent and Australia's is 25 percent.

As noted earlier, immigrants have not settled evenly across the nation. As shown in the map in Figure 4.3, the six states of California, New York, Florida, Texas, New Jersey, and Illinois account for 70 percent of the nation's total foreign-born population but less than 40 percent of the nation's total population.

Cities in these states are the focus of the foreign-born population. Almost half (43.3 percent) live in the central city of a metropolitan area, compared with about one-quarter (27.0 percent) of the nation's population. More than one-third of residents in the cities of Miami, Los Angeles, San Francisco, San Jose, and New York City are now foreign-born (Camarota 2007b).

The third pattern of immigration is that the source of immigrants has changed. The majority of today's 37.9 million foreign-born people are from Latin America. Primarily, they are from Central America and, more specifically, Mexico. By contrast, Europeans, who dominated the early settlement of the United States, now account for fewer than one in seven of the foreign-born today.

Early Immigration

European explorers of North America were soon followed by settlers, the first immigrants to the Western Hemisphere. The Spanish founded St. Augustine, Florida, in 1565, and the English founded Jamestown, Virginia, in 1607. Protestants from England emerged from the colonial period as the dominant force numerically, politically, and socially. The English accounted for 60 percent of the 3 million White Americans in 1790. Although exact statistics are lacking for the early years of the United States, the English were soon outnumbered by other nationalities as the numbers of Scotch-Irish and Germans, in particular, swelled. However, the English colonists maintained their dominant position, as Chapter 5 will examine.

Throughout American history, immigration policy has been politically controversial. The policies of the English king, George III, were criticized in the U.S. Declaration of Independence for obstructing immigration to the colonies. Toward the end of the nineteenth century, the American republic itself was criticized for enacting immigration restrictions. In the beginning, however, the country encouraged immigration. Legislation initially fixed the residence requirement for naturalization at five years, although briefly,

FIGURE 4.3
**Foreign-Born Population
for States, 2006**

Source: Author's estimate based
on census bureau data in the
American Community Survey
2006. Bureau of the Census
2007c.

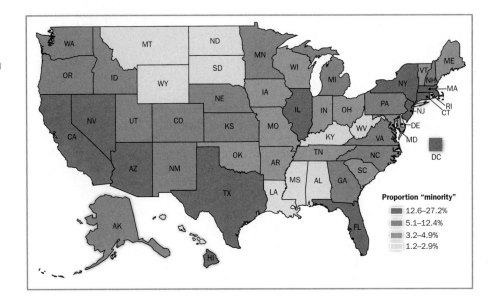

under the Alien Act of 1798, it was fourteen years, and so-called dangerous people could be expelled. Despite this brief harshness, immigration was unregulated through most of the 1800s, and naturalization was easily available. Until 1870, naturalization was limited to "free white persons" (Calavita 2007).

Besides holding the mistaken belief that concerns about immigration are something new, we also assume that immigrants to the United States rarely reconsider their decision to come to a new country. Analysis of available records, beginning in the early 1900s, suggests that about 35 percent of all immigrants to the United States eventually emigrated back to their home country. The proportion varies, with the figures for some countries being much higher, but the overall pattern is clear: about one in three immigrants to this nation eventually chooses to return home (Wyman 1993).

The relative absence of federal legislation from 1790 to 1881 does not mean that all new arrivals were welcomed. **Xenophobia** (the fear or hatred of strangers or foreigners) led naturally to **nativism** (beliefs and policies favoring native-born citizens over immigrants). Although the term *nativism* has largely been used to describe nineteenth-century sentiments, anti-immigration views and organized movements have continued into the twenty-first century. Political scientist Samuel P. Huntington (1993, 1996) articulated the continuing immigration as a "clash of civilizations" that could be remedied only by significantly reducing legal immigration, not to mention to close the border to illegal arrivals. His view, which enjoys support, was that the fundamental world conflicts of the new century are cultural in nature rather than ideological or even economic (Citrin et al. 2007; Schaefer 2008b).

Historically, Roman Catholics in general and the Irish in particular were among the first Europeans to be ill-treated. We will look at how organized hostility toward Irish immigrants eventually gave way to their acceptance into the larger society in our next chapter.

However, the most dramatic outbreak of nativism in the nineteenth century was aimed at the Chinese. If there had been any doubt by the mid-1800s that the United States could harmoniously accommodate all and was some sort of melting pot, debate on the Chinese Exclusion Act would negatively settle the question once and for all.

The Anti-Chinese Movement

xenophobia
The fear or hatred of
strangers or foreigners.

nativism
Beliefs and policies favoring native-born citizens
over immigrants.

Before 1851, official records show that only 46 Chinese had immigrated to the United States. Over the next 30 years, more than 200,000 came to this country, lured by the discovery of gold and the opening of job opportunities in the West. Overcrowding, drought, and warfare in China also encouraged them to take a chance in the United States. Another important factor was improved oceanic transportation; it was actually cheaper to travel from Hong Kong to San Francisco than from Chicago to San Francisco. The frontier communities of the West, particularly in California, looked on the Chinese as a valuable resource to fill manual jobs. As early as 1854, so many Chinese wanted to emigrate that ships had difficulty handling the volume.

In the 1860s, railroad work provided the greatest demand for Chinese labor until the Union Pacific and Central Pacific railroads were joined at Promontory Summit, Utah, in 1869. The Union Pacific relied primarily on Irish laborers, but 90 percent of the Central Pacific's labor force was Chinese because Whites generally refused to do the backbreaking work over the Western terrain. Despite the contribution of the Chinese, White workers physically prevented them from attending the driving of the golden spike to mark the joining of the two railroads.

With the dangerous railroad work largely completed, people began to rethink the wisdom of encouraging Chinese to immigrate to do the work no one else would do. Reflecting their xenophobia, White settlers found the Chinese immigrants and their customs and religion difficult to understand. Indeed, few people actually tried to understand these immigrants from Asia. Although they had had no firsthand contact with Chinese Americans, Easterners and legislators were soon on the anti-Chinese bandwagon as they read sensationalized accounts of the lifestyle of the new arrivals.

Even before the Chinese immigrated, stereotypes of them and their customs were prevalent. American traders returning from China, European diplomats, and Protestant missionaries consistently emphasized the exotic and sinister aspects of life in China. The **sinophobes**, people with a fear of anything associated with China, appealed to the racist theory developed during the slavery controversy that non-Europeans were subhuman. Similarly, Americans were beginning to be more conscious of biological inheritance and disease, so it was not hard to conjure up fears of alien genes and germs. The only real challenge the anti-Chinese movement had was to convince people that the negative consequences of unrestricted Chinese immigration outweighed any possible economic gain. Perhaps briefly, racial prejudice had earlier been subordinated to industrial dependence on Chinese labor for the work that Whites shunned, but acceptance of the Chinese was short-lived. The fear of the "yellow peril" overwhelmed any desire to know more about Asian peoples and their customs (Takaki 1989).

Employers were glad to pay the Chinese low wages, but laborers came to direct their resentment against the Chinese rather than against their compatriots' willingness to exploit the Chinese. Only a generation earlier, the same concerns had been felt about the Irish, but with the Chinese, the hostility reached new heights because of another factor.

Although many arguments were voiced, racial fears motivated the anti-Chinese movement. Race was the critical issue. The labor market fears were largely unfounded, and

sinophobes
People with a fear of anything associated with China.

"IT SAYS THIS ORANGE JUICE IS MADE WITH FRUIT PICKED ENTIRELY BY AMERICAN WORKERS. IT'S 43 DOLLARS."

Immigrant labor plays a significant role in many ways. Many immigrants are paid with low wages that keep prices lower for the consumer.

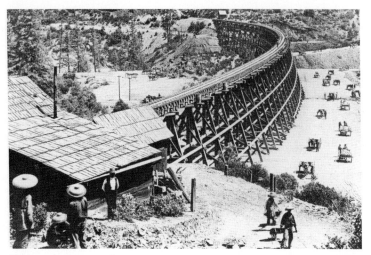

Chinese workers, such as these pictured in 1844, played a major role in building railroads in the West.

most advocates of restrictions at that time knew that. There was no possibility that the Chinese would immigrate in numbers that would match those of Europeans at that time, so it is difficult to find any explanation other than racism for their fears (Winant 1994).

From the sociological perspective of conflict theory, we can explain how the Chinese immigrants were welcomed only when their labor was necessary to fuel growth in the United States. When that labor was no longer necessary, the welcome mat for the immigrants was withdrawn. Furthermore, as conflict theorists would point out, restrictions were not applied evenly: Americans focused on a specific nationality (the Chinese) to reduce the overall number of foreign workers in the nation. Because decision making at that time rested in the hands of the descendants of European immigrants, the steps to be taken were most likely to be directed against the least powerful: immigrants from China who, unlike Europeans seeking entry, had few allies among legislators and other policy makers.

In 1882, Congress enacted the Chinese Exclusion Act, which outlawed Chinese immigration for 10 years. It also explicitly denied naturalization rights to the Chinese in the United States; that is, they were not allowed to become citizens. There was little debate in Congress, and discussion concentrated on how suspension of Chinese immigration could best be handled. No allowance was made for spouses and children to be reunited with their husbands and fathers in the United States. Only brief visits of Chinese government officials, teachers, tourists, and merchants were exempted.

The rest of the nineteenth century saw the remaining loopholes allowing Chinese immigration closed. Beginning in 1884, Chinese laborers were not allowed to enter the United States from any foreign place, a ban that also lasted 10 years. Two years later, the Statue of Liberty was dedicated, with a poem by Emma Lazarus inscribed on its base. To the Chinese, the poem welcoming the tired, the poor, and the huddled masses must have seemed a hollow mockery.

In 1892, Congress extended the Exclusion Act for another 10 years and added that Chinese laborers had to obtain certificates of residence within a year or face deportation. After the turn of the century, the Exclusion Act was extended again. Two decades later, the Chinese were not alone; the list of people restricted by immigration policy had expanded many times.

Restrictionist Sentiment Increases

As Congress closed the door to Chinese immigration, the debate on restricting immigration turned in new directions. Prodded by growing anti-Japanese feelings, the United States entered into the so-called gentlemen's agreement, which was completed in 1908. Japan agreed to halt further immigration to the United States, and the United States agreed to end discrimination against the Japanese who had already arrived. The immigration ended, but anti-Japanese feelings continued. Americans were growing uneasy that the "new immigrants" would overwhelm the culture established by the "old immigrants." The earlier immigrants, if not Anglo-Saxon, were from similar groups such as the Scandinavians, the Swiss, and the French Huguenots. These people were more experienced in democratic political practices and had a greater affinity with the dominant Anglo-Saxon culture. By the end of the nineteenth century, however, more and more immigrants were neither English-speaking nor Protestant and came from dramatically different cultures.

The National Origin System

Beginning in 1921, a series of measures were enacted that marked a new era in American immigration policy. Whatever the legal language, the measures were drawn up to block the growing immigration from southern Europe (from Italy and Greece, for example) and also were drawn to block all Asian immigrants by establishing a zero quota for them.

Anti-immigration sentiment, combined with the isolationism that followed World War I, caused Congress to severely restrict entry privileges not only of the Chinese and Japanese but also of Europeans. The national origin system was begun in 1921 and remained the basis of immigration policy until 1965. This system used nationality to determine whether a person could enter as a legal alien, and the number of previous immigrants and their descendants was used to set the group's annual immigration cap.

To understand the effect of the national origin system on immigration, it is necessary to clarify the quota system. The quotas were deliberately weighted in favor of immigration from northern Europe. Because of the ethnic composition of the country in 1920, the quotas placed severe restrictions on immigration from the rest of Europe and other parts of the world. Immigration from the Western hemisphere (i.e., Canada, Mexico, Central and South America, and the Caribbean) continued unrestricted. The quota for each nation was set at 3 percent of the number of people descended from each nationality recorded in the 1920 census. Once the statistical manipulations were completed, almost 70 percent of the quota for the Eastern hemisphere went to just three countries: Great Britain, Ireland, and Germany.

The absurdities of the system soon became obvious, but it was nevertheless continued. British immigration had fallen sharply, so most of its quota of 65,000 went unfilled. However, the openings could not be transferred, even though countries such as Italy, with a quota of only 6,000, had 200,000 people who wanted to enter. However one rationalizes the purpose behind the act, the result was obvious: any English person, regardless of skill and whether related to anyone already here, could enter the country more easily than, say, a Greek doctor whose children were American citizens. The quota for Greece was 305, with the backlog of people wanting to come reaching 100,000.

By the end of the 1920s, annual immigration had dropped to one-fourth of its pre–World War I level. The worldwide economic depression of the 1930s decreased immigration still further. A brief upsurge in immigration just before World War II reflected the flight of Europeans from the oppression of expanding Nazi Germany. The war virtually ended transatlantic immigration. The era of the great European migration to the United States had been legislated out of existence.

Ellis Island
Although it was not opened until 1892, New York harbor's Ellis Island—the country's first federal immigration facility—quickly became the symbol of all the migrant streams to the United States. By the time it was closed in late 1954, it had processed 17 million immigrants. Today their descendants number over 100 million Americans. A major renovation project was launched in 1984 to restore Ellis Island as a national monument and a tourist destination.

The 1965 Immigration and Nationality Act

The national origin system was abandoned with the passage of the 1965 Immigration and Nationality Act, signed into law by President Lyndon B. Johnson at the foot of the Statue of Liberty. The primary goals of the act were to reunite families and to protect the American labor market. The act also initiated restrictions on immigration from Latin America. After the act, immigration increased by one-third, but the act's influence was primarily on the composition rather than the size of immigration. The sources of immigrants now included Italy, Greece, Portugal, Mexico, the Philippines, the West Indies, and South America. The effect is apparent when we compare the changing sources of immigration over the last 180 years, as shown in Figure 4.4. The most recent period shows that Asian and Latin American immigrants combined to account for 81 percent of the people who were permitted entry. This contrasts sharply with early immigration, which was dominated by arrivals from Europe.

The nature of immigration laws is exceedingly complex and is subjected to frequent, often minor, adjustments. In 2000 and 2006, between 840,000 and 1,270,000 people were legally admitted each year. For the most recent year, people were admitted for the following reasons:

Relatives of citizens	55%
Relatives of legal residents	9%
Employment based	13%
Refugees/people seeking political asylum	17%
Diversity (lottery among applications from nations historically sending few immigrants)	3%
Other	3%

Overall, two-thirds of the immigrants come to join their families, one-seventh because of skills needed in the United States, and another one-seventh because of special refugee status (Office of Immigration Statistics 2007, Table 7).

Contemporary Social Concerns

Although our current immigration policies are less restrictive than other nations', they are the subjects of great debate. Table 4.1 summarizes the benefits and concerns regarding immigration to the United States. Now we consider five continuing criticisms relating to our immigration policy: the brain drain, population growth, mixed status, English language acquisition, and illegal immigration. All five, but particularly illegal immigration, have provoked heated debates on the national level and continuing efforts to resolve them with new policies. We will then consider the economic impact of immigration, followed by the nation's policy toward refugees, a group distinct from immigrants.

TABLE 4.1
Immigration Benefits and Concerns

Potential Benefits	Areas of Concern
Provide needed skills	Drain needed resources from home country
Contribute to taxes	Send remittances home
May come with substantial capital to start business	Less-skilled immigrants compete with those already disadvantaged
Maintain growth of consumer market	Population growth
Diversify the population (intangible gain)	Language differences
Maintain ties with countries throughout the world	May complicate foreign policy by lobbying the government
	Illegal immigration

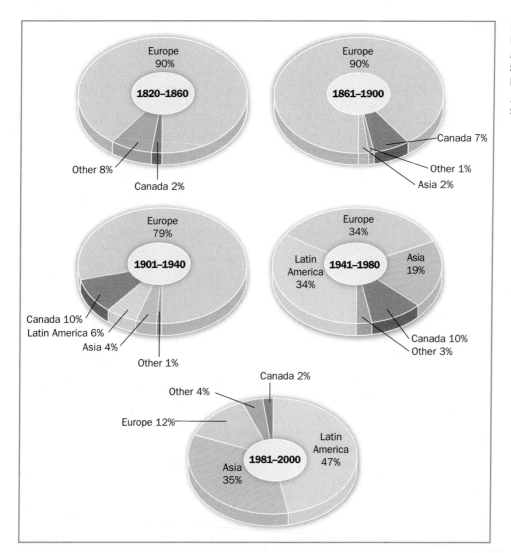

FIGURE 4.4
Legal Immigrants Admitted to the United States by Region of Last Residence, 1820–2000

Source: Office of Immigration Statistics. 2006, 10–13.

The Brain Drain

How often have you identified your science or mathematics teacher or your physician as someone who was not born in the United States? This nation has clearly benefited from attracting human resources from throughout the world, but this phenomenon has had its price for the nations of origin.

Brain drain is the immigration to the United States of skilled workers, professionals, and technicians who are desperately needed by their home countries. In the mid–twentieth century, many scientists and other professionals from industrial nations, principally Germany and Great Britain, came to the United States. More recently, however, the brain drain has pulled emigrants from developing nations, including India, Pakistan, the Philippines, and several African nations. They are eligible for H-1B visas that qualify them for permanent work permits.

One out of four physicians in the United States is foreign-born and plays a critical role in serving areas with too few doctors. Thousands of skilled, educated Indians now seek to enter the United States, pulled by the economic opportunity. The pay differential is so great that, beginning in 2004, when foreign physicians were no longer favored with entry to the United States, physicians in the Philippines were retraining as nurses so that they could immigrate to the United States where, employed as nurses, they would make four times what they would as doctors in the Philippines (Mullen 2005; *New York Times* 2005b).

Many foreign students say they plan to return home. Fortunately for the United States, many do not and make their talents available in the United States. One study showed that

brain drain
Immigration to the United States of skilled workers, professionals, and technicians who are desperately needed by their home countries.

the majority of foreign students receiving their doctorates in the sciences and engineering remain here four years later. Critics note, however, that this foreign supply means that this country overlooks its own minority scholars. Currently, for every two minority doctorates, five foreign citizens are receiving this degree. In the physical sciences, for every doctorate issued to a minority citizen, foreign citizens receive 11. More encouragement needs to be given to African Americans and Latinos to enter high-tech career paths.

Conflict theorists see the current brain drain as yet another symptom of the unequal distribution of world resources. In their view, it is ironic that the United States gives foreign aid to improve the technical resources of African and Asian countries while maintaining an immigration policy that encourages professionals in such nations to migrate to our shores. These are the very countries that have unacceptable public health conditions and need native scientists, educators, technicians, and other professionals. In addition, by relying on foreign talent, the United States is not encouraging native members of subordinate groups to enter these desirable fields of employment (Hoffer et al. 2001; Pearson 2006; Wessel 2001).

Population Growth

The United States, like a few other industrial nations, continues to accept large numbers of permanent immigrants and refugees. Although such immigration has increased since the passage of the 1965 Immigration and Nationality Act, the nation's birthrate has decreased. Consequently, the contribution of immigration to population growth has become more significant. As citizen "baby boomers" age, the country has increasingly depended on the economically younger population fueled by immigrants (Meyers 2007).

Immigration, legal and illegal, accounted for about 45 percent to 60 percent of the nation's growth in the early years of the twenty-first century. To some observers, the United States is already overpopulated. The respected environmentalist group Sierra Club debated for several years whether to take an official position favoring restricting immigration, recognizing that greater numbers of people put greater strain on the nation's natural resources. Thus far, the majority of the club's members have indicated a desire to keep a neutral position rather than enter the politically charged immigration debate (Barringer 2004; Camarota 2007b; Passel and Cohn 2008).

The patterns of uneven settlement by immigrants in the United States are expected to continue so that future immigrants' impact on population growth will be felt much more in certain areas: say, California and New York rather than Wyoming or West Virginia. Although immigration and population growth may be viewed as national concerns, their impact is localized in certain areas such as Southern California and large urban centers nationwide (Bean et al. 2004).

Mixed-Status Families

Very little is simple when it comes to immigration, and this is particularly true to the challenge of "mixed status." **Mixed status** refers to families in which one or more members are citizens and one or more are noncitizens. This especially becomes problematic when the noncitizens are illegal or undocumented immigrants.

The problem of mixed status clearly emerges on two levels. On the macro level, when policy debates are made about issues that seem clear to many people—such as whether illegal immigrants should be allowed to attend state colleges or whether illegal immigrants should be immediately deported—the complicating factor of mixed-status families quickly emerges. On the micro level, the daily toll on members of mixed-status households is very difficult. Often the legal resident or even the U.S. citizen in a household finds daily life limited for fear of revealing the undocumented status of a parent or brother or even a son.

There are almost 7 million families in which the head of the household or spouse is an illegal immigrant. Yet in about one-third of these families, one or more of the children are U.S. citizens. This means that some of the issues facing illegal immigrants, whom we

mixed status
Families in which one or more members are citizens and one or more are noncitizens.

will discuss later, will also affect the citizens in the families because they are reluctant to bring attention to themselves for fear of revealing the legal status of their mother or father (Brewington 2008; Fix and Zimmerman 1999; Passel 2005).

Language Barriers

For many people in the United States, the most visible aspect of immigration are non–English speakers, businesses with foreign-language storefronts, and even familiar stores assuring potential customers that their employees speak Spanish or Polish or Chinese or some other foreign language.

About 19 percent of the population speaks a language other than English, as shown in Figure 4.5. Indeed, 32 different languages are spoken at home by at least 200,000 residents (Shin and Bruno 2003). As of 2006, about half of the

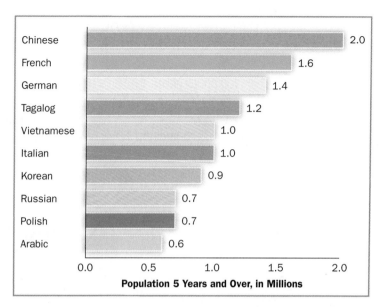

FIGURE 4.5
Ten Languages Most Frequently Spoken at Home, Other Than English and Spanish

Source: Data for 2000 released in 2003 in Shin and Bruno 2003.

37 million people born abroad spoke English less than "very well." This rises to 75 percent among those born in Mexico. Nationally, about 70 percent of Latino schoolchildren report speaking Spanish at home (Brodie et al. 2002; Bureau of the Census 2003a, 158, 2007c, Table S0506).

The myth of Anglo superiority has rested in part on language differences. (The term *Anglo* in the following text is used to mean all non-Hispanics but primarily Whites.) First, the criteria for economic and social achievement usually include proficiency in English. By such standards, Spanish-speaking pupils are judged less able to compete until they learn English. Second, many Anglos believe that Spanish is not an asset occupationally. Only recently, as government agencies have belatedly begun to serve Latino people and as businesses recognize the growing Latino consumer market, have Anglos recognized that knowing Spanish is not only useful but also necessary to carry out certain tasks

Until the last 40 years, there was a conscious effort to devalue Spanish and other languages and to discourage the use of foreign languages in schools. In the case of Spanish, this practice was built on a pattern of segregating Hispanic schoolchildren from Anglos. In the recent past in the Southwest, Mexican Americans were assigned to Mexican schools to keep Anglo schools all-White. These Mexican schools, created through de jure school segregation, were substantially underfunded compared with the regular public schools. Legal action against such schools dates back to 1945, but it was not until 1970 that the U.S. Supreme Court ruled, in *Cisneros v. Corpus Christi Independent School District*, that the de jure segregation of Mexican Americans was unconstitutional. Appeals delayed implementation of that decision, and not until September 1975 was the de jure plan forcibly overturned in Corpus Christi, Texas (Commission on Civil Rights 1976).

Is it essential that English be the sole language of instruction in schools in the United States? **Bilingualism** is the use of two or more languages in places of work or educational facilities, according each language equal legitimacy. Thus, a program of **bilingual education** may instruct children in their native language (such as Spanish) while gradually introducing them to the language of the dominant society (English). If such a program is also bicultural, it will teach children about the culture of both linguistic groups. Bilingual education allows students to learn academic material in their own language while they are learning a second language. Proponents believe that, ideally, bilingual education programs should also allow English-speaking pupils to be bilingual, but generally they are directed only at making non–English speakers proficient in more than one language.

Do bilingual programs help children learn English? It is difficult to reach firm conclusions on the effectiveness of the bilingual programs in general because they vary so widely in their approach to non–English-speaking children. The programs differ in the length of the transition to English and how long they allow students to remain in bilingual classrooms. A major study released in 2004 analyzed more than three decades of

bilingualism
The use of two or more languages in places of work or education and the treatment of each language as legitimate.

bilingual education
A program designed to allow students to learn academic concepts in their native language while they learn a second language.

The United States has a long history of receiving immigrants who do not speak English very well, and the response recently has included both bilingual programs as well as calls for a constitutional amendment to make English the official language.

research, combining 17 different studies, and found that bilingual education programs produce higher levels of student achievement in reading. The most successful are paired bilingual programs—those offering ongoing instruction in a native language and English at different times of the day (Slavin and Cheung 2003, Soltero 2008).

Attacks on bilingualism in both voting and education have taken several forms and have even broadened to question the appropriateness of U.S. residents using any language other than English. Federal policy has become more restrictive. Local schools have been given more authority to determine appropriate methods of instruction; they have also been forced to provide more of their own funding for bilingual education. In the United States, 30 states as of 2008 have made English their official language. Repeated efforts have been made to introduce a constitutional amendment declaring English as the nation's official language. Even such an action would not completely outlaw bilingual or multilingual government services. It would, however, require that such services be called for specifically as in the Voting Rights Act of 1965, which requires voting information to be available in multiple languages (U.S. English 2008).

Non–English speakers cluster in certain states, but bilingualism attracts nationwide passions. The release in 2006 of "Nuestro Himno," the Spanish-language version of "The Star-Spangled Banner," led to a strong reaction, with 69 percent of people saying it was appropriate to be sung only in English. Yet at least one congressman who decried the Spanish version sang the anthem himself in English with incorrect lyrics. Similarly, a locally famous restaurant owner in Philadelphia posted signs at his Philly steak sandwich diner announcing he would accept orders only in English. Passions remain strong as policy makers debate how much support should be given to people who speak other languages (Carroll 2006; Koch 2006b).

Illegal Immigration

The most bitterly debated aspect of U.S. immigration policy has been the control of illegal or undocumented immigrants. These immigrants and their families come to the United States in search of higher-paying jobs than their home countries can provide.

Because by definition, illegal immigrants are in the country illegally, the exact number of these undocumented or unauthorized workers is subject to estimates and disputes. Based on the best available information, there are more than 11 million illegal or unauthorized immigrants in the United States. This compares with about 4 million in 1992. Today, about 7.2 million are employed, accounting for about 5 percent of the entire civilian labor force (Camarota 2007b; Jenness et al. 2008; Passel 2006).

Illegal immigrants, and even legal immigrants, have become tied by the public to almost every social problem in the nation. They become the scapegoats for unemployment; they are labeled as "drug runners" and, especially since September 11, 2001, "terrorists." Their vital economic and cultural contribution to the United States is generally overlooked, as it has been for more than a hundred years.

The cost of the federal government's attempt to police the nation's borders and locate illegal immigrants is sizable. There are significant costs for aliens—that is, foreign-born noncitizens—and for other citizens as well. Civil rights advocates have expressed concern that the procedures used to apprehend and deport people are discriminatory and deprive many aliens of their legal rights. American citizens of Hispanic or Asian origin, some of whom were born in the United States, may be greeted with prejudice and distrust, as if their names automatically imply that they are illegal immigrants. Furthermore, these citizens and legal residents of the United States may be unable to find work because employers wrongly believe that their documents are forged.

In the context of this illegal immigration, Congress approved the Immigration Reform and Control Act of 1986 (IRCA) after debating it for nearly a decade. The act marked a historic change in immigration policy compared with earlier laws, as summarized in Table 4.2. Amnesty was granted to 1.7 million illegal immigrants who could document that they had established long-term residency in the United States. Under the IRCA, hiring illegal aliens became illegal, subjecting employers to fines and even prison sentences. Little workplace enforcement occurs for the hiring of undocumented workers. In 2007, fewer than 100 executives or hiring managers were arrested, and only 4,100 unauthorized workers were apprehended nationwide (Preston 2008).

Many illegal immigrants continue to live in fear and hiding, subject to even more severe harassment and discrimination than before. From a conflict perspective, these immigrants, primarily poor and Hispanic or Asian, are being firmly lodged at the bottom of the nation's social and economic hierarchies. However, from a functionalist perspective, employers, by paying low wages, are able to produce goods and services that are profitable for industry and more affordable to consumers. Despite the poor working conditions often experienced by illegal immigrants here, they continue to come because it is still in their best economic interest to work here in disadvantaged positions rather than seek wage labor unsuccessfully in their home countries.

Although never a priority, prosecuting those who hire illegal immigrants has fallen to the point where only about 100 employers are arrested annually, involving about 4,000 workers nationwide (Hsu 2008).

Amidst heated debate, Congress reached a compromise and passed the Illegal Immigration Reform and Immigrant Responsibility Act of 1996, which emphasized making more effort to keep immigrants from entering the country illegally. The act prevented illegal immigrants from having access to such programs as Social Security and welfare. Legal immigrants would still be entitled to such benefits, although social service agencies were now required to verify their legal status. Another significant element was to increase border control and surveillance.

TABLE 4.2
Major Immigration Policies

Policy	Target Group	Impact
Chinese Exclusion Act, 1882	Chinese	Effectively ended all Chinese immigration for more than 60 years
National origin system, 1921	Southern Europeans	Reduced overall immigration and significantly reduced likely immigration from Greece and Italy
Immigration and Nationality Act, 1965	Western hemisphere and the less skilled	Facilitated entry of skilled workers and relatives of U.S. residents
Immigration Reform and Control Act of 1986	Illegal immigrants	Modest reduction of illegal immigration
Illegal Immigration Reform and Immigrant Responsibility Act of 1996	Illegal immigrants	Greater border surveillance and increased scrutiny of legal immigrants seeking benefits

Illegal aliens or undocumented workers are not necessarily transient. A 2006 estimate indicated 60 percent had been here for at least five years. Many have established homes, families, and networks with relatives and friends in the United States whose legal status might differ. These are the mixed-status households noted earlier. For the most part, their lives are not much different from legal residents, except when they seek services that require citizenship status to be documented (Passel 2006).

Policy makers continue to avoid the only real way to stop illegal immigration: discourage employment opportunities. The public often thinks in terms of greater surveillance at the border. After the terrorist attacks of September 11, 2001, greater control of border traffic took on a new sense of urgency, even though almost all the men who took over the planes had entered the United States legally. It is very difficult to secure the vast boundaries that mark the United States on land and sea.

Reflecting the emphasis on heightened security, a potentially major shake-up took place in 2003. Since 1940, the Immigration and Naturalization Service (INS) had been in the Department of Justice, but now it was transferred to the newly formed Department of Homeland Security. The various functions of the INS were split into three agencies with a new Bureau of Citizenship and Immigration Services and two other units separately concerned with customs and border protection. For years, immigrant advocates had argued for the separation of border enforcement from immigration, but the placement of immigrant services in the office responsible for protecting the United States from terrorists has sent a chilling message to immigrants.

Numerous civil rights groups and migrant advocacy organizations have expressed alarm over the large numbers of people now crossing into the United States illegally who perish in their attempt. Some die in deserts, in isolated canyons, and while concealed in containers or locked in trucks during smuggling attempts. Several hundred die annually in the Southwest, seeking more and more dangerous crossing points, as border control has increased. However, this death toll has received little attention, causing one journalist to liken it to a jumbo jet crashing between Los Angeles and Phoenix every year without anyone giving it much notice (Del Olmo 2003; Sullivan 2005).

What certainly was noticed in 2006 was the public debate over how to stop further illegal immigration and what to do about illegal immigrants already inside the United States. Proposals to harden the border by erecting a 700-mile-long double concrete wall brought concerns that desperate immigrants would take even more chances with their lives in order to work in the United States. A congressional proposal to make assisting an illegal immigrant already here a felony led to strong counterdemonstrations that drew tens of thousands of marchers in cities across the Untied States. Meanwhile, the federal government, as it has for a century, struggled between addressing the need to attract workers to do jobs many people here legally would not do and enforcing the laws governing legal immigration (Tumulty 2006).

When it comes to issues of race and ethnicity, South Africa usually evokes past images of apartheid and the struggle to overcome generations of racial separation—both important topics to be considered in Chapter 16. However, in Global View, we consider the contemporary challenge of dealing with immigration.

Path to Citizenship: Naturalization

In **naturalization**, citizenship is conferred on a person after birth, a process that has been outlined by Congress and extends to foreigners the same benefits given to native-born U.S. citizens. Naturalized citizens, however, cannot serve as president.

Until the 1970s, most people who were naturalized had been born in Europe. Reflecting changing patterns of immigration, Asia and Latin America are now the largest sources of new citizens. In fact, in 2006, the number of naturalized citizens from Mexico came close to matching those from all of Europe. In recent years, the number of new citizens going through the naturalization process has been between one-half million and one million a year (Simanski 2007).

naturalization
Conferring of citizenship on a person after birth.

A Global View

IMMIGRATION AND SOUTH AFRICA

With its nearly 50 million people, the Republic of South Africa is not rich by global standards, but its economy is very attractive to most of the African continent. For example, South Africa has a gross national income per person of $9,560, compared to well under $1,000 in neighboring Zimbabwe. Even when South Africa was ruled by a White-supremacist government, Black Africans from throughout the continent came to the country fleeing violence and poverty in their home countries and to work, often in the mining of coal and diamonds. In the post-apartheid era, the numbers of immigrants, legal and illegal, have skyrocketed. Today's government is caught between compassion for those seeking entry and the growing inability of the economy to absorb those who seek work and shelter.

In 2008, the world took notice as riots broke out between poor South Africans taking out their rage on even more impoverished foreigners. The growing xenophobia took the government, which advocates racial harmony, by surprise as it tried to quell violence among Black Africans divided by citizenship status and nationality. In a matter of months in early 2008, some 32,000 immigrants had been driven from their homes, with attackers seizing all of their belongings. Some immigrants returned to their home countries—including Burundi, Ethiopia, Ghana, Malawi, Mozambique, and Zimbabwe—but most settled temporarily in camps.

South Africa, with limited government resources, deported 260,000 in 2006–2007, a proportion nearly comparable to that of the United States (with six times the population), which reported 1.2 million deportations during the same period. However, estimates of the total number of illegal immigrants in South Africa range from 3 million to 5 million—a much higher proportion than estimated in the Untied States.

The scapegoating of immigrants, or "border jumpers" as they often are called in South Africa, is not unique to this nation, but for the global community that still relishes Nelson Mandela's peaceful ascent to power, it has been a reminder of immigration's challenge throughout the world.

Sources: Dixon 2007; Haub 2008; Koser 2008; Nevin 2008; Roodt 2008; Office of Immigration Statistics 2007 South African Institute of Race Relations 2007.

To become a naturalized U.S. citizen, a person must meet the following general conditions:

- be 18 years of age;
- have continually resided in the United States for at least 5 years (3 years for the spouses of U.S. citizens);
- have good moral character as determined by the absence of conviction of selected criminal offenses;
- be able to read, write, speak, and understand words of ordinary usage in the English language; and
- pass a test in U.S. government and history.

Table 4.3 offers a sample of the types of questions immigrants face on the citizenship test. As of 2009, the fee for applying for citizenship is $675, compared with $95 in 1998.

Although we often picture the United States as having a very insular, nativistic attitude toward foreigners living here, the country has a rather liberal policy toward people maintaining the citizenship of their old countries. Although most countries do not allow people to maintain dual (or even multiple) citizenships, the United States does not forbid it.

TABLE 4.3
So You Want to Be a Citizen?

Try these sample questions from the naturalization test (answers below).

1. What do the stripes on the flag represent?

2. How many changes, or amendments, are there to the Constitution?

3. Who is the chief justice of the Supreme Court?

4. What are some of the requirements to be eligible to become president?

5. What are inalienable rights?

6. What is the introduction to the Constitution called, and what year was it written?

7. Name one right or freedom guaranteed by the First Amendment.

8. What group of essays supported passage of the U.S. Constitution?

Answers:

(1) The first 13 states; (2) 27; (3) John Roberts; (4) Candidates for president must be natural-born citizens, be at least 35 years old, and have lived in the United States for at least 14 years; (5) Individual rights that people are born with; (6) The Preamble and 1787; (7) The rights are freedom of speech, religion, assembly, and press, and freedom to petition the government; (8) *The Federalist Papers*.

Source: Bureau of Citizenship and Immigrant Services (CIS) 2008. Sample reflects changes proposed by CIS as of January 2008.

Dual citizenship is most common when a person goes through naturalization after already being a citizen of another country or is a U.S.-born citizen and goes through the process of becoming a citizen of another country—for example, after marrying a foreigner (Department of State 2008).

The Economic Impact of Immigration

There is much public and scholarly debate about the economic effects of immigration, both legal and illegal. Varied, conflicting conclusions have resulted from research ranging from case studies of Korean immigrants' dominance among New York City greengrocers to mobility studies charting the progress of all immigrants and their children. The confusion results in part from the different methods of analysis. For example, the studies do not always include political refugees, who generally are less prepared than other refugees to become assimilated. Sometimes, the research focuses only on economic effects, such as whether people are employed or on welfare; in other cases, it also considers cultural factors such as knowledge of English.

In Listen to Our Voices, sociologist Tomás Jiménez of the University of California–San Diego considers the role that immigration has played in the United States in shaping the nation's identity.

Perhaps the most significant factor in determining the economic impact of immigration is whether a study examines the national impact of immigration or only its effects on a local area. Overall, we can conclude from the research that immigrants adapt well and are an asset to the local economy. In some areas, heavy immigration may drain a community's resources. However, it can also revitalize a local economy. Marginally employed workers, most of whom are either themselves immigrants or African Americans, often experience a negative impact by new arrivals. With or without immigration, competition for low-paying jobs in the United States is high, and those who gain the most from this competition are the employers and the consumers who want to keep prices down (Steinberg 2005; Zimmerman 2008).

The impact of immigration on African Americans deserves special attention. Given that African Americans are a large minority and many continue to be in the underclass, many people, including some Blacks themselves, perceive immigrants as advancing at the expense of the African American community. There is evidence that in the very lowest paid jobs—for example, workers in chicken-processing plants—wages have dropped with the availability of unskilled immigrants to perform them, and Blacks have left these jobs for good. Many of these African Americans do not necessarily move to better or even equivalent jobs. This pattern is repeated in other relatively low-paying undesirable employment sectors, so Blacks are not alone in being impacted; but given other job opportunities, the impact is longer lasting (Borjas, Grogger, and Hanson 2006; Holzer 2008).

About 70 percent of illegal immigrant workers pay taxes of one type or another. Many of them do not file to receive entitled refunds or benefits. For example, in 2005, the Social Security Administration identified thousands of unauthorized workers contributing about $7 billion to the fund but that could not be credited properly (Porter 2005).

Social science studies generally contradict many of the negative stereotypes about the economic impact of immigration. A variety of recent studies found that immigrants are a net economic gain for the population in times of economic boom as well as in periods of recession. But despite national gains, in some areas and for some groups, immigration may be an economic burden or create unwanted competition for jobs (Kochhar 2006).

What about the immigrants themselves? Considering contemporary immigrants as a group, we can make the following conclusions that show a mix of success and challenges to adaptation.

Less Encouraging

- Although immigrants have lower divorce rates and are less likely to form single-parent households than natives, their rates equal or exceed these rates by the second generation.
- Children in immigrant families tend to be healthier than U.S.-born children, but the advantage declines. We will consider this in greater detail later in this chapter.
- Immigrant children attend schools that are disproportionately attended by other poor children and students with limited English proficiency, so they are ethnically, economically, and linguistically isolated.

Positive Signs

- Immigrant families and, more broadly, noncitizen households are more likely to be on public assistance, but their time on public assistance is less and they receive fewer benefits. This is even true when considering special restrictions that may apply to noncitizens.
- Second-generation immigrants (i.e., children of immigrants) are overall doing as well as or better than White non-Hispanic natives in educational attainment, labor force participation, wages, and household income.
- Immigrants overwhelmingly (65 percent) continue to see learning English as an ethical obligation of all immigrants.

These positive trends diverge among specific immigrant groups, with Asian immigrants doing better than European immigrants, who do better than Latino immigrants (Capps et al. 2002; Zimmerman 2008; Farkas 2003; Fix et al. 2001; Myers et al. 2004).

One economic aspect of immigration that has received increasing attention is the role of **remittances**, or the monies that immigrants return to their countries of origin. The amounts are significant and measure in the hundreds of millions of dollars flowing from the United States to a number of countries where they provide substantial support for families and even venture capital for new businesses. Although some observers express concern over this outflow of money, others counter that it probably represents a small price to pay for the human capital that the United States is able to use in the form of the immigrants themselves. Immigrants in the United States send billions to their home countries and worldwide remittances bring about $300 billion to all the world's developing countries, easily surpassing all other forms of foreign aid (International Fund for Agricultural Development 2007).

The concern about immigration today is both understandable and perplexing. The nation has always been uneasy about new arrivals, especially those who are different from the more affluent and the policy makers. In most of the 1990s, we had paradoxical

remittances
The monies that immigrants return to their country of origin.

THE NEXT AMERICANS

Tomás R. Jiménez

"How immigrants and their descendants see themselves will change over time, and they will simultaneously transform many aspects of what it means to be an American. This is undoubtedly an uncomfortable process, fraught with tension between newcomers and established Americans that can occasionally become explosive. But the real issue is whether the United States can provide opportunities for upward mobility so that immigrants can, in turn, fortify what is most essential to our nation's identity.

History is instructive on whether immigrants will create a messy patchwork of ethnicities in the U.S. About a century ago, a tide of Southern and Eastern European immigrants arriving on our shores raised fears similar to those we hear today. Then, as now, Americans worried that the newcomers were destroying American identity. Many were certain that Catholic immigrants would help the pope rule the United States from Rome, and that immigrants from Southern Europe would contaminate the American gene pool.

None of this came to pass, of course. The pope has no political say in American affairs, the United States is still a capitalist democracy, and there is nothing wrong with the American gene pool. The fact that these fears never materialized are often cited as proof that European-origin immigrants and their descendants successfully assimilated into an American societal monolith.

However, as sociologists Richard Alba and Victor Nee point out, much of the American identity as we know it today was shaped by previous waves of immigrants. For instance, they note that the Christian tradition of the Christmas tree and the leisure Sunday made their way into the American mainstream because German immigrants and their descendants brought these traditions with them. Where religion was concerned, Protestantism was the clear marker of the nonsecular mainstream. But because of the assimilation of millions of Jews and Catholics, we today commonly refer to an American "Judeo-Christian tradition," a far more encompassing notion of American religious identity than the one envisioned in the past. . . .

Even in Los Angeles County, where 36% of the population is foreign-born and more than half speak a language other than English at home, English is not losing out in the long run. According to a recent study by

concerns about immigrants hurting the economy despite strong economic growth. With the economic downturn beginning in 2008, it was clear that low-skilled immigrants (legal or illegal) took the hardest hit and, as a result, remittances immediately declined.

Women and Immigration

Immigration is presented as if all immigrants are similar, with the only distinctions being made concerning point of origin, education, and employment prospects. Another significant distinction is whether immigrants travel with or without their families. We often think that historical immigrants to the United States were males in search of work. Men dominate much of the labor migration worldwide, but because of the diversified labor force in the United States and some policies that facilitate relatives coming, immigration to the

social scientists Rubén Rumbaut, Douglas Massey, and Frank Bean, published in the Population and Development Review, the use of non-English languages virtually disappears among nearly all U.S.-born children of immigrants in the county. Spanish shows more staying power among the U.S.-born children and grandchildren of Mexican immigrants, which is not surprising given that the size of the Spanish-speaking population provides near-ubiquitous access to the language. But the survival of Spanish among U.S.-born descendants of Mexican immigrants does not come at the expense of their ability to speak English and, more strikingly, English overwhelms Spanish-language use among the grandchildren of these immigrants.

An equally telling sign of how much immigrants and their children are becoming "American" is how different they have become from those in their ethnic homelands. Virtually all of today's immigrants stays connected to their countries of origin. They send money to family members who remain behind. Relatively inexpensive air, rail, and bus travel and the availability of cheap telecommunication and e-mail enable them to stay in constant contact, and dual citizenship allows their political voices to be heard from abroad. These enduring ties might lead to the conclusion that continuity

between here and there threatens loyalty to the Stars and Stripes.

But ask any immigrant or their children about a recent visit to their country of origin, and they are likely to tell you how American they felt. The family and friends they visit quickly recognize the prodigal children's tastes for American styles, their American accents and their declining cultural familiarity with life in the ethnic homeland—all telltale signs that they've Americanized. As sociologist David Fitzgerald puts it, their assimilation into American society entails a good deal of "dissimilation" from the countries the immigrants left behind.

American identity is absorbing something quite significant from immigrants and being changed by them. Language, food, entertainment and holiday traditions are palpable aspects of American culture on which immigrants today, as in the past, are leaving their mark. Our everyday lexicon is sprinkled with Spanish words. We are now just as likely to grab a burrito as a burger. Hip-hop is tinged with South Asian rhythms. And Chinese New Year and Cinco de Mayo are taking their places alongside St. Patrick's Day as widely celebrated American ethnic holidays.

Source: Jiménez 2007.

United States generally has been fairly balanced. Actually, most immigration historically appears to be families. For example, from 1870 through 1940, men entering the United States exceeded women by only about 10 percent to 20 percent. Since 1950, women immigrants have actually exceeded men by a modest amount (Gibson and Jung 2006).

The second-class status women normally experience in society is reflected in immigration. Most dramatically, women citizens who married immigrants who were not citizens actually lost their U.S. citizenship from 1907 through 1922 with few exceptions. However, this policy did not apply to men (Johnson 2004).

Immigrant women face not only all the challenges faced by immigrant men but also additional ones. Typically, they have the responsibility of navigating the new society when it comes to services for their family and, in particular, their children. Many new immigrants view the United States as a dangerous place to raise a family and therefore remain particularly vigilant of what happens in their children's lives.

Immigration is a challenge to all family members, but immigrant women must navigate a new culture and a new country not only for themselves but also for their children, such as in this household in Colorado.

Caring for the health of their households falls mainly on women in their social roles as mother, wife, and caregiver for aging parents. In Research Focus, we consider the most recent research on how immigrants are doing in the United States in terms of health. The outcome may not be what one expects.

Male immigrants are more likely to be consumed with work, leaving the women to navigate the bureaucratic morass of city services, schools, medical facilities, and even everyday concerns such as stores and markets. Immigrant women are often reluctant to seek outside help whether they are in need of special services for medical purposes or they are victims of domestic violence. Yet immigrant women are more likely to be the liaison for the household, including adult men, to community associations and religious organizations (Hondagneu-Sotelo 2003).

Women play a critical role in overseeing the household; for immigrant women, the added pressures of being in a new country and trying to move ahead in a different culture heighten this social role.

The Global Economy and Immigration

Immigration is defined by political boundaries that bring the movement of peoples crossing borders to the attention of government authorities and their policies. Within the United States, people may move their residence, but they are not immigrating. For residents in the member nations of the European Union, free movement of people within the union is also protected.

Yet, increasingly, people recognize the need to think beyond national borders and national identity. As noted in Chapter 1, **globalization** is the worldwide integration of government policies, cultures, social movements, and financial markets through trade, movement of people, and the exchange of ideas. In this global framework, even immigrants are less likely to think of themselves as residents of only one country. For generations, immigrants have used foreign-language newspapers to keep in touch with events in their home countries. Today, cable channels carry news and variety programs from their home countries, and the Internet offers immediate access to the homeland and kinfolk thousands of miles away.

globalization
Worldwide integration of government policies, cultures, social movements, and financial markets through trade, movements of people, and the exchange of ideas.

transnationals
Immigrants who sustain multiple social relationships that link their societies of origin and settlement.

Although it helps in bringing the world together, globalization has also highlighted the dramatic economic inequalities between nations. Today, people in North America, Europe, and Japan consume 32 times more resources than the billions of people in developing nations. Thanks to tourism, media, and other aspects of globalization, the people of less-affluent countries are aware of such affluent lifestyles and, of course, often aspire to enjoy them (Diamond 2003).

Transnationals are immigrants who sustain multiple social relationships that link their societies of origin and settlement. Immigrants from the Dominican Republic, for example, not only identify themselves with Americans but also maintain very close ties to their

ASSIMILATION MAY BE HAZARDOUS TO YOUR HEALTH

Immigrants come to the United States seeking a better life, but the transition can be very difficult. We are familiar with the problems new arrivals experience in finding good jobs, but we may be less aware of how pervasive the challenges are.

Researchers continuously show that immigrants often encounter health problems as they leave behind old health networks and confront the private-pay system of medical care in the United States. The outcome is that the health of immigrants often deteriorates. Interestingly, this occurs with Puerto Ricans, who are citizens upon arrival and obviously do not experience as much culture shock as other new arrivals. Scholars Nancy Landale, R. S. Orapesa, and Bridget Gorman looked at the implications for infant mortality of migration from Puerto Rico to the United States. Their analysis showed that children of migrants have lower rates of infant mortality than do children of mainland-born Puerto Rican women. This means that babies of Puerto Rican mothers who are born in the United States are more likely to die than those of mothers who migrated from Puerto Rico.

Why does this happen? Immigrants generally are still under the protection of their fellow travelers. They are still networked with other immigrants, who assist them in adapting to life in the United States. However, as life in a new country continues, these important social networks break down as people learn to navigate the new social system—in this example, the health care system. They are more likely to be uninsured and unable to afford medical care except in emergencies. The researchers do note that Puerto Ricans in the United States, regardless of recency of arrival, still experience better health than those in Puerto Rico. Of course, this finding only further indicates the legacy of the colonial relationship of Puerto Rico to the United States and the health care system there on the island.

Source: King 2007; Landale et al. 2000; Lara et al. 2005; Read and Emerson 2005.

Caribbean homeland. They return for visits, send remittances, and host extended stays of relatives and friends. Back in the Dominican Republic, villages reflect these close ties, as shown in billboards promoting special long-distance services to the United States and by the presence of household appliances sent by relatives. The volume of remittances worldwide is easily the most reliable source of foreign money going to poor countries, far outstripping foreign aid programs.

The growing number of transnationals, as well as immigration in general, directly reflects the world systems analysis we considered in Chapter 1. Transnationals are not new, but the ability to communicate and transfer resources makes the immigration experience today different from that of the nineteenth century. The sharp contrasts between the industrial "have" nations and the developing "have-not" nations only encourages movement across borders. The industrial haves gain benefits from such movement even when they seem to discourage it. The back-and-forth movement only serves to increase globalization and help create informal social networks between people who seek a better life and those already enjoying increased prosperity.

The transnationals themselves maintain a multithreaded relationship between friends and relatives in the United Sates, their home country, and perhaps other countries where relatives and friends have resettled. Besides the economic impact of remittances described above, scholars are increasingly giving attention to "social remittances" that include ideas, social norms, and practices (religious and secular) throughout this global social network (Levitt and Jaworsky 2007).

Refugees

refugees
People living outside their country of citizenship for fear of political or religious persecution.

asylees
Foreigners who have already entered the United States and now seek protection because of persecution or a well-founded fear of persecution.

Refugees are people living outside their country of citizenship for fear of political or religious persecution. Enough refugees exist to populate an entire "nation." There are approximately 11 million to 12 million refugees worldwide. That makes the nation of refugees larger than Belgium, Sweden, or Cuba. The United States has touted itself as a haven for political refugees. However, as we shall see, the welcome to political refugees has not always been unqualified.

The United States makes the largest financial contribution of any nation to worldwide assistance programs. The United States resettles about 70,000 refugees annually and served as the host to a cumulative 1 million refugees between 1990 and 2003. The post-9/11 years have seen the procedures become much more cumbersome for foreigners to acquire refugee status and gain entry to the United States. Many other nations much smaller and much poorer than the United States have many more refugees than the United States, with Jordan, Iran, and Pakistan hosting more than 1 million refugees each (Cumming-Bruce 2008; Jefferys 2007).

The United States, insulated by distance from wars and famines in Europe and Asia, has been able to be selective about which and how many refugees are welcomed. Since the arrival of refugees uprooted by World War II, the United States through the 1980s had allowed three groups of refugees to enter in numbers greater than regulations would ordinarily permit: Hungarians, Cubans, and Southeast Asians.

Despite periodic public opposition, the U.S. government is officially committed to accepting refugees from other nations. According to the United Nations treaty on refugees, which our government ratified in 1968, countries are obliged to refrain from forcibly returning people to territories where their lives or liberty might be endangered. However, it is not always clear whether a person is fleeing for his or her personal safety or to escape poverty. Although people in the latter category may be of humanitarian interest, they do not meet the official definition of refugees and are subject to deportation.

Refugees are people who are granted the right to enter a country while still residing abroad. **Asylees** are foreigners who have already entered the United States and now seek protection because of persecution or a well-founded fear of persecution. This persecution may be based on the individual's race, religion, nationality, membership in a particular social group, or political opinion. Asylees are eligible to adjust to lawful permanent resident status after one year of continuous presence in the United States. Asylum is granted to about 13,000 people annually.

As these Haitians now in detention facilities awaiting processing and most likely deportation found, the United States is often reluctant to accept refugees seeking to escape desperate conditions in their own countries.

Because asylees, by definition, are already here, the outcome is either to grant them legal entry or to return them to their home country. It is the practice of deporting people who are fleeing poverty that has been the subject of criticism. There is a long tradition in the United States of facilitating the arrival of people leaving Communist nations, such as the Cubans. Mexicans who are refugees from poverty, Liberians fleeing civil war, and Haitians running from despotic rule are not similarly welcomed. The plight of Haitians has become one of particular concern.

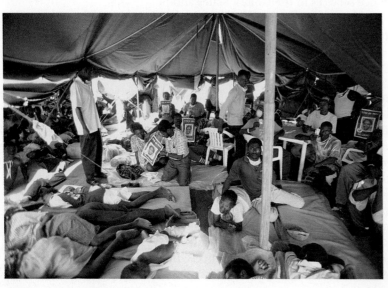

Haitians began fleeing their country, often on small boats, in the 1980s. The U.S. Coast Guard intercepted many Haitians at sea, saving some of these boat people from death in their rickety and overcrowded wooden vessels. The Haitians said they feared detentions, torture, and execution if they remained in Haiti. Yet both Republican and Democratic administrations viewed most of the Haitian exiles as economic migrants rather than political refugees and opposed granting them asylum and permission to enter the United States. Once apprehended, the Haitians are returned. In 1993, the U.S. Supreme Court, by an 8–1 vote, upheld the government's right to intercept Haitian refugees at sea and return them to their homeland without asylum hearings.

African Americans and others have denounced the Haitian refugee policy as racist. They have contrasted it to the "wet foot, dry foot" policy toward Cuban refugees. If the government intercepts Cubans at sea, they are returned; but if they escape detection and make it to the mainland, they may apply for asylum. About 75 percent of Cubans seeking asylum are granted refugee status, compared with only 22 percent of Haitians.

Even with only about a thousand Haitians successfully making it into the United States each year, there is an emerging Haitian American presence, especially in southern Florida. As of 2000, about 70,000 immigrants and their descendants live in metropolitan Miami. Despite continuing obstacles, the community exhibits pride in those who have succeeded, from a Haitian American Florida state legislator to hip-hop musician Wyclef Jean (Alvarez 2008; Dahlburg 2001; U.S. Committee for Refugees 2003).

New foreign military campaigns often bring new refugee issues. The occupation of Iraq, beginning in 2003, had been accompanied by large movements of Iraqis throughout the country and the region. Hopefully, most will return home, but some clearly are seeking to relocate to the United States. As was true in Vietnam, many Iraqis who have aided the U.S.-led mission have increasingly sought refuge in the West, fearing for their safety if they were to remain in Iraq or even in the Middle East. Gradually, the United States has begun to offer refugee status to Iraqis; some 2,700 arrived in 2008 to join an Iraqi American community of 90,000. The diverse landscape of the United States takes on yet another nationality group in large numbers (Bennett 2008; Klein 2008).

Conclusion

For its first hundred years, the United States allowed all immigrants to enter and become permanent residents. However, the federal policy of welcome did not mean that immigrants would not encounter discrimination and prejudice. The possibility of a melting pot, which had always been a fiction, was legislated out of existence.

In the 1960s and again in 1990, the policy was liberalized so that the importance of nationality was minimized, and a person's work skills and relationship to an American were emphasized. This liberalization came at a time when most Europeans no longer wanted to emigrate to the United States.

Throughout the history of the United States, as we have seen, there has been intense debate over the nation's immigration and refugee policies. In a sense, this debate reflects the deep value conflicts in the U.S. culture and parallels the "American dilemma" identified by Swedish social economist Gunnar Myrdal (1944). One strand of our culture, epitomized by the words "Give us your tired, your poor, your huddled masses," has emphasized egalitarian principles and a desire to help people in their time of need. One could headly have anticipated at the time the Statue of Liberty was dedicated in 1886, that more than a century later that Barack Obama, the son of a Kenyan immigrant, would be elected President of the United States.

At the same time, however, hostility to potential immigrants and refugees, whether the Chinese in the 1880s, European Jews in the 1930s and 1940s, or Mexicans, Haitians, and Arabs today, reflects not only racial, ethnic, and religious prejudice but also a desire to maintain the dominant culture of the in-group by keeping out those viewed as outsiders. The conflict between these cultural values is central to the American dilemma of the twenty-first century.

The current debate about immigration is highly charged and emotional. Some people see it in economic terms, whereas others see the new arrivals as a challenge to the very culture of our society. Clearly, the general perception is that immigration presents a problem rather than a promise for the future.

Today's concern about immigrants follows generations of people coming to settle in the United States. This immigration in the past produced a very diverse country in terms of both nationality and religion, even before the immigration of the last 50 years. Therefore, the majority of Americans today are not descended from the English, and Protestants are just more than half of all worshipers. This diversity of religious and ethnic groups is examined in Chapter 5.

Summary

1. Immigration to the United States has been consistent since the country achieved its independence, but in the last 30 years the number of legal immigrants has even exceeded the numbers of the early 1900s.

2. Immigration has been regulated by United States; the first significant restriction was the Chinese Exclusion Act in 1882.

3. Subsequent legislation through the national origins system favored northern and western Europeans. Not until 1965 were quotas by nation largely lifted.

4. Immigration policy is impacted by economic demands for workers who cannot be found among citizens. These workers may be professionals, but they also include large numbers of people who are prepared to do hard labor for wages deemed too low for most citizens but which are attractive to many people outside the United States.

5. Issues such as population growth, the brain drain, mixed-status households, and English-language acquisition influence contemporary immigration policy.

6. Illegal immigration remains formidable and heightened by new concerns about securing our borders since the September 11, 2001, terrorist attacks.

7. Economically, immigration impacts local communities differently, but the new arrivals typically pay taxes and energize the national economy.

8. Refugees present a special challenge to policy makers who balance humanitarian values against an unwillingness to accept all those who are fleeing poverty and political unrest.

Key Terms

asylees 108
bilingual education 97
bilingualism 97
brain drain 95
chain immigration 87

globalization 106
mixed status 96
nativism 90
naturalization 100
refugees 108

remittances 103
sinophobes 91
transnationals 106
xenophobia 90

Review Questions

1. What are the functions and dysfunctions of immigration?

2. What were the social and economic issues when public opinion mounted against Chinese immigration to the United States?

3. Ultimately, what do you think is the major concern people have about contemporary immigration to the United States: the numbers of immigrants, their legal status, or their nationality?

4. What principles appear to guide U.S. refugee policy?

Critical Thinking

1. What is the immigrant root story of your family? Consider how your ancestors arrived in the United States and also how your family's past has been shaped by other immigrant groups.

2. Can you find evidence of the brain drain in terms of the professionals with whom you come in contact? Do you regard this as a benefit? What groups in the United States may not have been encouraged to fill such positions by the availability of such professionals?

3. What challenge does the presence of people in the United States speaking languages other than English present for them? For schools? For the workplace? For you?

Ethnicity
and Religion

THE UNITED STATES INCLUDES A MULTITUDE OF ETHNIC AND religious groups. Do they coexist in harmony or in conflict? How significant are they as sources of identity for their members? Because White is a race, significant attention has been given to the social construction of race as it applies to White people. Many White ethnic groups have transformed their ethnic status into Whiteness. In the 1960s and 1970s, there was a resurgence of interest in White ethnicity, partly in response to the renewed pride in the ethnicity of Blacks, Latinos, and Native Americans. We have an ethnicity paradox in which White ethnics seem to enjoy their heritage but at the same time seek to assimilate into the larger society. Major White ethnic groups such as German, Irish, Italian, and Polish Americans have experienced similar, yet distinctive, social circumstances in the United States. We can make some tentative comparisons from their experiences and what we could expect among today's immigrants. Religious diversity continues and expands with immigration and growth in the followings of non-Christian faiths. Religious minorities experience intolerance in the present as they have in the past. Constitutional issues such as school prayer, secessionist minorities, creationism, and public religious displays are regularly taken to the Supreme Court. The Amish are presented as a case study of the experience of a specific religious group in the United States.

The very complexity of relations between dominant and subordinate groups in the United States today is partly the result of its heterogeneous population. No one ethnic origin or religious faith encompasses all the inhabitants of the United States. Even though our largest period of sustained immigration is three generations past, an American today is surrounded by remnants of cultures and practitioners of religions whose origins are foreign to this country. Ethnicity and religion continue to be significant in defining a person's identity.

In Listen to Our Voices, Albanian immigrant Harallamb Terba speaks of his efforts to attend Truman College, the Chicago city college, and become part of the American society. His experience may not be identical to the many immigrant experiences we will consider in this chapter, but it reflects the constant awareness of making decisions about "fitting in" to a new society.

Ethnic Diversity

The ethnic diversity of the United States at the beginning of the twenty-first century is apparent to almost everyone. Passersby in New York City were undoubtedly surprised once when two street festivals met head-to-head. The procession of San Gennaro, the patron saint of Naples, marched through Little Italy, only to run directly into a Chinese festival originating in Chinatown. Teachers in many public schools often encounter students who speak only one language, and it is not English. Students in Chicago are taught in Spanish, Greek, Italian, Polish, German, Creole, Japanese, Cantonese, or the language of a Native American tribe. In the Detroit metropolitan area, classroom instruction is conveyed in 21 languages, including Arabic, Portuguese, Ukrainian, Latvian, Lithuanian, and Serbian. In many areas of the United States, you can refer to a special yellow pages and find a driving instructor who speaks Portuguese or a psychotherapist who will talk to you in Hebrew.

Germans are the largest ancestral group in the United States; the 2000 census showed almost one-sixth of Americans saying they had at least some German ancestry. Although most German Americans are assimilated, it is possible to see the ethnic tradition in some areas, particularly in Milwaukee, whose population has 48 percent German ancestry. There, three Saturday schools teach German, and one can affiliate with 34 German American clubs and visit a German library that operates within the public library system. Just a bit to the south in River Forest, a Chicago suburb, kinderwerkstatt meets weekly to help parents and children alike to maintain German culture (Carvajal 1996; Freedman 2004; Johnson 1992; Usdansky 1992).

Germany is one of 20 European nations from which at least 1 million people claim to have ancestry. The numbers are striking when one considers the size of some of the sending countries. For example, there are more than 36 million Irish Americans, and the Republic of Ireland had a population of 4 million in 2008. Similarly, more than 4 million people claim Swedish ancestry, and 9 million people live in Sweden today. Of course, many Irish Americans and Swedish Americans are of mixed ancestry, but not everyone in Ireland is Irish, nor is everyone in Sweden Swedish.

Why Don't We Study Whiteness?

Race is socially constructed, as we learned in Chapter 1. Sometimes we come to define race in a clear-cut manner. A descendant of a Pilgrim is White, for example. But sometimes race is more ambiguous: people who are the children of an African American and Vietnamese

Listen to Our Voices

I WAS BORN IN TIRANA

My name is Harallamb Terba. I was born in Tirana, Albania, in November 21, 1965. I came here exactly in March 25, 1996. It was afternoon, 5:00 Chicago time, but my watch say 12:00 in the night because it is seven hours different from my country to here. [Laughs.]

Harallamb Terba

I'm in college now. My major is computer information system. I think after I will be graduating from school, I'm gonna start working, maybe for a company. I love working in computer, computer programming, designing and building programs, applications. I think my life is gonna be good. I always think about that. My wife is in school, too. She's taking sign language. She loves working with deaf people. So I think she is gonna get a good job. . . .

Home is the place where you live. I think about my home in my country. It's the place where you born. But this is the life. The life change. You have to move. You have to try and when you try for the best, it's better for you. I like my country. I like the people there, but I feel this is my home now. I don't feel that about Albania now. I feel that when I was in Albania, I have this thought in my mind that, "I will go. One day I will go in the United States. Everything that I did here it's nothing. I have to get my education. I have to work. I have to do, but everything it's gonna start when I go in the United States." That's why I wish to came here younger.

I think to have my own home, years after. I think about that. It's not important, but I always loved having my own home, my yard. I always loved that because I have been grow up with big home with a yard in front, so that's why I love that. But now I'm living in apartment and everything is OK. I like that.

In the future I want plan for to have children. I'm going to tell my children in the future that they will be American because they will be born here, but I always am gonna tell them from where they are, their parents are. So they have to know about their country because this was the country that grow us, their father and their mother. So they have to know about their culture. Maybe I'm gonna advise them that when they go in Albanian, to be more Albanian than Albanians are, because Albanians are gonna see them just, "Hey, you are from America. You're American." You know what happens.

America to me means freedom, and the land where everyone can do what he dreams. Dreams come true. It's a hard work to do what you want, but finally you can do that. I came from one country that you want to do something, but no one lets you to do that. You can only do what they say to you. So here, if you want to do that, if you like to do that, you can do that. It's hard. I know it's hard. Nothing is easy in our life today, but you can do that. And this is more important for our life, to do what we want.

Source: Excerpt from Terba 2004, 194–195.

American union are biracial or "mixed," or whatever they come to be seen as by others. Our recognition that race is socially constructed has sparked a renewed interest in what it means to be White in the United States. Two aspects of White as a race are useful to consider: the historical creation of Whiteness and how contemporary White people reflect on their racial identity.

When the English immigrants established themselves as the political founders of the United States, they also came to define what it meant to be White. Other groups that today are regarded as White—such as Irish, Germans, Norwegians, or Swedes—were not always considered White in the eyes of the English. Differences in language and religious worship, as well as past allegiance to a king in Europe different from the English monarch, all caused these groups to be seen not so much as Whites in the Western hemisphere but more as nationals of their home country who happened to be residing in North America.

The old distrust in Europe, where, for example, the Irish were viewed by the English as socially and culturally inferior, continued on this side of the Atlantic Ocean. Karl Marx, writing from England, reported that the average English worker looked down on the Irish the way poor Whites in the U.S. South looked down on Black people (Ignatiev 1994, 1995; Roediger 1994).

Whiteness

As European immigrants and their descendants assimilated to the English and distanced themselves from other oppressed groups such as American Indians and African Americans, they came to be viewed as White rather than as part of a particular culture. Writer Noel Ignatiev (1994, 84), contrasting being White with being Polish, argues, "Whiteness is nothing but an expression of race privilege." This strong statement argues that being White, as opposed to being Black or Asian, is characterized by being a member of the dominant group. Whiteness, although it may often be invisible, is aggressively embraced and defended (Giroux 1997).

Whites as people do not think of themselves as a race or have a conscious racial identity. The only occasion when a White racial identity emerges is momentarily when Whites fill out a form asking for self-designation of race or one of those occasions when they are culturally or socially surrounded by people who are not White.

Many immigrants who were not "White on arrival" had to "become White" in a process long forgotten by today's White Americans. The long documented transparent racial divide that engulfed the South during slavery allowed us to ignore how Whiteness was constructed.

Therefore, contemporary White Americans generally give little thought to "being White." Consequently, there is little interest in studying "Whiteness" or considering "being White" except that it is "not being Black." Unlike non-Whites, who are much more likely to interact with Whites, take orders from Whites, and see Whites as the leading figures in the mass media, Whites enjoy the privilege of not being reminded of their Whiteness.

Unlike racial minorities, Whites downplay the importance of their racial identity although they are willing to receive the advantages that come from being White. This means that advocacy of a "color-blind" or "race-neutral" outlook permits the privilege of Whiteness to prevail (Bonilla-Silva 2002; Feagin and Cobas 2008; Yancey 2003).

The new scholarly interest seeks to look at Whiteness but not from the vantage point of a White supremacist. Rather, focusing on White people as a race or on what it means today to be White goes beyond any definition that implies superiority over non-Whites. It is also recognized that "being White" is not the same experience for all Whites any more than "being Asian American" or "being Black" is the same for all Asian Americans or all Blacks. Historian Noel Ignatiev observes that studying Whiteness is a necessary stage to the "abolition of whiteness"—just as, in Marxist analysis, class consciousness is a necessary stage to the abolition of class. By confronting Whiteness, society grasps the all-encompassing power that accompanies socially constructed race (Lewis 2004; McKinney 2003; Roediger 2006).

White Privilege

Whiteness carries with it a sense of identity of being White as opposed to being, for example, Asian or African. For many people, it may not be easy to establish a social identity of Whiteness, as in the case of biracial children. However, one can argue that the social identity of Whiteness exists if one enjoys the privilege of being White.

White privilege
Rights or immunities granted as a particular benefit or favor for being White.

White privilege refers to the rights or immunities granted as a particular benefit or favor for being White. This advantage exists unconsciously and is often invisible to the very White people who enjoy it (Ferber 2008).

Scholar Peggy McIntosh of the Wellesley College Center for Research on Women looked at the privilege that comes from being White and the added privilege of being male. The other side of racial oppression is the privilege enjoyed by dominant groups. Being White or being successful in establishing a White identity carries with it distinct advantages. Among those that McIntosh (1988) identified were the following:

- being considered financially reliable when using checks, credit cards, or cash;
- taking a job without having co-workers suspect it came about because of your race;
- never having to speak for all the people of your race;
- watching television or reading a newspaper and seeing people of your own race widely represented;
- speaking effectively in a large group without being called a credit to your race; and
- assuming that if legal or medical help is needed, your race will not work against you.

Whiteness does carry privileges, but most White people do not consciously think of them except on the rare occasions when they are questioned. We will return to the concepts of Whiteness and White privilege, but let us also consider the rich diversity of religion in the United States, which parallels the ethnic diversity of this nation.

Typically, White people do not see themselves as privileged in the way many African Americans and Latinos see themselves as disadvantaged. When asked to comment on their "Whiteness," White people are most likely to see themselves devoid of ethnicity ("no longer Irish" for example), stigmatized as racist, and victims of reverse discrimination. Privilege for many White people may be easy to exercise in one's life, but it is exceedingly difficult to acknowledge (McKinney 2008).

The Rediscovery of Ethnicity

Robert Park (1950, 205), a prominent early sociologist, wrote in 1913 that "a Pole, Lithuanian, or Norwegian cannot be distinguished, in the second generation, from an American, born of native parents." At one time, sociologists saw the end of ethnicity as nearly a foregone conclusion. W. Lloyd Warner and Leo Srole (1945) wrote in their often-cited *Yankee City* series that the future of ethnic groups seemed to be limited in the United States and that they would be quickly absorbed. Oscar Handlin's *Uprooted* (1951) told of the destruction of immigrant values and their replacement by American culture. Although Handlin was among the pioneers in investigating ethnicity, assimilation was the dominant theme in his work.

Many writers have shown almost a fervent hope that ethnicity would vanish. The persistence of ethnicity was for some time treated by sociologists as dysfunctional because it meant a continuation of old values that interfered with the allegedly superior new values. For example, to hold on to one's language delayed entry into the larger labor market and the upward social mobility it afforded. Ethnicity was expected to disappear not only because of assimilation but also because aspirations to higher social class and status demanded that it vanish. Somehow, it was assumed that one could not be ethnic and middle class, much less affluent.

The Third-Generation Principle

Historian Marcus Hansen's (1952) **principle of third-generation interest** was an early exception to the assimilationist approach to White ethnic groups. Simply stated, Hansen maintained that in the third generation—the grandchildren of the original immigrants—ethnic interest and awareness would actually increase. According to Hansen, "What the son wishes to forget, the grandson wishes to remember."

Hansen's principle has been tested several times since it was first put forth. John Goering (1971), in interviewing Irish and Italian Catholics, found that ethnicity was more important to members of the third generation than it was to the immigrants themselves. Similarly, Mary Waters (1990), in her interviews of White ethnics living in suburban San Jose, California, and suburban Philadelphia, Pennsylvania, observed that many grandchildren wanted to study their ancestors' language, even though it would be a foreign language to

principle of third-generation interest Marcus Hansen's contention that ethnic interest and awareness increase in the third generation, among the grandchildren of immigrants.

symbolic ethnicity
Herbert Gans's term that describes emphasis on ethnic food and ethnically associated political issues rather than deeper ties to one's heritage.

them. They also expressed interest in learning more of their ethnic group's history and a desire to visit the homeland.

Social scientists in the past were quick to minimize the ethnic awareness of blue-collar workers. In fact, ethnicity was viewed as merely another aspect of White ethnics' alleged racist nature, an allegation that will be examined later in this chapter. Curiously, the very same intellectuals and journalists who bent over backward to understand the growing solidarity of Blacks, Hispanics, and Native Americans refused to give White ethnics the academic attention they deserved (Kivisto 2008; Wrong 1972).

The new assertiveness of Blacks and other non-Whites of their rights in the 1960s unquestionably presented White ethnics with the opportunity to reexamine their own position. "If solidarity and unapologetic self-consciousness might hasten Blacks' upward mobility, why not ours?" asked the White ethnics, who were often only a half-step above Blacks in social status. The African American movement pushed other groups to reflect on their past. The increased consciousness of Blacks and their positive attitude toward African culture and the contributions worldwide of African Americans are embraced in what we called the *Afrocentric perspective* (Chapter 1). Therefore, the mood was set in the 1960s for the country to be receptive to ethnicity. By legitimizing Black cultural differences from White culture, along with those of Native Americans and Hispanics, the country's opinion leaders legitimized other types of cultural diversity.

Symbolic Ethnicity

Observers comment on both the evidence of assimilation and the signs of ethnic identity that seem to support a pluralistic view of society. How can both be possible?

First, there is the visible evidence of **symbolic ethnicity**, which may lead us to exaggerate the persistence of ethnic ties among White Americans. According to sociologist Herbert Gans (1979), ethnicity today increasingly involves the symbols of ethnicity, such as eating ethnic food, acknowledging ceremonial holidays such as St. Patrick's Day, and supporting specific political issues or the issues confronting the old country. One example was the push in 1998 by Irish Americans to convince state legislatures to make it compulsory in public schools to teach about the Irish potato famine, which was a significant factor in immigration to the United States. This symbolic ethnicity may be more visible, but this type of ethnic heritage does not interfere with what people do, read, or say or even whom they befriend or marry.

The ethnicity of the twenty-first century, embraced by English-speaking Whites, is largely symbolic. It does not include active involvement in ethnic activities or participation in ethnic-related organizations. In fact, sizable proportions of White ethnics have gained large-scale entry into almost all clubs, cliques, and fraternal groups. Such acceptance is a key indicator of assimilation. Ethnicity has become increasingly peripheral to the lives of the members of the ethnic group. Although today's White ethnics may not relinquish their ethnic identity, other identities become more important.

Second, the ethnicity that does exist may be more a result of living in the United States than actual importing of practices from the past or the old country. Many so-called ethnic foods or celebrations, for example, began in the United States. The persistence of ethnic consciousness, then, may not depend on foreign birth, a distinctive language, and a unique way of life. Instead, it may reflect the experiences in the United States of a unique group that developed a cultural tradition distinct from that of the mainstream. For example, in Poland, the szlachta, or landed gentry, rarely mixed socially with the peasant class. In the United States, however, even with those associations still fresh, szlachta and peasants interacted

White privilege, as described by Peggy McIntosh, includes holding a position in a company without co-workers suspecting it came about because of your race.

together in social organizations as they settled in concentrated communities segregated physically and socially from others (Lopata 1994; Winter 2008).

Third, maintaining ethnicity can be a critical step toward successful assimilation. This ethnicity paradox facilitates full entry into the dominant culture. The ethnic community may give its members not only a useful financial boost but also the psychological strength and positive self-esteem that will allow them to compete effectively in a larger society. Thus, we may witness people participating actively in their ethnic enclave while trying to cross the bridge into the wider community (Lal 1995).

Therefore, ethnicity gives continuity with the past in the form of an effective or emotional tie. The significance of this sense of belonging cannot be emphasized enough. Whether reinforced by distinctive behavior or by what Milton Gordon (1964) called a sense of *peoplehood*, ethnicity is an effective, functional source of cohesion. Proximity to fellow ethnics is not necessary for a person to maintain social cohesion and in-group identity. Fraternal organizations or sports-related groups can preserve associations between ethnics who are separated geographically. Members of ethnic groups may even maintain their feelings of in-group solidarity after leaving ethnic communities in the central cities for the suburban fringe.

The German Americans

Germany is the largest single source of ancestry of people in the United States today, even exceeding the continents of either Africa or Asia. Yet except in a few big city neighborhood enclaves, the explicit presence of German culture seems largely relegated to bratwurst, pretzels, and Kris Kringle.

Settlement Patterns

In the late 1700s, the newly formed United States experienced the arrival of a number of religious dissenters from Germany (such as the Amish) who were attracted by the proclaiming of religious freedom as well as prospects for economic advancement. At the time of the American Revolution, immigrants from Germany (as well as German-speaking Swill) accounted for about one in eight White residents. German colonial subjects split their loyalty between the revolutionaries and the British, but were united in their optimistic view of the opportunities the New World would present.

Although Pennsylvania was the center of early settlements, German Americans, like virtually all other Europeans, moved out west (Ohio, Michigan, and beyond), where land was abundant. In many isolated communities, they established churches and parochial schools, and, in some instances, ethnic enclaves that in selected areas spoke of creating "New Germanys."

Beginning in the 1830s through 1890, Germans represented at least one-quarter of the immigration, ensuring their destiny in the settlement of the United States (see Figure 5.1). Their major urban presence was in Milwaukee, Chicago, Cleveland, Detroit, and Cincinnati.

Early in the history of Americas, German immigrant cultural influence was apparent. Although the new United States never voted on making German

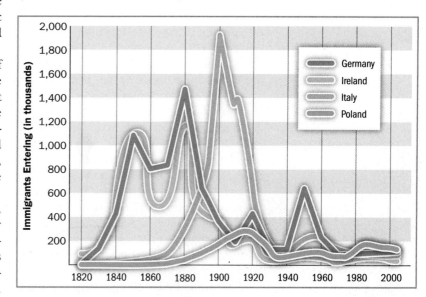

FIGURE 5.1

Immigration from Germany, Ireland, Italy, and Poland

Note: Immigration after 1925 from Northern Ireland is not included. No separate data is included for Poland from 1900 to 1920.

Source: Office of Immigration Statistics 2006, Table 2.

Anti-German sentiment spread in the United States during World War I, escalating dramatically after the United States entered the war in April 1917. A wave of verbal and physical attacks on German Americans was accompanied by a campaign to repress German culture. In this photograph from 1917, a group of children stand in front of an anti-German sign posted in Chicago, Illinois. As the sign suggests, some people in the United States questioned the loyalty of their German American neighbors.

the national language, publications of the proceedings of the Continental Congress were published in German and English. Yet even in those early years, the fear of foreigners—that is non-Anglos—prevented German, even temporarily, from ever getting equal footing with English.

German Americans, perhaps representing 10 percent of the population, established bilingual programs in many public schools, but the rise of Germany as a military foe in the twentieth century ended that movement (Harzig 2008; Nelson 1973).

Twentieth-Century German America

In 1901, The German-American National Alliance (Deutsche-Amerikanischer National-Bund) was founded to speak for all Germans in the United States but especially urban Protestant middle-class German Americans. As time passed, it sought to commemorate the contributions to the nation's development but also sought to block prohibition. With the rise of German military power, many German Americans sought to argue for U.S. neutrality. But these efforts ended quickly, and the organization actually disbanded after the United States declared war on Germany in 1917.

With World War I and especially the rise of the Nazi era and the war years of the 1930s and 1940s, most German Americans sought to distance themselves from the politics in their homeland. There were anti-German incidents of harassment and intimidation. About 11,000 German Americans (out of 5 million) were interned, but the stigmatization did not come close to that felt by Japanese Americans. By comparison, many more German Americans enlisted and played important roles (none more so than Dwight Eisenhower, whose ancestors immigrated to Pennsylvania from Germany in 1741).

German Americans made the group transition into core society. Indeed, Horace Kallen, who popularized the term *pluralism*, held up German America as a success in finding a place in United States. With the end of wartime tensions, German Americans moved from having multiple identities that included being somewhat marginalized as "Germans" to an identity of "American" and, less explicitly, White (Carlson 2003; Kazal 2004; Krammer 1997; Olzmann 2000).

By the latter half of the twentieth century, the animosity toward Germany seemed a part of the distant past. Germany and its people became emblematic of stalwart friends of the United States, as reflected with appearances beginning with John F. Kennedy in Berlin in 1963 and Ronald Reagan in 1987. Both spoke of the U.S. commitment to uniting Germany, and presidential candidate Barack Obama in 2008 spoke in Berlin of a united Europe.

In the last 10 years, immigration from Germany, a country of 82 million, has fluctuated between 5,000 and 10,000 annually. The steady immigration for decades placed Germany in the 2000 census as the tenth-largest source of foreign-born residents, with more than 700,000 (only about 170,000 behind Cuba and Korea). Yet the broad dispersion of these immigrants and their bilingual capability means the numbers are insufficient to create (or re-create) a German cultural presence. Rather, today's German American community is characterized by postwar and historical ties that have long since overshadowed the lingering bitterness of World Wars I and II (Harzig 2008; Office of Immigration Statistics 2006).

Famous German Americans include industrialist John D. Rockefeller, General John Pershing, baseball players Babe Ruth and Lou Gehrig, and actors Clark Gable and Kirsten Dunst.

The Irish Americans

The Irish presence in the United States stretches back to the 1600s and reflects a diversity based on time of entry, settlement area, and religion. Irish Americans have been visible both in a positive way in terms of playing a central role in American life and in a negative way at certain historical periods, being victimized like so many other immigrant groups.

Irish Immigration

The Protestants dominated the early Irish immigration to the colonies even though these Presbyterians from Ireland of Scottish descent accounted for nearly one out of seven of the island of Ireland's residents in the eighteenth century. Motivating the early immigrants was the lure of free land in North America, which was in sharp contrast to Ireland, where more and more tenants had to compete for land. The powerful landlords there took full advantage by squeezing more and more profits out of the tenants, making migration to colonial America attractive.

The Roman Catholics among the early immigrants were a diverse group. Some were extensions of the privileged classes seeking even greater prosperity. Protestant settlers of all national backgrounds were united in their hatred of Catholicism. In most of the colonies, Catholics could not practice their faith openly and either struggled inwardly or converted to Anglicanism. Other Roman Catholics and some Protestants came from Europe as an alternative to prison or after signing articles of indenture and arriving bound to labor for periods of customarily 3 to 5 years and sometimes as long as 7 years (Meagher 2005).

The American Revolution temporarily stopped the flow of immigration, but deteriorating economic conditions in Ireland soon spurred even greater movement to North America. British officials, by making passage to the newly formed republic of the United States expensive, diverted many immigrants to British North America (Canada). Yet the numbers to the United States remained significant and, although still primarily Protestant, drew from a broader spectrum of Ireland both economically and geographically.

Many people mistakenly overlook this early immigration and begin with Irish immigration during the Great Famine. Yet the Irish were the largest group after the English among immigrants during the colonial period. The historical emphasis on the famine immigrants is understandable, given the role it played in Ireland and its impetus for the massive transfer of population from Ireland to the United States.

In 1845, a fungus wiped out the potato crop of Ireland, as well as that of much of western Europe and even coastal America. Potatoes were particularly central to the lives of the Irish, and the devastating starvation did not begin to recede until 1851. Mortality was high, especially among the poor and in the more agricultural areas of the island. Predictably, to escape catastrophe, some 2 million Irish fled mostly to England, but then many continued on to the United States. From 1841 through 1890, more than 3.2 million Irish arrived in the United States (Figure 5.1).

This new migration fleeing the old country was much more likely to consist of families rather than single men. The arrival of entire households and extended kinship networks increased significantly the rapid formation of Irish social organizations in the United States. This large influx of immigrants led to the creation of ethnic neighborhoods, complete with parochial schools and parish churches serving as focal points. Fraternal organizations such as the Ancient Order of Hibernians, corner saloons, local political organizations, and Irish nationalist groups seeking the ouster of Britain from Ireland rounded out neighborhood social life.

Even in the best of times, the lives of the famine Irish would have been challenging in the United States, but they arrived at a very difficult time. Nativist—that is, anti-Catholic and anti-immigrant—movements were already emerging and being embraced by politicians. Antagonism was not limited to harsh words. From 1834 to 1854, mob violence against Catholics across the country led to death, the burning of a Boston convent, the destruction of a Catholic church and the homes of Catholics, and the use of Marines and state militia to bring peace to American cities as far west as St. Louis.

In retrospect, the reception given to the Irish is not difficult to understand. Many immigrated after the potato crop failure and famine in Ireland. They fled not so much to a better life as from almost certain death. The Irish Catholics brought with them a celibate clergy, who struck the New England aristocracy as strange and reawakened old religious hatreds. The Irish were worse than Blacks, according to the dominant Whites, because unlike the slaves and even the freed Blacks, who "knew their place," the Irish did not suffer their maltreatment in silence. Employers balanced minorities by judiciously mixing immigrant groups to prevent unified action by the laborers. For the most part, nativist efforts only led the foreign born to emphasize their ties to Europe.

Mostly of peasant backgrounds, the Irish arriving were ill prepared to compete successfully for jobs in the city. Their children found it much easier to improve their occupational status over that of their fathers as well as experienced upward mobility in their own lifetimes.

Becoming White

Ireland had a long antislavery tradition, including practices that prohibited Irish trade in English slaves. Some 60,000 Irish signed an address in 1841, petitioning Irish Americans to join the abolitionist movement in the United States. Many Irish Americans already opposed to slavery applauded the appeal, but they were soon drowned out by fellow immigrants who denounced or questioned the authenticity of the petition.

The Irish immigrants, subjected to derision and menial jobs, sought to separate themselves from the even lower classes, particularly Black Americans and especially the slaves. It was not altogether clear that the Irish were "White" during the antebellum period. Irish character was rigidly cast in negative racial typology. Although the shared experiences of oppression could have led Irish Americans to ally with Black Americans, they grasped for Whiteness at the margins of their life in the United States. Direct competition was not common between the two groups. For example, in 1855, Irish immigrants made up 87 percent of New York City's unskilled laborers, whereas free Blacks accounted for only 3 percent (Greeley 1981; Ignatiev 1995; Roediger 1994).

As Irish immigration continued in the latter part of the nineteenth century until Irish independence in 1921, they began to see themselves favorably in comparison to the initial waves of Italian, Polish, and Slovak Roman Catholic immigrants. The Irish Americans began to assume more leadership positions in politics and labor unions. Loyalty to the church still played a major role. By 1910, the priesthood was the professional occupation of choice for second-generation men. Irish women were more likely than their German and English immigrant counterparts to become schoolteachers. In time, Irish Americans' occupational profiles diversified, and they began to experience slow advancement and gradually were welcomed into the White working class as their identity as "White" overcame any status as "immigrant."

With mobility came social class distinctions within Irish America. The immigrants and their children who began to move into the more affluent urban areas were derogatorily referred to as the "lace-curtain Irish." The lower-class Irish immigrants they left behind, meanwhile, were referred to as the "shanty Irish." But as immigration from Ireland slowed and upward mobility quickened, fewer and fewer Irish qualified as the poor cousins of their predecessors.

For the Irish American man, the priesthood was viewed as a desirable and respected occupation. Irish Americans furthermore played a leadership role in the Roman Catholic Church in the United States. The Irish dominance persisted long after other ethnic groups swelled the ranks of the faithful (Fallows 1979; Lee and Bean 2007; Lee and Casey 2006).

The Contemporary Picture

By 2006, 36 million people identified themselves as having Irish ancestry—second only to German ancestry and nine times the current population of Ireland itself. Massachusetts has the largest concentration of Irish Americans, with 24 percent of the state indicating Irish ancestry (Bureau of the Census 2008c).

Contemporary Irish immigration is relatively slight, accounting for perhaps one out of 1,000 legal arrivals today, compared with more than one-third of all immigrants in the 1840s and 1850s. About 202,000 people in the United States were born in Ireland—comparable to the number of Portuguese born in the United States. Today's Irish American typically enjoys the symbolic ethnicity of food, dance, and music. Gaelic language instruction is limited to fewer than 30 colleges. Visibility as a collective ethnic group is greatest with the annual St. Patrick's Day celebrations, when everyone seems to be Irish, or with the occasional fervent nationalism aimed at curtailing Great Britain's role in Northern Ireland. Yet some stereotypes remain concerning excessive drinking despite available

For many Irish American participants in a St. Patrick's Day parade, this is their most visible expression of symbolic ethnicity during an entire year.

data indicating that alcoholism rates are no higher and sometimes lower among people of Irish ancestry compared to descendants of other European immigrant groups.

St. Patrick's Day celebrations, as noted previously, offer an example of how ethnic identity evolves over time. The Feast of St. Patrick has a long history, but the public celebrations with parties, concerts, and parades originated in the United States, which were then exported to Ireland in the latter part of the twentieth century. Even today, the large Irish American population often defines what is authentic Irish globally. For example, participants in Irish step dancing in the United States have developed such clout in international competitions that they have come to define many aspects of cultural expression, much to the consternation of the Irish in Ireland (Hassrick 2007; Bureau of the Census 2008c).

Well-known Irish Americans can be found in all arenas of American society, including the celebrity chef Bobby Flay, actor Philip Seymour Hoffman, comedian Conan O'Brien, and author Frank McCourt as well as the political dynasties of the Kennedys in Massachusetts and the Daleys in Chicago. Reflecting growing rates of intermarriage, Irish America also includes singer Mariah Carey (her mother Irish and her father African American and Venezuelan).

The Irish were the first immigrant group to encounter prolonged organized resistance. However, strengthened by continued immigration, facility with the English language, building on strong community and family networks, and familiarity with representative politics, Irish Americans became an integral part of the United States.

The Italian Americans

Although each European country's immigration to the United States has created its own social history, the case of Italians, though not typical of every nationality, offers insight into the White ethnic experience. Italians immigrated even during the colonial period, coming from what was a highly differentiated land, because Italian states did not unify as one nation and escaped foreign domination until 1848.

Early Immigration

Italian Americans from the beginning played prominent roles during the American Revolution and the early days of the republic. Mass immigration began in the 1880s, peaking in the first 20 years of the twentieth century, when Italians accounted for one-fourth of European immigration (refer to Figure 5.1).

Italian immigration was concentrated not only in time but also by geography. The majority of the immigrants were landless peasants from rural southern Italy, the Mezzogiorno. Although many people in the United States assume that Italians are a nationality with a single culture, this is not true either culturally or economically. The Italian people recognize multiple geographic divisions reflecting sharp cultural distinctions. These divisions were brought with the immigrants to the New World.

Many Italians, especially in the early years of mass immigration in the nineteenth century, received their jobs through an ethnic labor contractor, the padrone. Similar arrangements have been used by Asian, Hispanic, and Greek immigrants, where the labor contractors, most often immigrants, have mastered sufficient English to mediate for their compatriots. Exploitation was common within the padrone system through kickbacks, provision of inadequate housing, and withholding of wages. By World War I, 90 percent of Italian girls and 99 percent of Italian boys in New York City were leaving school at age 14 to work, but by that time, Italian Americans were sufficiently fluent in English to seek out work on their own, and the padrone system had disappeared. Still, by comparison to the Irish, the Italians in the United States were slower to accept formal schooling as essential to success (Sassler 2006).

Along with manual labor, the Catholic Church was a very important part of Italian Americans' lives at that time. Yet they found little comfort in a Catholic church dominated by an earlier immigrant group: the Irish. The traditions were different; weekly attendance for Italian Americans was overshadowed by the religious aspects of the feste (or festivals) held throughout the year in honor of saints (the Irish viewed the feste as practically a form of paganism). These initial adjustment problems were overcome with the establishment of ethnic parishes, a pattern repeated by other non-Irish immigrant groups. Thus, parishes would be staffed by Italian priests, sometimes imported for that purpose. Although the hierarchy of the Church adjusted more slowly, Italian Americans were increasingly able to feel at home in their local parish church. Today, more than 70 percent of Italian Americans identify themselves as Roman Catholics (Luconi 2001).

Constructing Identity

As assimilation proceeded, Italian Americans began to construct a social identity as a nationality group rather than viewing themselves in terms of their village or province. As shown in Figure 5.2, over time, Italian Americans shed old identities for a new one. As immigration from Italy declined, the descendants' ties became more nationalistic. This move from local or regional to national identity was followed by Irish and Greek Americans. The changing identity of Italian Americans reflected the treatment they received in the United States, whereas non-Italians did not make those regional distinctions. However, they were not treated well. For example, in turn-of-the-century New Orleans, Italian Americans established special ties with the Black community because both groups were marginalized in Southern society. Gradually, Italian Americans became White and enjoyed all the privileges that came with it. Today, it would be inconceivable to imagine that Italian Americans of New Orleans would reach out to the African American community as their natural allies on social and political issues (Guglielmo and Salerno 2003; Luconi 2001).

A controversial aspect of the Italian American experience involves organized crime, as typified by Al Capone (1899–1947). Arriving in U.S. society in the bottom layers, Italians lived in decaying, crime-ridden neighborhoods that became known as Little Italy. For a

FIGURE 5.2

Constructing Social Identity Among Italian Immigrants

Over time, Italian Americans moved from seeing themselves in terms of their provincial or village identity to their national identity, and then they successfully became indistinguishable from other Whites.

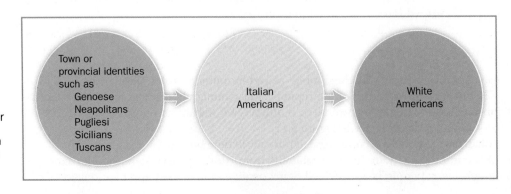

small segment of these immigrants, crime was a significant means of upward social mobility. In effect, entering and leading criminal activity was one aspect of assimilation, though not a positive one. Complaints linking ethnicity and crime actually began in colonial times with talk about the criminally inclined Irish and Germans, and they continue with contemporary stereotyping about groups such as Colombian drug dealers and Vietnamese street gangs. Yet the image of Italians as criminals has persisted from Prohibition-era gangsters to the view of mob families today. As noted earlier, it is not at all surprising that groups have been organized to counter such negative images.

The fact that Italians often are characterized as criminal, even in the mass media, is another example of what we have called respectable bigotry toward White ethnics. The persistence of linking Italians, or any other minority group, with crime probably is attributable to attempts to explain a problem by citing a single cause: the presence of perceived undesirables. Many Italian Americans still see their image tied to old stereotypes. A 2001 survey of Italian American teenagers found that 39 percent felt the media presented their ethnic group as criminal or gang members and 34 percent as restaurant workers (Girardelli 2004; National Italian American Foundation 2006; Parrillo 2008).

The immigration of Italians was slowed by the national origins system, described in Chapter 4. As Italian Americans settled permanently, the mutual aid societies that had grown up in the 1920s to provide basic social services began to dissolve. More slowly, education came to be valued by Italian Americans as a means of upward mobility. Even becoming more educated did not ward off prejudice, however. In 1930, for example, President Herbert Hoover rebuked Fiorello La Guardia, then an Italian American member of Congress from New York City, stating that "the Italians are predominantly our murderers and bootleggers" and recommending that La Guardia "go back to where you belong" because, "like a lot of other foreign spawn, you do not appreciate this country which supports you and tolerates you" (Baltzell 1964, 30).

Although U.S. troops, including 500,000 Italian Americans, battled Italy during World War II, some hatred and sporadic violence emerged against Italian Americans and their property. However, they were not limited to actions against individuals. Italian Americans were even confined by the federal government in specific areas of California by virtue of their ethnicity alone, and 10,000 were relocated from coastal areas. In addition, 1,800 Italian Americans who were citizens of Italy were placed in an internment camp in Montana. The internees were eventually freed on Columbus Day 1942 as President Roosevelt lobbied the Italian American community to gain full support for the impending land invasion of Italy (Department of Justice 2001a; Fox 1990).

In Research Focus we consider how social scientists examine the economic experience of these early Italian immigrants and their children in the United States and compare it to how Mexican immigrants are faring today.

The Contemporary Picture

In politics, Italian Americans have been more successful, at least at the local level, where family and community ties can be translated into votes. However, political success did not come easily because many Italian immigrants anticipated returning to their homeland and did not always take neighborhood politics seriously. It was even more difficult for Italian Americans to break into national politics.

Not until 1962 was an Italian American named to a cabinet-level position. Geraldine Ferraro's nomination as the Democratic vice presidential candidate in 1984 was every bit as much an achievement for Italian Americans as it was for women. The opposition to the nomination of Judge Samuel Alito to the Supreme Court in 2006 struck many as bordering on anti–Italian American sentiments in the manner the opposition was advanced. Numerous critics used the phrase "Judge Scalito" in obvious reference to the sitting Italian American on the Court, Justice Antonio Scalia (Cornacchia and Nelson 1992; National Italian American Foundation 2006).

There is no paucity of famous Italian Americans. They include athletes such as Joe DiMaggio and Joe Paterno, politician Rudolph Giullani, film director Francis Ford

IMMIGRANTS: YESTERDAY AND TODAY

Anyone thinking about the future of today's immigrants might reflect back on the experiences of those who came a century ago. It is widely agreed that, despite difficult times and often harsh treatment by those already here, the immigrants of the late nineteenth and early twentieth century ultimately fared well. Certainly their descendants are doing well today. So can we generalize from this experience to today's immigrants?

Sociologist Joel Perlmann and other scholars have considered the experience of immigrants from southern, central, and eastern Europe who were predominantly low-skilled workers. A significant component were Italian and Poles. Based on his analysis and that of other sociologists, we find that these earlier immigrant workers earned typically only between 60 percent and 88 percent in wages as that of nonimmigrant Whites in the same occupational groups.

Contrary to an often commonly held belief, these immigrants did not end up in well-paying jobs in manufacturing that led them into the middle class in their own lifetime. Rather, they firmly remained working class until after World War II. Upward mobility occurred across generations typically, not within the lifetime of the arriving Italian, Polish, and other southern, central, and eastern European immigrants. This would mean economic parity took about three or four generations and not a decade as some writers have romantically portrayed it.

Taking these data, Perlmann looks at contemporary Mexican immigrants. In may ways the deck is stacked against this current immigrant group, which is by far the largest. Unlike their European counterparts of a

---

Coppola, singer Madonna, comedian Jay Leno, writer Mario Puzo, actor Nicholas Cage, chef Rachel Ray, and auto racing legend Mario Andretti.

In 2000, the 15.9 million people of Italian ancestry accounted for about 6 percent of the population, although only a small fraction of them had actually been born in Italy. Italian Americans still remain the seventh-largest immigrant group. Just how ethnically conscious is the Italian American community? Although the number is declining, 1 million Americans speak Italian at home; only six languages are spoken more frequently at home: Spanish, French, Chinese, Vietnamese, Tagalog (Philippines), and German. For another 14-plus million Italian Americans, however, the language tie to their culture is absent, and, depending on their degree of assimilation, only traces of symbolic ethnicity may remain. In a later section, we will look at the role that language plays for many immigrants and their children (Shin and Bruno 2003).

The Polish Americans

Immigrants from Poland have had experiences similar to those of the Irish and Italians. They had to overcome economic problems and personal hardships just to make the journey. Once in the United States, they found themselves often assigned to the jobs many citizens had not wanted to do. They had to adjust to a new language, a familiar yet different culture. And always they were looking back to the family members left behind who either wanted to join them in the United States or, in contrast, never wanted them to leave in the first place.

Like other arrivals, many Poles sought improvement in their lives, a migration that was known as Za Chlebem (For Bread). The Poles who came were, at different times, more

century ago, many arrivals from Mexico (about 55 percent) are having to labor as illegal immigrants, which obviously curtails the opportunities available to them and their family members. Particularly harmful to rapid upward mobility is that today's second-generation Mexicans in the United States are lagging further behind in education compared to most people than were the comparable generation of the turn-of-the century European immigrants. This is particularly challenging given the much greater importance that formal schooling has today for economic success compared to a century ago.

Language acquisition does not appear to be an issue, even given the large concentrations of Spanish-speaking neighborhoods that might seem to work against Hispanics becoming fluent English speakers. Although 23 percent of the Hispanic immigrants as a group speak English very well, the percentage of these immigrants who are fluent in English rises to 88 percent among their U.S.-born children and then to 94 percent in the third generation.

It is early to make firm direct comparisons because the second-generation Mexican American is just coming of age, much less having full labor force experience and creating their own families. Although the complete entry of today's immigrants into economy is likely to come based on analysis of the situation today, comparisons to White ethnics suggests that it may take the immigrants longer by at least an additional generation.

Sources: Bean and Stevens 2003; Camarota 2007a; Dickson 2006; Hakimzadeh and Cohn 2007; Katz et al. 2007; Perlmann 2005; Portes 2006; Portes and Rumbaut 2006; Zaldez 2006.

likely than many other European immigrants to see themselves as forced immigrants and were often described by, and themselves adopted, the terminology directly reflecting their social roles—exiles, refugees, displaced persons, or émigrés. The primary force for this exodus was the changing political status of Poland through most of the nineteenth and twentieth centuries, which was as turbulent as the lives of the new arrivals.

Early Immigration

Polish immigrants were among the settlers at Jamestown, Virginia, in 1608, to help develop the colony's timber industry, but it was the Poles who came later in that century who made a lasting mark. The successful exploits of Polish immigrants such as cavalry officer Casimir Pulaski and military engineer Thaddeus Kosciuszko are still commemorated today in communities with large Polish American populations. As we can see in Figure 5.1, it was not until the 1890s that Polish immigration was significant in comparison to some other European arrivals. Admittedly, it is difficult to exactly document the size of this immigration because at various historical periods Poland or parts of the country became part of Austria-Hungary, Germany (Prussia), and the Soviet Union so that the migrants were not officially coming from a nation called "Poland."

Many of the Polish immigrants were adjusting not only to a new culture but also to a more urban way of life. Sociologists William I. Thomas and Florian Znaniecki, in their classic study *The Polish Peasant in Europe and America,* traced the path from rural Poland to urban America. Many of the peasants did not necessarily come directly to the United States but first traveled through other European countries. This pattern is not unique and reminds us that, even today, many immigrants have crossed several countries, sometimes establishing themselves for a period of time before finally settling in the United States (1996, 1918–1920).

Like the Germans, Italians, and Irish, Poles arrived at the large port cities of the East Coast but, unlike the other immigrant groups, these were more likely to settle in cities further inland or work in mines in Pennsylvania. In such areas, they would join kinfolk or acquaintances through the process of chain migration (described in the previous chapter).

The reference to coal mining as an occupation reflects the continuing tendency of immigrants to work in jobs avoided by most U.S. citizens because they paid little, were dangerous, or both. For example, in September 1897, a group of miners in Lattimer, Pennsylvania, marched to demand safer working conditions and an end to special taxes placed only on foreign-born workers. In the ensuing confrontation with local officials, police officers shot at the protesters, killing 19 people, most of whom were Polish, the others Lithuanians and Slovaks (Duszak 1997).

Polonia

With growing numbers, the emergence of Polonia (meaning Polish communities outside of Poland) became more common in cities throughout the Midwest. Male immigrants who came alone often took shelter through a system of inexpensive boarding houses called *tryzmanie bortnków* (brother keeping), which allowed the new arrival to save money and send it back to Poland to support his family. These funds eventually provided the financial means necessary to bring family members over, adding to the size of Polonia in cities such as Buffalo, Cleveland, Detroit, Milwaukee, Pittsburgh, and, above all, Chicago, where the population of Poles was second only to Warsaw, Poland.

Religion has played an important role among the Polish immigrants and their descendants. Most of the Polish immigrants who came to the United States before World War I were Roman Catholic. They quickly established their own parishes where new arrivals could feel welcome. Although religious services at that time were in the Latin language, as they had been in Poland, the many service organizations around the parish, not to mention the Catholic schools, kept the immigrants steeped in the Polish language and the latest happenings back home. Jewish Poles began immigrating during the first part of the twentieth century to escape the growing hostility they felt in Europe that culminated in the Holocaust. Their numbers swelled greatly until movement from Poland stopped with the invasion of Poland by Germany in 1939; it resumed after the war.

Although the Jewish–Catholic distinction may be the most obvious distinguishing factor among Polish Americans, there are other divisions as well. Regional subgroups such as the Kashubes, the Górali, and the Mazurians have often carried great significance. Some Poles emigrated from areas where German actually was the language of origin.

As with other immigrant groups, Polish Americans could make use of a rich structure of self-help voluntary associations that was already well established by the 1890s. Not all organizations smoothly cut across different generations of Polish immigrants. For example, the Poles who came immediately after World War II as political refugees fleeing Soviet domination were quite different in their outlook than the descendants of the economic refugees from the turn of the century. These kinds of tensions in an immigrant community are not unusual even if they go unnoticed by the casual observer who lumps all immigrants of the same nationality together (Jaroszyńska-Kirchmann 2004).

Like many other newcomers, Poles have been stigmatized as outsiders and also stereotyped as simple and uncultured—the typical biased view of working-class White ethnics. Their struggles in manual occupations placed them in direct competition with other White ethnics and African Americans, which occasionally led to labor disputes and longer-term tense and emotional rivalries. "Polish jokes" continue now to have a remarkable shelf life in casual conversation well into the twenty-first century. Jewish Poles suffer the added indignities of anti-Semitism (Dolan and Stotsky 1997).

The Contemporary Picture

Today, Polonia in the United States exceeds 10 million. Although this may not seem significant in a country of more than 300 million, we need to recall that today Poland itself has a population of only about 39 million. Whether it was to support the efforts of Lech Walesa, the Solidarity movement leader who confronted the Soviet Union in the 1980s, or to celebrate the elevation of Karol Józef Wojtyla as Pope John Paul II in 1978, Polish Americans are a central part of the global Polish community.

Richie Sambora, guitarist with the rock group Bon Jovi, is one of many well-known Polish Americans.

Many Polish Americans have retained little of their rich cultural traditions and may barely acknowledge even symbolic ethnicity. Others are still immersed in Polonia, and their lives still revolve around many of the same religious and social institutions that were the center of Polonia a century ago. For example, as of 2006, 54 Roman Catholic churches in the metropolitan Chicago area still offer Polish-language masses. Although in many of these parishes there may be only one service in Polish serving a declining number of celebrants, a few traditional "Polish" churches actually still have Polish-speaking priests in residence. Even with the decline in Polish-language service, Pole seminarians are actively recruited by the Roman Catholic Church although now English-language training is often emphasized.

In the latter part of the twentieth century, some of the voluntary associations relocated or built satellite centers to serve the outlying Polish American populations. To sustain their activities financially, these social organizations also reached out of the central cities in order to tap into the financial resources of suburban Poles. Increasingly, people of Polish descent also have now made their way into the same social networks populated by German, Irish, Italian, and other ethnic Americans (Bukowcyk 1996; Erdmans 1998, 2006; Lopata 1994; Mocha 1998; Polzin 1973; Stone 2006).

Among the many Polish Americans well known or remembered today are actor Adrien Brody, home designer Martha (Kostyra) Stewart, comedian Jack Benny (Benjamin Kubelsky), guitarist Richie Sambora of the rock group Bon Jovi, actress Jane Kaczmarek of *Malcolm in the Middle*, entertainer Liberace, *Wheel of Fortune* host Pat Sajak, baseball star Stan Musial, football star Mike Ditka, novelist Joseph Conrad (Józef Korzeniowski), singer Bobby Vinton (Stanley Ventula, Jr.), polio vaccine pioneer Albert Sabin, and motion picture director Stanley Kubrick.

Religious Pluralism

Religion plays a fundamental role in society, even affecting those who do not practice or even believe in organized religion. *Religion* refers to a unified system of beliefs and practices relative to sacred that encompasses elements beyond everyday life that inspire awe, respect, and even fear (Durkheim [1912] 2001).

In popular speech, the term *pluralism* has often been used in the United States to refer explicitly to religion. Although certain faiths figure more prominently in the worship scene, there has been a history of greater religious tolerance in the United States than in most other nations. Today there are more than 1,500 religious bodies in the United States, ranging from the more than 66 million members of the Roman Catholic Church to sects with fewer than 1,000 adherents. In virtually every region of the country, religion is being expressed in greater variety, whether it be the Latinization of Catholicism and some Christian faiths or the de-Europeanizing of some established Protestant faiths as

denomination
A large, organized religion not officially linked with the state or government.

with Asian Americans or the de-Christianizing of the overall religious landscape with Muslims, Buddhists, Hindus, Sikhs, and others (Roof 2007).

How do we view the United States in terms of religion? There is an increasingly non-Christian presence in the United States. In 1900, an estimated 96 percent of the nation was Christian; slightly more than 1 percent was nonreligious, and approximately 3 percent held other faiths. In 2007, it was estimated that the nation was 82 percent Christian, nearly 11 percent nonreligious, and another 7 percent all other faiths. The United States has a long Jewish tradition, and Muslims number close to 5 million. A smaller but also growing number of people adhere to such Eastern faiths as Hinduism, Buddhism, Confucianism, and Taoism (Newport 2007).

Sociologists use the word **denomination** for a large, organized religion that is not linked officially with the state or government. By far, the largest denomination in the United States is Catholicism, yet at least 25 other Christian religious denominations have 1 million or more members (Table 5.1).

There are also at least four non-Christian religious groups in the United States whose numbers are comparable to any of these large denominations: Jews, Muslims, Buddhists,

TABLE 5.1
Churches with More Than a Million Members

Denomination Name	Inclusive Membership
The Roman Catholic Church	67,515,016
Southern Baptist Convention	16,306,246
The United Methodist Church	7,995,456
The Church of Jesus Christ of Latter-day Saints	5,779,316
The Church of God in Christ	5,499,875
National Baptist Convention, U.S.A., Inc.	5,000,000
Evangelical Lutheran Church in America	4,774,203
National Baptist Convention of America, Inc.	3,500,000
Presbyterian Church (U.S.A.)	3,025,740
Assemblies of God	2,836,174
Progressive National Baptist Convention, Inc.	2,500,000
African Methodist Episcopal Church	2,500,000
National Missionary Baptist Convention of America	2,500,000
The Lutheran Church—Missouri Synod (LCMS)	2,414,997
Episcopal Church	2,154,572
Churches of Christ	1,639,495
Greek Orthodox Archdiocese of America	1,500,000
Pentecostal Assemblies of the World, Inc.	1,500,000
African Methodist Episcopal Zion Church	1,443,405
American Baptist Churches in the U.S.A.	1,371,278
United Church of Christ	1,218,541
Baptist Bible Fellowship International	1,200,000
Christian Churches and Churches of Christ	1,071,616
The Orthodox Church in America	1,064,000
Jehovah's Witness	1,069,533
Church of God	1,032,550

Note: Most recent data as of 2008. Membership reporting year ranges from 1992 to 2007.

Source: Eileen Lindner (ed.) 2008. Yearbook of American and Canadian Churches 2008. Nashville: Abingden Press. Reprinted by permission from Yearbook of American and Canadian Churches 2008. Copyright © National Council of Churches of Christ in the USA.

and Hindus. In the United States each numbers more than 1 million members. Within each of these groups are branches or sects that distinguish themselves from each other. For example, as we examine in greater detail later in this chapter, in the United States and the rest of the world, some Muslims are Sunni and others Shia. There are further divisions within these groups, just as there are among Protestants, and, in turn, among Baptists.

Even if religious faiths have broad representation, they tend to be fairly homogeneous at the local church level. This is especially ironic, given that many faiths have played critical roles in resisting racism and in trying to bring together the nation in the name of racial and ethnic harmony (Orfield and Liebowitz 1999).

Broadly defined faiths represent a variety of ethnic and racial groups. In Figure 5.3, we consider the interaction of White, Black, and Hispanic races with religions. Muslims, Pentecostals, and Jehovah's Witnesses are much more diverse than Presbyterians or Lutherans. Religion plays an even more central role for Blacks and Latinos than Whites. A 2004 national survey indicated that 65 percent of African Americans and 51 percent of Latinos attend a religious service every week, compared to 44 percent of White non-Hispanics (Winseman 2004).

It would also be mistaken to focus only on older religious organizations. Local churches that developed into national faiths in the 1990s, such as the Calvary Chapel, Vineyard, and Hope Chapel, have created a following among Pentecostal believers, who embrace a more charismatic form of worship devoid of many traditional ornaments, with pastors and congregations alike favoring informal attire. New faiths develop with increasing rapidity in what can only be called a very competitive market for individual religious faith. In addition, many people, with or without religious affiliation, become fascinated with spiritual concepts such as angels or become a part of loose-knit fellowships such as the Promise Keepers, an all-male movement of evangelical Christians founded in 1990. Religion in the United States is an ever-changing social phenomenon. Other non-mainstream faiths emerge in new arenas, as evidenced by the campaign of Mitt Romney, a Mormon, to win the Republican nomination for president in 2008 or the visible role of celebrities promoting the Church of Scientology (Dudley and Roozen 2001; Schaefer and Zellner 2008).

Divisive conflicts along religious lines are muted in the United States compared with those in, say, the Middle East. Although not entirely absent, conflicts about religion in the United States seem to be overshadowed by civil religion. **Civil religion** is the religious dimension in the United States that merges the public life with sacred beliefs. It also reflects that no single faith is privileged over all others.

Sociologist Robert Bellah (1967) borrowed the phrase *civil religion* from eighteenth-century French philosopher Jean-Jacques Rousseau to describe a significant phenomenon in the contemporary United States. Civil religion exists alongside established religious faiths, and it embodies a belief system that incorporates all religions but is not associated specifically with any one. It is the type of faith to which presidents refer in inaugural speeches and to which American Legion posts and Girl Scout troops swear allegiance. In 1954, Congress added the phrase *under God* to the pledge of allegiance as a legislative recognition of religion's significance. Elected officials in the United States, beginning with Ronald Reagan, often concluded even their most straightforward speeches with "God bless the United States of America," which in effect evokes the civil religion of the nation.

Functionalists see civil religion as reinforcing central American values that may be more expressly patriotic than sacred in nature. Often, the mass media, following major societal upheavals, from the 1995 Oklahoma City bombing to the 2001 terrorist attacks, show church services with clergy praying and asking for national healing. Bellah (1967) sees no sign that the importance of civil religion has diminished in promoting collective identity, but he does acknowledge that it is more conservative than during the 1970s.

In the following sections, we will explore the diversity among the major Christian groups in the United States, such as Roman Catholics and Protestants, as well as how Islam has emerged as a significant religious force in the United States and can no longer be regarded as a marginal faith in terms of followers.

civil religion
The religious dimension in American life that merges the state with sacred beliefs.

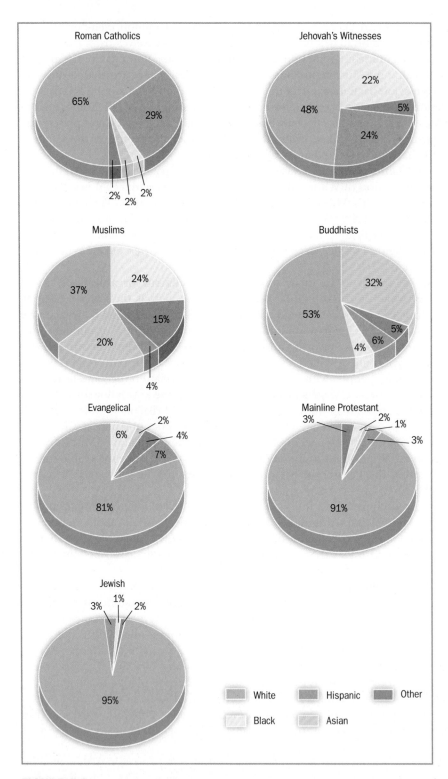

FIGURE 5.3

Racial and Ethnic Makeup of Selected Religions in the United States

Note: "Other" includes self-identified mixed race. Evangelical includes Baptist, Lutheran (Missouri and Wisconsin Synods), and Pentecostal among others. Mainline Protestant includes Methodist, Lutheran (ELCA), Presbyterian, Episcopal, and United Church of Christ, among others, but excludes historically Black Churches. Based on a national survey of 35,556 adults conducted in August 2007.

Source: Pew Forum on Religion and Public Life 2008, 120.

Diversity among Roman Catholics

Social scientists have persistently tended to ignore the diversity within the Roman Catholic Church in the United States. Recent research has not sustained the conclusions that Roman Catholics are melding into a single group, following the traditions of the American Irish Catholic model, or even that parishioners are attending English-language churches. Religious behavior has been different for each ethnic group within the Roman Catholic Church. The Irish and French Canadians left societies that were highly competitive both culturally and socially. Their religious involvement in the United States is more relaxed than it was in Ireland and Quebec. However, the influence of life in the United States has increased German and Polish involvement in the Roman Catholic Church, whereas Italians have remained largely inactive. Variations by ethnic background continue to emerge in studies of contemporary religious involvement in the Roman Catholic Church (Eckstrom 2001).

Since the mid-1970s, the Roman Catholic Church in America has received a significant number of new members from the Philippines, Southeast Asia, and particularly Latin America. Although these new members have been a stabilizing force offsetting the loss of White ethnics, they have also challenged a church that for generations was dominated by Irish, Italian, and Polish parishes. Perhaps the most prominent subgroup in the Roman Catholic Church is the Latinos, who now account for one-third of all Roman Catholic parishioners. In the 2006 new class of priests ordained, nearly one-third were foreign-born. Some Los Angeles churches in or near Latino neighborhoods must schedule 14 masses each Sunday to accommodate the crowds of worshipers. By 2006, Latinos constituted 44 percent of Roman Catholics nationwide (*Chicago Tribune* 2006; Murphy and Banerjee 2005).

The Roman Catholic Church, despite its ethnic diversity, has clearly been a powerful force in reducing the ethnic ties of its members, making it also a significant assimilating force. The irony in this role of Catholicism is that so many nineteenth-century Americans heaped abuse on Catholics in this country for allegedly being un-American and having a dual allegiance. The history of the Catholic Church in the United States may be portrayed as a struggle within the membership between the Americanizers and the anti-Americanizers, with the former ultimately winning. Unlike the various Protestant churches that accommodated immigrants of a single nationality, the Roman Catholic Church had to Americanize a variety of linguistic and ethnic groups. The Catholic Church may have been the most potent assimilating force after the public school system. Comparing the assimilationist goal of the Catholic Church and the current diversity in it leads us to the conclusion that ethnic diversity has continued in the Roman Catholic Church despite, not because of, this religious institution.

Diversity among Protestants

Protestantism, like Catholicism, often is portrayed as a monolithic entity. Little attention is given to the doctrinal and attitudinal differences that sharply divide the various denominations in both laity and clergy. However, several studies document the diversity. Unfortunately, many opinion polls and surveys are content to learn whether a respondent is a Catholic, a Protestant, or a Jew. Stark and Glock (1968) found sharp differences in religious attitudes within Protestant churches. For example, 99 percent of Southern Baptists had no doubt that Jesus was the divine Son of God as contrasted to only 40 percent of Congregationalists. We can identify four "generic theological camps":

1. *Liberals:* United Church of Christ (Congregationalists) and Episcopalians
2. *Moderates:* Disciples of Christ, Methodists, and Presbyterians
3. *Conservatives:* American Lutherans and American Baptists
4. *Fundamentalists:* Missouri Synod Lutherans, Southern Baptists, and Assembly of God

FIGURE 5.4
Income and Denominations

Denominations attract different income groups. All groups have both affluent and poor members, yet some have a higher proportion of members with high incomes while others are comparatively poor.

Source: General Social Survey, 1996 through 2006. See Davis et al. 2007.

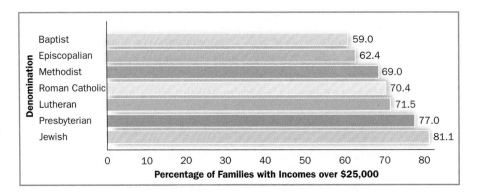

Roman Catholics generally hold religious beliefs similar to those of conservative Protestants, except on essentially Catholic issues such as papal infallibility (the authority of the spiritual role in all decisions regarding faith and morals). Whether or not there are four distinct camps is not important: the point is that the familiar practice of contrasting Roman Catholics and Protestants is clearly not productive. Some differences between Roman Catholics and Protestants are inconsequential compared with the differences between Protestant sects.

Secular criteria as well as doctrinal issues may distinguish religious faiths. Research has consistently shown that denominations can be arranged in a hierarchy based on social class. As Figure 5.4 reveals, members of certain faiths, such as Episcopalians, Jews, and Presbyterians, have a higher proportion of affluent members. Members of other faiths, including Baptists, tend to be poorer. Of course, all Protestant groups draw members from each social stratum. Nonetheless, the social significance of these class differences is that religion becomes a mechanism for signaling social mobility. A person who is moving up in wealth and power may seek out a faith associated with a higher social ranking. Similar contrasts are shown in formal schooling in Figure 5.5.

Protestant faiths have been diversifying, and many of their members have been leaving them for churches that follow strict codes of behavior or fundamental interpretations of biblical teachings. This trend is reflected in the gradual decline of the five mainline churches: Baptist, Episcopalian, Lutheran, Methodist, and Presbyterian. In 2006, these faiths accounted for about 58 percent of total Protestant membership, compared with 65 percent in the 1970s. With a broader acceptance of new faiths and continuing immigration, it is unlikely that these mainline churches will regain their dominance in the near future (Davis et al. 2007, 171–172).

Although Protestants may seem to define the civil religion and the accepted dominant orientation, some Christian faiths feel they, too, experience the discrimination usually associated with non-Christians such as Jews and Muslims. For example, representatives of the liberal and moderate faiths dominate the leadership of the military's chaplain corps. There are 16 Presbyterian soldiers for every Presbyterian chaplain, 121 Full Gospel worshippers for every Full Gospel chaplain, and 339 Muslim soldiers for every Muslim chaplain (Cooperman 2005).

As another example of denominational discrimination, in 1998, the Southern Baptist Convention amended its basic theological statements of beliefs to include a strong statement on family life. However, the statement included a declaration that a woman should "submit herself graciously" to her husband's leadership. There were widespread attacks on this position, which many Baptists felt was inappropriate because they were offering guidance for their denomination's members. In some respects, Baptists felt this was a form of respectable bigotry. It was acceptable to attack them for their views on social issues even though such criticism would be much more muted for many more liberal faiths that seem free to tolerate abortion (Bowman 1998; Niebuhr 1998).

Religion and the Courts

Religious pluralism owes its existence in the United States to the First Amendment declaration that "Congress shall make no law respecting an establishment of religion, or prohibiting the free exercise thereof." The U.S. Supreme Court has consistently interpreted this wording to mean not that government should ignore religion but that it should follow a policy of neutrality to maximize religious freedom. For example, the government may not help religion by financing a new church building, but it also may not obstruct religion by denying a church adequate police and fire protection. We will examine four issues that continue to require clarification: school prayer, secessionist minorities and their rituals, creationism (including intelligent design), and the public display of religious (or sacred) symbols.

School Prayer Among the most controversial and continuing disputes has been whether prayer has a role in the schools. Many people were disturbed by the 1962 Supreme Court decision in *Engel v. Vitale,* which disallowed a purportedly nondenominational prayer drafted for use in the New York public schools. The prayer was "Almighty God, we acknowledge our dependence upon Thee, and we beg Thy blessings upon us, our parents, our teachers, and our country." Subsequent decisions overturned state laws requiring Bible reading in public schools, laws requiring recitation of the Lord's Prayer, and laws permitting a daily one-minute period of silent meditation or prayer. Despite such judicial pronouncements, children in many public schools in the United States are led in regular prayer recitation or Bible reading.

What about prayers at public gatherings? In 1992, the Supreme Court ruled 5–4 in *Lee v. Weisman* that prayer at a junior high school graduation in Providence, Rhode Island, violated the U.S. Constitution's mandate of separation of church and state. A rabbi had given thanks to God in his invocation. The district court suggested that the invocation would have been acceptable without that reference. The Supreme Court did not agree with the school board that a prayer at a graduation was not coercive. The Court did say in its opinion that it was acceptable for a student speaker voluntarily to say a prayer at such a program (Marshall 2001).

Public schools and even states have mandated a "moment of silence" at the start of the school day in what critics contend is a transparent attempt to get around *Lee v. Weisman.* The Supreme Court had struck down such actions earlier, but then prayer was clearly intended by legislators when they created these "moments." More recent mandates such as those in Illinois in 2007 have not had such explicit provisions, but more legal actions are expected to challenge such actions in public schools (Robelen 2007).

Secessionist Minorities Several religious groups have been in legal and social conflict with the rest of society. Some can be called *secessionist minorities* in that they reject both assimilation and coexistence in some form of cultural pluralism. The Amish are one such group that comes into conflict with outside society because of its beliefs and way of life. The Old Order Amish shun most modern conveniences, and later in this chapter we will consider them as a case study of maintaining a lifestyle dramatically different from that of larger society.

Are there limits to the free exercise of religious rituals by secessionist minorities? Today, tens of thousands of members of Native American religions believe that ingesting the powerful drug peyote is a sacrament and that those who partake of peyote will enter into direct contact with God. In 1990, the Supreme Court ruled that prosecuting people who

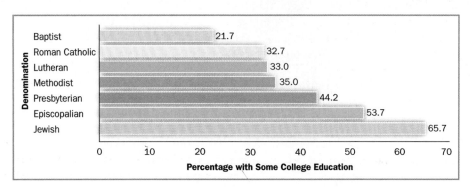

FIGURE 5.5
Education and Denominations

There are sharp differences in the proportion of those with some college education by denomination.

Source: General Social Survey, 1996 through 2006. See Davis et al. 2007.

creationists
People who support a literal interpretation of the biblical book of Genesis on the origins of the universe and argue that evolution should not be presented as established scientific thought.

intelligent design
View that life is so complex that it must have been created by a higher intelligence.

use illegal drugs as part of a religious ritual is not a violation of the First Amendment guarantee of religious freedom. The case arose because Native Americans were dismissed from their jobs for the religious use of peyote and were then refused unemployment benefits by the state of Oregon's employment division. In 1991, however, Oregon enacted a new law permitting the sacramental use of peyote by Native Americans (*New York Times* 1991).

In another ruling on religious rituals, in 1993, the Supreme Court unanimously overturned a local ordinance in Florida that banned ritual animal sacrifice. The High Court held that this law violated the free-exercise rights of adherents of the Santeria religion, in which the sacrifice of animals (including goats, chickens, and other birds) plays a central role. The same year, Congress passed the Religious Freedom Restoration Act, which said the government may not enforce laws that "substantially burden" the exercise of religion. Presumably, this action will give religious groups more flexibility in practicing their faiths. However, many local and state officials are concerned that the law has led to unintended consequences, such as forcing states to accommodate prisoners' requests for questionable religious activities or to permit a church to expand into a historic district in defiance of local laws (Greenhouse 1996).

Creationism and Intelligent Design   The third area of contention has been whether the biblical account of creation should be or must be presented in school curricula and whether this account should receive the same emphasis as scientific theories. In the famous "monkey trial" of 1925, Tennessee schoolteacher John Scopes was found guilty of teaching the scientific theory of evolution in public schools. Since then, however, Darwin's evolutionary theories have been presented in public schools with little reference to the biblical account in Genesis. People who support the literal interpretation of the Bible, commonly known as **creationists**, have formed various organizations to crusade for creationist treatment in U.S. public schools and universities.

In a 1987 Louisiana case, *Edwards v. Aguillard*, the Supreme Court ruled that states may not require the teaching of creationism alongside evolution in public schools if the primary purpose of such legislation is to promote a religious viewpoint. Nevertheless, the teaching of evolution and creationism has remained a controversial issue in many communities across the United States (Applebome 1996).

Beginning in the 1980s, those who believe in a divine hand in the creation of life have advanced **intelligent design** (ID), the idea that life is so complex it could only have been created by a higher intelligence. Although not explicitly drawn on the biblical account, creationists feel comfortable with ID and advocate that it is a more accurate account than Darwinism or, at the very least, that it be taught as an alternative alongside the theory of evolution. In 2005, a federal judge in *Kitzmiller v. Dove Area School District* ended a Pennsylvania school district intention to require the presentation of ID. In essence, the judge found ID to be "a religious belief" that was only a subtler way of finding God's fingerprints in nature than traditional creationism. Because the issue continues to be hotly debated, future court cases are certain to come (Clemmitt 2005; Goodstein 2005).

Public Displays   The fourth area of contention has been a battle over public displays that depict symbols of religion or appear to others to be sacred representations. Can manger scenes be erected on public property? Do people have a right to be protected from large displays such as a cross or a star atop a water tower

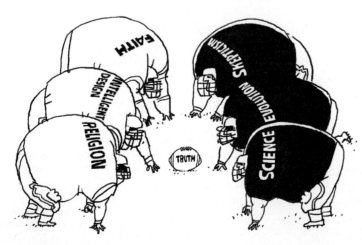

Competing interests argue over the inclusion of intelligent design as a valid aspect of science curriculum in public schools.

overlooking an entire town? In a series of decisions in the 1980s through 1995, the Supreme Court ruled that tax-supported religious displays on public government property may be successfully challenged but may be permissible if made more secular. Displays that combine a crèche, the Christmas manger scene depicting the birth of Jesus, or the Hanukkah menorah and also include Frosty the Snowman or even Christmas trees have been ruled secular. These decisions have been dubbed "the plastic reindeer rules." In 1995, the Court clarified the issue by stating that privately sponsored religious displays may be allowed on public property if other forms of expression are permitted in the same location.

The final judicial word has not been heard, and all these rulings should be viewed as tentative because the Court cases have been decided by close votes. Changes in the Supreme Court's composition in the next few years also may alter the outcome of future cases (Bork 1995; Hirsley 1991; Mauro 1995).

Limits of Religious Freedom: The Amish

The Amish began migrating to North America early in the eighteenth century and settled first in eastern Pennsylvania, where a large settlement is still found. Those who continued the characteristic lifestyle of the Amish are primarily members of the Old Order Amish Mennonite Church representing the most visible remnant of early German immigration. By 2003, there were about 1,400 Old Order Amish settlements in the United States and Canada. Estimates place this faith and other Amish groups at about 200,000, with the majority living in three states: Ohio, Pennsylvania, and Indiana.

The Amish Way of Life

Amish practice self-segregation, living in settlements divided into church districts that are autonomous congregations composed of about 75 baptized members. If the district becomes much larger, it is again divided because the members meet in each other's homes. There are no church buildings. Amish homes are large, with the main floor often having removable walls so a household can take its periodic turn hosting the Sunday service.

Each Amish district has a bishop, two to four preachers, and an elder, but there are no general conferences, mission groups, or cooperative agencies. The Amish differ little from the Mennonites in formal religious doctrine. Holy Communion is celebrated twice each year, and both groups practice washing of feet. Adults are baptized when they are admitted to formal membership in the church, around the ages of 17 to 20. Old Order Amish services are conducted in German with a mixture of English, commonly known as *Pennsylvania Dutch* (from *Deutsch*, the German word for "German").

The Amish are best known for their plain clothing and their nonconformist way of life. Sociologists sometimes use the term **secessionist minorities** to refer to groups such as the Amish, who reject assimilation and practice coexistence or pluralism with the rest of society primarily on their own terms. The practice of Meidung, or shunning, persists, and sociologists view it as central to the Amish system of social control. The social norms of this secessionist minority that have evolved over the years are known as the Ordnung. These oral "expectations" or "understandings" specify the color and style of clothing, color and style of buggies, the use of horses for fieldwork, the use of the Pennsylvania Dutch dialect, worship services in the homes, unison singing without instruments, and marriage within the church, to name a few.

The Amish shun telephones and electric lights, and they drive horses and buggies rather than automobiles. The Ordnung also prohibits filing a lawsuit, entering military service, divorce, using air transportation, and even using wall-to-wall carpeting. They are generally considered excellent farmers, but they often refuse to use modern farm machinery. Concessions have been made but do vary from one Amish settlement to another. Among common exceptions to the Ordnung is the use of chemical fertilizers, insecticides, and pesticides; the use of indoor bathroom facilities; and modern medical and dental practice. Some Amish subgroups tolerate exceptions such as the use of bicycles, milking machines, and power lawn mowers, to name a few.

secessionist minority
Groups, such as the Amish, that reject both assimilation and coexistence.

The Amish have made relatively few accommodations with the larger culture—the culture of outsiders referred collectively to by the Amish as the "English."

The Amish and Larger Society

The Amish have made some concessions to the dominant society, but larger society has made concessions to the Amish to facilitate their lifestyle. For example, in 1972, the U.S. Supreme Court, in *Yoder v. Wisconsin,* allowed Wisconsin Amish to escape prosecution from laws that required parents to send their children to school until age 18. Amish education ends at about age 13 because the community feels its members have received all the schooling necessary to prosper as Amish people. States waive certification requirements for Amish teaching staff (who are other Amish people), minimum wage requirements for the teachers, and school building requirements.

The Amish today do not totally reject social change. For example, until the late 1960s, church members could be excommunicated for being employed in other than agricultural pursuits. Now their work is much more diversified. Although you will not find Amish computer programmers, there are Amish engaged as blacksmiths, harness makers, buggy repairers, and carpenters. Non-Amish often hire these craftspeople as well.

The movement by the Amish into other occupations is sometimes a source of tension with larger society, or the "English," as the Amish refer to non-Amish people. Conflict theorists observe that as long as the Amish remained totally apart from dominant society in the United States, they experienced little hostility. As they entered the larger economic sector, however, intergroup tensions developed in the form of growing prejudice. The Amish today may underbid their competitors.

The Amish entry into the commercial marketplace has also strained the church's traditional teaching on litigation and insurance, both of which are to be avoided. Mutual assistance has been the historical path taken, but that does not always mesh well with the modern businessperson. After legal action taken on their behalf, Amish businesses typically have been allowed to be exempt from paying Social Security and workers' compensation, another sore point with English competitors.

Children are not sent to high schools. This practice caused the Amish some difficulty because of compulsory school attendance laws, and some Amish parents have gone to jail rather than allow their children to go to high school. Eventually, as noted earlier, in *Yoder v. Wisconsin,* the Supreme Court upheld a lower court's decision that a Wisconsin compulsory education law violated the Amish right to religious freedom. However, not all court rulings have been friendly to Amish efforts to avoid the practices and customs of the non-Amish. In another case, efforts by the Amish to avoid using the legally mandated orange triangles for marking slow-moving vehicles (such as their buggies) was rejected. If you travel through Amish areas, you can now see their horse-drawn buggies displaying this one symbol of modernity.

Living alongside this modernity, Amish youth often test their subculture's boundaries during a period of discovery called Rumspringa, a term that means "running around." Amish young people attend barn dances where taboos such as drinking, smoking, and driving cars are commonly broken. Parents often react by looking the other way, sometimes literally. For example, when they hear radio sounds from a barn or motorcycle entering their property in the middle of the night, they do not immediately investigate and punish their offspring. Instead, they pretend not to notice, secure in the comfort that their children almost always return to the traditions of the Amish lifestyle. In 2004, the UPN television network aired the "Amish in the City" reality program featuring five

Amish youths, allegedly on Rumspringa, moving in with six city-wise young adults in Los Angeles. Critics on behalf of the Amish community noted that this exploitation showed how vulnerable the Amish are because no program was developed to try to show the conversion of Muslim or Orthodox Jewish youth.

A growing area of Amish–English legal clashes is over the custom of young Amish children working as laborers. Amish families in western and central Pennsylvania in 1998 protested the federal government's enforcement of labor laws that are intended to protect children from workplace hazards. The Amish are turning to new businesses, such as sawmills and woodshops, as their available farmland begins to disappear. That means more children on the shop floor. The Amish contend that their religious and cultural traditions hold that children should work, but the U.S. Department of Labor had taken a different view. The Amish argued that letting children work alongside their fathers instills core values of hard work, diligence, cooperation, and responsibility, values that they say are central to their faith. Non-Amish businesses see this underage employment as another form of unfair competition by the Amish. In 2004, Congress passed the law with the Amish in mind that exempted such child labor as long as machinery is not operated and adults are present.

The Old Order Amish have developed a pluralistic position that has become increasingly difficult to maintain as their numbers grow and as they enter the economy in competition with the English, or the non-Amish (Dart 1998; *The Economist* 2004a; Kraybill 2001, 2003, 2008; Kraybill and Nolt 1995; Public Broadcasting System 1998; Schaefer and Zellner 2008).

ethnicity paradox
The maintenance of one's ethnic ties in a way that can assist with assimilation in larger society.

Conclusion

Considering ethnicity and religion reinforces our understanding of the spectrum of intergroup relations first presented in Chapter 1. The figure on the next page shows the rich variety of relationships as defined by people's ethnic and religious identity. The profiles of German, Irish, Italian, and Polish Americans reflect the variety of White ethnic experiences.

Any study of life in the United States, especially one that focuses on dominant and subordinate groups, cannot ignore religion and ethnicity. The two are closely related, as certain religious faiths predominate in certain nationalities. Both religious activity and interest by White ethnics in their heritage continue to be prominent features of the contemporary scene. People have been and continue to be ridiculed or deprived of opportunities solely because of their ethnic or religious affiliation. To get a true picture of people's place in society, we need to consider both ethnicity and social class in association with their religious identification.

Religion is changing in the United States. As one commercial recognition of this fact, Hallmark created its first greeting card in 2003 for the Muslim holiday Eid-al-fitr, which marks the end of the month-long fast of Ramadan. The issue of the persistence of ethnicity is an intriguing one. Some people may only casually exhibit their ethnicity and practice what has been called *symbolic ethnicity*. However, can people immerse themselves in their ethnic culture without society punishing them for their will to be different? The tendency to put down White ethnics through respectable bigotry continues. Despite this intolerance, ethnicity remains a viable source of identity for many citizens today. There is also the **ethnicity paradox**, which finds that practicing one's ethnic heritage often strengthens people and allows them to move successfully into the larger society.

The issue of religious expression in all its forms also raises a variety of intriguing questions. How can a country that is increasingly populated by diverse and often non-Christian faiths maintain religious tolerance? How might this change in the decades ahead? How will the courts and society resolve the issues of religious freedom? This is a particularly important issue in areas such as school prayer, secessionist minorities, creationism, intelligent design, and public religious displays. Some examination of religious ties is fundamental to completing an accurate picture of a person's social identity.

Ethnicity and religion are a basic part of today's social reality and of each individual's identity. The emotions, disputes, and debate over religion and ethnicity in the United States are powerful indeed.

SPECTRUM OF INTERGROUP RELATIONS

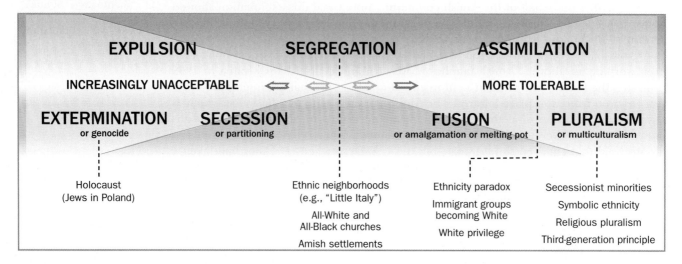

EXPULSION SEGREGATION ASSIMILATION

INCREASINGLY UNACCEPTABLE ⬅⇦ ⇦ ⇨ ⇨ MORE TOLERABLE

EXTERMINATION SECESSION FUSION PLURALISM
or genocide or partitioning or amalgamation or melting pot or multiculturalism

Holocaust
(Jews in Poland)

Ethnic neighborhoods
(e.g., "Little Italy")

All-White and
All-Black churches

Amish settlements

Ethnicity paradox

Immigrant groups
becoming White

White privilege

Secessionist minorities

Symbolic ethnicity

Religious pluralism

Third-generation principle

Summary

1. While considering race an ethnicity in the United States, we often ignore how White people come to see themselves as a group and in relationship to others.

2. Typically unconsciously, White people accept privilege automatically extended them in everyday life.

3. Feelings of ethnicity may be fading among the descendants of Europeans, but it may remerge as reflected in either the third-generation principle or, in a more limited fashion, through symbolic ethnicity.

4. Even though the historical circumstances and settlement patterns differ, there are definite similarities in the experiences of German, Irish, Italian, and Polish Americans.

5. Research shows that historically, at least, a generation passes before immigrants experienced upward mobility. Contemporary immigrants seem to follow the same pattern, with most speaking English fluently by the second generation and virtually all third-generation members doing so.

6. The ethnic diversity of the United States is matched by the many denominations among Christians as well as the sizable Jewish and Muslim presence.

7. In its interpretation of the First Amendment, the Supreme Court has tried to preserve religious freedom, but critics have argued that the Court has served to stifle religious expression.

8. The self-segregated Amish are an example of a religious group that immigrated to the United States and continues to thrive by practicing its different lifestyle.

Key Terms

civil religion 131
creationists 136
denomination 130
ethnicity paradox 139

intelligent design 136
principle of third-
   generation interest 117
secessionist minority 137

symbolic ethnicity 118
White privilege 116

Review Questions

1. In what respects are ethnic and religious diversity in the United States related to each other?
2. Is assimilation automatic within any given ethnic group?
3. Apply "Whiteness" to German, Irish, Italian, and Polish Americans.
4. To what extent has a non-Christian tradition been developing in the United States?
5. How have court rulings affected religious expression?

Critical Thinking

1. When do you see ethnicity becoming more apparent? When does it appear to occur only in response to other people's advancing their own ethnicity? From these situations, how can ethnic identity be both positive and perhaps counterproductive or even destructive?
2. Why do you think we are so often reluctant to show our religion to others? Why might people of certain faiths be more hesitant than others?
3. How does religion reflect conservative and liberal positions on social issues? Consider services for the homeless, the need for child care, the acceptance or rejection of gay men and lesbians, and a woman's right to terminate a pregnancy versus the fetus's right to survive.

6

Native Americans

THE ORIGINAL INHABITANTS OF NORTH AMERICA WERE THE first to be subordinated by the Europeans. The Native Americans who survived contact with the non-Indian people usually were removed, often far away, from their ancestral homes. The U.S. government weakened tribal institutions through a succession of acts, beginning with the Allotment Act of 1887. Even efforts to strengthen tribal autonomy, such as the 1934 Reorganization Act, did so by encouraging Native Americans to adopt White society's way of life. More recent relations between Native Americans and non-Indians have been much the same, as shown by such measures as the Termination Act and the Employment Assistance Program. Today, the pan-Indian movements speak for a diverse Native American people with many needs: settlement of treaty violations, economic development, improved educational programs, effective health care, religious and spiritual freedom, control over natural resources, and greater self-rule.

143

Dustina Abrahamson Edmo (pictured on page 143) has reason to be happy. A member of the Shoshone-Bannock tribe, she is graduating from Haskell Indian Nations University in Kansas. She had participated the year before in a student exchange program in Siberia. After graduation, she traveled to Siberia again and participated in a program sponsored by the National Science Foundation to monitor water quality in the U.S. Southwest. Along the way she has been a champion women's traditional dancer and in 2008 served on the school board of Shoshone-Bannock High School on the Fort Hill Indian Reservation, Idaho. Hers is one face of native peoples in the United States.

William Blackie's money ran out near midnight on a June day in 2005 in Farmington, New Mexico. A 46-year-old Navaho, he made his way home on foot only to encounter three White youths who offered to give him a ride if he would buy them beer with their money. Actually, as they admitted later, they were looking for a victim. Soon the boys headed out of town, dragged him out of the car, and beat him while shouting racial epithets at him. Eventually, the attackers tired of hitting Blackie and left him in the desert. Fortunately, he was able to soon contact the police who eventually found the attackers through anonymous tips. The attackers were eventually all convicted of felony assault and kidnapping, although hate crime charges were dropped. William Blackie is also one face of the native peoples of the United States (Buchanan 2006; Edmo-Suppah 2008; Perotti 2004; Saunders 2007).

Although our focus in this chapter is on the Native American experience in the United States, the pattern of land seizure, subjugation, assimilation, and resistance to domination has been repeated with indigenous people in nations throughout the world. Indeed, in Chapter 16, we will consider the experiences of the tribal people in Brazil, Mexico and Canada. Hawaiians, another native people who fell under the political, economic, and cultural control of the United States, are considered in Chapter 12. Later in this chapter we will consider the experience of the Aboriginal people of Australia. Indigenous peoples on almost every continent are familiar with the patterns of subjugation and the pressure to assimilate. So widespread is this oppression that the United Nations (1997) and even its precursor organization, the League of Nations, have repeatedly considered this issue.

The common term *American Indians* tells us more about the Europeans who explored North America than it does about the native people. The label reflects the initial explorers' confusion in believing that they had arrived in "the Indies" of the Asian continent. However, reference to the diversity of tribal groups either by American Indians or Native Americans comes as a result of the forced subordination to the dominant group. Today, most American Indians preference for self-identification is to use their tribal affiliation such as "Cherokee" or affiliations such as "Cheyenne Arapaho" if one has mixed ancestry. For collective reference to all tribal people, we will use *Native Americans* and *American Indians* interchangeably.

An estimated 2,357,544 Native Americans/and Alaskan natives lived in the United States in 2006. This represents an increase of about 40 percent over the 1990s. In addition to this 2.4 million people who gave American Indian or Alaskan Native as their sole racial identification, another 1.4 million people listed multiple responses that included American Indian. As was shown in Figure 1.8, *American Indian* and *White* was the most common dual racial response given in Census 2000 (American Community Survey 2006).

Early European Contacts

Native Americans have been misunderstood and ill treated by their conquerors for several centuries. Assuming that he had reached the Indies, Christopher Columbus called the native residents "people of India." The European immigrants who followed Columbus did not understand them any more than the Native Americans could have anticipated the destruction of their way of life. But the Europeans had superior weaponry, and the diseases they brought wiped out huge numbers of indigenous people throughout the Western hemisphere.

The first explorers of the Western hemisphere came long before Columbus and Leif Eriksson. The ancestors of today's Native Americans were hunters in search of wild game, including mammoths and long-horned bison. For thousands of years, these people spread through the Western hemisphere, adapting to its many physical environments. Hundreds of cultures evolved, including the complex societies of the Maya, Inca, and Aztec (Deloria 1995, 2004).

It is beyond the scope of this chapter to describe the many tribal cultures of North America, let alone the ways of life of Native Americans in Central and South America and the islands of the Caribbean. We must appreciate that the term *Indian culture* is a convenient way to gloss over the diversity of cultures, languages, religions, kinship systems, and political organizations that existed—and, in many instances, remain—among the peoples referred to collectively as *Native Americans* or *American Indians*. For example, in 1500, an estimated 700 distinct languages were spoken in the area north of Mexico. For simplicity's sake, we will refer to these many cultures as *Native American*, but we must be always mindful of the differences this term conceals. Similarly, we will refer to non–Native Americans as *non-Indians*, recognizing in this context that this term encompasses many groups, including Whites, African Americans, and Hispanics in some instances (J. Schwartz 1994; Swagerty 1983).

The number of Native Americans north of the Rio Grande, estimated at about 10 million in 1500, gradually decreased as their food sources disappeared and they fell victim to diseases such as measles, smallpox, and influenza. By 1800, the Native American population was about 600,000; by 1900, it had been reduced to less than 250,000. This loss of human life can only be judged as catastrophic. The United States does not bear total responsibility. The pattern had been well established by the early Spaniards in the Southwest and by the French and English colonists who sought to gain control of the eastern seaboard.

Native Americans did have warfare between tribes, which presumably reduces the guilt for European-initiated warfare. However, their conflicts differed significantly from those of the conquerors. The Europeans launched large campaigns against the tribes, resulting in mass mortality. In contrast, in the Americas, the tribes limited warfare to specific campaigns designed for very specific purposes such as recapturing a resource or avenging a loss.

Not all the initial contacts led to deliberate loss of life. Some missionaries traveled well in advance of settlement in efforts to Christianize the Native Americans before they came into contact with other less-tolerant Europeans. Fur trappers, vastly outnumbered by Native Americans, were forced to learn their customs, but these trappers established routes of commerce that more and more non-Indians were to follow (Snipp 1989; Swagerty 1983; Thornton 1991).

Gradually, the policies directed from Europe toward the indigenous peoples of North America resembled the approach described in the world systems theory. As introduced in Chapter 01, the **world systems theory** takes the view that the global economic system is divided between nations that control wealth and those that provide natural resources and labor. The indigenous peoples and, more important to the Europeans, the land they occupied were regarded as targets of exploitation by Spain, England, France, Portugal, and other nations with experience as colonizers in Africa and Asia (Chase-Dunn and Hall 1998).

Treaties and Warfare

The United States formulated a policy during the nineteenth century toward Native Americans that followed the precedents established during the colonial period. The government policy was not to antagonize the Native Americans unnecessarily. Yet if the needs of

world systems theory
A view of the global economic system as divided between nations that control wealth and those that provide natural resources and labor.

tribes interfered with the needs, or even the whims, of non-Indians, then Whites were to have precedence.

Tribes were viewed as separate nations to be dealt with by treaties arrived at through negotiations with the federal government. Fair-minded as that policy might seem, it was clear from the very beginning that the non-Indian people's government would deal harshly with the tribal groups that refused to agree to treaties. Federal relations with the Native Americans were the responsibility of the secretary of war. Consequently, when the Bureau of Indian Affairs was created in 1824 to coordinate the government's relations with the tribes, it was placed in the Department of War. The government's primary emphasis was on maintaining peace and friendly relations along the frontier. Nevertheless, as settlers moved the frontier westward, they encroached more and more on land that Native Americans had inhabited for centuries.

The Indian Removal Act, passed in 1830, called for the relocation of all Eastern tribes across the Mississippi River. The Removal Act was very popular with non–American Indians because it opened more land to settlement through annexation of tribal land. Almost all non-Indians felt that the Native Americans had no right to block progress—which was defined as movement by White society. Among the largest groups relocated were the five tribes of the Creek, Choctaw, Chickasaw, Cherokee, and Seminole, who were resettled in what is now Oklahoma. The movement, lasting more than a decade, has been called the Trail of Tears because the tribes left their ancestral lands under the harshest conditions. Poor planning, corrupt officials, little attention to those ill from a variety of epidemics, inadequate supplies, and the deaths of several thousand Native Americans characterized the forced migration (Remini 2001).

The Removal Act disrupted Native American cultures but didn't move the tribes far enough or fast enough to stay out of the path of the ever-advancing non-American Indian settlers. After the Civil War, settlers moved westward at an unprecedented pace. The federal government negotiated with the many tribes but primarily enacted legislation that affected them with minimal consultation. The government's first priority was almost always to allow the settlers to live and work regardless of Native American claims. Along with the military defeat of the tribes, the federal government tried to limit the functions of tribal leaders. If tribal institutions were weakened, it was felt, the Native Americans would assimilate more rapidly. The government's intention to merge the various tribes into White society was unmistakably demonstrated in the 1887 Dawes, or General Allotment, Act. This failure to assist Native American people was followed by a somewhat more admirable effort, the Indian Reorganization Act of 1934. The Allotment Act and the Reorganization Act established the government's paternalistic approach.

The more significant federal actions that continue up to the present are summarized in Table 6.1.

These early policies also reflect the oppression of **internal colonialism**. As presented in Chapter 1, internal colonialism is the treatment of subordinate groups like colonial subjects by those in power. Native Americans found themselves to be the subordinate group on land that they once occupied alone. Now they were being treated like a colonized people by the newly formed government, which itself had successfully broken from the colonial hold of Great Britain. Ironically, the former colony was practicing internal colonialism toward the indigenous people of the new land.

The Case of the Sioux

The nineteenth century was devastating for every Native American tribe in the areas claimed by the United States. No tribe was the same after federal policy touched it. The treatment of the Great Sioux Nation was especially cruel and remains fresh in the minds of tribal members even today.

In an effort to safeguard non-Indian settlers, the United States signed the Fort Laramie Treaty of 1868 with the Sioux, who were then led by Red Cloud. The government agreed to keep non-Indians from hunting or settling on the newly established

internal colonialism
The treatment of subordinate peoples as colonial subjects by those in power.

TABLE 6.1
Major Federal Policies

Year	Policy	Central Feature
1830	Removal Act	Relocated Eastern tribes westward
1887	Allotment Act	Subdivided tribal lands into individual household plots
1934	Reorganization Act	Required tribes to develop election-based governments and leaders
1934	Johnson-O'Malley Act	Aided public school districts with Native American enrollments
1946	Indian Claims Commission	Adjudicated litigation by tribes against the federal government
1952	Employment Assistance Program	Relocated reservation people to urban areas for jobs
1953	Termination Act	Closed reservations and their federal services
1971	Alaska Native Settlement Act	Recognized legally the lands of tribal people
1974	Indian Financing Act	Fostered economic development
1975	Indian Self-Determination and Education Assistance Act	Increased involvement by tribal people and governments
1986	Indian Gaming Regulation Act	Allowed states to negotiate gaming rights to reservations
1990	Native American Graves and Repatriation Act	Returned Native remains to tribes with authentic claims
1990	Indian Arts and Crafts Act	Monitored authenticity of crafts
1994	American Indian Religious Freedom Act	Sought to protect tribal spirituality including use of peyote

Great Sioux Reservation, which included all of the land that is now South Dakota, west of the Missouri River. In exchange, the Sioux relinquished most of the remaining land they occupied at that time. The first few years saw relative peace, except for some raids by warrior bands under the leadership of medicine man Sitting Bull. Red Cloud even made a much-publicized trip to Washington and New York in 1870.

A flood of non-Indian people eventually entered the Sioux territory, spurred on by Colonel George Custer's exaggerated 1874 reports of gold in the Black Hills. Hostilities followed, and bands of Native Americans were ordered to move during the winter, when travel was impossible. When the Sioux failed to move, Custer moved in to pacify them and the neighboring Cheyenne. Relying on Crow scouts, Custer underestimated the strength of the Sioux warriors under the leadership of Crazy Horse. The ensuing Battle of the Little Big Horn in 1876 was the last great Sioux victory. After the battle, the large encampment of warriors scattered throughout the plains into small bands and were defeated one by one by a Congress and an Army more determined than ever to subdue the Sioux.

In 1876, the Sioux reluctantly sold the Black Hills and agreed to the reduction of the Great Sioux Reservation to five much smaller ones. Unable to hunt game as they traditionally had, the Sioux found life unbearable on the reservation. They sought escape through the supernatural Ghost Dance, a religion that included dances and songs proclaiming the return of the buffalo and the resurrection of dead ancestors in a land free of non-Indian people. The religion soon became what social scientists call a **millenarian movement**, a movement founded on the belief that a cataclysmic upheaval would occur in the immediate future, followed by collective salvation. The movement originated among the Paiutes of Nevada and, ironically, spread northward to the Plains Indians via the cornerstone of the government's assimilationist policy: the schools. The English that Native Americans learned in the mission or government schools gave them the means to overcome the barriers of tribal languages and communicate with one another. By 1890, about 65 percent of the tribes in the West, according to sociologist Russell Thornton (1981), were involved in this movement.

From a functionalist perspective, this millenarian movement can be viewed as a means of coping with the domination of non-Indian intruders. Although the Ghost Dance was harmless to non-Indians, they feared that the new tribal solidarity encouraged by the movement would lead to renewed warfare. As a result, more troops were summoned to areas where the Ghost Dance had become popular.

millenarian movements Movements, such as the Ghost Dance, that prophesy a cataclysm in the immediate future, to be followed by collective salvation.

In late December 1890, anticipating that a massive Ghost Dance would be staged, a cavalry division arrived at an encampment of Teton Sioux at Wounded Knee Creek on the Pine Ridge, South Dakota, reservation. When the soldiers began to disarm the warriors, a random shot was fired at the soldiers, touching off a close-range battle. The cavalry then turned its artillery on men, women, and children. Approximately 300 Sioux and 25 government soldiers were killed in the ensuing fighting, which is now called the Battle of Wounded Knee. One Sioux witness later recalled, "We tried to run, but they shot us like we were a buffalo. I know there are some good white people, but the soldiers must be mean to shoot children and women" (D. Brown 1971, 417).

For the federal government, what it considered the Indian problem remained. Despite the effects of disease and warfare, nearly 250,000 Indians still lived, according to the 1890 census. The reservation system constructed in the last decades of the nineteenth century to provide settlements for Native American peoples has formed the basis of the relationship of Native Americans to the government from then until the present.

The Allotment Act

The Allotment Act of 1887 bypassed tribal leaders and proposed to make individual landowners of tribal members. Each family was given as many as 160 acres under the government's assumption that, with land, Native Americans would become more like the White homesteaders who were then flooding the not-yet-settled areas of the West.

The effect of the Allotment Act, however, was disastrous. To guarantee that they would remain homesteaders, the act prohibited the Native Americans from selling the land for 25 years. Yet no effort was made to acquaint them with the skills necessary to make the land productive. Many tribes were not accustomed to cultivating land and, if anything, considered such labor undignified, and they received no assistance in adapting to homesteading.

Much of the land initially deeded under the Allotment Act eventually came into the possession of White landowners. The land could not be sold legally, but it could be leased with the Bureau of Indian Affairs (BIA) serving as the trustee. In this role, the federal government took legal title that included the duty to collect on behalf of the tribal members any revenues generated by non-Indians through mining, oil, timber operations, grazing, or similar activities. The failure of the government to carry this out has been an issue for well over a century.

Large parcels of land eventually fell into the possession of non-Indians. For Native Americans who managed to retain the land, the BIA required that, upon the death of the owner, the land be divided equally among all descendants, regardless of tribal inheritance customs. In documented cases, this division resulted in as many as 30 people trying to live off an 80-acre plot of worthless land. By 1934, Native Americans had lost approximately 90 million of the 138 million acres in their possession before the Allotment Act. The land left was generally considered worthless for farming and marginal even for ranching (Blackfeet Reservation Development Fund 2006; Deloria and Lytle 1983).

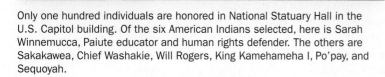

Only one hundred individuals are honored in National Statuary Hall in the U.S. Capitol building. Of the six American Indians selected, here is Sarah Winnemucca, Paiute educator and human rights defender. The others are Sakakawea, Chief Washakie, Will Rogers, King Kamehameha I, Po'pay, and Sequoyah.

The Reorganization Act

The assumptions behind the Allotment Act and the missionary activities of the nineteenth century were that it was best for Native Americans to assimilate into the White society, and each individual was best considered apart

By Jeff Kerr © 1999 *Indian Country Today.*

from his or her tribal identity. Very gradually, in the twentieth century, government offi-cials have accepted the importance of tribal identity. The Indian Reorganization Act of 1934, known as the Wheeler-Howard Act, recognized the need to use, rather than ignore, tribal identity. But assimilation, rather than movement toward a pluralistic society, was still the goal.

Many provisions of the Reorganization Act, including revocation of the Allotment Act, benefited Native Americans. Still, given the legacy of broken treaties, many tribes at first distrusted the new policy. Under the Reorganization Act, tribes could adopt a written constitution and elect a tribal council with a head. This system imposed for-eign values and structures. Under it, the elected tribal leader represented an entire reservation, which might include several tribes, some hostile to one another. Further-more, the leader had to be elected by majority rule, a concept alien to many tribes. Many full-blooded Native Americans resented the provision that mixed-bloods were to have full voting rights. The Indian Reorganization Act did facilitate tribal dealings with government agencies, but the dictation to Native Americans of certain proce-dures common to White society and alien to the tribes was another sign of forced assimilation.

As had been true of earlier government reforms, the Reorganization Act sought to as-similate Native Americans into the dominant society on the dominant group's terms. In this case, the tribes were absorbed within the political and economic structure of the larger society. Apart from the provision about tribal chairmen who were to oversee reservations with several tribes, the Reorganization Act solidified tribal identity. Unlike the Allotment Act, it recognized the right of Native Americans to approve or reject some actions taken on their behalf. The act still maintained substantial non–Native American control over the reservations. As institutions, the tribal governments owed their existence not to their people but to the BIA. These tribal governments rested at the bottom of a large adminis-trative hierarchy (Cornell 1984; Deloria 1971; McNickle 1973; Washburn 1984; Wax and Buchanan 1975).

In 2000, on the 175th anniversary of the BIA, its director, Kevin Guer, a Pawnee, declared that it was "no occasion for celebration as we express our profound sorrow for what the agency has done in the past." A formal apology followed (Stout 2000). The United States is not the only country expressing regret over past actions with its indigenous peoples as we see in A Global View.

Reservation Life and Federal Policies

Today, more than one-third of Native Americans live on 557 reservations and trust lands in 33 states, which account for a bit more than 2 percent of the land throughout the United States. Even for those Native Americans who reside far away from the tribal lands, the reser-vations play a prominent role in their identity (Ogunwole 2006) (Figure 6.1).

More than any other segment of the population, with the exception of the military, the Native American living on the reservation finds his or her life determined by the federal government. From the condition of the roads to the level of fire protection to the qual-ity of the schools, the federal government through such agencies as the BIA and the Public Health Service effectively controls reservation life. Tribes and their leaders are

A Global View

AUSTRALIA'S ABORIGINAL PEOPLE

The indigenous people of Australia have continuously inhabited the continent for at least 50,000 years. Today they constitute about 2.4 percent of the total population and, although small in number, their presence based on this long legacy is highly visible. The terms *Aboriginal* and *indigenous people* are used here interchangeably.

Aboriginals make up many clans, language groups, and communities with little interconnections except those that are occasionally created through kinship or trade. The cultural practices of these indigenous peoples have historically been very diverse. At the time Europeans arrived, an estimated 600 to 700 groups spoke 200 to 250 separate languages as distinct from one another as French is to German. In addition, there were many more dialects of a language that could be more or less understood by others.

Reflecting this diversity is the spirituality of the people. Although belief systems vary in ways that reflect the changing terrain from the Outback to rainforests, Aboriginals see themselves as having arisen from the land itself and ultimately returning to the land. Collectively, these beliefs are commonly referred to as *Dreaming* or *Dreamtime* and sometimes take on a style that Westerners view or label as a cosmology or oral folklore.

As was the case with American Indians, the size of Australia's indigenous population declined dramatically after European settlement as a result of the colonialism.

The impact of new diseases, some of which were not life threatening to Europeans, had devastating effects on indigenous communities because they lacked immunity. The number of indigenous people also decreased as a result of their mistreatment, the dispossession of their land, and the disruption and disintegration of their culture.

Legally, there historically was little recognition of indigenous people. Only in 1967, Australian citizenship and voting rights were extended to the indigenous people, allowing them access to welfare and unemployment benefits. It would be misleading to view Aboriginal people as passive either in colonial days or more contemporary times with respect to their position in Australia. They have taken an active part in efforts to secure their rights.

Reflecting the low regard that White Australians had for the indigenous people, thousands of Aboriginal children were forcibly taken from their families and raised by Whites because it was thought that bringing them into the dominant society's culture was best for them. The government program affected somewhere between 10 percent and 30 percent of all Aboriginal children from 1910 to 1970. Finally in 2008, the Australian government expressed its regret for "the Stolen Generations" and committed to improve the living conditions and future prospects of all Aboriginal people.

Sources: Anderson 2003; Attwood 2003; Schaefer 2008a.

now consulted more than in the past, but the ultimate decisions rest in Washington, D.C., to a degree that is not true for the rest of the civilian population.

Many of the policies instituted by the BIA in the twentieth century have been designed with this purpose in mind. Most Native Americans and their organizations do not quarrel with this goal. They may only wish that the government and the White people had never gotten into the Indian business in the first place. Disagreement between the BIA and the tribes and among Native Americans themselves has focused on *how* to reduce federal control and subsidies, not on whether they *should be* reduced. The government has taken three steps in this direction since World War II. Two of these measures have been the formation of the Indian Claims Commission and the passage of the Termination Act. The

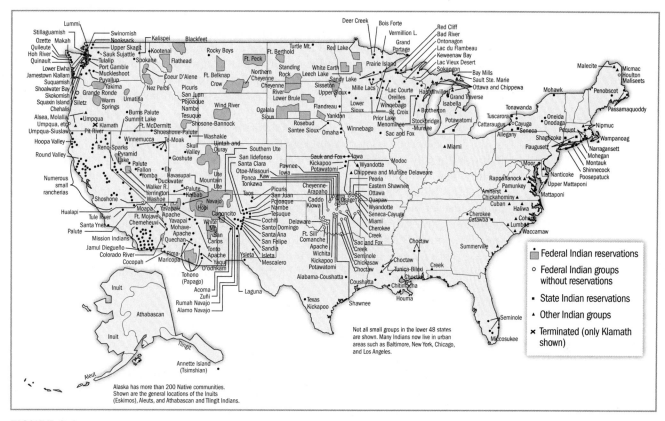

FIGURE 6.1
Native American Lands and Communities
Source: Bureau of Indian Affairs 1986, 12–13.

following section shows how the third step, the Employment Assistance Program, has created a new meeting place for Native Americans in cities, far from their native homelands and the reservations.

Native American Legal Claims

Native Americans have had a unique relationship with the federal government. As might be expected, little provision was ever made for them as individuals or tribes to bring grievances against the government. From 1863 to 1946, Native Americans could bring no claim against the government without a special act of Congress, a policy that prevented most charges of treaty violations. Only 142 claims were heard during those 83 years.

In 1946, Congress created the Indian Claims Commission and gave it authority to hear all tribal cases against the government. The three-member commission was also given a 5-year deadline. During the first 5 years, however, nearly three times as many claims were filed as had been filed during the 83 years of the old system. Therefore, the commission's term was extended and extended again, and its size was expanded. The commission was disbanded in 1978, with its cases now being heard by the U.S. Court of Federal Claims. As of 1997, the commission and the court, over a period of more than 50 years, paid claims totaling an average of $1,000 for each American Indian for all treaty violations and related claims. In 2006, Congress was trying to settle cases left over from the commission almost 30 years after being disbanded (Associated Press 2006; Drabelle 1997; Nagel 1996).

In 1986, Eloise Corbell, a member of the Blackfeet tribe in Montana, brought a class-action lawsuit on behalf of a half-million American Indians, charging that the government had cheated them of billions in royalties under the trust arrangements created by the Allotment Act of 1887. The courts ruled that the BIA and other government agencies had extremely poor records even from recent times, much less going back in time. How difficult had been the federal government defense in the *Corbell* case? The BIA shut down its Web site over fear that any information it gave out about almost anything could be wrong. The Department of Interior, by its own accounts, is spending more than $100 million annually in attempts to clean up the record keeping in a manner that will allow it to defend itself in court eventually. Eventually the court granted the tribal people $445 million, much less than was originally sought (IndianTrust 2008).

In specific land issues apart from the *Corbell* class action lawsuit, Native Americans often express a desire to recover their land rather than accept any financial settlements. After numerous legal decisions favoring the Sioux Indians, including a ruling of the U.S. Supreme Court, Congress finally agreed to pay $106 million for the land that was illegally seized in the aftermath of the Battle of the Little Big Horn described earlier. The Sioux rejected the money and lobbied for measures such as the 1987 Black Hills Sioux Nation Act in Congress, to return the land to the tribe. No positive action has yet been taken on these measures. In the meantime, however, the original settlement, the subsequent unaccepted payments, and the accrued interest brought the 1991 total of funds being held for the Sioux to more than $330 million. Despite the desperate need for housing, food, health care, and education, the Sioux still would prefer to regain the land lost in the 1868 Fort Laramie Treaty and, as of 2006, have not accepted payment.

The Termination Act

The Termination Act of 1953 initiated the most controversial government policy toward reservation Native Americans in the twentieth century. Like many such policies, the act originated in ideas that were meant to benefit Native Americans. The BIA commissioner, John Collier, had expressed concern in the 1930s over extensive government control of tribal affairs. In 1947, congressional hearings were held to determine which tribes had the economic resources to be relieved of federal control and assistance. The policy proposed at that time was an admirable attempt to give Native Americans greater autonomy while at the same time reducing federal expenditures, a goal popular among taxpayers.

The services the tribes received, such as subsidized medical care and college scholarships, should not have been viewed as special and deserving to be discontinued. These services were not the result of favoritism but merely fulfilled treaty obligations. The termination of the Native Americans' relationship to the government then came to be viewed by Native Americans as a threat to reduce services rather than a release from arbitrary authority. Native Americans might be gaining greater self-governance but at a high price.

Unfortunately, the Termination Act as finally passed in 1953 emphasized reducing costs and ignored individual needs. Recommendations for a period of tax immunity were dropped. According to the act, federal services such as medical care, schools, and road equipment were supposed to be withdrawn gradually. Instead, when the Termination Act's provisions began to go into effect, federal services were stopped immediately, with minimal coordination between local government agencies and the tribes to determine whether the services could be continued by other means. The effect of the government orders on the Native Americans was disastrous, with major economic upheaval on the affected tribes, who were unable to establish some of the most basic services—such as road repair and fire protection—which the federal government had previously provided. The federal government resumed these services in 1975 with congressional action that signaled the end of another misguided policy intended to be good for tribal peoples (Deloria 1969; Fixico 1988; Tyler 1973; Wax and Buchanan 1975).

Employment Assistance Program

The depressed economic conditions of reservation life might lead us to expect government initiatives to attract business and industry to locate on or near reservations. The government could provide tax incentives that would eventually pay for themselves.

However, such proposals have not been advanced. Rather than take jobs to the Native Americans, the federal government decided to lead the more highly motivated away from the reservation. This policy has further devastated the reservations' economic potential.

In 1952, the BIA began programs to relocate young Native Americans. One of these programs, after 1962, was called the Employment Assistance Program (EAP). Assistance centers were created in Chicago, Cleveland, Dallas, Denver, Los Angeles, Oakland, San Jose, Oklahoma City, Tulsa, and Seattle. In some cities, the Native American population increased as much as five-fold in the 1950s, primarily because of the EAP. By 1968, more than 100,000 people had participated in the program, and 200,000, or one-fourth of the Native American population, had moved to urban areas.

The EAP's primary provision was for relocation, individually or in families, at government expense, to urban areas where job opportunities were greater than those on the reservations. The BIA stressed that the EAP was voluntary, but this was a fiction given the viable economic alterna-

In this famous Alexander Gardner photograph at the time of the 1868 Fort Laramie Treaty talks, the military leaders are identified by name, shown sitting on chairs, and facing the camera. Reflecting the hierarchy of the situation, tribal leaders are not identified, seated on the ground and with their backs to the camera.

tives open to American Indians. The program was not a success for the many Native Americans who found the urban experience unsuitable or unbearable. By 1965, one-fourth to one-third of the people in the EAP had returned to their home reservations. So great was the rate of return that in 1959 the BIA stopped releasing data on the percentage of returnees, fearing that they would give too much ammunition to critics of the EAP (Bahr 1972).

The movement of Native Americans into urban areas has had many unintended consequences. It has further reduced the labor force on the reservation. Those who leave tend to be better educated, creating the Native American version of the brain drain described in Chapter 4. Urbanization unquestionably contributed to the development of an intertribal network, or pan-Indian movement, which we describe later in this chapter. The city became the new meeting place of Native Americans, who learned of their common predicament both in the city and on the federally administered reservations. Government agencies also had to develop a policy of continued assistance to nonreservation Native Americans; despite such efforts, the problems of Native Americans in cities persist.

Programs have emerged to meet the needs of city-dwelling Native Americans. Founded in 1975, the Native American Education Service College in Chicago is an independent, accredited college trying to partially provide for the education of that city's 10,000 Native Americans, who represent 100 tribes. It offers college degrees, with specialized courses in Native American language and history. The college emphasizes small classes and individualized instruction. This institution is unusual not only in higher education but also in offering urban Native Americans a pluralistic solution to being an American Indian in White America (Lauerman 1993).

Collective Action

Native Americans have worked collectively through tribal or reservation government action and across tribal lines. As we noted in Chapter 1, the panethnic development of solidarity among ethnic subgroups has been reflected in the use of such terms as *Hispanic,*

Latino, and *Asian American.* **Pan-Indianism** refers to intertribal social movements in which several tribes, joined by political goals but not by kinship, unite in a common identity. Today, these pan-Indian efforts are most vividly seen in cultural efforts and political protests of government policies (Cornell 1996; Jolivette 2008).

Proponents of this movement see the tribes as captive nations or internal colonies. They generally see the enemy as the federal government. Until recently, pan-Indian efforts usually failed to overcome the cultural differences and distrust between tribal groups. However, some efforts to unite have succeeded. The Iroquois made up a six-tribe confederation dating back to the seventeenth century. The Ghost Dance briefly united the Plains tribes in the 1880s, some of which had earlier combined to resist the U.S. Army. But these were the exceptions. It took nearly a century and a half of BIA policies to accomplish a significant level of unification.

The National Congress of American Indians (NCAI), founded in 1944 in Denver, Colorado, was the first national organization representing Native Americans. The NCAI registered itself as a lobby in Washington, D.C., hoping to make the Native American perspective heard in the aftermath of the Reorganization Act described earlier. Concern about "White people's meddling" is reflected in the NCAI requirement that non-Indian members pay twice as much in dues. The NCAI has had its successes. Early in its history, it played an important role in creating the Indian Claims Commission, and it later pressured the BIA to abandon the practice of termination. It is still the most important civil rights organization for Native Americans and uses tactics similar to those of the NAACP, although the problems facing African Americans and Native Americans are legally and constitutionally different.

A later arrival was the more radical American Indian Movement (AIM), the most visible pan-Indian group. The AIM was founded in 1968 by Clyde Bellecourt (of the White Earth Chippewa) and Dennis Banks (of the Pine Ridge Oglala Sioux), both of whom then lived in Minneapolis. Initially, AIM created a patrol to monitor police actions and document charges of police brutality. Eventually, it promoted programs for alcohol rehabilitation and school reform. By 1972, AIM was nationally known not for its neighborhood-based reforms but for its aggressive confrontations with the BIA and law enforcement agencies.

Protest Efforts

Fish-ins began in 1964 to protest interference by Washington State officials with Native Americans who were fishing, as they argued, in accordance with the 1854 Treaty of Medicine Creek and were not subject to fine or imprisonment, even if they did violate White society's law. The fish-ins had protesters fishing en masse in restricted waterways. This protest was initially hampered by disunity and apathy, but several hundred Native Americans were convinced that civil disobedience was the only way to bring attention to their grievances with the government. Legal battles followed, and the U.S. Supreme Court confirmed the treaty rights in 1968. Other tribes continued to fight in the courts, but the fish-ins brought increased public awareness of the deprivations of Native Americans. These fishing rights battles continue today with the Chippewas in Wisconsin and Nez Perce in Idaho among others (Bobo and Tuan 2006; Johnson 2005).

The fish-ins were only the beginning. After the favorable Supreme Court decision in 1968, other events followed in quick succession. In 1969, members of the San Francisco Indian Center seized Alcatraz Island in San Francisco Bay. The 13-acre island was an abandoned maximum-security federal prison, and the federal government was undecided about how to use it. The Native Americans claimed "the excess property" in exchange for $24 in glass beads and cloth, following the precedent set in the sale of Manhattan more than three centuries earlier. With no federal response and the loss of public interest in the demonstration, the protesters left the island more than a year later. The activists' desire to transform it into a Native American cultural center was ignored. Despite the

pan-Indianism
Intertribal social movements in which several tribes, joined by political goals but not by kinship, unite in a common identity.

fish-ins
Tribes' protests over government interference with their traditional rights to fish as they like.

outcome, the event gained international publicity for their cause. Red Power was born, and Native Americans who sympathized with the BIA were labeled "Uncle Tomahawks" or "apples" (red on the outside, white on the inside).

The federal government did not totally ignore calls for a new policy that involved Native Americans in its formulation. Nevertheless, no major breakthroughs came in the 1960s. One significant step was passage of the Alaska Native Settlement Act of 1971. Alaskan Native American people—the 100,000 Inuit Eskimo and other Aleuts—have maintained their claim to the land since Alaska was purchased from Russia in 1867. The federal government had allowed the natives to settle on about one-third of the land they claimed but had not even granted them title to that land. The discovery of huge oil reserves in 1969 made the issue more explosive as the state of Alaska auctioned off mineral rights, ignoring Inuit occupation of the land.

The Alaskan Federation of Natives (AFN), the major native-Alaskan group, which had been organized in 1967, moved quickly to stop "the biggest land grab in the history of the U.S.," as the AFN called it. An AFN-sponsored bill was revised, and a compromise, the Native Claims Settlement Act, was passed in late 1971. The final act, which fell short of the requests by the AFN, granted control and ownership of 44 million acres to Alaska's 53,000 Inuits, Aleuts, and other peoples and gave them a cash settlement of nearly $1 billion. Given the enormous pressures from oil companies and conservationists, the Native Claims Settlement Act can be regarded as one of the more reasonable agreements reached between distinctive tribal groups of Native Americans and the government. Further reforms in 1988 helped to safeguard the original act, but as a major trade-off the Alaska Native Americans surrendered future claims to all aboriginal lands (Cornell and Kalt 2003; Ogunwole 2002).

The most dramatic confrontation between Native Americans and the government came early the next year in what some people have termed the Battle of Wounded Knee II. In January 1973, AIM leader Russell Means led an unsuccessful drive to impeach Richard Wilson as tribal chairman of the Oglala Sioux tribe on the Pine Ridge Reservation. In the next month, Means, accompanied by some 300 supporters, started a 70-day occupation of Wounded Knee, South Dakota, site of the infamous cavalry assault in 1890 and now part of the Pine Ridge Reservation. The occupation received tremendous press coverage.

However, the coverage did not affect the outcome. Negotiations between AIM and the federal government on the occupation itself brought no tangible results. Federal prosecutions were initiated against most participants. AIM leaders Russell Means and Dennis Banks eventually faced prosecution on a number of felony charges, and both men were imprisoned. AIM had less visibility as an organization then. Russell Means wryly remarked in 1984, "We're not chic now. We're just Indians, and we have to help ourselves" (Hentoff 1984, 23; also see Janisch 2008; Nagel 1988, 1996).

The most visible recent AIM activity has been its efforts to gain clemency for one of its leaders, Leonard Peltier. Imprisoned since 1976, Peltier was given two life sentences for murdering two FBI agents the year before on the embattled Sioux reservation of Pine Ridge, South Dakota. Fellow AIM leaders such as Dennis Banks organized a 1994 Walk for Justice to bring attention in Washington, D.C., to the view that Peltier is innocent. This view was supported in two 1992 movie releases: the documentary *Incident at Oglala*, produced by Robert Redford, and the more entertaining but fictionalized *Thunderheart*. To date, clemency appeals to the president to lift the federal sentence have gone unheeded, but this issue remains the rallying point for today's remnants of AIM (Matthiessen 1991; Sandage 2008).

Most reservations today have a measure of self-government through an elected tribal council. Pictured is the Navaho tribal council at work.

FIGURE 6.2
Ten Largest American Indian Tribal Groupings, 2000

Source: Ogunwole 2002, 10.

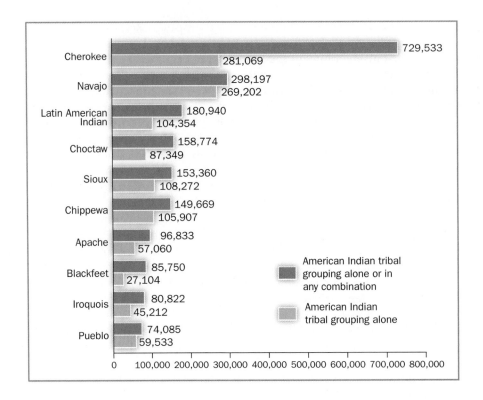

Collective Action: An Overview

Protest activities have created a greater solidarity among Native Americans as they seek solutions to common grievances with government agencies. Research shows that tribal people born since the collective action efforts of the 1960s are more likely to reject negative and stereotypic representations of American Indians than those born before the self-determination efforts. Whether through moderate groups such as the NCAI or the more activist AIM, these pan-Indian developments have awakened Whites to the real grievances of Native Americans and have garnered the begrudging acceptance of even the most conservative tribal members, who are more willing to cooperate with government action (Schulz 1998).

However, the results of collective action have not all been productive, even when viewed from a perspective sympathetic to Native American self-determination. The national organizations are dominated by Plains tribes, not only politically but also culturally. Powwow styles of dancing, singing, and costuming derived from the Plains tradition are spreading nationwide as common cultural traits (see Figure 6.2 for the ten largest tribes).

The growing visibility of **powwows** is symbolic of Native Americans in the 1990s. The phrase *pau wau* referred to the medicine man or spiritual leader of the Algonquian tribes, but Europeans who watched medicine men dance thought that the word referred to entire events. Over the last hundred years, powwows have evolved into gatherings in which Native Americans of many tribes come to dance, sing, play music, and visit. More recently, they have become organized events featuring competitions and prizes at several thousand locations. The general public sees them as entertainment, but for Native Americans, they are a celebration of their cultures (Eschbach and Applebaum 2000).

powwows
Native American gatherings of dancing, singing, music playing, and visiting, accompanied by competitions.

American Indian Identity

Today American Indian Identity occurs on two levels: macro and micro. At the macro level is the recognition of tribes; at the micro level is how individuals come to view themselves as American Indian and how this perception is recognized.

Sovereignty

Sovereignty refers in this context to tribal self-rule. Supported by every U.S. president since the 1960s, sovereignty is recognition that tribes have vibrant economic and cultural lives. At the same time, numerous legal cases, including many at the level of the Supreme Court, continue to clarify to what extent a recognized tribe may rule itself and to what degree it is subject to state and federal laws. In 2004, the U.S. Supreme Court ruled 7–2 in *United States v. Lara* that a tribe has the inherent right to prosecute all American Indians, regardless of affiliation, for crimes that occur on the reservation. However, other cases in lower courts continue to chip away at tribal self-government (Indianz.com 2004).

This legal relationship can be quite complex. For example, tribal members always pay federal income, Social Security, unemployment, and property taxes but do not pay state income tax if they live and work only on the reservation. Whether tribal members on reservations pay sales, gasoline, cigarette, or motor vehicle taxes has been negotiated on a reservation-by-reservation basis in many states.

Focused on the tribal group, sovereignty remains linked to both the actions of the federal government and the actions of individual American Indians. The government ultimately determines which tribes are recognized, and although tribal groups may argue publicly for their recognition, self-declaration carries no legal recognition. This has always been an issue, but given the rise of casino gambling (discussed shortly), the determination of who constitutes a sovereign tribe and who does not may carry significant economic benefits.

The federal government takes this gate-keeping role of sovereignty very seriously—the irony of the conquering people determining who are "Indians" is not lost on many tribal activists. In 1978, the Department of the Interior established what it called the *acknowledgment process* to decide whether any more tribes should have a government-to-government relationship. They must show that they were a distinct group and trace continuity since 1900. Through 2004, 294 groups have sought sovereignty, with just 16 acknowledged and another 9 receiving it though special congressional action.

sovereignty
Tribal self-rule.

Individual Identity

Most people reflect on their ancestry as a way to find roots or to self-identify themselves. For an individual who perceives themselves to be an American Indian, the process is defined by legalistic language. Recognized tribes establish a standard of ancestry or what some tribes call "blood quantum." to determine who is a tribal member or "enrolled" as on the "tribal rolls." Understandably, there is some ambivalence about this procedure because it applies some racial purity measures. Still, tribes see it as an important way to guard against potential "wannabes" (Fitzgerald 2008).

This process may lead some individuals or entire extended families to be disenrolled. For these people, who perceive themselves as worthy of recognition by a tribe but are denied this coveted "enrollment" status, disputes have resulted that are rarely resolved satisfactorily for all parties involved. This has been occurring for generations but has become contentious recently for those tribes who profit from casino gambling and must determine who is entitled to share in any profits that could be distributed to those on tribal rolls (Beiser 2006; Campbell 2008a).

In Listen to Our Voices, Charles Trimble ponders the issue of identifying as an Indian. His experience and feelings are similar to those of many people of mixed ancestry.

Native Americans Today

The United States has taken most of the land originally occupied by or deeded to Native Americans, restricted their movement, unilaterally severed agreements, created a special legal status for them, and, after World War II, attempted to move them again. As a result of these efforts and generally poor economic conditions of most reservations, substantial numbers of Native Americans live in the nation's most populated urban areas.

Listen to Our Voices

IYESKA: NOTES FROM MIXED-BLOOD COUNTRY

I am an Iyeska, a mixed-blood—Oglala Lakota and bits of European nationalities, mostly Irish and English. Over the years we were called *half-breeds* or *breeds*, as well as various other names from both sides of our ancestry, many of them unprintable.

Iyeska in Lakota translates as "speaks white," but through the years has taken on the generic term for "mixed blood." What I write here comes from my own experiences as an Iyeska, and from what I have observed among Iyeskas I have known.

Whether or not we admit it, most of the mixed-blood kids that I knew in the Indian boarding school I attended and in my home village on the Pine Ridge Reservation through the 1940s and '50s wished sometimes that we were not Indian at all. That came perhaps from seeing movies and reading books in which the White guys always won, had all the money, nice cars and girls. Indians were always the bad guys, killing innocent settlers who only wanted us dead and our land theirs. And in most towns on the reservation, the stores and other businesses were owned by Whites. In reservation border towns, we often faced discrimination. In short, our futures sometimes didn't look all that promising as Indians.

So we bought into what was being pushed on us anyway—assimilation—and we acted out what was expected of us to get jobs and fit into the larger society. . . .

In the schools, there was often a sense of superiority among Iyeskas over the full-bloods, and sometimes there was tension between them. "Buck" was a common term used to describe a person who the Iyeska

Charles A. Trimble

considered backward—mainly full-bloods. But an Iyeska didn't say it too loudly, because many of the best athletes and the toughest boys were full-bloods.

It seems to me that during our growing-up years, we used our white characteristics to our advantage in getting scholarships and employment opportunities, and now that there are more opportunities for Indians—especially from casino earnings—we want to take back our Indianness, at least in our fantasies.

Admittedly, what I have written above could be seen as cynical or even mean. I admit that the scenario applies to me to a greater or lesser degree, or I would not have written it. It is true that most Iyeskas who stayed on the reservation are very comfortable in their status, and their relations in their communities. And many Iyeskas are very serious in their search to find their roots and a culture they may feel to have been deprived of. For whatever reason they may have "returned to the blanket," some are happy in finding that special goodness and peace that can be found in traditional life.

But for many of us Iyeskas, I think that perhaps it's time to quit trying to impress White people and younger generations of Indians with fantasy stories of another life, or blaming someone else for having given up a culture that was largely peripheral to our lives anyway. We need to take pride in our Indianness, no matter how thin our tribal blood quantum; but we also need to give some credit to our White or Latino or Black forebears. The inner peace of living a real life, with a true life story, is worth it.

Source: Trimble 2008, 5.

How are Native Americans being treated today? A very public insult is the continuing use of American Indian names as mascots for athletic teams, including high schools, colleges, and many professional sports teams in the United States. Almost all American Indian organizations, including AIM, have brought attention to the use of Native Americans as the mascots of sports teams, such as the Washington Redskins, and to such spectator practices as the "Tomahawk chop" associated with the Atlanta Braves baseball team.

TABLE 6.2
Urban Native Americans, 2006

According to the Bureau of the Census, 16 metropolitan areas each have more than 45,000 Native Americans. By comparison, only four reservations have that many residents.

Los Angeles/Long Beach	128,755
New York City	100,040
Phoenix/Mesa/Scottsdale	103,185
Tulsa	97,989
Oklahoma City	82,171
Seattle/Tacoma	68,295
Dallas/Ft. Worth	64,881
Albuquerque	57,568
Gallup, NM	54,008
Portland, OR/Vancouver, WA	52,247
Farmington, NM	50,934
San Francisco/Oakland	50,640
Lumberton, NC	48,337
Chicago	46,989
Tucson	45,793

Source: Based on data from the American Community Survey 2006, released in 2007 by the Bureau of the Census.

Many sports fans and college alumni find it difficult to understand why Native Americans take offense at a name such as "Braves" or even "Redskins" if it is meant to represent a team about which they have positive feelings. For Native Americans, however, the use of such mascots trivializes their past and their presence today. This at best puzzles if not infuriates most Native people, who already face a variety of challenges today. The National Collegiate Athletic Association (NCAA), which oversees college athletics, has asked colleges to "explain" their use of mascot names, nicknames, or logos such as "savages," "braves," "warriors," "chieftains," "redmen," and "Indians" to name a few. In some cases, the NCAA has already banned the appearance of students dressed as such mascots in tournaments. Typically, college alumni and most students wonder what the fuss is about, while most Native people question why should they be so "honored" if they don't want to be (NCAA 2003a, 2003b; Weiberg 2006).

Any discussion of Native American socioeconomic status today must begin with an emphasis on the diversity of the people. Besides the variety of tribal heritages already noted, the contemporary Native American population is split between those on and off reservations and those who live in small towns or central cities. Life in these contrasting social environments is quite different, but enough similarities exist to warrant some broad generalizations on the status of Native Americans in the United States today.

The sections that follow summarize the status of contemporary Native Americans in economic development, education, health care, religious and spiritual expression, and the environment.

Economic Development

Native Americans are an impoverished people. Even to the most casual observer of a reservation, the poverty is a living reality, not merely numbers and percentages. Some visitors seem unconcerned, arguing that because Native Americans are used to hardship and lived a simple life before the Europeans arrived, poverty is a familiar and traditional way of life. In an absolute sense of dollars earned or quality of housing, Native Americans are no worse off now. But in a relative sense that compares their position with that of non-Indians, they are dismally behind on all standards of income and occupational status. A 1995 national survey showed that overall unemployment is more than 30 percent. Among those who do have jobs, one-third earned less than $10,000.

Given the lower incomes and higher poverty rates, it is not surprising that the occupational distribution of Native Americans is similarly bleak. Those who are employed are less likely to be managers, professionals, technicians, salespeople, or administrators. This pattern of low-wage employment is typical of many racial and ethnic minorities in the United States, but Native Americans differ in three areas: their roles in tourism, casino gambling, and government employment.

Tourism Tourism is an important source of employment for many reservation residents, who either serve the needs of visitors directly or sell souvenirs and craft items. Generally, such enterprises do not achieve the kind of success that improves the tribal economy significantly. Even if they did, sociologist Murray Wax (1971, 69) argued, "It requires a special type of person to tolerate exposing himself and his family life to the gaze of tourists, who are often boorish and sometimes offensively condescending in their attitudes."

Tourism, in light of exploitation of tribal people, is a complex interaction of the outside with Native American. Interviews with tourists visiting museums and reservations found that, regardless of the presentation, many visitors interpreted their brief experiences to be consistent with their previously held stereotypes of and prejudices toward Native Americans. Yet, at the other extreme, some contemporary tourists conscious of the historical context are uncomfortable taking in Native foods and purchasing crafts at tribal settlements despite the large economic need many reservations have for such commerce (Laxson 1991; Padget 2004).

Craftwork rarely realizes the profits that most Native Americans desire and need. The trading-post business has also taken its toll on Native American cultures. Many craft workers have been manipulated by other Native Americans and non-Indians to produce what the tourists want. Creativity and authenticity often are replaced by mechanical duplication of "genuine Indian" curios. There continues to be concern and controversy surrounding art such as paintings and pottery that may not be produced by real Native Americans. In 1935, the federal government had created the Indian Arts and Crafts Board to promote tribal arts. The influx of fraudulent crafts was so great that Congress added to its responsibilities the Indian Arts and Crafts Act, which severely punishes anyone who offers to sell an object as produced by a Native American artisan when it was not. The price of both economic and cultural survival is very high (McCoy 2004).

Casino Gambling A more recent source of significant income and some employment has been the introduction of gambling on reservations. Forms of gambling, originally part of tribal ceremonies or celebrations, existed long before Europeans arrived in the Western hemisphere. Today, however, commercial gambling is the only viable source of employment and revenue available to several tribes.

Under the 1988 Indian Gaming Regulatory Act, states must negotiate gambling agreements with reservations and cannot prohibit any gambling already allowed under state law. By 2008, 225 tribal governments in 28 states were operating a variety of gambling operations, including off-track betting, casino tables such as blackjack and roulette, lotteries, sports betting, video games of chance, telephone betting, slot machines, and high-stakes bingo. The gamblers, almost all non–Native Americans, sometime travel long distances for the opportunity to wager money. The actual casinos are a form of tribal government enterprise as opposed to private business operations.

The economic impact on some reservations has been enormous, and nationwide receipts amounted to $265 billion in 2007 from reservation casino operations—more than Las Vegas and Atlantic City combined. However, the wealth is uneven: about two-thirds of the recognized Indian tribes have no gambling ventures. A few successful casinos have led to staggering windfalls, such as the profits to the 820 members of the Connecticut Mashantucket Pequot Indians, whose Foxwoods Resort Casino, with annual gambling receipts far exceeding $1.5 billion, provides generous benefits to anyone who can establish that he or she is at least one-sixteenth Pequot. Gaming money from the 25 or so highly successful operations not only supports tribal members but also has been used to buy back tribal lands and even to help underwrite the cost of the Smithsonian Museum of the American Indian, which opened in 2004 (Katel 2006; National Indian Gaming Association 2008; Werner 2008).

The more typical picture is of moderately successful gambling operations associated with tribes whose social and economic needs are overwhelming. Tribes that have opened casinos have experienced drops in unemployment and increases in household income not seen on nongaming reservations. However, three important factors need to be considered.

- First, the tribes do pay taxes. They pay $6 billion in gambling-generated taxes to local, state, and federal governments. That still leaves significant profits that can be paid out to tribal members or reinvested in collective tribal operations.

- Second, nationwide the economic and social impact of this revenue is limited. The tribes that make substantial revenue from gambling are a small fraction of all Native American people.

- Third, even on the reservations that benefit from gambling enterprises, the levels of unemployment are substantially higher and the family income significantly lower than for the nation as a whole (Bartlett and Steele 2002; Katel 2006, 365; National Indian Gaming Association 2006; Sahagun 2004; Taylor and Kalt 2005).

Criticism is not hard to find, even among Native Americans, some of whom oppose gambling both on moral grounds and because it is marketed in a form that is incompatible with Native American cultures. Opponents are concerned about the appearance of compulsive gambling among some tribal members. The majority of the gamblers are not Native Americans, and almost all of the reservation casinos, though owned by the tribes, are operated by non-Indian–owned businesses. Some tribal members feel that the casinos trivialize and cheapen their heritage. The issue of who shares in gambling profits also has led to heated debates in some tribal communities about who is a member of the tribe. In addition, established White gaming interests lobby Congress to restrict the tribes, even though Native Americans generate only 23 percent of the nation's total of legal gambling revenue, including lotteries and racing (National Indian Gaming Association 2006).

Native Americans' voting clout is very weak compared to that of even African Americans and Latinos, but their lobbying power has become significant. Casino money fueled the 2006 scandal involving lobbyist Jack Abramoff, who cheated several tribes by pretending to lobby on their behalf. Although many of the political donations Native Americans make are aimed at protecting reservation casinos, tribes' political agendas include obtaining federal grants for education, roads, housing, and other projects.

Although income from gambling has not dramatically changed the lifestyle of most Native Americans, it has been a magnet of criticism from outsiders. Critics question the special status being afforded to Native Americans and contend that there should be an even playing field. This view certainly would have been endorsed by tribal members, because most of what passed for government policies over the last 200 years placed tribes at a major disadvantage. Attention is drawn to some tribes that had made contributions to politicians involved in policies concerning gambling laws. Although some of these contributions may have been illegal, the national media attention was far more intense than was warranted in the messy area of campaign financing. It is another example of how the notion that Native Americans are now playing the White man's game of capitalism "too well" becomes big news (Drinkard 2006; Glionna 2004).

Government Employment Another major source of employment for Native Americans is the government, principally the BIA, but also other federal agencies, the military, and state and local governments. As recently as 1970, one of every four employed Native Americans worked for the federal government. More than half the BIA's employees have tribal ancestry. In fact, since 1854, the BIA has had a policy of giving employment preference to Native Americans over non-Indians. This policy has been questioned, but the U.S. Supreme Court (*Morton v. Mancari*) upheld it in 1974. Although this is a significant source of employment opportunity, other tribe members have leveled many criticisms at Native American government workers, especially federal employees.

These government employees form a subculture in Native American communities. They tend to be Christians, educated in BIA schools, and sometimes the third generation born into government service. Discrimination against Native Americans in private industry makes government work attractive, and once a person is employed and has seniority, he or she is virtually guaranteed security. Of course, this security may lead some people (whether Native Americans or Whites) to work inefficiently (Bureau of Indian Affairs 1970; Rachlin 1970).

We have examined the sources of economic development such as tourism, government service, and legalized gambling, but the dominant feature of reservation life is, nevertheless, unemployment. A government report issued by the Full Employment Action Council opened with the statement that such words as *severe, massive,* and *horrendous* are appropriate to describe unemployment among Native Americans. Official unemployment figures for reservations range from 23 percent to 90 percent. It is little wonder that the 1990 census showed that the poorest county in the nation was wholly on tribal lands: Shannon County, South Dakota, of the Pine Ridge Reservation, had a 63 percent poverty rate. Unemployment rates for urban-based Indians are also very high; Los Angeles reports more than 40 percent, and Minneapolis, 49 percent (Cornell and Kalt 1990; Kanamine 1992; Knudson 1987; Sullivan 1986).

The economic outlook for Native Americans need not be bleak. A single program is not the solution; the diversity of both Native Americans and their problems demands a multifaceted approach. The solutions need not be unduly expensive; indeed, because the Native American population is very small compared with the total population, programs with major influence may be financed without significant federal expenditures. Murray Wax (1971) observed that reformers viewing the economically depressed position of Native Americans often seize on education as the key to success. As the next section shows, improving educational programs for Native Americans would be a good place to start.

Education

Government involvement in the education of Native Americans dates as far back as a 1794 treaty with the Oneida Indians. In the 1840s, the federal government and missionary groups combined to start the first school for American Indians. By 1860, the government was operating schools that were free of missionary involvement. Today, laws prohibit federal funds for Native American education from going to sectarian schools. Also, since the passage of the Johnson-O'Malley Act in 1934, the federal government has reimbursed public school districts that include Native American children.

Federal control of the education of Native American children has had mixed results from the beginning. Several tribes started their own school systems at the beginning of the nineteenth century, financing the schools themselves. The Cherokee tribe developed an extensive school system that taught both English and Cherokee, the latter using an alphabet developed by the famed leader Sequoyah. Literacy for the Cherokees was estimated by the mid-1800s at 90 percent, and they even published a bilingual newspaper. The Creek, Chickasaw, and Seminole also maintained school systems. But by the end of the nineteenth century, all these schools had been closed by federal order. Not until the 1930s did the federal government become committed to ensuring an education for Native American children. Despite the push for educational participation, by 1948 only one-quarter of the children on the Navajo reservation, the nation's largest, were attending school (Pewewardy 1998).

Educational Attainment A serious problem in Native American education has been the unusually low level of enrollment. Many children never attend school, or they leave while in elementary school and never return. Enrollment rates are as low as 30 percent for Alaskan Eskimos (or Inupiats). This high dropout rate is at least 50 percent higher than that of Blacks or Hispanics and nearly three times that of Whites. The term *dropout* is misleading because many tribal American schoolchildren have found their educational experience so hostile that they have no choice but to leave. In 2005, the South Dakota Supreme Court ruled that a school serving the Lakota Sioux tribe was routinely calling in the police to deal with the slightest misbehavior. The youth soon developed a juvenile record leading to what was termed "school-to-discipline pipeline" (Dell'Angela 2005; James et al. 1995).

Rosalie Wax (1967) conducted a detailed study of the education among the Sioux on the Pine Ridge Reservation of South Dakota. She concluded that terms such as **kickout** or **pushout** are more appropriate. The children are not so much hostile toward school as they are set apart from it; they are socialized by their parents to be independent and not to embarrass their peers, but teachers reward docile acceptance and expect schoolchildren to correct one another in public. Socialization is not all that separates home from school. Teachers often are happy to find parents not "interfering" with their job. Parents do not visit the school, and teachers avoid the homes, a pattern that only furthers the isolation of school from home. This lack of interaction results partly from the predominance of non–Native American teachers, many of whom do not recognize the learning styles of American Indian students, although the situation is improving (Hilberg and Tharp 2002).

Quality of Schooling The quality of Native American education is more difficult to measure than the quantity. How does one measure excellence? And excellence for what? White society? Tribal life? Both? Chapter 1 discussed the disagreement over measuring intellectual achievement (how much a person has learned) and the greater hazards in measuring intellectual aptitude (how much a person is able to learn). Studies of reservation children, using tests of intelligence that do not require a knowledge of English, consistently show scores at or above the levels of middle-class urban children. Yet in the upper grades, a **crossover effect** appears when the tests used assume lifelong familiarity with English. Native American students drop behind their White peers and so would be classified by the dominant society as underachievers (Bureau of Indian Affairs 1988; Coleman et al. 1966; Fuchs and Havighurst 1972).

Preoccupation with such test results perhaps avoids the more important question: educational excellence for what? It would be a mistake to assume that the tribal peoples have reached a consensus. However, they do want to see a curriculum that, at the very least, considers the unique aspects of their heritage. Charles Silberman (1971, 173) reported visiting a sixth-grade English class in a school on a Chippewa reservation where the students were all busily at work writing a composition for Thanksgiving: "Why We Are Happy the Pilgrims Came." A 1991 Department of Education report titled *Indian Nations at Risk* still found the curriculum presented from a European perspective. It is little wonder that in 2004, only 1 percent of Native American high school seniors even attempted the SATs, compared to 63 percent of White seniors. In Figure 6.3, we compare educational attainment of the largest tribal groups with all-White non-Hispanics (Henig 2006).

kickouts or pushouts
Native American school dropouts who leave behind an unproductive academic environment.

crossover effect
An effect that appears as previously high-scoring Native American children score below average in intelligence when tests are given in English rather than their native languages.

FIGURE 6.3
Educational Attainment 2000
Source: Ogunwole 2006, 8.

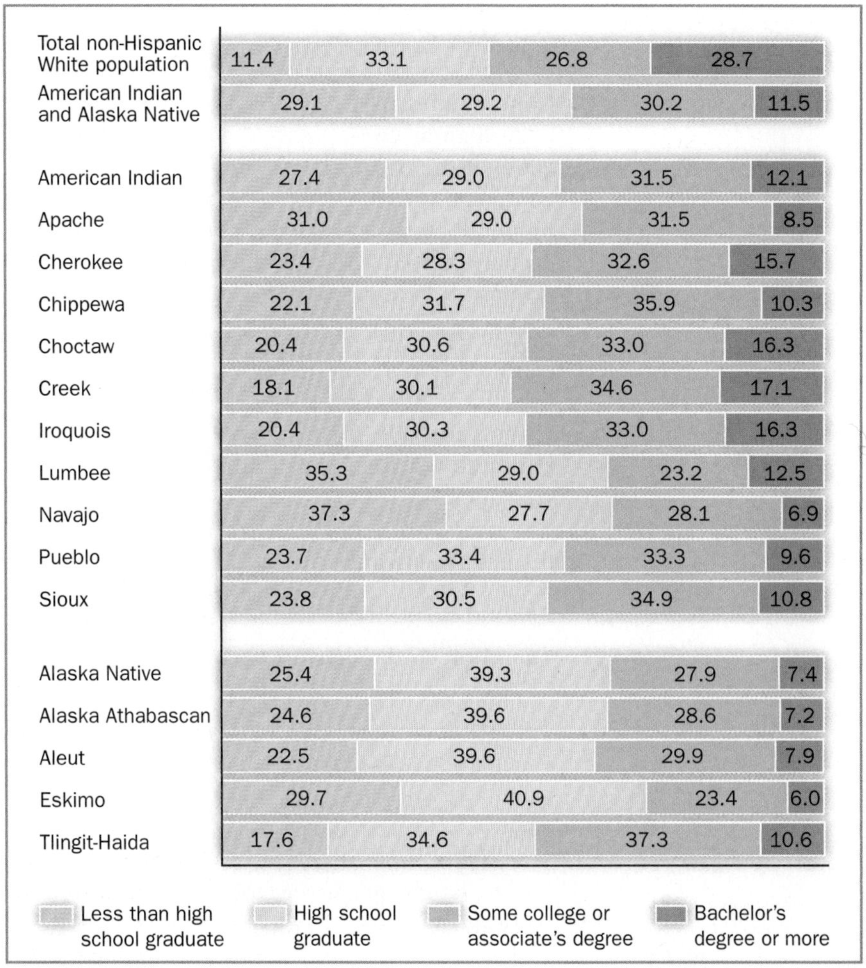

	Less than high school graduate	High school graduate	Some college or associate's degree	Bachelor's degree or more
Total non-Hispanic White population	11.4	33.1	26.8	28.7
American Indian and Alaska Native	29.1	29.2	30.2	11.5
American Indian	27.4	29.0	31.5	12.1
Apache	31.0	29.0	31.5	8.5
Cherokee	23.4	28.3	32.6	15.7
Chippewa	22.1	31.7	35.9	10.3
Choctaw	20.4	30.6	33.0	16.3
Creek	18.1	30.1	34.6	17.1
Iroquois	20.4	30.3	33.0	16.3
Lumbee	35.3	29.0	23.2	12.5
Navajo	37.3	27.7	28.1	6.9
Pueblo	23.7	33.4	33.3	9.6
Sioux	23.8	30.5	34.9	10.8
Alaska Native	25.4	39.3	27.9	7.4
Alaska Athabascan	24.6	39.6	28.6	7.2
Aleut	22.5	39.6	29.9	7.9
Eskimo	29.7	40.9	23.4	6.0
Tlingit-Haida	17.6	34.6	37.3	10.6

Some positive changes are occurring in education. About 23 percent of the students in BIA-funded schools receive bilingual education. There is growing recognition of the need to move away from past policies that suppressed or ignored the native language and to acknowledge that educational results may be optimized when the native language is included. In Research Focus, we consider the importance of incorporating native teachings and cultures (Bureau of Indian Affairs 1988; James et al. 1995; Reese 1996; Wells 1991).

Higher Education The picture for Native Americans in higher education is decidedly mixed, with some progress and some promise. Enrollment in college increased steadily from the mid-1970s through the beginning of the twenty-first century, but degree completion, especially the completion of professional degrees, may actually be declining. The economic and educational background of Native American students, especially reservation residents, makes the prospect of entering a predominantly White college a very difficult decision. Native American students may soon feel isolated and discouraged, particularly if the college does not help them understand the alien world of American-style higher education. Even at campuses with large numbers of Native Americans in their student bodies, only a few Native American faculty members or advisors are present to serve as role models. About 53 percent of the students leave at the end of their first year (Carnegie Foundation for the Advancement of Teaching 1990; Wells 1989).

Another encouraging development in higher education in recent years has been the creation of tribally controlled colleges, usually two-year community colleges. The Navajo Community College (now called Diné College), the first such institution, was established in 1968, and by 2008 there were 36 tribal colleges in 14 states, with more than 30,000 students enrolled. Besides serving in some rural areas as the only educational institution for many miles, these colleges also provide services such as counseling and child care. Tribal colleges enable the students to maintain their cultural identity while training them to succeed outside the reservation (American Indian Higher Education Consortium 2008).

At higher levels, Native Americans largely disappear from the educational scene. In 2004, of the 35,605 doctorates awarded to U.S. citizens, 217 went to Native Americans, compared with more than 12,000 that went to citizens of foreign countries. This production of doctorates among Native Americans has not changed significantly since at least as far back as 1981 (Bureau of the Census 2007a, 183).

Summary "Diné bizaad beeyashti!" Unfortunately, this declaration of "I speak Navajo!" is not commonly heard from educators. Gradually, schools have begun to encourage the preservation of native cultures. Until the 1960s, BIA and mission schools forbade speaking in the native languages, so it will take time to produce an educated teacher corps that is knowledgeable in and conversant with native cultures (Linthicum 1993).

As we have seen, there are many failures in our effort to educate, not just assimilate, the first Americans. The problems include

- underenrollment at all levels, from the primary grades through college;
- the need to adjust to a school with values that are sometimes dramatically different from those of the home;
- the need to make the curriculum more relevant;
- the underfinancing of tribal community colleges;
- the unique hardships encountered by reservation-born Native Americans who later live in and attend schools in large cities; and
- the language barrier faced by the many children who have little or no knowledge of English.

Research Focus

LEARNING THE NAVAJO WAY

What leads to academic success? Often the answer is a supportive family, but this has not always been said about Native Americans. Educators rooted in the European education traditions often argue that American Indian families whose children are faithful to the traditional cultures cannot succeed in schools. This assimilationist view argues that to succeed in larger White-dominated society, it is important to begin to shed the "old ways" as soon as possible. Interestingly, research done in the last 10 years has questioned the assimilationist view, concluding that American Indian students can improve their academic performance through educational programs that are less assimilationist and use curricula that build on what the Native American youth learn in their homes and communities.

Representative of this growing research is the study completed by sociologist Angela A. A. Willeto among her fellow Navajo tribal people. She studied a random sample of 451 Navajo high school students from 11 different Navajo Nation schools. She examined the impact of the students' orientation toward traditional Navajo culture on their performance. The prevailing view has been that all that is inherently Navajo in a child must be eliminated and replaced with mainstream White society beliefs and lifestyles.

The Navajo tradition was measured by a number of indicators, such as participating in Navajo dances, consulting a medicine man, entering a sweat bath to cleanse oneself spiritually, weaving rugs, living in a traditional hogan, and using the Navajo language. School performance was measured by grades, commitment to school, and aspirations to attend college. Willeto found that the students who lived a more traditional life among the Navajo succeeded in school just as well and were just as committed to success in school and college as high schoolers leading a more assimilated life.

These results are important because even many Native Americans accept an assimilationist view. Even within the Navajo Nation, where Navajo language instruction has been mandated in all reservation schools since 1984, many Navajos still equate learning only with the mastery of White society's subject matter.

Sources: Reyhner 2001; Willeto 1999, 2007.

Other problems include lack of educational innovation (the BIA had no kindergartens until 1967) and a failure to provide special education to children who need it.

Health Care

For Native Americans, "health care" is a misnomer, another broken promise in the long line of unmet pledges the government has made. Compared to other groups, Native Americans are more likely to have poorer health and unmet medical needs and not be able to afford the care. They are more likely to have higher levels of diabetes, trouble hearing, and activity limitations and to have experienced serious psychological distress (Barnes et al. 2005; Campbell 2008b).

In 1955, amidst criticism even then, the responsibility for health care through the Indian Health Service (IHS) transferred from the BIA to the Public Health Service.

By either name, gaming or gambling has become big business for a few of the nation's tribes. Shown here are patrons at Mystic Lake Casino, which is operated by the Shakopee Mdewakanton Sioux outside Minneapolis, Minnesota.

Although the health of Native Americans has improved markedly in absolute terms since the mid-1960s, their overall health is comparatively far behind all other segments of the population. The Commission on Civil Rights (2003) found that the federal per capita expenditure for health care of prison inmates was 50 percent higher than it was for Native Americans. With the pressure to assimilate Native Americans in all aspects of their lives, there has been little willingness to recognize their traditions of healing and treating illnesses. Native treatments tend to be noninvasive, with the patient encouraged to contribute actively to the healing benefits and prevent future recurrence. In the 1990s, a pluralistic effort was slowly emerging to recognize alternative forms of medicine, including those practiced by Native Americans. In addition, reservation health care workers began to accommodate traditional belief systems as they administered the White culture's medicine (Angier 1993; Fox 1992; *Indian Country* 1999).

Contributing to the problems of health care and mortality on reservations are often high rates of crime, not all of which is reported. Poverty and few job opportunities offer an excellent environment for the growth of youth gangs and drug trafficking. All the issues associated with crime can be found on the nation's reservations. There are 171 tribal enforcement agencies operating nearly 70 jails or detention facilities. As with other minority communities dealing with poverty, Native Americans strongly support law enforcement but at the same time contend that their people are being abused by the very individuals who have been selected to protect them. As with efforts for improving health care, the isolation and vastness of some of the reservations make them uniquely vulnerable to crime (Duthu 2008; Reynolds 2006).

Religious and Spiritual Expression

Like other aspects of Native American cultures, the expression of religion is diverse, reflecting the variety of tribal traditions and the assimilationist pressure of the Europeans. Initially, missionaries and settlers expected Native Americans simply to forsake their traditions for European Christianity, and, as in the case of the repression of the Ghost Dance, sometimes force was used to do so. Today, many Protestant churches and Roman Catholic parishes with large tribal congregations incorporate customs such as the sacred pipe ceremony, native incenses, sweat lodges, ceremonies affirming care for the Earth, and services and hymns in native languages.

Whether traditional in nature or reflecting the impact of Europeans, Native people typically embrace a broad world of spirituality. Whereas Christians, Jews, and Muslims adhere to a single deity and often confine spiritual expression to designated sites, traditional American Indian people see considerably more relevance in the whole of the world, including animals, water, and the wind.

After generations of formal and informal pressure to adopt Christian faiths and their rituals, in 1978 Congress enacted the American Indian Religious Freedom Act, which declares that it is the government's policy to "protect and preserve the inherent right of American Indians to believe, express, and practice their traditional religions." However, the act contains no penalties or enforcement mechanisms. For this reason, Hopi leader Vernon Masayesva (1994, 93) calls it "the law with no teeth." Therefore, Native Americans are lobbying to strengthen this 1978 legislation. They are seeking protection for religious worship services for military personnel and incarcerated Native Americans, as well as better access to religious relics, such as eagle feathers, and better safeguards against the exploitation of sacred lands (Burgess 1992; Deloria 1992; Friends Committee on National Legislation 1993).

A major spiritual concern is the stockpiling of Native American relics, including burial remains. Contemporary Native Americans are increasingly seeking the return of their ancestors' remains and artifacts, a demand that alarms museums and archeologists. The Native American Graves Protection and Repatriation Act of 1990 requires an inventory of such collections and provides for the return of materials if a claim can be substantiated. This has had significant impact on many anthropological and archaeological collections.

Many scholars believe the ancient bones and burial artifacts to be valuable clues to humanity's past. In part, however, this belief reflects a difference in cultural traditions. Yet the return, or repatriation, of these remains has been very uplifting to tribes and individual Native American families, who often greet the arrival with elaborate and emotionally touching ceremonies (Campbell 2008c; G. Johnson 2005).

In recent years, significant publicity has been given to an old expression of religion: the ritual use of peyote, which dates back thousands of years. The sacramental use of peyote was first observed by Europeans in the 1640s. In 1918, the religious use of peyote, a plant that creates mild psychedelic effects, was organized as the Native American Church (NAC). At first a Southwest-based religion, the NAC has spread since World War II among northern tribes. The use of the substance is a small part of a long and moving ritual. The exact nature of NAC rituals varies widely. Clearly, the church maintains the tradition of ritual curing and the seeking of individual visions. However, practitioners also embrace elements of Christianity, representing a type of religious pluralism of Indian and European identities.

Peyote is a hallucinogen, however, and federal and state governments have been concerned about its use by NAC members. Several states passed laws in the 1920s and 1930s prohibiting the use of peyote. In the 1980s, several court cases involved the prosecution of Native Americans who were using peyote for religious purposes. Finally, in 1994, Congress amended the American Indian Religious Freedom Act to allow Native Americans the right to use, transport, and possess peyote for religious purposes (J. Martin 2001).

Today's Native Americans are asking that their traditions be recognized as an expression of pluralist rather than assimilationist coexistence. These traditions are also closely tied to religion. The sacred sites of Native Americans, as well as their religious practices, have been under attack. In the next section, we will focus on aspects of environmental disputes that are anchored in the spiritualism of Native Americans (Kinzer 2000; Mihesuah 2000).

Paul Moss is giving an Arapaho name to his newborn great-grandson, Raphael, who lies in his arms. The name he chose to give the infant is the one his own deceased son held, Himookoonit, or Golden Eagle. At his feet are cloth goods and cash offerings given to the elder who has given the name.

Environment

environmental justice
Efforts to ensure that hazardous substances are controlled so that all communities receive protection regardless of race or socioeconomic circumstances.

Environmental issues bring together many of the concerns we have previously considered for Native Americans: stereotyping, land rights, environmental justice, economic development, and spiritualism.

First, we can find in some of today's environmental literature stereotypes of Native peoples as the last defense against the encroachment of "civilization." This image tends to trivialize native cultures, making them into what one author called a "New Age savage" (Waller 1996).

Second, many environmental issues are rooted in continuing land disputes arising from treaties and agreements more than a century old. Reservations contain a wealth of natural resources and scenic beauty. In the past, Native Americans often lacked the technical knowledge to negotiate beneficial agreements with private corporations—and even when they did have this ability, the federal government often stepped in and made the final agreements more beneficial to the non–Native Americans than to the residents of the reservations. The Native peoples have always been rooted in their land. It was their land that became the first source of tension and conflict with the Europeans. At the beginning of the twenty-first century, it is not surprising that land and the natural resources it holds continue to be major concerns. In 1967, the Council of Energy Resource Tribes (CERT) was formed by the leaders of 25 of the West's largest tribes. This new council reasoned that by organizing, it could ensure more revenue from the tribes' vast mineral resources. CERT, which by 2008 represented 59 tribes in the United States and Canada, has provided numerous services to tribes. Working with consultants, CERT helps them develop their resources by marketing natural gas more effectively and dealing with the deregulation of utilities. One recent positive development has been the creation of ways to harness the wind for electrical power. Some Plains American Indian tribes are starting to create wind farms that not only provide power for their own needs but also even allows them to sell extra power (Archuleta 1998; Barringer 2008; CERT 2008).

Third, environmental issues reinforce the tendency to treat the first inhabitants of the Americas as inferior. This is manifested in **environmental justice**—a term introduced in Chapter 3 to describe efforts to ensure that hazardous substances are controlled so that all communities receive protection regardless of race or socioeconomic circumstances. Reservation representatives often express concern about how their lands are used as dumping grounds. For example, the Navajo reservation is home to almost 1,100 abandoned uranium mines. After legal action, the federal government finally provided assistance in 2000 to Navajos who had worked in the mines and were showing ill effects from radiation exposure. Although compensation has been less than was felt necessary, the Navajos continue to monitor closely new proposals to use their land. Few reservations have escaped negative environmental impact, and some observers contend that Native American lands are targeted for nuclear waste storage. Critics see this as a de facto policy of nuclear colonialism, whereby reservations are forced to accept all the hazards of nuclear energy, but the Native American people have seen few of its benefits (Daitz 2003).

Fourth, environmental concerns by American Indians often are balanced against economic development needs, just as they are in the larger society. On some reservations, authorization by timber companies to access hardwood forests led to very conflicted feelings among American Indians. However, such arrangements often are the only realistic source of needed revenue, even if they mean entering into arrangements that more affluent people would never consider. The Skull Valley Goshute tribe of Utah has tried to attract a nuclear waste dump over state government objections. Eventually, the federal government rejected the tribe's plans. Even on the Navajo reservation, a proposed new uranium mine has its

Role models for success in schooling are vital to today's young Native Americans. Here Astronaut John Herrington, Chickasaw, speaks to children attending a weeklong space and aviation academy in Oklahoma.

supporters—those who consider the promises of royalty payments coupled with alleged safety measures sufficient to offset the past half-century of radiation problems (Bryan 2006; Foy 2006).

Fifth, spiritual needs must be balanced against demands on the environment. For example, numerous sacred sites lie in such public areas as the Grand Canyon, Zion, and Canyonlands National Parks that, though not publicized, are accessible to outsiders. Tribal groups have sought vainly to restrict entry to such sites. The San Carlos Apaches unsuccessfully tried to block the University of Arizona from erecting an observatory on their sacred Mt. Graham. Similarly, Plains Indians have sought to ban tourists from climbing Devil's Tower, long the site of religious visions, where prayer bundles of tobacco and sage were left behind by Native peoples (Campbell 2008d; Martin 2001).

Conclusion

Native Americans have to choose between assimilating to the dominant non-Indian culture and maintaining their identity. In the figure on the next page we revisit the Spectrum of Intergroup Relations as it relates to Native Americans. Recently there is evidence of pluralism, but the desire to improve themselves economically usually drives them toward assimilation.

Maintaining one's tribal identity outside a reservation is not easy. One's cultural heritage must be consciously sought out while under the pressure to assimilate. Even on a reservation, it is not easy to integrate being Native American with elements of contemporary society. The dominant society needs innovative approaches to facilitate pluralism.

The reservations are economically depressed, but they are also the home of the Native American people spiritually and ideologically, if not always physically. Furthermore, the reservation isolation means that the frustrations of reservation life and the violent outbursts against them do not alarm large numbers of Whites, as do disturbances in urban centers. Native Americans today, except in motion pictures, are out of sight and out of mind. Ever since the BIA's creation in 1824, the federal government has had much greater control over Native Americans than over any other civilian group in the nation. For Native Americans, the federal government and White people are virtually synonymous. However, the typical non-Indian tends to be more sympathetic, if not paternalistic, toward Native Americans than toward African Americans.

Subordinate groups in the United States, including Native Americans, have made tremendous gains and will continue to do so in the years to come. But the rest of the population is not standing still. As Native American income rises, so does White income. As Native American children stay in school longer, so do White children. American Indian health care improves, but so does White health care. Advances have been made, but the gap remains between the descendants of the first Americans and those of later arrivals. Low incomes, inadequate education, and poor health care spurred relations between Native Americans and non-Indians to take a dramatic turn in the 1960s and 1970s, when Native Americans demanded a better life in America.

As Chapter 7 will show, African Americans have achieved a measure of recognition in Washington, D.C., that Native Americans have not. Only 5 percent as numerous as the Black population, Native Americans have a weaker collective voice even with casino money fueling lobbying efforts. Only a handful of Native Americans have ever served in Congress, and many of the non-Indians representing states with large numbers of Native Americans have emerged as their biggest foes rather than their advocates.

The greatest challenge to and asset of the descendants of the first Americans is their land. More than 130 years after the Allotment Act, Native American peoples are still seeking what they feel is theirs. The land they still possess, although only a small slice of what they once occupied, is an important asset. It is barren and largely unproductive agriculturally, but some of it is unspoiled and often rich in natural resources. No wonder many large businesses, land developers, environmentalists, and casino managers covet their land for their own purposes. For Native Americans, the land they still occupy, as well as much of that occupied by other Americans, represents their roots, their homeland.

One Thanksgiving Day, a scholar noted that, according to tradition, at the first Thanksgiving in 1621 the Pilgrims and the Wampanoag ate together. The descendants of these celebrants increasingly sit at distant tables with equally distant thoughts of equality. Today's Native Americans are the "most undernourished, most short-lived, least educated, least healthy." For them, "that long ago Thanksgiving was not a milestone, not a promise. It was the last full meal" (Dorris 1988, A23).

SPECTRUM OF INTERGROUP RELATIONS

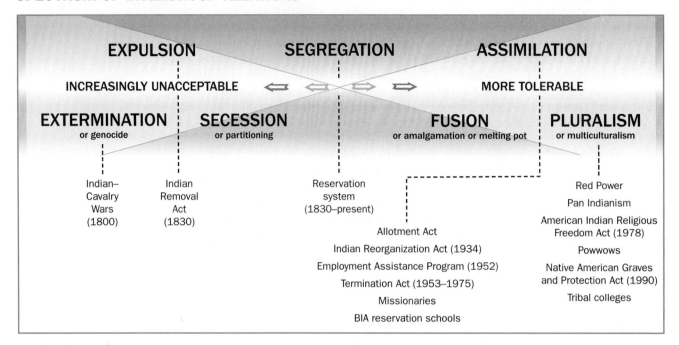

Summary

1. Early European Americans usually did not intend to antagonize the Native peoples unnecessarily, but the needs of the settlers always ruled.

2. Policies of the reservation era such as the Allotment, Reorganization, and Termination acts and the Employment Assistance Program reflected a treatment of tribal people akin to internal colonialism.

3. Native Americans have consistently resisted mistreatment through their tribes and reservation organizations and collectively across boundaries through pan-Indian efforts.

4. American Indians' identity issues emerge today through sovereignty questions at the macro level and self-identification and tribal enrollment at the micro level.

5. Despite gains over the last couple of generations, Native Americans trail the rest of the country in economic development, employment levels, and access to quality health care.

6. Quality education continues to be a challenge to American Indians. Efforts to bring native cultures to the curriculum and bolster tribal colleges seek to overcome a century of neglect.

7. Diversity of American Indian cultures is reflected in religious and spiritual expression.

8. Despite the loss of so much of their historical settlement areas, Native Americans struggle to achieve environmental justice.

Key Terms

crossover effect 163
environmental justice 168
fish-ins 154
internal colonialism 146

kickouts or pushouts 163
millenarian movements 147
pan-Indianism 154
powwows 156

sovereignty 157
world systems theory 145

Review Questions

1. Identify three policies or actions taken by the federal government that have significant impact today in the daily lives of Native Americans.

2. How have land rights been a continuing theme in White–Native American relations?

3. How much are Native Americans expected to shed their cultural heritage to become a part of contemporary society?

4. Do casinos and other gaming outlets represent a positive force for Native American tribes today?

5. What challenges are there to reservation residents receiving effective health care?

Critical Thinking

1. Consider Independence Day and Thanksgiving Day. How do these national holidays remind Native Americans today of their marginal status?

2. Chronicle how aspects of leisure time, from schoolyard games to Halloween costumes to team mascots, trivialize Native Americans. What experience have you had with such episodes, or what have you seen in the mass media?

3. Why do you think that many people in the United States hold more benevolent attitudes toward Native Americans than they do toward other subordinate groups such as African Americans and Latinos?

The Making of African Americans in a White America

THE AFRICAN PRESENCE IN THE UNITED STATES BEGAN ALMOST simultaneously with permanent White settlement. Unlike most Europeans, however, the African people were brought involuntarily and in bondage. The end of slavery heralded new political rights during Reconstruction, but this was a short-lived era of dignity. Despite advocacy of nonviolence by leaders such as the Reverend Martin Luther King, Jr., the civil rights movement met violent resistance throughout the South. In the mid-1960s, the nation's attention was diverted to urban violence in the North and the West. Blacks responded to their relative deprivation and rising expectations by advocating Black Power, which in turn met with White resistance. Although African Americans have made significant gains, the gap between Blacks and Whites remains remarkably unchanged in the last half century. Religion continues to be a major force in the African American community. In recent years, Black America has been diversified with immigration from Africa and the Caribbean.

173

The Gee's Bend Ferry resumed service crossing the Alabama River in 2006. This is especially noteworthy because it represented the end of several decades of keeping Blacks from voting in Camden, Alabama. In 1962, as Blacks began to vote in larger numbers, no ferry service meant that a key concentration of 700 African American citizens would have to travel an hour rather than 15 minutes to get to the county seat to register to vote.

In 2003, the city council of Zephyrhills, a community of 11,000 people 35 miles northeast of Tampa, Florida, voted to rename a street in honor of Martin Luther King, Jr. In taking this step, they joined company with about 650 other cities in 41 states that have renamed streets in honor of the civil rights worker. Although a few responded to the creation of Martin Luther King, Jr., Avenue with pleasure, the city council was unprepared for the strong protest that accompanied its decision. Protesters became more vocal over the action, with critics saying they did not want to have to change their address. Observers noticed that all the townspeople who spoke against the policy were White, and most of the supporters were African American. In May, the council reversed itself, and King Avenue again became Sixth Avenue. This is not the story of just one town, because this has occurred again and again. Efforts to recognize significant figures in African American history have often been controversial. The people of San Diego were so incensed about renaming a street after Martin Luther King, Jr., that they successfully got the issue on the ballot in 1987 and had the former name restored. More recently, in 2003, the people of Muncie, Indiana, defeated the idea of renaming a street after the slain civil rights leader, and similarly in Portsmouth, New Hampshire, the suggestion to name a city park after King did not succeed (Goodnough 2004; Linn 2006).

Relationships between Whites and Blacks in the United States have been marked by many episodes like these, sometimes a step backward and occasionally a step forward.

The United States, with more than 38 million Blacks, has the eighth-largest Black population in the world. Only Brazil, Congo, Ethiopia, Nigeria, South Africa, Sudan, and Tanzania have larger Black populations.

To a significant degree, the history of African Americans is the history of the United States. Black people accompanied the first explorers, and a Black man was among the first to die in the American Revolution. The enslavement of Africans was responsible for the South's wealth in the nineteenth century and led to the country's most violent domestic strife. After Blacks were freed from slavery, their continued subordination led to sporadic outbreaks of violence in the rural South and throughout urban America. This chapter concentrates on the history of African Americans into the beginning of the twenty-first century. Their contemporary situation is the subject of Chapter 8.

The Black experience in what came to be the United States began as something less than citizenship yet slightly better than slavery. In 1619, 20 Africans arrived in Jamestown as indentured servants. Their children were born free people. These Blacks in the British colonies were not the first in the New World, however; some Blacks had accompanied European explorers, perhaps even Columbus. But all this is a historical footnote. By the 1660s, the British colonies had passed laws making Africans slaves for life, forbidding interracial marriages, and making children of slaves bear the status of their mother regardless of their father's race. Slavery had begun in North America; more than three centuries later we still live with its legacy.

Slavery

Slavery seems far removed from the debates over issues that divide Whites and Blacks today. However, contemporary institutional and individual racism, which is central to today's conflicts, has its origins in the institution of slavery. Slavery was not merely a single aspect of American society for three centuries; it has been an essential part of our country's life. For nearly half of this country's history, slavery was not only tolerated but also legally protected by the U.S. Constitution as interpreted by the U.S. Supreme Court.

In sharp contrast to the basic rights and privileges enjoyed by White Americans, Black people in bondage lived under a system of repression and terror. For several decades, nearly one out five people were Black and enslaved in the United States (see Table 7.1). Because the institution of slavery was so fundamental to our culture, it continues to influence Black–White relations in the twenty-first century.

slave codes
Laws that defined the low position held by slaves in the United States.

Slave Codes

Slavery in the United States rested on five central conditions: slavery was for life, the status was inherited, slaves were considered mcre property, slaves were denied rights, and coercion was used to maintain the system (Noel 1972). As slavery developed in colonial America and the United States, so did **slave codes**, laws that defined the low position of slaves in the United States. Although the rules varied from state to state and from time to time and were

---

TABLE 7.1
Black Population, 1790–2050

Blacks accounted for a decreasing proportion of the total population until the 1940s, primarily because White immigration to the United States far outdistanced population growth by Blacks.

Census	Black Population (in Thousands)	Black Percentage (of Total Population)
1790	757	19.3
1810	1,378	19.0
1830	2,329	18.1
1850	3,639	15.7
1870	4,880	12.7
1890	7,489	11.9
1910	9,828	10.7
1930	11,891	9.7
1950	15,042	10.0
1970	22,580	11.1
1990	29,986	12.1
2000	35,818	12.7
2010 (projection)	40,454	13.1
2050 (projection)	61,361	14.6

Source: Bureau of the Census 2002a, 2004b, table 1a.

not always enforced, the more common features demonstrate how completely subjugated the Africans were:

1. A slave could not marry or even meet with a free Black.
2. Marriage between slaves was not legally recognized.
3. A slave could not legally buy or sell anything except by special arrangement.
4. A slave could not possess weapons or liquor.
5. A slave could not quarrel with or use abusive language toward Whites.
6. A slave could not possess property (including money) except as allowed by his or her owner.
7. A slave could neither make a will nor inherit anything.
8. A slave could not make a contract or hire him- or herself out.
9. A slave could not leave a plantation without a pass noting his or her destination and time of return.
10. No one, including Whites, was to teach a slave (and in some areas even a free Black) to read or write or to give a slave a book, including the Bible.
11. A slave could not gamble.
12. A slave had to obey established curfews.
13. A slave could not testify in court except against another slave.

Violations of these rules were dealt with in a variety of ways. Mutilation and branding were not unknown. Imprisonment was rare; most violators were whipped. An owner was largely immune from prosecution for any physical abuse of slaves. Because slaves could not testify in court, a White's actions toward enslaved African Americans were practically above the law (ACLU 1996; Elkins 1959; Franklin and Moss 2000; Stampp 1956).

Slavery, as enforced through the slave codes, controlled and determined all facets of the lives of the enslaved Africans. The organization of family life and religious worship were no exceptions. Naturally, the Africans had brought to America their own cultural traditions. In Africa, people had been accustomed to a closely regulated family life and a rigidly enforced moral code. Slavery rendered it impossible for them to retain these family ties in the New World.

Through the research of W. E. B. Du Bois and many others, we know that the slave families had no standing in law. Marriages between slaves were not legally recognized, and masters rarely respected them in selling adults or children. Slave breeding—a deliberate effort to maximize the number of offspring—was practiced with little attention to the emotional needs of the slaves themselves. The slaveholder, not the parents, decided at what age children should begin working in the fields. The slave family could not offer its children shelter or security, rewards or punishments. The man's only recognized family role was that of siring offspring, being the sex partner of a woman. In fact, slave men often were identified as if they were the woman's possession, for example, as "Nancy's Tom." Southern law consistently ruled that "the father of a slave is unknown to our law." This does not imply that the male slave did not occupy an important economic role. Men held almost all the managerial positions open to slaves (Du Bois 1970; Stampp 1956).

For many generations, Africans were treated by their White slave owners as property, yet they tried to maintain a sense of family life. This 1862 image shows five generations of a family whose members were all born on a plantation in Beaufort, South Carolina.

Unlike the family structure, to which slavery dealt near-mortal blows, a strong religious tradition survived. In fact, a slaveholder wanting to do "God's work on Earth" would encourage the slave church, finding it functional in dominating the slaves. Of course, African religions were forbidden, and the White people's Christianity flourished, but Blacks still used West African concepts in the new way of life that slavery brought. The preacher maintained an intense relationship with the congregation, similar to the role played by the elder in West Africa. The Christianity to which the slaves were introduced stressed obedience to their owners. Complete surrender to Whites meant salvation and eternal happiness in the hereafter. In contrast, to question God's will or to fight slavery caused everlasting damnation. Obviously, this twisted version of Christianity was intended to make slaves acquiesce to their holders' wishes in return for reward after death. To some degree, however, religion did keep the desire for freedom alive in slaves, and to some extent it formed the basis of their struggle for freedom: nightly prayer meetings and singing gave them a sense of unity and common destiny necessary for that struggle. On a more personal level, religion made the slaves' daily lives more bearable (Frazier 1964; Rawick 1972; Stampp 1956).

African Americans and Africa

The importance of Africa to Black Americans can be seen in the aspects of African culture that became integral parts of Blacks' lives in the United States. Black scholars W. E. B. Du Bois (1939) and Carter Woodson (1968) and respected White anthropologist Melville Herskovits (1941) have all argued persuasively for the continued influence of the African heritage.

Scholars debate to what degree African culture was able to persist despite efforts by slaveholders to replace any vestige of African tradition. The survival of African culture can be most easily documented in folklore, religion, language, and music. It is difficult to clarify the degree of survival, however, because Africans came from many different cultures. When we think of ethnic origins, our thoughts turn to European groups such as Poles or Greeks, but within Africa are the Ibos, Gas, and Yorubas, to name a few of the sources of slaves from Africa (see Figure 7.1). Thus, to speak of a single source of African culture ignores the complexity of social life on that continent. Furthermore, as the **Afrocentric perspective** argues, some aspects of African culture, such as certain art forms, have so permeated Western culture that we mistakenly believe their origins are European.

Africa has had and will always have an importance to Blacks that many Blacks and most Whites do not appreciate, and this importance is unlikely to be changed by the continued debate over which aspects of Black life today can be traced back to African culture. The significance of Africa to Black Americans is one of the most easily identifiable themes in the Black experience. During certain periods (the 1920s and the late 1960s), the Black cultural tradition was the rallying point of many Blacks, especially those living in the cities. Studies continue to document the survival of African culture in North America.

Research has identified remnants of grammar and sentence construction in the speech patterns of low-income and rural Blacks. **Ebonics** is the distinctive dialect, with a complex language structure, that is found among Black Americans. Although the term *Ebonics* (*ebony* and *phonics*) was coined in the 1970s, there has long been a recognition of a distinctive language pattern, sometimes called "Black English," that includes some vocabulary and grammar rules that reflect the West African origins of Black Americans. In 1996, Ebonics became a national issue after the Oakland, California, school board's recognition of it as the primary language of schoolchildren who were then learning mainstream American English. This debate aside, there is consensus that, a century after slavery, remnants of African cultural traditions survive (Applebome 1997).

The Attack on Slavery

Although the slave was vulnerable to his or her owner's wishes, slavery as an institution was vulnerable to outside opinion. For a generation after the American Revolution,

Afrocentric perspective
An emphasis on the customs of African cultures and how they have pervaded the history, culture, and behavior of Blacks in the United States and around the world.

Ebonics
Distinctive dialect with a complex language structure found among many Black Americans.

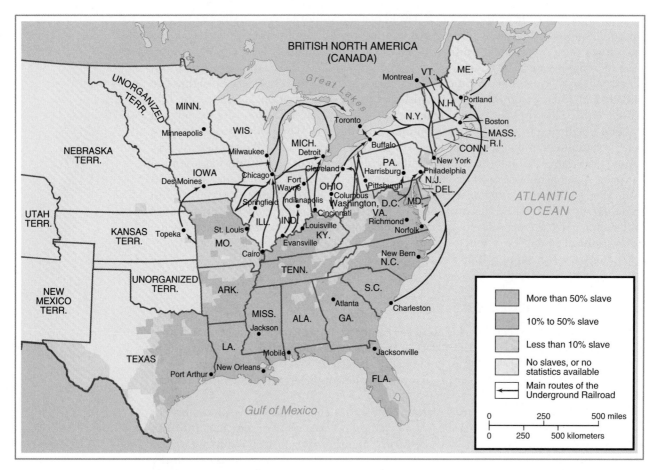

FIGURE 7.1

Slave Concentration, 1860

Slavery was so dominant in the South that slaves outnumbered the White population in many areas. Yet even as the Civil War approached, slaves risked their lives to navigate the underground railroad to freedom in the North or Canada.

Source: Brands et al. 2009, 311.

restrictions on slaves increased as Southerners accepted slavery as permanent. Slave revolts and antislavery propaganda only accelerated the intensity of oppression. This change led to the ironic situation that as slavery was attacked from within and without, its conditions became harsher and its defenders became more outspoken in asserting what they saw as its benefits.

Antislavery advocates, or **abolitionists**, included both Whites and free Blacks. Many Whites who opposed slavery, such as Abraham Lincoln, did not believe in racial equality. In their minds, even though slavery was a moral evil, racial equality was still unimaginable. This apparent inconsistency did not lessen the emotional fervor of the efforts to end slavery. Antislavery societies had been founded even before the American Revolution, but the Constitution dealt the antislavery movement a blow. To appease the South, the framers of the Constitution recognized and legitimized slavery's existence. The Constitution even allowed slavery to increase Southern political power. A slave was counted as three-fifths of a person in determining population representation in the House of Representatives.

Abolitionists, both Black and White, continued to speak out against slavery and the harm it was doing not only to the slaves but also to the entire nation, which had become economically dependent on bondage. Frederick Douglass and Sojourner Truth, both freed slaves, became very visible in the fight against slavery through their eloquent speeches and publications. Harriet Tubman, along with other Blacks and sympathetic Whites, developed the Underground Railroad to convey escaping slaves to freedom in the North and Canada (Franklin and Moss 2000).

abolitionists
Whites and free Blacks who favored the end of slavery.

Another aspect of Black enslavement was the slaves' own resistance to servitude. Slaves did revolt, and between 40,000 and 100,000 actually escaped from the South and slavery. Yet fugitive slave acts provided for the return even of slaves who had reached free states. Enslaved Blacks who did not attempt escape, at least in part because failure often led to death, resisted slavery through such means as passive resistance. Slaves feigned clumsiness or illness; pretended not to understand, see, or hear; ridiculed Whites with a mocking, subtle humor that their owners did not comprehend; and destroyed farm implements and committed similar acts of sabotage. As illustrated in Figure 7.1, the most dramatic form of resistance was to flee enforced servitude by escaping through the Underground Railroad that linked safe houses and paths to freedom in the North and Canada (Kimmons 2008; Williams Jr. 2008).

Slavery's Aftermath

On January 1, 1863, President Lincoln issued the Emancipation Proclamation. The document created hope in slaves in the South, but many Union soldiers resigned rather than participate in a struggle to free slaves. The proclamation freed slaves only in the Confederacy, over which the president had no control. Six months after the surrender of the Confederacy in 1865, abolition became law when the Thirteenth Amendment abolished slavery throughout the nation.

From 1867 to 1877, during the period called Reconstruction, Black–White relations in the South were unlike anything they had ever been. The Reconstruction Act of 1867 put each Southern state under a military governor until a new state constitution could be written, with Blacks participating fully in the process. Whites and Blacks married each other, went to public schools and state universities together, and rode side by side on trains and streetcars. The most conspicuous evidence of the new position of Blacks was their presence in elected office. In 1870, the Fifteenth Amendment was ratified, prohibiting the denial of the right to vote on grounds of race, color, or previous condition of servitude. Black men put their vote to good use; Blacks were elected as six lieutenant governors, 16 major state officials, 20 members of the House of Representatives, and two U.S. senators. Despite accusations that they were corrupt, Black officials and Black-dominated legislatures created new and progressive state constitutions. Black political organizations, such as the Union League and the Loyal League, rivaled the church as the focus of community organization (Du Bois 1969b; Foner 2006).

Reconstruction was ended as part of a political compromise in the election of 1876; consequently, segregation became entrenched in the South. Evidence of Jim Crow's reign was

Jim Crow
Southern laws passed in the late nineteenth century that kept Blacks in their subordinate position.

White primary
Legal provisions forbidding Black voting in election primaries, which in one-party areas of the South effectively denied Blacks their right to select elected officials.

slavery reparation
The act of making amends for the injustices of slavery.

apparent by the close of the nineteenth century. The term **Jim Crow** appears to have its origin in a dance tune, but by the 1890s it was synonymous with segregation and referred to the statutes that kept African Americans in an inferior position. Segregation often preceded Jim Crow laws and in practice often went beyond their provisions. The institutionalization of segregation gave White supremacy its ultimate authority. In 1896, the U.S. Supreme Court ruled in *Plessy v. Ferguson* that state laws requiring "separate but equal" accommodations for Blacks were a "reasonable" use of state government power (Cheng 2008; Woodward 1974).

It was in the political sphere that Jim Crow exacted its price soonest. In 1898, the Court's decision in *Williams v. Mississippi* declared constitutional the use of poll taxes, literacy tests, and residential requirements to discourage Blacks from voting. In Louisiana that year, 130,000 Blacks were registered to vote. Eight years later only 1,342 were. Even all these measures did not deprive all African Americans of the vote, and so White supremacists erected a final obstacle: the **White primary** that forbade Black voting in election primaries. By the turn of the century, the South had a one-party system, making the primary the significant contest and the general election a mere rubber stamp. Beginning with South Carolina in 1896 and spreading to 12 other states within 20 years, statewide Democratic party primaries were adopted. The party explicitly excluded Blacks from voting, an exclusion that was constitutional because the party was defined as a private organization that was free to define its own membership qualifications. The White primary brought an end to the political gains of Reconstruction (Lacy 1972; Lewinson 1965; Woodward 1974).

Reparations for Slavery

The legacy of slavery lives on more than 150 years after its end in the United States. We can see it in the nation's Capitol and the White House, which were built with slave labor, but we can also see it in the enduring poverty that grips a large proportion of the descendants of slavery.

For more than 30 years, there has been serious discussion about granting reparations for slavery. **Slavery reparation** refers to the act of making amends for the injustice of slavery. Few people would argue that slavery was wrong and continues to be wrong where it is practiced in parts of the world even today. However, what form should the reparations take? Since 1989, Congressman John Conyers, a Black Democrat from Detroit, has annually introduced in Congress a bill to acknowledge the "fundamental injustice, cruelty, brutality, and inhumanity of slavery" and calls for the creation of a commission to examine the institution and to make recommendations on appropriate remedies. This bill has never made it out of committee, but the discussion continues outside the federal government.

There has not been an official government apology for slavery even though the U.S. government has apologized for injustices to the American Indians and to the Japanese Americans placed in internment camps during World War II. The absence of an official apology angers many African Americans today and those sympathetic to the reparation issue, but the true controversy surrounds what form a remedy should take. Should the government develop and fund some major program to assist the African American community? Should there be direct payments to all African Americans or only to people who can prove that they are descended from enslaved people? Each possibility raises a variety of questions about fairness and equity, but many people object in principle to giving any money to those who were not enslaved themselves.

Beginning in the late 1990s, legal researchers raised yet another issue as documentation emerged that private companies that still exist today benefited from slavery. Although it is not too difficult to see how much of the plantation economy of the South was built on enslaved people, the corporate profits from slavery go well beyond the cotton fields. The railroad industry depended heavily on slave labor for the construction of railway systems still in use today. Insurance companies even in the North during slavery collected a substantial number of insurance premiums from slaveholders who insured their slaves, much as they would other forms of property. Proponents of slavery reparations argue that these companies owe payments to today's slavery descendants, similar to efforts to get reparations to Jews and their descendants from German companies that profited from the Holocaust during World War II (Cox 2002; Dawson and Popoff 2004; Foner 2006; Salzberger and Turck 2004).

The Challenge of Black Leadership

The institutionalization of White supremacy precipitated different responses from African Americans, just as slavery had. In the late 1800s and early 1900s, a number of articulate Blacks attempted to lead the first generation of freeborn Black Americans. Most prominent were Booker T. Washington and W. E. B. Du Bois. The personalities and ideas of these two men contrasted with one another. Washington was born a slave in 1856 on a Virginia plantation. He worked in coal mines after emancipation and attended elementary school. Through hard work and driving ambition, Washington became the head of an educational institute for Blacks in Tuskegee, Alabama. Within 15 years, his leadership brought the Tuskegee Institute national recognition and made him a national figure. Du Bois, on the other hand, was born in 1868 of a free family in Massachusetts. He attended Fisk University and the University of Berlin and became the first Black to receive a doctorate from Harvard. Washington died in 1915, and Du Bois died in self-imposed exile in Africa in 1963.

The Politics of Accommodation

Booker T. Washington's approach to White supremacy is called the *politics of accommodation*. He was willing to forgo social equality until White people saw Blacks as deserving of it. Perhaps his most famous speech was made in Atlanta on September 18, 1895, to an audience that was mostly White and mostly wealthy. Introduced by the governor of Georgia as "a representative of Negro enterprise and Negro civilization," Washington (1900) gave a 5 minute speech in which he pledged the continued dedication of Blacks to Whites:

> As we have proved our loyalty to you in the past, in nursing your children, watching by the sick-bed of your mothers and fathers, and often following them with tear-dimmed eyes to their graves, so in the future, in our humble way, we shall stand by you with a devotion that no foreigner can approach, ready to lay down our lives, if need be, in defense of yours. *(221)*

The speech catapulted Washington into the public forum, and he became the anointed spokesperson for Blacks for the next 20 years. President Grover Cleveland congratulated Washington for the "new hope" he gave Blacks. Washington's essential theme was compromise. Unlike Frederick Douglass, who had demanded the same rights for Blacks as for Whites, Washington asked that Blacks be educated because it would be a wise investment for Whites. He called racial hatred "the great and intricate problem which God has laid at the doors of the South." The Blacks' goal should be economic respectability. Washington's accommodating attitude ensured his popularity with Whites. His recognition by Whites contributed to his large following of Blacks, who were not used to seeing their leaders achieve fame among Whites.

It is easy in retrospect to be critical of Washington and to write him off as simply a product of his times. Booker T. Washington entered the public arena when the more militant proposals of Douglass had been buried. Black politicians were losing political contests and influence. To become influential as a Black, Washington reasoned, required White acceptance. His image as an accommodator allowed him to fight discrimination covertly. He assisted Presidents Roosevelt and Taft in appointing Blacks to patronage positions. Washington's goal was for African Americans eventually to have the same rights and opportunities as Whites. Just as people disagree with leaders today, some Blacks disagreed over the means that Washington chose to reach that goal. No African American was more outspoken in his criticism of the politics of accommodation than W. E. B. Du Bois (Conyers 1996; Harlan 1972; Hawkins 1962; Meier and Rudwick 1966).

The Niagara Movement

The rivalry between Washington and Du Bois has been exaggerated. Actually, they enjoyed fairly cordial relations for some time. In 1900, Washington recommended Du Bois, at his request, for superintendent of Black schools in Washington, D.C. By 1905, however, relations between the two had cooled. Du Bois spoke critically of Washington's influence, arguing that his power was being used to stifle African Americans who spoke out against the politics of accommodation. He also charged that Washington had caused the transfer of funds from academic programs to vocational education. Du Bois's greatest objection to Washington's statements was that they encouraged Whites to place the burden of the Blacks' problems on the Blacks themselves (Du Bois 1961; Hawkins 1962).

As an alternative to Washington's program, Du Bois (1903) advocated the theory of the *talented tenth*, which reflected his atypical educational background. Unlike Washington, Du Bois was not at home with both intellectuals and sharecroppers. Although the very phrase *talented tenth* has an elitist ring, Du Bois argued that these privileged Blacks must serve the other nine-tenths. This argument was also Du Bois's way of criticizing Washington's emphasis on vocational education. Although he did not completely oppose the vocational approach, Du Bois thought education for African Americans should emphasize academics, which would be more likely to improve their position. Drawing on the talented tenth, Du Bois invited 29 Blacks to participate in a strategy session near Niagara Falls in 1905. Out of a series of meetings came several demands that unmistakably placed the responsibility for the problems facing African Americans on the shoulders of Whites.

The Niagara Movement, as it came to be called, was closely monitored by Booker T. Washington. Du Bois encountered difficulty gaining financial support and recruiting prominent people, and Du Bois (1968) himself wrote, "My leadership was solely of ideas. I never was, nor ever will be, personally popular" (303). The movement's legacy was the education of a new generation of African Americans in the politics of protest. After 1910, the Niagara Movement ceased to hold annual conventions. In 1909, however, the National Association for the Advancement of Colored People (NAACP), with White and Black members, was founded by the Niagara Movement leaders. It was through the work of the NAACP that the Niagara Movement accomplished most of the goals set forth in 1905. The NAACP also marked the merging of White liberalism and Black militancy, a coalition unknown since the end of the abolition movement and Reconstruction (Rudwick 1957; Wortham 2008).

Remarkably, as Du Bois agitated for social change, he continued to conduct ground-breaking research into race relations. He oversaw the Atlanta Sociological Laboratory; its work at the time was generally ignored by the White-dominated academic institutions but is now gradually being rediscovered (Wright II 2006).

In 1900, 90 percent of African Americans lived in the South. Blacks moved out of the South and into the West and North, especially the urban areas in those regions, during the post–Civil War period and continued to migrate through the 1950s and 1960s. By the 1980s and 1990s, a migration to the South began as job opportunities grew in that part of the country and most vestiges of Jim Crow vanished in what had been the states of the Confederacy. By 2000, 55 percent of African Americans lived in the South, compared to 33 percent of the rest of the population (Figure 7.2).

The pattern of violence, with Blacks usually the victims, started in the South during Reconstruction and continued into the twentieth century, when it also spread northward. In 1917, a riot in East St. Louis, Illinois, claimed the lives of 39 Blacks and nine Whites. The several days of violence resulted from White fear of social and economic gains made by Blacks. The summer of 1919 saw so much violence that it is commonly called the "red summer." Twenty-six riots broke out throughout the country as White soldiers who returned from World War I feared the new competition that Blacks represented. This period of violence against African Americans also saw a resurgence of the Ku Klux Klan, which at its height had nearly 9 million members (Grimshaw 1969; Schaefer 1971, 1980).

By no stretch of the imagination, and certainly as documented by historians and sociologists, the South had no monopoly on racism. In Research Focus we consider the evidence of communities called sundown towns that kept Blacks out at night and were found throughout the North beginning in 1890 and continuing well into the last quarter of the twentieth century.

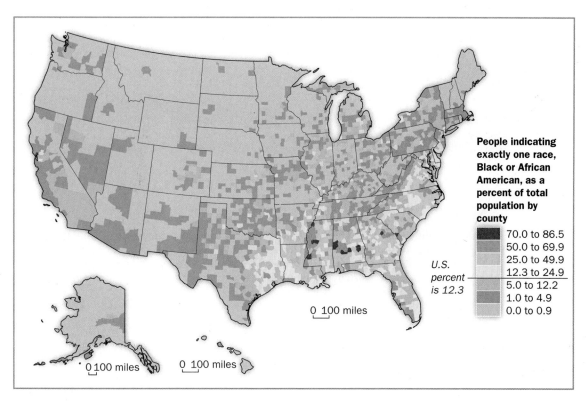

FIGURE 7.2
Black Population, 2000
Source: Bureau of the Census data map in C. Brewer and Suchan 2001.

Reemergence of Black Protest

American involvement in World War II signaled improved economic conditions for both Whites and Blacks. Nearly a million African Americans served in the military in rigidly segregated units. Generally, more Blacks could participate in the armed services in World War II than in previous military engagements, but efforts by Blacks to contribute to the war effort at home were hampered by discriminatory practices in defense plants.

A. Philip Randolph, president of the Brotherhood of Sleeping Car Porters, threatened to lead 100,000 Blacks in a march on Washington in 1941 to ensure their employment. Randolph's proposed tactic was nonviolent direct action, which he modeled on Mahatma Gandhi's practices in India. Randolph made it clear that he intended the march to be an all-Black event because he saw it as neither necessary nor desirable for Whites to lead Blacks to their own liberation. President Franklin Roosevelt responded to the pressure and agreed to issue an executive order prohibiting discrimination if Randolph would call off the march. Although the order and the Fair Employment Practices Commission it set up did not fulfill the original promises, a precedent had been established for federal intervention in job discrimination (Garfinkel 1959).

Racial turmoil during World War II was not limited to threatened marches. Racial disturbances occurred in cities throughout the country, the worst riot occurring in Detroit in June 1943. In that case, President Roosevelt sent in 6,000 soldiers to quell the violence, which left 25 Blacks and nine Whites dead. The racial disorders were paralleled by a growth in civil disobedience as a means to achieve equality for Blacks. The Congress of Racial Equality (CORE) was founded in 1942 to fight discrimination with nonviolent direct action. This interracial group used sit-ins to open restaurants to Black patrons in Chicago, Baltimore, and Los Angeles (Grimshaw 1969; Meier and Rudwick 1966).

The war years and the postwar period saw several U.S. Supreme Court decisions that suggested the Court was moving away from tolerating racial inequities. The White primary

Research Focus

SUNDOWN TOWNS, USA

Sundown towns are communities from which non-Whites were systematically excluded from living. They emerged in the late nineteenth century and persisted for a hundred years into the late twentieth century. Sundown towns existed throughout the nation, but more often they were located in Northern states that were not pre–Civil War slave states. Although the precise number of sundown towns in the United States is unknown, it is estimated that there were several thousand such towns throughout the nation.

The term *sundown town* comes from signs once posted at the city limits reading "Nigger, Don't Let the Sun Set on YOU." In addition to excluding African Americans from many small towns, Chinese Americans, Japanese Americans, Mexican Americans, Jews, and Native Americans—citizens and noncitizens alike—were also subject to such exclusions. In some cases, the exclusion was official town policy. In others cases, the racism policy was enforced through intimidation. This intimidation could occur in a number of ways, including harassment by law enforcement officers with the blessing of the local citizens.

Although the thought of sundown towns may seem a relic of the past to many of us today, sociologist James Loewen estimates that by 1970, still *more than half* of all incorporated communities outside the traditional South probably excluded African Americans. Many of these communities had no history of Blacks in residence. Such laws persisted even throughout the era of the civil rights movement. The city council of New Market, Iowa, for example, suspended its sundown ordinance for one night in the mid-1980s to allow an interracial band to play at a town festival, but it went back into effect the next day.

So what is it like today in these communities? Few sundown towns today have significant populations of excluded people. Some towns where colleges are located have benefited from efforts to desegregate their hometown. Such has been the case with initiatives by Lawrence University in Appleton, Wisconsin. What Loewen calls "recovering" sundown towns face continuing challenges to developing good race relations to attract African American families, including biased school curricula and overwhelmingly White teaching staffs. Practices that discourage desegregation persist across the country.

Source: Loewen 2005, 2008; Loewen and Schaefer 2008.

---

elections endorsed in Jim Crow's formative period were finally challenged in the 1944 *Smith v. Allwright* decision. The effectiveness of the victory was limited; many states simply passed statutes that used new devices to frustrate African American voters.

A particularly repugnant legal device for relegating African Americans to second-class status was the **restrictive covenant**, a private contract entered into by neighborhood property owners stipulating that property could not be sold or rented to certain minority groups, thus ensuring that they could not live in the area. In 1948, the Supreme Court finally declared in *Shelley v. Kramer* that restrictive covenants were not constitutional, although it did not actually attack their discriminatory nature. The victory was in many ways less substantial than it was symbolic of the new willingness by the Supreme Court to uphold the rights of Black citizens.

The Democratic administrations of the late 1940s and early 1950s made a number of promises to Black Americans. The party adopted a strong civil rights platform in 1948, but its provisions were not enacted. Once again, union president Randolph threatened Washington, D.C., with a march. This time he insisted that as long as Blacks were subjected

sundown towns
Communities where non-Whites were systematically excluded from living.

restrictive covenant
A private contract or agreement that discourages or prevents minority-group members from purchasing housing in a neighborhood.

to a peacetime draft, the military must be desegregated. President Truman responded by issuing an executive order on July 26, 1948, that desegregated the armed forces. The U.S. Army abolished its quota system in 1950, and training camps for the Korean War were integrated. Desegregation was not complete, however, especially in the reserves and the National Guard, and even today charges of racial favoritism confront the armed forces. Whatever its shortcomings, the desegregation order offered African Americans an alternative to segregated civilian life (Moskos and Butler 1996).

de jure segregation
Children assigned to schools specifically to maintain racially separated schools.

The Civil Rights Movement

It is difficult to say exactly when a social movement begins or ends. Usually, a movement's ideas or tactics precede the actual mobilization of people and continue long after the movement's driving force has been replaced by new ideals and techniques. This description applies to the civil rights movement and its successor, the continuing struggle for African American freedom. Before 1954, there were some confrontations of White supremacy: the CORE sit-ins of 1942 and efforts to desegregate buses in Baton Rouge, Louisiana, in 1953. The civil rights movement gained momentum with a Supreme Court decision in 1954 that eventually desegregated the public schools, and it ended as a major force in Black America with the civil disorders of 1965 through 1968. However, beginning in 1954, toppling the traditional barriers to full rights for Blacks was the rule, not the exception.

Struggle to Desegregate the Schools

For the majority of Black children, public school education meant attending segregated schools. Southern school districts assigned children to school by race rather than by neighborhood, a practice that constituted **de jure segregation**, or segregation that results from children being assigned to schools specifically to maintain racially separate schools. It was this form of legal humiliation that was attacked in the landmark decree of *Linda Brown et al. v. Board of Education of Topeka, Kansas.*

Seven-year-old Linda Brown was not permitted to enroll in the grade school four blocks from her home in Topeka, Kansas. Rather, school board policy dictated that she attend the Black school almost two miles away. This denial led the NAACP Legal Defense and Educational Fund to bring suit on behalf of Linda Brown and 12 other Black children. The NAACP argued that the Fourteenth Amendment was intended to rule out segregation in public schools. Chief Justice Earl Warren of the Supreme Court wrote the unanimous opinion that "in the field of public education the doctrine of 'separate but equal' has no place. Separate educational facilities are inherently unequal."

The freedom that African Americans saw in their grasp at the time of the *Brown* decision essentially amounted to a reaffirmation of American values. What Blacks sought was assimilation into White American society. The motivation for the *Brown* suit did not come merely because Black schools were inferior, although they were. Blacks were assigned to poorly ventilated and dilapidated buildings, with overcrowded classrooms and unqualified teachers. Less money was spent on Black schools than on White schools throughout the South in both rural and metropolitan areas. The issue was not such tangible factors, however, but the intangible effect of not being allowed to go to school with Whites. All-Black schools could not be equal to all-White schools. Even in this victory, Blacks were reaffirming White society and the importance of an integrated educational experience.

Although *Brown* marked the beginning of the civil rights movement, the reaction to it showed just how deeply prejudice

In this often-reproduced photograph, civil rights hero Rosa Parks is shown defying de jure segregation by sitting in the White section of the bus that launched the Montgomery, Alabama, bus boycott in 1955. Actually, although the event was very real, no journalists were present at the time, and this iconic photography was a re-creation with an Associated Press reporter seated behind Rosa Parks.

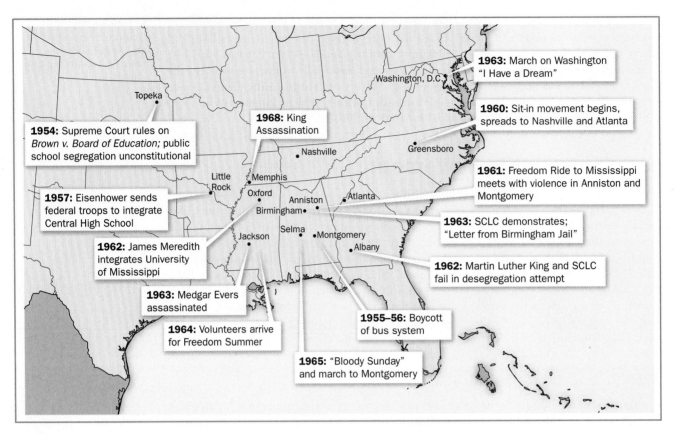

FIGURE 7.3
Major Events of the Civil Rights Movement

was held in the South. Resistance to court-ordered desegregation took many forms: some people called for impeachment of all the Supreme Court justices; others petitioned Congress to declare the Fourteenth Amendment unconstitutional; cities closed schools rather than comply; and the governor of Arkansas used the state's National Guard to block Black students from entering a previously all-White high school in Little Rock (Figure 7.3).

The issue of school desegregation was extended to higher education, and Mississippi state troopers and the state's National Guard confronted each other over the 1962 admission of James Meredith, the first African American accepted by the University of Mississippi. Scores of people were injured, and two were killed in this clash between segregationists and the law. A similar defiant stand was taken a year later by Governor George Wallace, who "stood in the schoolhouse door" to block two Blacks from enrolling in the University of Alabama. President Kennedy federalized the Alabama National Guard to guarantee admission of the students. *Brown* did not resolve the school controversy, and many questions remain unanswered. More recently, the issue of school segregation resulting from neighborhood segregation has been debated. In Chapter 8, another form of segregation—*de facto segregation*—is examined more closely (Bell 2004, 2007).

Civil Disobedience

The success of a yearlong boycott of city buses in Montgomery, Alabama, dealt Jim Crow another setback. On December 1, 1955, Rosa Parks defied the law and refused to give her seat on a crowded bus to a White man. Her defiance led to the organization of the Montgomery Improvement Association, headed by 26-year-old Martin Luther King, Jr., a Baptist minister with a Ph.D. from Boston University. The bus boycott was the first of many instances in which Blacks used nonviolent direct action to obtain the rights that Whites already enjoyed. The boycott eventually demanded the end of segregated seating.

The *Brown* decision woke up all of America to racial injustice, but the Montgomery boycott marked a significant shift away from the historical reliance on NAACP court battles (Killian 1975).

Civil disobedience is based on the belief that people have the right to disobey the law under certain circumstances. This tactic was not new; it had been used before in India and also by Blacks in the United States. Under King's leadership, however, civil disobedience became a widely used technique and even gained a measure of acceptability among some prominent Whites. King distinguished clearly between the laws to be obeyed and those to be disobeyed: "A just law is a man-made law of God. An unjust law is a code that is out of harmony with the moral law" (1963, 82). In disobeying unjust laws, King (1958) developed this strategy:

- actively but nonviolently resisting evil,
- not seeking to defeat or humiliate opponents but to win their friendship and understanding,
- attacking the forces of evil rather than the people who happen to be doing the evil,
- being willing to accept suffering without retaliating,
- refusing to hate the opponent,
- acting with the conviction that the universe is on the side of justice (101–107)

King, like other Blacks before him and since, made it clear that passive acceptance of injustice was intolerable. He hoped that by emphasizing nonviolence, Southern Blacks would display their hostility to racism in a way that would undercut violent reaction by Whites.

The pattern had now been established and a method devised to confront racism. But civil disobedience did not work quickly. The struggle to desegregate buses in the South, for example, took 7 years. Civil disobedience was also not spontaneous. The success of the civil rights movement rested on a dense network of local efforts. People were spontaneously attracted to the efforts, but organized tactics and targets were crucial to dismantling racist institutions that had existed for generations (Payne 1995).

Beginning in April 1963, the Southern Christian Leadership Conference, founded by King, began a series of marches in Birmingham to demand fair employment opportunities, desegregation of public facilities, and the release of 3,000 people arrested for participating in the marches. King, himself arrested, tells in Listen to Our Voices why civil disobedience and the confrontations that followed were necessary. In May, the Birmingham police used dogs and water from high-pressure hoses on the marchers, who included many schoolchildren.

Congress had still failed to enact any sweeping federal barrier to discrimination. Following the example of A. Philip Randolph in 1941, Blacks organized the March on Washington for Jobs and Freedom on August 28, 1963. With more than 200,000 people participating, the march was the high point of the civil rights movement. The mass of people, middle-class Whites and Blacks looking to the federal government for support, symbolized the struggle. However, a public opinion poll conducted shortly before the march documented the continuing resentment of the majority of Whites: 63 percent were opposed to the rally (G. Gallup 1972).

King (1971, 351) delivered his famous "I Have a Dream" speech before the large crowd; he looked forward to a time when all Americans "will be able to join hands and sing in the words of the old Negro spiritual, 'Free at last! Free at last! Thank God Almighty, we are free at last!'" Just 18 days later, a bomb exploded in a Black church in Birmingham, killing four little girls and injuring 20 other people.

Despair only increased as the November 1963 elections saw segregationists successful in their bids for office. Most distressing was the assassination of President Kennedy on November 22. As president, Kennedy had appealed to Blacks despite his previously mediocre legislative record in the U.S. Senate. His death left doubt as to the direction and pace of future actions on civil rights by the executive branch under President Lyndon Baines Johnson. Two months later, however, the Twenty-Fourth Amendment was ratified, outlawing the poll tax that had long prevented Blacks from voting. The

civil disobedience
A tactic promoted by Martin Luther King, Jr., based on the belief that people have the right to disobey unjust laws under certain circumstances.

Listen to Our Voices

LETTER FROM BIRMINGHAM JAIL

You may well ask: "Why direct action? Why sit-ins, marches and so forth? Isn't negotiation a better path?" You are quite right in calling for negotiation. Indeed, this is the very purpose of direct action. Nonviolent direct action seeks to create such a crisis and foster such a tension that a community that has constantly refused to negotiate is forced to confront the issue. It seeks so to dramatize the issue that it can no longer be ignored. My citing the creation of tension as part of the work of the nonviolent-resister may sound rather shocking. But I must confess that I am not afraid of the word "tension." I have earnestly opposed violent tension, but there is a type of constructive, nonviolent tension which is necessary for growth. Just as Socrates felt that it was necessary to create a tension in the mind so that individuals could rise from the bondage of myths and half-truths to the unfettered realm of creative analysis and objective appraisal, so must we see the need for nonviolent gadflies to create the kind of tension in society that will help men rise from the dark depths of prejudice and racism to the majestic heights of understanding and brotherhood.

The purpose of our direct-action program is to create a situation so crisis-packed

Martin Luther King, Jr.

that it will inevitably open the door to negotiation. I therefore concur with you in your call for negotiation. Too long has our beloved Southland been bogged down in a tragic effort to live in monologue rather than dialogue. . . .

You express a great deal of anxiety over our willingness to break laws. This is certainly a legitimate concern. Since we so diligently urge people to obey the Supreme Court's decision of 1954 outlawing segregation in the public schools, at first glance it may seem rather paradoxical for us consciously to break laws. One may well ask: "How can you advocate breaking some laws and obeying others?" The answer lies in the fact that there are two types of laws: just and unjust. I would be the first to advocate obeying just laws. One has not only a legal but a moral responsibility to obey just laws. Conversely, one has a moral responsibility to disobey unjust laws. I would agree with St. Augustine that "an unjust law is no law at all."

Source: King Jr. Copyright © 1963 by Martin Luther King, Jr. Renewed 1991 by Coretta Scott King. Reprinted by arrangement with The Estate of Martin Luther King, Jr., c/o Writer's House as agents for the proprietor.

enactment of the Civil Rights Act on July 2, 1964, was hailed as a major victory and provided, at least for awhile, what historian John Hope Franklin called "the illusion of equality" (Franklin and Moss 2000).

In the months that followed the passage of the act, the pace of the movement to end racial injustice slowed. The violence continued, however, from the Bedford-Stuyvesant section of Brooklyn to Selma, Alabama. Southern state courts still found White murderers of Blacks innocent, and they had to be tried and convicted in federal civil, rather than criminal, court on the charge that by killing a person one violates that person's civil rights. Government records, which did not become public until 1973, revealed a systematic campaign by the FBI to infiltrate civil rights groups in an effort to discredit them in the belief that such activist groups were subversive. It was in such an atmosphere that the Voting Rights Act was passed in August 1965, but this significant, positive event was somewhat overshadowed by violence in the Watts section of Los Angeles in the same week (Blackstock 1976).

Urban Violence and Oppression

Riots involving Whites and Blacks did not begin in the 1960s. As we saw earlier in this chapter, urban violence occurred after World War I and even during World War II, and violence against Blacks in the United States is nearly 350 years old. But the urban riots of the 1960s influenced Blacks and Whites in the United States and throughout the world so extensively that they deserve special attention. However, we must remember that most violence between Whites and Blacks has not been large-scale collective action but has involved only a small number of people.

The summers of 1963 and 1964 were a prelude to riots that gripped the country's attention. Although most people knew of the civil rights efforts in the South and legislative victories in Washington, everyone realized that the racial problem was national after several cities outside the South experienced violent disorders. In April 1968, after the assassination of Martin Luther King, Jr., more cities exploded than had in all of 1967. Even before the summer of 1968 began, there were 369 civil disorders. Communities of all sizes were hit (Oberschall 1968).

As the violence continued and embraced many ghettos, a popular explanation was that riot participants were mostly unemployed youths who had criminal records, often involving narcotics, and who were vastly outnumbered by the African Americans who repudiated the looting and arson. This explanation was called the **riff-raff theory** or the rotten-apple theory because it discredited the rioters and left the barrel of apples, White society, untouched. On the contrary, research shows that the Black community expressed sympathetic understanding toward the rioters and that the rioters were not merely the poor and uneducated but included middle-class, working-class, and educated residents (Sears and McConahay 1969, 1973; Tomlinson 1969; R. Turner 1994).

Several alternatives to the riff-raff theory explain why Black violent protest increased in the United States at a time when the nation was seemingly committed to civil rights for all. Two explanations stand out. One ascribes the problem to Black frustration with rising expectations in the face of continued deprivation relative to Whites.

The standard of living of African Americans improved remarkably after World War II, and it continued to do so during the civil rights movement. However, White income and occupation levels also improved, so the gap between the groups remained. Chapter 3 showed that feelings of relative deprivation often are the basis for perceived discrimination. **Relative deprivation** is the conscious feeling of a negative discrepancy between legitimate expectations and current actualities (W. Wilson 1973).

It is of little comfort to African Americans that their earning power matches that of Whites 10 or more years earlier. As shown in Figure 7.4, Black family income has increased significantly, but so has that of White families, leaving the gap between the two largely unchanged. Relative to Whites, most Blacks made no tangible gains in housing, education, jobs, or economic security. African Americans were doing better in absolute numbers, but not relative to Whites.

At the same time that African Americans were feeling relative deprivation, they were also experiencing growing discontent. **Rising expectations** refers to the increasing sense of frustration that legitimate needs are being blocked. Blacks felt that they had legitimate aspirations to equality, and the civil rights movement reaffirmed that discrimination had blocked upward mobility. As the horizons of African

riff-raff theory
Also called the rotten-apple theory; the belief that the riots of the 1960s were caused by discontented youths rather than by social and economic problems facing all African Americans.

relative deprivation
The conscious experience of a negative discrepancy between legitimate expectations and present actualities.

rising expectations
The increasing sense of frustration that legitimate needs are being blocked.

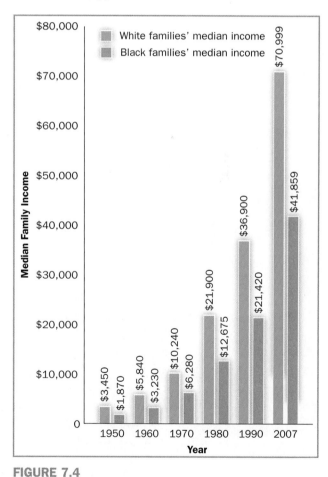

FIGURE 7.4
Black–White Income Gap

For the more than 50 years of available data, median Black family income has been only about half that of White family income.

Note: 2007 data are for White non-Hispanic households.

Sources: Bureau of the Census 1975, 297; 2002; DeNavas-Walt et al. 2008. HINC.

Americans broadened, they were more likely to make comparisons with Whites and feel discontented. The civil rights movement gave higher aspirations to Black America, yet for the majority, life remained basically unchanged. Not only were their lives unchanged but also the feeling was widespread that the existing social structure held no prospect for improvement (Garner 1996; Sears and McConahay 1970; Thomas and Thomas 1984).

Black Power

The riots in the Northern ghettos captured the attention of Whites, and Black Power was what they heard. Appropriately enough, Black Power was born not of Black but of White violence. On June 6, 1966, James Meredith was carrying out a one-person march from Memphis to Jackson, Mississippi, to encourage fellow African Americans to overcome their own fears and vote after the passage of the Voting Rights Act. During that march, an unidentified assailant shot and wounded Meredith. Blacks from throughout the country immediately continued the march. During the march, Stokely Carmichael of the Student Nonviolent Coordinating Committee proclaimed to a cheering Black crowd, "What we need is Black Power." King and others later urged "Freedom Now" as the slogan for the march. A compromise dictated that no slogan would be used, but the mood of Black America said otherwise (King 1967; Lomax 1971).

In retrospect, it may be puzzling that the phrase *Black Power* frightened Whites and offended so many Blacks. It was not really new. The National Advisory Commission on Civil Disorders (1968) correctly identified it as old wine in new bottles: Black consciousness was not new, even if the phrase was.

By advocating Black Power, Carmichael was distancing himself from the assimilationism of King. Carmichael rejected the goal of assimilation into White middle-class society. Instead, he said, Blacks must create new institutions. To succeed in this endeavor, Carmichael argued that Blacks must follow the same path as the Italians, Irish, and other

Since the riots of the 1960s, inner-city neighborhoods such as South Central Los Angeles (renamed South Los Angeles in 2003 to symbolically erase the stigma) have undergone only modest redevelopment, and much less than originally anticipated by the residents. Santa Ana Pines development, pictured here, is one of the few examples of economic investment in the community.

White ethnic groups. "Before a group can enter the open society, it must first close ranks . . . . Group solidarity is necessary before a group can operate effectively from a bargaining position of strength in a pluralistic society" (Ture and Hamilton 1992, 44). Prominent Black leaders opposed the concept; many feared that Whites would retaliate even more violently. King (1967) saw Black Power as a "cry of disappointment" but acknowledged that it had a "positive meaning."

Eventually Black Power gained wide acceptance among Blacks and even many Whites. Although it came to be defined differently by nearly every new proponent, support of Black Power generally implied endorsing Black control of the political, economic, and social institutions in Black communities. One reason for its popularity among African Americans was that it gave them a viable option for surviving in a segregated society. The civil rights movement strove to end segregation, but the White response showed how committed White society was to maintaining it. Black Power presented restructuring society as the priority item on the Black agenda (Carmichael and Thelwell 2003).

One aspect of Black Power clearly operated outside the conventional system. The Black Panther Party was organized in October 1966 in Oakland, California, by Huey Newton, age 24, and Bobby Seale, age 30, to represent urban Blacks in a political climate that the Panthers felt was unresponsive. The Panthers were controversial from the beginning, charging police brutality and corruption among government officials. They engaged in violent confrontations with law enforcement officers. From 1969 to 1972, internal weaknesses, a long series of trials involving most of its leaders, intraparty strife, and several shoot-outs with police combined to bring the organization to a standstill.

Although the Black Panthers were often portrayed as the most separatist of the Black militant movements, the Panthers were willing to form alliances with non-Black organizations, including Students for a Democratic Society, the Peace and Freedom Party, the Young Lords, the Young Patriots, and the Communist Party of the United States. Despite, or perhaps because of, such coalitions, the Panthers were not a prominent force in shaping contemporary Black America. Newton himself admitted in 1973 that the party had alienated Blacks and had become "too radical" to be accepted by the Black community (Cleaver 1982; Joseph 2006).

The militant Black Panthers encountered severe difficulties in the 1970s and fell victim to both internal political problems and external surveillance. The role of spokesperson for a minority group in the United States is exhausting, and people who have assumed that role for a time often turn to more conventional, less personally demanding roles, especially if public support for their programs wanes.

The Religious Force

It is not possible to overstate the role religion has played, good and bad, in the social history of African Americans. Historically, Black leaders have emerged from the pulpits to seek out rights on behalf of all Blacks. Churches have served as the basis for community organization in neighborhoods abandoned by businesses and even government. Religion may be a source of antagonism as well.

As we saw earlier in this chapter, because the Africans who were brought involuntarily to the Western hemisphere were non-Christian, they were seen as heathens and barbarians. To "civilize" the slaves in the period before the Civil War, Southern slaveholders encouraged and often required their slaves to attend church and embrace Christianity. The Christian churches to which Blacks were introduced in the United States encouraged them to accept the inferior status enforced by Whites, and the religious teaching that the slaves received equated Whiteness with salvation, presenting Whiteness as an acceptable, if not preferred, object of reverence.

Despite being imposed in the past by Whites, the Christian faiths are embraced by most African Americans today. As shown in Figure 7.5, African Americans are overwhelmingly Protestant, with the majority belonging to historically Black churches.

Du Bois (1996, 2003) wrote of the importance of the church in the Black community but was also critical that the church failed at times to be more than a social organization often stratified by class boundaries.

Black churches continue to be socially involved in their communities. About 12 percent of Black Americans, compared to 16 percent of Whites, indicated in a 2007 survey that they were religiously unaffiliated, atheistic, or agnostic. Even when upwardly mobile African Americans move out of the central city, many travel long distances to return to their congregations to support them financially and spiritually (Pew Forum on Religion and Public Life 2008; Watson 2004).

Despite their second-class status until well after World War II, African Americans have contributed to every war effort. Notable were the Tuskegee Airmen, an all-Black unit of pilots who flew during World War II and received numerous decorations for valor. Surviving members continue to gather in celebratory reunions.

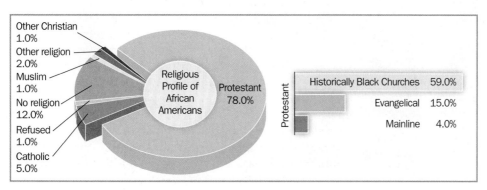

Other Christian 1.0%
Other religion 2.0%
Muslim 1.0%
No religion 12.0%
Refused 1.0%
Catholic 5.0%

Religious Profile of African Americans

Protestant 78.0%

Protestant:
Historically Black Churches	59.0%
Evangelical	15.0%
Mainline	4.0%

FIGURE 7.5
Religious Profile of African Americans 2007

Source: Pew Forum on Religion and Public Life, 2008.

However, a variety of non-Christian groups have exerted a much greater influence on African Americans than the reported numbers of their followers suggest. The Nation of Islam, for example, which became known as the Black Muslims, has attracted a large number of followers and received the most attention. We will look at this group in greater detail in Chapter 11 when we consider the large Muslim community in the United States.

The New Immigration

When they think of the upsurge of arrivals in the United States seeking permanent residency, most people imagine immigrants from Latin America and Asia. Yet another dramatic flow has come from Africa and the Caribbean. This is all the more dramatic because there had been little immigration of Black people to the United States for the first 100 years after the Civil War. Obviously, the world's Black population was acutely aware of how people of color had been treated in the United States. Furthermore, restrictive legislation made it difficult for people to immigrate from Africa.

Improved living conditions for Black people made the United States an attractive destination for Black people as it had been for generations for people from Europe. The increase is startling: from 125,000 foreign-born Blacks in 1960 to 816,000 in 1980 and to 2.8 million in 2005. About two-thirds were born in the Caribbean, with Jamaica and Haiti representing the majority. The other third of foreign-born Blacks are from Africa, with 30 percent born in either Nigeria or Ethiopia.

This new addition to the African American community is a diverse group, including newcomers who first came to study, others to join relatives, and some who came as refugees. They and their descendants are often not taking long to make their presence felt, as witnessed by Colin Powell, the son of Jamaican immigrants, and President Barack Obama, whose father was a Kenyan immigrant.

To many people in the United States, the sheer size of this group has gone unnoticed. This is probably because of the relative concentration of the immigrants in certain urban areas. Nearly two-thirds of Caribbean Blacks live in either the New York City or Miami–Fort Lauderdale metropolitan areas. African-born Blacks are more dispersed, but local efforts to make refugees feel welcome have led to selected settlement patterns in cities such as Minneapolis, where one out of five Blacks are African-born.

These new immigrants experience all the problems of transitioning into a new society experienced by other immigrants. Similarly, many foster ties to home and to fellow countrymen. Yet these Black immigrants are confronted by a society still deeply divided by race. Although they typically were aware of divisions before immigrating, trying to navigate racial formation as it has emerged often presents daily challenges to these newcomers (Bennett 2008; Kent 2007; Traoré 2008).

Especially in urban centers, recent immigrants from Africa have begun to provide a new diversity to the Black community in the United States. This Senegalese restaurateur is shown in front of her Philadelphia restaurant.

Conclusion

The dramatic events affecting African Americans today have their roots in the forcible bringing of their ancestors to the United States as slaves. In the South, whether as slaves or later as victims of Jim Crow, Blacks were not a real threat to any but the poorest Whites, although even affluent Whites feared the perceived potential threat that Blacks posed. During their entire history here, Blacks have been criticized when they rebelled and praised when they went along with the system. During the time of slavery, revolts were met with increased suppression; after emancipation, leaders who called for accommodation were applauded.

The Black migration to the urban North helped to define a new social order. Yet many of the communities in which they may have settled were sundown towns where the welcome mat had been replaced with covert and overt racism. Whites found it more difficult to ignore Blacks as residents of the ghetto than as sharecroppers in the rural South. No longer excluded by the White primary as in the South, the Black urban voter had potential power. The federal government and city halls slowly began to acknowledge the presence of Blacks. From the Black community came voices that spoke of pride and self-help: Douglass, Tubman, Washington, Du Bois, King, and Malcolm X.

Most people today look back at the civil rights movement and accept the significance of its legacy but, like so many things in society, Black and White perceptions differ. A national survey found that 46 percent of Whites, compared to 75 percent of Blacks, felt the movement was extremely important. Half of Whites felt that most of the goals of the civil rights movement have been achieved, while only 30 percent of African Americans were similarly convinced (Ludwig 2004).

Blacks, in their efforts to bring about change, have understandably differed in their willingness to form coalitions with Whites. African Americans who resisted in the days of either slavery or the civil rights movement (see the intergroup relations continuum in the figure at the bottom of this page) would have concurred with Du Bois's (1903) comment that a Black person "simply wishes to make it possible to be both a Negro and an American, without being cursed and spit upon by his fellows, without having the door of opportunity closed roughly in his face" (3–4). The object of Black protest seems simple enough, but for many people, including presidents, the point was lost.

How much progress has been made? When covering several hundred years, beginning with slavery and ending with rights recognized constitutionally, it is easy to be impressed. Yet let us consider Topeka, Kansas, the site of the 1954 *Brown v. Board of Education* case. Linda Brown, one of the original plaintiffs, was recently touched by another segregation case. In 1992, the courts held that Oliver Brown, her grandchild, was being victimized because the Topeka schools were still segregated, now for reasons of residential segregation. The remedy to separate schools in this Kansas city is still unresolved (Hays 1994).

Chapter 8 assesses the status of African Americans today. Recall the events chronicled in this chapter as you consider the advances that have been made. These events are a reminder that any progress has followed years—indeed, generations—of struggle by African Americans, enlisting the support of Whites seeking to end second-class status for African Americans in the United States.

SPECTRUM OF INTERGROUP RELATIONS

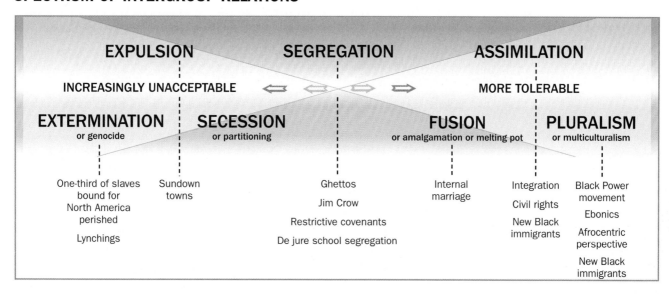

Summary

1. Slavery was a system that defined the people forcibly brought from Africa, and their descendants, as property of their masters with no rights, governed by a series of slave codes.

2. Despite the total restrictiveness of slavery as an institution, slaves often sought to resist the system as abolitionists worked for their freedom.

3. Throughout history, many individuals have emerged as leaders within the African American community. Particularly noteworthy were Booker T. Washington and W. E. B. Du Bois, both of whom, although they took different approaches, expressed dissatisfaction with the second-class status of being Black in America.

4. The end of slavery was followed by a long period of subjugation through the practice of Jim Crow and de jure segregation. Only gradually after *Brown v. Board of Education* did these practices begin to fade.

5. Major social change did not come voluntarily by White Americans but was granted in response to years of civil disobedience through the civil rights movement and the example set by Martin Luther King, Jr. The pace of change was limited, as reflected in the calls for Black Power that came from more-youthful members of the movement.

6. Although many White Americans felt that the civil rights movement had accomplished real change, this illusion was dramatically shattered as urban violence and growing militancy occurred not in the South, which had been the battleground of the civil rights movement, but in Northern central cities.

7. Historically, the church has been a major force in the Black community and continues to be a major part of the social culture.

8. A significant recent trend in the long history of Black people in the United States has been the increase in immigration from Africa and the Caribbean.

Key Terms

abolitionists 178
Afrocentric perspective 177
civil disobedience 187
de jure segregation 185
Ebonics 177

Jim Crow 180
relative deprivation 189
restrictive covenant 184
riff-raff theory 189
rising expectations 189

slave codes 175
slavery reparation 180
sundown towns 184
White primary 180

Review Questions

1. In what ways were slaves defined as property?
2. How did slavery provide a foundation for both White and Black America today?
3. If civil disobedience is nonviolent, then why has so much violence been associated with it?
4. How did observers of the urban riots tend to dismiss any social importance to the outbreaks?
5. Why has religion proved to be a force for both unity and disunity among African Americans?

Critical Thinking

1. How much time do you recall spending in school thus far learning about the history of Europe? How about Africa? What do you think this says about the way education is delivered or what we choose to learn?
2. What would you consider the three most important achievements in civil rights for African Americans since 1900? What roles did Whites and Blacks play in making these events happen?
3. Growing numbers of Blacks are immigrating to the United States (especially to the eastern United States) from the Caribbean. What impact might this have on what it means to be Black or African American in the United States? What would the social construction of race say about this development?

African Americans Today

AFRICAN AMERICANS HAVE MADE SIGNIFICANT PROGRESS IN many areas, but they have not kept pace with White Americans in many sectors. African Americans have advanced in formal schooling to a remarkable degree, although in most areas residential patterns have left many public schools predominantly Black or White. Higher education also reflects the legacy of a nation that has operated two schooling systems: one for Blacks and another for Whites. Gains in earning power have barely kept pace with inflation, and the gap between Whites and Blacks has remained largely unchanged. African American families are susceptible to the problems associated with a low-income group that also faces discrimination and prejudice. Housing in many areas remains segregated, despite growing numbers of Blacks in suburban areas. African Americans are more likely to be victims of crimes and to be arrested for violent crimes. The subordination of Blacks is also apparent in health care delivery. African Americans have made substantial gains in elective office but still are underrepresented compared with their numbers in the general population.

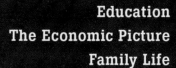

John and Glenn are alike in almost every way: about the same age, Big Ten college graduates, similar jobs, and active sports enthusiasts. But they find that they have very dissimilar experiences in such everyday activities as walking into a shopping mall to buy shoes or looking over the latest CDs. John typically receives instant attention when he walks even near the shoe department, but the same salesperson fails to acknowledge Glenn even though he has been waiting five minutes. A little later John casually picks up some CDs in a record store. At the very same time, Glenn is engaged in exactly the same behavior in the same store, but he is closely shadowed by a store employee, who observes Glenn's every move.

John is White and Glenn is Black, which makes all the difference even in this everyday shopping behavior. They were part of an experiment conducted by the television newsmagazine *Primetime Live* in St. Louis to assess the impact of race on the day-to-day lives of average African Americans and Whites. Over a period of three weeks, the program closely monitored the two researchers, who had been trained to present themselves in an identical manner in a variety of situations.

In a televised report on this experiment, *Primetime Live* host Diane Sawyer acknowledged that, at times, the two men were treated equally. However, Sawyer added that not once or twice but "every single day," there were instances of differential treatment. At an employment agency, Glenn was lectured on laziness and told that he would be monitored "real close." John, by contrast, was encouraged to pursue job leads, and staff members made it clear that he could expect to find a suitable position (ABC News 1992).

Race is socially constructed, but that does not mean that being Black does not have consequences and being White carries privileges. Despite the publicity given to obvious discrimination that has persisted well into the present, a superficial sense of complacency about the position of African Americans in the United States exists now in the twenty-first century.

As you read this chapter, try to keep in perspective the profile of African Americans in the United States today. This chapter will assess education, the economy, family life, housing, criminal justice, health care, and politics among the nation's African Americans. Progress has occurred, and some of the advances are nothing short of remarkable. The deprivation of the African American people relative to Whites remains, however, even if absolute deprivation has been softened. A significant gap remains between African Americans and the dominant group, and to this gap a price is assigned: the price of being African Americans in the United States.

Education

The African American population in the United States has placed special importance on acquiring education, beginning with its emphasis in the home of the slave family and continuing through the creation of separate schools for Black children because the public schools were closed to them by custom or law. Today, long after the old civil rights coalition has disbanded, education remains a controversial issue. Because racial and ethnic groups realize that formal schooling is the key to social mobility, they want to maximize this opportunity for upward mobility and, therefore, want better schooling. White Americans also appreciate the value of formal schooling and do not want to do anything that they perceive will jeopardize their own position.

Quality and Quantity of Education

Several measures document the inadequate education received by African Americans, starting with the quantity of formal education. The gap in educational attainment between

Blacks as a group and Whites as a group has always been present. Despite programs directed at the poor, such as Head Start, White children are still more likely to have formal prekindergarten education than are African American children. Later, Black children generally drop out of school sooner and, therefore, are less likely to receive high school diplomas, let alone college degrees. Table 8.1 shows the gap in the amount of schooling African Americans receive compared to Whites. It also illustrates progress in reducing this gap in recent years. Despite this progress, however, the gap remains substantial, with nearly twice the proportion of Whites holding a college degree as Blacks in 2007.

A second aspect of inadequate schooling, many educators argue, is that many students drop out of school because of the inadequacies of their education. Among the deficiencies noted have been insensitive teachers, poor counseling, overcrowded classes, and dilapidated school facilities.

Although several of these problems can be addressed with more adequate funding, some are stalemated by disagreements over what changes would lead to the best outcome. For example, there is significant debate among educators and African Americans in general over the content of curriculum that is best for minority students. Some schools have developed academic programs that take an Afrocentric perspective and immerse students in African American history and culture. Yet a few of these programs have been targeted as ignoring fundamentals. On other occasions, the Afrocentric curriculum has even been viewed as racist against Whites. The debates over a few controversial programs attract a lot of attention, clouding the widespread need to reassess the curriculum for racial and ethnic minorities.

Middle- and upper-class children occasionally face these barriers to a high-quality education, but they are more likely than the poor to have a home environment that is favorable to learning. Even African American schoolchildren who stay in school are not guaranteed equal opportunities in life. Many high schools do not prepare students who are interested in college for advanced schooling. The problem is that schools are failing

TABLE 8.1
Years of School Completed (Percentages of People 25 Years and Older)

	1960	1980	2007
COMPLETING HIGH SCHOOL (%)			
Black			
Male	18.2	50.8	81.8
Female	21.8	51.5	82.5
White			
Male	41.6	69.6	90.1
Female	44.7	68.1	91.0
COMPLETING COLLEGE (%)			
Black			
Male	2.8	8.4	18.0
Female	3.3	8.3	19.0
White			
Male	10.3	21.3	33.2
Female	6.0	13.3	30.6

Note: Data for Whites are for White non-Hispanics.

Source: Bureau of the Census 2005a, 147; 2007d.

to meet the needs of students, not that students are failing in school. Therefore, the problems with schooling were properly noted as a part of the past discrimination component of total discrimination illustrated in Figure 3.1 on page 63.

School Segregation

It has been more than 50 years since the U.S. Supreme Court issued its unanimous ruling in *Brown v. Board of Education of Topeka, Kansas* that separate educational facilities are inherently unequal. What has been the legacy of that decision? Initially, the courts, with the support of the federal government, ordered Southern school districts to end racial separation. But as attention turned to larger school districts, especially in the North, the challenge was to have integrated schools even though the neighborhoods were segregated. In addition, some city school districts were predominantly African American and Hispanic, surrounded by suburban school districts that were predominantly White. This type of school segregation, which results from residential patterns, is called **de facto segregation**.

Initially, courts sought to overcome de facto segregation just as they had de jure school segregation in the *Brown* case. Typically, students were bused within a school district to achieve racial balance, but in a few cases Black students were bused to predominantly White suburban schools and White children were bused into the city. In 1974, however, the Supreme Court ruled in *Millikin v. Bradley* that it was improper to order Detroit and the suburbs to have a joint metropolitan busing solution. These and other Supreme Court decisions have effectively ended initiatives to overcome residential segregation, once again creating racial isolation in the schools. Indeed, even in Topeka, one-third of the schools are segregated (Orfield et al. 1996).

Racial diversity in individual schools was still largely absent in schools in 2000. White students typically attend public schools that on the average are 80 percent White. Trend data since the 1960s indicate that public schools are increasingly becoming all White, all Black, or all Hispanic. New initiatives such as charter schools to provide better education, as well as increases in homeschooling, contribute to greater school segregation.

School segregation has been so enduring that the term *apartheid schools* has been coined to refer to schools that are all Black. An analysis released in 2003 by the Civil Rights Project of Harvard University documented that one in six of the nation's Black students attends an **apartheid school**, and this proportion rose to one out of four in the Northeast and Midwest. If there has been any trend, it is that the typical African American student was less likely to have White classmates in 2000 than in 1970 (Frankenberg et al. 2003; Renzulli and Evans 2005).

Although studies have shown positive effects of integration, a diverse student population does not guarantee an integrated, equal schooling environment. For example, **tracking** in schools, especially middle and high schools, intensifies segregation at the classroom level. Tracking is the practice of placing students in specific curriculum groups on the basis of test scores and other criteria. It also has the effect of decreasing White–Black classroom interaction as African American children are disproportionately assigned to general classes, and more White children are placed in college-preparatory classes. It is estimated that about 60 percent of elementary schools in the United States and about 80 percent of secondary schools use some form of tracking. Studies indicate that African American students are more likely than White students to be classified as learning disabled or emotionally disturbed. Although there are successes in public education, integration clearly is not one of them (Ellison 2008; Hallinan 2003).

Acting White, Acting Black, or Neither

A common view advanced by some educators is that the reason African Americans, especially males, do not succeed in school is that they do not want to be caught "**acting White**." That is, they avoid at all costs taking school seriously and do not accept the authority of teachers and administrators. Whatever the accuracy of such a generalization, acting White clearly shifts the responsibility of low school attainment from the school to the individual and,

de facto segregation
Segregation that is the result of residential patterns.

apartheid schools
All-Black schools.

tracking
The practice of placing students in specific curriculum groups on the basis of test scores and other criteria.

acting White
Taking school seriously and accepting the authority of teachers and administrators

therefore, can be seen as yet another example of blaming the victim. Acting White is also associated with speaking proper English or cultural preferences like listening to rock music rather than hip-hop (Ferguson 2007; Fordham and Ogbu 1986; Fryer 2006; Ogbu 2004; Ogbu with Davis 2003).

The issue of acting White sparks strong emotions. In 2004, comedian Bill Cosby sparked the latest round of debates on the subject in a NAACP-sponsored speech he made to mark the fiftieth anniversary of the *Brown* decision. He criticized Black families for tolerating their children not taking school seriously. Social scientists and pundits quickly weighed in not only to deal with the issue but also to question the appropriateness of a Black person criticizing other Blacks in public.

To what extent do Blacks not want to act White in the context of high achievers? Many scholars have noted that individuals' efforts to avoid looking like they want an education has a long history and is hardly exclusive to any one race. Students of all colors may hold back for fear of being accused of "too hardworking."

Back in the 1950s, one heard disparaging references to "teacher's pet" and "brown nosing." Does popularity come to high school debaters and National Honor Society students or to cheerleaders and athletes? Academic-oriented classmates are often viewed as social misfits, nerds, and geeks and are seen as socially inept even if their skill building will later make them more economically independent and often more socially desirable. For minority children, including African Americans, to take school seriously means they must overcome their White classmates' same desire to be cool and not a nerd. In addition, Black youth must also come to embrace a curriculum and respect teachers who are much less likely to look or sound like them (Chang and Demyan 2007; Ferguson 2007; Tyson et al. 2005).

Is there a difference between Black and White schoolchildren in achievement orientation? Although some people feel that African American youth avoid acting White, research points to no difference in this respect. Members of high school science clubs, whether Black or White, are equally likely to overcome being regarded as "geeks" or "nerds."

The acting-White thesis overemphasizes personal responsibility rather than structural features such as quality of schools, curriculum, and teachers. Therefore, it locates the source of Black miseducation—and by implication, the remedy—in the African American household. As scholar Michael Dyson (2005) observes, "When you think the problems are personal, you think the solutions are the same." If we could only get African American parents to encourage their children to work a little harder and act better (i.e., White), everything would be fine. As Dyson notes, "It's hard to argue against any of these things in the abstract; in principle such suggestions sound just fine."

Of course, not all Whites act White. To equate acting White with high academic achievement has little empirical or cultural support. Although more Whites between ages 18 and 19 are in school, the differences are modest—68 percent of Whites compared to 63 percent of Blacks. Studies comparing attitudes and performance show that Black students have the same attitudes—good and bad—about achievement as their White counterparts. Too often we tend to view White slackers who give a hard time to the advanced placement kids as "normal," but when low-performing African Americans do the same thing, it becomes a systemic pathology undermining everything good about schools. The primary stumbling block is not acting White or acting Black but being presented with similar educational opportunities (Bureau of the Census 2007a, 211; Downey 2008; Tough 2004; Tyson et al. 2005).

Higher Education

Higher education for Blacks reflects the same pattern: the overall picture of African American higher education is not promising. Although strides were made in the period after the civil rights movement, a plateau was reached in the mid-1970s. African Americans are more likely than Whites to be part-time students and to need financial aid, which began to be severely cut in the 1980s. They are also finding the social climate on predominantly White campuses less than positive. As a result, the historically Black colleges and universities (HBCUs) are once again playing a significant role in educating African Americans. For a century, they were the only real source of college degrees for Blacks. Then, in the 1970s, predominantly White colleges began to recruit African Americans. As of 2006, however, the 105 HBCUs still accounted for about one-quarter of all Black college graduates (White House Initiative 2006).

As shown in Table 8.1, although African Americans are more likely today to be college graduates, the upward trend has declined. Several factors account for this reversal in progress:

1. Reductions in financial aid and more reliance on loans than on grants-in-aid, coupled with rising costs, have tended to discourage students who would be the first members of their families to attend college.

2. Pushing for higher standards in educational achievement without providing remedial courses has locked out many minority students.

3. Employment opportunities, though slight for African Americans without some college, have continued to lure young people who must contribute to their family's income and who otherwise might have gone to college.

4. Negative publicity about affirmative action may have discouraged some African Americans from even considering college.

5. Attention to what appears to be a growing number of racial incidents on predominantly White college campuses has also been a discouraging factor.

Colleges and universities seem uneasy about these problems; publicly, the schools appear committed to addressing them.

There is little question that special challenges face the African American student at a college with an overwhelmingly White student body, faculty, advisors, coaches, and administrators. The campus culture may be neutral at best, and it is often hostile to members of racial minorities. The high attrition rate of African American students on predominantly White college campuses confirms the need for a positive environment.

Because fewer African Americans complete their higher education, fewer are available to fill faculty and administrative positions. This means that despite increases in the numbers of Blacks who enter college, there are no more, and perhaps fewer, role models in college classrooms for students from subordinate groups to see.

The disparity in schooling becomes even more pronounced at the highest levels, and the gap is not closing. Only 5.8 percent of all doctorates awarded in 2005 were to native-born African Americans, reflecting a modest increase from 3.9 percent in 1981 (Bureau of the Census 2007a, 185).

In summary, the picture of education for Black Americans is uneven—marked progress in absolute terms (much better educated than a generation ago), but relative to Whites the gap in educational attainment remains at all levels. Fifty years ago, the major issue appeared to be school desegregation, but the goal was to improve the quality of education received by Black schoolchildren. Today the concerns of African American parents and most educators are similar—quality education. W. E. B. Du Bois advanced the same point in 1935—that what a Black student needs "is neither segregated schools nor mixed schools. What he needs is Education" (335).

Thus far, few but now growing in numbers, African Americans are entering positions that few people of any color reach. Ayana Howard, with a doctorate in electrical engineering sits beside SmartNav, a prototype for the Mars rover, on a large-scale model of the planet at NASA's Jet Propulsion Laboratory in California.

The Economic Picture

The general economic picture for African Americans has been gradual improvement over the last 50 years, but this improvement is modest compared with that of Whites, whose standard of living has also increased. Therefore, in terms of absolute deprivation, African Americans are much better off today but have experienced much less significant improvement with respect to their relative deprivation to Whites on almost all economic indicators. We will consider income and wealth, employment, and African American–owned businesses.

Income and Wealth

There are two useful measures of the overall economic situation of an individual or household: income and wealth. **Income** refers to salaries, wages, and other money received; **wealth** is a more inclusive term that encompasses all of a person's material assets, including land and other types of property.

There is a significant gap between the incomes of Black and White households in the United States. As we saw in Figure 7.4 on page 189, Black income has been increasing steadily, but so has that of Whites. In 2007, the median income of Black families was $37,005, compared with $64,663 for White non-Hispanic households. Another way to consider the gap is that Black income today resembles that of Whites more than 10 years ago. This lag has been present since World War II. In Figure 8.1, we look at the overall distribution of Black and White household income. Even a casual glance at the figure will show very different income profiles for Blacks and Whites today.

The underside of the income picture is people trapped in poverty. In 2007, 19.5 percent of Black people lived below the poverty level, compared with 10.4 percent of White non-Hispanics. Low incomes are counterbalanced to some extent by Medicare, Medicaid, public assistance, and food stamps. However, that an African American family is three times more likely to be poor shows that social inequality is staggering (DeNavas-Walt et al. 2008, 22; G. Wilson 2007).

Wealth is more difficult to measure because it takes more effort to determine accurately how much people own and owe, as opposed to how much they earn in a given year. Yet wealth is very important in that it protects individuals against financial hardship and may offer a way to pass money or property to future generations, giving them a good start. On the other hand, the lack of wealth or even the presence of debt can place young people at a severe disadvantage as they seek to become independent.

The wealth picture in the United States shows even greater disparity between Whites and Blacks than does income. Sociologists Melvin Oliver and Thomas Shapiro (1996) drew on data from more than 12,000 households and conducted in-depth interviews with a range of Black and White families. There is clearly a significant difference in wealth patterns because generations of social inequality have left African Americans, as a group, unable to accumulate the kind of wealth that Whites, as a group, have. This is particularly true in the ability to own a home, most people's biggest asset.

income
Salaries, wages, and other money received.

wealth
An inclusive term encompassing all of a person's material assets, including land and other types of property.

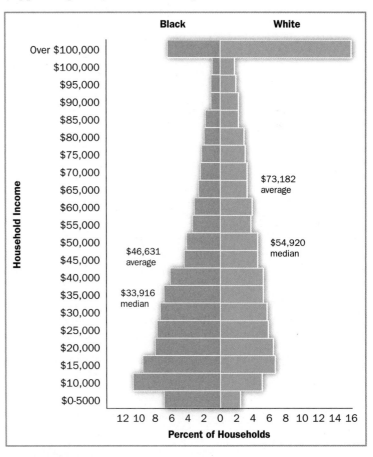

FIGURE 8.1

Income Distribution: Black versus White

Note: Income data for 2007 were reported in 2008, and these data are for White non-Hispanics.

Source: DeNavas-Walt et al. 2008:Table HINC-01.

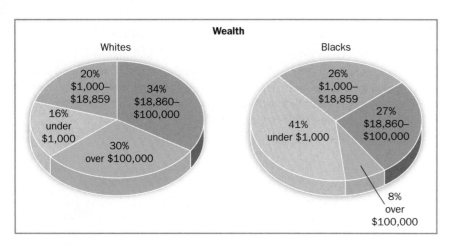

FIGURE 8.2
Wealth Distribution: Black versus White
Note: The wealth data for 1988 were reported in 1996.
Source: Oliver and Shapiro. Primetime Copyright © 1996. Reproduced by permission of Routledge/Taylor & Francis Books, Inc.

The inability of many Blacks to own a home and develop this asset results not only from lower incomes but also from discriminatory lending practices, which we consider later in this chapter. Of course, there are poor Whites and very rich Blacks, but the group differences that the researchers documented are unmistakable. The most striking differences are seen when we compare Blacks and Whites in their thirties and when we compare the most educated Blacks with the most educated Whites. Both the young adults and the more-educated African Americans would have benefited the most from efforts to reduce inequality, but the gap remains (Shapiro 2004).

As shown in Figure 8.2, most Whites are not in debt in terms of assets, and 30 percent have a net worth that is more than $100,000. In contrast, more than 40 percent of African Americans have a net worth of less than $1,000, with only 8 percent showing assets worth more than $100,000. Assets are valuable as a means to protect people from falling into poverty if all sources of income are interrupted. About 57 percent of all Whites can stay out of poverty for at least six months if all income ends, but only 17 percent of African Americans are in a similar situation.

Assets are important both to insulate households against short-term crises and to help other family members, whether for furthering their education, paying insurance premiums, buying the latest computer, or even starting to furnish their first home.

Employment

This precarious situation for African Americans—the lack of dependable assets—is particularly relevant as we consider their employment picture. Higher unemployment rates for Blacks have persisted since the 1940s, when statistics were first documented. Since 1990, the national unemployment rate for Whites has ranged from 3.5 percent to 5.2 percent, whereas for Blacks it has ranged from 7.6 percent to 11.4 percent. This means that, even in the best economic times, the Black unemployment rate is still significantly higher than it is for Whites during recessions. Obviously, when there is a national economic downturn, the results for the African American community are disastrous. Recessions take a heavy toll on African Americans (Bureau of the Census 2007a, 396).

The employment picture is especially grim for African American workers aged 16 to 24. Many live in the central cities and fall victim to the unrecorded, irregular—perhaps illegal—economy outlined in Chapter 3. Many factors have been cited by social scientists to explain why official unemployment rates for young African Americans exceed 30 percent:

■ many African Americans live in the depressed economy of the central cities,

■ immigrants and illegal aliens present increased competition,

■ White middle-class women have entered the labor force, and

■ illegal activities at which youths find they can make more money have become more prevalent.

None of these factors is likely to change soon, so depression-like levels of unemployment probably will persist.

The picture grows even more somber when we realize that we are considering only official unemployment. The federal government's Bureau of Labor Statistics counts as unemployed only people who are actively seeking employment. Therefore, to be counted as unemployed, a person must not hold a full-time job, must be registered with a government employment agency, and must be engaged in writing job applications and seeking interviews.

Quite simply, the official unemployment rate leaves out millions of Americans, Black and White, who are effectively unemployed. It does not count people so discouraged that they have temporarily given up looking for employment. The problem of unemployment is further compounded by **underemployment**, or working at a job for which one is overqualified, involuntarily working part time instead of full-time, or being employed only intermittently.

Studies continue to show the deepening plight economically for young Black men. In the nation's inner cities, especially, young Black men often lack necessary schooling and find appropriate jobs few and far between. In many cities, they face increased competition from immigrants who are often willing to accept jobs at low pay and without benefits or job security. The official unemployment rate for African American male high school dropouts is about 72 percent, well above the 25 percent jobless rate for the nation as a whole during the depression of the 1930s and the 34 percent unemployment rate of White dropouts. Again, such official statistics do not include youths who have dropped out of the system: those who are not at school, not at work, and not looking for a legitimate job. If we add to the official figures the discouraged job seeker, the rate of unemployment and underemployment of African American teenagers in central-city areas climbs to 90 percent (Eckholm 2006; W. Wilson 1996).

Although a few African Americans have crashed through the glass ceiling and made it into the top echelons of business or government, more have entered a wider variety of jobs. The taboo against putting Blacks in jobs in which they would supervise Whites has weakened, and the percentage of African Americans in professional and managerial occupations rose from 4 percent in 1949 to 8.4 percent in 2006, a remarkable improvement. However, most of this advancement came before 1980. Little advancement has occurred since then.

As shown in Table 8.2, African Americans, who constitute 13 percent of the population, are underrepresented in high-status, high-paying occupations. Less than 6 percent of lawyers, judges, physicians, financial managers, public relations specialists, architects, pharmacists, and dentists are African American. On the other hand, they account for more than 15 percent of cooks, health aides, hospital orderlies, maids, janitors, and stock handlers.

underemployment
Working at a job for which the worker is overqualified, involuntary working part time instead of full time, or being intermittently employed.

TABLE 8.2
Percentages of African American Employees in Selected Occupations, 1972 and 2006

Occupation	1972 (%)	2006 (%)
Engineers	2	5
Lawyers and judges	2	5
Physicians	3	5
Registered nurses	6	11
College teachers	4	7
Other teachers	8	9
Social workers	16	23
Managers	3	6
Sales workers	3	11
Service workers	17	16
Cleaners and servants	64	20
Firefighters	4	10
Police and detectives	8	15

Source: Bureau of the Census 2007a, 388–390.

Even when they enter highly paid, prestigious positions, Black men typically earn less than their White male colleagues in similar positions. For example, Black lawyers make 79 cents to the "White dollar" and 80 cents compared to White physicians. This is not to say they don't do well. African American physicians enjoy high wages—$134,000 annually in 2001—but this compares to $166,890 among White male physicians. Although they have high prestige, such professionals must build a client base, and a White professional is at an advantage as he seeks to gain the respect of high-paying, largely White potential clients (Grodsky and Pager 2001; Tran 2001).

Family Life

In its role as a social institution providing for the socialization of children, the family is crucial to its members' life satisfaction. The family also reflects the influence, positive or negative, of income, housing, education, and other social factors. For African Americans, the family reflects both amazing stability and the legacy of racism and low income across many generations.

Challenges to Family Stability

Although it is the conventional view that a female heads the typical African American family, most children are still in two-parent households. More than one-third of African American children had both a father and a mother present in 2007 (see Figure 8.3). Although single-parent African American families are common, they are not universal. In comparison, such single-parent arrangements were also present in about one in five White families.

It is as inaccurate to assume that a single-parent family is necessarily deprived as it is to assume that a two-parent family is always secure and happy. Nevertheless, life in a single-parent family can be extremely stressful for all single parents and their children and not just for those who are members of subordinate groups. Because the absent parent is more often the father, the lack of a male presence almost always means the lack of a male income. This monetary impact on a single-parent household cannot be overstated (A. Hacker 1995; Tucker and Mitchell-Kernan 1995).

For many single African American women living in poverty, having a child is an added burden. However, the tradition of extended family among African Americans eases this burden somewhat. The absence of a husband does not mean that no one shares in child

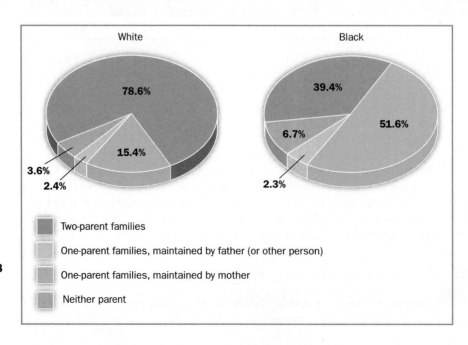

FIGURE 8.3
Living Arrangements for Children Younger Than 18
Note: Data for 2007 reported in 2008.

Source: Bureau of the Census 2008c, Table C3.

care: out-of-wedlock children born to Black teenage mothers live with their grandparents and form three-generation households.

No one explanation accounts for the rise in single-parent households. Sociologists attribute the rapid expansion in the number of such households primarily to shifts in the economy that have kept Black men, especially in urban areas, out of work. The phenomenon certainly is not limited to African Americans. Increasingly, both unmarried White and Black women bear children. More and more parents, both White and Black, divorce, so even children born into a two-parent family might end up living with only one parent.

Strengths of African American Families

In the midst of ever-increasing single parenting, another picture of African American family life becomes visible: success despite discrimination and economic hardship. Robert Hill (1999), of the National Urban League and Morgan State University, listed the following five strengths of African American families that allow them to function effectively in a hostile (racist) society.

1. *Strong kinship bonds*: Blacks are more likely than Whites to care for children and the elderly in an extended family network.

2. *A strong work orientation*: poor Blacks are more likely to be working, and poor Black families often include more than one wage earner.

3. *Adaptability of family roles*: in two-parent families, the egalitarian pattern of decision making is the most common. The self-reliance of Black women who are the primary wage earners best illustrates this adaptability.

4. *Strong achievement orientation*: working-class Blacks indicate a greater desire for their children to attend college than do working-class Whites. Even a majority of low-income African Americans want to attend college.

5. *A strong religious orientation*: since the time of slavery, Black churches have been the impetus behind many significant grassroots organizations.

Social workers and sociologists have confirmed through social research the strengths that Hill noted first in 1972. In the African American community, these are the sources of family strength (Hudgins 1992).

Increasingly, social scientists are learning to look at both the weaknesses and the strengths of African American family life. Expressions of alarm about instability date back to 1965, when the Department of Labor issued the report *The Negro Family: The Case for National Action*. The document, commonly known as the Moynihan Report, after its principal author, sociologist Daniel Patrick Moynihan, outlined a "tangle of pathology" with the Black family at its core. More recently, two studies—the Stable Black Families Project and the National Survey of Black Americans—sought to learn how Black families encounter problems and resolve them successfully with internal resources such as those that Hill outlined in his highly regarded work (Department of Labor 1965; Furstenberg 2007).

The most consistently documented strength of African American families is the presence of an extended family household. The most common feature is having grandparents residing in the home. Extended living arrangements are much more common among Black households than among White ones. These arrangements are recognized as having the important economic benefit of pooling limited economic resources. Because of the generally lower earnings of African American heads of household, income from second, third, and even fourth wage earners is needed to achieve a desired standard of living or, in all too many cases, simply to meet daily needs (Bryson and Casper 1999).

The African American Middle Class

Many characterizations of African American family life have been attacked because they overemphasize the poorest segment of the African American community. An opposite error

Family reunions are important annual events for many African Americans.

is the exaggeration of the success African Americans have achieved. Social scientists face the challenge of avoiding a selective, one-sided picture of Black society. The problem is similar to viewing a partially filled glass of water. Does one describe it as half empty and emphasize the need for assistance? Or does one describe the glass as half full to give attention to what has been accomplished? The most complete description would acknowledge both perspectives (Gouldner 1970).

A clearly defined African American middle class has emerged. In 2007, nearly one-quarter of African Americans earned more than the median income for White non-Hispanics. At least 23 percent of Blacks, then, are middle class or higher. Many observers have debated the character of this middle class. E. Franklin Frazier (1957), a Black sociologist, wrote an often critical study of the African American middle class in which he identified its overriding goal as achieving petty social values and becoming acceptable to White society (DeNavas-Walt et al. 2008, PINC-03).

African Americans are still aware of their racial subordination even when they have achieved economic equality. The Black middle class may not be militant, but its newest members do not forget their roots. They are more likely than Whites to be first-generation middle class, dependent on two or more sources of income, and precariously close to the lower class both financially and residentially. Yet with their relative success has come a desire to live in better surroundings. The migration of middle-class African Americans out of the ghetto in the 1970s and 1980s has left a vacuum. They may still care about the problems of the Black poor, but they are no longer present as role models.

Directing attention to the Black middle class also requires that we consider the relative importance of race and social class The degree to which affluent Blacks identify themselves in class terms or racial terms is an important ideological question. W. E. B. Du Bois (1952) argued that . . . argued that when racism decreases, class issues become more important. As Du Bois saw it, exploitation would remain, and many of the same people would continue to be subordinate. Black elites might become economically successful, either as entrepreneurs (Black capitalists) or professionals (Black white-collar workers), but they would continue to identify with and serve the dominant group's interest.

In the Listen to Our Voices box, sociologist Mary Pattillo describes the tension across social class boundaries as a Black neighborhood on Chicago's South Side experiences gentrification as more affluent African Americans move into a neighborhood that for a generation had been economically depressed.

class
As defined by Max Weber, people who share similar levels of wealth.

Social scientists have long recognized the importance of class. **Class** is a term used by sociologist Max Weber to refer to people who share a similar level of wealth and income. The significance of class in people's lives is apparent to all. In the United States today,

Listen to Our Voices

DIVIDED

"No more blacks." That was the forecast of a resident of the Oakland community when asked about the future of her South Side neighborhood.

"No more blacks?" I responded, worried in no small part because my research is about black gentrification.

Mary Pattillo

"[A] couple of blacks" would be left, the woman then allowed. "They got money." . . .

The gentrifying black middle and upper classes recognize a shared history of oppression and the lingering effects of racism. They tend to be grounded by an upbringing to more humble black surroundings. Yet our society prizes individual success. It promoted aspirations to one day becomes The Man.

This creates a tension that few in the white middle class know much about. It tears at the middleman's allegiances and alliances. And it means that, sometimes, in the pursuit of racial solidarity, we black professionals act in ways contrary to our own interests.

For example, by deciding to move into North Kenwood-Oakland, many black professionals pit their class and racial interests against each other: Wanting to take part in the renaissance of a historic black community, many sacrifice the greater home value and appreciation that would more reliably come from buying in whiter areas of the city.

Source: Pattillo 2008.

roughly half the lower-class population suffers from chronic health conditions that limit their activity, compared with only one in 11 among the affluent. The poor are more likely to become victims of crime, and they are only about half as likely as the affluent to send their children to colleges or vocational schools. When considering class difference, remarkable similarities exist in child-rearing practices between Black and White households (Lareau 2002).

The complexity of the relative influence of race and class was apparent in the controversy surrounding the publication of sociologist William J. Wilson's *The Declining Significance of Race* (1980). Pointing to the increasing affluence of African Americans, Wilson concluded that "class has become more important than race in determining black life-chances in the modern world" (150). The policy implications of his conclusion are that programs must be developed to confront class subordination rather than ethnic and racial discrimination. Wilson did not deny the legacy of discrimination reflected in the disproportionate number of African Americans who are poor, less educated, and living in inadequate and overcrowded housing. However, he pointed to "compelling evidence" that young Blacks were competing successfully with young Whites.

Critics of Wilson comment that focusing attention on this small educated elite ignores vast numbers of African Americans relegated to the lower class (Pinkney 1984; Willie 1978, 1979). Wilson himself was not guilty of such an oversimplification and indeed expressed concern over the plight of lower-class, inner-city African Americans as they seemingly fall even further behind, like those who become a part of the irregular economy discussed in Chapter 3. He pointed out that the poor are socially isolated and have shrinking economic opportunities (1988, 1996). However, it is easy to conclude superficially that because educated Blacks are entering the middle class, race has ceased to be of concern.

Zoning laws that may stipulate expensive building materials help keep out the less affluent, who are more likely to be African American home buyers.

Housing

Housing plays a major role in determining the quality of a person's life. For African Americans, as for Whites, housing is the result of personal preferences and income. However, African Americans differ from Whites in that their housing has been restricted through discrimination in a manner that it has not for Whites. We devote significant attention to housing because, for most people, housing is critical to their quality of life and often represents their largest single asset.

Although Black housing has improved—as indicated by statistics on home ownership, new construction, density of living units, and quality as measured by plumbing facilities—African Americans remain behind Whites on all these standards. The quality of Black housing is inferior to that of Whites at all income levels, yet Blacks pay out a larger proportion of their income for shelter.

Housing was the last major area to be covered by civil rights legislation. The delay was not caused by its insignificance; quite the contrary, it was precisely because housing touches so many parts of the American economy and relates to private property rights that legislators were slow to act. After an executive order by President Kennedy, the government required nondiscrimination in federally assisted housing, but this ruling included only 7 percent of the housing market. In 1968, the federal Fair Housing Act (Title VIII of the 1968 Civil Rights Act) and the U.S. Supreme Court decision in *Jones v. Mayer* combined to outlaw all racial discrimination in housing. Enforcement has remained weak, however, and many aspects of housing, real estate customs, and lending practices remain untouched.

Residential Segregation

Typically in the United States, as noted, White children attend predominantly White schools, Black children attend predominantly Black schools, and Hispanic children attend predominantly Hispanic schools. This school segregation is not only the result of the failure to accept busing but also the effect of residential segregation. In their studies on segregation, Douglas Massey and Nancy Denton (1993) concluded that racial separation "continues to exist because white America has not had the political will or desire to dismantle it." (8). In Chapter 1, we noted the pervasiveness of residential segregation as reflected in Census 2000 (refer back to Figure 1.5). This racial isolation in neighborhoods has not improved since the beginnings of the civil rights movement in the 1950s (Massey 2008).

What factors create residential segregation in the United States? Among the primary factors are the following:

- Because of private prejudice and discrimination, people refuse to sell or rent to people of the "wrong" race, ethnicity, or religion.
- The prejudicial policies of real estate companies steer people to the "correct" neighborhoods.
- Government policies enforce antibias legislation ineffectively.
- Public housing policies today, as well as past construction patterns, reinforce housing for the poor in inner-city neighborhoods.
- Policies of banks and other lenders create barriers based on race to financing home purchasing.

This last issue of racial-basis financing deserves further explanation. In the 1990s, new attention was given to the persistence of **redlining**, the practice of discrimination against people trying to buy homes in minority and racially changing neighborhoods. As we noticed in Listen to Our Voices in Chapter 3, Patricia Williams eloquently spoke about her being a victim of discrimination in housing lending practices.

It is important to recall the implications of this discrimination in home financing for the African American community. Earlier in the chapter, we noted the great disparity between

redlining
The pattern of discrimination against people trying to buy homes in minority and racially changing neighborhoods.

Black and White family wealth and the implications this had for both the present and future generations. The key factor in this inequality was the failure of African Americans to accumulate wealth through home buying. Now we see that discrimination plays a documented role in this barrier: in 2007, 47.2 percent of Blacks were homeowners, compared with 75.2 percent of White non-Hispanics (Bureau of the Census 2007e).

A dual housing market is part of today's reality, although attacks continue against the remaining legal barriers to fair housing. In theory, **zoning laws** are enacted to ensure that specific standards of housing construction will be satisfied. These regulations can also separate industrial and commercial enterprises from residential areas. However, some zoning laws in suburbs have seemed to curb the development of low- and moderate-income housing that would attract African Americans who want to move out of the central cities.

For years, the construction of low-income public housing in the ghetto has furthered racial segregation. The courts have not ruled consistently in this matter in recent years so, as with affirmative action, public officials lack clear guidance. Even if court decisions continue to dismantle exclusionary housing practices, the rapid growth of integrated neighborhoods is unlikely. In the future, African American housing probably will continue to improve and remain primarily in all-Black neighborhoods. This gap is greater than can be explained by differences in social class.

Criminal Justice

A complex, sensitive topic affecting African Americans is their role in criminal justice. It was reported in 2007 that Blacks constitute 5 percent of all lawyers, 14.9 percent of police officers, 17.6 percent of detectives, and 29.8 percent of security guards but 39 percent of jail inmates.

Data collected annually in the FBI's Uniform Crime Report show that Blacks account for 28 percent of arrests, even though they represent only about 13 percent of the nation's population. Conflict theorists point out that the higher arrest rate is not surprising for a group that is disproportionately poor and, therefore, much less able to afford private attorneys, who might be able to prevent formal arrests from taking place. Even more significantly, the Uniform Crime Report focuses on index crimes (mainly property crimes), which are the type of crimes most often committed by low-income people.

These numbers are staggering but, as dramatic as they are, it is not unusual to hear exaggerations presented as facts, such as "more Black men are in prison than in college." The reality is sobering enough. About one in 16 White males can expect to go to a state or federal prison during his lifetime, yet for Black males this lifetime probability is one out of three (Bureau of the Census 2007a, 202, 339, 389; Gaines 2005).

Most (actually 70 percent) of all the violent crimes against Whites are perpetrated by Whites, according to the FBI. In contrast to popular misconceptions about crime, African Americans and the poor are especially likely to be the victims of serious crimes. This fact is documented in **victimization surveys**, which are systematic interviews of ordinary people carried out annually to reveal how much crime occurs. These Department of Justice statistics show that African Americans are 35 percent more likely to be victims of violent crimes than are Whites (Catalano 2006).

Central to the concern that minorities often express about the criminal justice system is **differential justice**—that is, Whites are dealt with more leniently than are Blacks, whether at the time of investigation, arrest, indictment, conviction, sentencing, incarceration, or parole. Studies demonstrate that police often deal with African American youths more harshly than with White youngsters. Law is a public social institution and in many ways reproduces the inequality experienced in life (Rosich 2007; Sandefur 2008).

There is also a reluctant acceptance that the government cannot be counted on to address inner-city problems. In crimes involving African Americans, scholars of the legal system have observed **victim discounting**, or the tendency to view crime as less socially significant if the victim is viewed as less worthy. For example, the numerous killings of Black youth going to and from school attracts much less attention than a shooting spree that takes five lives in a suburban school. When a schoolchild walks into a cafeteria or schoolyard with automatic weapons and kills a dozen children and

zoning laws
Legal provisions stipulating land use and the architectural design of housing, often used to keep racial minorities and low-income people out of suburban areas.

victimization surveys
Annual attempts to measure crime rates by interviewing ordinary citizens who may or may not have been crime victims.

differential justice
Whites being dealt with more leniently than Blacks, whether at the time of arrest, indictment, conviction, sentencing, or parole.

victim discounting
Tendency to view crime as less socially significant if the victim is viewed as less worthy.

Research Focus

MEDICAL APARTHEID

Even when medical care is accessible, numerous studies have documented the reluctance of African Americans to trust the medical establishment. Whether it's seeking medical care or even donating blood or signing up for organ donation programs, Black Americans are underrepresented.

There is good reason—a long history of mistreatment up to the present. Some is the result of explicit discrimination—banned from medical schools, denied access to "White blood" as soldiers in the military until after World War II, and even, until the 1960s, prohibited from joining the American Medical Association. But it has more to do with the way Black Americans have been looked upon.

Many people, White as well as Black, are familiar with the notorious Tuskegee syphilis study. In this federal government study, which began in 1932, Black men in Alabama were deliberately infected with syphilis so that researchers could observe the progression of the disease. Despite the discovery of effective treatments in 1945, the men were not given any medical assistance until the press uncovered the program in 1972. Such events caused contemporary African Americans to be particularly leery of the medical establishment.

Regrettably, this was neither an isolated incident nor the first or last abuse of African Americans with respect to health care. For generations, the role of medical practitioners with respect to people of color was either to verify their worth as slaves or to determine for their masters whether their property was really sick or just trying to get out of doing slave labor.

A 1991 experiment implanted the now-defunct birth control device Norplant into African American teenagers in Baltimore in a program that was applauded by some observers as a way to "reduce the underclass." From 1992 to 1997, Columbia University undertook a study that sought to determine whether there is a biological or genetic basis that might cause violent behavior to run in families—and all the boys recruited for the study were Black. Researchers had misled the parents, claiming their children were simply coming in for a series of tests and questions when, in fact, they were given potentially risky doses of the same drug found in the controversial Fen-pfen weight loss pill, which was later banned when it was found to have caused heart irregularities.

All of these episodes make the Black community's suspicions of medicine fairly understandable—but perhaps most telling has been the actual avoidance of the community when it should have been considered. Only 1 percent of the nearly 20 million Americans enrolled in biomedical studies or clinical trials are Black. This means that African Americans have often missed out on the latest breakthroughs. For example, virtually no Blacks were included in the original studies of the HIV inhibitor AZT, so when the drug came into widespread use in 1991, the Food and Drug Administration had little evidence of its impact on Blacks and erroneously reported that it was not effective for Black patients.

Sources: Centers for Disease Control and Prevention 2007; Head 2007; Jecker 2000; Reverby 2000; H. Washington 2007.

teachers, it becomes a case of national alarm, as with Columbine. When children kill each other in drive-by shootings, it is viewed as a local concern, reflecting the need to clean up a dysfunctional neighborhood. Many African Americans note that the main difference between these two situations is not the death toll but who is being killed: middle-class Whites in the schoolyard shootings and Black ghetto youth in the drive-bys.

Health Care

The price of being an African American took on new importance with the release of a shocking study in a prestigious medical journal revealing that two-thirds of boys in Harlem, a predominantly Black neighborhood in New York City, can expect to die young or in mid-adulthood—that is, before they reach age 65. In fact, they have less chance of surviving even to age 45 than their White counterparts nationwide have of reaching age 65. The medical researchers noted that it is not the stereotyped images of AIDS and violence that explain the staggering difference. Black men are much more likely to fall victim to unrelenting stress, heart disease, and cancer (Fing et al. 1996).

The morbidity and mortality rates for African Americans as a group, and not just Harlem men, are equally distressing. Compared with Whites, Blacks have higher death rates from diseases of the heart, pneumonia, diabetes, and cancer. The death rate from strokes was twice as high among African Americans as for Whites. Such epidemiologic findings reflect in part the higher proportion of Blacks found among the nation's lower classes. White Americans can expect to live 75.7 years if male and 80.8 years if female. By contrast, life expectancy for African Americans is only 69.5 years for males and 76.5 years for females (National Center for Health Statistics 2007, Table 27).

Drawing on the conflict perspective, sociologist Howard Waitzkin (1986) suggests that racial tensions contribute to the medical problems of African Americans. In his view, the stress resulting from racial prejudice and discrimination helps to explain the higher rates of hypertension found among African Americans (and Hispanics) than among Whites. Death resulting from hypertension is twice as common in Blacks as in Whites; it is believed to be a critical factor in Blacks' high mortality rates from heart disease, kidney disease, and strokes. Although medical experts disagree, some argue that the stress resulting from racism and suppressed hostility exacerbates hypertension among African Americans (Cooper et al. 1999; A. Green et al. 2007).

A very troubling history of how the medical establishment has treated African Americans in the United States continues to have implications for health care delivery today, as we consider in this chapter's Research Focus, "Medical Apartheid."

Related to the health care dilemma is the problem of environmental justice, which was introduced in Chapter 3 and again in Chapter 6 with reference to Native Americans. Problems associated with toxic pollution and hazardous garbage dumps are more likely to be faced by low-income Black communities than by their affluent counterparts. This disproportionate exposure to environmental hazards can be viewed as part of the complex cycle of discrimination faced by African Americans and other subordinate groups in the United States.

Just how significant is the impact of poorer health on the lives of the nation's less-educated people, less-affluent classes, and subordinate groups? Drawing on a variety of research studies, population specialist Evelyn Kitagawa (1972) estimated the "excess mortality rate" to be 20 percent. In other words, 20 percent more people were dying than otherwise might have because of poor health linked to race and class. Using Kitagawa's model, we can calculate that if every African American in the United States were White and had at

A NATIONAL ACADEMY OF SCIENCE'S INSTITUTE OF MEDICINE REPORT FINDS MINORITIES ARE LESS LIKELY TO RECEIVE PROPER MEDICAL CARE THAN WHITES.

...BACK OF THE AMBULANCE, BUB!...

U.S. HEALTH CARE SYSTEM

AMBULANCE

www.cagle.com
©2002

Jeff Parker of Florida Today, April 9, 2002

gerrymandering
Redrawing districts
bizarrely to create
politically advantageous
outcomes.

least one year of college education, some 57,000 fewer Blacks would have died in 2007 and in each succeeding year (author's estimate based on Bureau of the Census 2007a).

Politics

Despite, Barack Obama entering the White House as president in 2009, African Americans have not received an equal share of the political pie. After Reconstruction, it was not until 1928 that a Black was again elected to Congress. Now, more than 70 years and several civil rights acts later, there are still only 38 African American congressional representatives. With Obama's election to the presidency, there is once again no African American elected to the U.S. Senate. Recent years have brought some improvement. In fact, between 1970 and 2002, the number of Black elected officials has increased more than fivefold (Figure 8.4).

Obama's electoral victory was impressive, and while not a landside victory, his winning margin enjoyed widespread support. Expectedly, he had 95 percent of Black voters backed Obama, but he also had 6 percent of all voters under 30 and 69 percent of first-time voters were prepared to vote for the first African American president (Connelly 2008).

Yet there are major problems in the continued success of African American politicians. Locally elected Black officials find it difficult to make the jump to statewide office. Voters, particularly non-Black voters, have difficulty seeing Black politicians as anything other than representatives of the Black community and express concern that the views of Whites and other non-Blacks will not be represented by an African American.

The political gains by African Americans, as well as Hispanics, had been placed in jeopardy by legal actions that questioned race-based districts. Boundaries for elective office, ranging from city council positions to the U.S. House of Representatives, have been drawn in such a way so as to concentrate enough members of a racial or ethnic group to create a "safe majority" to make it likely a member of that group will get elected.

The creation of these minority districts redrawn in this manner raised cries of **gerrymandering**. A practice dating from 1810, gerrymandering is the bizarre outlining of districts to create politically advantageous outcomes. Although creating race-based districts may seem discriminatory, boundaries have routinely been drawn based on a commonality of interests, such as rural versus urban interests, or even to maximize the likelihood of electing

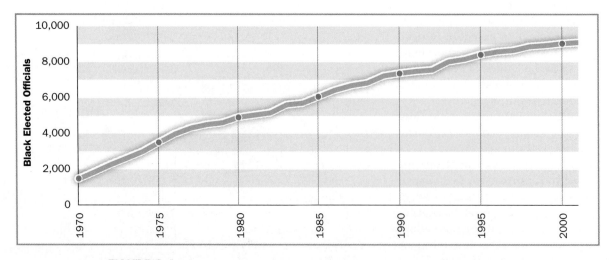

FIGURE 8.4
Black Elected Officials, 1970–2002
Although the rate of increase has leveled off, the number of Black elected officials has steadily increased over three decades.

Source: Reprinted by permission of the Joint Center for Political and Economic Studies.

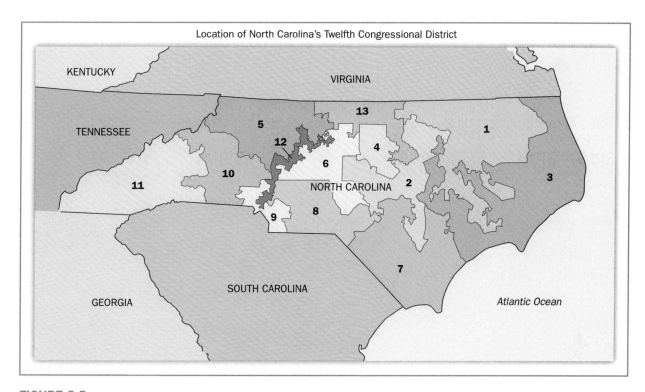

FIGURE 8.5
Developing a Minority District: North Carolina's Twelfth

In areas with a history of keeping African Americans from voting, courts have approved oddly drawn districts to increase the likelihood of a Black being elected to office. The twelfth congressional district in North Carolina zigzags along Interstate 85 from Charlotte to Winston-Salem to create a district that is 45 percent Black and has consistently elected a Black candidate to the U.S. House of Representatives.

a representative from a certain political party. For more than a decade, the legality of these actions has been debated; finally, in 2003, the Supreme Court ruled 5–4 that a state might consider overall minority influence in the political process. In Figure 8.5, we look at the admittedly bizarre shape of one congressional district.

In 2006, President George W. Bush signed into law the Fannie Lou Hamer, Rosa Parks, and Coretta Scott King Voting Rights Reauthorization and Amendments Act of 2006. Congress and the president rejected attempts to dilute the original intent of the bill and passed a "clean" reauthorization bill that renews key provisions of the Voting Rights Act, dating back to 1965, that would have otherwise expired in 2007. For example, one potent provision requires jurisdictions, whether a school district or an entire state, with significant histories of discrimination in voting to get federal approval of any new voting practices or procedures and to show that these procedures do not have a discriminatory purpose or effect.

The changing racial and ethnic landscape can be expected to have an impact on future strategies to elect African Americans to office, especially in urban areas. However, now that the number of Hispanics exceeds the number of Blacks nationwide, observers wonder how this might play out in the political world. A growing number of major cities, including Los Angeles and Chicago, are witnessing dramatic growth in the Hispanic population. Latinos often settle near Black neighborhoods or even displace Blacks who move out into suburbs, making it more difficult to develop safe African American districts. For example, South Central Los Angeles, the site of rioting in 1992 described in the previous chapter, is now largely a Latino neighborhood. The full impact has not been felt yet because the Latino population tends to be younger, with many not yet reaching voting age. Even more significant, many Latino adults have not yet obtained their citizenship. As the Hispanic population becomes eligible to vote, the impact is going to be particularly felt by African Americans, who have just begun to enjoy success in local elections.

SPECTRUM OF INTERGROUP RELATIONS

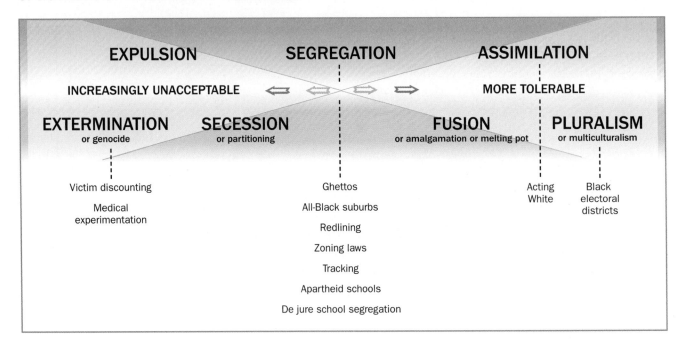

Conclusion

Black and White Americans have dealt with the continued disparity between the two groups by endorsing several ideologies, as shown in the figure above. Assimilation was the driving force behind the civil rights movement, which sought to integrate Whites and Blacks into one society. People who rejected contact with the other group endorsed separatism. As Chapter 2 showed, both Whites and Blacks generally lent little support to separatism. In the late 1960s, the government and various Black organizations began to recognize cultural pluralism as a goal, at least paying lip service to the desire of many African Americans to exercise cultural and economic autonomy. Perhaps on no other issue is this desire for control more evident than in the schools.

Twice in this nation's history, African Americans have received significant attention from the federal government and, to some degree, from the larger White society. The first period extended from the Civil War to the end of Reconstruction. The second period was during the civil rights movement of the 1960s. In both periods, the government acknowledged that race was a major issue, and society made commitments to eliminate inequality. As noted in Chapter 7, Reconstruction was followed by decades of neglect, and on several measures the position of Blacks deteriorated in the United States. Although the 1980s and 1990s were not without their successes, race is clearly not a major issue on today's national agenda. Even inner-city violence only diverts much of the nation's attention for a few fleeting moments, whereas attacks on school integration and affirmative action persist.

The gains that have been made are substantial, but will the momentum continue? Improvement has occurred in a generation inspired and spurred on to bring about change. If the resolve to continue toward that goal lessens in the United States, then the picture may become bleaker, and the rate of positive change may decline further.

Summary

1. African Americans have made gains in all levels of formal schooling but still fall behind the gains made by others. Debate continues over the appropriateness of the notion that Black youths avoid appearances of acting White.
2. Income and wealth disparities persist between Black and White Americans, with African Americans facing the challenge of accumulating assets.
3. Typically, Black Americans are underrepresented in high-wage, high-status occupations and overrepresented in low-wage, low-status occupations.
4. Family life among Black Americans has many identifiable strengths. A particular challenge faces the growing proportion of households that are moving into the middle class.
5. While de jure segregation has faded, residential segregation persists.
6. Blacks are more likely to be victims of crime as well as more likely to be arrested and imprisoned. Critics question whether minorities are subjected to differential justice.
7. Health care statistics reveal significantly higher morbidity and mortality rates for African Americans.
8. Black Americans have made great strides in being elected to office but remain under-represented nationally despite some districts being gerrymandered to their advantage.

Key Terms

acting White 200
apartheid schools 200
class 208
de facto segregation 200
differential justice 211

gerrymandering 214
income 203
redlining 210
tracking 200
underemployment 205

victim discounting 211
victimization surveys 211
wealth 203
zoning laws 211

Review Questions

1. To what degree have the civil rights movement initiatives in education been realized, or do they remain unmet?
2. What challenges face the African American middle class?
3. What are the biggest assets and problems facing African American families?
4. What are the similarities in the experiences of African Americans in the criminal justice and health care systems?
5. How is race-based gerrymandering related to affirmative action?

Critical Thinking

1. Without the comparison to John, Glenn might have taken the shoe salesman to be merely incompetent at his job rather than purposefully avoiding selling to African Americans. Drawing on the case of John and Glenn, what are other types of situations in which people may be victims of discrimination but be unaware of it?
2. What has been the ethnic and racial composition of the neighborhoods you have lived in and the schools you have attended? Consider how the composition of one may have influenced the other. What steps would have been necessary to ensure more diversity?
3. How are the problems in crime, housing, and health interrelated?

9

Hispanic Americans

THE GROUP LABEL *HISPANIC* OR *LATINO AMERICAN* LINKS a diverse population that mostly shares a common language heritage but otherwise has many significant differences. The language barrier in an assimilation-oriented society has been of major significance to Hispanics. For generations, schools made it difficult for Spanish-speaking children to succeed. The United States has only recently made any effort to recognize its bilingual, bicultural heritage and to allow those whose native language is not English to use it as an asset rather than as a liability. Latinos include several major groups, of which Mexican Americans, Puerto Ricans, and Cubans are the largest in the United States. Cuban Americans constitute a significant presence in southern Florida. Increasingly, immigrants and refugees from Central and South America have also established communities throughout the United States.

L ike those in some other small towns in Nevada, Pahrump's brothels are legal. The town council accepts tax money from the Chicken Ranch but hands voted to make English as the official language and has banned the flying of foreign flags in this town where one in eight residents are Latinos. Many community Latinos and sympathetic non-Hispanics deeply resented the measure amidst reports that school officials were even harassing students using Spanish in casual, private conversations. Facing lawsuits that such actions violated freedom of speech, a newly elected council repealed the action.

Yet the pull toward pluralism is also present. In growing numbers of predominantly Hispanic communities, Latino developers are avoiding taquerias (small restaurants) and "amigo stores" targeting immigrants, in favor of Chili's, Starbucks, Trader Joe's, and Applebee's. As councilwoman Marlen Garcia of Baldwin Park, California (which has a population that is three-fourths Latino) said, "We're not against our culture, nothing like that. But we want something that speaks to every culture" (Becerra 2008, A16; Freiss 2007, 2008).

The governor of the state that has the largest Latino presence declares that Puerto Ricans and Cubans are particularly feisty because of their mixed Black and Latino "blood." What was Arnold Schwarzenegger thinking of when he made these statements? He soon apologized when they became public, but what is interesting is not so much his political misstep but rather the fact that we have a German-speaking, Austrian-born man who did not immigrate to the United States until he was 20 years old became a naturalized citizen in 1983—becoming who has so assimilated that he readily and nonchalantly expressers old-fashioned American stereotype among friends (Blood 2006).

More than one in eight people in the U.S. population are of Spanish or Latin American origin. Collectively, this group is called *Hispanics* or *Latinos,* two terms that we use interchangeably in this book. The Bureau of the Census (2008d) estimates that by the year 2050, Hispanics will constitute about 30 percent of the U.S. population. This growth is fueled by births among Latinos here, continuing legal immigration, and sustained illegal or unauthorized immigration from throughout Latin America.

By 2006, population data showed that 41.9 million Latinos outnumbered the 39 million African Americans. The Latino population is very diverse. Today, nearly 27 million, or two-thirds of Hispanics in the United States, are Mexican Americans, or Chicanos. The diversity of Latinos and their national distribution in the United States are shown in Figures 9.1 and 9.2.

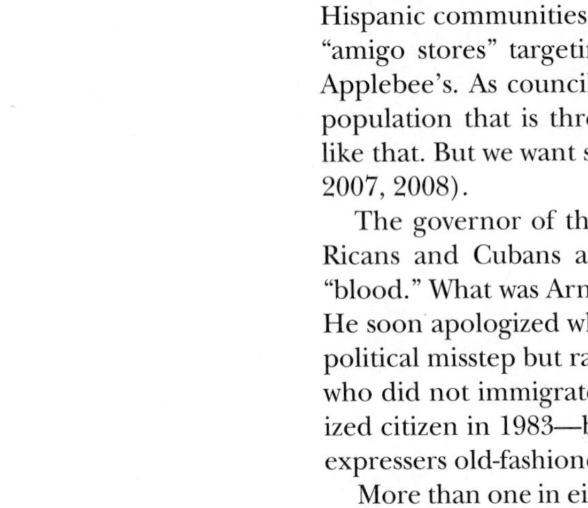

Except for Puerto Ricans, who are citizens by birth, legal status looms as a major issue within the Latino community. The specter of people questioning Latinos about their legal status looms even over legal residents. According to a national survey, the majority of Hispanic adults in the United States worry that they, a family member, or a close friend could be deported. Nearly two-thirds say the failure of Congress to enact an immigration reform bill has made life more difficult for all Latinos (Pew Hispanic Center 2007).

Some of the prevailing images of Hispanic settlements in the United States are no longer accurate. Latinos do not live in rural areas. They are generally urban dwellers: 91 percent live in metropolitan areas; only 78 percent of White non-Hispanics do. In addition, some Hispanics have moved away from their traditional areas of settlement. Many Mexican Americans have left the

FIGURE 9.1

Hispanic Population of the United States by Origin

Note: "Other Hispanic" includes Spanish Americans and Latinos identified as mixed ancestry as well as other Central and South Americans not otherwise indicated by specific country.

Source: Author estimates based on American Community Survey 2007, released in 2008 by the Bureau of the Census at factfinder.census.gov.

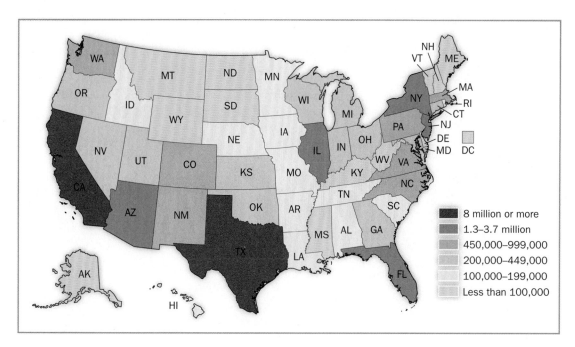

FIGURE 9.2
Where Most Hispanic Americans Live

Source: Author estimates based on American Community Survey 2007, released in 2008 by the Bureau of the Census at factfinder.census.gov.

Southwest, and many Puerto Ricans have left New York City. In 1940, 88 percent of Puerto Ricans residing in the United States lived in New York City, but by the 2000 census the proportion had dropped to less than one-third (J. Logan 2001a; Ramirez and de la Cruz 2003).

Latino Identity

Is there a common identity among Latinos? Is a panethnic identity emerging? **Panethnicity** is the development of solidarity between ethnic subgroups. Hispanics do not share a common historical or cultural identity. We noted in Chapter 1 that ethnic identity is not self-evident in the United States and may lead to heated debates even among those who share the same ethnic heritage. Non-Hispanics often give a single label to the diverse group of native-born Latino Americans and immigrants. This labeling by the out-group is similar to the dominant group's way of viewing "American Indians" or "Asian Americans" as one collective group. For example, sociologist Clara Rodríquez has noted that Puerto Ricans, who are American citizens, are often mistakenly viewed as an immigrant group and lumped together with all Latinos or Hispanics. She observes that to most Anglos, "[a]ll Hispanics look alike. It's the tendency to see all Latinos as the same. It's an unfortunate lack of attention to U.S. history" (Rodríquez 1994, 32).

Are Hispanics or Latinos themselves developing a common identity? Indicators vary. Sharp divisions remain among Hispanics on the identity issue. Only a minority, about 24 percent, prefers to use panethnic names such as *Hispanic* or *Latino*. In Miami, Florida, bumper stickers proclaim "No soy Hispano, soy Cubano": "I am not Hispanic, I am Cuban." Among U.S.-born Latinos, there is clearly a move away from using the native country as a means of identity. Among this segment of the Latino population, 46 percent say they either first use or only use *American* to describe themselves, and 29 percent use their parents' country of origin. This contrasts sharply with foreign-born Latinos, a group

panethnicity
The development of solidarity between ethnic subgroups, as reflected in the terms *Hispanic* and *Asian American*.

Mural art can be found in many Latino neighborhoods across the United States. This 32-foot long mural delivers the poignant message "We Are Not a Minority" in East Los Angeles. It was painted in 1978 and then repainted in 1996.
Source: Corbis

in which only 21 percent use *American* and 54 percent use *Mexican* or *Colombian* or a similar national term of reference. Immigrants from Central and South America, including even their U.S.-born children, are less likely to endorse a panethnic identity (Brodie et al. 2002; Masuoka 2006).

An even trickier issue is how Latinos identify themselves in racial terms now and in the future. Typically, the sharp White–Black divide is absent in their home countries, where race, if socially constructed, tends to be along a color gradient. A **color gradient** places people along a continuum from light to dark skin color rather than in two or three distinct racial groupings. The presence of color gradients is yet another reminder of the social construction of race. Terms such as *mestizo Hondurans, mulatto Colombians,* or *African Panamanians* reflect this continuum of a color gradient. In the United States, Latinos tend to avoid taking on the label of being "White" or "Black," although lighter-skinned Hispanics generally distinguish themselves from Black Americans. Social scientists speculate whether in time, like the Irish almost a century ago, Latinos will come to be viewed as "White" rather than as some sort of third collective group in addition to White and Black Americans (Bonilla-Silva 2004; Feagin and Cobas 2008).

The Economic Picture

Although there are many indicators of how well a group is doing economically in the United States, income is probably the best one. As we can see in Figure 9.3, the median household income of Latinos has gradually increased over the last 25 years, with some fluctuations. However, relative to White non-Hispanics, the income gap has remained. Generally, over recent years, Latino households can expect to earn about 70 cents to the dollar that their White counterparts earn.

Income is just part of the picture. Low levels of wealth—total assets minus debt—is characteristic of Hispanic households. Although they appear to have slightly higher levels of median wealth than African American households, Hispanic households average less than 10 cents for every dollar in wealth owned by White households. Also the trend is not encouraging. During a recent five-year period, Latino wealth increased by 14 percent, compared to 17 percent for White non-Hispanics. So Latinos not only are likely to earn much less annually but also have fewer financial resources to fall back on (Kochhar 2004; Pew Hispanic Center 2006a).

color gradient
The placement of people on a continuum from light to dark skin color rather than in distinct racial groupings by skin color.

The trend in poverty rate reflects the income pattern. At the beginning of 2006, 21.8 percent of Latinos were below the poverty level, compared to 8.3 percent of White non-Hispanics. Latinos were impoverished. For example, this would mean that a household of two adults and two children would earn less than $19,806. Typically, over the last quarter century, the proportion of Latinos in poverty has been two or three times that of White non-Hispanics (see Figure 9.4).

By looking at income and poverty trends of Latino households, we can see how much—but also how little—has been accomplished to reduce social inequality between ethnic and racial groups. Although the income of Latinos has gradually increased over the last 30 years, so has White income. The gap between the two groups in both income and poverty level has remained relatively constant. Indeed, the income of the typical Latino household in 2005 was more than $10,000 behind the typical 1972 White non-Hispanic household.

Previously, in Chapter 8, we noted the growing proportion of poor African Americans who find it increasingly difficult to obtain meaningful work. Although this also has been said of today's poor Latinos, their situation is much more difficult to predict. On the one hand, as a group, poor Latinos are more geographically mobile than poor African Americans, which offers them some prospect of a brighter future. On the other hand, nearly half of Latinos send money abroad to help relatives, which obviously puts a greater strain on supporting themselves in the United States (Latino Coalition 2006).

Language acquisition is key to the future economic development of Hispanics, as it is for immigrants from most countries. In Research Focus on pages 226–227, we consider the latest data on immigrants, and their descendants' fluency in English.

FIGURE 9.3
Household Income Trends, 1972–2007

Source: Bureau of the Census data in DeNavas-Walt et al. 2008.

The Growing Political Presence

Over the last 30 years, both major political parties have begun to acknowledge that Latinos form a force in the election process. This recognition has come primarily through the growth of the Hispanic population and also through policies that have facilitated non-English voters.

In 1975, Congress moved toward recognizing the multilingual background of the U.S. population. Federal law now requires bilingual or even multilingual ballots in voting districts where at least 5 percent of the voting-age population or 10,000 people do not speak English. Even before Congress acted, federal courts had been ordering cities such as Chicago, Miami, and New York City to provide bilingual ballots where necessary. In the November 2002 elections, some 296 counties and municipalities in 30 states issued multilingual ballots (*Migration News* 2002b).

These voting reforms did not have the impact that many of their advocates had hoped for. The turnout was poor because, although Hispanics were interested in voting, many were ineligible to vote under the U.S. Constitution because they were noncitizens. At the time of the 2008 presidential election, Hispanics accounted for 15 percent of the total population but only 9 percent of the eligible electorate.

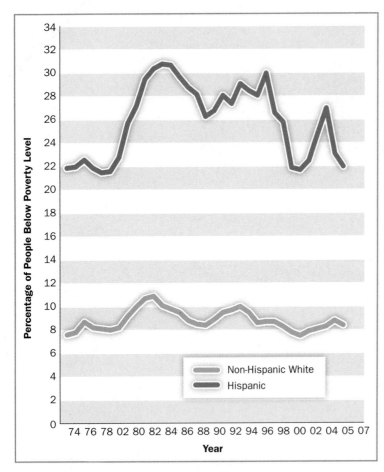

FIGURE 9.4
People in Poverty Trends, 1973–2007

Source: Bureau of the Census data in DeNavas-Walt et al. 2008.

borderlands
The area of a common culture along the border between Mexico and the United States.

maquiladoras
Foreign-owned companies on the Mexican side of the border with the United States.

The potential for a greater Latino political presence is strong. Anticipating the greater turnout, political parties are advancing more Hispanic candidates. Generally, the Democrats have been more successful in garnering the Hispanic vote. A national survey in 2008 showed that only 26 percent of registered Latino voters said they typically leaned toward a Republican candidate; 65 percent leaned toward the Democratic candidate. The one exception to the Democratic-leaning Latino voter are Cuban Americans, who have generally been supportive of the Republicans because of the party's stronger position in isolating Castro-controlled Cuba. The 2008 election, however, showed that some gains were being made even here by Democrats (Lopez and Minuskin 2008; Padgett 2008).

Unlike the Black vote, the major political parties are somewhat more likely to see the Latino vote still in play. The 2004 Bush–Cheney ticket heavily promoted the "agenda del Presidente" while Kerry–Edwards encouraged "contribuya al Partido Democrático." Four years later, Republican candidate John McCain and Democratic candidate Barack Obama made back-to-back appearances before the annual meeting of the National Association of Latino Elected and Appointed Officials. Yet ultimately 67 percent of Latinos backed Democrat candidate Obama—a victory margin comparable to that enjoyed by any Democrat of the last 10 presidential elections. The Hispanic community's rapidly growing population, higher proportions of voter registration, and higher participation in elections guarantee future efforts by politicians to elicit their support (Connelly 2008; Kiely 2008; Pew Hispanic Center 2006c; Suro and Escobar 2006).

Like African Americans, many Latinos resent the fact that every four years political movers and shakers rediscover they exist. Between major elections, little effort is made to court their interest except by Latino elected officials.

The Borderlands

"The border is not where the U.S. stops and Mexico begins," said Mayor Betty Flores of Laredo, Texas. "It's where the U.S. blends into Mexico" (Gibbs 2001, 42). The term **borderlands** here refers to the area of a common culture along the border between Mexico and the United States (see Figure 9.6 on page 228). Though particularly relevant to Mexicans and Mexican Americans, the growing Mexican influence is relevant to the other Latino groups that we will discuss.

Legal and illegal emigration from Mexico to the United States, day laborers crossing the border regularly to go to jobs in the United States, the implementation of the North American Free Trade Agreement (NAFTA), and the exchange of media across the border all make the notion of separate Mexican and U.S. cultures obsolete in the borderlands.

The economic position of the borderlands is complex in terms of both businesses and workers. Very visible on the Mexican side are **maquiladoras**. These foreign-owned operations are exempt from paying Mexican taxes and are not required to provide insurance or benefits for their workers. Pay at $3.00 an hour is considered very good by prevailing

The GOP (the Republican Party) has literally tangled itself up in its strong position on curbing illegal immigration, which has hampered its candidates from getting support from the Latino community.

wage standards in Mexico. However, this one example of international trade soon was trumped by another aspect of globalization. As low as these hourly wages seem to people in industrial countries, multinational corporations soon found even lower wages in China. More than 40 percent of the 700,000 maquiladora jobs created in the 1990s had been eliminated by 2003 (Cañas et al. 2007).

Immigrant workers have a significant economic impact on their home country while employed in the United States. Many Mexicans, as well as other Hispanic groups we discuss in this chapter, send some part of their earnings back to family members remaining in their native country. This substantial flow of money, sometimes called **remittances**, totals an estimated $24 billion annually. Most of the money is spent to pay for food, clothing, and housing, but increasingly a growing proportion is being invested to create small businesses (Airola 2007; *Migration News* 2008).

The close cultural and economic ties to the home country that are found in the borderlands also can be found with other Latino groups. Such economic and political events continue to have a prominent role in the lives of immigrants and their children, and even grandchildren, in the United States. In recent years, Mexicans have also turned their attention to their other borders as migrants from other Latin American countries enter Mexico, sometimes illegally, to either settle there or move north to the United States.

Inland from the borders, **hometown clubs** (or associations) have sprung up in northern cities with large settlements of Mexicans. Hometown clubs typically are nonprofit organizations that maintain close ties to immigrants' hometowns in Mexico and other Latin American countries. Hometown clubs collect money for improvements in hospitals and schools that are beyond the means of the local people back home. The impact of hometown clubs has become so noticeable that some states in Mexico have begun programs whereby they will match funds from hometown clubs to encourage such public-spirited efforts. The work of more than 1,500 hometown clubs in the United States and Mexican communities alone reflects the blurring of border distinctions within the Latino community (Korecki 2003; *Migration News* 2000).

As we have noted, the Latino or Hispanic community comprises several nationalities. Mexican Americans, the people of the borderlands and beyond, and Puerto Ricans are by far the two largest communities and are considered separately in Chapter 10. We will continue in this chapter by considering the other Latino groups: Cuban Americans, Central Americans, and South Americans.

remittances
The monies that immigrants return to their countries of origin.

hometown clubs
Nonprofit organizations that maintain close ties to immigrants' hometowns in Mexico and other Latin American countries.

Maquiladoras are foreign-owned manufacturers located in Mexico along the United States border. Workers assemble components for export to the United States at a plant in Nuevo Laredo, Mexico.

ENGLISH-LANGUAGE ACQUISITION

Few issues swirling around the everyday life of Latinos in the United States are more heated than fluency in English. As we saw in Chapter 3, political efforts to declare English the official language continue, and the funding of bilingual programs is constantly in jeopardy, Native English speakers often resent hearing even accented English in the workplace or in public. Ironically, people who proudly see themselves as Latino but do not speak Spanish experience resentment from some Hispanics who feel they are too assimilated.

Yet these tensions occur against a backdrop where English language acquisition is not an issue among immigrants themselves. A 2007 survey showed that 59 percent of Latinos even support the notion that immigrants should be required to be proficient in English to remain in the country. They see this as vital to advancement because other surveys have documented that those who lack fluency have greater problems in the job market and even have more limited exposure to newer technologies such as the Internet.

The reality is that most immigrants and their offspring quickly become fluent in English and abandon their mother tongue. In Figure 9.5, we look at data from Southern California, a region with a high proportion of immigrants. Given this high concentration of non–English speakers, we might anticipate that there may be little motivation to learn English. Yet these data document a steady and rapid move toward use of English in preference to the mother tongue. Even Spanish-speaking immigrants from Mexico, El Salvador, and Guatemala become English speakers despite the presence of large Latino enclaves in their communities.

Latinos cite language skills as more of an explanation for discrimination they have experienced than immigration status, income, education, or skin color. In summary, language continues to be a hot issue, but largely by the second generation, and certainly by the third generation, proficiency in the language of the host society becomes dominant.

Sources: Carroll 2007; Fox and Livingston 2007; Hakimzadeh and Cohn 2007; Rumbaut, Massey, and Bean 2006.

Cuban Americans

Third in numbers only to Mexican Americans and Puerto Ricans, Cuban Americans are a significant ethnic Hispanic minority in the United States. Their presence in this country has a long history, with Cuban settlements in Florida dating back to as early as 1831. These settlements tended to be small, close-knit communities organized around a single enterprise such as a cigar-manufacturing firm.

Until recently, however, the number of Cuban Americans was very modest. The 1960 census showed that 79,000 people who had been born in Cuba lived in the United States. By 2006, more than 1.5 million people of Cuban birth or descent lived here. This tremendous increase followed Fidel Castro's assumption of power after the 1959 Cuban Revolution.

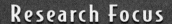

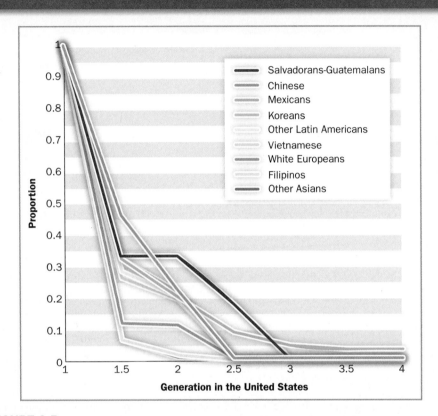

FIGURE 9.5
Proportion of Immigrant Group Members Speaking Mother Tongue by Generation

Note: Based on 5,703 surveyed in metropolitan Los Angeles and San Diego 2000–2004. The 1.5 generation are those who came to the United States to live before the age of 15. The 2 generation are those born in the United States and who had at least one parent who was foreign born. The 3+ generation represents those who, with their parents, were born in the United States but had one or more foreign-born grandparents.

Source: Rumbaut, Massey, and Bean 2006, 456.

Immigration

Cuban immigration to the United States since the 1959 revolution has been continuous, but there were three significant influxes of large numbers of immigrants through the 1980s. First, the initial exodus of about 200,000 Cubans after Castro's assumption of power lasted about three years. Regular commercial air traffic continued despite the United States' severing of diplomatic relations with Cuba. This first wave stopped with the missile crisis of October 1962, when all legal movement between the two nations was halted.

An agreement between the United States and Cuba in 1965 produced the second wave through a program of freedom flights: specially arranged charter flights from Havana to Miami. Through this program, more than 340,000 refugees arrived between 1965 and 1973. Despite efforts to encourage these arrivals to disperse into other parts of the United States, most settled in the Miami area (M. Abrahamson 1996).

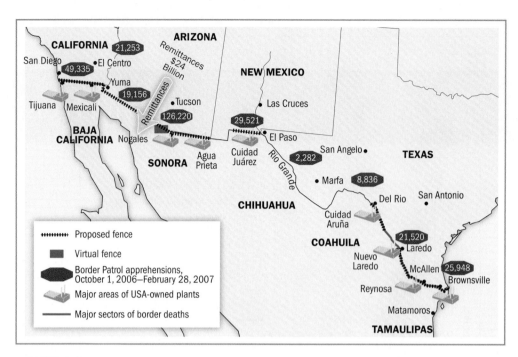

FIGURE 9.6

The Borderlands

In search of higher wages, undocumented Mexicans often attempt to cross the border illegally, risking their lives in the process. Maquiladoras located just south of the U.S.–Mexican border employ Mexican workers at wages far lower than those earned by U.S. workers. The Mexican workers and Mexican Americans send large amounts of money, called *remittances*, to assist kinfolk and communities in Mexico. Simultaneously, the U.S. government continues to harden the border and has even experimented with a "virtual fence" in which a system of radar towers and ground sensors have been set along a 28-mile stretch of the Arizona desert.

Source: Prepared by author based on Archibold and Preston 2008; Cañas et al. 2007; Marosi 2007; Romero and Ramirez 2007; Thompson 2001.

The third major migration, the 1980 Mariel boatlift, has been the most controversial. In 1980, more than 124,000 refugees fled Cuba in the "freedom flotilla." In May of that year, a few boats from Cuba began to arrive in Key West, Florida, with people seeking asylum in the United States. President Carter, reflecting the nation's hostility toward Cuba's communist government, told the new arrivals and anyone else who might be listening in Cuba that they were welcome "with open arms and an open heart." As the number of arrivals escalated, it became apparent that Castro had used the invitation as an opportunity to send prison inmates, patients from mental hospitals, and drug addicts. However, the majority of the refugees were neither marginal to the Cuban economy nor social deviants.

Other Cubans soon began to call the refugees of this migration **Marielitos**. The word, which implies that these refugees were undesirable, refers to Mariel, the fishing port west of Havana from which the boats departed and where Cuban authorities herded people into boats. The term *Marielitos* remains a stigma in the media and in Florida. Because of their negative reception by longer-established Cuban immigrants and the group's modest skills and lack of formal education, these immigrants had a great deal of difficulty in adjusting to their new lives in the United States (Masud-Piloto 2008).

Now a Chicago real estate broker, Alfredo Jimenez tells in Listen to Our Voices of the experience he had as a young child being taken by his family and leaving everything behind in Cuba to go to the United States.

The difficult transition for many members of this freedom flotilla also has other reasons. Unlike the earlier waves, they grew up in a country bombarded with anti-American images. Despite these problems, their eventual acceptance by the Hispanic community has been impressive, and many members of this third significant wave have found employment. Most have applied for permanent resident status. Government assistance to these immigrants was limited, but help from some groups of Cuban Americans in the Miami

Marielitos
People who arrived from Cuba in the third wave of Cuban immigration, most specifically those forcibly deported by way of Mariel Harbor. The term is generally reserved for refugees seen as especially undesirable.

Listen to Our Voices

LEAVING CUBA

Alfredo Jimenez

At the age of eight I first realized my family was planning on leaving Cuba when my mother went to my second grade school in Havana to inform the principal that my brother and I would not be returning. I remember my teacher was not surprised that we were leaving but was surprised that we were *gusanos,* literally meaning worms or political dissidents. I returned home as my family waited to receive word that we were allowed to leave.

We waited about a week when a policeman knocked at our door in the middle of the night on May 17, 1980, and handed my father a document granting permission to leave Cuba. Within hours we had to get to the processing center, so my parents woke us up and prepared my grandmother, who was in a wheelchair. At the center, the Cuban government confiscated our passports, searched us, keeping all valuables, including my parents' wedding rings. From there it was to Mariel Port, three hours away, by a special bus.

The trip on the bus was tough for an eight-year-old as people along the entire route beat on our bus with bats, sticks, stones, eggs, and tomatoes. Once at the port, my brother and I managed to get away from the adults to play with other children at the beach, where I remember playing with small crabs in the sand. My parents got very upset when our pant legs got wet. They had written on the inside of our pant legs the names, addresses, and phone numbers of friends and family in the United States and Spain.

Days of waiting, and we were finally able to board an overcrowded boat headed for Florida. Already filled to the brim, the boat in the middle of the night rescued 12 people from another boat that was sinking. After 12 hours, we arrived in Key West to be greeted by waving American flags. Soon we headed on to Tampa to live with an aunt and her family—she had come to America soon after Fidel Castro assumed power.

The entire trip was an experience that my family values very much to this day. As young as my brother and I were, we didn't appreciate how difficult it was for my parents to leave everything behind.

Source: Alfredo Jimenez 2005.

area was substantial. However, for a small core group, adjustment was impossible. The legal status of a few of these detainees (i.e., arrivals who were held by the government pending clarification of their refugee or immigrant status) was ambiguous because of alleged offenses committed in Cuba or in the United States (Peréz 2001).

Since 1994, the United States has a **dry foot, wet foot** policy with respect to arrivals from Cuba. Government policy generally allows Cuban nationals who manage to actually reach the United States ("dry foot") to remain, whereas those who are picked up at sea ("wet foot") are sent back to Cuba. Unfortunately, many Cubans have taken great risks in crossing the Florida Straits, and an unknown number have perished before reaching the mainland or being intercepted by the Coast Guard.

The Current Picture

Compared with other recent immigrant groups and with Latinos as a whole, Cuban Americans are doing well. As shown in Table 9.1, Cuban Americans have college completion

dry foot, wet foot
Policy toward Cuban immigrants that allows those who manage to reach the United States (dry foot) to remain but sends those who are picked up at sea (wet foot) back to Cuba.

TABLE 9.1

Selected Social and Economic Characteristics of Cubans and South Americans, 2004

	Total White Non-Hispanic	Total Hispanic	Cuban	Central American	South American
Percentage citizens	96.2	60.8	36.7	32.3	30.3
Percentage completing college, 25 years and older	29.7	12.7	25.3	10.8	29.3
Percentage of households that are married couples	57.3	50.8	51.9	48.8	55.6
Percentage living below poverty level	8.8	22.0	15.2	17.6	12.9
Median household income ($)	48,784	35,929	38,256	36,369	43,788

Source: Bureau of the Census 2007f, 8, 11, 15, 17, 18.

rates that are twice those of other Latinos. In this and all other social measures, the pattern is similar. Cuban Americans in 2000 compared favorably with other Hispanics, although recent arrivals as a group trail behind White Americans.

The presence of Cubans has been felt in urban centers throughout the United States but most notably in the Miami area. Throughout their various immigration phases, Cubans have been encouraged to move out of southern Florida, but many have returned to Dade County (metropolitan Miami), with its warm climate and proximity to other Cubans and Cuba itself. As of 2000, 55 percent of all Cuban Americans lived in the Miami area; another 15 percent lived elsewhere in Florida. Metropolitan Miami itself now has a Hispanic majority of 57 percent of the total population, compared with a Hispanic presence of only 4 percent in 1950 (J. Logan 2001a).

Probably no ethnic group has had more influence on the fortunes of a city in a short period of time than have the Cubans on Miami. Most people consider the Cubans' economic influence to be positive. With other Latin American immigrants, Cubans have transformed Miami from a quiet resort to a boomtown. To a large degree, they have re-created the Cuba they left behind. Today, the population of Miami is more than 59 percent foreign born—more than any other city. Residents like to joke that one of the reasons they like living in Miami is that it is close to the United States (N. Malone et al. 2003).

The relations between Miami's Cuban Americans and other groups have not been perfect. For example, other Hispanics—including Venezuelans, Ecuadorians, and Colombians—resent being mistaken for Cubans and feel that their own distinctive nationalities are being submerged. Cubans now find that storefronts in Miami's Little Havana area advertise Salvadoran corn pancakes and that waitresses hail from El Salvador. Cuban Miamians are also slowly adjusting to sharing their influence with the growing diversity of Hispanics. One obvious symbol is the investment of the park district in building more and more soccer fields—Cubans traditionally play baseball (Dahlburg 2004a).

All Cuban immigrants have had much to adjust to, and they have not been able to immediately establish the kind of life they sought. Although some of those who fled Cuba were forced to give up their life's savings, the early immigrants of the first wave were generally well educated, had professional or managerial backgrounds, and therefore met with greater economic success than later immigrants. However, regardless of the occupations the immigrants were able to enter, there was tremendous adjustment for their families. Women who typically did not work outside the home often had to seek employment. Immigrant parents found their children being exposed to a foreign culture. All the challenges typically faced by immigrant households were complicated by the uncertain fates of those they left behind in Cuba.

The primary adjustment among south Florida's Cuban Americans has been more to each other than to Whites, African Americans, or other Latinos. The prolonged immigration now stretching across two generations has led to differences between Cuban Americans in terms of ties to Cuba, social class, and age. There is no single Cuban American lifestyle.

The long-range prospects for Cubans in the United States depend on several factors. Of obvious importance are events in Cuba; many exiles have publicly proclaimed their desire to return to Cuba if the communist government is overturned. A powerful force in politics in Miami is the Cuban American National Foundation, which takes a strong anti-Castro position. The organization has actively opposed any proposals that the United States develop a more flexible policy toward Cuba. More-moderate voices in the Cuban exile community have not been encouraged to speak out. Indeed, sporadic violence has even occurred within the community over U.S.–Cuban relations. In addition, artists or speakers who come from Cuba receive a cold reception in Miami unless they are outspoken critics of Fidel Castro (Bostillo and Williams 2008).

Cuban Americans have selectively accepted Anglo culture. Cuban culture itself has been tenacious; the Cuban immigrants do not feel they need to forget Spanish while establishing fluency in English, the way other immigrant children have shunned their linguistic past. Still, a split between the original exiles and their children is evident. Young people are more concerned about the Miami Dolphins football team than they are about what is happening in Havana. They are more open to reestablishing relations with a Castro-led Cuba. However, the more recent wave of immigrants, the *recién llegados* (recently arrived), have again introduced more openly anti-Castro feelings even as the presidency transferred from Fidel Castro to his brother Raúl in 2008 (Masud-Piloto 2008a).

Central and South Americans

The immigrants who have come from Central and South America are a diverse population that has not been closely studied. Indeed, most government statistics treat its members collectively as "other" and rarely differentiate among them by nationality. Yet people from Chile and Costa Rica have little in common other than their hemisphere of origin and the Spanish language, if that. Still others may come from indigenous populations, especially in Guatemala and Belize, and have a social identity apart from any national allegiance. Also, not all Central and South Americans even have Spanish as their native tongue; for example, immigrants from Brazil speak Portuguese, immigrants from French Guyana speak French, and those from Suriname speak Dutch.

Many of the nations of Central and South America have a complex system of placing people into myriad racial groups. Their experience with a color gradient necessitates an adjustment when they come to the Black–White racial formation of the United States.

Added to language diversity and the color gradient are social class distinctions, religious differences, urban-versus-rural backgrounds, and differences in dialect even among those who speak the same language. Social relations among Central and South American groups with each other, Latinos, and non-Latinos defy generalization. Central and South Americans do not form, nor should they be expected to form, a cohesive group, nor do they naturally form coalitions with Cuban Americans, Mexican Americans, or Puerto Ricans (Orlov and Ueda 1980).

Immigration

Immigration from the various Central and South American nations has been sporadic, influenced by both our immigration laws and social forces operating in the home countries. Perceived economic opportunities escalated the northward movement in the 1960s. By 1970, Panamanians and Hondurans represented the largest national groupings, most of them being identified in the census as "nonwhite." By 2000, El Salvador, Columbia, and Guatemala were the top countries of origin. Immigration often comes through Mexico, which may serve as a brief stop along the way or represent a point of settlement for six months to three years or even longer (Horton 2008; López 2004; Zell and Skop 2008).

Since the mid-1970s, increasing numbers of Central and South Americans have fled unrest. Although Latinos as a whole are a fast-growing minority, the numbers of Central and South Americans increased even faster than the numbers of Mexicans or any other group in the 1980s. In particular, from about 1978, war and economic chaos in El Salvador,

brain drain
Immigration to the United States of skilled workers, professionals, and technicians who are desperately needed by their home countries.

Nicaragua, and Guatemala prompted many to seek refuge in the United States. The impact of the turmoil cannot be exaggerated. It is estimated that anywhere from 13 percent in Guatemala to 32 percent in El Salvador of the total population left the country. Not at all a homogeneous group, they range from Guatemalan Indian peasants to wealthy Nicaraguan exiles. These latest arrivals probably had some economic motivation for migration, but this concern was overshadowed or at least matched by their fear of being killed or hurt if they remained in their home country (Camarillo 1993; López 2004).

In a Global View, we look at the close relationship between the people of El Salvador and the United States.

The Current Picture

Two issues have clouded the recent settlement of Central and South Americans. First, many of the arrivals are illegal immigrants. Among those uncovered as undocumented workers, citizens from El Salvador, Guatemala, and Colombia are outnumbered only by Mexican nationals. Second, significant numbers of highly trained and skilled people have left these countries, which are in great need of professional workers. We noted in Chapter 4 how often immigration produces a **brain drain**: immigration to the United States of skilled workers, professionals, and technicians.

As a group, Central and South Americans are better educated than most Hispanics, as shown in Table 9.1. This reflects the plight that often faces recent immigrants. When relocating to a new country, they initially experience downward mobility in terms of occupational status.

The challenges to immigrants from Latin America are reflected in the experience of Colombians, who number more than a half million in the United States. The initial arrivals from this South American nation after World War I were educated middle-class people who quickly assimilated to life in the United States. Rural unrest in Colombia in the 1980s, however, triggered large-scale movement to the United States, where these newer Colombian immigrants had to adapt to a new culture and to urban life. The adaptation of this later group has been much more difficult. Some have found success by catering to other Colombians. For example, enterprising immigrants have opened bodegas (grocery stores) to supply traditional, familiar foodstuffs. Similarly, Colombians have established restaurants, travel agencies, and real estate firms that serve other Colombians. However, many immigrants are obliged to take menial jobs and to combine the income of several family members to meet the high cost of urban life. Colombians of mixed African descent face racial as well as ethnic and language barriers (Guzmán 2001).

Latinos rarely appear on television in central roles, much less on successful television programs. Although animated, *Dora the Explorer* on Nickelodeon is an exception to this rule.

What is likely to be the future of Central and South Americans in the United States? Although much will depend on future immigration, they could assimilate over the course of generations. One alternative is that they will become trapped with Mexican Americans as a segment of the dual labor market for those urban areas where they have taken up residence. A more encouraging possibility is that they will retain an independent identity, like the Cubans, while also establishing an economic base. For example, nearly 600,000 Dominicans (from the Dominican Republic) settled in the New York City area, where they make up a significant 7 percent of the population. In some neighborhoods, such as Washington Heights, one can easily engage in business, converse, and eat just as if one were in the Dominican Republic. People continue to remain attentive to events in Dominican politics, which often command greater attention than

A Global View

THE SALVADORAN CONNECTION

El Salvador is a Central American country with nearly 6 million people. Like many other Latin American countries, most Salvadorans are mestizo (mixed Native American and Spanish origin), with maybe one in 10 of Spanish ancestry viewing themselves as "White." An even smaller group is indigenous native people who have held on to their native cultures, including distinctive languages.

Political unrest, hurricanes, and volcanic eruptions have propelled people to emigrate in search of better opportunities. Salvadorans immigrated to the United States not so much out of a desire to be a citizen of another country but largely out of fear of remaining in their home country. Reliance on coffee as an export, which was controlled by a small elite, also limited upward mobility by those who sought to improve their lives. Early in the twentieth century, emigration to neighboring countries such as Honduras was the goal, but by the 1980s, immigration patterns had expanded to include not only the region but also Canada, Australia, and, in particular, the United States.

As of 2006, nearly 1.4 million Salvadorans were in the United States, a number nearly equivalent to one-fourth of the population of their country. About two-thirds were born in El Salvador; the balance were born in the United States of Salvadoran immigrants. Economically, they are doing much better than their counterparts back home, but their an income is approximately 14 percent less than that of the general U.S. population. Poverty rates run about 50 percent higher than the general population.

Most people think of assimilation in positive or neutral terms. An immigrant acquires the language of the host society or adjusts their attire to "fit in" a bit more. Assimilation means taking on the characteristics of the dominant culture, even though some of those behaviors and traits may actually be negative, as we noted in Chapter 4 when we saw that the health of immigrants' children and grandchildren actually deteriorates (see p. 107).

Media coverage in both the United States and El Salvador has drawn attention to some young Salvadorans who have returned to the Central American nation and reestablished gang organizations to which they belonged in the United States. The Immigration and Customs Enforcement (ICE), part of the U.S. Department of Homeland Security, has cracked down on foreign-born residents involved in criminal activities and quickly deported them. This get-tough policy has led to a deportation-and-return cycle as Salvadoran police report that 90 percent of the gang members return to the United States. Critics of the ICE policy argue that most arrests are for immigration offenses and not criminal actions and that many suspected "associates" are often lumped in with hard-core gang members, which only reinforces gang ties.

In contrast and perhaps more typical of the Salvadoran–U.S. connection is the hamlet of Brentwood on Long Island. The Salvadoran presence is unmistakable in Brentwood's fish stores, markets, and 40 restaurants whose culinary offerings range from Salvadoran pupusas to Italian dishes such as chicken francese. In the 1980s, as Salvadorans fled civil war in their home country, they were attracted to the wooded landscape of Long Island and the presence of Spanish-speaking Puerto Ricans. Ironically, the Salvadorans now find a measure of friction as local Puerto Ricans express concern about illegal immigrants in their community.

Like Mexican Americans, the Salvadorans have created hometown clubs or associations that relate to a specific village that receives remittances. Salvadorans have the highest level among Hispanics in sending money back home—70 percent of Salvadoran Americans make remittances, compared to 48 percent of Mexican Americans and 39 percent of Cuban Americans. In some cases, these immigrant-created organizations have specific objectives of improving the quality of life back home so that people are less likely to want or need to leave El Salvador. The process of movement between the United States and El Salvador is very complex indeed.

Sources: Berger 2008; Bureau of the Census 2007g; Cordova 2005; Hernández-Arias 2008; Quirk 2008; Waldinger 2007.

events in the United States. However, within their local neighborhoods, Dominicans here are focused on improving employment opportunities and public safety (J. Logan 2001a; Pessar 1995; Suro 1998).

Conclusion

The signals are mixed. Many movies and television programs and much music have a Hispanic flavor. Candidates for political office seek Latino votes and sometimes even speak Spanish to do so. Yet the poverty rate of Latino families reported in 2007 was more than 22 percent, compared with less than 8 percent for White Americans.

This mixture of positive and negative trends is visible in other areas. Ballots are printed in Spanish and other languages. Many Latinos feel that to be bilingual is not to be less a part of the United States. Espousing pluralism rather than assimilation is not un-American.

The contrast of images and substance will be evident again in Chapter 10. "In World War II, more Latinos won Medals of Honor than any other ethnic group," said Democratic Representative Matthew Martinez, a former U.S. Marine who represented part of Los Angeles. "How much blood do you have to spill before you prove you are a part of something?" (Whitman 1987, 49).

Much more recently, we might not be surprised to know that many of the soldiers in Iraq are Hispanic. Perhaps a bit surprising to the general public would be to learn that at least 22 Mexican citizens resident in the United States died in the military during the first two years of the Iraq War for their adopted country. Typically, Congress passes a resolution making these fallen soldiers citizens after their death. Under a new rule, the families can now use their deceased as a sponsor for their own residency papers (P. Jonsson 2006; McKinley 2005). Still, a contrasting image is offered by the refrain "Si usted no habla inglés puede quedarse rezagado": "If you don't speak English, you might be left behind."

Summary

1. Latinos are a growing presence throughout the United States, and even though people of Mexican descent represent the majority, significant numbers of Latino immigrants come from throughout Latin America.

2. Latinos do not share a common cultural or historical identity, yet a panethnic identity emerges in many aspects of life in the United States.

3. Economically, life for Latinos continues to improve—but relative to non-Hispanics, the gap has hardly changed over the last two generations.

4. Research documents the acquisition of fluency in English among virtually all immigrants, including Spanish-speaking residents, by the third generation.

5. A part of the assimilation as well as pluralism among Latinos has been growing involvement in electoral politics, which has been recognized by both the Democratic and Republican parties.

6. The long land border between the United States and Mexico divides an area that shares a common culture and an economic market that is fostered by both nations despite a hardening of the boundary by the United States.

7. Although they account for only 3 percent of the Hispanic population, Cuban Americans are a major presence in southern Florida and continue to exert a significant political force on U.S. policy toward Cuba.

8. Diversity is a key aspect of the varied cultures represented by immigrants from Central and South America.

Key Terms

borderlands 224

brain drain 232

color gradient 222

dry foot, wet foot 229

hometown clubs 225

maquiladoras 224

Marielitos 228

panethnicity 221

remittances 225

Review Questions

1. What different factors seem to unite and divide the Latino community in the United States?

2. How do Hispanics view themselves as a group? How are they viewed by others?

3. Identify the factors that contribute to and limit the political power of Latinos as a group in the United States.

4. To what extent has the Cuban migration been positive, and to what degree do significant challenges remain?

5. How have Central and South Americans contributed to the diversity of the Hispanic peoples in the United States?

Critical Thinking

1. Language and culture are almost inseparable. How do you imagine your life would change if you were not permitted to speak your native language? Or how has it been affected if you have been expected to speak some other language?

2. How have you witnessed the presence of a different culture in the United States? At what times have you found it to be interesting and intriguing? Are there times you felt threatened by it or felt its presence to be unfair?

3. Why do you think the U.S.–Mexico border region have been the subject of such close scrutiny, whereas there is little attention to similar areas along the U.S.–Canada border?

10

Mexican Americans and Puerto Ricans

THE HISTORY OF MEXICAN AMERICANS IS CLOSELY TIED TO immigration, which has been encouraged (for example, the *bracero* program) when Mexican labor is in demand and discouraged (repatriation and Operation Wetback) when Mexican workers are unwanted. The Puerto Rican people are divided between those who live in the island commonwealth and those who live on the mainland. Puerto Ricans who migrate to the mainland most often come in search of better jobs and housing. As groups, both Mexican Americans and Puerto Ricans have lower incomes, less formal education, and greater health problems than White Americans. Both family and religion are sources of strength for the typical Puerto Rican or Mexican American.

Citizenship is the basic requirement for receiving one's legal rights and privileges in the United States. However, for both Mexican Americans and Puerto Ricans, citizenship has been an ambiguous concept at best. Mexican Americans (or Chicanos) have a long history in the United States, stretching back before the nation was even formed, to the early days of European exploration. Santa Fe, New Mexico, was founded more than a decade before the Pilgrims landed at Plymouth. The Mexican American people trace their ancestry to the merging of Spanish settlers with the Native Americans of Central America and Mexico. This ancestry reaches back to the brilliant Mayan and Aztec civilizations, which attained their height about C.E. 700 and 1500, respectively. However, roots in the land do not guarantee a group dominance over it. Over several centuries, the Spaniards conquered the land and merged with the Native Americans to form the Mexican people. In 1821, Mexico obtained its independence, but this independence was short-lived, for domination from the north began less than a generation later (Meier and Rivera 1972).

Today, Mexican Americans are creating their own destiny in the United States while functioning in a society that is often concerned about immigration, both legal and illegal. In the eyes of some, including a few in positions of authority, to be Mexican American is to be suspected of being in the country illegally or, at least, of knowingly harboring illegal aliens.

For no other minority group in the United States is citizenship so ambiguous as it is for Puerto Ricans. Even Native Americans, who are subject to some unique laws and are exempt from others because of past treaties, have a future firmly dominated by the United States. This description does not necessarily fit Puerto Ricans. Their island home is the last major U.S. colonial territory and, for that matter, one of the few colonial areas remaining in the world. Besides assessing the situation of Puerto Ricans on the mainland, we will also need to consider the relationship of the United States to Puerto Rico.

Mexican Americans

Wars play a prominent part in any nation's history. The United States was created as a result of the colonies' war with England to win their independence. In the 1800s, the United States acquired significant neighboring territory in two different wars. The legacy of these wars and the annexation that resulted were to create the two largest Hispanic minorities in the United States: Mexican Americans and Puerto Ricans.

A large number of Mexicans became aliens in the United States without ever crossing any border. These people first became Mexican Americans with the conclusion of the Mexican–American War. This two-year war culminated with a U.S. occupation of 11 months. Today Mexicans visit the Museum of Interventions in Mexico City, which outlines the war and how Mexico permanently gave up half its country. The war is still spoken of today as "the Mutilation" (T. Weiner 2004).

In the war-ending Treaty of Guadalupe Hidalgo, signed February 2, 1848, Mexico acknowledged the annexation of Texas by the United States and ceded California and most of Arizona and New Mexico to the United States for $15 million. In exchange, the United States granted citizenship to the 75,000 Mexican nationals who remained on the annexed land after one year. With citizenship, the United States was to guarantee religious freedom, property rights, and cultural integrity—that is, the right to continue Mexican and Spanish cultural traditions and to use the Spanish language.

The beginnings of the Mexican experience in the United States were as varied as the people themselves. Some Mexican Americans were affluent, with large land holdings. Others were poor peasants barely able to survive. Along such rivers as the Rio Grande, commercial towns grew up around the increasing river traffic. In New Mexico and Arizona, many Mexican American people welcomed the protection that the U.S. government offered against several Native American tribes. In California, life was quickly dominated by the gold miners, and Anglos controlled the newfound wealth. One generalization can be made about the many segments of the Mexican American population in the nineteenth century: they were regarded as a conquered people. In fact, even before the war, many Whites who traveled into the West were already prejudiced against people of mixed blood (in this instance, against Mexicans). Whenever Mexican American and Anglo interests conflicted, Anglo interests won.

A pattern of second-class treatment for Mexican Americans emerged well before the twentieth century. Gradually, the Anglo system of property ownership replaced the Native American and

The Roman Catholic Church has a long history among Mexicans and Mexican Americans. The Mission San Xavier del Bac in Arizona was founded in 1700.

Hispanic systems. Mexican Americans who inherited land proved no match for Anglo lawyers. Court battles provided no protection for poor Spanish-speaking landowners. Unscrupulous lawyers occasionally defended Mexican Americans successfully, only to demand half the land as their fee. Anglo cattle ranchers gradually pushed out Mexican American ranchers. By 1892, the federal government was granting grazing privileges on public grasslands and forests to anyone except Mexican Americans. Effectively, the people who were now Mexican *Americans* had become outsiders in their own homeland. The ground was laid for the social structure of the Southwest in the twentieth century, an area of growing productivity in which minority groups have increased in size but remain largely subordinate.

The Immigrant Experience

Nowhere else in the world do two countries with such different standards of living and wage scales share such an open border. Immigration from Mexico is unique in several respects. First, it has been a continuous large-scale movement for most of the last hundred years. The United States did not restrict immigration from Mexico through legislation until 1965. Second, the proximity of Mexico encourages past immigrants to maintain strong cultural and language ties with the homeland through friends and relatives. Return visits to the old country are only one- or two-day bus rides for Mexican Americans, not once-in-a-lifetime voyages, as they were for most European immigrants. The third point of uniqueness is the aura of illegality that has surrounded Mexican migrants. Throughout the twentieth century, the suspicion in which Anglos have held Mexican Americans has contributed to mutual distrust between the two groups.

The years before World War I brought large numbers of Mexicans into the expanding agricultural industry of the Southwest. The Mexican revolution of 1909–1922 thrust refugees into the United States, and World War I curtailed the flow of people from Europe, leaving the labor market open to the Mexican Americans. After the war, continued political turmoil in Mexico and more prosperity in the Southwest brought still more Mexicans across the border.

Simultaneously, corporations in the United States, led by agribusiness, invested in Mexico in such a way as to maximize their profits but minimize the amount of money

repatriation
The 1930s program of deporting Mexicans.

bracero
Contracted Mexican laborers brought to the United States during World War II.

mojados
"Wetbacks"; derisive slang for Mexicans who enter illegally, supposedly by swimming the Rio Grande.

remaining in Mexico to provide needed employment. Conflict theorists view this investment as part of the continuing process in which American businesses, with the support and cooperation of affluent Mexicans, have used Mexican people when it has been in corporate leaders' best interests. The Mexican workers are used either as cheap laborers in their own country by their fellow Mexicans and by Americans or as undocumented workers here who are dismissed when they are no longer judged to be useful (Guerin-Gonzales 1994).

Beginning in the 1930s, the United States embarked on a series of measures aimed specifically at Mexicans. The Great Depression brought pressure on local governments to care for the growing number of unemployed and impoverished. Government officials developed a quick way to reduce welfare rolls and eliminate people seeking jobs: ship Mexicans back to Mexico. This program of deporting Mexicans in the 1930s was called **repatriation**. As officially stated, the program was constitutional because only illegal aliens were to be repatriated. Mexicans and even people born in the United States of Mexican background were deported to relieve the economic pressure of the depression. The legal process of fighting a deportation order was overwhelming, however, especially for a poor Spanish-speaking family. The Anglo community largely ignored this outrage against the civil rights of those deported and did not show interest in helping repatriates to ease the transition (Balderrama and Rodriguez 2006).

When the depression ended, Mexican laborers again became attractive to industry. In 1942, when World War II was depleting the labor pool, the United States and Mexico agreed to a program allowing migration across the border by contracted laborers, or **braceros**. Within a year of the initiation of the bracero program, more than 80,000 Mexican nationals had been brought in; they made up one-eleventh of the farm workers on the Pacific Coast. The program continued with some interruptions until 1964. It was devised to recruit labor from poor Mexican areas for U.S. farms. In a program that was supposed to be supervised jointly by Mexico and the United States, minimum standards were to be maintained for the transportation, housing, wages, and health care of the braceros. Ironically, these safeguards placed the braceros in a better economic situation than Mexican Americans, who often worked alongside the protected Mexican nationals. The Mexicans were still regarded as a positive presence by Anglos only when useful, and the Mexican American people were merely tolerated.

Like many policies of the past relating to disadvantaged racial and ethnic groups, the bracero program lives on. After decades of protests, the Mexican government finally issued checks of $3,500 to former braceros and their descendants. The payments were to resolve disputes over what happened to the money the U.S. government gave to the Mexican government to assist in resettlement. To say this has been regarded as too little, much too late is an understatement.

Another crackdown on illegal aliens was to be the third step in dealing with the perceived Mexican problem. Alternately called Operation Wetback and Special Force Operation, it was fully inaugurated by 1954. The term *wetbacks*, or **mojados**—the derisive slang for Mexicans who enter illegally—refers to those who secretly swim across the Rio Grande. Like other roundups, this effort failed to stop the illegal flow of workers. For several years, some Mexicans were brought in under the bracero program while other Mexicans were being deported. With the end of the bracero program in 1964 and stricter immigration quotas for Mexicans, illegal border crossings increased because legal crossings became more difficult (J. Kim 2008).

More dramatic than the negative influence that continued immigration has had on employment conditions in the Southwest is the effect on the

Mexican migrants harvest strawberries in California.

Mexican and Mexican American people themselves. Routinely, the rights of Mexicans, even the rights to which they are entitled as illegal aliens, are ignored. Of the illegal immigrants deported, few have been expelled through formal proceedings. The Mexican American Legal Defense and Education Fund (MALDEF) has repeatedly expressed concern over the government's handling of illegal aliens.

Against this backdrop of legal maneuvers is the tie that the Mexican people have to the land both in today's Mexico and in the parts of the United States that formerly belonged to Mexico. *Assimilation* may be the key word in the history of many immigrant groups, but for Mexican Americans the key term is **La Raza**, literally "the people" or "the race." Among contemporary Mexican Americans, however, the term connotes pride in a pluralistic Spanish, Native American, and Mexican heritage. Mexican Americans cherish their legacy and, as we shall see, strive to regain some of the economic and social glory that once was theirs (Delgado 2008a).

Despite the passage of various measures designed to prevent illegal immigration, neither the immigration nor the apprehension of illegal aliens is likely to end. Mexican Americans will continue to be more closely scrutinized by law enforcement officials because their Mexican descent makes them more suspect as potential illegal aliens. The Mexican American community is another group subject to racial profiling that renders their presence in the United States suspect in the eyes of many Anglos.

In the United States, Mexican Americans have mixed feelings toward the illegal Mexican immigrants. Many are their kin, and Mexican Americans realize that entry into the United States brings Mexicans better economic opportunities. However, numerous deportations only perpetuate the Anglo stereotype of Mexican and Mexican American alike as surplus labor. Mexican Americans, largely the product of past immigration, find that the continued controversy over illegal immigration places them in the ambivalent role of citizen and relative. Mexican American organizations opposing illegal immigration must confront people to whom they are closely linked by culture and kinship, and they must cooperate with government agencies they deeply distrust.

La Raza
Literally meaning 'the people," the term refers to the rich heritage of Mexican Americans; it is therefore used to denote a sense of pride among Mexican Americans today.

The Economic Picture

As shown in Table 10.1, both Mexican Americans and Puerto Ricans have higher unemployment rates, higher rates of poverty, and significantly lower incomes than White Americans. Seven percent of all managerial and professional positions are held by Latinos. When we consider Latinos' economic situation, two topics deserve special attention: the debate over what has been called the culture of poverty and the effort to improve the status of migrant workers (Bureau of the Census 2007a, 388).

The Culture of Poverty Like the African American families described in Chapter 8, Mexican American families are labeled as having traits that, in fact, describe poor families rather than specifically Mexican American families. Indeed, as long ago as 1980, a

TABLE 10.1
Selected Social and Economic Characteristics of Mexican Americans and Puerto Ricans, 2004

	Total White Non-Hispanic	Total Hispanic	Mexican Americans	Puerto Ricans
Percentage having citizenship	96.2	60.8	60.6	98.7
Percentage completing college, 25 years and older	28.1	12.7	8.6	16.2
Percentage households of married couples	57.3	50.8	52.7	40.6
Percentage living below poverty level	8.8	22.0	23.6	23.7
Median family income ($)	48,784	35,929	35,185	34,092

Source: Bureau of the Census 2007f, 8, 11, 15, 17, 18.

culture of poverty
A way of life that involves no future planning, no enduring commitment to marriage, and no work ethic; this culture follows the poor even when they move out of the slums or the barrio.

report of the Commission on Civil Rights (1980, 8) stated that the two most prevalent stereotypical themes appearing in works on Hispanics showed them as exclusively poor and prone to commit violence.

Social scientists have also relied excessively on the traits of the poor to describe an entire subordinate group such as Mexican Americans. Anthropologist Oscar Lewis (1959, 1966), in several publications based on research conducted among Mexicans and Puerto Ricans, identified the **culture of poverty**. According to its theorists, the culture of poverty embraces a deviant way of life that involves no future planning, no enduring commitment to marriage, and absence of the work ethic. This culture supposedly follows the poor, even when they move out of the slums or the barrio.

The culture-of-poverty view is another way of blaming the victim: the affluent are not responsible for social inequality, nor are the policy makers; it is the poor who are to blame for their own problems. This stance allows government and society to attribute the failure of antipoverty and welfare programs to Mexican Americans and other poor people rather than to the programs themselves. These are programs designed and too often staffed by middle-class, English-speaking Anglo professionals. Conflict theorists, noting a similar misuse of the more recent term *underclass,* argue that it is unfair to blame the poor for their lack of money, low education, poor health, and low-paying jobs (Ryan 1976).

Lewis's hypothesis about the culture of poverty came to be used indiscriminately to explain continued poverty. Critics argue that Lewis sought out exotic, pathological behavior, ignoring the fact that even among the poor, most people live fairly conventionally and strive to achieve goals similar to those of the middle class. A second criticism challenges the use of the term *culture of poverty* to describe an entire ethnic group. Because Lewis's data were on poor people, social scientists have increasingly stressed that his conclusions may be correct as far as the data permit, but the data cannot be generalized to all Latinos. His sample was not a representative cross section drawn from different economic and educational levels (Gans 1995; Valentine 1968).

More-recent social science research, unlike Lewis's research, does sample Mexican American families across a broad range of socioeconomic levels. This research shows that when Anglo and Mexican American families of the same social class are compared, they differ little in family organization and attitudes toward child rearing. In addition, comparisons of work ethics find no significant differences between Mexican Americans and Anglos. Poverty is present among Mexican Americans; there is no doubt about that. However, that does not mean there is a culture of poverty or a permanent underclass. Institutions such as the family and the Church seem viable, but the schools are in despair, and the picture on businesses is mixed. However, to question the label *culture of poverty* does not deny the poor life chances facing many Mexican Americans (Aponte 1991; Moore and Pinderhughes 1993; Ryo 2008).

Labor leader Cesar Chavez advocating a boycott of grapes until workers receive better wages and improved working conditions.

Chávez and the Farm Laborers The best-known Hispanic labor leader for economic empowerment was César Chávez, the Mexican American who crusaded to organize migrant farm workers. Efforts to organize agricultural laborers date back to the turn of the twentieth century, but Chávez was the first to enjoy any success. These laborers had never won collective bargaining rights, partly because their mobility made it difficult for them to organize into a unified group.

In 1962, Chávez, then 35 years old, formed the National Farm Workers Association, later to become the United Farm Workers (UFW). Organizing migrant farm workers was not easy because they had no savings to pay for organizing or to live on while striking. Growers could rely on an almost limitless supply of Mexican laborers to replace the Mexican Americans and Filipinos who struck for higher wages and better working conditions.

FARM WORKERS' SANITATION FACILITIES...

Recently, farm workers have protested their working conditions and the pesticide use that may threaten their lives.

Source: © Gary Huck/UE, Huck/Konopacki Labor Cartoons.

Despite initial success, Chávez and the UFW were plagued with continual opposition by agribusiness and many lawmakers. This was about the time the UFW was also trying to heighten public consciousness about the pesticides used in the fields. Research into the long-term effects of pesticides had only begun. Although Chávez's 1988 fast to bring attention to this issue was widely publicized, his efforts did not gain the support he had hoped for.

Chávez had difficulty fulfilling his objectives. By 1993, union membership had dwindled from a high of 80,000 in 1970 to 21,000 (it stood at 27,000 in 2004). Nevertheless, what he and the UFW accomplished was significant. First, they succeeded in making federal and state governments more aware of the exploitation of migrant laborers. Second, the migrant workers, or at least those organized in California, developed a sense of their own power and worth that will make it extremely difficult for growers to abuse them in the future as they had in the past. Third, working conditions improved. California agricultural workers were paid an average of less than $2 an hour in the mid-1960s. By 1987, they were being paid an average of about $5.85 an hour (Mandelbaum 2000; Pawel 2006; Sanchez 1998; Triplett 2004).

Migrant workers still face a very harsh life. An ongoing study of agricultural workers found they are much more likely to suffer from high blood pressure, dental disease, anemia, and poor nutrition, which is ironic because they are harvesting the nation's food. About 70 percent of the workers lack health insurance, and most make less than $10,000 a year, which makes obtaining health care very difficult. Women have far better access to medical treatment because of special maternal and child health services, but a third of the men surveyed said they had never been to a physician or a clinic (Rainey 2000).

César Chávez died in 1993. Although his legacy is clear, many young people, when they hear mention of Chávez, are more likely to think of professional boxer Julio Cesar Chavez. By the beginning of the twenty-first century, the primary challenge came from efforts to permit more foreign workers, primarily from Mexico and Central America, to enter the United States temporarily at even lower wages. About three-quarters of all farm workers are Mexican or Mexican American. The problems of migrant farm workers are inextricably tied to the lives of both Latinos and Latin Americans (Franklin 2007; Triplett 2004).

Political Organizations

Chicanismo
An ideology emphasizing pride and positive identity among Mexican Americans.

As noted in Chapter 9, Latinos are becoming more involved in party politics in the United States. Though tending to support Democratic candidates (with the exception of Cuban Americans, who typically back Republicans), Latinos are showing a willingness to be more independent voters. As one might expect, given their growing numbers and greater voting power, more Latinos are successfully seeking elective office. This has not always been the case. Politically oriented Mexican Americans such as Rodolfo "Corky" Gonzales in Denver turned to grassroots community organizing. Frustrated by the lack of responsiveness of established politicians, Mexican Americans for a brief period created their own independent party in Texas. La Raza Unida was a third party supporting candidates who offered alternatives to the Democratic and Republican parties (Hero 1995; Rosales 1996).

The social protests that characterized much of the political activity in the United States of the mid-1960s touched the Mexican American community as well. In Southern California in 1966, young Chicanos in college were attracted to the ideology of **Chicanismo** (or *Chicanozaje*) and joined what is popularly called the *Chicano movement*. Like Black Power, Chicanismo has taken on a variety of meanings, but all definitions stress a positive self-image and place little reliance on conventional forms of political activity. Followers of Chicanismo, unlike the more assimilation-oriented older generations, have been less likely to accept the standard claim that the United States is equally just to all.

Besides a positive self-image, Chicanismo and the movement of La Raza include renewed awareness of the plight of Chicanos at the hands of Anglos. Mexican Americans are a colonial minority, as Joan Moore (1970) wrote, because their relationship with Anglos was originally involuntary. Mexican culture in the United States has been either transformed or destroyed by Anglos, and the Mexican American people themselves have been victims of racism. The colonial model points out the ways in which societal institutions have failed Mexican Americans and perpetuated their problems. Militant Mexican Americans refer to assimilationists, who they say would sell out to the White people, as *vendidos*, or traitors. The ultimate insult is the term *Malinche*, the name of the Mexican American woman who became the mistress of Spanish conqueror Cortés. Many in the Chicano movement believe that if one does not work actively in the struggle, one is working against it (Delgado 2008b; Rosales 1996).

Perhaps as well as any recent Mexican American, Reies López Tijerina captures the spirit of Chicanismo. Born in a cotton field worked by migrant farmers, Tijerina became a Pentecostal preacher and in the late 1950s took an interest in old Spanish land grants. From research in Mexico, Spain, and the Southwest, he concluded that the Mexican Americans—and, more specifically, the Hispanos—had lost significant tracts of land through quasi-legal and other questionable practices. In 1963, he formed the Alianza Federal de Mercedes (Federal Alliance of Land Grants), whose purpose is to recover the lost land. To publicize his purpose when few Anglos would pay attention, he seized part of the Kit Carson National Forest in New Mexico. Tijerina spent the next few years either in jail or awaiting trial. Tijerina's quest for restoration of land rights has been accompanied by violence, even though he advocates civil disobedience. However, the violence led him to be criticized by some Hispanics as well as Anglos (Nabokov 1970; Rosales 1996).

Thirty years later, Tijerina's arguments, which had seemed outrageous to most, were beginning to be endorsed by politicians. In 1997, Republican members of Congress introduced the Guadalupe-Hidalgo Treaty Claims Act to review Latino land claims, especially as they relate to government-held forestland. Clearly, the Republicans were trying to garner support from Hispanic voters, but most important, this action showed that the goals of Tijerina and his followers were finally being considered seriously.

Organized in 1967, the Mexican American Legal Defense and Education Fund has emerged as a potent force to protect Mexican Americans' constitutional rights. Although it does not endorse candidates, MALDEF has made itself felt in the political arena, much as the NAACP has for African Americans. On the education side, it has addressed segregation, biased testing, inequities in school financing, and failure to promote bilingualism.

MALDEF has been involved in litigation concerning employment practices, immigration reform, and voting rights. It has emerged as the primary civil rights group for Mexican Americans and other Latinos (Alvarez-Smith 2008).

The late 1990s saw the Mexican community in the United States faced with a new political challenge. Beginning in 1998, Mexicans in the United States could acquire rights as Mexican nationals under Mexico's new dual nationality law. Their children, even if U.S. born, are also eligible for Mexican nationality. The United States does not prohibit dual nationality, and it is estimated that anywhere from 5 million to 10 millionMexican Americans are eligible for such dual nationality. Although many dual-nationality people will not be allowed to vote in Mexico's elections, this measure is likely to further their interest in political life south of the border. As we will now see with Puerto Rico, Latinos in the United States find political issues of importance outside the 50 states (*Migration News* 1998).

Puerto Ricans

Puerto Ricans' current association with the United States, like that of the Mexican people, began as the result of the outcome of a war. The island of Borinquén, subsequently called Puerto Rico, was claimed by Spain in 1493. The native inhabitants, the Taino Indians, were significantly reduced in number by conquest, slavery, and genocide. Although for generations the legacy of the Taino was largely thought to be archaeological in nature, recent DNA tests revealed that more than 60 percent of Puerto Ricans today have a Taíno ancestor (Cockburn 2003, 41).

After Puerto Rico had been ruled by Spain for four centuries, the island was seized by the United States in 1898 during the Spanish–American War. Spain relinquished control of it in the Treaty of Paris. The value of Puerto Rico for the United States, as it had been for Spain, was mainly its strategic location, which was advantageous for maritime trade (Figure 10.1).

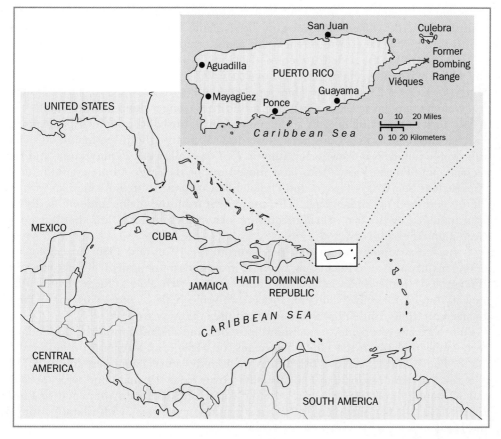

FIGURE 10.1
Puerto Rico

The beginnings of rule by the United States quickly destroyed any hope that Puerto Ricans—or Boricua, as Puerto Ricans call themselves—had for self-rule. All power was given to officials appointed by the president, and any act of the island's legislature could be overruled by Congress. Even the spelling was changed briefly to Porto Rico to suit North American pronunciation. English, previously unknown on the island, became the only language permitted in the school systems. The people were colonized—first politically, then culturally, and finally economically (Aran et al. 1973; Christopulos 1974).

Citizenship was extended to Puerto Ricans by the Jones Act of 1917, but Puerto Rico remained a colony. This political dependence altered in 1948, when Puerto Rico elected its own governor and became a commonwealth. This status, officially Estado Libre Asociado, or Associated Free State, extends to Puerto Rico and its people privileges and rights different from those of people on the mainland. Although Puerto Ricans are U.S. citizens and elect their own governor, they may not vote in presidential elections and have no voting representation in Congress. They are subject to military service, Selective Service registration, and all federal laws. Puerto Ricans have a homeland that is and at the same time is not a part of the United States.

The Bridge between the Island and the Mainland

Despite their citizenship, Puerto Ricans are occasionally challenged by immigration officials. Because other Latin Americans attempt to enter the country posing as Puerto Ricans, Puerto Ricans find their papers scrutinized more closely than do other U.S. citizens.

Puerto Ricans came to the mainland in small numbers in the first half of the century, often encouraged by farm labor contracts similar to those extended to Mexican braceros. During World War II, the government recruited hundreds of Puerto Ricans to work on the railroads, in food-manufacturing plants, and in copper mines on the mainland. But migration has been largely a post–World War II phenomenon. The 1940 census showed fewer than 70,000 Puerto Ricans on the mainland. By 2006, more than 4 million Puerto Ricans lived on the mainland and 3.9 million residents lived on the island.

Among the factors that have contributed to migration are the economic pull away from the underdeveloped and overpopulated island, the absence of legal restrictions against travel, and the growth of cheap air transportation. As the migration continues, the mainland offers the added attraction of a large Puerto Rican community in New York City, which makes adjustment easier for new arrivals.

New York City still has a formidable population of Puerto Ricans (770,000), but significant changes have taken place. First, Puerto Ricans no longer dominate the Latino scene in New York City, making up only a little more than a third of the city's Hispanic population. Second, Puerto Ricans are now more dispersed throughout the mainland's cities, with sizable numbers in New Jersey, Illinois, Florida, California, Pennsylvania, and Connecticut. The Puerto Ricans who have moved out of the large ethnic communities in cities such as New York, Chicago, and Philadelphia are as a group more familiar with U.S. culture and the English language. This movement from the major settlements also has been hastened by the loss of manufacturing jobs in these cities, a loss that hits Puerto Rican men especially hard.

As the U.S. economy underwent recessions in the 1970s and 1980s, unemployment among mainland Puerto Ricans, always high, increased dramatically. This increase shows in migration. In the 1950s, half of the Latino arrivals were Puerto Rican. By the 1970s, they accounted for only 3 percent. Indeed, in some years of the 1980s, more Puerto Ricans went from mainland to the island than the other way around.

Puerto Ricans returning to the island have become a significant force. Indeed, they have come to be given the name **Neoricans**, or *Nuyoricans*, a term the islanders also use for Puerto Ricans in New York. Longtime islanders direct a modest amount of hostility toward these Neoricans. They usually return from the mainland with more formal schooling, more money, and a better command of English than native Puerto Ricans have. Not too surprisingly, Neoricans compete very well with islanders for jobs and land.

Neoricans
Puerto Ricans who return to the island to settle after living on the mainland of the United States (also Nuyoricans).

The ethnic mix of the nation's largest city has gotten even more complex over the last 10 years as Mexican and Mexican American arrivals in New York City have far outpaced any growth among Puerto Ricans. New York City is now following the pattern of other cities such as Miami, where the Latino identity is no longer defined by a single group.

neocolonialism
Continuing dependence of former colonies on foreign countries.

The Island of Puerto Rico

Puerto Rico, located about a thousand miles from Miami, has never been the same since Columbus discovered it in 1493. The original inhabitants of the island were wiped out in a couple of generations by disease, tribal warfare, hard labor, unsuccessful rebellions against the Spanish, and fusion with their conquerors. These social processes are highlighted in the Spectrum of Intergroup Relations that summarizes the experience of Latinos in the United States (see figure on page 257).

Among the institutions imported to Puerto Rico by Spain was slavery. Although slavery in Puerto Rico was not as harsh as in the southern United States, the legacy of the transfer of Africans is present in the appearance of Puerto Ricans today, many of whom are seen by people on the mainland as Black.

The commonwealth period that began in 1948 has been a significant one for Puerto Rico. Change has been dramatic, although whether it has all been progress is debatable. On the positive side, Spanish has been reintroduced as the language of classroom instruction, but the study of English is also required. The popularity in the 1980s of music groups such as Menudo shows that Puerto Rican young people want to maintain ties with their ethnicity. Such success is a challenge because Puerto Rican music is almost never aired on non-Hispanic radio stations. The Puerto Rican people have had a vibrant and distinctive cultural tradition, as seen clearly in their folk heroes, holidays, sports, and contemporary literature and drama. Dominance by the culture of the United States makes it difficult to maintain their culture on the mainland and even on the island itself.

Puerto Rico and its people reflect a phenomenon called **neocolonialism**, which refers to continuing dependence of former colonies on foreign countries. Initially, this term was introduced to refer to African nations that, even after gaining their political independence from Great Britain, France, and other European nations, continued to find their destiny in the hands of the former colonial powers. Although most Puerto Ricans today are staunchly proud of their American citizenship, they also want to have their own national identity independent of the United States. This has not been and continues not to be easy.

Puerto Ricans generally maintain dual identity proudly, celebrating Puerto Rican Day each June by observing the island's independence from Spain.

From 1902, English was the official language of the island, but Spanish was the language of the people, reaffirming the island's cultural identity independent of the United States. In 1992, however, Puerto Rico also established Spanish as an additional official language.

In reality, the language issue is related more to ideology than to substance. Although English is once again required in primary and secondary schools, textbooks may be written in English although the classes are conducted in Spanish. Indeed, Spanish remains the language of the island; 8 percent of the islanders speak only English, and among Spanish-speaking adults about 15 percent speak English "very well" (Bureau of the Census 2007h).

Issues of Statehood and Self-Rule   Puerto Ricans have consistently argued and fought for independence for most of the 500 years since Columbus landed. They continue to do so in even in the twenty-first century. The contemporary commonwealth arrangement is popular with many Puerto Ricans, but others prefer statehood, whereas some call for complete independence from the United States. In Table 10.2, we summarize the advantages and disadvantages of the current status as a territory or commonwealth and the alternatives of statehood and independence.

The arguments for continued commonwealth status include both the serious and the trivial. Among some island residents, the idea of statehood invokes the fear of higher taxes and an erosion of their cultural heritage. Some even fear the end of separate Puerto Rican

TABLE 10.2
Puerto Rico's Future

Continuing Territorial Status (Status Quo)

Pros	Cons
■ Island is under U.S. protection.	■ United States has ultimate authority over island matters.
■ Islanders enjoy U.S. citizenship with a distinct national identity.	■ Residents cannot vote for president.
■ Residents don't pay federal income taxes (they do pay into Social Security, Medicare, and 32% to island tax collectors).	■ Residents who work for any company or organization that is funded by the United States must pay federal income taxes.
■ United States provides federal funds in the sum of $22 billion annually and offers other tax advantages.	■ Although Puerto Rico has a higher standard of living compared to other Caribbean islands, it has half the per capita income of the poorest U.S. states.
■ Island retains representation in the Miss Universe Pageant and Olympic Games.	■ Island cannot enter into free-trade agreements.

Statehood

Pros	Cons
■ Permanent and guaranteed U.S. citizenship and an end to U.S. colonial rule over the island.	■ Possibility of English-only requirements (loss of cultural or national identity).
■ The island would receive federal money to build the infrastructure.	■ An increased standard of living could result in greater economic deterioration because of the current muddled economic situation.
■ The island would be able to enjoy open-market trade with U.S. allies.	■ Businesses that take advantage of certain tax benefits could leave the island, and future businesses might not consider working there.
■ The island would acquire six seats in the House of Representatives and two seats in the Senate, enabling the island to have more political clout and the right to vote in presidential elections.	■ Island would lose representation in the Miss Universe Pageant and Olympic Games.

Independence

Pros	Cons
■ Island would retain language and culture.	■ Lose U.S. citizenship.
■ Island would be able to participate in the global economy.	■ Lose U.S. protection.
■ End of U.S. colonial rule over the island.	■ Lose federal funds.

Sources: Author, based on *Let Puerto Rico Decide* 2005; President's Task Force on Puerto Rico's Status 2005; C. J. Williams 2006a, 2007.

participation in the Olympic Games and the Miss Universe Pageant. On the other hand, although independence may be attractive, commonwealth supporters argue that it includes too many unknown costs, so they embrace the status quo. Others view statehood as a key to increased economic development and expansion for tourism.

Proponents of independence have a long, vocal history of insisting on the need for Puerto Rico to regain its cultural and political autonomy. Some of the supporters of independence have even been militant. In 1950, nationalists attempted to assassinate President Truman, killing a White House guard in the process. Four years later, another band of nationalists opened fire in the gallery of the U.S. House of Representatives, wounding five members of Congress. Beginning in 1974, a group calling itself the Armed Forces of National Liberation (FALN, for Fuerzas Armadas de Liberación Nacional) took responsibility for more than 100 explosions that continued through 1987. The FALN is not alone; at least four other militant groups advocating independence were identified as having been at work in the 1980s. The island itself is occasionally beset by violent demonstrations, often reacting to U.S. military installations there—a symbol of U.S. control (Santos-Hernanández 2008).

For more than 60 years, a portion of Puerto Rico has been as a bombing target by the military and is seen by many Puerto Ricans as an obvious example of colonial oppression. Protests for years focused on the bombing practice runs over Viéques, an island located six miles off its southeastern coast (see Figure 10.1). Residents were evicted with little compensation. Long after this exodus, residents of remaining areas of Viéques objected to continued bombing. The death of a civilian hit by a misguided bomb in 1999 launched a series of marches, sit-ins, blockades, and other acts of civil disobedience reminiscent of the civil rights era (Ayala and Carro-Figueroa 2006; Colón Morera and Santana 2006).

The federal government ended the bombing in 2003, but islanders continue to be upset that more has not been done sooner to clean up the leftover bombs. In Listen to Our Voices, poet and professor Martín St. Espada questions the continued bombing and urges people on the mainland to join Puerto Ricans on the island in calling for an immediate halt to the military exercises (Quintanilla 2006).

The issue of Puerto Rico's political destiny is, in part, ideological. Independence is the easiest way for the island to retain and strengthen its cultural and political identity. Some nationalists express the desire that an autonomous Puerto Rico develop close political ties with communist Cuba. The crucial arguments for and against independence probably are economic. An independent Puerto Rico would no longer be required to use U.S. shipping lines, which are more expensive than those of foreign competitors. However, an independent Puerto Rico might be faced with a tariff wall when trading with its largest current customer, the mainland United States. Also, Puerto Rican migration to the mainland could be restricted.

Puerto Rico's future status most recently faced a vote in 1998. In the latest nonbinding referendum, 50 percent of residents favored continuing commonwealth status, and 47 percent backed statehood. Less than 3 percent favored independence. Interestingly, a 1998 survey of people on the mainland found the population evenly split, with a third favoring each option. Given the lack of overwhelming feelings for statehood on the island, it is unlikely that there will be sufficient support in Congress to move toward statehood. Yet with half the island population expressing a preference for a change, it is clear that discontent with the current arrangement prevails and remains a "colonial dilemma" (Navarro 1998; Saad 1998).

The Social Construction of Race The most significant difference between the meaning of race in Puerto Rico and on the mainland is that Puerto Rico, like so many other Caribbean societies, has a **color gradient**, a term that describes distinctions based on skin color made on a continuum rather than by sharp categorical separations. The presence of a color gradient reflects past fusion between different groups (see figure on page 257). Rather than being either "Black" or "White," people are judged in such societies as "lighter" or "darker" than others. Rather than seeing people as either black or white in skin color, Puerto Ricans perceive people as ranging from pale white to very black. Puerto Ricans are more sensitive to degrees of difference and make less effort to pigeonhole a person into one of two categories.

color gradient
The placement of people on a continuum from light to dark skin color rather than in distinct racial groupings by skin color.

Listen to Our Voices

¡VIVA VIEQUES!

More than eighty years ago, Puerto Rican poet and political leader Jose de Diego wrote, "Puerto Ricans do not know how to say no." And yet, he pointed out, "The no of the oppressed has been the word, the genesis, of the liberation of peoples." De Diego warned: "We must learn to say no."

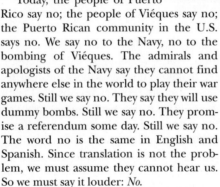

Martín St. Espada

Today, the people of Puerto Rico say no; the people of Viéques say no; the Puerto Rican community in the U.S. says no. We say no to the Navy, no to the bombing of Viéques. The admirals and apologists of the Navy say they cannot find anywhere else in the world to play their war games. Still we say no. They say they will use dummy bombs. Still we say no. They promise a referendum some day. Still we say no. The word no is the same in English and Spanish. Since translation is not the problem, we must assume they cannot hear us. So we must say it louder: *No.*

Viéques is an offshore island municipality of Puerto Rico. It is controlled, like the rest of Puerto Rico, by the United States. More than 9,300 people live in Viéques. Yet since 1941, the U.S. Navy has occupied two-thirds of this inhabited island for war games and live-ammunition target practice. According to journalist Juan Gonzalez, "Practice at the range goes on for as many as 200 days a year. Combat planes bomb and strafe the island. Destroyers bomb it from the sea. . . . Maneuvers have included, on occasion, practice with depleted uranium shells, napalm, and cluster bombs."

Federal tax dollars go directly to the military budget, and thus to support the Navy presence in Viéques. We share a responsibility to the people of Viéques to protest the injustice our dollars make possible. Keep in mind, too, that Puerto Rico lacks a voting representative in Congress. Given the absence of democratic representation for the people of Puerto Rico, the people of the United States must speak for them.

We Puerto Ricans must keep saying no. And by saying no, we say yes. As Eduardo Galeano has written, "By saying no to the devastating empire of greed whose center lies in North America, we are saying yes to another possible America. . . . In saying no to a peace without dignity, we are saying yes to the sacred right of rebellion against injustice."

Source: St. Espada 2000, 27–29.
Copyright © 2000 by *The Progressive.*
Reprinted by permission of *The Progressive,*
409 E. Main Street, Madison, WI 53703. www.
progressive.org.

The presence of a color gradient rather than two or three racial categories does not necessarily mean that prejudice is less. Generally, however, societies with a color gradient permit more flexibility, and therefore, are less likely to impose specific sanctions against a group of people based on skin color alone. Puerto Rico has not suffered interracial conflict or violence; its people are conscious of different racial heritages. Studies disagree on the amount of prejudice in Puerto Rico, but all concur that race is not as clear-cut an issue on the island as it is on the mainland.

Racial identification in Puerto Rico depends a great deal on the attitude of the individual making the judgment. If one thinks highly of a person, then he or she may be seen as a member of a more acceptable racial group. A variety of terms is used in the color gradient to describe people racially: *blanco* (white), *trigueño* (bronze- or wheat-colored), *moreno* (dark-skinned), and *negro* (black) are a few of these. Factors such as social class and social position determine race, but on the mainland race is more likely to determine social class. This situation may puzzle people from the mainland, but racial etiquette on the mainland may be just as difficult for Puerto Ricans to comprehend and accept. Puerto Ricans arriving in the United States may find a new identity thrust on them by the dominant society (Denton and Villarrubia 2007; Landale and Oropesa 2002; Loveman and Muniz 2007; Sánchez 2007).

The Island Economy

The United States' role in Puerto Rico has produced an overall economy that, though strong by Caribbean standards, remains well below that of the poorest areas of the United States. For many years, the federal government exempted U.S. industries locating in Puerto Rico from taxes on profits for at least 10 years. In addition, the federal government's program of enterprise zones, which grants tax incentives to promote private investment in inner cities, has been extended to Puerto Rico. Unquestionably, Puerto Rico has become attractive to mainland-based corporations. Skeptics point out that as a result, the island's agriculture has been largely ignored. Furthermore, the economic benefits to the island are limited. Businesses have spent the profits gained on Puerto Rico back on the mainland.

Puerto Rico's economy is in severe trouble compared with that of the mainland. Its unemployment rate in 2006 was 15.7 percent, compared with 6.4 percent for the mainland—about three times that of the mainland. In addition, the median household income is one-third of what it is in the United States. In 2007, 45.5 percent of the population was below the poverty rate, compared with 13 percent in the nation as a whole and 20.6 percent in Mississippi, the state with the highest level. Efforts to raise the wages of Puerto Rican workers only make the island less attractive to labor-intensive businesses, that is, those that employ larger numbers of unskilled people. Capital-intensive companies, such as the petrochemical industries, have found Puerto Rico attractive, but they have not created jobs for the semiskilled. A growing problem is that Puerto Rico is emerging as a major gateway to the United States for illegal drugs from South America, which has led the island to experience waves of violence and the social ills associated with the drug trade (Bureau of the Census 2007h, 2008e; Collins, Bosworth, and Soto-Class 2006).

Puerto Rico is an example of the world systems theory initially presented in Chapter 1. **World systems theory** is the view of the global economic system as divided between certain industrialized nations that control wealth and developing countries that are controlled and exploited. Although Puerto Rico may be well off compared with many other Caribbean nations, it clearly is at the mercy of economic forces in the United States and, to a much lesser extent, other industrial nations. Puerto Rico continues to struggle with the advantages of citizenship and the detriment of playing a peripheral role in the economy of the United States.

New challenges continue to face Puerto Rico. First, with congressional approval in 1994 of the North American Free Trade Agreement, Mexico, Canada, and the United States became integrated into a single economic market. The reduction of trade barriers with Mexico, coupled with that nation's lower wages, combined to undercut Puerto Rico's commonwealth advantage. Second, many more island nations now offer sun-seeking tourists from the mainland alternative destinations to Puerto Rico. In addition, cruise ships present another attractive option for tourists. Given the economic problems of the island, it is not surprising that many Puerto Ricans migrate to the mainland (Rivera-Batiz and Santiago 1996; Rohter 1993).

For years, circular migration between the mainland and island has served as a safety valve for Puerto Rico's population, which has grown annually at a rate 50 percent faster than that of the rest of the United States. Typically, migrants from Puerto Rico represent a broad range of occupations. There are seasonal fluctuations as Puerto Rican farm workers leave the island in search of employment. Puerto Ricans, particularly agricultural workers, earn higher wages on the mainland, yet a significant proportion return despite the higher wages (Meléndez 1994; Torres 2008).

world systems theory
A view of the global economic system as divided between nations that control wealth and those that provide natural resources and labor.

The Contemporary Picture of Mexican Americans and Puerto Ricans

tracking
The practice of placing students in specific curriculum groups on the basis of test scores and other criteria.

We will now consider the major social institutions of education, the family, health care, and religion, noting the similarities in their organization between Puerto Ricans and Mexican Americans.

Education

Both Mexican Americans and Puerto Ricans, as groups, have experienced gains in formal schooling but still lag behind White Americans in many standards of educational attainment. As is apparent in Table 10.1, both groups are also well behind other Latinos. Although bilingual education is still endorsed in the United States, the implementation of effective, high-quality programs has been difficult, as Chapter 9 showed. In addition, attacks on the funding of bilingual education have continued into the present.

Latinos, including Mexican Americans and Puerto Ricans, have become increasingly isolated from non-Latinos. In 1968, 55 percent of all Hispanics attended predominantly minority schools—that is, schools in which at least half of the students were members of minorities. Four decades later, this had increased to 76 percent. By 2003, the typical Latino student was still in a school that was 54 percent Hispanic, with only 30 percent of the students White non-Hispanic. Furthermore, as we noted in Chapter 1, the separation continues, with the highest patterns of residential segregation occurring in the cities with the largest number of Hispanics (Frankenburg et al. 2003; Orfield 2002; Orfield and Lee 2005).

Three factors explain this increasing social isolation of Mexican Americans and Puerto Ricans from other students in school. First, Latinos are increasingly concentrated in the largest cities, where minorities dominate. Second, the numbers of Latinos have increased dramatically since the 1970s, when efforts to desegregate schools began to lose momentum. Third, schools once desegregated have become resegregated as the numbers of school-aged Mexican Americans in an area have increased and as the determination to maintain balances in schools has lessened.

Even where Anglos and Latinos live in the same school district, the problem of social isolation in the classroom is often furthered through tracking. **Tracking** is the practice of placing students in specific classes or curriculum groups on the basis of test scores and other criteria. Tracking begins very early in the classroom, often in reading groups during first grade. These tracks may reinforce the disadvantages of Hispanic children from less-affluent families and non–English-speaking households that have not been exposed to English reading materials in their homes during early childhood (Rodríguez 1989).

Students see few teachers and administrators like themselves because few Latino university students have been prepared to serve as teachers and administrators. In 2006, only 51 percent of Mexican Americans and 64 percent of Puerto Ricans aged 25 or older had completed high school, compared with 88 percent of White non-Hispanics (see Table 10.1). Mexican Americans and Puerto Ricans who do choose to continue their education beyond high school are more likely to select a technical school or community college to acquire work-related skills (Ellison 2008).

Mexican Americans and Puerto Ricans are underrepresented in higher education in all roles. Recent reports have documented the absence of Hispanics among college teachers and administrators: less than 5 percent of all college teachers were Latino in 2006. The situation is similar in this respect to

Latino college students look for the same social experiences as do non-Hispanics. Fraternities and sororities oriented to attracting Hispanics have experienced tremendous increases in the last decade. Here are members of Lambda Upsilon Lambda fraternity at Rutgers University.

that of Blacks; however, there are no Latino counterparts to historically Black colleges, such as the Tuskegee Institute, to provide a source of leaders (Bureau of the Census 2007a, 389).

Motivation does not appear to be the barrier to school achievement, at least among Mexican immigrants. A Harvard University study of the attitudes of Mexican immigrant adolescents showed that 84 percent felt that school was the most important thing, compared with 40 percent of White teenagers. Again, 68 percent of immigrant children felt that doing their homework was more important than helping a friend, compared with only 20 percent of White adolescents who held the same priorities. However, there is evidence that as these children assimilate, they begin to take on the prevailing White views. The same survey showed second-generation Mexican Americans still giving education a higher priority but not as high as their immigrant counterparts. We will consider shortly how assimilation has a similar effect on health (Crosnoe 2005; Woo 1996).

With respect to higher education, Latinos face challenges similar to those that Black students meet on predominantly White campuses. Given the social isolation of Latino high schools, Mexican Americans are likely to have to adjust for the first time to an educational environment almost totally populated by Anglos. They may experience racism for the first time, just as they are trying to adjust to a heavier academic load.

Family Life

The most important organization or social institution among Latinos, or for that matter any group, is the family. The structure of the Mexican American family differs little from that of all families in the United States, a statement remarkable in itself, given the impoverishment of a significant number of Mexican Americans.

Latino households are described as laudably more familistic than others in the United States. **Familism** means pride and closeness in the family, which results in family obligation and loyalty coming before individual needs. The family is the primary source of both social interaction and caregiving. In Research Focus, we look at familism more closely.

Familism has been viewed as both a positive and a negative influence on individual Mexican Americans and Puerto Ricans. It has been argued to have the negative effect of discouraging youths with a bright future from taking advantage of opportunities that would separate them from their family. Familism is generally regarded as good, however, because an extended family provides emotional strength in times of crisis. Close family ties maintain the mental and social well-being of the elderly. Most Latinos, therefore, see the intact, extended family as a norm and as a nurturing unit that provides support throughout a person's lifetime. The many significant aspects of familism include the importance of *campadrazgo* (the godparent–godchild relationship), the benefits of the financial dependency of kin, the availability of relatives as a source of advice, and the active involvement of the elderly in the family.

Health Care

Earlier, in Chapter 5, we introduced the concept of **life chances**, which are people's opportunities to provide themselves with material goods, positive living conditions, and favorable life experiences. We have consistently seen Latino groups as having more limited life chances. Perhaps in no other area does this apply so much as in the health care system.

Hispanics as a group are locked out of the health care system more often than any other racial or ethnic group. Although federal law requires that emergency medical treatment be available to all people, even illegal immigrants, many Hispanics—even those with legal residency but who have relatives here illegally—are wary of seeking medical treatment. A third had no health insurance (or other coverage such as Medicaid) for all of 2007, compared with 11.2 percent of White non-Hispanics and 19.3 percent of Blacks. Predictably, the uninsured are less likely to have a regular source of medical care. This means that they wait for a crisis before seeking care. Fewer are immunized, and rates of preventable diseases such as lead poisoning are higher. No coverage is increasing, a circumstance that may reflect a further breakdown in health care

familism
Pride and closeness in the family that result in placing family obligation and loyalty before individual needs.

life chances
People's opportunities to provide themselves with material goods, positive living conditions, and favorable life experiences.

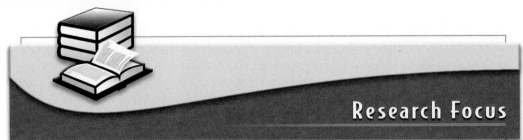

Research Focus

THE LATINO FAMILY CIRCLE: FAMILISM

Familism within the Latino community is associated with a sense of obligation to fellow family members, the placement of family interests over individual desires, and exclusiveness of the family even over friends and work. Familism has been likened to a *thick* social network where everyday social interaction is defined by one's family.

Familism for the U.S.-born Latino is also associated with familiarity with Spanish so that one can truly relate to the older relatives for whom English may remain very much a foreign language. Being nominally if not practicing Roman Catholic is another means of maintaining strong family ties.

U.S. Hispanic families are undergoing transition with the growth of more multigenerational families born in the United States as well as simultaneously continuing arrival of new immigrants. This is all complicated by the **mixed status** present in so many Latino extended families (with the obvious exception of Puerto Ricans, for whom citizenship is automatic). As explained in Chapter 4, mixed status refers to families in which one or more is a citizen and one or more is a noncitizen. This especially becomes problematic when the noncitizens are illegal or undocumented immigrants. All the usual pressures within a family become magnified when there is mixed status.

Although immigration makes generalizing about Latinos as a group very difficult at any one point in time, analysis of available data indicates that Hispanic households are taking on more of the characteristics of larger society. For example, cohabiting couples with or without children were relatively uncommon among Hispanic groups but now are coming to resemble the pattern of non-Hispanics. Similarly, Mexican-born women in the United States are more likely to enter marriage earlier, but now later generations are more likely to start marriage later. The same was true for Puerto Rican women born on the island, compared with those born on the mainland.

In the future, the greatest factor that may lead to a decline in familism is marriage across ethnic lines. Continuing immigration from Mexico has tended to slow out-group marriage, but during periods of lessened migration, immigrants have been more likely to form unions with different Latino groups or with non-Hispanics.

Today we still see a more collective orientation or familism rather than an individualistic orientation that is more likely to encourage family members to move away from their relatives or, more dramatically, lead to desertion or divorce. Studies with other established, longer-term immigrant groups suggest that family members become more individualistic in their values and behavior. People both within and outside the Latino community are very interested to see if Hispanics will follow this pattern and whether the familism that is so characteristic of much of the Latino community will fade.

Source: Jacobson, England, and Barrus 2008; Landale and Oropesa 2007 to 2002; Landale, Oropesa, and Bradatan 2006; Lichter, Brown, Qian, and Carmalt 2007; Sarkistan, Gerena, and Gerstel 2007.

delivery or may be a result of continuing immigration (DeNavas-Walt et. al. 2008, 22; Ortega et al. 2007).

The health care problem facing Mexican Americans and other Hispanic groups is complicated by the lack of Hispanic health professionals. Hispanics accounted for 6 percent or less of dentists and physicians, yet as a group Hispanics are about 15 percent of the population. Obviously, one does not need to be administered health care by someone in one's own ethnic group, but the paucity of Hispanic professionals increases the likelihood that the group will be underserved (Bureau of the Census 2007a, 389).

Some Mexican Americans and many other Latinos have cultural beliefs that make them less likely to use the medical system. They may interpret their illnesses according to

mixed status
Families in which one or more members are citizens and one or more are noncitizens.

folk practices or **curanderismo**: Latino folk medicine, a form of holistic health care and healing. This orientation influences how one approaches health care and even how one defines illness. Most Hispanics probably use folk healers, or *curanderos*, infrequently, but perhaps 20 percent rely on home remedies. Although these are not necessarily without value, especially if a dual system of folk and establishment medicine is followed, reliance on natural beliefs may be counterproductive. Another aspect of folk beliefs is the identification of folk-defined illnesses such as *susto* (or fright sickness) and *atague* (or fighting attack). Although these complaints, alien by these names to Anglos, often have biological bases, they must be dealt with carefully by sensitive medical professionals who can diagnose and treat illnesses accurately (Belliard and Ramirez-Johnson 2005; Dansie 2004; Lara et al. 2005).

curanderismo
Hispanic folk medicine.

Religion

The most important formal organization in the Hispanic community is the Church. Most Puerto Ricans and Mexican Americans express a religious preference for the Catholic Church. In 2007, about 58 percent of Hispanics were Catholic. In Figure 10.2, we examine a more detailed background of specific religious affiliations indicated by Latinos.

The Roman Catholic Church took an assimilationist role in the past, whether with Hispanic Catholics or with other minority Catholics. The Church has only sporadically involved itself in the Chicano movement, and rarely in the past did the upper levels of the Church hierarchy support Chicanismo. For example, only with some prodding did the Roman Catholic Church support the United Farm Workers, a group whose membership was predominantly Catholic.

Recently, the Roman Catholic Church has become more community oriented, seeking to identify Latino, or at least Spanish-speaking, clergy and staff to serve Latino parishes. The lack of Spanish-speaking priests has been complicated by a smaller proportion of a declining number of men who are training for the priesthood and who speak Spanish (Ramirez 2000; Rosales 1996).

Not only is the Catholic Church important to Hispanics, but also Hispanics play a significant role for the Church. The population growth of Mexican Americans and other Hispanics has been responsible for the Catholic Church's continued growth in recent years, whereas mainstream Protestant faiths have declined in size. Hispanics account for more than a third of Catholics in the United States. The Church is trying to adjust to Hispanics' more expressive manifestation of religious faith, with frequent reliance on their own patron saints and the presence of special altars in their homes. Catholic churches in some parts of the United States are even starting to accommodate observances of the Mexican Día de los Muertos, or Day of the Dead. Such practices are a tradition from rural Mexico, where religion was followed without trained clergy. Yet even today in the United States, Hispanics continue to be underrepresented among priests, with only 4.4 percent nationwide being Hispanic (O'Connor 1998).

Although Latinos are predominantly Catholic, their membership in Protestant and other Christian faiths is growing. According to a national survey by the University of

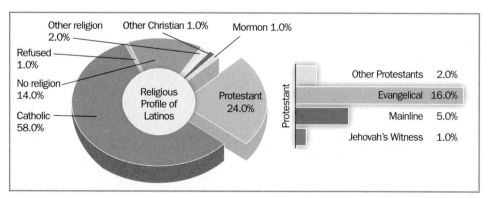

FIGURE 10.2
Religious Profile of Latinos

Source: Pew Forum on Religion and Public Life, 2008.

Pentecostalism
A religion similar in many respects to evangelical faiths that believes in the infusion of the Holy Spirit into services and in religious experiences such as faith healing.

Notre Dame, first-generation Latinos are 74 percent Catholic, but by the third generation only 62 percent are Catholic (Watanabe and Enriquez 2005).

Pentecostalism, a type of evangelical Christianity, is growing in Latin America and is clearly making a significant impact on Latinos in the United States. Adherents to Pentecostal faiths hold beliefs similar to those of the evangelicals but also believe in the infusion of the Holy Spirit into services and in religious experiences such as faith healing. Pentecostalism and similar faiths are attractive to many because they offer followers the opportunity to express their religious fervor openly. Furthermore, many of the churches are small and, therefore, offer a sense of community, often with Spanish-speaking leadership. Gradually, the more-established faiths are recognizing the desirability of offering Latino parishioners a greater sense of belonging (Hunt 1999).

Conclusion

David Gomez (1971) described Mexican Americans as "strangers in their own land." Puerto Ricans, on the other hand, are still debating what should be the political destiny of their island nation. All of this makes nationality a very real part of the destiny of Mexican Americans and Puerto Ricans. Can they also preserve their cultures along with a sense of national fervor, or will these be a casualty of assimilation?

As we have seen, even when we concentrate on just Mexican Americans or Puerto Ricans out of the larger collective group of Hispanics or Latinos, diversity remains. As shown in Table 10.3, large concentrations of Latinos live in a number of the largest U.S. metropolitan areas.

Mexican Americans are divided among the Hispanos and the descendants of earlier Mexican immigrants and the more recent arrivals from Mexico. Puerto Ricans can be divided by virtue of residency and the extent to which they identify with the island culture. For many Puerto Ricans, the identity dilemma is never truly

resolved: "No soy de aquí ni de allá": "I am not from here nor from there" (Comas-Díaz et al. 1998).

Economic change is also apparent. Poverty and unemployment rates are high, and new arrivals from Mexico and Puerto Rico are particularly likely to enter the lower class, or working class at best, upon arrival. However, there is a growing middle class within the Hispanic community.

Mexican culture is alive and well in the Mexican American community. Some cultural practices that have become more popular here than in Mexico are being imported back to Mexico, with their distinctive Mexican American flavor. All this is occurring in the midst of a reluctance to expand bilingual education and a popular move to make English the official language. In 1998, Puerto Rico observed its 500th anniversary as a colony: four centuries under Spain and another century under the United States. Its dual status as a colony and as a developing nation has been the defining issue for Puerto Ricans, even those who have migrated to the mainland.

TABLE 10.3
Metropolitan Areas with the Largest Latino Concentrations, 2006

Metropolitan Area	Number of Latinos	Proportion of City's Population (%)
Los Angeles–Long Beach	5,694,422	44.0
New York City	3,985,375	21.2
Miami	2,093,306	38.3
Chicago	1,828,296	19.2
Houston	1,823,830	32.9
Riverside–San Bernardino	1,774,114	44.1
Dallas	1,590,786	26.5
Phoenix	1,209,591	29.9
San Antonio	1,026,189	52.7

Note: San Juan metropolitan area, Puerto Rico, reported 2,556,467 Latinos, which accounted for 98 percent of its population in 2006.

Source: Author, based on American Community Survey 2006 in Bureau of the Census 2007i.

SPECTRUM OF INTERGROUP RELATIONS

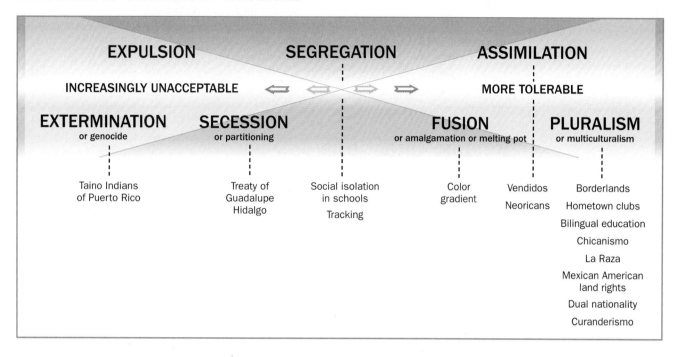

Summary

1. As a result of the 1848 Treaty of Guadalupe Hidalgo, which ended the Mexican–American War, the United States acquired a significant amount of Mexican territory, starting the long history of Latinos in the United States.

2. Federal policies such as repatriation, the bracero program, Operation Wetback, and Special Force Operation reflect that the United States regards Mexico and its people as a low-wage labor supply to be encouraged or shut off as dictated by U.S. economic needs.

3. The lowly status of migrant farm workers was dramatically changed by the collective efforts led by César Chávez.

4. Grassroots community organizations have marked the efforts of Mexican Americans seeking equity in the United States.

5. Puerto Ricans have enjoyed citizenship by birth since 1917 but have commonwealth status on the island. The future status of Puerto Rico remains the key political issue within the Puerto Rican community.

6. Like much of the rest of the Caribbean and Latin America, Puerto Rico has more of a color gradient in terms of race than the sharp Black–White dichotomy of the mainland.

7. Mexican Americans and Puerto Ricans have experienced some improvement in education and health care but remain well behind non-Hispanics.

8. Religion plays an important role in the lives of Latinos who, although most remain Roman Catholic, are increasingly becoming members of Pentecostal faiths.

Key Terms

bracero 240
Chicanismo 244
color gradient 249
culture of poverty 242
curanderismo 255
familism 253

La Raza 241
life chances 253
mixed status 254
mojados 240
neocolonialism 247
Neoricans 246

Pentecostalism 256
repatriation 240
tracking 252
world systems theory 251

Review Questions

1. In what respects has Mexico been viewed as both a source of workers and as a place to leave unwanted laborers?

2. In what respects are Hispanic families similar to and different from Anglo households?

3. How does Chicanismo relate to the issue of Hispanic identity?

4. How does the case of Puerto Rico support the notion of race as a social concept?

5. What role does religion play in the Latino community?

Critical Thinking

1. Consider what it means to be patriotic and loyal in terms of being a citizen of the United States. How do the concerns that Puerto Ricans have for the island's future and the Mexican concept of dual nationality affect those notions of patriotism and loyalty?

2. The phrase *territorial minorities* has been used to apply to subordinate groups that have special ties to their land, such as Native American tribes. How would you apply this to Mexican Americans?

3. The family is often regarded by observers as a real strength in the Latino community. How can this strength be harnessed to address some of the challenges that Mexican Americans and Puerto Ricans face in the United States?

4. Are Mexican Americans assimilated, and are recent Mexican immigrants likely to assimilate over time?

Muslim and Arab Americans: Diverse Minorities

MUSLIM AND ARAB AMERICANS ARE DIFFERENT GROUPS IN THE United States. Although the two groups overlap, with some Muslim Americans being of Arab ancestry, they are distinct from each other. Most Arab Americans are not Muslim, and most Muslim Americans are not of Arab background. Within each group is significant diversity that can be seen by differences in forms of religious expression, ancestral background, and how recently they arrived in the United States. Both groups have been seen and stereotyped in the West through the lens of orientalism. This stigmatizing of people grew more all-encompassing with the outbreak of terrorism and specifically the events of September 11, 2001. Even without these violent events, it is a challenge for Muslim and Arab Americans to sort out their identity, but nonetheless both function in strong and growing communities in the United States.

261

Amidst the roller coasters, out come the prayer rugs. In 2008, several theme parks from New Jersey and Georgia to Illinois and California once again had a Muslim Day where facilities were set aside so the faithful could kneel and worship. Caterers bring in food that conforms to dietary restrictions that are appropriate to observant Muslims. The parks also allow Muslim women to wear loose-fitting pants and shirts rather than swimsuits in the pool. Female park attendants are assigned to rides to make sure that such garments do not get caught in the equipment.

Refugees and immigrants are a part of the nation's landscape, including Boise, Idaho. This is one of 130 U.S. cities from Anchorage, Alaska, to Stone Mountain, Georgia, that have accepted a federal initiative to welcome refugees from war-torn Iraq. By 2008, Boise, one of the cities accepting refugees, already had three mosques. True, one of these mosques saw anti-Muslim graffiti after the 9/11 attacks, yet now the city of Boise boasts an Islamic community center, English classes designed for Arabic speakers, translators at hospitals, and instruction in immigration law.

At a political rally in Houston, Texas, during the 2004 presidential campaign, Black Muslims and Muslim immigrants joined together in a get-out-the-vote campaign because many issues, such as U.S. foreign policy and racial profiling, are ones in which they have a common interest. Yet in 2008 as presidential candidate Barack Obama secured the Democratic nomination, Muslims wondered why he regularly spoke at churches and temples but seemed to avoid photo opportunities that might place him standing near a mosque (Basu 2004; Elliott 2008; Horan 2008; Stone 2008).

orientalism
The simplistic view of the people and history of the Orient with no recognition of change over time or the diversity within its many cultures.

There are two reasons to consider Arab and Muslim Americans together in this chapter. One is to clarify the distinctions between two groups that are often incorrectly referred to as a single population. The second is to overcome the prism of orientalism through which many contemporary Americans view the Arab and Muslim world. **Orientalism** is the simplistic view of the people and history of the Orient (generally, the region of the Middle East to East Asia), with no recognition of change over time or the diversity within its many cultures. Palestinian American literary scholar Edward Said (1978) stressed how so many people in North America and Europe came to define, categorize, and study the Orient and therefore created a static stereotype of hundreds of millions of people stretched around the globe.

The diversity of Arabs and Muslims is thereby discounted, which allows the outsider to come up with simplistic descriptions and often simplistic policies. Orientalism has led people to see a sweeping unity in both Arab and Muslim societies. It is also an unchanging and a clearly nonmodern image. One must focus on smaller culturally consistent groups or countries rather than surrender to the temptation of a single broad generalization.

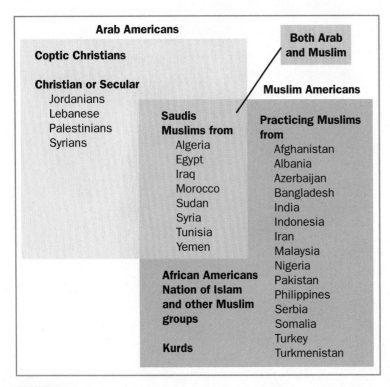

FIGURE 11.1

Relationship between Muslim and Arab Americans

Many Arab Americans are not Muslims, and most Muslim Americans are not Arabs.

The Arab American and Muslim American communities are among the most rapidly growing subordinate groups in the United States. Westerners often confuse the two groups. Actually, Arabs are an ethnic group, and Muslims are a religious group. Typically, Islam is the faith (like Christianity), and a Muslim is a believer of that religion (like a Christian). Worldwide, many Arabs (12 million) are not Muslims, and most Muslims (85 percent) are not Arabs (David and Ayouby 2004).

This relationship between religion and an ethnic group that crosses many nationalities is illustrated in Figure 11.1. As we can see, one cannot accurately identify the Muslim faithful by nationality alone, and clearly being Arab does not define one as being a follower of Islam.

Arab Americans

The name *Arab Americans* refers to the immigrants and their descendants from the countries that now make up the Arab world (see Figure 11.2). As defined by the membership of the League of Arab States, these are the 22 nations of North Africa and what is popularly called the Middle East, including Morocco, Syria, Iraq, Saudi Arabia, and Somalia. Not

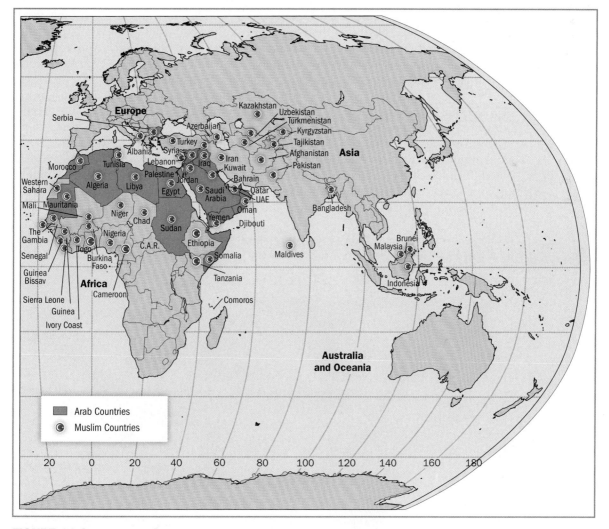

FIGURE 11.2
Arab and Muslim Countries

Source: Author, based on Chambers 2005 and Coogan 2003.

all people living in these countries are necessarily Arab (e.g., the Kurds of Iraq), and some Arab Americans may have immigrated from non-Arab countries such as Great Britain or France, where their families have lived for generations.

Further complicating the use of collective terms of identity such as *Arab* and *Muslim* is evoking the term *Middle Eastern* (Middle Eastern American). Although it is also frequently used, the *Middle East* is an ambiguous geographic designation that includes large numbers of people who are neither Muslim nor Arab (such as Israeli Jews). Collectively, in the view of orientalism, Middle Easterners are lumped together and collectively subjected to prejudice and discrimination but are not eligible for supportive efforts such as affirmative action (Marvasti 2005; Marvasti and McKinney 2004; Tehranian 2008; Wald 2008).

The Arabic language is the single most unifying force among Arabs, although not all Arabs and certainly not all Arab Americans can read and speak Arabic. As the language has evolved over the centuries, people in different parts of the Arab world speak with a different dialect, using their own choices of vocabulary and pronunciation. Although most Arab Americans are not Muslim, the fact that the Qur'an was originally in Arabic 1,400 years ago gives the knowledge of Arabic special importance. This is similar to many Jews' reading of the Torah in Hebrew; and it is unlike Christians, who almost always read the Bible in a translation that is in their native tongue.

Estimates of the size of the Arab American community differ widely. Despite efforts of the census bureau to enlist the assistance of experts, census results are widely thought to severely undercount the Arab American community. The government counts only those individuals who have identified their ancestry from the countries of the Arab world and, therefore, would not include those descended from other large overseas Arab communities. The Arab American community doubled in size during the 1990s; even by the official census count, it would be equivalent to that of Greek Americans.

By some estimates, there are as many as 3 million people with Arab ancestry in the United States. Among those who identify themselves as Arab American, the largest single source of ancestry was Lebanon, followed by Syria, Egypt, and Palestine. These four groups accounted for two-thirds of Arab Americans in 2000. As with other racial and ethnic groups, Arab Americans, as shown in Figure 11.3, are not uniformly distributed throughout the United States. This rising population has led to the development of Arab retail centers in several cities, including Los Angeles, Chicago, New York City, Washington, D.C., and Dearborn and Detroit, Michigan (Brittingham and de la Cruz 2005).

Diversity underlies virtually everything about Arab Americans. First, there are variations in time of arrival. Many Arab Americans have lived for several generations in the

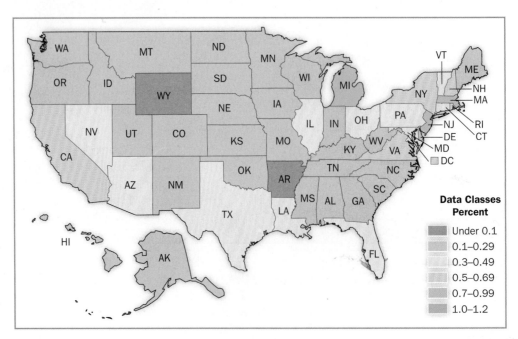

FIGURE 11.3
Arab American Population, 2000

Source: U.S. Bureau of the Census data reported in Brittingham and de la Cruz 2005.

United States, whereas others are foreign born. A second aspect of diversity is point of origin, which ranges from urban Cairo, Egypt, to rural Morocco. Third, there is a rich variety of religious tradition that can include Christian or Muslim, practicing or nonpracticing, and so forth. It becomes impossible to characterize Arab Americans having a family type or a gender role or an occupational pattern (Dallo, Ajouch, and Al-Shih 2008; David 2004).

As with any ethnic or immigrant community, divisions arise over who can truly be counted as a member of the community. Sociologist Gary David (2003, 2007) developed the concept of the **deficit model of ethnic identity**. This states that one's identity is viewed by others as a factor of subtracting away characteristics corresponding to some ideal ethnic type. Each factor encompassing a perfect ethnic identity missing from a person's background or identity leads the person to be viewed by others as more assimilated and less ethnic. In the case of Arab Americans, if they are unable to speak Arabic, then they are less Arab to some people; if they are married to non-Arabs, then they are less ethnic; if they have never been to the home country, then they are less ethnic. Depending on one's perspective, an Arab American can come to regard another Arab American as either "too American" or "too Arab." Arab American organizations, magazines, and associations may seek to cater to the entire Arab American community, but, more likely, cater to certain segments based on nationality, religion, and degree of assimilation. Organization may also be found by groups that gravitated to one another because they share the same sense of what it means be Arab American.

deficit model of ethnic identity
One's ethnicity is viewed by others as a factor of subtracting away the characteristics corresponding to some ideal ethnic type.

hajj
Pilgrimage to Mecca to be completed at least once in a Muslim's lifetime.

Muslim Americans

Islam, with approximately 1.3 billion followers worldwide, is second to Christianity among the world's religions. Although news events and a worldview of orientalism suggest an inherent conflict between Christians and Muslims, the two faiths are similar in many ways. Both are monotheistic (i.e., based on a single deity) and indeed worship the same God. Allah is the Arabic word for God and refers to the God of Moses, Jesus, and Muhammad. Both Christianity and Islam include a belief in prophets, an afterlife, and a judgment day. In fact, Islam recognizes Jesus as a prophet, though not the son of God. Islam reveres both the Old and New Testaments as integral parts of its tradition. Both faiths impose a moral code on believers, which varies from fairly rigid proscriptions for fundamentalists to relatively relaxed guidelines for liberals.

Although it has some beliefs in common with Christianity, Islam is guided by the teachings of the Qur'an (or Koran), which Muslims believe was revealed to the seventh-century Prophet Muhammad. The Qur'an includes the collected sayings, or *hadeeth*, and deeds of Muhammad, which are called *Sunnah*, or the way of the prophet. Muhammad grew up an orphan and became a respected businessman who rejected the widespread polytheism of his day and turned to the one god (Allah) as worshipped by the region's Christians and Jews. Islam says that he was visited by the angel Gabriel, who began reciting the word of Allah, the Qur'an. Muslims see Muhammad as the last in a long line of prophets; he was preceded by Abraham, Moses, and Jesus. Islam is communal, encompassing all aspects of one's life. Consequently, in countries that are predominantly Muslim, the separation of religion and the state is not considered necessary or even desirable. In fact, governments in Muslim countries often reinforce Islamic practices through their laws. Muslims do vary in their interpretation of several traditions, some of which—such as the requirement for women to wear face veils—are disputed.

Like other religious systems, certain rituals referred to as the "pillars of wisdom" characterize Islam. Muslims fast during the month of Ramadan, which marks the revelation of the Qur'an to the Prophet Muhammad; they pray to Allah, facing Mecca, five times a day; they make charitable donations; and they say, where possible, Friday afternoon prayers within their community. They also undertake the **hajj**, the pilgrimage to Mecca, at least once in their lifetime. This city in contemporary Saudi Arabia is home of the House of Allah, or Ka'aba, which was built by Abraham and his son Ishmael. Muslims perform the hajj in accordance with the Qur'an and in the manner prescribed by the Prophet Muhammed in his Sunnah.

Although the Muslim presence in the United States has only very recently been recognized by the general public, it has a long history. Yarrow Marmout, an African Muslim and former slave, was painted in this portrait by famed artist Charles Wilson Peele in 1819. (Courtesy of The Historical Society of Pennsylvania Collection, Atwater Kent Museum of Philadelphia).

jihad
Struggle against the enemies of Allah, usually taken to mean one's own internal struggle.

Islamic believers are divided into a variety of faiths and sects such as Sunnis and Shi'is (or Shiites). These divisions sometimes result in antagonisms between the members, just as there are religious rivalries between Christian denominations. The large majority of Muslims in the United States are Sunni Muslims—literally, those who follow the Sunnah, the way of the prophet. Compared to other Muslims, they tend to be more moderate in their religious orthodoxy. The Shi'is (primarily from Iraq, Iran, and southern Lebanon) are the second-largest group. The two groups differ on who should have been the *caliph*, or ruler, after the death of the Prophet Muhammad. This disagreement resulted in different understandings of beliefs and practices, concluding in the Sunni and Shi'is worshipping separately from each other. They worship separately even if it means crossing national and linguistic lines to do so—provided there are sufficient numbers of Shi'is to support their own mosque, or *masjid*.

There are many other expressions of Islamic faith and even divisions among Sunnis and Shi'is, so to speak of Muslims as Sunni or Shi'i would be akin to speaking of Christians as Roman Catholic or Baptist, forgetting that there are other denominations as well as sharp divisions within the Roman Catholic and Baptist faiths. Furthermore, there are Muslim groups unique to the United States; later we will focus on the largest one—Islam among African Americans.

Verses in the Qur'an prescribe to Muslims **jihad**, or struggle against the enemies of Allah. Typically, jihad is taken by Muslims to refer to their internal struggle for spiritual purity. Today, a very visible minority of Muslims in the world sees this as a pretext to carry out an armed struggle against what they view as the enemies of the Palestinians, such as Israel and the United States. Such interpretations, even if held by a few, cannot be dismissed, because Islam is a faith without an established hierarchy; there is no Muslim pope to deliver the one true interpretation, and there is no provision for excommunication. Individual *imams*, leaders or spiritual guides of a mosque, can offer guidance and scholarship, but Islam's authority rests with the scripture and the teachings of the prophet (Belt 2002).

Based on the most recent studies, there are at least 1.9 million and perhaps as many as 3 million Muslims in the United States. About two-thirds are U.S.-born citizens. In terms of ethnic and racial background, the more-acceptable estimates still vary widely. Estimates range as follows:

- 20–42 percent African American,
- 24–33 percent South Asian (Afghan, Bangladeshi, Indian, and Pakistani),
- 12–32 percent Arab, and
- 15–22 percent "other" (Bosnian, Iranian, Turk, and White and Hispanic converts)

There appears to be total agreement that the Muslim population in the United States is growing rapidly through immigration and conversion (Grossman 2008; Pew Forum on Religion and Public Life 2008).

Malcolm X, reflecting his conversion to Islam, made a pilgrimage to the Muslim holy city of Mecca. On this trip in 1964, the year before his assassination in New York City, he also met with area leaders such as Prince Faisal al-Saud of Saudi Arabia.

Reflecting the growth of the Muslim population in the United States, the number of mosques has grown to more than 1,700. Mosques (more properly referred to as a *masjids*) do not maintain identifiable membership rolls as do churches, but scholars have observed that mosques and their imams are today taking on some of the characteristics of a congregation. To maintain their tax-exempt status, mosques are forced to incorporate boards and bylaws. Imams in the United States are more likely to take on a pastoral role relating to nonreligious functions, such as helping immigrants adjust, and representing the Muslim community to other nonprofit groups serving the larger community.

However common mosques are in the United States, these symbols of faith and houses of worship still attract a different kind of attention than a steeple atop a Lutheran church. For many people in the United States, the mosque does not represent religious freedom and diversity or even a curiosity but a foreign threat in yet another example of orientalism. Mosques are occasionally the focus of either government-initiated surveillance or police protection from anti-Muslim attacks. Muslim groups have found some communities blocking their efforts to build religious centers. Local authorities may require that the building be stripped of cultural symbols and even forgo the traditional dome.

Existing mosques have also seen city councils blocking their efforts to publicly broadcast their call to prayer over loudspeakers even when neighboring churches just as loudly ring bells to signal the start of worship. Even after accepting some community-driven changes, mosques or Islamic centers often are victims of vandalism. However, there are also signs of acceptance. College campuses are adjusting to growing numbers of Muslims by hiring part-time imams to minister to their needs, dedicating space for Muslims' prayers to be said five times a day, and providing for the restrictions of the Muslim diet (Ba-Yunus and Kone 2004; Leinwand 2004; Leonard 2003; S. Simon 2004; Wilgoren 2001).

In summary, Muslim Americans reflect a **blended identity**—that is, a self-image and worldview that is a combination of religious faith, cultural background based on nationality, and the status of being a resident of the United States. As shown in Figure 11.4, Muslims often find their daily activities defined by their faith, their nationality, and their status as American, however defined in terms of citizenship. Younger Muslims especially can move freely among the different identities. In Chicago, Muslim college students perform hip-hop in Arabic with lyrics like "La ilaha ila Allah" ("There is no God but Allah"). In Fremont, California, high school Muslim girls and some of their non-Muslim girlfriends hold an alternative prom, decked out in silken gowns, dancing to both 50 Cent and Arabic music, dining on lasagna, but pausing at sunset to face toward Mecca and pray (Abdo 2004a; P. Brown 2003; Mostofi 2003).

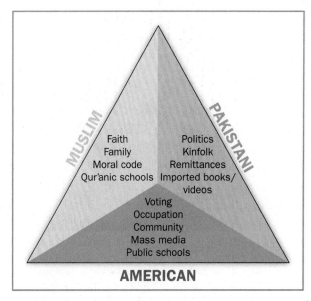

FIGURE 11.4
Blended Identity of Muslim Americans

Muslim Americans, as shown in this illustration representing the life/experience of a Pakistani Muslim living in the United States, form their identity by bringing together three different identities: their faith, their homeland, and the United States.

There is one remaining but basic question: what, if anything, is different about being Muslim in the United States as opposed to an Islamic country? In the United States, we have a Muslim population that numbers in the millions but reflects the diversity of the worldwide Islamic faith, and it practices its rituals and beliefs in a nation where the expression of Christianity dominates culturally. Some scholars of Islam argue that the experience of democracy and the history of religious diversity and free expression have facilitated a stronger and even more correct Islamic practice—uninhibited by the more totalitarian regimes many Muslims find in their homelands. Certainly there is disagreement over what is correct, but there is little pressure outside the Muslim community in the United States about how to precisely follow the teachings of the Prophet Muhammad.

Other scholars contend that what makes the American Muslim experience unique is that followers must place an even stronger focus on Islam in order to survive in a culture that is so permissive and, indeed, encourages so much behavior that is prohibited by either Islamic law or cultural traditions.

Black Muslims

African Americans who embrace Islam form a significant segment within the Muslim American community. Islam is also a significant expression of religious beliefs among Black Americans. They number around 1.6 to 1.7 million, or about 5 percent of all African Americans, yet they are estimated to account for 90 percent of all converts to Islam in the United States.

blended identity
Self-image and
that is a co
religio
backgr
national
residency

Colleges and employers are increasingly setting aside areas in which Muslim students and employees can carry out their daily prayers. Here at the Massachusetts Institute of Technology in Cambridge, Massachusetts, worshippers gather for afternoon prayers.

The history of Black American Islam begins in the seventeenth century, when members of some Muslim tribes were forcibly brought to the American colonies. It is estimated that 10 percent of African slaves were Muslim. Slave owners discouraged anything that linked them culturally to Africa, including their spiritual beliefs. Furthermore, many in the South saw making slaves Christians as part of their mission in civilizing the enslaved people. Enslaved Muslims in the colonies and elsewhere often resisted the pressure to assimilate to the dominant group's faith and maintained their dedication to Islam (Ba-Yunus and Kone 2004; Leonard 2003; McCloud 1995).

It was exceedingly difficult, if not impossible, for a collective Muslim community to survive slavery. Organized Muslim groups within the African American community grew and dispersed in the late nineteenth century and the first half of the twentieth century. Resurgence of Islam among Black Americans often centered around the leadership of charismatic people such as West Indian–born Edward Wilmot Blyden and North Carolinian Noble Drew Ali, who founded the Moorish Science Temple. Typically, followers of the movements dispersed at the death of the central leader; but with each movement, the core of converts to Islam grew within the African American community (R. Turner 2003).

Like other Muslims, generally African Americans who follow Islam are not tightly organized into a single religious fellowship. However, most today trace their roots either to the teachings of W. Fard Muhammad or, just as significantly, to those who responded against his version of the faith. Little is known of the early years of the immigrant W. Fard Muhammad, who arrived in Detroit around 1930, introducing the teaching of Islam to poor African Americans. He spoke strongly against adultery and alcohol consumption (which are forbidden by Islamic tradition) and smoking and dancing (which are prohibited among some Muslims). However, he also spoke of the natural superiority of Black people, which would cause them to win out in the inevitable struggle between Blacks and Whites—but only if they adopted their "natural religion" and reclaimed their identities as Muslims (Lincoln 1994; R. Turner 2003).

Malcolm X, originally a member of the Nation of Islam, became the most powerful and brilliant voice of Black self-determination in the 1960s. He was an authentic folk hero to his sympathizers then and remains so to many people today, more than a generation after his death. Besides his own followers, he commanded an international audience and is still referred to in a manner befitting a prophet. Indeed, Spike Lee's 1993 movie, based on the *Autobiography of Malcolm X*, reintroduced him to another generation. Malcolm X was highly critical of the civil rights movement in general and of Martin Luther King, Jr., in particular.

Malcolm X is remembered for his sharp attacks on other Black leaders, for his break with the Nation of Islam, and for his apparent shift to support the formation of coalitions with progressive Whites. He is especially remembered for taking the position that Blacks must resist violence "by any means necessary," which greatly concerned supporters of nonviolence. By the last year of his life, Malcolm X (by then known as Malik El-Shabazz) had taken on a very different orientation. He created the secular Organization of Afro-American Unity, which was meant to internationalize the civil rights movement. Malcolm X's life was ended by three assassins in 1964. "His philosophy can be summarized as pride in Blackness, the necessity of knowing Black history, Black autonomy, Black unity, and self-determination for the Black community" (Pinkney 1975, 213; see also Dyson 1995; Kieh 1995).

In recent years, Minister Louis Farrakhan, despite leading a small proportion of Black Muslims, has been the most visible spokesperson among the various Muslim groups in the African American community. Farrakhan broke with the successors of Elijah Muhammad and named his group Nation of Islam, adopting, along with the name used by the earlier group, the more unorthodox-to-Islam ideas of Elijah Muhammad, such as Black moral superiority. Farrakhan jumped into the limelight, although his public statements about Jews and Israel have given his teachings an anti-Semitic taint (Abdo 2004b; Henry 1994; Lincoln 1994).

Although Farrakhan's statements against Whites—Jews in particular—and his anti-Israeli foreign policy have attracted the media's attention, many of his speeches and writings reflect the basic early tenets of the Nation of Islam. Abortion, drugs, and homosexuality are condemned. Self-help, bootstrap capitalism, and strict punishment are endorsed. Farrakhan is not pessimistic about the future of race relations in the United States. As leader of the 1995 Million Man March, he encouraged both marchers and African Americans nationwide to register to vote and work for positive change (Bositis 1996; Loury 1996).

Traditionally, there has been little contact at best and actually some friction between the African American Muslim community, particularly those who adhere to the Nation of Islam, and immigrant Muslims and their descendants. Black Muslims may feel that the larger Islamic community does not speak to what they feel is the unique oppression faced by people who are Black and Muslim in the United States. Meanwhile, other Muslims often assume incorrectly that all African American Muslims embrace the Black superiority view and do not follow orthodox Muslim traditions. It is likely that a single dominating voice of Islam will not emerge among African Americans. That is not surprising because a pluralistic interpretation of faith is common to Muslims worldwide just as it is to Christians and Jews (Abdo 2004; McCloud 2004).

Immigration to the United States

The history of both Muslims and Arabs in the United States is a long one, but their visibility as a true immigrant presence is more of a twentieth-century phenomenon. As has already been noted, a significant proportion of African slaves were followers of Islam. Even earlier, Spanish Muslims accompanied explorers and conquistadores to the Americas. In the nineteenth century, contingents of Arabs made dramatic impressions at a series of world's fairs held in Philadelphia, St. Louis, and Chicago, where millions of fairgoers had certainly their first contact and probably their first awareness of Arab culture. Although often viewed through the lens of orientalism, fairgoers came away with an awareness of cultures previously unknown to them. Positive reports of the recep-

tion of these delegations began to encourage Arabs, particularly those from Syria and Lebanon, to immigrate to the United States. At about the same time, other Arabs immigrated as the result of encouragement from U.S.-funded missionary programs in the Middle East.

Just as immigration of Arabs and, to a lesser extent, practicing Muslims began to annually number in the thousands in the early twentieth century, World War I intervened; and then the restrictive national origin system (see Chapter 4), with its pro-Western and Northern Europe bias, slowed the movement to the United States. As with so many other immigrant groups, the pattern was for immigration to be disproportionately male and the destination to be cities of the East Coast. Pressure to assimilate caused many newcomers to try to reduce the differences between themselves and the host country.

Like all other immigrants, Muslim Americans incorporate U.S. tradi[...] daily lives. Here Girl Scout troop leader Farheen Hakeem (righ[...] dogs that are hallal—that is, dietarily acceptable—during a G[...] Minneapolis. Most of these troop members are Somali immigra[...] children.

Muslim Americans represent a diverse group with diverse interests. Kareem Salama grew up in rural Oklahoma of Egyptian immigrants. He entered law school but is now best known as a country and western singer.

So, for example, many women ceased to cover their heads—a practice common to both Christian Arab and Muslim women.

In the wake of professional-preference clauses within the 1965 Immigration and Nationality Act, immigration increased among both Muslims and Arabs. This movement of skilled workers greatly benefited the United States, as the law intended, but obviously contributed to the brain drain experienced throughout the Arab and Muslim worlds. With the Arab defeat in the 1967 Arab–Israeli War, there was a noticeable rise in immigration, with many Arab and Muslim Americans seeking to bring family members to join them from throughout the Middle East (Naff 1980). Since 1970, an increasing proportion of the Arabs who have immigrated have been Muslim. In addition, as some countries restricted their immigration policies, notably Great Britain, more Muslims came from non-Arab countries such as Pakistan and Bangladesh as well as from Muslim areas of Africa (Camarota 2002).

The immediate aftermath of 9/11 led to a decline of about 30 percent of Arabs and Muslims immigrating to the United States because of apprehension over the reception they would receive and increased scrutiny of their entry documents by the federal government. For example, the numbers of tourists and students declined nearly by half. However, recently numbers have begun to rebound. In 2005, more than 40,000 arrivals from Muslim countries sought permanent residency, resulting in the highest annual numbers of Muslim immigrants since 2000. Some new residents even argue they are better off in post–9/11 America because Islamic centers are more organized and free legal help is more accessible (Elliott 2006).

The growth and continuing vibrancy of an Arab presence in the Dearborn, Michigan, area is a unique development in the history of Arab immigration. A few Lebanese immigrants in the late nineteenth century were joined by fellow countrymen and women. Also came immigrants from Lebanon who were largely Christian, as well as from Yemen, who were typically Sunni Muslims. With the expansion of the automobile industry during the 1910s, Arabs came to work in the area's many factories. These immigrants were pleased by their treatment and wages, so more immigrants joined them. By 1919, the first mosque was established, and a variety of service agencies began to serve the needs of the immigrant community.

The mosques in the metropolitan Detroit area serve an estimated 200,000 Muslims. With at least 40 percent of the Detroit area's population of Arab ancestry today, it is hard for a visitor not to see the evidence of this century-long immigration. Business establishments often feature greetings for Christmas, Ramadan, New Year's, and the two Islamic holidays (called *Eids*) in both English and Arabic. Today, metropolitan Detroit has by far the largest concentration of Arab Americans as well as Muslims. Indeed, this is probably the largest Arab community outside of the Arab world (Abraham and Shryock 2000; Bagby 2004; David and Ayouby 2004; S. Gold 2001).

Contemporary Life in the United States

As has already been noted, Arab Americans tended to immigrate to urban areas. There they have filled a variety of occupational roles, and immigrants, since the 1965 Immigration and Naturalization Act, have been filling skilled and professional roles in the United States. Another area in which Arab Americans often find opportunities for upward mobility is to become self-employed merchants or entrepreneurs. They typically are financially unable to buy into prosperous businesses or high-end retail stores. Rather, they have tended to become involved in precisely those businesses that privileged Whites have long since left behind or avoided altogether. To some degree, Arabs follow a pattern of Jewish and Korean immigrant entrepreneurs, operating stores in low-income areas of central cities that major retailers ignore. Opportunities for success are great, but it also means that the Arab American merchant faces the challenges of serving a low-income population with few consumer choices and a history of being exploited by outsiders (Cainkar 2006).

Family Life and Gender

As with any people, the family plays a central role in the lives of both Muslim and Arab Americans. Given the diversity within both groups, it is impossible to generalize about typical patterns. Traditionally, Islam permitted men to have multiple wives—a maximum of four. The Qur'an admonished Muslim men to do justice economically and emotionally to their wives, and if they could not, then they should have only one wife. In some non-Islamic countries, this practice of multiple marriages is legal, but it is exceedingly rare for Muslim households in countries where the law is not supportive.

In the United States, for those who are recent immigrants or the children of immigrants, family patterns are more likely to be affected by the traditions of their homeland than by the fact that they are Muslim or Arab. Certainly, the role of women receives a great deal of attention because their outer clothing is a conspicuous symbol that to some non-Muslims and non-Arabs seems to represent repression of women in society. There is a full range of views of women among Muslims and Arabs, just as there is among Christians and other ethnicities. However, Islam does stress that women need to be protected and should present themselves modestly in public. This code is operationalized very differently among countries where Muslims dominate, and it varies within Muslim populations in the United States (Haeri 2004).

Sexism and sexist behavior are universal. However, the perception of gender practices in Muslim societies has received special attention in the Western media. Individually, all Muslims, men and women alike, must cover themselves and avoid revealing clothes that are designed to accentuate contours of the body and to emphasize its physical beauty. According to the Qur'an, more-revealing garments can be worn in private with one's family or before members of the same sex, so in some Muslim countries some beaches and public pools are designated for use by men only or by women only.

The Prophet Muhammad indicated in his Sunnah that the female body should be covered except the face, hands, and feet. Hence, traditional Muslim women should wear head coverings. The **hijab** refers to a variety of garments that allow women to follow the guidelines of modest dress. It may include head coverings or a face veil and can take the form of a headscarf rather than something that actually covers the face; the latter would be dictated by a cultural tradition, not Islam. U.S. Muslims select from an array of traditional garments from Muslim countries. These garments include long, loose tailored coats or a loose black overgarment along with a scarf and perhaps a face veil. U.S. Muslim women are just as apt to wear long skirts or loose pants and overblouses that they may buy at any local retail outlet (Haeri 2004).

When it comes to the hijab, or outer garments, research has identified three perspectives among Muslim women in the United States and other settlements outside Islamic countries. Younger, better-educated women who support wearing the hijab in public draw on Western ideas of individual rights, arguing in favor of veiling as a form of personal expression. In contrast, older, less-educated women who also support the wearing of hijab tend to make their arguments without any reference to Western ideology. They cannot see why veiling should be an issue in the first place. A

hijab
A variety of garments that allow women to follow guidelines of modest dress.

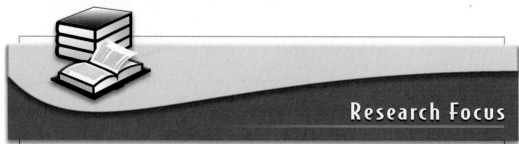

Research Focus

CHRISTIAN AND MUSLIM ARAB AMERICAN WOMEN'S GENDER ROLES

Few issues concerning Islam and Arabs spark more discussion than the role of women. Images of both groups tend to assume women's role is very limited and that any deviation from that role is heavily sanctioned. Sociologist Jen'nan Ghazal Read conducted a national survey of Arab American women in 2000. She was able to compare attitudes on gender roles between Christian and Muslim Arab Americans. Differing opinions on gender roles highlighted varying responses on such issues as attitudes on marital roles (who should make the decisions), parenting (mothers with preschool children working full-time), and nontraditional public roles such as women leading religious services.

Read found that Muslim women were more gender traditional than their non-Muslim peers in the Arab American community. However, she also noted that the Muslim respondents were more likely to be immigrants, to have an Arab spouse, and to be more conservative in their faith compared to Christian Arab women. Once she considered these differences, being Muslim seemed to have no impact on how the women viewed gender roles. For example, both the Bible and Qur'an encourage women to be more domestic and less public. Hence, she found that devout Christian and devout Muslim women were conservative in their gender attitudes compared to those of both faiths who were less inclined to accept their holy scripture literally.

Research into the views of Arab and Muslim Americans is just beginning, and Read's research underscores the importance of considering immigrant status and commitment to one's faith. The next step is to collect such data while including a comparable non-Muslim, non-Arab sample.

Sources: Marshall and Read 2003; Read 2003, 2004, 2007.

third group of women, of all ages and educational backgrounds, oppose the hijab. Some countries, notably France, have come under fire for taking official positions banning the hijab or headscarf in public schools. Generally, this has not been an issue in the United States; however, one 11-year-old girl had to go to federal court to be able to attend school in Muskogee, Oklahoma, wearing a headscarf. Interestingly, the Department of Justice supported the girl in her lawsuit (C. Killian 2003; *Religious Diversity News* 2004).

In Research Focus, sociologist Jen'nan Ghazal Read reports on research showing how Christian and Muslim Arab American women view gender roles.

Gender-role differences among Muslims are not limited to the home and the family. There are differences in the role of women within the faith and in the mosque, or masjid. In part, this reflects the differences in Islamic practices worldwide. For example, in Pakistan and Bangladesh, women are rarely allowed to enter most mosques. However, in Mecca and Medina, Saudi Arabia, the most holy mosques in Islam, women pray apart from the men but not in separate areas or behind curtains. In the United States, it is not unusual for women to be members of the boards of mosques. In many mosques, the explanation for segregating the sexes is the lack of space necessary to maintain modesty while kneeling for prayer, and it is true that many mosques are little more than small storefronts. However, even newly built mosques do not necessarily accommodate women worshippers in the same way they do men. In mosques that attract more U.S.-born Muslims, these issues remain points of contention and anxiety within the Muslim community (Goodstein 2004).

Education

Muslim and Arab Americans recognize the importance of education, and many of the recent immigrants have high levels of formal education and have benefited by the immigration policy that gave preference to those having job skills needed to enter the United States. Muslims also value formal instruction in their faith, and there are several hundred elementary and secondary schools, the majority attached to mosques, that offer what has been referred to in other religious contexts as a parochial school education. Increasing numbers of Muslims are turning to home schooling either out of a desire to adhere to their customs in a way that is difficult to do in public schools or out of a concern over the prejudice their children may experience (Brittingham and de la Cruz 2005).

Schools are specific to particular expressions of Islam and specific nationalities, and some schools serve principally Black Muslims. Qur'anic or Sunday schools also coexist, offering specifically religious instruction either to those attending mosque schools or as a supplement for children enrolled in public schools. A major growth industry has emerged in North America that provides curriculum materials and software to serve these schools, which range from preschool and continue through college, including graduate education (K. Leonard 2003; MacFarquhar 2008).

Children attending public schools encounter the type of adjustment experienced by those of a religious faith different from the dominant one of society. Although public schools are intended to be secular, it is difficult to escape the orientation of many activities to Christmas and Easter or dietary practices that may not conform to the cultural tradition of the children's families. In some school districts with larger Muslim student populations, strides have been made to recognize the religious diversity. A few have granted Eid-al-Fitr, the day marking the end of Ramadan, as an official school holiday for all students (Avila 2003).

By Jeff Parker for *Florida Today*. It appeared in the *Washington Post* National Weekly Edition.

Politics

Muslim and Arab Americans are politically aware and often active. For those who identify with their homeland, politics may take the form of closely monitoring international events as they affect their home country and perhaps their kinfolk who still live there. Admittedly, because U.S. foreign policy often is tilted against some areas such as Palestine, the concerns that Arab Americans may have about events abroad may not be relieved by statements and actions taken by U.S. government officials. On a different level, Muslims and Arab Americans are increasingly involved in politics in the United States. Certainly the most visible Arab American in politics has been consumer advocate Ralph Nader, who has tried to open up presidential politics to consider a true alternative to the two-party system.

Within the traditional two-party system, Arab and Muslim Americans have moved away from the conservative family values policy of the Republicans because of the continuing concerns about government actions and policies in countries such as Afghanistan, Iraq, Lebanon, and the occupied territories of Palestine. By 2007, a national survey indicated 63% of Muslim leaders to be Democrats compared to only 11 percent toward the Republicans. In 2006, Keith Ellison, an African American Democrat from Minneapolis, was elected to the House of Representatives, becoming the first Muslim American to serve—and marking a new age (Pew Research Center 2007).

Muslims in the United States often express the view that their faith encourages political participation. They note that as the Prophet Muhammad lay on his deathbed, he explicitly refused to name a successor to his rule, preferring that the people choose their own leaders. Individual Arabs and Muslims have sought elective office and have been appointed to high-level positions. As voters, they are eagerly sought out by the major parties because they are concentrated in states such as Michigan, Pennsylvania, Ohio, and Florida that often play a critical role in close presidential elections.

There is a clear distancing that one can observe between the major parties and Muslims and Arab Americans. Although there are frequent official welcoming statements of support, close identification as might be shown in routine dinners and convention appearances are rare. This represents a contrast to how politicians cater to African Americans and Latinos to gain votes and more closely resembles the arm's-length relationship with gay and lesbian voters. As charges have escalated in the last decade that some organizations and charities in the Arab and Muslim community were financially assisting overseas groups unfriendly to Israel or even supportive of terrorist objectives, U.S. politicians began to take the safe position of refusing campaign money from virtually any group linked to the Muslim or Arab community. Needless to say, this did not make U.S. citizens who also happen to be of Arab decent or followers of Islam feel very welcomed in the political process. Some Muslims were also annoyed about how vociferous the Barack Obama campaign was to deny charges he was a Muslim, as his late Kenyan-born father had been, as if to be a Muslim was akin to being a Communist or, even worse, a terrorist.

Despite often being ignored presently by politicians, Arab and Muslim Americans are seeking to organize themselves as voters. For example, the Washington-based Muslim American Society (2008) has stepped up efforts to register Muslims to vote. Arab and Muslim Americans are following the time-honored tradition of other racial and ethnic minority groups by making themselves heard in electoral politics.

Being a part of a Muslim minority in someplace other than the United States can create challenges, as we consider in A Global View, "Muslims in France."

Although many Muslim children attend public schools in the United States, others attend private or parochial schools. A teacher at the American Islamic Academy in Dearborn, Michigan, reminds her young students to be quiet when walking through school hallways.

A Global View

MUSLIMS IN FRANCE

Historically, France has not been a destination of immigrants especially from outside Europe. In the efforts to rebuild France following World War II, workers came to France from its colonies in North Africa; many of them were Muslim. As countries such as Algeria, Morocco, and Tunisia (refer back to Figure 11.2) gained their independence in the 1950s and 1960s, immigration grew. Today's Muslim population totals perhaps 5 percent of the general population and comprises both continuing immigration and the children and grandchildren of immigrants. Members of this latter group—those born in France—see their status especially in comparison to other French men and women rather than the people in North Africa.

In 1989, the French government banned Muslim girls in public school from wearing headscarves, taking the position that religious symbols have no place being displayed in schools. Critics argued that Muslims were being targeted while Christian children continued to wear crosses. Although the enforcement of the headscarf ban has been problematic, many Muslims saw it as an act of bigotry rather than an act promoting secular freedom. Ironically, rising numbers of Muslims have been welcomed in Roman Catholic schools, where their headscarves are accepted. By 2008, Muslims accounted for more than 10 percent of Catholic school enrollment.

More dramatic than these policy clashes have been the riots since the 1980s by immigrants protesting poor economic and social conditions and marginalization from mainstream French society as well as elements of lawlessness. The worst riots in recent years occurred in 2005, with the widespread burning of cars and public buildings. Although riot participants have been a diverse cross section of working and lower classes, they have been widely seen and portrayed as immigrant, if not immigrant Muslim, in origin.

Whatever may be the challenges of being Muslim in the United States, many observers in Europe contrast the sense of alienation that Muslims feel there with the perception of most Muslims in the United States that they at least fit in and that some may be enjoying success.

Sources: Bennhold 2008; *Economist* 2008; Mann 2008; C. Smith 2005; Woesthoff 2008.

News events have fueled anti-Arab, anti-Muslim feeling. Activities carried out by Arabs or Muslims, including the 1972 terrorist raid at the Munich Olympics and the 1998 bombings of the U.S. embassies in Kenya and Tanzania, contributed to the negative image. The attack of September 11, 2001, engineered by Arab Muslim terrorists, caused many Americans to associate Arab and Muslim Americans with America's enemy in the war against terrorism. As the economy softened and taxpayers paid for increased security, Arab and Muslim Americans became scapegoats. Vandalism of mosques, attacks on Arab-speaking people, and calls for widespread dragnets based on ethnicity or religion were common. Terrorism, even domestic terrorism, often is the product of homegrown troublemakers, as evidenced by hundreds of attacks on abortion clinics and the 1995 bombing of the federal building in Oklahoma City, Oklahoma.

The events of September 11, 2001, catapulted the United States to focus on segments of the population with a scrutiny that had not been witnessed since the attack on Pearl Harbor 60 years earlier. Speaking from the Washington, D.C., Islamic Center within days

racial profiling
Any arbitrary police-initiated action based on race, ethnicity, or natural origin rather than a person's behavior.

of the hijacking of four airliners, President George W. Bush (2001) assured the nation that "the face of terror is not the true faith of Islam. . . . Islam is peace" and that "Muslims make an incredibly valuable contribution to our country." However, much harm had already been done. Follow-up remarks in the days to come were made by the president and other administrative officials in front of mosques or in the presence of representatives of the Muslim and Arab American community. Even the USA PATRIOT Act passed in October 2001, which has been sharply criticized for contributing to fear within the Arab and Muslim communities, has specific provisions condemning discrimination against Arab and Muslim Americans. Although these were positive symbols of reaching out, the further stigmatization of Muslim and Arab Americans was unstoppable. In addition, Muslims and Arabs became one indistinguishable and homogenous group (Winter and Watanable 2007).

In light of these suspicions, some citizens have found themselves under special surveillance because of racial profiling at airports and border checkpoints. As noted earlier, in Chapter 2, **racial profiling** is any police-initiated action based on race, ethnicity, or national origin rather than a person's behavior. Profiling of Arabs and Muslims became especially intense after September 11, 2001. Although it first denied the program's existence, the Los Angeles Police Department (LAPD) later dropped a "counterterrorism project" to identify "Muslim neighborhoods." Critics not only questioned this venture into religious profiling but also noted that it showed the ignorance of the LAPD to even assume there were enclaves of Muslims. Citizens find it difficult to understand these attitudes in a nation of immigrants that is grounded in religious freedom (Byng 2008; Musabji and Abraham 2007).

In those weeks after 9/11, surveys showed that both Muslim and Arab Americans supported the president's policy of going after terrorists. At the same time, they were fearful that continued military action would hurt how the United States is viewed. In the wake of 9/11, expressions and proof of loyalty were forced on Arab and Muslim Americans.

In an effort to locate domestic terrorists, the U.S. Department of Justice required that all foreign-born Muslim men report to the Bureau of Citizenship and Immigration Services to be photographed, fingerprinted, and interviewed. Some questions were mundane: Where did they work? Were they married? Did they have children? Some were more pointed: Had they been asked by any Arabs or Muslims to teach them to fly airplanes? With very little public notice, 144,513 Muslim men from 25 countries reported during a five-month period ending in 2003. Of those who reported, about 13,000 faced deportation because of visa violations such as overstaying their visas, and 11 remained in custody because they were suspected terrorists.

The registration deepened fear and disillusionment among the many law-abiding Muslims in the United States. Many of the more than 144,000 men interviewed were embarrassed to even be questioned because their code of behavior (no drinking or illegal drugs) meant they were less likely to have faced routine encounters with law enforcement officials. Immigration advocates argued that the government was selectively enforcing immigration laws, but the courts have upheld the process and the right of the government to keep secret the names of those deported or detained (King 2004c; N. Lewis 2003; *Migration News* 2003b).

Consider the particular case of some 100,000 Afghan Americans, typically Muslim but, like the people of Afghanistan, not considered Arabs. After September 11, Afghan Americans found themselves specially targeted for prejudice and were understandably concerned when the United States bombed Afghanistan in search of terrorist groups. Some Afghan Americans talk of leaving for Afghanistan, generally out of a desire to reestablish family ties. Like other Muslim immigrants, Afghan Americans generally came to the United States seeking better education, improved housing, and a higher standard of living in a country they perceived as tolerant of religious diversity. Most came in the 1970s and now have children who are more American than Afghan. Increasingly, their family ties, not just the economic ones, are in the United States (Brittingham and de la Cruz 2005; Ritter and Squitieri 2002).

Issues of Prejudice and Discrimination

"Al tikrar biallem il hmar": "By repetition even the donkey learns."

Media scholar Jack Shaheen (2003, 171) uses this Arab proverb to underscore how the media has reinforced the negative image of Arabs and Muslims. Motion pictures such as *The Sheik* (1921), *The Mummy* (1932), *True Lies* (1994), and *The Mummy Returns* (2001) uniformly show Arabs and Muslims as savages and untrustworthy. Even Disney's 1995 animated film *Aladdin* referred to Arabs as "barbaric" and depicted, contrary to Islamic law, a guard threatening to cut off a young girl's hand for stealing food. In what ways do prejudice and discrimination manifest themselves with respect to Muslim and Arab Americans? In form and magnitude, they are much like what is shown toward other subordinate groups. Regrettably, the situation appears to have gone beyond orientalism, in which one sees people as "the other" and somewhat frightening. **Islamophobia** refers to a range of negative feelings toward Muslims and their religion that ranges from generalized intolerance to hatred. What makes current expressions of hostility strikingly different is that the events of the twenty-first century have been given a decidedly patriotic fervor; that is, for many who overtly express their anti-Muslim or anti-Arab feeling, they also believe themselves to be pro-American (Halsted 2008).

In Listen to Our Voices, opinion pollster and founder of the Arab American Institute, James Zogby, raises his concerns about the continuing presence of hate crimes against Arab and Muslim Americans and how the government pursues those cases.

Perhaps even more troubling to many Arab and Muslim Americans are the portrayals and images in the news and general information programming on television. To some, there is an overemphasis on the extreme representations, such as the wearing of opaque face veils by women, with little social context offered.

There are very few normalizing or positive images. Rarely are Arab and Muslim Americans shown doing "normal" behavior such as shopping, attending a sporting event, or even just eating without a subtext of terrorism lurking literally in the shadows. This is similar to the media portrayal of Native Americans. Like Arab and Muslim Americans, tribal people are rarely depicted just going about their daily routine as citizens. Furthermore, the interests of the United States are depicted either as leaning against the Arabs and Muslims, as in the Israeli-Palestinian violence, or presented as hopelessly dependent on them, in the case of our reliance on foreign oil production.

Evidence of hate crimes and harassment toward Arab and Muslim Americans rose sharply after 9/11, compared to studies done in the mid-1990s. It continued to remain high through 2008, according to more-recent studies. Incidents have ranged from beatings to vandalism of mosques to organized resistance to opening of Arabic schools. Evidence of a backlash also includes Muslim Americans getting unwarranted eviction notices (Bosman 2007).

Surveys show a complex view in the United States of Arab and Muslim Americans. Surveys since 2001 show one in four people believe a number of anti-Muslim stereotypes such as the idea that Islam teaches violence and hatred. Curiously, while harboring these views, people do recognize that Arab Americans are poorly treated. In 2006, 47 percent of White non-Hispanics felt that Arab Americans were ill treated. Yet about 40 percent would require Muslim citizens of the United States to carry special identification and be subjected to greater surveillance (Council on American-Islamic Relations 2004; Jones 2006; Saad 2006a).

Arab Americans and Muslim Americans, like other subordinate groups, have not responded passively to their treatment. Organizations have been created in their communities to counter negative stereotypes and to offer schools material responding to the labeling that has occurred. As with other groups that have been disadvantaged and do not have clear access to the top levels of decision making in the public and private sectors, nonprofit organizations, such as the Council of American-Islamic Relations, the American Muslim Alliance, the Muslim Public Affairs Council, and the American Arab Anti-Discrimination Committee, have formed to represent their interests and promote understanding as well as to bring attention to discrimination and expressions of prejudice in public life and the mass media.

Islamophobia
A range of negative feelings toward Muslims and their religion that ranges from generalized intolerance to hatred.

HATE CRIME PUNISHED

On Friday, July 11, 2008, a resident of Arlington, Virginia, was sentenced to two concurrent one year prison terms for threatening my life and using hate-filled threats to violate my civil rights and those of my staff at the Arab American Institute. Upon release, he will be under supervised probation for three more years and be required both to perform community service and undergo psychiatric counseling.

James Zogby

A simple enough story, on the surface. But there are a number of back stories here that need to be told.

While the Department of Justice (DOJ) has not been well-led during the past eight years, the career attorneys in the DOJ's Civil Rights Division and the FBI agents who work with them investigating rights violations deserve significant credit for tracking down and prosecuting hate crimes against Arab Americans and American Muslims.

Arab Americans, myself included, have been subjected to threats and violence for decades now. But never before have the agencies of the U.S. government been so committed to hunting down these criminals and punishing them. Since 2001, in all, the Civil Rights Division has convicted 166 such criminals. I know of their work, first-hand, since three of these cases involved individuals who threatened me.

While credit is due to the above-mentioned law enforcement officials, serious questions must be raised about the behavior of the U.S. State Department (DOS) in this affair. The person who was sentenced last week was a 25-year career foreign service officer at DOS who had twice been stationed in Lebanon.

His two phone calls and four email messages to my office were so obscene and so violent that I cannot reprint them in full. Sent to me, and some members of my staff, in the midst of the Israeli-Lebanese war of 2006, he said, in part, "The only good Lebanese is a dead Lebanese. The only good Arab is a dead Arab;" called me and my staff "wicked and evil", said that "we should burn in the fires of hell for all eternity" and that the "U.S. would be safer without" us. There was worse. Much worse.

The messages were frightening, and of concern. Even more disturbing was when I was informed by the investigating law enforcement officers that the perpetrator worked at the State Department. More troubling still was the fact that after DOS officials were notified of his behavior, they did nothing and allowed the individual to remain at his job for another nine months until he was able to retire with full pension.

Conclusion

We have seen the diversity within the Native American tribal community and among Latinos. Prejudice, discrimination, and responses of resistance have typified these groups and African Americans' long history in the United States. Now we can see in a special way that Arab Americans and Muslim Americans share this experience. Not very numerous in absolute terms until the latter part of the twentieth century, both Arabs and Muslims have built on a fragmented history that in the United States literally goes back 200 years. When Muslims were less numerous, it was difficult to maintain any sense of communal identity, but as their numbers increased, identifiable groups emerged (see the figure on page 280).

Listen to Our Voices

Perhaps worst of all was the fact, revealed in court, that the convicted foreign service officer had engaged in other anti-Arab behavior earlier in his career, and that nothing was done by the DOS to censure or stop him. That the Department did nothing to correct this bigoted and criminal behavior is unacceptable, for many reasons—not least of which is that it compromises the work of so many fine career foreign service officers, dedicated public servants who both serve America well and respect the people of the Arab world.

Finally, a word about hate crimes. There are some who argue that obscene, hateful and threatening language should not be punished, since to do so would be a violation of free speech. (This, in fact, was the initial defense raised by the individual in this case, before he ultimately pled guilty to the charges against him.)

They are wrong. Such behavior is a crime, and individuals who commit these crimes do so precisely because they seek to violate the free speech of others. And though their targets are individuals, the intended victims are entire communities who the hate criminals seek to intimidate into silence.

Hate crimes are an extension of bigotry and political exclusion. Blacks, Jews, gays, and others have been repeatedly targeted by these crimes, and so, too, have Arab Americans and American Muslims. There were those who discriminated against and defamed Arab Americans (as terrorist supporters), and pressed political leaders to exclude Arab Americans from the mainstream—all of this contributing to the climate that would incite some to threaten or commit acts of violence.

My friend Alex Odeh, California Director of the American-Arab Anti-Discrimination Committee, was murdered in 1985. He had been threatened on a number of occasions by phone and by mail. I personally brought Alex's complaints to the FBI. Tragically, at the time, they did not respond. And to this day, no one has been indicted for Alex's murder.

Over the past 38 years, I have, on many occasions, been a target. I have been threatened, attacked, and—at one point—my office was firebombed. And for most of this time, law enforcement did little to intervene. Thankfully, this has changed. While the number of these threats and acts of violence may have increased since September 11, 2001, because of the work of the Civil Rights unit at DOJ, and FBI agents working on hate crimes, the number of convictions has gone up even more.

The vigorous work of law enforcement and, in particular, the sentence meted out in this case, sends a clear message that these crimes will not be tolerated. For that I and my staff, and my community, are thankful.

Source: Zogby 2008.

Diversity has marked both Arab Americans and Muslim Americans in the United States. For the descendants of earlier Arab settlers, their identity as Arabs may be discounted by recent Arab immigrants through a process of the deficit model of ethnic identity. For the Muslim community, the divisions within the faith overseas are reproduced in the United States, with the added significant presence of African Americans who have embraced Islam.

The world and domestic events of recent years, and especially in the early years of the twenty-first century, have created some new challenges. In some respects, the continuing conflict in Israel and Palestine has served to create an Arab identity that was largely missing a few generations ago when more strictly nationalistic agendas prevailed. Similarly, the agenda of fundamentalist and militant Muslims has created an us–them mentality found both

SPECTRUM OF INTERGROUP RELATIONS

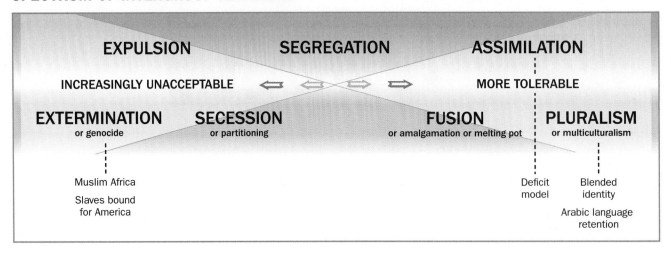

in international organizations and on street corners of the United States. This lack of true understanding of one another is not totally new but is built on the orientalism that has its roots in the initial contacts between Europeans and the people of the Middle East and South Asia.

For many Arab and Muslim Americans, this is all ancient history. They, like other U.S. citizens, are seeking to define themselves and move ahead in their society. The challenges for them to do this seem measurably greater than they were just a few years ago, but their efforts to create bridges are also significant.

Summary

1. Views of Muslim and Arab Americans are distorted through orientalism and Islamophobia.

2. Arabs (an ethnic group) and Muslims (a religious group) overlap but are not the same; many Muslims (such as Indonesians) are not Arabs, and many Arabs (such as Coptic Christians) are not Muslim.

3. Many Arab Americans are judged by their fellow ethnic members as being less Arab if they do not speak Arabic.

4. Many of the early Muslims in the Americas came as slaves; a significant component of African Americans today have accepted Islam as their faith.

5. Muslim Americans often have a blended identity of their nationality, religion, and status as residents of the United States.

6. Muslims and Arab Americans are both diverse groups among whom there are differing patterns for approaching the family and gender roles. Some of these roles do not conform to the social norm of the United States.

7. Politics is becoming a growing aspect of both the Arab and the Muslim community and is expanding beyond issues specific to the Middle East.

8. The position of being Arab or Muslim in the United States grew more complex and contentious in the wake of the events of September 11, 2001, despite the public efforts of many Arabs and Muslims to proclaim their loyalty to the United States.

Key Terms

blended identity 267

deficit model of ethnic
  identity 265

hijab 271

hajj 265

Islamophobia 277

jihad 266

orientalism 262

racial profiling 276

Review Questions

1. What are the dimensions of diversity among Arab Americans and among Muslims?

2. What distinguishes African American Muslims from other practicing Muslims in the United States?

3. How has the immigration of Muslims and Arabs been influenced by the governmental policies of the United States?

4. What would you identify as the four most important differences between being a Christian in the United States and being a Muslim in this country?

Critical Thinking

1. Identify groups other than Arab Americans and Muslim Americans that have recently been subjected to prejudice, perhaps in your own community.

2. Apply the deficit model of ethnic identity to another group besides Arab Americans.

3. What are some characteristics associated with Muslim and Arab Americans that have come to be viewed as negatives but when practiced by Christian Whites are seen as positives?

4. How are the Arab and Muslim communities composed of differences by language, social class, citizenship status, nationality, and religion?

12

Asian Americans: Growth and Diversity

ASIAN AMERICANS AND PACIFIC ISLANDERS ARE A DIVERSE group that is one of the fastest-growing segments of the U.S. population. Asian Americans often are viewed as a model minority that has successfully overcome discrimination. This inaccurate image disguises lingering maltreatment and anti–Asian American violence. Furthermore, it denies Asian Americans the assistance afforded other racial minorities. Immigration is the primary source of growth among Asian Indians, Filipinos, Southeast Asians, and Koreans. All Asian groups, along with Blacks and Whites (or *Haoles*, as they are known there), coexist in Hawai'i.

283

M adison Nguyen won election to the city council of San Jose, California, the nation's tenth-largest city, in 2006. This was a significant event because she became the city council's first Vietnamese American member. Although San Jose has a large Asian American community, she attracted a lot of White, African American, and Latino voters as well. Was her Vietnamese ancestry an issue? That leads us to the second remarkable aspect of her election, because attorney Madison Nguyen defeated another Vietnamese American, Linda Nguyen, who directs the popular New Year's Tet parade in the city.

Pulitzer Prize–winning writer Jhumpa Lahiri has lived all 39 years of her life in the United States, except for her first two in London. She still sees her home being as much in Calcutta as in Rhode Island, where she grew up. Still to this day, despite all the success her writing has had in English, she sees her life as a shifting equation between being a Bengali Indian and an American (Lahiri 2006; Vuong 2006).

Madison Nguyen and Jhumpa Lahiri, despite being public figures, could be speaking for all Asian Americans who are often aware of the country from which they or their parents came and their position in the United States. An elected official and a successful writer both remind us that the legacy of immigration to the United States is not merely quaint turn-of-the-century black-and-white photos taken at Ellis Island. It is not merely a thickly accented elderly person reminiscing about the "old country." Immigration, race, and ethnicity are being lived out among people of all ages, and for no collective group is this truer than for Asian Americans who are living throughout the United States (Figure 12.1).

Asian Americans include groups such as Chinese Americans and Filipinos, whose nationality groups also include different linguistic groups and identifiable ethnic groups

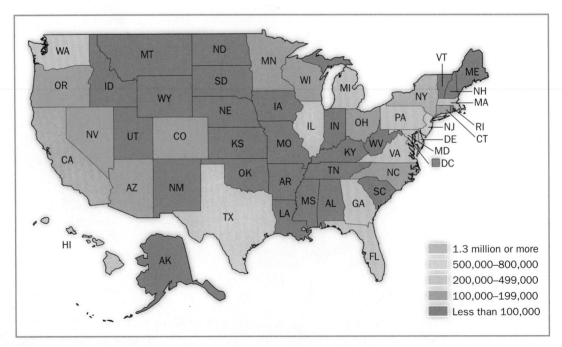

FIGURE 12.1
Where Most Asian Pacific Islanders Live, 2006

Source: Author, based on American Community Survey 2006, Table B01001D.

(Figure 12.2). Asian Americans also include ethnic groups, such as the Hmong, that do not correspond to any one nation. Finally, the U.S. population also includes Pacific Islanders, including Hawaiians, Samoans, Tongans, and many smaller groups. Collectively, Asian Pacific Islanders in 2006 numbered 13.5 million—a 27-percent increase over 2000, compared with an overall population increase of only 6 percent.

Despite these large numbers—which are equivalent to the total African American population after World War II—Asian Americans feel ignored. They see "race and ethnicity" in America framed as a Black–White issue or, more recently, as a "triracial" issue that includes Hispanics. But where are the Asian Americans in these pictures of the United States? For example, tens of thousands of Asian Americans, especially Vietnamese Americans, were displaced by Hurricane Katrina in 2005, but they received little media notice. Immigration issues understandably focus on Latin America, but what about challenges facing Asians who seek legal entry to the United States or the Asian Americans who are already here?

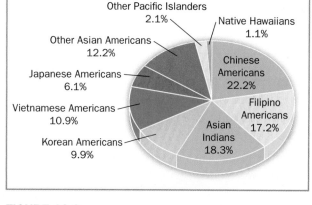

FIGURE 12.2
Asian Pacific Islanders, 2006
Source: Author, based on American Community Survey 2006. Tables B02006, B02007.

To comprehend better the collective picture of Asian Americans, we will first consider the powerful image that many people have of Asian Americans constituting some kind of perfect, model minority. We will then turn our attention to the role they play politically in the United States and the degree to which a pan-Asian identity is emerging.

We will then consider four of the larger groups—Filipinos, Asian Indians, Southeast Asians, and Koreans—in greater depth. The chapter concludes by examining the coexistence of a uniquely mixed group of peoples—Hawaiians—among whom Asian Americans form the numerical majority. Chapter 13 concentrates on the Chinese and the Japanese, the two Asian groups with the longest historical tradition in the United States.

The "Model-Minority" Image Explored

"Asian Americans are a success! They achieve! They succeed! There are no protests, no demands. They just do it!" This is the general image that people in the United States so often hold of Asian Americans as a group. They constitute a **model** or **ideal minority** because, although they have experienced prejudice and discrimination, they seem to have succeeded economically, socially, and educationally without resorting to political or violent confrontations with Whites. Some observers point to the existence of a model minority as a reaffirmation that anyone can get ahead in the United States. Proponents of the model-minority view declare that because Asian Americans have achieved success, they have ceased to be subordinate and are no longer disadvantaged. This labeling is only a variation of blaming the victim; with Asian Americans, it is "praising the victim." An examination of aspects of their socioeconomic status will allow a more thorough exploration of this view (Chang and Demyan 2007; Fong 2002; Hurh and Kim 1989; Thrupkaew 2002).

Education and the Economy

Asian Americans, as a group, have impressive school enrollment rates in comparison to the total population. In 2004, 48.2 percent of Asian Americans 25 years old or older held bachelor's degrees, compared with 29.7 percent of the White population (Table 12.1). These rates vary among Asian American groups; Asian Indians, Filipino Americans, Korean Americans, Chinese Americans, and Japanese Americans have higher levels of educational

model or **ideal minority**
A group that, despite past prejudice and discrimination, succeeds economically, socially, and educationally without resorting to political or violent confrontations with Whites.

TABLE 12.1
Selected Social and Economic Characteristics of Asian Americans

	White Non-Hispanics	Asian Americans	Pacific Islanders	Asian Indians	Filipino Americans	Korean Americans
Percentage completing college, 25 years old and older	29.70	48.20	13.80	67.90	47.90	50.80
Households with a single parent (%)	12.40	13.60	24.50	8.00	17.60	10.80
People living below poverty level (%)	8.80	11.80	18.10	9.70	5.20	14.90
Median household income ($)	48,784	56,161	47,442	68,771	65,700	43,195
Citizenship status (%)	98.30	69.50	85.00	58.70	76.10	65.70
Foreign born (%)	3.80	67.40	21.90	73.30	66.20	75.80

Note: Data are for 2004. Excludes people selecting multiple race designations.

Source: Bureau of the Census 2007c 10, 11, 15, 17, 18; Bureau of the Census 2007j 8, 10, 12, 14, 16, 17.

achievement than others. Yet other groups such as Vietnamese Americans and Pacific Islanders, including Native Hawaiians, fare much worse than White Americans.

This encouraging picture does have some qualifications, however, that call into question the optimistic model-minority view. According to a study of California's state university system, although Asian Americans often are viewed as successful overachievers, they have unrecognized and overlooked needs and experience discomfort and harassment on campus. As a group, they also lack Asian faculty and staff members to whom they can turn for support. They confront many identity issues and have to do a "cultural balancing act" along with all the usual pressures faced by college students. The report noted that an "alarming number" of Asian American students appear to be experiencing intense stress and alienation, problems that have often been "exacerbated by racial harassment" (Ohnuma 1991; Zhou 2004).

Even the positive stereotype of Asian American students as "academic stars" or "whiz kids" can be burdensome to the people so labeled. Asian Americans who do only modestly well in school may face criticism from their parents or teachers for their failure to conform to the "whiz kid" image. Some Asian American youths disengage from school when faced with these expectations or receive little support for their interest in vocational pursuits or athletics (Kibria 2002; Maddux et al. 2008).

As a group, Asian Americans work in the same occupations as Whites, which suggests that they have been successful, and many have been. However, the pattern shows some differences. Asian immigrants, like other minorities and immigrants before them, are found disproportionately in the low-paying service occupations. At the same time, they are also concentrated at the top in professional and managerial positions. Yet, as we will see, they rarely reach the very top. They hit the glass ceiling (as described in Chapter 3) or, as some others say, try to "climb a broken ladder" before they reach management. In 2002, only 2 percent of 11,500 people who serve on the boards of the nation's 1,000 largest corporations were Asian American (G. Strauss 2002; Omi 2008).

The absence of Asian Americans as top executives also indicates that their success is not complete. Asian Americans have done well in small businesses and modest agricultural ventures. Although self-employed and managing their own businesses, Asian Americans have had very modest-sized operations. Because of the long hours, the income from such a business may be below prevailing wage standards, so even when they are business owners, they may still constitute cheap labor, although they also get the profits. Chinese restaurants, Korean American cleaning businesses and fruit and vegetable stores, and motels, gasoline stations, and newspaper vending businesses operated by Asian Indians fall into this category.

Another misleading sign of the apparent success of Asian Americans is their high incomes as a group. Like other elements of the image, however, this deserves closer inspection. Asian American family income approaches parity with that of Whites because of their greater achievement than Whites in formal schooling. If we look at specific educational levels, however, Whites earn more than their Asian counterparts of the same age. Asian Americans' average earnings increased by at least $2,300 for each additional year of schooling whereas Whites gained almost $3,000. As we see in Table 12.1, Asian Americans as a group have significantly more formal schooling but actually have lower household family income. We should note that to some degree, some Asian Americans' education is from overseas and, therefore, may be devalued by U.S. employers. Yet in the end, educational attainment does pay off as much if one is of Asian descent as it does for White non-Hispanics (F. Wu 2002; Zeng and Xie 2004; Zhou and Kamo 1994).

There are striking contrasts among Asian Americans. Nevertheless, for every Asian American family with an annual income of $75,000 or more, another earns less than $10,000 a year. In New York City's Chinatown neighborhood, about one-quarter of all families live below the poverty level. In San Diego, dropout rates were close to 60 percent among Southeast Asians in 1997. Even successful Asian Americans continue to face obstacles because of their racial heritage. According to a study of three major public hospitals in Los Angeles, Asian Americans account for 34 percent of all physicians and nurses but fill only 11 percent of management positions at these hospitals (Dunn 1994; Reeves and Bennett 2003; Sengupta 1997).

At first, one might be puzzled to see criticism of a positive generalization such as "model minority." Why should the stereotype of adjusting without problems be a disservice to Asian Americans? The answer is that this incorrect view helps to exclude Asian Americans from social programs and conceals unemployment and other social ills. When representatives of Asian groups do seek assistance for those in need, people who have accepted the model-minority stereotype resent them. This is especially troubling given that problems of substance abuse and juvenile delinquency need to be addressed within the Asian American community.

If a minority group becomes viewed as successful, its members will no longer be included in any program designed to alleviate the problems they encounter as minorities. The positive stereotype reaffirms the United States system of mobility. New immigrants as well as established subordinate groups ought to achieve more merely by working within the system. At the same time, viewed from the conflict perspective outlined in Chapter 1, this becomes yet another instance of **blaming the victim**: if Asian Americans have succeeded, then Blacks and Latinos must be responsible for their own low status rather than recognizing society's responsibility (Bascara 2008; Choi and Lahey 2006; Maddux et al. 2008; Ryan 1976).

blaming the victim
Portraying the problems of racial and ethnic minorities as their fault rather than recognizing society's responsibilities.

SECRET ASIAN MAN by Tak Toyoshima

Discussions of race and ethnicity often leave out Asian Americans, yet Asian Americans too are subject to stereotypes today, such as the model-minority image.

The Door Half Open

Despite the widespread belief that they constitute a model minority, Asian Americans are victims of both prejudice and violence. Reports released annually by the National Asian Pacific American Legal Consortium (2002) have chronicled incidents of suspected and proven anti–Asian American incidents. After the terrorist attacks of September 11, 2001, anti-Asian violence increased dramatically for several months in the United States. The first fatality was an Asian Indian American who was shot and killed by a gunman in Mesa, Arizona, shouting, "I stand for America all the way."

This anti–Asian American feeling is built on a long cultural tradition. The term *yellow peril* dates back to the view of Asian immigration, particularly from China, as unwelcome. **Yellow peril** came to refer to the generalized prejudice toward Asian people and their customs. The immigrants were characterized as heathen, morally inferior, drug addicted, savage, or lustful. Although the term was first used around the turn of the twentieth century, this anti-Asian sentiment is very much alive today. Many contemporary Asian Americans find this intolerance very unsettling given their conscientious efforts to extend their education, seek employment, and conform to the norms of society. Hate crimes against Asian Americans persist and have even risen in recent years (Hurh 1994; Lee, Vue, Seklecki, and Ma 2007).

What explains the increase in violence against Asian Americans? Prejudice against Asian Americans is fueled by how they are represented in the media. The Asian American Journalists Association (2000) annually conducts a "media watch" to identify how mainstream news media use ethnic slurs and stereotypes, demonstrate insensitivity, and otherwise exhibit bias in reporting. We can identify several ways in which this occurs—some subtle, some overt.

- **Inappropriate use of clichés:** News reports use the term *Asian invasion* even when referring to a small number of Asian Americans. For example, a 1994 *Sports Illustrated* article about Asians trying out for major league baseball teams was billed "Orient Express" and "Asian Invasion," yet the story noted only two Asians as examples.

- **Mistaken identity:** Not only are Asians identified by the wrong nationality but also American citizens of Asian descent are presented as if they were foreigners.

- **Overgeneralization:** Inappropriate assumptions are made and too widely applied. For example, a newspaper article discussing the growth of Chinatown was headlined "There Goes the Neighborhood," implying that any increase in the number of Chinese Americans was undesirable.

- **Ethnic slurs:** Although the print media generally take great pains to avoid racially derogatory terms, radio talk shows offer frequent examples of racism. Comedians often mock Asian names and, in a derisive manner, mimic patterns of Asian American speech.

- **Inflammatory reporting:** Unbalanced coverage of such events as World War II or Asian investment in the United States can needlessly contribute to ill feelings. The identification of the 2007 Virginia Tech shooter as a Korean American led to extended treatment of adjustment problems for some immigrant households.

- **Asian bashing:** News accounts may unfairly blame Asian nations for economic problems in the United States. For example, the low production costs of China-based industries are seen as responsible for job loss in the United States even though they make many goods much more affordable to consumers in North America.

- **Media invisibility:** News reports may ignore Asian Americans and rarely seek their views on issues related to Asia, much less general global issues.

- **Model minority:** This positive portrayal can also have a negative effect.

yellow peril
A term denoting a generalized prejudice toward Asian people and their customs.

In its own way, each bias contributes to the unbalanced view we have developed of the large, diverse Asian American population.

The resentment against Asian Americans is not limited to overt expressions of violence. Like other subordinate groups, Asian Americans are subject to institutional discrimination.

For example, some Asian American groups have large families and find themselves subject to zoning laws stipulating the number of people per room, which make it difficult for family members to live together. Kinfolk are unable to take in family members legally. Whereas we may regard these family members as distant relatives, many Asian cultures view cousins, uncles, and aunts as relatives to whom they have a great deal of familial responsibility.

The marginal status of Asian Pacific Islanders leaves them vulnerable to both selective and collective oppression. In 1999, news stories implicated Wen Ho Lee, a nuclear physicist at Los Alamos National Laboratory in New Mexico, as a spy for China. Subsequent investigation, during which Lee was imprisoned under very harsh conditions, concluded that the naturalized citizen scientist had indeed downloaded secret files to an unsecured computer, but there was no evidence that the information ever went further.

In the aftermath of the Wen Ho Lee incident, a new form of racial profiling emerged. We introduced **racial profiling** in Chapter 2 as any police-initiated action that relies on race, ethnicity, or national origin rather than a person's behavior. Despite Lee's being found not guilty, Asian Americans were viewed as security risks. A survey found that 32 percent of the people in the United States felt that Chinese Americans are more loyal to China than to the United States. In fact, the same survey showed that 46 percent were concerned about Chinese Americans passing secrets to China. Subsequent studies found that Asian Americans were avoiding top-secret science labs for employment because they became subject to racial profiling at higher security levels (Committee of 100 2001; Department of Energy 2000; Lee with Zia 2006; F. Wu 2002).

For young Asian Americans, life in the United States often is a struggle for identity when their heritage is so devalued by those in positions of influence. Sometimes identity means finding a role in White America; other times, it involves finding a place among Asian Americans collectively and then locating oneself within one's own racial or ethnic community.

Asian Americans are subject to stereotypes, one of which, "straight-A student," reflects the model-minority image. (© 2001 Oliver Chin. Reprinted by permission of Oliver Chin.)

Political Activity and Pan-Asian Identity

Against this backdrop of prejudice, discrimination, and a search for identity, it would not be surprising to see Asian Americans seeking to recognize themselves. Historically, Asian Americans have followed the pattern of other immigrant groups: they bring organizations from the homeland and later develop groups to respond to the special needs identified in the United States.

Rather than being docile, as Asian Americans are often labeled, they have organized in labor unions, played a significant role in campus protests, and been active in immigration rights issues. Recently, given a boost by anti-alien feelings after 9/11, Asian Americans staged demonstrations in several cities, seeking to persuade people to become citizens and register to vote (Chan 1991; Chang 2007).

These efforts, similar to the recent steps taken by Hispanic groups discussed in previous chapters, have also met with mixed success. Asians' and Pacific Islanders' political clout is still developing; many still are not citizens. At the time of the 2006 election, 33 percent were not citizens and were, therefore, ineligible to vote, compared with 40 percent of Hispanics and 2 percent of White non-Hispanics (T. File 2008).

For newly arrived Asians, grassroots organizations and political parties are a new concept. With the exception of Asian Indians, the immigrants come from nations where political participation was unheard of or looked upon with skepticism and sometimes fear. Using the sizable Chinese American community as an example, we can see why Asian Americans have been slow to achieve political mobilization. At least six factors have been

racial profiling
Any arbitrary police-initiated action based on race, ethnicity, or natural origin rather than a person's behavior.

Democrat Tammy Duckworth was named Illinois Director of Veterans' Affairs after an unsuccessful campaign for Congress. Duckworth, a trained helicopter pilot who lost both her legs in the Iraq War and where she rose to the rank of major, is of mixed European, Thai, and Chinese ancestry.

identified that explain why Chinese Americans—and, to a large extent, Asian Americans in general—have not been more active in politics:

1. To become a candidate means to take risks, invite criticism, be assertive, and be willing to extol one's virtues. These traits are alien to Chinese culture.

2. Older people remember when discrimination was blatant, and they tell others to be quiet and not attract attention.

3. Many recent immigrants have no experience with democracy and arrive with a general distrust of government.

4. Like many new immigrant groups, Chinese Americans have concentrated on getting ahead economically and educating their children rather than thinking in terms of the larger community.

5. The brightest students tend to pursue careers in business and science rather than law or public administration and, therefore, are not prepared to enter politics.

6. Chinatowns notwithstanding, Chinese and other Asian American groups are dispersed and cannot control the election of even local candidates.

On the other hand, both Democrats and Republicans are increasingly regarding Asian Americans as a future political force in the United States. During the last five national elections, the Republicans and Democrats seemed to evenly share the electorate. Yet in 2008, 66 percent of Asian American voters backed Democrat Obama—a partisan margin not seen before. Whether this reflects a permanent shift to the Democrats or speaks to the popularity of Barack Obama will be closely watched in coming elections (Connelly 2008).

Despite the diversity among groups of Asian Americans and Asian Pacific Islanders, they have spent generations being treated as a monolithic group. Out of similar experiences have come panethnic identities in which people share a self-image, as do African Americans or Whites of European descent. As we noted in Chapter 1, **panethnicity** is the development of solidarity between ethnic subgroups. Are Asian Americans finding a panethnic identity? In Listen to Our Voices, New York-based writer Jean Han, born in the United States and the daughter of immigrants from Korea, tackles this question head on.

It is true that in the United States, extremely different Asian nationalities have been lumped together in past discrimination and current stereotypes. Asian Americans now see the need to unify their diverse subgroups. After centuries of animosity between ethnic groups in Asia, any feelings of community among Asian Americans must develop anew here; they bring none with them. Some observers contend that a

panethnicity
The development of solidarity between ethnic subgroups, as reflected in the terms *Hispanic* and *Asian American.*

Listen to Our Voices

ASIAN AMERICA STILL DISCOVERING ELUSIVE IDENTITY

It's not easy to figure out the collective identity of a community.

An annual lift in spirits comes around the month of May designated as APA Heritage Month, which has become an opportunity to observe the history of Asians in America through a calendar full of cultural events and celebrations.

But the month also serves as a springboard for many Asian Americans to grapple with identity on a personal and communal level outside of these organized events.

Jean Han

Having a political voice, for example, still remains a challenge for Asians, say Ann Surapruik, who serves on the Washington D.C. chapter board of the national Asian Pacific American Women's Forum. According to Surapruik, when groups of high-level people gather, very often Asian Americans are not represented. "Our biggest issue is visibility," she says.

Visibility also extends to the different deeds of ethnic groups within the "Asian Pacific Islander" description. For example, a February *Seattle Times* article details the battle against the misperception by potential scholarship funders that because Asian Pacific Islander students are doing well as a group, they do not need extra help—yet there are wide disparities in standardized test performance between Japanese American and Samoan American students.

And this may prove one of the ways APA Heritage Month can be most useful: to spotlight how the APA community is cohesive, but not homogeneous. Events that come and go, like APA Heritage month, can seem "generic," says Ben de Guzman, national campaign coordinator for the Asian Pacific American Labor Alliance. "But I think the usefulness of it is our ability to say in an official way that this is [Asian America] in all of its diversity."

APA Heritage month can also create a diversity of public forums for important Asian American issues, says Deepa Iyer, executive director of South Asian Americans Leading Together, a nonprofit community-building organization in Maryland. "Different forums exist, whether it's a corporate affinity group or a local high school, or even [looking at] Asian American history," Iyer says. "There are many different ways in which we can take a closer look at our community."

The month can also be a time for more personal reflection. Attorney Courtney Chappell, a Korean American adoptee, says her questions of Asian identity did not surface fully until college. "I'm still sort of figuring out what it means," she adds.

Chappell recalls the difficulty of finding an Asian American role model or someone who could empathize with her identity struggles. "When I face racism and discrimination, it was hard to share that with my parents, who would try but couldn't relate," she explains.

For Chappell, celebrating a heritage that is mostly foreign to her is empowering: "I celebrate by being part of a movement that is larger than me."

What it means to be Asian American on a personal level, then, may often be placed within a larger context of community. At the same time, understanding what the larger community needs means identifying its smaller parts. "Our community is so diverse," de Guzman concludes, "it exceeds our ability to describe it."

Source: J. Han 2008.

move toward pan-Asian identity represents a step in assimilation by downplaying cultural differences.

Yet pan-Asian identity often serves to solidify and strengthen organizing at the grassroots level when trying to bring about change in neighborhoods and communities where they are outnumbered and underrepresented in the corridors of political power. From this perspective, pan-Asian unity is a necessity and urgency for all Asian groups (Cheng and Yang 2000; Mitra 2008; Võ 2004).

Diversity among Asian Americans

The political activity of Asian Pacific Islanders occurs within a complex segment of the population: Asian Americans who reflect the diversity of their native lands. Asia is a vast region, holding more than half the world's population. The successive waves of immigrants to the United States from that continent have comprised a large number of nationalities and cultures. In addition to the seven groups listed in Figure 12.2, the U.S. Bureau of the Census enumerates 47 groups, as shown in Table 12.2. Given this variety among Asian Pacific Islanders, we can apply to Asian Americans several generalizations made earlier about Native Americans. Both groups are a collection of diverse peoples with distinct linguistic, social, and geographic backgrounds.

Asian Americans, like Native Americans, are not evenly distributed across the United States. To lump these people together ignores the sharp differences between them. Any examination of Asian Americans quickly reveals their diversity, which will be apparent as we focus on individual Asian American groups, beginning with Asian Indians.

TABLE 12.2
Asian Pacific Islander Groups in the United States

Asian	Pacific Islander
Asian Indian	Carolinian
Bangladeshi	Chuukese
Bhutanese	Fijian
Burmese	Guamanian or Chamorro
Cambodian	I-Kiribati
Chinese	Kosraean
Filipino	Mariana Islander
Hmong	Marshallese
Indo Chinese	Melanesian
Indonesian	Micronesian
Iwo Jiman	Native Hawaiian
Japanese	Ni-Varnualu
Korean	Palauan
Laotian	Papua New Guinean
Malaysian	Pohnpeian
Maldivian	Polynesian
Nepalese	Saipanese
Okinawan	Samoan
Pakistani	Solomon Islander
Singaporean	Tahitian
Sri Lankan	Tokelauan
Taiwanese	Tongan
Thai	Yapese
Vietnamese	

Note: Groups as enumerated separately in the 2000 census.
Source: Barnes and Bennett 2002; Grieco 2001.

Asian Indians

The second-largest Asian American group (after Chinese Americans) is composed of immigrants from India and their descendants and numbers more than 2.3 million. Sometimes immigrants from Pakistan, Bangladesh, and Sri Lanka are also included in this group.

Immigration

Like several other Asian immigrant groups, Asian Indians (or East Indians) are recent immigrants. Only 17,000 total came from 1820 to 1965, with the majority of those arriving before 1917. These pioneers were subjected to some of the same anti-Asian measures that restricted Chinese immigration. In the 10 years after the Immigration and Naturalization Act, which eliminated national quotas, more than 110,000 arrived (Takaki 1989).

Immigration law, although dropping nationality preferences, gave priority to the skilled, so the Asian Indians arriving in the 1960s through the 1980s tended to be urban, educated, and English-speaking. More than twice the proportion of Asian Indians aged 25 and older had a college degree, compared with the general population. These families experienced a smooth transition from life in India to life in the United States. They usually settled here in urban areas or located near universities or medical centers. Initially, they flocked to the Northeast, but by 1990, California had edged out New York as the state with the largest concentration of Asian Indians. The growth of Silicon Valley's information technology industry furthered the increase of Asian Indian professionals in Northern California (Bureau of the Census 2007c).

More-recent immigrants, sponsored by earlier immigrant relatives, are displaying less facility with English, and the training they have tends to be less easily adapted to the U.S. workplace. They are more likely to work in service industries, usually with members of their extended families. They are often in positions that many Americans reject because of the long hours, the seven-day workweek, and vulnerability to crime. Consequently, Asian Indians are as likely to be cab drivers or managers of motels or convenience stores as they are to be physicians or college teachers. Asian Indians see the service industries as transitional jobs to acclimatize them to the United States and to give them the money they need to become more economically self-reliant (Kalita 2003; Levitt 2004; Varadarajan 1999).

The Current Picture

It is difficult to generalize about Asian Indians because, like all other Asian Americans, they reflect a diverse population. With more than 1 billion people in 2000, India will soon be the most populous nation in the world. Diversity governs every area. The Indian government recognizes 18 official languages, each with its own cultural heritage. Some can be written in more than one type of script. Hindus are the majority in India and also among the immigrants to the United States, but significant religious minorities include Sikhs, Muslims, Jains, and Zoroastrians.

Religion among Asian Indians presents an interesting picture. Among initial immigrants, religious orthodoxy often is stronger than it is in India. Immigrants try to practice the Hindu and Muslim faiths true to their practices in India rather than joining the Caribbean versions of these major faiths already established in the United States by other immigrant groups. Although other Indian traditions are maintained, older immigrants see challenges not only

Asian Americans are rarely featured in motion pictures except where martial arts are a central focus. Exceptions to that are Kal Penn (on the right), born of Asian Indian immigrants, and Korea-born John Cho, both of whom have starred in the successful *Harold and Kumar* movies.

desi
Colloquial name for people who trace their ancestry to South Asia, especially India and Pakistan.

from U.S. culture but also from pop culture from India, which is imported through motion pictures and magazines. It is a very dynamic situation as the Asian Indian population moves into the twenty-first century (Kurien 2004; Rangaswamy 2005).

Maintaining traditions within the family household is a major challenge for Asian Indian immigrants to the United States. These ties remain strong, and many Asian Indians see themselves as more connected to their relatives 10,000 miles away than Americans are to their kinfolk less than a hundred miles away. Parents are concerned about the erosion of traditional family authority among the desi. **Desi** (pronounced "DAY-see") is a colloquial name for people who trace their ancestry to South Asia, especially India.

Asian Indian children, dressed like their peers, go to fast-food restaurants and eat hamburgers while out on their own, yet both Hindus and many Asian Indian Muslims are vegetarian by practice. Sons do not feel the responsibility to the family that tradition dictates. Daughters, whose occupation and marriage could, in India, be closely controlled by the family, assert their right to choose work and, in an even more dramatic break from tradition, select their husbands.

In Research Focus, we consider one cultural practice faced by Asian Indian and some other immigrant groups not a part of American mainstream culture: arranged marriages.

About six of 10 Asian Indian Americans are citizens, and their political impact is beginning to be felt by this, the second-largest Asian American community. Most well known is Louisiana governor Bobby Jindel, the son of immigrants. More at the grassroots level is Harvinder Anand, mayor of the upscale Long Island community of Laurel Hollow, which is 95 percent White. As evidenced by these two elected officials, successful Asian Indian politicians are reaching well beyond their Asian American base (Vitello 2007).

Filipino Americans

Little has been written about the Filipinos, although they are the third-largest Asian American group in the United States, with 2.2 million people now living here. Social science literature considers them Asians for geographic reasons, but physically and culturally, they also reflect centuries of Spanish colonial rule and the more-recent U.S. colonial and occupation governments.

Immigration Patterns

Immigration from the Philippines has been documented since the eighteenth century; it was relatively small but significant enough to create a "Manila Village" along the Louisiana coast around 1750. Increasing numbers of Filipino immigrants came as American nationals when, in 1899, the United States gained possession of the Philippine Islands at the conclusion of the Spanish–American War. In 1934, the islands gained commonwealth status. The Philippines gained their independence in 1948 and with it lost their unrestricted immigration rights. Despite the close ties that remained, immigration was sharply restricted to only 50 to 100 people annually until the 1965 Immigration Act lifted these quotas. Before the restrictions were removed, pineapple growers in Hawai'i lobbied successfully to import Filipino workers to the islands.

Besides serving as colonial subjects of the United States, Filipinos played another role in this country. The U.S. military accepted Filipinos in selected positions. In particular, the Navy put Filipino citizens to work in kitchens. Filipino veterans of World War II believed that their U.S. citizenship would be expedited. This proved untrue; the problem was only partially resolved by a 1994 federal court ruling. However, many of these veterans felt they were regarded not as former Navy employees but as unwanted immigrants (*AsianWeek* 2007; Padilla 2008a).

Filipino immigration can be divided into four distinct periods:

1. The first generation, which immigrated in the 1920s, was mostly male and employed in agricultural labor.

2. A second group, which also arrived in the early twentieth century, immigrated to Hawai'i to serve as contract workers on Hawai'i's sugar plantations.

ARRANGED MARRIAGES IN AMERICA

The question becomes not does he or she love me but who do my parents want me to marry. An **arranged marriage** is when others choose the marital partners not based on any preexisting mutual attraction. Indeed, typically in arranged marriages the couple does not even know one another.

The idea of arranged marriages seems strange to most youth growing up in the United States whose culture romanticizes finding Mr. or Ms. Right. In an arranged marriage, the boy and girl start off on neutral ground, with no expectations of each other. Then understanding develops between them as the relationship matures. The couple selected is assumed to be compatible because they are chosen from very similar social, economic, and cultural backgrounds.

In an arranged marriage, the couple works to achieve the mutual happiness they expect to find. In contrast, in a romantic or sentimental marriage, couples start off from a high ground of dreams and illusions from which there is little likelihood for things to get better and there are great chances of failure, as some of the dreams do not materialize after marriage.

Historically, arranged marriages are not unusual and even today are common in many parts of Asia and Africa. In cultures where arranged marriage is common, young people tend to be socialized to expect and look forward to such unions. But what happens in cultures that send very different messages? For example, immigrants from India, Pakistan, and Bangladesh may desire that their children enter an arranged union, but their children are growing up in culture where most of their schoolmates are obsessed with dating as a prelude to marriage and endlessly discuss the latest episodes of *Bachelor* and *Bachelorette*.

Studies of young people, in countries such as Canada and the United States, whose parents still cling to the tradition of arranging their children's marriages document the challenges this represents. Many young people do still embrace the tradition of their parents. As one first-year female Princeton student of Asian Indian ancestry puts it, "In a lot of ways it's easier. I don't have pressure to look for a boyfriend" (Herschthal 2004). Young people like her will look to their parents and other relatives to finalize a mate or even accept a match with a partner who has been selected in the country of their parents. Systematic, nationwide studies are lacking, but available research points to a trend away from arranged marriages toward romantic marriages, even when the couples enter such unions over family objections.

Change has brought with it some variations as the expectation for formally arranged marriages has been modified to *assisted marriages* in which parents identify a limited number of possible mates based on what is referred to as "bio-data"—screening for caste, family background, and geography. Children get final veto power but rarely head out on their own when seeking a mate. Young men and women may date on their own but, when it comes to marrying, they limit themselves to a very narrow field of eligibles brought to them by their parents. The combination of arranged and assisted marriages has meant that Asian Indian immigrants have the highest rates of ethnic endogamy of any major immigrant group in the United States—about 90 percent in-group marriage.

Sources: Bellafante 2005; Herschthal 2004; Talbani and Hasanali 2000; Zaidi and Shuraydi 2002.

---

3. The post–World War II arrivals included many war veterans and wives of U.S. soldiers.

4. The newest immigrants, who include many professionals (physicians, nurses, and others), arrived under the 1965 Immigration Act. More than 40 percent of Filipino Americans have immigrated since 1990 (Bureau of the Census 2007c; Min 2006; Posadas 1999).

arranged marriage
When one's marital partner is chosen by others and the relationship is not based on any preexisting mutual attraction.

Filipino American World War II veterans protested in 1997 for full veterans' benefits for Filipinos who served in World War II.

As in other Asian groups, the people are diverse. Besides these stages of immigration, the Filipinos can also be defined by various states of immigration (different languages, regions of origin, and religions), distinctions that sharply separate people in their homeland as well. In the Philippines and among Filipino immigrants to the United States, eight distinct languages with an estimated 200 dialects are spoken. Yet assimilation is under way; a 1995 survey showed that 47 percent of younger Filipino Americans speak only English and do not speak Tagalog, the primary language of the Philippine people (Bonus 2000; Kang 1996; Pido 1986).

The Current Picture

The Filipino population increased dramatically when restrictions on immigration were eased in 1965. More than two-thirds of the new arrivals qualified for entry as professional and technical workers, but like Koreans, they have often worked at jobs ranked below those they left in the Philippines. Surprisingly, U.S.-born Filipinos often have less formal schooling and lower job status than the newer arrivals. They come from poorer families that are unable to afford higher education, and they have been relegated to unskilled work, including migrant farm work. Their poor economic background means that they have little start-up capital for businesses. Therefore, unlike other Asian American groups, Filipinos have not developed small business bases such as retail or service outlets that capitalize on their ethnic culture.

A significant segment of the immigration from the Philippines, however, constitutes a more professional educated class in the area of health professionals. Although a positive human resource for the United States, it has long been a brain drain on the medical establishment of the Philippines. This is apparent when we consider areas in the United States that reflect Filipino settlement in the last 40 years. For example, in metropolitan Chicago, Filipino Americans have household incomes 30 percent higher than the general population and higher than that of Asian Indians. When the United States ceased giving preference to physicians from abroad, doctors in the Philippines began to enter the United States retrained as nurses, which dramatically illustrates the incredible income differences between the United States and the Philippines. They also send significant money back as remittances to help members of the extended family (DeParle 2007; Espiritu and Wolf 2001; Lau 2006; Zarembro 2004).

Despite their numbers, no significant single national Filipino social organization has formed, for several reasons. First, Filipinos' strong loyalty to family (*sa pamilya*) and church, particularly Roman Catholicism, works against time-consuming efforts to create organizations that include a broad spectrum of the Filipino community. Second, their diversity makes forming ties here problematic. Divisions along regional, religious, and linguistic lines present in the Philippines persist in the United States. Third, although Filipinos have organized many groups, they tend to be clublike or fraternal. They do not seek to represent the general Filipino population and, therefore, remain largely invisible to Anglos. Fourth, although Filipinos initially stayed close to events in their homeland, they show every sign of seeking involvement in broader non-Filipino organizations and avoiding group exclusiveness. Three-quarters of Filipino America are citizens, which is a larger proportion than most Asian American groups. The two political terms of Filipino American Benjamin Cayetano as governor of Hawai'i from 1994 to 2002 are an example of such involvement in mainstream political organizations (Bonus 2000; Kang 1996; Lau 2006; Padilla 2008a; Posadas 1999).

Southeast Asian Americans

The people of Southeast Asia—Vietnamese, Cambodians, and Laotians—were part of the former French Indochinese Union. *Southeast Asian* is an umbrella term used for convenience; the peoples of these areas are ethnically and linguistically diverse. Ethnic Laotians constitute only half of the Laotian people, for example; a significant number of Mon-Khmer, Yao, and Hmong form minorities. Numbering more than 2.1 million in 2005, Vietnamese Americans are the largest group, with more than 1.4 million members, or nearly 11 percent of the total Asian American population (see Figure 12.2).

gook syndrome
David Riesman's phrase describing Americans' tendency to stereotype Asians and to regard them as all alike and undesirable.

The Refugees

The problem of U.S. involvement in Indochina did not end when all U.S. personnel were withdrawn from South Vietnam in 1975. The final tragedy was the reluctant welcome given to the refugees from Vietnam, Cambodia, and Laos by Americans and people of other nations. One week after the evacuation of Vietnam in April 1975, a Gallup poll reported that 54 percent of Americans were against giving sanctuary to the Asian refugees, with 36 percent in favor and 11 percent undecided. The primary objection to Vietnamese immigration was that it would further increase unemployment (Schaefer and Schaefer 1975).

Many Americans offered to house refugees in their homes, but others declared that the United States had too many Asians already and was in danger of losing its "national character." This attitude toward the Indochinese has been characteristic of the feeling that Harvard sociologist David Riesman called the **gook syndrome**. *Gook* is a derogatory term for an Asian, and the syndrome refers to the tendency to stereotype these people in the worst possible light. Riesman believed that the American news media created an unflattering image of the South Vietnamese and their government, leading the American people to believe they were not worth saving (Luce 1975).

The initial 135,000 Vietnamese refugees who fled in 1975 were joined by more than a million running from the later fighting and religious persecution that plagued Indochina. The United States accepted about half of the refugees, some of them the so-called boat people, primarily Vietnamese of ethnic Chinese background, who took to the ocean in overcrowded vessels, hoping that some ship would pick them up and offer sanctuary. Hundreds of thousands were placed in other nations or remain in overcrowded refugee camps administered by the United Nations.

The Current Picture

Like other immigrants, the refugees from Vietnam, Laos, and Cambodia face a difficult adjustment. Few expect to return to their homelands for visits, and fewer expect to return permanently. Therefore, many look to the United States as their permanent home and the home of their children. However, the adult immigrants still accept jobs well below their occupational positions in Southeast Asia; geographic mobility has been accompanied by downward social mobility. For example, only a small fraction of refugees employed as managers in Vietnam have been employed in similar positions in the United States.

Language is also a factor in adjustment by the refugees; a person trained as a manager cannot hold that position in the United States until he or she is fairly fluent in English. The available data indicate that refugees from Vietnam have increased their earnings rapidly, often by working long hours. Partly because Southeast Asians comprise significantly different subgroups, assimilation and acceptance are not likely to occur at the same rate for all.

Although most refugee children spoke no English upon their arrival here, they have done extremely well in school. Studies indicate that immigrant parents place great emphasis on education and are pleased by the prospect of their children going to college—something very rare in their homelands. The children do very well with this encouragement, which is not unlike that offered by Mexican immigrants to their children, as we discussed in Chapter 10. It remains to be seen whether this motivation will decline as members of the next young generation look more to their American peers as role models.

The picture for young Southeast Asians in the United States is not completely pleasant. Crime is present in almost all ethnic groups, but some observers fear that in this case it has two very ugly aspects. Some of this crime may represent reprisals for the war: anti-Communists and Communist sympathizers who continue their conflicts here. At the same

Vietnamese Americans are sometimes divided over their loyalty to their "home country." Some Vietnamese in the United States make a point of displaying the "heritage flag" on the left that was last used by South Vietnam. They regard those who display the flag pictured on the right—the flag of Vietnam and formerly North Vietnam—as embracing the past injustices committed under Communism.

time, gangs are emerging as young people seek the support of close-knit groups even if they engage in illegal and violent activities. Of course, this pattern is very similar to that followed by all groups in the United States. Indeed, defiance of authority can be regarded as a sign of assimilation. Another unpleasant but well-documented aspect of the current picture is the series of violent episodes directed at Southeast Asians by Whites and others expressing resentment over their employment or even their mere presence (Alvord 2000; Zhou and Bankston 1998).

In 1995, the United States initiated normal diplomatic relations with Vietnam, which is leading to more movement between the nations. Gradually, Vietnamese Americans are returning to visit but generally not to take up permanent residence. **Viet Kieu**, Vietnamese living abroad, are making the return—some 270,000 in 1996, compared with only 80,000 four years earlier. Generational issues are also emerging as time passes. In Vietnamese communities from California to Virginia, splits emerge over a powerful symbol—under what flag to unite a nationality. Merchants, home residents, and college Vietnamese student organizations take a stand by whether they decide to display the yellow-with-red-bars flag of the now-defunct South Vietnam, sometimes called the "heritage flag," or the red-with-yellow-star flag of the current (and Communist) Vietnam (Tran 2008).

Meanwhile, for the more than 1.4 million Vietnamese Americans who remain, settlement patterns here vary. Little Saigons can be found in major cities in the United States long after the former South Vietnam capital of Saigon became Ho Chi Min City. Like many other immigrant groups in the second generation, some Vietnamese have moved into suburbs where residential patterns tend to be rather dispersed but one can still spot mini-malls with Vietnamese restaurants and grocery stores—some even sporting a sloping red-tiled roof. Other Vietnamese Americans remain in rural areas— for example, the Gulf Coast fishermen who were rendered homeless by Hurricane Katrina in 2005. Perhaps one sign of how settled Vietnamese Americans have become is that some of the same organizations that helped the refugees learn English are now helping younger Vietnamese Americans learn Vietnamese (Olivo 2007; Pfeifer 2008b).

Case Study: A Hmong Community

Wausau (population 38,000) is a community in rural Wisconsin that is best known, perhaps, for the insurance company bearing its name. To sociologists, it is distinctive for its sizable Hmong (pronounced "Mong") population. The Hmong come from rural areas of Laos and Vietnam, where they had been recruited to work for the CIA during the Vietnam War. This association made life very difficult for them after the United States pulled out. Hence, many immigrated, and the United States has maintained a relatively open policy to their becoming permanent residents. Wausau finds itself with the greatest percentage of Hmong of any city in Wisconsin. Hmong and a few other Southeast Asians

Viet Kieu
Vietnamese living abroad, such as in the United States.

account for 12 percent of the city's population and 25 percent of its public school students (Chan 1991; T. Jones 2003; Torriero 2004a).

The Hmong, who numbered 186,000 as of 2000, immigrated to the United States from Laos and Vietnam after the end of the U.S. involvement in Vietnam in April 1975. The transition for the Hmong was difficult since they were typically farmers with little formal education. Poverty levels have been high and home ownership has been uncommon. Hmong have tended to form tight-knit groups organized around community leaders. Nationwide divisions exist along generational lines as well as dialect spoken and whether they are veterans of military service. Typically cultural traditions surrounding marriage and funerals remain strong Hmong Americans. Some are giving up Hmong traditional worship of spirits for Christian faiths. Perhaps reflecting their entry into mainstream culture, Hmong culture and the challenges faced by the Hmong in the United States was explored in Clint Eastwood's 2008 fictional film Gran Torino (Pfeifer 2008a).

Like other refugees from South Asia at the time, the first Hmong came to Wausau at the invitation of religious groups. Others followed as they found the surrounding agricultural lands were places they could find work. Coming from a very rural peasant society, the immigrants faced dramatic adjustment upon arrival in the United States (Hein 2000; T. Jones 2003).

Wausau school officials believed that progress in teaching the Hmong English was stymied because the newcomers continued to associate with each other and spoke only their native tongue. In the fall of 1993, the Wausau school board decided to distribute the Hmong and other poor students more evenly by restructuring its elementary schools in a scheme that required two-way busing.

Recalls of elected officials are rare in the United States, but in December 1993, opponents of the busing plan organized a special election that led to the removal of the five board members. This left the Wausau board with a majority who opposed the busing plan that had integrated Asian American youngsters into mostly White elementary schools. By 2006, neighborhood schools played an important role in Wausau so that among elementary schools, the proportion of Hmong children ranged from 2 percent to 52 percent (Seibert 2002; Wausau School District 2006).

How events will unfold in Wausau is unclear. However, positive signs are identifiable in Wausau and other centers of Hmong life in the United States. Immigrants and their children are moving into nonagricultural occupations. Enrollment in citizenship classes is growing. The Wausau Area Hmong Mutual Association, funded by a federal grant and the local United Way, offers housing assistance. Although many of these immigrants struggle to make a go of it economically, large numbers have been able to move off public assistance. Language barriers and lack of formal schooling still are barriers encountered by older Hmong residents, but the younger generation is emerging to face some of the same identity and assimilation questions experienced by other Asian American groups. To help facilitate the adjustment, some Wausau residents are learning Hmong through a special program at a local college (Menchaca 2008; Peckham 2002).

The challenges facing the Hmong extend well beyond Wausau, Wisconsin. In other cities with concentrations of Hmong immigrants, disputes break out over contemporary U.S. policies. Hmong were recruited by U.S. military intelligence in the Vietnam War to gather information about Communists. To this day, occasional violence occurs in the Hmong community over whether the United States might lift trade barriers with the Communist-run government of Laos. Finally in 2004, the United States, recognizing the special role that the Hmong people played in the Vietnam conflict era, agreed to accept thousands of Hmong people who had been in overseas refugee camps for 30 years (Pfeifer 2008a).

Korean Americans

The population of Korean Americans, with more than 1.2 million in 2005 (see Figure 12.2), is now the fifth-largest Asian American group, yet Korean Americans often are overlooked in studies in favor of groups such as Chinese Americans and Japanese Americans, who have a longer historical tradition in the United States.

Historical Background

Today's Korean American community is the result of three waves of immigration. The initial wave of a little more than 7,000 immigrants came to the United States between 1903 and 1910, when laborers migrated to Hawai'i. Under Japanese colonial rule (1910–1945), Korean migration was halted except for a few hundred "picture brides" allowed to join their prospective husbands.

The second wave took place during and after the Korean War, accounting for about 14,000 immigrants from 1951 through 1964. Most of these immigrants were war orphans and wives of American servicemen. Little research has been done on these first two periods of immigration.

The third wave was initiated by the passage of the 1965 Immigration Act, which made it much easier for Koreans to immigrate. In the four years before the passage of the act, Koreans accounted for only seven of every 1,000 immigrants. In the first four years after the act's passage, 38 of every 1,000 immigrants to the United States were Korean. This third wave, which continues today, reflects the admission priorities set up in the 1965 immigration law. These immigrants have been well educated and have arrived in the United States with professional skills. More than 40 percent of Korean Americans have arrived in the United States since 1990 (Bureau of the Census 2007c; Kim and Yoo 2008; Min 2006).

However, many of the most recent immigrants must at least initially settle for positions of lower responsibility than those they held in Korea and must pass through a period of economic adjustment and even disenchantment for several years. This problems documented reflect the pain of adjustment: stress, loneliness, alcoholism, family strife, and mental disorders. Korean American immigrants who accompanied their parents to the United States when young now occupy a middle, marginal position between the cultures of Korea and the United States. They have also been called the **ilchomose**, or "1.5 generation." Today, they are middle-aged, remain bilingual and bicultural, and tend to form the professional class in the Korean American community (Hurh 1998; Kim 2006).

The Current Picture

Today's young Korean Americans face many of the cultural conflicts common to any initial generation born in a new country. The parents may speak the native tongue, but the signs on the road to opportunity are in the English language, and the road itself runs through U.S. culture. It is very difficult to maintain a sense of Korean culture in the United States; the host society is not particularly helpful. Although the United States fought a war there and U.S. troops remain in South Korea, Korean culture is very foreign to contemporary Americans. In the few studies of attitudes toward Koreans, White Americans respond with vague, negative attitudes or simply lump Korean Americans with other Asian groups.

Studies by social scientists indicate that Korean Americans face many problems typical for immigrants, such as difficulties with language—only one in four are U.S.-born. In Los Angeles, home to the largest concentration, more than 100 churches have only Korean-language services, and local television stations feature several hours of Korean programs. The Korean immigrants' high level of education should help them cope with the challenge. Although Korean Americans stress conventional Western schooling as a means to success, Korean schools have also been established in major cities. Typically operated on Saturday afternoons, they offer classes in Korean history, customs, music, and language to help students maintain their cultural identity (Bureau of the Census 2007c; Hurh and Kim 1984).

Korean American women commonly participate in the labor force, as do many other Asian American women. About 60 percent of U.S.-born Korean American women and half the women born abroad work in the labor force. These figures may not seem striking compared with the data for White women, but the cultural differences make the figures more significant. Korean women come here from a family system with established, well-defined marital roles: the woman is expected to serve as homemaker and mother only. Although these roles are carried over to the United States, because of their husbands' struggles to establish themselves, women are pressed to help support their families financially as well.

ilchomose
The 1.5 generation of Korean Americans—those who immigrated into the United States as children.

Many Korean American men begin small service or retail businesses and gradually involve their wives in the business. Wages do not matter as the household mobilizes to make a profitable enterprise out of a marginal business. Under economic pressure, Korean American women must move away from traditional cultural roles. However, the move is only partial; studies show that despite the high rate of participation in the labor force by Korean immigrant wives, first-generation immigrant couples continue in sharply divided gender roles in other aspects of daily living.

Korean American businesses are seldom major operations; most are small. They do benefit from a special form of development capital (or cash) used to subsidize businesses called a **kye** (pronounced "kay"). Korean Americans pool their money through the kye, an association that grants members money on a rotating basis to allow them to gain access to additional capital. Kyes depend on trust and are not protected by laws or insurance, as bank loans are. Kyes work as follows: say, for example, that 12 people agree to contribute $500 a year. Then, once a year, one of these individuals receives $6,000. Few records are kept, because the entire system is built on trust and friendship. Rotating credit associations are not unique to Korean Americans; West Indians and Ethiopians have used them in the United States, for example. Not all Korean business entrepreneurs use the kye, but it does represent a significant source of capital. Ironically, these so-called mom and pop entrepreneurs, as they encounter success, feel competitive pressure from national chains that come into their areas after Korean American businesses have created a consumer market (Reckard 2007; Watanabe 2007).

A number of recent Korean immigrants, some of whom are here illegally, lack the resources to consider kyes. Like their counterparts in other ethnic groups, they experience health care problems, substandard housing, and very limited employment opportunities (Korean Immigrant Workers Alliance 2007).

In the early 1990s, nationwide attention was given to the friction between Korean Americans and other subordinate groups, primarily African Americans but also Hispanics. In New York City, Los Angeles, and Chicago, Korean American merchants confronted African Americans who were allegedly robbing them. The African American neighborhood groups sometimes responded with hostility to what they perceived as the disrespect and arrogance of the Korean American entrepreneurs toward their Black customers. Such friction is not new; earlier generations of Jewish, Italian, and Arab merchants encountered similar hostility from what to outsiders seems an unlikely source—another oppressed subordinate group. The contemporary conflict was dramatized in Spike Lee's 1989 movie *Do the Right Thing*, in which African Americans and Korean Americans clashed. The situation arose because Korean Americans are the latest immigrant group prepared to cater to the needs of the inner city, which has been abandoned by those who have moved up the economic ladder (Hurh 1998; New American Media 2007b).

Among Korean Americans, the church is the most visible organization holding the group together. Half of the immigrants were affiliated with Christian churches before immigrating. One study of Koreans in Chicago and Los Angeles found that 70 percent were affiliated with Korean ethnic churches, mostly Presbyterian, with small numbers of Catholics and Methodists. Korean ethnic churches are the fastest-growing segment of the Presbyterian and Methodist faiths. The church performs an important function, apart from its religious one, in giving Korean Americans a sense of attachment and a practical way to meet other Korean Americans. The churches are much more than simply sites for religious services; they assume multiple secular roles for the Korean community. As the second generation seeks a church with which to affiliate as adults, they may find the ethnic church and its Korean-language services less attractive, but for now, the fellowship in which Korean Americans participate is both spiritual and ethnic (Kim and Pyle 2004; Kwon et al. 2001).

kye
Rotating credit system used by Korean Americans to subsidize the start-up costs of businesses.

Hawai'i and Its People

The entire state of Hawai'i appears to be the complete embodiment of cultural diversity. Nevertheless, despite a dramatic blending of different races living together, prejudice, discrimination, and pressure to assimilate are very much present in Hawai'i. As we will see, life

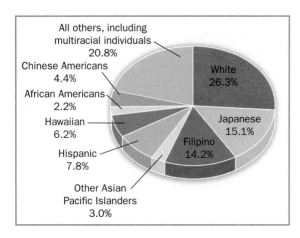

FIGURE 12.3
Hawai'i: Racial Composition, 2005

Source: Author, based on the American Community Survey 2005, Bureau of the Census.

on the island is much closer to that in the rest of the country than to the ideal of a pluralistic society. Hawai'i's population is unquestionably diverse, as shown in Figure 12.3. To grasp contemporary social relationships, we must first understand the historical circumstances that brought races together on the islands: the various Asian peoples and the **Haoles** (pronounced "hah-oh-lehs"), the term often used to refer to Whites in Hawai'i (Ledward 2008).

Historical Background

Geographically remote, Hawai'i was initially populated by Polynesian people who had their first contact with Europeans in 1778, when English explorer Captain James Cook arrived. The Hawaiians (who killed Cook) tolerated the subsequent arrival of plantation operators and missionaries. Fortunately, the Hawaiian people were united under a monarchy and received respect from the European immigrants, a respect that developed into a spirit of goodwill. Slavery was never introduced, even during the colonial period, as it was in so many areas of the Western hemisphere. Nevertheless, the effect of the White arrival on the Hawaiians themselves was disastrous. Civil warfare and disease had reduced the number of full-blooded natives to fewer than 30,000 by 1900, and the number is probably well under 10,000 now. Meanwhile, large sugarcane plantations imported laborers from China, Portugal, Japan, and, in the early 1900s, the Philippines, Korea, and Puerto Rico.

In 1893, a revolution encouraged by foreign commercial interests overthrew the monarchy. During the revolution, the United States landed troops, and five years later, Hawai'i was annexed as a territory to the United States. The 1900 Organic Act guaranteed racial equality, but foreign rule dealt a devastating psychological blow to the proud Hawaiian people. American rule had mixed effects on relations between the races. Citizenship laws granted civil rights to all those born on the islands, not just the wealthy Haoles. However, the anti-Asian laws still applied, excluding the Chinese and Japanese from political participation.

The twentieth century witnessed Hawai'i's transition from a plantation frontier to the fiftieth state and an integral part of the national economy. During that transition, Hawai'i became a strategic military outpost, although that role has had only a limited effect on race relations. Even the attack on Pearl Harbor had little influence on Japanese Americans in Hawai'i.

The Current Picture

Hawai'i has achieved some fame for its good race relations. Tourists, who are predominantly White, have come from the mainland and have seen and generally accepted the racial harmony. Admittedly, Waikiki Beach, where large numbers of tourists congregate, is atypical of the islands, but even there tourists cannot ignore the differences in intergroup relations. If they look closely, they will see that the low-wage workers in the resorts and tourist industry tend to be disproportionately of Asian descent (Adler and Adler 2004).

One clear indication of the multicultural nature of the islands is the degree of exogamy: marrying outside one's own group. The out-group marriage rate varies annually but seems to be stabilizing; about 45 percent of all marriages performed in the state involving residents are exogamous. The rate varies by group, from a low of 41 percent among Haoles to 62 percent among Chinese Americans (Hawaii Department of Health 2001, Table 80).

Prejudice and discrimination are not alien to Hawai'i. Attitudinal surveys show definite racial preferences and sensitivity to color differences. Housing surveys taken before the passage of civil rights legislation showed that many people were committed to nondiscrimination, but racial preferences were still present. Certain groups sometimes dominate residential neighborhoods, but there are no racial ghettos. The various racial groups are not distributed uniformly among the islands, but they are clustered rather than sharply segregated.

Haoles
Native Hawaiians' term for Caucasians.

The multiracial character of the islands will not change quickly, but the identity of the Native Hawaiians has already been overwhelmed. Although they have a rich cultural heritage, they tend to be very poor and often view the U.S. occupation as the beginning of their cultural and economic downfall. For centuries they traditionally placed the earthly remains of their loved ones in isolated caves. However, as these "archaeological sites" were found by Haoles, the funeral remains made their way to the Bishop Museum, which is the national historical museum located in Honolulu. Now Native Hawaiians are using the Native American Graves and Protection Act to get the remains back and rebury them appropriately (LaDuke 2006).

A 2008 occupation of the historic Iolani Palace in Honolulu brought attention to the grievances of Native Hawaiians who feel they have not received enough attention for their problems despite there being the descendants of the Kingdom of Hawai'i, which became a U.S. possession in the nineteenth century and the fiftieth state in 1959.

"E Heluuelu Kaqkou," Nako'hlani Warrington tells her third graders ("Let's read together"). She has no need to translate because she is teaching at the public immersion school where all instruction is in the Hawaiian language. Not too long ago it was assumed that Hawaiian would be spoken only by linguistic scholars, but efforts to revive it in general conversation have resulted in its use well beyond "Aloha." In 1983, only 1,500 people were considered native speakers; now native speakers number 68,000. This goes well beyond symbolic ethnicity. Language perpetuity is being combined with a solid grade school education, and a supportive doctoral program in the Hawaiian language was introduced in 2007 (*Indian Country Today* 2007; Kana'iaupuni 2008).

The **sovereignty movement** is the effort by the indigenous people of Hawai'i to secure a measure of self-government and restoration of their lands. Its roots and significance to the people are very similar to the sovereignty efforts by tribal people on the continental United States. The growing sovereignty movement has also sought restoration of the Native Hawaiian land that has been lost to Anglos over the last century, or at least compensation for it. Sometimes, the Native Hawaiians successfully form alliances with environmental groups that want to halt further commercial development on the islands. In 1996, a Native Hawaiian vote was held, seeking a response to the question, "Shall the Hawaiian people elect delegates to propose a Native Hawaiian government?" The results indicated that 73 percent voting were in favor of such a government structure. Since then, the state Office of Hawaiian Affairs has sought to create a registry of Hawaiians that is only about halfway to having all the estimated 200,000 people of significant Hawaiian descent on the islands come forward (Halvalani 2002; Staton 2004a).

Up to the present, Hawai'i's congressional delegation has sought passage of the Native Hawaiian Government Reorganization Act, or the Akaka Bill, after U.S. Senator Daniel Akaka. It would give people of Hawaiian ancestry more say over resources, provide affordable housing, take steps to preserve culture, and create a means by which they could better express their grievances. As of 2008, the measure had passed the House but was never discussed on the floor of the Senate (Akaka 2008).

In 2008, a Native Hawaiian independence group seized the historic royal palace in Honolulu to protest the U.S.-backed overthrow of the Hawaiian government more than a century ago. Although the occupation barely lasted a day, the political discontentment felt by many Native Hawaiians persists (Magin 2008).

In an absolute sense, Hawai'i is not a racial paradise. Certain occupations and even social classes tend to be dominated by a single racial group. Hawai'i is not immune to intolerance, and it is expected that the people will not totally resist prejudice as the island's isolation is reduced. However, newcomers to the islands do set aside some of their old stereotypes and prejudices. The future of race relations in Hawai'i is uncertain, but relative to the mainland and much of the world, Hawai'i's race relations are characterized more by harmony than by discord.

sovereignty movement
Effort by the indigenous people of Hawai'i to secure a measure of self-government and restoration of their lands.

Conclusion

Asian Americans are a rapidly growing group. Despite striking differences between them, they are often viewed as if they arrived all at once and from one culture. Also, they are often characterized as a successful or model minority. However, individual cases of success and some impressive group data suggest that the diverse group of peoples who make up the Asian American community are not uniformly successful. Indeed, despite high levels of formal schooling, Asian Americans earn far less than Whites with comparable education and continue to be victims of discriminatory employment practices.

The diversity within the Asian American community belies the similarity suggested by the panethnic label *Asian American*. Chinese and Japanese Americans share a history of several generations in the United States. Filipinos are veterans of a half century of direct U.S. colonization and a cooperative role with the military. In contrast, Vietnamese, Koreans, and Japanese are associated in a negative way with three wars. Korean Americans come from a nation that still has a major U.S. military presence and a persisting "cold war" mentality. Korean Americans and Chinese Americans have taken on middleman roles, whereas Filipinos, Asian Indians, and Japanese Americans tend to avoid the ethnic enclave pattern.

Who are the Asian Americans? This chapter has begun to answer that question by focusing on four of the larger groups: Asian Indians, Filipino Americans, Southeast Asian Americans, and Korean Americans. Hawai'i is a useful model because its harmonious social relationships cross racial lines. Although it is not an interracial paradise, Hawai'i does illustrate that, given proper historical and economic conditions, continuing conflict is not inevitable. Chinese and Japanese Americans, the subjects of Chapter 13, have experienced problems in American society despite striving to achieve economic and social equality with the dominant culture.

Summary

1. Often Asian Americans are labeled as a model minority, which overlooks the many problems they face and serves to minimize the challenges of succeeding despite prejudice and discrimination.

2. Asian Americans have been active politically through collective action and recently through seeking elected office. They continue to embrace both their unique identity as well as a broader pan-Asian identity.

3. Asian Indians are a diverse group culturally and, although most are Hindu, embrace a number of faiths.

4. Filipino Americans have a long historical connection to the United States, with today's immigrants including both professionals as well as the descendants of those who have served in the U.S. military.

5. Southeast Asians' presence in the United States has typically resulted from waves of refugees. They have created significant settlements throughout the United States and often have dispersed throughout the larger population.

6. The Hmong, originally from Laos and Vietnam, are a distinctive ethnic group that took up residence in the United States following their loyal support of the war effort in Vietnam in the 1960s and 1970s.

7. Korean Americans have settled largely in urban areas, where many have become successful entrepreneurs.

8. Hawai'i and its Native Hawaiians present a different multiracial pattern from that of the mainland but not one without both prejudice and discrimination.

Key Terms

arranged marriage 295
blaming the victim 287
desi 294
gook syndrome 297
Haoles 302

ilchomose 300
kye 301
model or ideal
  minority 285
panethnicity 290

racial profiling 289
sovereignty movement 303
Viet Kieu 298
yellow peril 288

Review Questions

1. How is the model-minority image a disservice to both Asian Americans and other subordinate racial and ethnic groups?
2. In what respects has the mass media image of Asian Americans been both undifferentiated and negative?
3. How has the tendency of many Korean Americans to help each other been an asset but also viewed with suspicion by those outside their community?
4. What critical events or legislative acts increased each Asian American group's immigration into the United States?
5. To what degree do race relations in Hawai'i offer both promise and a chilling dose of reality to the future of race and ethnicity on the mainland?

Critical Thinking

1. How is the model-minority image reinforced by images in the media?
2. Coming of age is difficult for anyone, given the ambiguities of adolescence in the United States. How is it doubly difficult for the children of immigrants? How do you think the immigrants themselves, such as those from Asia, view this process?
3. *American Indians, Hispanics,* and *Asian Americans* are all convenient terms to refer to diverse groups of people. Do you see these broad umbrella terms as being more appropriate for one group than for the others?

Chinese Americans and Japanese Americans

PRESENT-DAY CHINESE AMERICANS ARE DESCENDANTS OF BOTH immigrants who came before the Chinese Exclusion Act and those who immigrated after World War II. Although Chinese Americans are associated with Chinatown and its glitter of tourism, this facade hides the poverty of the newly arrived Chinese and the discontent of U.S.-born Chinese Americans. Japanese Americans encountered discrimination and ill treatment in the early twentieth century. The involuntary wartime internment of 113,000 Japanese Americans was the result of sentencing without charge or trial. During wartime, merely being of Japanese ancestry was reason enough to be suspected of treason. A little more than a generation later, Japanese Americans did very well, with high educational and occupational attainment. Today, Chinese Americans and Japanese Americans experience both prejudice and discrimination despite a measure of economic success.

307

As years and generations pass, how is identity maintained—or is it? And what if you throw a party and few come? In 2007, Japanese Americans in Los Angeles's Little Tokyo threw a day-long party of Asian hip-hop along with traditional martial arts demonstrations to bring Japanese Americans scattered across Southern California back for a day. Debbie Hazama, 35, a homemaker with three children, drove with her husband from the suburbs because she recognizes there are not many Japanese Americans where she lives, so she wants her children "to stay connected."

Three years earlier, the Los Angeles Japanese American festival was in full swing in mid-July 2004 when, during the opening ceremonies, a 24-year-old South Pasadena woman grabbed a heavy mallet and took a swing at a drum just as she had practiced doing for months. Nicole Miyako Cherry, the daughter of a Japanese American mother and a White American father, had not had much interest in her Japanese roots except for wearing a kimono for Halloween as a youngster. Yet in the last couple of years, she had begun to take interest in all things Japanese, including visiting Japan. Looking to her future as a social work therapist, she says she would like her own children to learn Japanese, go to Japanese festivals, play in Japanese sports leagues, and have Japanese first names (M. Navarro 2004; Watanabe 2007 B13).

Debbie's children and Nicole's experience are examples of the principle of third-generation interest—that ethnic awareness may increase among the grandchildren. But Nicole is of mixed ancestral background, so she is obviously making a choice to maintain her Japanese American identity as an important part of her future. But for many other Asian Americans, particularly recent immigrants, they are just trying to survive and accumulate savings for their family here and kinfolk in the old country.

Many people in the United States find it difficult to distinguish between Japanese Americans and Chinese Americans physically, culturally, and historically. As we will see in this chapter, the two groups differ in some ways but also share similar patterns in their experiences in the United States.

Chinese Americans

China, the most populous country in the world, has been a source of immigrants for centuries. Many nations have a sizable Chinese population whose history can be traced back more than five generations. The United States is such a nation. Even before the great migration from Europe began in the 1880s, more than 100,000 Chinese already lived in the United States. Today, Chinese Americans number more than 3 million, as noted in Table 13.1.

Early Settlement Patterns

From its beginning, Chinese immigration has aroused conflicting views among Americans. In one sense, Chinese immigration was welcome because it brought to these shores needed hardworking laborers. At the same time, it was unwelcome because the Chinese brought with them an alien culture that the European settlers were unwilling to tolerate. There was also a perception of economic competition by people in the western United States, and the Chinese newcomers proved to be very convenient and powerless scapegoats. As detailed in Chapter 4, the anti-Chinese mood led to the passage of the Chinese Exclusion Act in 1882, which was not repealed until 1943. Even then, the group that lobbied for repeal, the Citizens' Committee to Repeal Chinese Exclusion, encountered the old racist arguments against Chinese immigration (Pfaelzer 2007).

TABLE 13.1

Chinese American and Japanese American Population, 1860–2006

Year	Chinese Americans	Japanese Americans
1860	34,933	—
1880	105,465	148
1900	89,863	24,326
1930	74,954	138,834
1950	117,629	141,768
1960	237,292	464,332
1970	435,062	591,290
1980	806,027	700,747
1990	1,640,000	847,562
2000	2,314,533	796,700
2006	3,090,453	829,767

Note: Data beginning with 1960 include Alaska and Hawai'i.

Source: Barnes and Bennett 2002; S. Lee 1998, 15. Data for 2006 from American Community Survey of the Bureau of the Census, American Community Survey 2007b.

Very gradually, the Chinese were permitted to enter the United States after 1943. Initially, the annual limit was 105. Then several thousand wives of servicemen were admitted, and college students were later allowed to remain after finishing their education. Not until after the 1965 Immigration Act did Chinese immigrants arrive again in large numbers, almost doubling the Chinese American community. Immigration continues to exert a major influence on the growth of the Chinese American population. It has approached 100,000 annually. The influx was so great in the 1990s that the number of new arrivals in that decade exceeded the total number of Chinese Americans present in 1980.

As the underside of immigration, illegal immigration is also functioning in the Chinese American community. The lure of perceived better jobs and a better life leads overseas Chinese to seek alternative routes to immigration if legal procedures are unavailable to them. The impact of illegal entry in some areas of the country can be significant. For example, every month in 2002, 340 illegal Chinese immigrants were apprehended at Chicago's O'Hare Airport and taken to a rural jail (Starks 2002).

A small but socially significant component of Chinese in the United States are those who have been adopted by American non-Chinese couples. Beginning in 1991, China loosened its adoption laws to address the growing number of children, particularly girls, who were abandoned under the country's one-child policy. This policy strongly encourages couples to have only one child; having more children can impede promotions and even force a household to accept a less-roomy dwelling. The numbers of adopted Chinese were small, but in recent years about 7,000 have been adopted annually. This policy of was tightened significantly in 2008 by the Chinese government, reducing the number of annual adoptions. Although most are still young, they and their adopting parents face the complex issues of cultural and social identity. Organized efforts now exist to reconnect these children with their roots back in China, but for most of their lives they are adjusting to being Chinese American in a non-Chinese American family (Department of State 2008; Olemetson 2005).

It is also important to appreciate that even *Chinese American* is a collective term. There is diversity within this group represented by nationality (China versus Taiwan, for example), language, and region of origin. It is not unusual for a church serving a

Before and after the Chinese Exclusion Act, settlers attacked Chinese enclaves throughout the West on 183 separate occasions, driving the immigrants eastward where they created Chinatowns, some of which still are thriving today. This engraving depicts the Denver riot of 1880, which culminated in one Chinese man being hanged. The lynchers were identified but released the next year. There was no restoration for the damage done by the estimated mob of 3,000 men (Ellis 2004; Pfaelzer 2007).

Chinese American community to have five separate services, each in a different dialect. These divisions can be quite sharply expressed. For example, near the traditional Chinatown of New York City, a small neighborhood has emerged of Chinese from China's Fujian Province. In this area, job postings include annotations in Chinese that translate as "no north," meaning people from the provinces north of Fujian are not welcome. Throughout the United States, Chinese Americans often divide along pro-China and pro-Taiwan allegiances (K. Guest 2003; Lau 2008; Louie 2004; Sachs 2001).

Occupational Profile of Chinese Americans

By many benchmarks, Chinese Americans are doing well. As we can see in Table 13.2, as a group they have higher levels of formal schooling and household income compared to all Asian Americans and even to White non-Hispanics. Note that the Chinese American poverty rate is high—an issue we will return to later.

As we might expect, given the high income levels, half of all Chinese Americans serve in management, professional, and related occupations, compared to only a third of the general population. This reflects two patterns: first, entrepreneurial development by Chinese Americans who start their own businesses; second, the immigration of skilled overseas Chinese as well as Chinese students who chose to remain in the United States following the completion of their advanced degrees (Bureau of the Census 2007c).

The background of the contemporary Chinese American labor force lies in Chinatown. For generations, Chinese Americans were largely barred from working elsewhere. The Chinese Exclusion Act was only one example of discriminatory legislation. Many laws were passed that made it difficult or more expensive for Chinese Americans to enter certain occupations. Whites did not object to Chinese in domestic service occupations or in the laundry trade because most White men were uninterested in such menial, low-paying work. When given the chance to enter better jobs, as they were in wartime, Chinese Americans jumped at the opportunities. Where such opportunities were absent, however, many Chinese Americans sought the relative safety of Chinatown. The tourist industry and the restaurants dependent on it grew out of the need to employ the growing numbers of idle workers in Chinatown.

Chinatowns Today

Chinatowns represent a paradox. The casual observer or tourist sees them as thriving areas of business and amusement, bright in color and lights, exotic in sounds and sights. Behind this facade, however, they have large poor populations and face the problems associated with all slums. Most Chinatowns are older, deteriorating sections of cities. There are exceptions, such as Monterey Park outside Los Angeles, where Chinese Americans dominate the economy. However, in the older enclaves, the problems of Chinatowns include the entire range of the social ills that affect low-income areas but with even greater difficulties because the glitter sometimes conceals the problems from outsiders and even social planners. A unique characteristic of Chinatowns, one that distinguishes them from other ethnic enclaves, is the variety of social organizations they encompass.

Organizational Life The Chinese in this country have a rich history of organizational membership, much of it carried over from China. Chief among such associations are the clans, or *tsu*; the benevolent associations, or *hui kuan*; and the secret societies, or *tongs*.

TABLE 13.2

	White Non-Hispanics	Asian Americans	Chinese Americans	Japanese Americans
Percentage completing college, 25 years old and older	29.70	48.20	50.20	43.70
Households with a single parent (%)	12.40	13.60	24.50	9.10
People living below poverty level (%)	8.80	11.80	13.40	8.70
Median household income ($)	48,784	56,161	57,433	53,763
Citizenship status (%)	98.30	69.50	70.60	69.50
Foreign born (%)	3.80	67.40	29.30	30.50

Note: Data for 2004. Excludes people selecting multiple race designations.

Source: Bureau of the Census 2007c, 10, 11, 15, 17, 18.

The clans, or **tsu**, that operate in Chinatown have their origins in the Chinese practice in which families with common ancestors unite. At first, immigrant Chinese continued to affiliate themselves with those sharing a family name, even if a blood relationship was absent. Social scientists agree that the influence of clans is declining as young Chinese become increasingly acculturated. The clans in the past provided mutual assistance, a function increasingly taken on by government agencies. The strength of the clans, although diminished today, still points to the extended family's important role for Chinese Americans. Social scientists have found parent–child relationships stronger and more harmonious than those among non–Chinese Americans. Just as the clans have become less significant, however, so has the family structure changed. The differences between family life in Chinese and non-Chinese homes are narrowing with each new generation (Li 1976; Lyman 1986; Sung 1967).

The benevolent associations, or **hui kuan** (or *huiguan*), help their members adjust to a new life. Rather than being organized along kinship ties like the clans, hui kuan membership is based on the person's district of origin in China. Besides extending help with adjustment, the *hui kuan* lend money to and settle disputes between their members. They have thereby exercised wide control over their members. The various *hui kuan* are traditionally, in turn, part of an unofficial government in each city was called the Chinese Six Companies, a name later changed to the Chinese Consolidated Benevolent Association (CCBA). The president of the CCBA is sometimes called the mayor of a Chinatown. The CCBA often protects newly arrived immigrants from the effects of racism. The organization works actively to promote political involvement among Chinese Americans and to support the democracy movement within the People's Republic of China. Some members of the Chinese community have resented, and still resent, the CCBA's authoritarian ways and its attempt to speak as the sole voice of Chinatown.

The Chinese have also organized in **tongs**, or secret societies. The secret societies' membership is determined not by family or locale but by interest. Some have been political, attempting to resolve the dispute over which China (the People's Republic of China or Taiwan) is the legitimate government, and others have protested the exploitation of Chinese workers. Other *tongs* provide illegal goods and services, such as drugs, gambling, and prostitution. Because they are secret, it is difficult to determine accurately the power of *tongs* today. Most observers concur that their influence has dwindled over the last 60 years and that their functions, even the illegal ones, have been taken over by elements less closely tied to Chinatown.

Some conclusions can be reached about these various social organizations. First, all have followed patterns created in traditional China. Even the secret societies had antecedents in China, organizationally and historically. Second, all three types have performed similar functions, providing mutual assistance and representing their members' interests to a sometimes hostile dominant group. Third, because all these groups have had similar purposes and have operated in the same locale, conflict between them has been

tsu
Clans established along family lines and forming a basis for social organization by Chinese Americans.

hui kuan
Chinese American benevolent associations organized on the basis of the district of the immigrant's origin in China.

tongs
Chinese American secret associations.

Chinatowns, even if most Chinese Americans do not live in them, are an important focal point for Chinese immigrants and their descendants in the United States.

inevitable. Such conflicts were very violent in the nineteenth century, but in the twentieth century they tended to be political. Fourth, the old associations have declined in significance, notably since the mid-1970s, as new arrivals from Asian metropolises bring little respect for the old rural ways to which such organizations were important. Fifth, when communicating with the dominant society, all these groups have downplayed the problems that afflict Chinatowns. Only recently has the magnitude of social problems become known (Adams 2006; Lyman 1974, 1986; Soo 1999; Tong 2000; Wei 1993; Zhao 2002).

Social Problems It is a myth that Chinese Americans and Chinatowns have no problems. We saw some indication of that in the data in Table 13.2. Although overall household income levels ran 20 percent ahead of White non-Hispanics, the poverty of Chinese Americans as a group was 13.4 percent, compared to only 8.8 percent of Whites. Obviously, many Chinese Americans are doing very well, but a significant group is doing very poorly.

The false impression of Chinese American success grows out of our tendency to stereotype groups as being all one way or the other, as well as the Chinese people's tendency to keep their problems within their community. The false image is also reinforced by the desire to maintain tourism. The tourist industry is a double-edged sword. It provides needed jobs, even if some of them pay substandard wages. But it also forces Chinatown to keep its problems quiet and not seek outside assistance, lest tourists hear of social problems and stop coming. Slums do not attract tourists. This parallel between Chinese Americans and Native Americans finds both groups depending on the tourist industry even at the cost of hiding problems (Light et al. 1994).

In the late 1960s, White society became aware that all was not right in the Chinatowns. This awareness grew not because living conditions suddenly deteriorated in Chinese American settlements but because the various community organizations could no longer maintain the facade that hid Chinatowns' social ills. Despite Chinese Americans' remarkable achievements as a group, the inhabitants suffered by most socioeconomic measures. Poor health, high suicide rates, run-down housing, rising crime rates, poor working conditions, inadequate care for the elderly, and the weak union representation of laborers were a few of the documented problems.

These problems have grown more critical as Chinese immigration has increased. For example, the population density of San Francisco's Chinatown already by the late 1980s was 10 times that of the city as a whole. The problems faced by elderly Chinese are also exacerbated by the immigration wave because the proportion of older Chinese immigrants is more than twice that of older people among immigrants in general. The economic gap between Chinatown residents and outsiders is growing. As Chinese Americans become more affluent, they move out of Chinatowns. Census data showed that household income for Chinese Americans in New York City's Chinatown was significantly lower than those who lived outside the ethnic enclave. Although half of Chinatown's households earn less than $20,000 per year, only 23 percent of Asian Americans do so outside of Manhattan's Chinatown. Barely 5 percent of Chinatown's residents earn over $100,000 annually, but 25 percent living elsewhere in Manhattan do so (Logan et al. 2002; Wong 2006).

Life in Chinatown may seem lively to an outsider, but beyond the neon signs the picture can be quite different. Chinatown in New York City remained a prime site of sweatshops well into the 1990s. Dozens of women labor over sewing machines, often above restaurants. These small businesses, often in the garment industry, consist of workers sewing 12 hours a day, six or seven days a week, and earning about $200 weekly—well below minimum wage. The workers, most of whom are women, can be victimized because they are either illegal immigrants who may owe labor to the smugglers who brought them into the United States, or legal residents unable to find better employment (Finder 1994; Kwong 1994).

The attacks on the World Trade Center in 2001 made the marginal economy of New York's Chinatown even shakier. Although not located near the World Trade Center, the economy was close enough to feel the drop in customary tourism and a significant decline in shipments to the garment industry. Initially, emergency relief groups ruled out assistance to Chinatown, but within a couple of months, agencies opened up offices in Chinatown. Within two months, 42,000 people had received relief as 60 percent of businesses cut staff. Like many other minority neighborhoods, New York City's Chinatown may be economically viable, but it always is susceptible to severe economic setbacks that most other areas could withstand much more easily (J. Lee 2001; Swanson 2004).

Increasingly, Chinese neither live nor work in Chinatowns; most have escaped them or have never experienced their social ills. Chinatown remains important for many of those who now live outside its borders, although less so than in the past. For many Chinese, movement out of Chinatown is a sign of success. Upon moving out, however, they soon encounter discriminatory real estate practices and White parents' fears about their children playing with Chinese American youths.

The movement of Chinese Americans out of Chinatowns parallels the movement of White ethnics out of similar enclaves. It signals the upward mobility of Chinese Americans, coupled with their growing acceptance by the rest of the population. This mobility and acceptance are especially evident in the presence of Chinese Americans in managerial and professional occupations.

Chinatowns, and ethnic enclaves among other groups, have deserved and received attention from researchers. In Research Focus, we examine the application of the concepts of social capital and cultural capital in better understanding these communities and the role they play both for immigrants and their children and grandchildren.

Even with their problems and constant influx of new arrivals, we should not forget that first and foremost, Chinatowns are communities of people. Originally, in the nineteenth century, they emerged because the Chinese arriving in the United States had no other area in which they were allowed to settle. Today, Chinatowns represent cultural decompression chambers for new arrivals and an important symbolic focus for long-term residents. Even among many younger Chinese Americans, these ethnic enclaves serve as a source of identity.

Family Life

Family life is the major force that shapes all immigrant groups' experience in the United States. Generally, with assimilation, cultural behavior becomes less distinctive. Family life and religious practices are no exceptions. For Chinese Americans, the latest immigration wave has helped preserve some of the old ways, but traditional cultural patterns have undergone change even in the People's Republic of China, so the situation is very fluid.

The contemporary Chinese American family often is indistinguishable from its White counterpart except that it is victimized by prejudice and discrimination. Older Chinese Americans and new arrivals often are dismayed by the more American behavior patterns of Chinese American youths. Change in family life is one of the most difficult cultural changes to accept. Children questioning parental authority, which Americans grudgingly accept, is a painful experience for the tradition-oriented Chinese.

Where acculturation has taken hold less strongly among Chinese Americans, the legacy of China remains. Parental authority, especially the father's, is more absolute, and the extended family is more important than is typical in White middle-class families. Divorce is rare, and attitudes about sexual behavior tend to be strict because the Chinese generally frown on public expressions of emotion. We noted earlier that Chinese immigrant women in Chinatown endure a harsh existence. A related problem beginning to surface is domestic violence. Although the available data do not indicate that Asian American men are any more abusive than men in other groups, their wives, as a rule, are less willing to talk about their plight and to seek help. The nation's first shelter for Asian women was established in Los Angeles in 1981, but the problem is increasingly being recognized in more cities (Banerjee 2000; Tong 2000).

CULTURAL CAPITAL, SOCIAL CAPITAL, AND CHINATOWNS TODAY

In trying to comprehend the persistence of inequality among racial and ethnic groups, sociologists and other social scientists have found it useful to think in terms of the role played by social and cultural capital. This is particularly relevant to understanding the importance of ethnic enclaves such as Chinatowns. Popularized by the French sociologist Pierre Bourdieu, these concepts refer to assets that are not necessarily economic but do impact one's family and future.

Cultural capital refers to noneconomic forces such as family background and past investments in education, which are then reflected in knowledge about the arts and language. It is not necessarily book knowledge but the kind of education valued by the elites. Chinese immigrants have faced challenges because of English not being spoken at home. Data show that only 17 percent of all Chinese Americans speak only English at home. The general historical pattern has been for immigrants, especially those who came in large numbers and settled in ethnic enclaves, to take two or three generations to reach educational parity. Knowledge of Chinese cuisine is culture,

but it is not the culture that is valued and prestigious. Society privileges or values some lifestyles over others. This is not good, but it is social reality. Differentiating between types of dumplings will not get you to the top of corporate America as fast as will differentiating among wines. This is, of course, not unique to the United States. Someone settling in China would have to deal with the cultural capital valued there. In virtually all countries except for the United States, you are much better off following the run-up to the World Cup rather than the contenders for the next Super Bowl.

Social capital refers to the collective benefit of durable social networks and their patterns of reciprocal trust. Much has been written about the strength of family and friendship networks among all racial and ethnic minorities. Kinfolk within Chinatowns are not merely acquaintances but truly living assets upon which one depends or, at the very least, feels comfortable to repeatedly call on. Networks outside the family are critical to coping in a society that often seems to be determined to keep anyone who looks like you down. But given past as well as current discrimination and

---

cultural capital
Noneconomic forces such as family background and past investments in education that are then reflected in knowledge about the arts and language.

social capital
Collective benefits of durable social networks and their patterns of reciprocal trust.

Another problem for Chinese Americans is the rise in gang activity since the mid-1970s. Battles between opposing gangs have taken their toll, including the lives of some innocent bystanders. Some trace the gangs to the *tongs* and, thus, consider them an aspect, admittedly destructive, of the cultural traditions some groups are trying to maintain. However, a more realistic interpretation is that Chinese American youths from the lower classes are not part of the model minority. Upward mobility is not in their future. Alienated, angry, and with prospects of low-wage work in restaurants and laundries, they turn to gangs such as the Ghost Shadows and Flying Dragons and force Chinese American shopkeepers to give them extortion money. Asked why he became involved in crime, one gang member replied, "To keep from being a waiter all my life" (Takaki 1989, 451; see also Chin 1996).

Japanese Americans

The nineteenth century was a period of sweeping social change for Japan: it brought the end of feudalism and the beginning of rapid urbanization and industrialization. Only a few pioneering Japanese came to the United States before 1885 because Japan prohibited

prejudice, these social networks may help you become a restaurant worker, but they are less likely to get you into a board room. Yet social capital extends beyond the family, and Chinatowns host numerous social organizations that provide support for everything from job referral to child care to youth-oriented crisis-prevention services.

Thus, Chinatowns are an important means of helping immigrants and their children adjust and take advantage of social and cultural capital. But in time, it may become dysfunctional to hold on to all of one's cultural traditions to become fully a part of the larger economy. Perhaps accelerating this transition will be the tendency for successful Chinese Americans to be more likely to network with up-and-coming members of Chinatown while Whites are more likely to be more comfortable, even complacent, with the next generation making it on their own. We are increasingly appreciative of the importance of aspirations and motivation, which are often much more present among people with poor or immigrant backgrounds than those born of affluence. We know that

bilingualism is an asset, not a detriment. Children who have translated for their parents when interacting with everyone from landlords to doctors develop "real-world" skills at a much earlier age than their monolingual English counterparts.

Considering cultural and social capital does leave room for measured optimism. Chinese Americans as well as other racial and ethnic groups have shared their cultural capital whether it is the music we dance to or the food we eat. As the barriers to privilege weaken and eventually fall, people of all colors will be able to advance. The particular strength that arriving immigrants bring to the table is that they also have the ability to resist and to refuse to accept second-class status. The role that cultural and social capital play also points to the need to embrace strategies of intervention that will increasingly acknowledge the skills and talents found in a pluralistic society.

Source: Aguilera 2008; Bauder 2003; Bourdieu 1983; Bourdieu and Passeron 1990; DiMaggio 2005; Lau 2008; Monkman et al. 2005; Portes 1998; Wong 2006; Yosso 2005; Zhou 2000; Zhou and Logan 1989.

emigration. After 1885, the numbers remained small relative to the great immigration from Europe at the time.

Early Japanese Immigration

With little consideration of the specific situation, the American government began to apply to Japan the same prohibitions it applied to China. The early feelings of yellow peril were directed at the Japanese as well. The Japanese who immigrated into the United States in the 1890s took jobs as laborers at low wages under poor working conditions. Their industriousness in such circumstances made them popular with employers but unpopular with unions and other employees.

Japanese Americans distinguish sharply between themselves according to the number of generations a person's family has been in the United States. Generally, each succeeding generation is more acculturated, and each is successively less likely to know Japanese. The **Issei** (pronounced "EE-say") are the first generation, the immigrants born in Japan. Their children, the **Nisei** ("NEE-say"), are American-born. The third generation, the

Issei
First-generation immigrants from Japan to the United States.

Nisei
Children born of immigrants from Japan.

Sansei
The children of the Nisei—that is, the grandchildren of the original immigrants from Japan.

Yonsei
The fourth generation of Japanese Americans in the United States; the children of the Sansei.

Kibei
Japanese Americans of the Nisei generation sent back to Japan for schooling and to have marriages arranged.

Sansei ("SAHN-say"), must go back to their grandparents to reach their roots in Japan. The **Yonsei** ("YAWN-say") are the fourth generation. Because Japanese immigration is recent, these four terms describe almost the entire contemporary Japanese American population. Some Nisei are sent by their parents to Japan for schooling and to have marriages arranged, after which they return to the United States. Japanese Americans expect such people, called **Kibei** ("kee-bay"), to be less acculturated than other Nisei. These terms sometimes are used loosely, and occasionally *Nisei* is used to describe all Japanese Americans. However, we will use them as they were intended to differentiate the four generational groups (Yamashiro 2008).

The Japanese arrived just as bigotry toward the Chinese had been legislated in the harsh Chinese Exclusion Act of 1882. For a time after the act, powerful business interests on the West Coast welcomed the Issei. They replaced the dwindling number of Chinese laborers in some industries, especially agriculture. In time, however, anti-Japanese feeling grew out of the anti-Chinese movement. The same Whites who disliked the Chinese made the same charges about the new yellow peril. Eventually, a stereotype developed of Japanese Americans as lazy, dishonest, and untrustworthy.

The attack on Japanese Americans concentrated on limiting their ability to earn a living. In 1913, California enacted the Alien Land Act; amendments to the act in 1920 made it still stricter. The act prohibited anyone who was ineligible for citizenship from owning land and limited leases to three years. The anti-Japanese laws permanently influenced the form that Japanese American business enterprise was to take. In California, the land laws drove the Issei into cities. In the cities, however, government and union restrictions prevented large numbers from obtaining the available jobs, leaving self-employment as the only option. Japanese, more than other groups, ran hotels, grocery stores, and other medium-sized businesses. Although this specialty limited their opportunities to advance, it did give urban Japanese Americans a marginal position in the expanding economy of the cities (Bonacich 1972; Light 1973; Lyman 1986).

The Wartime Evacuation

Japan's attack on Pearl Harbor on December 7, 1941, brought the United States into World War II and marked a painful tragedy for the Issei and Nisei. Almost immediately, public pressure mounted to "do something" about the Japanese Americans living on the West Coast. Many White Americans feared that if Japan attacked the mainland, Japanese Americans would fight on behalf of Japan, making a successful invasion a real possibility. Pearl Harbor was followed by successful Japanese invasions of one Pacific island after another, and a Japanese submarine actually attacked a California oil tank complex early in 1943.

Rumors mixed with racism rather than facts explain the events that followed. Japanese Americans in Hawai'i were alleged to have cooperated in the attack on Pearl Harbor by using signaling devices to assist the pilots from Japan. Front-page attention was given to pronouncements by the Navy secretary that Japanese Americans had the greatest responsibility for Pearl Harbor. Newspapers covered in detail FBI arrests of Japanese Americans allegedly engaging in sabotage to assist the attackers. They were accused of poisoning drinking water, cutting patterns in sugarcane fields to form arrows directing enemy pilots to targets, and blocking traffic along highways to the harbor. None of these charges was substantiated, despite thorough investigations. It made no difference. In the 1940s, the treachery of the Japanese Americans was a foregone conclusion regardless of evidence to the contrary (Kashima 2003; Kimura 1988; Lind 1946; ten Brock et al. 1954).

Executive Order 9066 On February 13, 1942, President Franklin Roosevelt signed Executive Order 9066. It defined strategic military areas in the United States and authorized the removal from those areas of any people considered threats to national security. The events that followed were tragically simple. All people on the West Coast of at least one-eighth Japanese ancestry were taken to assembly centers for transfer to evacuation camps. These camps are identified in Figure 13.1. This order covered 90 percent of the 126,000 Japanese Americans on the mainland. Of those evacuated, two-thirds were citizens,

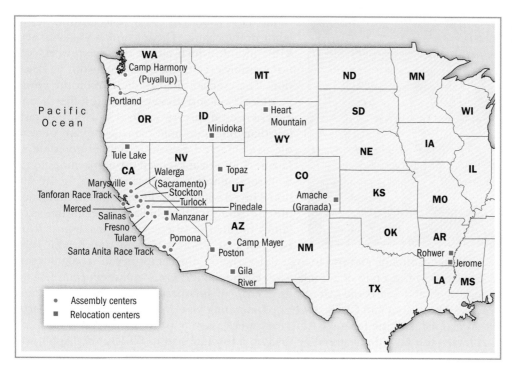

FIGURE 13.1

Japanese Americans were first ordered to report to "assembly centers," from which, after a few weeks or months, they were resettled in "relocation centers."

Source: Map "Evacuation Camps" in Weglyn 1976.

and three-fourths were under age 25. Ultimately, 120,000 Japanese Americans were in the camps. Of mainland Japanese Americans, 113,000 were evacuated, but to those were added 1,118 evacuated from Hawai'i, 219 voluntary residents (Caucasian spouses, typically), and, most poignantly of all, the 5,981 who were born in the camps (Weglyn 1976).

The evacuation order did not arise from any court action. No trials took place. No indictments were issued. Merely having a Japanese great-grandparent was enough to mark a person for involuntary confinement. The evacuation was carried out with little difficulty. For Japanese Americans to have fled or militantly defied the order would only have confirmed the suspicions of their fellow Americans. There was little visible objection initially from the Japanese Americans. The Japanese American Citizens League (JACL), which had been founded by the Nisei as a self-help organization in 1924, even decided not to arrange a court test of the evacuation order. The JACL felt that cooperating with the military might lead to sympathetic consideration later when tensions subsided (Iwamasa 2008b).

Even before reaching the camps, the **evacuees**, as Japanese Americans being forced to resettle came to be called officially, paid a price for their ancestry. They were instructed to carry only personal items. No provision was made for shipping their household goods. The federal government took a few steps to safeguard the belongings they left behind, but the evacuees assumed all risks and agreed to turn over their property for an indeterminate length of time. These Japanese Americans were destroyed economically. Merchants, farmers, and business owners had to sell all their property at any price they could get. Precise figures of the loss in dollars are difficult to obtain, but after the war the Federal Reserve Bank estimated it to be $400 million. To place this amount in perspective, one estimate stated that in 1995 dollars, the economic damages sustained, excluding personal income, would be more than $3.7 billion (Bureau of the Census 1996, 483; Commission on Wartime Relocation and Internment of Civilians 1982a, 1982b; Hosokawa 1969; Thomas and Nishimoto 1946).

The Camps Ten camps were established in seven states. Were they actually concentration camps? Obviously, they were not concentration camps constructed for the murderous purposes of those in Nazi Germany, but such a positive comparison is no compliment to the United States. To refer to them by their official designation as *relocation centers* ignores these facts: the Japanese Americans did not go there voluntarily, they had been charged with no crime, and they could not leave without official approval.

evacuees
Japanese Americans interned in camps for the duration of World War II.

Mournful Japanese Americans during World War II, as depicted in this present-day mural in Los Angeles.

Japanese Americans were able to work at wage labor in the camps. The maximum wage was set at $19 a month, which meant that camp work could not possibly recoup the losses incurred by evacuation. The evacuees had to depend on the government for food and shelter, a situation they had not experienced in prewar civilian life. More devastating than the economic damage of camp life was the psychological damage. Guilty of no crime, the Japanese Americans moved through a monotonous daily routine with no chance of changing the situation. Forced community life, with such shared activities as eating in mess halls, weakened the strong family ties that Japanese Americans, especially the Issei, took so seriously (Kitsuse and Broom 1956).

Amid the economic and psychological devastation, the camps began to take on some resemblance to U.S. cities of a similar size. High schools were established, complete with cheerleaders and yearbooks. Ironically, Fourth of July parades were held, with camp-organized Boy Scout and Girl Scout troops marching past proud parents. But the barbed wire remained, and the Japanese Americans were asked to prove their loyalty.

A loyalty test was administered in 1943 on a form all had to fill out, the "Application for Leave Clearance." Many of the Japanese Americans were undecided on how to respond to two questions:

> No. 27. Are you willing to serve in the armed forces of the United States on combat duty, wherever ordered?

> No. 28. Will you swear to abide by the laws of the United States and to take no action, which would in any way interfere with the war effort of the United States? (Daniels 1972, 113)

The ambiguity of the questions left many internees confused about how to respond. For example, if Issei said yes to the second question, would they then lose their Japanese citizenship and be left stateless? The Issei would be ending allegiance to Japan but were unable, at the time, to gain U.S. citizenship. Similarly, would Nisei who responded yes be suggesting that they had been supporters of Japan? For whatever reasons, 6,700 Issei and Nisei, many because of their unacceptable responses to these questions, were transferred to the high-security camp at Tule Lake for the duration of the war (Bigelow 1992).

Overwhelmingly, Japanese Americans showed loyalty to the government that had created the camps. In general, security in the camps was not a problem. The U.S. Army, which had overseen the removal of the Japanese Americans, recognized the value of the Japanese Americans as translators in the war ahead. About 6,000 Nisei were recruited to work as interpreters and translators, and by 1943, a special combat unit of 23,000 Nisei volunteers had been created to fight in Europe. The predominantly Nisei unit was unmatched, and it concluded the war as the most decorated of all American units.

Japanese American behavior in the concentration camps can be seen only as reaffirming their loyalty. True, some internees refused to sign an oath, but that was hardly a treasonous act. More typical were the tens of thousands of evacuees who contributed to the U.S. war effort.

A few Japanese Americans resisted the evacuation and internment. Several cases arising out of the evacuation and detention reached the U.S. Supreme Court during the war. Amazingly, the Court upheld lower court decisions on Japanese Americans without even raising the constitutionality of the whole plan. Essentially, the Court upheld the idea of an entire race's collective guilt. Finally, after hearing *Mitsuye Endo v. United States*, the Supreme Court ruled, on December 18, 1944, that the detainment was unconstitutional and consequently the defendant (and presumably all evacuees) must be granted freedom. Two weeks later, Japanese Americans were allowed to return to their homes for the first time in three years, and the camps were finally closed in 1946 (Asahina 2006; Iwamasa 2008a; ten Brock et al. 1954).

The immediate postwar climate was not pro–Japanese American. Whites terrorized returning evacuees in attacks similar to those against Blacks a generation earlier. Labor unions called for work stoppages when Japanese Americans reported for work. Fortunately, the most blatant expression of anti-Japanese feeling disappeared rather quickly. Japan stopped being a threat as the atomic bomb blasts destroyed Nagasaki and Hiroshima. For the many evacuees who lost relatives and friends in the bombings, however, it must have been a high price to pay for marginal acceptance (Maykovich 1972a, 1972b; Peterson 1971).

The Evacuation: What Does It Mean? The social significance of the wartime evacuation has often been treated as a historical exercise, but in the wake of the stigmatizing of Arab and Muslim Americans after 9/11, singling out people of Japanese descent almost 70 years ago takes on new meaning. Japanese American playwright Chay Yew reflected recently, "You think you can walk away from history and it takes you on the back" (Boehm 2004, E2). We will not know the consequences of the current focus on identifying potential disloyal Americans, but we do have some perspective on stigmatizing Japanese Americans during and after World War II.

The evacuation policy cost the U.S. taxpayers a quarter of a billion dollars in construction, transportation, and military expenses. Japanese Americans, as already noted, effectively lost at least several billion dollars. These are only the tangible costs to the nation. The relocation was not justifiable on any security grounds. No verified act of espionage or sabotage by a Japanese American was recorded. How could it happen?

Racism cannot be ignored as an explanation. Japanese Americans were placed in camps, but German Americans and Italian Americans were largely ignored. Many of those whose decisions brought about the evacuation were of German and Italian ancestry. The fact was that the Japanese were expendable. Placing them in camps posed no hardship for the rest of society, and, in fact, other Americans profited by their misfortune. That Japanese Americans were evacuated because they were seen as expendable is evident from the decision not to evacuate Hawai'i's Japanese. In Hawai'i, the Japanese were an integral part of the society; removing them would have destroyed the islands economically (Hosokawa 1969; Kimura 1988; Miyamoto 1973).

Some people argue that the Japanese lack of resistance made internment possible. This seems a weak effort to transfer guilt—to blame the victim. In the 1960s, some Sansei and Yonsei were concerned about the alleged timidity of their parents and grandparents when faced with evacuation orders. However, many evacuees, if not most, probably did not really believe what was happening. "It just cannot be that bad," they may have thought. At worst, the evacuees can be accused of being naive. But even if they did see clearly how devastating the order would be, what alternatives were open to them? None (Haak 1970; Kitano 1976; Takezawa 1991).

The Commission on Wartime Relocation and Internment of Civilians in 1981 held hearings on whether additional reparations should be paid to evacuees or their heirs. The final commission recommendation in 1983 was that the government formally apologize and give $20,000 tax-free to each of the approximately 82,000 surviving internees. Congress began hearings in 1986 on the bill authorizing these steps, and President Ronald Reagan signed the Civil Liberties Act of 1988, which authorized the payments. The payments, however, were slow in coming because other federal expenditures had higher priority. Meanwhile, the aging internees were dying at a rate of 200 a month. In 1990, the first checks were finally issued, accompanied by President Bush's letter of apology. Many Japanese Americans were disappointed by and critical of the begrudging nature of the compensation and the length of time it had taken to receive it (Commission on Wartime Relocation and Internment of Civilians 1982a, 1982b; Department of Justice 2000).

Six decades late! Ben Hara was a freshman at Lodi High School in May 1942 when he was taken and forced into an internment camp. In 2005, the California State Assembly authorized diplomas for the Japanese American internees.

Perhaps actor George Takei, of *Star Trek* fame, sums up best the wartime legacy of the evacuation of Japanese Americans. As a child, he had lived with his parents in the Tule Lake, California, camp. In 1996, on the fiftieth anniversary of the camp's closing and five years before 9/11 would turn the nation's attention elsewhere, he reflected on his arrival at the camp. "America betrayed American ideals at this camp. We must not have national amnesia; we must remember this" (S. Lin 1996, 10).

The Economic Picture

The socioeconomic status of Japanese Americans as a group is different from that of other Asian Americans. Japanese Americans as a group are even more educated and enjoy even higher incomes than Chinese Americans as well as White Americans (refer to Table 13.2). In contrast to other Asian Americans, the Japanese American community is more settled and less affected by new arrivals from the home country.

The camps left a legacy with economic implications; the Japanese American community of the 1950s was very different from that of the 1930s. Japanese Americans were more widely scattered. In 1940, 89 percent lived on the West Coast. By 1950, only 58 percent of the population had returned to the West Coast. Another difference was that a smaller proportion than before was Issei. The Nisei and even later generations accounted for 63 percent of the Japanese population. By moving beyond the West Coast, the Japanese Americans seemed less of a threat than if they had remained concentrated. Furthermore, by dispersing, Japanese American businesspeople had to develop ties to the larger economy rather than do business mostly with other Japanese Americans. Although ethnic businesses can be valuable initially, those who limit their dealings to those from the same country may limit their economic potential (Oliver and Shapiro 1996, 46).

After the war, some Japanese Americans continued to experience hardship. Some remained on the West Coast and farmed as sharecroppers in a role similar to that of the freed slaves after the Civil War. Sharecropping involved working the land of others, who provided shelter, seeds, and equipment and who also shared any profits at the time of harvest. The Japanese Americans used the practice to gradually get back into farming after being stripped of their land during World War II (Parrish 1995).

However, perhaps the most dramatic development has been the upward mobility that Japanese Americans collectively and individually have accomplished. By occupational and academic standards, two indicators of success, Japanese Americans are doing very well. The educational attainment of Japanese Americans as a group, as well as their family earnings, is higher than that of Whites, but caution should be used in interpreting such group data. Obviously, large numbers of Asian Americans, as well as Whites, have little formal schooling and are employed in poor jobs. Furthermore, Japanese Americans are concentrated in areas of the United States such as Hawai'i, California, Washington, New York, and Illinois, where both wages and the cost of living are far above the national average. Also, the proportion of Japanese American families with multiple wage earners is higher than that of White families. Nevertheless, the overall picture for Japanese Americans is remarkable, especially for a racial minority that had been discriminated against so openly and so recently (Inoue 1989; Kitano 1980; Nishi 1995).

The Japanese American story does not end with another account of oppression and hardship. Today, Japanese Americans have achieved success by almost any standard. However, we must qualify the progress that *Newsweek* (1971) once billed as their "Success Story: Outwhiting the Whites." First, it is easy to forget that several generations of Japanese Americans achieved what they did by overcoming barriers that U.S. society had created, not because they had been welcomed. However, many, if not most, have become acculturated. Nevertheless, successful Japanese Americans still are not wholeheartedly accepted into the dominant group's inner circle of social clubs and fraternal organizations. Second, Japanese Americans today may represent a stronger indictment of society than economically oppressed African Americans, Native Americans, and Hispanics. There are few excuses apart from racism that Whites can use to explain why they continue to look on Japanese Americans as different—as "them."

Family Life

The contradictory pulls of tradition and rapid change that are characteristic of Chinese Americans are very strong among Japanese Americans today. Surviving Issei see their grandchildren as very nontraditional. Change in family life is one of the most difficult cultural changes for any immigrant to accept in the younger generations.

As cultural traditions fade, the contemporary Japanese American family seems to continue the success story. The divorce rate has been low, although it is probably rising. Similar conclusions apply to crime, delinquency, and reported mental illness. Data on all types of social disorganization show that Japanese Americans have a lower incidence of such behavior than all other minorities; it is also lower than that of Whites. Japanese Americans find it possible to be good Japanese and good Americans simultaneously. Japanese culture demands high in-group unity, politeness, respect for authority, and duty to community—all traits that are highly acceptable to middle-class Americans. Basically, psychological research has concluded that Japanese Americans share the high-achievement orientation held by many middle-class White Americans. However, one might expect that as Japanese Americans continue to acculturate, the breakdown in traditional Japanese behavior will be accompanied by a rise in social deviance (Nishi 1995).

In the last 20 years, a somewhat different family pattern has emerged in what can almost be regarded as a second Japanese community forming. As Japan's economic engine took off in the later part of the twentieth century, corporate Japan sought opportunities abroad. Because of its large automobile market, the United States economy became one destination. Top-level executives and their families were relocated to look after these enterprises. This has created a small but significant community of Japanese in the United States. Although they are unlikely to stay, they are creating a presence that is difficult to miss. Several private schools have been established since 1966 in the United States, in which children follow Japanese curriculum and retain their native language and culture. Saturday school is maintained for Japanese American parents whose children attend public school during the week. Although these private academies are removed from the broader culture, they help to facilitate the creation nearby of authentic markets and Japanese bookstores. Researchers are interested to see what might be the lasting social implications of these households from Japan (Lewis 2008; Twohey 2007).

Remnants of Prejudice and Discrimination

The Fu Manchu image may be gone, but its replacement is not much better. In popular television series, Asian Americans, if they are present, usually are either karate experts or technical specialists involved in their work. Chinese Americans are ignored or misrepresented in history books. Even past mistakes are repeated. When the transcontinental railroad was completed in Utah in 1869, Chinese workers were barred from attending the ceremony. Their contribution is now well known and regarded as one of the stories of true heroism in the West. However, in 1969, when Secretary of Transportation John Volpe made a speech marking the 100th anniversary of the event, he neglected to mention the Chinese contribution. He exclaimed, "Who else but Americans could drill tunnels in mountains 30 feet deep in snow? Who else but Americans could chisel through miles of solid granite? Who else but Americans could have laid 10 miles of track in 12 hours?" (Yee 1973, 100). The Chinese contribution was once again forgotten.

Today, young Japanese Americans and Chinese Americans are very ambivalent about their cultural heritage. The pull to be American is intense, but so are the reminders that in the eyes of many others, Asian Americans are "they," not "we." College student Miku Ishii comments in Listen to Our Voices about the prejudice she has experienced both

FROM KAWASAKI TO CHICAGO

Miku Ishii

I was born a citizen of Japan in an area named Kawasaki, which is basically the suburbs of Tokyo. My parents raised me in a small apartment in Kawasaki until I was six years old. From then, my father's company decided to transfer him to the U.S., and my mother, my father, and my brother all moved to Illinois. Japanese is my native language, and as I came to America, I was forced to learn English. It took me four years in bilingual school to fully be able to speak English and get sent off to the "regular" school where there were no foreigners like me. Since we moved to the northwest suburbs of Chicago, I grew up with mostly Caucasian kids and a mediocre percentage of Asians. There were hardly any African American people in the town of Schaumburg. In elementary school, I was mistreated so badly at my "regular" school that I hardly spoke and was incredibly shy.

The very first time I had experienced the excruciating pain of pure racism was when I was only in the second grade. A Caucasian girl with big bright blue eyes and short bouncy blonde hair had a habit of picking at me constantly. She said it was because of my slanted slim slits of an eye. It was because of my dark jet-black pigtails that hung thick as horse tails around my face. One afternoon during recess, I climbed up a dome that she also happened to be on. As she saw me coming near, she jumped back down on the ground and ran to the teacher. The next thing I knew, my teacher was punishing me, saying that I should not be pushing this grinning blonde-haired blue-eyed girl. At the time, I was only a beginner in bilingual class, so I was barely able to say anything but "Where is the bathroom?" and "I don't know." I tried to explain to the teacher. But all that came out were words in Japanese. Of course they looked at me wide eyed as I tried to speak broken English with Japanese. Finally, the teacher, who could not understand me to hear my self-defense, banned me from

because she is Japanese American and sometimes because others just think of her as being "Asian" or even "Chinese."

Chinese Americans and Japanese Americans believe that prejudice and discrimination have decreased in the United States, but subtle reminders remain. Third-generation Japanese Americans, for example, feel insulted when they are told, "You speak English so well." Adopting new tactics, Asian Americans are now trying to fight racist and exclusionary practices (Lem 1976).

Marriage statistics also illustrate the effects of assimilation. At one time, 29 states prohibited or severely regulated marriages between Asians and non-Asians. Today, intermarriage, though not typical, is legal and certainly more common, and more than one-fourth of Chinese Americans under age 24 marry someone who is not Chinese. The degree of intermarriage is even higher among Japanese Americans: 1990 census data showed that two-thirds of all children born to a Japanese American had a parent of a different race.

The increased intermarriage indicates that Whites are increasingly accepting of Chinese Americans and Japanese Americans. It also suggests that Chinese and Japanese ties to their native cultures are weakening. As happened with the ways of life of European

Listen to Our Voices

going out to recess for a week. I was furious and embarrassed and felt ashamed of my race.

Even the bus ride to school and back could not be near peaceful for me. The back of the bus was where all the cool white kids sat. When I would try to sit in the back because there were no other seats, those kids would call me Chinese or chink and make that obnoxious sound which clearly mocked the language. Some days they threw chewed gum at me, not because I did anything to them but because I was a chink and they wanted to see how crazy I would react. I would always just ignore it and stay quiet. I wanted to make it seem like it did not bother me, but inside, it was breaking my heart. Heck, I was not even Chinese but I was always called that in such disdainful manner. Going to school became something I feared. I remember I felt so miserable and ashamed to death for being born "Chinese." All I wanted was to be white.

I stand here today still remembering those days very vividly. In all essence, those experiences have molded me into the person that I am today. I like to think that I am very open-minded and I love diversity. I love to learn about other cultures, and I have a very ethnic variety of friends. I would say relative to others, my multicultural experience has been rich because of the fact that I am an immigrant, a minority. And as I have expressed before, for many years when I first came to the United States, I have experienced so much hate and prejudice for just being born my race. I am still a citizen of Japan to this day, and I go back to Kawasaki about every two years. I feel that I have grown up in two different worlds. The experiences that I have undergone have made me accept people at face value. A lot of times for me, I forget about color because I never judge by race, but I am also not oblivious or blind to the fact that racism does exist. I think as sad as it sounds, that it is an evil that will never go away.

Source: Ishii 2006.

immigrants, the traditional norms are being cast aside for those of the host society. In one sense, these changes make Chinese Americans and Japanese Americans more acceptable and less alien to Whites. But this points to all the changes in Asian Americans rather than any recognition of diversity in the United States. As illustrated in the figure on the page 325, intermarriage patterns reflect the fusion of different racial groups; but, compared with examples of assimilation and pluralism, they are a limited social process at present (S. Fong 1965, 1973; Kibria 2002; Onishi 1995).

The Japanese American community struggles to maintain its cultural identity while also paying homage to those who were interned during World War II. Paradoxically, as many people see parallels between the collective guilt forced on people of Japanese ancestry during the 1940s and profiling of Arab and Muslim Americans, a few are seeking to justify the internment. Books and even a public middle school named after an internee in Washington state have been criticized; critics feel that when the subject of Japanese American internment was taught it was too biased and that arguments for internment being the correct action should be included. For many Japanese Americans, the more things change, the more they stay the same (Malkin 2004; Tizon 2004).

It would be incorrect to interpret assimilation as an absence of protest. Because a sizable segment of the college youth of the 1960s and early 1970s held militant attitudes, and because the Sansei are more heterogeneous than their Nisei and Issei relatives, it was to be expected that some Japanese Americans, especially the Sansei, would be politically active. For example, Japanese and other Asian Americans have emerged as activists for environmental concerns ranging from contaminated fish to toxic working conditions, and the targets of Japanese Americans' anger have included the apparent rise in hate crimes in the United States against Asian Americans in the 1990s. They also lobbied for passage of the Civil Rights Restoration Act, which extended reparations to the evacuees. They have expressed further activism through Hiroshima Day ceremonies that mark the anniversary of the detonation in World War II of the first atomic bomb over a major Japanese city. Also, each February, a group of Japanese American youths makes a pilgrimage to the site of the Tule Lake evacuation camp in a "lest we forget" observance. Such protests are modest, but they are a militant departure from the silent role played by the Nisei in the years immediately following the closing of the camps (Cart 2006).

Is pluralism developing? Japanese Americans show little evidence of wanting to maintain a distinctive way of life. The Japanese values that have endured are attitudes, beliefs, and goals shared by and rewarded by the White middle class in America. All Asian Americans, not only Japanese Americans, are caught in the middle. Any Asian American is culturally a part of a society that is dominated by a group that excludes him or her because of racial distinctions.

Conclusion

The presence of Asian and Pacific Islanders is unmistakable throughout much of the United States. As shown in Table 13.3, urban centers from coast to coast are homes of significant numbers of immigrants from Asia and their descendants.

Most White adults are confident that they can distinguish Asians from Europeans. Unfortunately, though, White Americans often cannot tell Asians apart from their physical appearance and are not disturbed about their confusion.

TABLE 13.3
Metropolitan Areas with the Largest Asian Pacific Islander Concentrations, 2006

City	Number of Asian Pacific Islanders	Proportion of City's Population (%)
Los Angeles–Long Beach	1,808,023	14.0
New York City	1,735,715	9.2
San Francisco–Oakland	938,874	22.4
San Jose	522,671	29.2
Chicago	494,999	5.2
Honolulu	474,418	52.1
Washington, D.C.	456,214	8.1
Seattle–Tacoma	357,668	11.0
Houston	315,858	5.9
San Diego	315,477	10.7
Dallas–Fort Worth	287,370	4.8
Boston–Cambridge	259,965	5.8

Source: American Community Survey 2006 data released in 2007, Tables C0200306 and C0200307.

SPECTRUM OF INTERGROUP RELATIONS

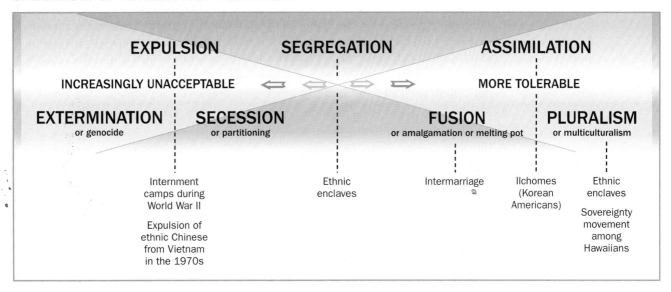

However, as we have seen, there are definite differences in the experience of the Chinese and the Japanese in the United States. One obvious difference is in the degree of assimilation. The Chinese Americans have maintained their ethnic enclaves more than the Japanese Americans have. Chinatowns live on, both as welcomed halfway points for new arrivals and as enclaves where many residents make very low wages. However, Little Tokyos are few because of the differences in the cultures of China and Japan. China was almost untouched by European influence, but even by the early 1900s, Japan had already been influenced by the West. Therefore, the Japanese arrived somewhat more assimilated than their Chinese counterparts. The continued migration of Chinese in recent years has also meant that Chinese Americans as a group have been less assimilated than Japanese Americans.

Both groups have achieved some success, but this success has not extended to all members. For Chinese Americans, a notable exception to success can be found in Chinatowns, which, behind the tourist front, are much like other poverty-stricken areas in American cities. Neither Chinese Americans nor Japanese Americans have figured prominently in the executive offices of the nation's large corporations and financial institutions. Compared with other racial and ethnic groups, Asian Americans have shown little interest in political activity on their own behalf.

However, the success of Asian Americans, especially that of the Japanese Americans, belongs to them, not to U.S. society. First, Asian Americans have been considered successful only because they conform to the dominant society's expectations. Their acceptance as a group does not indicate growing pluralism in the United States.

Second, the ability of the Nisei, in particular, to recover from the camp experience cannot be taken as a precedent for other racial minorities. The Japanese Americans left the camps a skilled group, ambitious to overcome their adversity and placing a cultural emphasis on formal education. They entered a booming economy in which Whites and others could not afford to discriminate even if they wanted to. African Americans after slavery and Hispanic immigrants have entered the economy without skills at a time when the demand for manual labor was limited. Many of them were forced to remain in a marginal economy, whether that of the ghetto, the barrio, or subsistence agriculture. For Japanese Americans, the post–World War II period marked the fortunate coincidence of their having assets and ambition when they could be used to full advantage.

Third, some Whites use the success of the Asian Americans to prop up their own prejudice. Bigoted people twist Asian American success to show that racism cannot possibly play a part in another group's subordination. If the Japanese or Chinese can do it, why cannot African Americans, the illogical reasoning goes. More directly, Japanese Americans' success may serve as a scapegoat for another's failure ("They advanced at my expense") or as a sign that they are clannish or too ambitious. Regardless of what a group does, a prejudiced eye will always view it as wrong.

As for other racial and ethnic minorities, assimilation seems to be the path most likely to lead to tolerance but not necessarily to acceptance. However, assimilation has a price that is well captured in the Chinese phrase "Zhancao zhugen": "To eliminate the weeds, one must pull out their roots." To work for acceptance means to uproot all traces of one's cultural heritage and former identity (Wang 1991).

Summary

1. Although welcomed for their labor in the nineteenth century, Chinese immigrants were shortly viewed as responsible for economic setbacks experienced by the nation, which culminated in the passage of the Chinese Exclusion Act.

2. Chinatowns are very visible signs of continued growth of the Chinese American population and represent both promise and problems for the immigrants.

3. The family is a central focus in the Chinese community and is critical to the successful adaptation of immigrants to the United States.

4. Immigrants from Japan, like so many others, were permitted to come when they fulfilled an economic niche but were quickly marginalized socially and legally.

5. The internment of people of Japanese ancestry during World War II is a clear instance of guilt by virtue of race.

6. The prosperity of Japanese Americans as a group reflects the willingness to endure post–World War II marginalization and continued investment in formal schooling for their children.

7. Despite competing effectively in the labor market, or perhaps because of it, Chinese and Japanese Americans continue to experience prejudice and discrimination in the twenty-first century.

8. With immigration from Japan decreasing over recent decades, it is more of a challenge for Japanese Americans to share their cultural heritage with the next generation than it is for Chinese Americans and other immigrant groups from the Asian continent.

Key Terms

cultural capital 314	Kibei 316	tongs 311
evacuees 317	Nisei 315	tsu 311
hui kuan 311	Sansei 316	Yonsei 316
Issei 315	social capital 314	

Review Questions

1. What has been the legacy of the "yellow peril"?

2. What made the placement of Japanese Americans in internment camps unique?

3. In what respects does diversity characterize Chinatowns?

4. How has Japanese American assimilation been blocked in the United States?

5. What are the most significant similarities between the Chinese American and Japanese American experiences? What are the differences?

Critical Thinking

1. Considering the past as well as the present, are the moves made to restrict or exclude Chinese and Japanese Americans based on economic or racist motives?

2. What events can you imagine that could cause the United States to again identify an ethnic group for confinement in some type of internment camps?

3. What stereotypical images of Chinese Americans and Japanese Americans can you identify in the contemporary media?

14

Jewish Americans: Quest to Maintain Identity

THE JEWISH PEOPLE ARE AN ETHNIC GROUP. THEIR IDENTITY rests not on the presence of physical traits or religious beliefs but on a sense of belonging that is tied to Jewish ancestry. The history of anti-Semitism is as ancient as the Jewish people themselves. Evidence suggests that this intolerance persists today in both thought and action. Jews in the United States may have experienced less discrimination than did earlier generations in Europe, but some opportunities are still denied them. Contemporary Jews figure prominently in the professions and as a group exhibit a strong commitment to education. Many Jews share a concern about either the lack of religious devotion of some members or the division within American Judaism over the degree of orthodoxy. Jews in the United States practice their faith as Orthodox, Conservative, or Reform. Paradoxically, the acceptance of Jews by Gentiles has made the previously strong identity of Jews weaker with each succeeding generation.

329

T wo events reflect the complexity of Jewish life in the United States; one began with a lawsuit and the other with violence.

On December 21, 2001, the federal Court of Appeals for the Second Circuit upheld earlier court decisions that ruled in favor of Yale University and against the "Yale Five." The case began in 1997 when three Orthodox Jews felt that the Yale housing policy that required unmarried freshmen and sophomores under age 21 to live on campus was discriminatory. The freshmen felt it would force Orthodox Jews to violate their faith's call for modesty in living, by expecting them to live in co-ed residence halls. Even a compromise offered by Yale to place them in rooms with bathrooms on single-sex floors was rejected. The students contended that the dormitory atmosphere of sexual promiscuity was irreconcilable with their deeply held religious beliefs. Two sophomores who had paid for university housing the year before while living off-campus soon joined their lawsuit. Many supported the Yale Five, but even other Orthodox Jewish students at Yale expressed anger over the lawsuit, feeling that they could be respectful to their faith and still conform to the housing standards of the university.

Billings, Montana, may have a Jewish population of only 300 or so, but it does have an established community of Jews. Until 1992, Billings had no history of visible anti-Jewish hostility. However, beginning that year, swastikas appeared outside a Jewish temple, tombstones in a Jewish cemetery were toppled, and bomb threats were made to a synagogue. Then, in the fall of 1993, rocks and bottles were thrown through the windows of homes of prominent members of the Jewish community in Billings. Police advised one of the victim households to remove the "Happy Hanukkah" pictures from their front windows. In light of this tension, local Christian ministers encouraged their members to place menorahs in their windows. Stores instantly sold out of them, and local newspapers printed color pictures of them for people to hang in their windows. As Christmas Day came in this overwhelmingly Christian community, home after home displayed symbols of Judaism, defying those who had attacked the Jews. The culprits were never identified, but they had succeeded in bringing a city together (Cohen 2006; Cohon 1995; Muller 2001; Sheskin and Dashefsky 2007).

The United States has the second-largest Jewish population in the world. This nation's approximately 5.3 million Jews account for 40 percent of the world's Jewish population. Jewish Americans not only represent a significant group in the United States but also play a prominent role in the worldwide Jewish community. The nation with the largest Jewish population, Israel, is the only one in which Jews are in the majority, accounting for 75 percent of the population, compared with 2 percent in the United States. Figure 14.1 depicts the worldwide distribution of Jews (DellaPergola 2007).

The Jewish people form a contrast to the other subordinate groups we have studied. At least 1,500 years had passed since Jews were the dominant group in any nation until Israel was created in 1948. Even there, Jews are in competition for power. American Jews superficially resemble Asian Americans in that both are largely free from poverty, compared to Chicanos or Puerto Ricans. Unlike those groups, however, the Jewish cultural heritage is not nationalistic in origin. Perhaps the most striking difference is that the history of anti-Jewish prejudice and discrimination (usually called **anti-Semitism**) is nearly as old as relations between Jews and Gentiles (non-Jews).

Without question, people in North America and Europe give the countries of the Southern hemisphere little attention unless they are directly impacted. To partially correct this pattern, we consider the Jewish community in Argentina in this chapter's A Global View.

anti-Semitism
Anti-Jewish prejudice or discrimination.

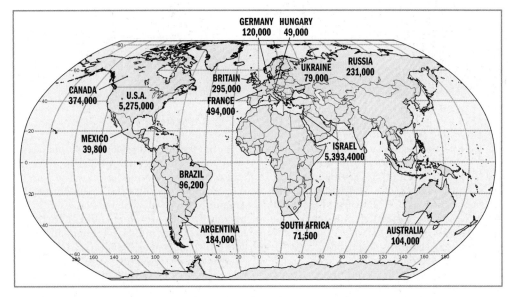

FIGURE 14.1
Worldwide Distribution of Jews, 2007

Note: Data include all nations with at least 35,000 Jews.

Source: DellaPergola 2007.

The most distinctive aspect of the Jewish population in the United States is its concentration in urban areas and in the Northeast. The most recent estimates place more than 44 percent of the Jewish population in the Northeast (see Figure 14.2 on the page 333). Jews are concentrated especially in the metropolitan areas of New York City, Los Angeles, and Miami, where altogether they account for half of the nation's Jewish population.

The Jewish People: Race, Religion, or Ethnic Group?

Jews are a subordinate group. They fulfill the criteria set forth in Chapter 1:

- Jewish Americans experience unequal treatment from non-Jews in the form of prejudice, discrimination, and segregation.
- Jews share a cultural history that distinguishes them from the dominant group.
- Jews do not choose to be Jewish, in the same way that Whites do not choose to be White or Mexican Americans to be Mexican American.
- Jews have a strong sense of group solidarity.
- Jewish men and women tend to marry one another rather than marry outside the group.

What are the distinguishing traits for Jewish Americans? Are they physical features, thus making Jews a racial group? Are these characteristics matters of faith, suggesting that Jews are best regarded as a religious minority? Or are they cultural and social, making Jews an ethnic group? To answer these questions, we must address the ancient and perennial question: what is a Jew?

The issue of what makes a Jew is not only a scholarly question; in Israel, it figures in policy matters. The Israel Law of Return defines who is a Jew and extends Israeli citizenship to all Jews. Currently, the law recognizes all converts to the faith, but pressure has grown recently to limit citizenship to those whose conversions were performed by Orthodox rabbis. Although the change would have little practical impact, symbolically this pressure shows the tension and lack of consensus even among Jews over who is a Jew.

A Global View

ARGENTINA'S JEWISH COMMUNITY

Jewish settlements are found throughout the world as a result of the dispersal, or *Diaspora*, from Palestine. Efforts to resettle in Europe often led to local and national actions over several centuries to expel the Jews, so sizable settlements eventually developed not only in North America but also in Argentina, especially after it obtained its independence from Spain. Argentina currently has the largest Jewish population in Latin America, which is estimated at 184,000.

The first Jews settled in Argentina shortly after their expulsion from Spain in 1492. Stigmatized, these early settlers often hid their faith from others and soon assimilated with other immigrants from Europe. By the nineteenth century, public vestiges of Jewish worship began to emerge in Argentina. One significant group of Jews from Russia settled in the frontier of Argentina, becoming cowboys or, as they are called there, *gauchos*.

The years after World War II were mixed times for Jews in Argentina because the country's leader, Juan Peron, had been sympathetic to the Nazis and welcomed Hitler's followers to the country. Yet Peron also established early on diplomatic relations with Israel, smoothing the way for Israeli Jews who wished to settle in Argentina. Later, human rights abuses during the dictatorship of 1976–1983 were anti-Semitic in character because certain abuses were coded that way (carving swastikas in people's bodies, for example) and Jews were targeted.

In the last three decades, Argentina has taken on a consistent pro-Israeli position and cooperated with efforts to locate Nazi war criminals who may still be hiding out. Argentine Jews have achieved some success in industry but are largely absent in the higher ranks of military, foreign affairs, and the court system. Visible Jewish buildings have been the targets of attacks, and many synagogues remain tightly guarded. Jewish immigration is now largely a factor of economic conditions. Downturns in the Argentine economy are associated with a migration to Israel and elsewhere while upswings lead to an influx of immigrants, including Jews. Evidence suggests that the Argentine Jewish population is aging and is not encountering growth.

The Jewish community resembles that of many other countries. Day schools provide instruction in Judaism and Hebrew and are attended by the majority of Jewish youth. McDonald's has even established its first kosher restaurant outside of Israel that, besides offering a menu conforming to dietary restrictions, closes for the Sabbath. Buenos Aires, with the largest urban Jewish population outside of Israel, North America, and Europe, is the center of Jewish life in today's Argentina and boasts numerous organizations and one of the world's four remaining daily Yiddish newspapers.

Source: DellaPergola 2007; Page 1983; Schwartz 2008; Schweimler 2007; Timerman 2002; Weiner 2008.

The definition of race used here is fairly explicit. The Jewish people are not physically differentiated from non-Jews. True, many people believe they can tell a Jew from a non-Jew, but actual distinguishing physical traits are absent. Jews today come from all areas of the world and carry a variety of physical features. Most Jewish Americans are descended from northern and eastern Europeans and have the appearance of Nordic and Alpine people. Many others carry Mediterranean traits that make them indistinguishable from Spanish or Italian Catholics. Many Jews reside in North Africa, and although they are not significantly represented in the United States, many people would view them only as a racial minority, Black. The wide range of variation among Jews makes it inaccurate to speak of a Jewish race in a physical sense (Gittler 1981; Montagu 1972).

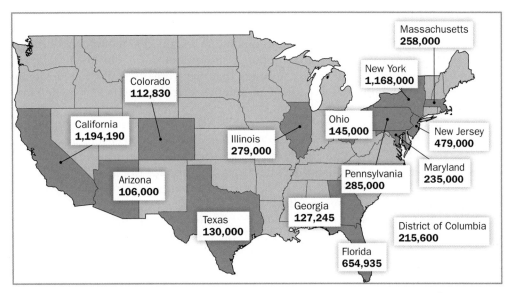

FIGURE 14.2
Jewish Population Distribution in the United States, 2007
Note: The highlighted states have Jewish populations estimated at more than 100,000 and are rounded off to nearest thousand.

Source: Ira and Donald Dashefsky 2007.

To define Jews by religion seems the obvious answer because there are Judaic religious beliefs, holidays, and rituals. But these beliefs and practices do not distinguish all Jews from non-Jews. To be a Jewish American does not mean that one is affiliated with one of the three religious groups: the Orthodox, the Reform, and the Conservative. A large segment of adult Jewish Americans, more than a third, do not participate in religious services or even belong, however tenuously, to a temple or synagogue. They have neither converted to Christianity nor ceased to think of themselves as Jews. Nevertheless, Jewish religious beliefs and the history of religious practices remain significant legacies for all Jews today, however secularized their everyday behavior. In a 1998 survey, half of all Jews felt that a "shared history or culture," much more so than religion, defined what it means to be Jewish (*Los Angeles Times* Poll 1998).

The trend for some time, especially in the United States, has been toward a condition called **Judaization**, the lessening importance of Judaism as a religion and the substitution of cultural traditions as the ties that bind Jews. Depending on one's definition, Judaization has caused some Jews to become so assimilated in the United States that very traditional Jews no longer consider them acceptable spouses (Gans 1956).

Jewish identity is ethnic. Jews share cultural traits, not physical features or uniform religious beliefs. The level of this cultural identity differs for the individual Jew. Just as some Apaches may be more acculturated than others, the degree of assimilation varies among Jewish people. Judaization may base identity on such things as eating traditional Jewish foods, telling Jewish jokes, and wearing the Star of David. For others, this cultural identity may be the sense of a common history of centuries of persecution. For still others, it may be an unimportant identification. They say, "I am a Jew," just as they say, "I am a resident of California."

The question of what constitutes Jewish identity is not easily resolved. The most appropriate explanation of Jewish identity may be the simplest. A Jew in contemporary America is a person who thinks of himself or herself as a Jew. That also means that being a Jew is a choice and, as we will return to later in the chapter, many Jews may not be making that choice (Abrahamson and Pasternak 1998; Himmelfarb 1982).

Judaization
The lessening importance of Judaism as a religion and the substitution of cultural traditions as the tie that binds Jews.

Immigration of Jews to the United States

As every schoolchild knows, 1492 was the year in which Christopher Columbus reached the Western hemisphere, exploring on behalf of Spain. That year also marked the expulsion of all Jews from Spain. The resulting exodus was not the first migration of Jews, nor was it the last. This is but one illustration of several of the social processes in the Spectrum of

Intergroup Relations illustrated in the figure on the page 352. Other examples will be presented throughout this chapter.

One of the most significant movements among Jews is the one that created history's largest concentration of Jews: the immigration to the United States. The first Jews arrived in 1654 and were of Sephardic origin, meaning that they were originally from Spain and Portugal. These immigrants sought refuge in America after they had been expelled from other European countries as well as from Brazil.

When the United States gained its independence from Great Britain, only 2,500 Jews lived here. By 1870 the Jewish population had climbed to about 200,000, supplemented mostly by Jews of German origin. They did not immediately merge into the older Jewish American settlements any more than the German Catholics fused immediately with native Catholics. Years passed before the two groups' common identity as Jews overcame nationality differences (Dinnerstein 1994; Jaher 1994).

The greatest migration of Jews to the United States occurred around the end of the nineteenth century and was simultaneous with the great European migration described in Chapter 4. Because they arrived at the same time does not mean that the movements of Gentiles and Jews were identical in all respects. One significant difference was that Jews were much more likely to stay in the United States; few returned to Europe. Although between 1908 and 1937, one-third of all European immigrants returned, only 5 percent of Jewish immigrants did. The legal status of Jews in Europe at the turn of the century had improved since medieval times, but their rights were still revoked from time to time (Sherman 1974).

Despite the legacy of anti-Semitism in Europe, past and present, most of the Jews who migrated to the United States up to the early twentieth century came voluntarily. These immigrants tended to be less pious and less observant of Judaic religious customs than those who remained in Europe. As late as 1917, there were only five small day schools, as Jewish parochial schools were called, in the entire nation. Nevertheless, although the earliest Jewish immigration was not a direct response to fear, the United States had special meaning for the Jewish arrivals. This nation had no history of anti-Semitism like that of Europe. Many Jews must have felt a new sense of freedom, and many clearly demonstrated their commitment to their new nation by becoming citizens at a rate unparalleled in other ethnic groups (Herberg 1983; Sklare 1971).

The immigration acts of the 1920s sharply reduced the influx of Jews, as they did for other European groups. Beginning in about 1933, the Jews arriving in the United States were not merely immigrants; they were also refugees. The tyranny of the Third Reich began to take its toll well before World War II. German and Austrian Jews fled Europe as the impending doom became more evident. Many of the refugees from Nazism in Poland, Hungary, and Ukraine tended to be more religiously orthodox and adapted slowly to the ways of the earlier Jewish immigrants, if they adapted at all. As Hitler's decline and fall came to pass, the concentration camps, the speeches of Hitler, the atrocities, the war trials, and the capture of Nazi leaders undoubtedly made all American Jews—natives and refugees, the secular and the orthodox—acutely aware of their Jewishness and the price one may be required to pay for ethnicity alone.

Because the U.S. Citizenship and Immigration Services do not identify an immigrant's religion, precise data are lacking for the number of people of Jewish background migrating recently to the United States. Estimates of 500,000 have been given for the number of Jews who made the United States their home in the 1960s and 1970s. The majority came from Israel, but 75,000 came from the Soviet Union and another 20,000 from Iran, escaping persecution in those

Jewish shoppers, many of them immigrants, crowd Orchard Street in New York City in 1923.

two nations. As the treatment of Jews in the Soviet Union improved in the late 1980s, U.S. immigration officials began to scrutinize requests for entry to see whether refugee status was still merited. Although some Soviet Jews had difficulty demonstrating that they had a "well-founded fear of persecution," the United States admitted more than 13,600 in 1988 (through the processing center in Rome alone). The situation grew more complicated with the collapse of the Soviet Union in 1991. Throughout the period, the immigrants' arrival increased the size of the Jewish community in the United States.

Anti-Semitism: Past and Present

The history of the Jewish people is a history of struggle to overcome centuries of hatred. Several religious observances, such as Passover, Hanukkah, and Purim, commemorate the past sacrifices or conflicts Jews have experienced. Anti-Jewish hostility, or anti-Semitism, has followed the struggle of the Jewish people since before the beginning of the Christian faith to the present.

Origins

Many anti-Semites justify their beliefs by pointing to the role of some Jews in the crucifixion of Jesus Christ, although he was also a Jew. For nearly 2,000 years, various Christians have argued that all Jews share in the responsibility of the Jewish elders who condemned Jesus Christ to death. Much anti-Semitism over the ages bears little direct relationship to the crucifixion, however, and has more to do with the persisting stereotype that Jews behave treacherously with members of the larger society in which they live.

A 2004 survey found that 26 percent of Americans felt Jews were "responsible for Christ's death"—a significant increase over a similar survey nine years earlier. At the time of the survey, many Jews felt that Mel Gibson's *The Passion of the Christ* reinforced such a view. Indeed, the same survey shows that among those who had seen the film, 36 percent held Jews responsible for the crucifixion (Pew Research Center 2004).

What truth is there in such stereotypes? Even prominent celebrities and political leaders have publicly expressed stereotyped opinions about Jews. In 2006, Gibson, a Hollywood director and actor, was stopped for drunk driving; he told the arresting officer, who happened to be Jewish, "The Jews are responsible for all wars in the world" (Cohen 2006). In 1974, the chairman of the Joint Chiefs of Staff of the U.S. armed forces declared that Jews "own, you know, the banks in this country" (*Time* 1974, 16). Yet the facts show that Jewish Americans are dramatically underrepresented in management positions in the nation's leading banks. Even in New York City, where Jews account for half the college graduates, Jewish Americans represent only 4 percent of that city's senior banking officials. Similarly, a 1998 national survey found that 8 percent of Jews were business owners, compared with 9 percent of the total U.S. population (Getlin 1998; Slavin and Pradt 1979, 1982).

If the stereotype that Jews are obsessed with money is false, how did it originate? Social psychologist Gordon Allport (1979), among others, advanced the **fringe-of-values theory**. Throughout history, Jews have occupied positions economically different from those of Gentiles, often because laws forbade them to farm or practice trades. For centuries, the Christian church prohibited the taking of interest in the repayment of loans, calling it the sin of usury. Consequently, in the minds of Europeans, the sinful practice of money lending was equated with the Jew. In reality, most Jews were not moneylenders, and most of those who were did not charge interest. In fact, many usurers were Christians, but because they worked in secret, it was only the reputation of the Jews that was damaged. To make matters worse, the nobles of some European countries used Jews to collect taxes, which only increased the ill feeling. To the Gentile, such business practices by the Jews constituted behavior on the fringes of proper conduct. Therefore, this theory about the perpetuation of anti-Semitism is called the *fringe-of-values theory* (American Jewish Committee 1965, 1966a, 1966b; *Time* 1974).

fringe-of-values theory
Behavior that is on the border of conduct that a society regards as proper and is often carried out by subordinate groups, subjecting those groups to negative sanctions.

in-group virtues
Proper behavior by one's own group that become unacceptable when practiced by outsiders (out-group vices).

out-group vices
In-group virtues that become unacceptable when practiced by outsiders.

Holocaust
The state-sponsored systematic persecution and annihilation of European Jewry by Nazi Germany and its collaborators.

A similar explanation is given for other stereotypes, such as the assertion that Jews are clannish, staying among themselves and not associating with others. In the ancient world, Jews in the Near East area often were attacked by neighboring peoples. Throughout history, Jews have also at times been required to live in closed areas, or ghettos. This experience naturally led them to unify and rely on themselves rather than others. More recently, the stereotype of clannishness has gained support because Jews have been more likely to interact with Jews than with Gentiles. But this behavior is reciprocal because Gentiles have tended to stay among their own kind too.

Being critical of others for traits for which you praise members of your own group is an example of **in-group virtues** becoming **out-group vices**. Sociologist Robert Merton (1968) described how proper behavior by one's own group becomes unacceptable when practiced by outsiders. For Christians to take their faith seriously is commendable; for Jews to withstand secularization is a sign of backwardness. For Gentiles to prefer Gentiles as friends is understandable; for Jews to choose other Jews as friends suggests clannishness. The assertion that Jews are clannish is an exaggeration and also ignores the fact that the dominant group shares the same tendency. It also fails to consider to what extent anti-Semitism has logically encouraged—and indeed, forced—Jews to seek out other Jews as friends and fellow workers (Allport 1979).

This only begins to explore the alleged Jewish traits, their origin, and the limited value of such stereotypes in accurately describing several million Jewish people. Stereotypes are only one aspect of anti-Semitism; another has been discrimination against Jews. In C.E. 313, Christianity became the official religion of Rome. Within another two centuries, Jews were forbidden to marry Christians or to try to convert them. Because Christians shared with Jews both the Old Testament and the origin of Jesus, they felt ambivalent toward the Jewish people. Gentiles attempted to purge themselves of their doubts about the Jews by projecting exaggerated hostility onto the Jews. The expulsion of the Jews from Spain in 1492 is only one example. Spain was merely one of many countries, including England and France, from which the Jews were expelled. In the mid-fourteenth century, the bubonic plague wiped out a third of Europe's population. Because of their social conditions and some of their religious prohibitions, Jews were less likely to die from the plague. Anti-Semites pointed to this as evidence that the Jews were in league with the devil and had poisoned the wells of non-Jews. Consequently, from 1348 to 1349, 350 Jewish communities were exterminated, not by the plague but by Gentiles.

The Holocaust

The injustices to the Jewish people continued for centuries. However, it would be a mistake to say that all Gentiles were anti-Semitic. History, drama, and other literature record daily, presumably friendly interaction between Jews and Gentiles. At particular times and places, anti-Semitism was an official government policy. In other situations, it was the product of a few bigoted individuals and sporadically became very widespread. Regardless of the scope, anti-Semitism was a part of Jewish life, something that Jews were forced to contend with. By 1870, most legal restrictions aimed at Jews had been abolished in Western Europe. Since then, however, Jews have again been used as scapegoats by opportunists who blame them for a nation's problems.

The most tragic example of such an opportunist was Adolf Hitler, whose "final solution" represented a dramatic example; his scapegoating of German Jews for Germany's problems led directly to the Holocaust. The **Holocaust** was the state-sponsored systematic persecution and annihilation of European Jewry by Nazi Germany and its collaborators. The move to eliminate Jews from the European continent started slowly, with Germany gradually restricting the rights of Jews: preventing them from voting, living outside the Jewish ghetto, and owning businesses. Much of the anti-Semitic cruelty was evident before the beginning of the war. If there was any doubt, *Kristallnacht*, or the "Night of Broken Glass," in Berlin on November 9, 1938, ended any doubt. Ninety Berlin Jews were murdered, hundreds of homes and synagogues were set on fire or ransacked, and thousands of Jewish store windows were broken.

Despite the obvious intolerance, Jews desiring to immigrate were turned back by government officials in the United States and elsewhere. Just a few months after

There are many stories from the Holocaust. Among the many remarkable ones is that of Dina Gottliebova Babbitt, who survived two years at the Auschwitz concentration camp by painting watercolors for the infamous Nazi Dr. Josef Mengele. Subsequently, she came to the United States and was an animator. She is still living, and many famous cartoonists have mounted a campaign to get her artwork back from Austria. As one part of this effort, a comic book has been produced, of which this is a section that relates her amazing story.

Kristallnacht, 903 Jewish refugees aboard the liner *St. Louis* were denied entry to Cuba. Efforts to gain entry in the United States, including special appeals to Congress and President Roosevelt, were useless. Ultimately the ship returned, and many of the Jews later died in the death camps. Between 1933 and 1945, two-thirds of Europe's total Jewish population was killed; in Poland, Germany, and Austria, 90 percent were murdered. Even today, there are still only 12 percent of the number of Jews who were present in 1938 (Institute for Jewish and Community Research 2008; DellaPergola 2007).

Many eyewitnesses to the events of the Holocaust remind us of the human tragedy involved. Among the most eloquent are the writings and speeches of Nobel Peace Prize winner, Romanian-born Elie Wiesel (pronounced "EL-ee Vee-SELL"). In Listen to Our Voices, he recalls the moments before he, age 16 at the time, and other Jews were freed from the Buchenwald concentration camp.

Despite the enormity of the tragedy, a small but vocal proportion of the world community are **Holocaust revisionists** who claim that the Holocaust did not happen. A controversial conference was held in 2006 in Iran that brought together revisionists from throughout the world. Debates also continue between those who contend that this part of modern history must be remembered and others, in the United States and Europe, who feel that it is time to put the Holocaust behind us and go on (Fathi 2006).

Despite these attacks on historical reality, the poignant statements by Holocaust survivors such as Wiesel and the release of such films as *Schindler's List* (1993), *Life Is Beautiful* (1998), and *The Pianist* (2002) keep the tragedy of the Holocaust in our minds (Cooper and Brackman 2001; Porter 2008; Stern 2001).

Anti-Semitism is definitely not just a historical social phenomenon in Europe. After the attacks on the United States on September 11, 2001, fresh outbreaks occurred throughout the continent. Newspapers reported Jewish worshippers being subjected to rock throwing and insults as they walked to services. A growing Arab and Muslim population in Europe is also serving to offer an audience for Christian-generated anti-Semitism, especially after the U.S. occupation of Iraq beginning in 2003 and the continued uncertainty of Palestine's future (J. Fleishman 2004).

U.S. Anti-Semitism: Past

Compared with the brutalities of Europe from the time of the early Christian church to the rule of Hitler, the United States cannot be described as a nation with a history of severe

Holocaust revisionists
People who deny the Nazi effort to exterminate the Jews or who minimize the numbers killed.

Listen to Our Voices

NIGHT

On April 10, [1945], there were still some twenty thousand prisoners in the camp, among them a few hundred children. It was decided to evacuate all of us at once. By evening. Afterward, they would blow up the camp.

And so we were herded into the huge *Appelplatz* [assembly square], in ranks of five, waiting for the gate to open. Suddenly, the sirens began to scream. Alert! We went back to the blocks. It was too late to evacuate us that evening. The evacuation was postponed to the next day.

Hunger was tormenting us; we had not eaten for nearly six days except for a few stalks of grass and some potato peels found on the grounds of the kitchens.

At ten o'clock in the morning, the SS took positions throughout the camp and began to herd the last of us toward the *Appelplatz*.

The resistance movement decided at that point to act. Armed men appeared from everywhere. Bursts of gunshots. Grenades exploding. We, the children stayed, remained flat on the floor of the block.

The battle did not last long. Around noon, everything was calm again. The SS had fled and the resistance had taken charge of the camp.

Elie Wiesel

At six o'clock that afternoon, the first American tank stood at the gates of Buchenwald.

Our first act as free men was to throw ourselves onto the provisions. That's all we thought about. No thought of revenge, or of our parents. Only of bread.

And then when we were no longer hungry, not one of us thought of revenge. The next day, a few of the young men ran into Weimar to bring back some potatoes and clothes—and to sleep with the girls. But still no trace of revenge.

Three days after the liberation of Buchenwald, I became very ill: some form of [food] poisoning. I was transferred to a hospital and spent two weeks between life and death.

One day when I was able to get up, I decided to look at myself in the mirror on the opposite wall. I had not seen myself since the ghetto.

From the depths of the mirror, a corpse was contemplating me.

The look in his eyes as he gazed at me has never left me.

Source: Wiesel 2006, 114–115. Originally published in 1958. Reprinted by permission of Hill & Wang, a division of Farrar, Straus & Giroux, LLC.

---

anti-Semitism. Nevertheless, the United States has also had its outbreaks of anti-Semitism, though none have begun to approach the scope or level of that seen in Western Europe. An examination of the status of Jewish Americans today indicates the extent of remaining discrimination against Jews. However, contemporary anti-Semitism must be seen in relation to past injustices.

In 1654, the year Jews arrived in colonial America, Peter Stuyvesant, governor of New Amsterdam (the Dutch city later named New York), attempted to expel them from the city. Stuyvesant's efforts failed, but they were the beginning of an unending effort to separate Jews from the rest of the population. Because the pre-1880 immigration of Jews was small, anti-Semitism was little noticed except, of course, by Jews. Most nineteenth-century movements against minorities were targeted at Catholics and Blacks and ignored Jews. In fact, Jews occasionally joined in such movements. By the 1870s, however, signs of a pattern of social discrimination against Jews had appeared. Colleges limited the number of Jewish students or excluded Jews altogether. The first

Jewish fraternity was founded in 1898 to compensate for the barring of Jews from campus social organizations. As Jews began to compete for white-collar jobs early in the twentieth century, job discrimination became the rule rather than the exception (Higham 1966; Selzer 1972).

The 1920s and the 1930s were periods of the most virulent and overt anti-Semitism. In these decades, the myth of an internationally organized Jewry took shape. According to a forged document titled *Protocols of the Learned Elders of Zion,* Jews throughout the world planned to conquer all governments, and the major vehicle for this rise to power was Communism, said by anti-Semites to be a Jewish movement. Absurd though this argument was, some respected Americans accepted the thesis of an international Jewish conspiracy and believed in the authenticity of the *Protocols.*

Henry Ford, founder of the automobile company that bears his name, was responsible for the publication of the *Protocols.* In his later years, Ford expressed regret for his espousal of anti-Semitic causes, but the damage had been done; he had lent an air of respectability to the most exaggerated charges against Jewish people.

It is not clear why Henry Ford, even for a short period of his life, so willingly accepted anti-Semitism. But Ford was not alone. Groups such as the Ku Klux Klan and the German American Bund, as well as radio personalities, preached about the Jewish conspiracy as if it were fact. By the 1930s, these sentiments expressed a fondness for Hitler. Even famed aviator Charles Lindbergh made speeches to gatherings claiming that Jews were forcing the United States into a war so that Jewish people could profit by wartime production. When the barbarous treatment of the Jews by Nazi Germany was exposed, most Americans were horrified by such events, and people such as Lindbergh were as puzzled as anyone about how some Americans could have been so swept up by the pre–World War II wave of anti-Semitism (N. Baldwin 2001; Meyers 1943; Selzer 1972).

Historical anti-Semitism is never far below the surface. The discredited *Protocols* was sold online by Wal-Mart through 2004 and described as "genuine" until protests made the large retailer rethink its sale. In 2006, a Spanish-language version published in Mexico City enjoyed wide distribution (*Intelligence Report* 2004; Rothstein 2006).

The next section examines anti-Semitic feelings in contemporary America. Several crucial differences between anti-Semitism in Europe and in the United States must be considered. First, and most important, the U.S. government has never promoted anti-Semitism. Unlike its European counterparts, the U.S. government has never embarked on an anti-Semitic program of expulsion or extermination. Second, because anti-Semitism was never institutionalized in the United States as it sometimes has been in Europe, American Jews have not needed to develop a defensive ideology to ensure the survival of their people. A Jewish American can make a largely personal decision about how much to assimilate or how secular to become.

Contemporary Anti-Semitism

Next to social research on anti-Black attitudes and behavior of Whites, anti-Semitism has been the major focus of studies of prejudice by sociologists and psychologists. Most of the conclusions described in Chapter 2 apply equally to the data collected on anti-Semitism. Little concern was

In order to combat anti-Semitism on college campuses, the U.S. Commission on Civil Rights launched a campaign that included this poster.

expressed by Jews in the United States about anti-Semitism immediately after World War II. From the late 1960s through the 1990s, however, anti-Semitism has again appeared to be a threat in many parts of the world. A 2007 national survey found that 27 percent of Jews felt anti-Semitism was a "very serious problem" and 60 percent "somewhat of a problem" in the United States. Looking at the statistical data, there is good reason to see this strong concern. More than two-thirds of reported religious hate crimes are against Jews (American Jewish Committee 2007; Chanes 2007).

The Anti-Defamation League (ADL) of B'nai B'rith, founded in 1913, makes an annual survey of reported anti-Semitic incidents. Although the number has fluctuated, the 1994 tabulation reached the highest level in the 22 years the ADL has been recording such incidents. Figure 14.3 shows the rise of harassment, threats, and assaults, which, adding episodes of vandalism, brings the total to 1,559 incidents for 2007. Some incidents were inspired and carried out by neo-Nazis or skinheads, groups of young people who champion racist and anti-Semitic ideologies.

In recent years, fewer anti-Semitic incidents have been reported from organized hate groups, but disturbing has been the growing number of reported anti-Semitic incidents on college campuses. Incidents continue to be reported. Anti-Jewish graffiti, anti-Semitic speakers, and swastikas affixed to predominantly Jewish fraternities were among the documented incidents. Another manifestation of it appears in editorial-style advertisements in college newspapers that argue that the Holocaust never occurred. A chilling development is the growing use of the Internet as a vehicle for anti-Semitism, either delivering such messages or serving as a means of reaching Web sites that spread intolerance (Anti-Defamation League 2008; Chanes 2007).

Acts of anti-Semitic violence in the United States, along with the continuing conflict in the Middle East and the expression of anti-Semitic themes by some African Americans, have prompted renewed national attention to anti-Semitism.

American Jews and Israel When the Middle East became a major hot spot in international affairs in the 1960s, a revival of 1930s levels of anti-Semitism occurred. Many Jewish Americans expressed concern that because Jews are freer in the United States than they have been in perhaps any other country in their history, they would ignore the struggle of other Jews. Israel's precarious status has proven to be a strong source of identity for Jewish Americans. Major wars in the Middle East in 1967, 1973, and 1991 reminded the

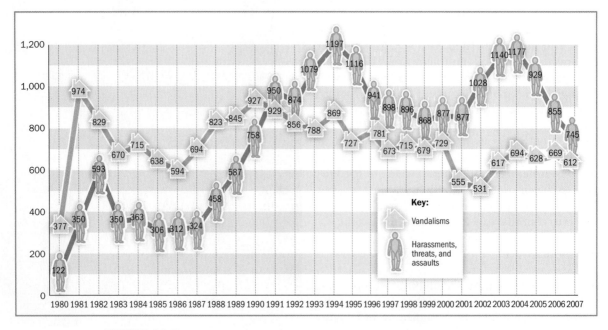

FIGURE 14.3
Anti-Semitic Incidents, 1980–2007

Source: Reprinted with permission of the Anti-Defamation League, www.adl.org.

world of Israel's vulnerability. Palestinian uprisings in the occupied territories and international recognition of the Palestine Liberation Organization (PLO) in 1988 and 2002 eroded the strong pro-Israeli front among the Western powers. Some Jewish Americans have shown their commitment to the Israeli cause by immigrating to Israel.

The majority of Jewish Americans feel the United States should remain active in world affairs, compared to 36 percent of the total U.S. population. However, even among Jews, support of Israel is not uniform. Although not all American Jews agree with Israel's actions, many Jews express support for Israel's struggles by contributing money and trying to influence American opinion and policy to be more favorable to Israel. A survey taken in 2007 showed that 30 percent of Jewish Americans feel "very close" to Israel and another 40 percent feel "fairly close." But that still leaves more than a quarter (29 percent) who feels distant from Israel. A similar proportion disagree that caring about Israel is an important part of being a Jew. It should be noted that there are those within the Jewish community who see Jews who did not totally back Israel as giving support to anti-Semitism (American Jewish Committee 2007; Rosenfeld 2007).

In the year after the oil embargo (1974), the United Nations General Assembly ignored American and Israeli objections and passed a resolution declaring that "Zionism is a form of racism and racial discrimination." **Zionism**, which initially referred to the old Jewish religious yearning to return to the biblical homeland, has been expressed in the twentieth century in the movement to create a Jewish state in Palestine. Ever since the **Diaspora**, the exile of Jews from Palestine several centuries before Christianity, many Jews have seen the destiny of their people only as the establishment of a Jewish state in the Holy Land.

The Zionism resolution, finally repealed by the United Nations in 1991, had no lasting influence and did not change any nation's foreign policy. However, it did increase Jewish fears of reawakened anti-Semitism thinly disguised as attacks on Zionist beliefs. Even the development of agreements between Israel and its Arab neighbors and the international recognition of Palestinian autonomy in Israel did not end the concern of Jewish Americans that continuing anti-Israeli feeling reflected anti-Semitism.

American Jews and African Americans There is no reason why anti-Semites should be exclusively White, but Jews have been especially troubled by some Black Americans expressing ethnic prejudices, given their own history of oppression. Why this special concern? Jewish Americans have been active in civil rights causes and have contributed generously to legal defense funds. Jewish neighborhoods and employers have also been quicker than their Gentile counterparts to accept African Americans. Therefore, there is a positive Black–Jewish alliance with a long history. For these reasons, some Jews find it especially difficult to understand why another group experiencing prejudice and discrimination should express anti-Semitic sentiments.

Beginning in the 1960s, some African American activists and the Black Panther Party supported the Arabs in the Middle East conflict and called on Israel to surrender. In the 1990s, unrelated events again seemed to draw attention to the relationship between Jews and African Americans. On several college campuses, invited African American speakers made anti-Israeli statements, inflaming the Jewish students in attendance. In a 1991 New York City incident, a Hasidic Jew ran a red light, killing an African American child, and the ambulance that regularly serves the Hasidic community did not pick up the child. In the emotional climate that resulted, an Australian Jewish researcher was stabbed to death, and several days of rioting in the Brooklyn neighborhood of Crown Heights followed (Morris and Rubin 1993).

In response to these and other events, many Jewish and African American leaders perceived a crisis in intergroup relations, and calls for unity became very public. For example, in 1994, the Reverend Jesse Jackson sought to distance himself from the statements of a Black Muslim leader, calling him "racist, anti-Semitic, divisive, untrue, and chilling." A similar countertrend is a 2008 estimate that 150,000 African Americans are practicing Jews (Finder 1994, 21; Johnston 2008).

African American resentment, in many situations attracting notoriety, has rarely been anti-Jewish as such but rather has been opposed to White institutions. As author James

Zionism
Traditional Jewish religious yearning to return to the biblical homeland, now used to refer to support for the state of Israel.

Diaspora
The exile of Jews from Palestine.

Baldwin (1967, 114) said, Blacks "are anti-Semitic because they're anti-White." That racial prejudice is deep in the United States is shown by the fact that two groups suffering discrimination, groups that might unite in opposition to the dominant society, fight each other instead.

An old Yiddish saying, "Schwer zu sein a Yid," means "It is tough to be a Jew." Anti-Semitism past and present is related. The old hostilities seem never to die. The atrocities of Nazi Germany have not been forgotten, nor should they be. Racial and ethnic hostility, against whatever group, unifies the group against its attackers, and Jewish Americans are no exception. The Jewish people of the United States have come together, regardless of nationality, to form a minority group with a high degree of group identity.

Position of Jewish Americans

Jewish Americans have an important role in contemporary America. They are active participants in the fight for civil rights and work on behalf of Israel. These efforts are important but only begin to describe their role in the United States. For a better perspective on Jewish people in the United States, the following summarizes their current situation with respect to employment and income, education, organizational activity, and political activity.

Employment and Income

Discrimination conditions all facets of a subordinate group's life. Jews have experienced, and to a limited extent still experience, differential treatment in the American job market. National surveys showed that most Jews viewed anti-Semitism as a problem in the United States, although not necessarily in hiring practices. As shown in Table 14.1, through perseverance and emphasis on education, Jewish Americans as a group have overcome barriers to full employment and now enjoy high incomes (American Jewish Committee 2007).

Using a variety of techniques, social science studies have documented declining discrimination against Jews in the business world. Sociologist Samuel Klausner interviewed business school graduates, comparing Jews with Protestants and Catholics who graduated

TABLE 14.1

Profile of Jews in the United States

	Jewish Americans (%)	All U.S. Residents (%)
INCOME		
Less than $30,000	14	31
More than $100,000	46	14
EDUCATION		
High school graduate	97	86
Age: over 50	51	41
U.S. born	89	88
SOCIAL POSITION		
Democrat/leaning Democrat	66	47
Favors legal abortions	84	51
Accepts homosexuality	79	50
Evolution not best explanation	17	45
Moderate	28	31
Conservative	23	40

Note: National representative sample of nearly 40,000 adults collected in summer 2007 and spring 2008.

Source: Pew Forum on Religion and Public Life 2008a, 39, 52, 56, 60; 2008b, 17, 85, 90, 92.

from the same university in the same year. Klausner (1988, 33) concludes, "(1) Jewish MBAs are winning positions in the same industries as their Catholic and Protestant classmates; (2) they are rising more rapidly in corporate hierarchies than their Catholic and Protestant colleagues; (3) they are achieving higher salaries than their Catholic and Protestant colleagues." Klausner adds that researchers tested seven indicators of discrimination and in each case failed to find evidence of discrimination against Jewish executives. Interestingly, however, this same study detected substantial discrimination against African Americans and women.

The economic success of the Jewish people as a group obscures the poverty of many individual Jewish families. We reached a similar conclusion in Chapter 12 from income data on Asian Americans and their image as a model minority. Sociologists largely agree that Jews in 1930 were as likely to be poverty stricken and living in slums as any minority group today. Most have escaped poverty, but what Ann Wolfe (1972) calls "the invisible Jewish poor" remain invisible to the rest of society. Like Chinese Americans, the Jewish poor were not well served by federal experiments to eradicate poverty in the 1960s and 1970s. Although the proportion of the poor among the Jews is not as substantial as among Blacks or Hispanics, it does remind us that not all Jewish families have affluent lifestyles (Gold 1965; Lavender 1977; Levine and Hochbaum 1974).

Education

Jews place great emphasis on education (see Table 14.1). This desire for formal schooling stems, it is argued, from the Judaic religion, which places the rabbi, or teacher, at the center of religious life.

In the United States today, all Jewish congregations emphasize religious instruction more than Protestants typically do. A 2008 estimate stated that there were 259 day schools with 230,000 pupils. Day schools are, in effect, private elementary schools with a substantial proportion of the curriculum given to Judaic studies and the learning of Hebrew. The less-religiously committed may attend instruction on Sundays or on weekday afternoons after attending public schools. Most Jews have received some form of formal Jewish education before they reach 30 years of age. The Jewish-sponsored component of higher education is not limited to strict religious instruction such as that found in rabbinical schools. Beginning in 1947, Jews founded graduate schools of medicine, education, social work, and mathematics, along with Brandeis University, which offers both undergraduate and graduate degrees. These institutions are nonsectarian (i.e., admission is not limited to Jews) and are conceived of as a Jewish-sponsored contribution to higher education (Rosenblatt 2008).

The religiously based tradition of lifelong study has left the legacy of a value system that stresses education. The poverty of Jewish immigrants kept them from devoting years to secular schooling, but they were determined that their children would do better. Despite their high levels of educational attainment, some members of the Jewish community express concern about Jewish education. They are disappointed with its highly secularized nature, not only because religious teaching has been limited but also because the Jewish sociocultural experience has been avoided altogether. It may even contribute to Judaization, the lessening importance of Judaization as a religion.

Political Activity

American Jews play a prominent role in politics as both voters and elected officials. Jews as a group are not typical in that they are more likely than the general population to label themselves Democrat (refer to Table 14.1). Also, most Jewish voters identify themselves as Democrat. Jewish voters have always backed the Democrat over the Republican presidential candidate for the last 10 elections, with Barack Obama receiving 78 percent of the vote, compared to only 21 percent for the Republican candidate John McCain. The one exception to this pattern of liberalism is gender issues related to the practice of Judaism, particularly among ultraorthodox Jews, whom we will consider later. Other Jewish religious traditions tend to be very open to egalitarian participation in most aspects of religious ritual, especially when compared to many Christian faiths (Connelly 2008; Fishman and Parmer 2008).

Jews have long been successful in being elected to office, but it was not until 1988 that an Orthodox Jew from Connecticut was elected to the U.S. Senate. Joseph Lieberman refrained from campaigning on the Sabbath (Shabbat) each week; his religious views were not an issue. He went on to be named as the vice presidential running mate of Al Gore. Even during the campaign, he honored the Sabbath and did not actively campaign, even avoiding dialing a telephone to potential supporters. Many view the positive response to his campaign as a sign of openness to devout Jews as political candidates (Issacson and Foltin 2001; Pew Charitable Trust 2000).

As in all subordinate groups, the political activity of Jewish Americans has not been limited to conventional electoral politics. The Jewish community has encompassed a variety of organizations since its beginnings. These groups serve many purposes: some are religious, and others are charitable, political, or educational. No organization, secular or religious, represents all American Jews, but there are more than 300 nationwide organizations (Chanes 2008).

Religious Life

Jewish identity and participation in the Jewish religion are not the same. Many Americans consider themselves Jewish and are considered Jewish by others even though they have never participated in Jewish religious life. The available data indicate that about half of American Jews are affiliated with a synagogue or temple, but only a small proportion consider participation in religious worship as extremely important. Even in Israel, only 30 percent of Jews are religiously observant. Nevertheless, the presence of a religious tradition is an important tie among Jews, even secular Jews (American Jewish Committee 2007; S. Cohen 1991).

The Judaic faith embraces several factions or denominations that are similar in their roots but marked by sharp distinctions. No precise data reveal the relative numbers of the three major groups. Part of the problem is the difficulty of placing individuals in the proper group. For example, it is common for a Jew to be a member of an Orthodox congregation but consider him- or herself Conservative. The following levels of affiliation are based on a December 2007 national survey of Jewish Americans:

- Orthodox—8 percent,
- Conservative—29 percent,
- Reconstructionist—2 percent,

Among those Jews in the United States who follow a more Orthodox religious tradition are the Hasidic Jews. A large Hasidic community is located in Brooklyn, New York.

- Reform—30 percent,
- just Jewish—29 percent, and
- not sure—2 percent.

kashrut
Laws pertaining to permissible (kosher) and forbidden foods and their preparation.

There are contradictory indications of whether observant Jews are more Orthodox or more moderate. Large Orthodox families, conversion to orthodoxy by other Jews, and immigration of traditional Jews to the United States lead to more conservative patterns of religion. Yet many Jewish households are attracted to the moderation of Reform Jews (American Jewish Committee 2005, 2007; Chanes 2008).

We will focus on two forms of Judaism at either end of the continuum: the Orthodox faith, which attempts to uphold a very traditional practice of Judaism; and the Reform faith, which accommodates itself to the secular world.

The Orthodox Tradition

The unitary Jewish tradition developed in the United States into three sects beginning in the mid–nineteenth century. The differences between Orthodox, Conservative, and Reform Judaism are based on their varying acceptance of traditional rituals. All three sects embrace a philosophy based on the Torah, the first five books of the Old Testament. The differences developed because some Jews wanted to be less distinguishable from other Americans. Another significant factor in explaining the development of different groups is the absence of a religious elite and bureaucratic hierarchy. This facilitated the breakdown in traditional practices.

Orthodox Jewish life is very demanding, especially in a basically Christian society such as the United States. Almost all conduct is defined by rituals that require an Orthodox Jew to constantly reaffirm his or her religious conviction. Most Americans are familiar with **kashrut**, the laws pertaining to permissible and forbidden foods. When strictly adhered to, kashrut governs not only what foods may be eaten (kosher) but also how the food is prepared, served, and eaten. Besides day-to-day practices, Orthodox Jews have weekly and annual observances. Women may not be rabbis among the Orthodox, although beginning in 2006, women were named to head a congregation, but only male members of the congregation could read publicly from the Torah (Luo 2006b).

Even Orthodox Jews differ in their level of adherence to traditional practices. Among the ultraorthodox are the Hasidic Jews, or Hasidim, who number some 200,000, with half residing chiefly in several neighborhoods in Brooklyn. To the Hasidim, following the multitude of *mitzvahs*, or commandments of behavior, is as important today as it was in the time of Moses. Their spiritual commitment extends well beyond customary Jewish law even as interpreted by Orthodox Jews.

Hasidic Jews wear no garments that mix linen and wool. Men wear a *yarmulke*, or skullcap, constantly, even while sleeping. Attending a secular college is frowned on. Instead, the men undertake a lifetime of study of the Torah and the accompanying rabbinical literature of the Talmud. Women's education consists of instruction on how to run the home in keeping with Orthodox tradition. Hasidic Jews, who themselves are organized in separate communities, have courts with jurisdiction recognized by the faithful in many matters, especially as they relate to family life.

One unlikely location for Orthodox Jews that has come to national attention has been rural Iowa. In Postville, Iowa, a community of barely 2,000, a group of Hasidic Jews built a large meat-processing plant that became the largest kosher meat-producing facility in the nation. Initially, there was a great deal of misunderstanding

A rabbi blesses a 13-year-old at her Bat Mitzvah in the temple. Jewish children often celebrate a coming-of-age ceremony. According to Jewish law, when Jewish children reach the age of maturity (12 years for girls, 13 years for boys), they become responsible for their actions. At this point a boy is said to become Bar Mitzvah; a girl is said to become Bat Mitzvah.

between local townspeople and the Hasidim households. As time passed, the factory expanded, but other problems arose independent of religious and cultural differences amid suspicions of unsafe working conditions. In 2008, the federal Immigration and Customs Enforcement agency conducted an immigration raid and apprehended 389 illegal immigrants, which affected many more family members living in the area. The very existence of the Postville kosher plant indicates the diversity of Jewish and Orthodox Jewish life across the country (Bloom 2000, 2008).

Orthodox children attend special schools in order to meet minimal New York State educational requirements. The devotion to religious study is reflected in this comment by a Hasidic Jew: "Look at Freud, Marx, Einstein—all Jews who made their mark on the non-Jewish world. To me, however, they would have been much better off studying in a yeshiva [a Jewish school]. What a waste of three fine Talmudic minds" (H. Arden 1975, 294). Although devoted to their religion, the Hasidim participate in local elections and politics and are employed in outside occupations. All such activities are influenced by their orthodoxy and a self-reliance rarely duplicated elsewhere in the United States.

The Reform Tradition

Reform Jews, although deeply committed to the religious faith, have altered many of the rituals. Women and men sit together in Reform congregations, and both sexes participate in the reading of the Torah at services. A few Reform congregations have even experimented with observing the Sabbath on Sunday. Circumcision for males is not mandatory. Civil divorce decrees are sufficient and recognized so that a divorce granted by a three-man rabbinical court is not required before remarriage. Reform Jews recognize the children of Jewish men and non-Jewish women as Jews with no need to convert. All these practices would be unacceptable to the Orthodox Jew.

Conservative Judaism is a compromise between the rigidity of the Orthodox and the extreme modification of the Reform. Because of the middle position, the national organization of Conservatives, the United Synagogue of America, strives to create its own identity and seeks to view its traditions as an appropriate, authentic approach to the faith.

Table 14.2 displays some results of a national survey on Jewish identification. The three sects here include both members and nonmembers of local congregations. Reform Jews are the least likely of the three religious groups to participate in religious events, to be involved in the Jewish community, or to participate in predominantly Jewish organizations. Yet in Reform temples, there has been an effort to observe religious occasions such as Rosh Hashanah (*Religion Watch* 1995b; Wertheimer 1996).

The one exception in Reform Jews' lower levels of participation is on issues concerning world Jewry, such as Israel or the treatment of Jews in such nations as the former Soviet Union and Iran. For the Orthodox Jew, these issues are less important than those strictly related to the observance of the faith. Although no nationwide organized movement advocates this, in recent years Reform Jews seem to have reclaimed traditions they once rejected.

TABLE 14.2
Jewish Identification by Group

Indices	Orthodox (%)	Conservative (%)	Reform (%)	"Just Jewish" (%)
Ethnic pride	86	79	73	65
Closeness to Jews	90	83	71	54
Observance of Jewish holidays	73	42	28	18
Observance of Christian holidays	6	6	17	28
Pro-Israel	78	71	56	50

Source: S. Cohen 1991, 58, 63, 74.

Unlike people of other faiths in the United States, Jews historically have not embarked on recruitment or evangelistic programs to attract new members. Beginning in the late 1970s, Jews, especially Reform Jews, debated the possibility of outreach programs. Least objectionable to Jewish congregations were efforts begun in 1978 aimed at non-Jewish partners and children in mixed marriages. In 1981, the program was broadened to invite conversions by Americans who had no religious connection, but these very modest recruitment drives are still far from resembling those that have been carried out by Protestant denominations for decades (Luo 2006a).

Like Protestant denominations, Jewish denominations are associated with class, nationality, and other social differences. The Reform Jews are the wealthiest and have the best formal education of the group, the Orthodox are the poorest and least educated in years of formal secular schooling, and the Conservatives occupy a position between the two. A fourth branch of American Judaism, Reconstructionism, an offshoot of the Conservative movement, has only recently developed an autonomous institutional structure with ritual practices similar to those of Reform Jews. Religious identification is associated with particular generations: immigrants and older Jews are more likely to be Orthodox, and their grandchildren are more likely to be Reform (*Los Angeles Times* Poll 1998).

Jewish Identity

Ethnic and racial identification can be positive or negative. Awareness of ethnic identity can contribute to a person's self-esteem and give that person a sense of group solidarity with similar people. When a person experiences an identity only as a basis for discrimination or insults, he or she may want to shed that identity in favor of one more acceptable to society. Unfavorable differential treatment can also encourage closer ties between members of the community being discriminated against, as it has for Jews.

Most would judge the diminishing of out-group hostility and the ability of Jews to leave the ghetto as a positive development (G. Friedman 1967). However, the improvement in Jewish–Gentile relations also creates a new problem in Jewish social identity. It has become possible for Jews to shed their "Jewishness," or **Yiddishkait**. Many retain their Yiddishkait even in suburbia, but it is more difficult there than in the ghetto. In the end, however, Jews cannot lose their identity entirely. Jews are still denied total assimilation in the United States no matter how much the individual ceases to think of him- or herself as Jewish. Social clubs may still refuse membership, and prospective non-Jewish in-laws may try to interfere with plans to marry.

Events in the world also remind the most assimilated Jew of the heritage left behind. A few such reminders in the past generation include Nazi Germany, the founding of Israel in 1948, the Six-Day War of 1967, Soviet interference with Jewish life and migration, the terrorist attack at the 1972 Munich Olympics, the Yom Kippur War of 1973, the 1973 oil embargo, the United Nations' 1974 anti-Zionism vote, and the Scud missile attacks during the 1991 Gulf War.

A unique identity issue presents itself to Jewish women, whose religious tradition has placed them in a subordinate position. For example, it was not until 1972 that the first female rabbi was ordained. Jewish feminism has its roots in the women's movement of the 1960s and 1970s, several of whose leaders were Jewish. There have been some changes in **halakha** (Jewish law covering obligations and duties), but it is still difficult for a woman to get a divorce recognized by the Orthodox Jewish tradition. Sima Rabinowicz of upstate New York has been hailed as the Jewish Rosa Parks for her recent bus battle. Rabinowicz refused to give up her seat in the women's section of a Hasidic-owned, publicly subsidized bus to Orthodox men who wanted to pray in private, segregated from women as required by halakha. The courts defended her right to ride as she wished, just as an earlier court had ruled with Rosa Parks in the Birmingham bus boycott. Jewish women contend that they should not be forced to make a choice between their identities as women and as Jews (Baum 1998; Frankel 1995).

We will now examine three factors that influence the ethnic identity of Jews in the United States: family, religion, and cultural heritage.

Yiddishkait
Jewishness.

halakha
Jewish laws covering obligations and duties.

Role of the Family

In general, the family works to socialize children, but for religious Jews it also fulfills a religious commandment. In the past, this compulsion was so strong that the *shadchan* (the marriage broker or matchmaker) fulfilled an important function in the Jewish community by ensuring marriage for all eligible people. The emergence of romantic love in modern society made the shadchan less acceptable to young Jews, but recent statistics show Jews more likely to marry than any other group.

Jews have traditionally remained in extended families, intensifying the transmission of Jewish identity. Numerous observers have argued that the Jewish family today no longer maintains its role in identity transmission and that the family is consequently contributing to assimilation. The American Jewish Committee released a report identifying 10 problems that are endangering "the family as the main transmission agent of Jewish values, identity, and continuity" (Conver 1976, A2). The following issues are relevant to Jews today:

- More Jews marry later than members of other groups.
- Most organizations of single Jews no longer operate solely for the purpose of matchmaking. These groups are now supportive of singles and the single way of life.
- The divorce rate is rising; there is no presumption of the permanence of marriage and no stigma attached to its failure.
- The birthrate is falling, and childlessness has become socially acceptable.
- Financial success has taken precedence over child raising in importance and for many has become the major goal of the family.
- The intensity of family interaction has decreased, although it continues to be higher than in most other religious and ethnic groups.
- There is less socializing across generation lines, partly as a result of geographic mobility.
- The sense of responsibility of family members to other family members has declined.
- The role of Jewishness is no longer central to the lives of Jews.
- Intermarriage has lessened the involvement of the Jewish partner in Jewish life and the emphasis on Jewish aspects of family life.

Data and sample surveys have verified these trends. Nevertheless, to use a term introduced in Chapter 10 in connection with the Latino family, Jewish Americans still have a higher than typical degree of *familism*. Jews are more likely than other ethnic or religious groups to be members of a household that interacts regularly with kinfolk. Nonetheless, the trend is away from familism, a trend that could further erode Jewish identity.

Without question, of the 10 problems cited by the American Jewish Committee, intermarriage has received the greatest attention from Jewish leaders. Therefore, it has been the subject of significant social research and not just idle speculation. This topic is the subject of our Research Focus.

Several trends come together to lead to a stabilization or decline in the number of active Jews in the United States. As shown in Figure 14.4 on page 350, the continuation of a Jewish tradition varies dramatically by denomination. Conservative and Orthodox Jews have larger families, encourage formal Jewish instruction, and are much less likely to witness intermarriage than Reform or unaffiliated ("just Jewish") Jewish Americans. Analysts of these data are concerned that Jews, especially if they are not Orthodox, cannot take it for granted that they will have grandchildren with whom to share seders, Sabbath, and other Jewish moments.

Role of Religion

Devotion to Judaism appears to be the clear way to preserve ethnic identity. Yet Jews are divided about how to practice their faith. Many of the Orthodox see Reform Jews as little better than nonbelievers. Even among the Orthodox, some sects such as the Lubavitchers try to awaken less-observant Orthodox Jews to their spiritual obligation.

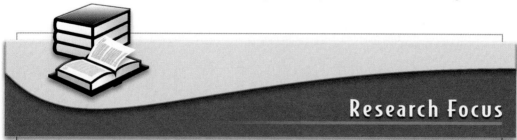

Research Focus

INTERMARRIAGE: THE FINAL STEP TO ASSIMILATION?

Sex and the City's Charlotte York, the quintessential WASP character, descends into a Jewish ritual bath, marking her conversion to Judaism. Although this fictional portrayal was welcomed by Jewish viewers, is it representative of what happens when Jews take a spouse today?

Since Christianity's influence has grown in Europe and North America, a persistent fear among Jews has been that their children or grandchildren would grow up ignorant of the Torah. Equally bad, a descendant might become *apikoros*, an unbeliever who engages in intellectual speculation about the relevance of Judaism. These concerns are growing as Jewish Americans' resistance to intermarriage declines. In 2005, two-thirds of Jews felt anti-Semitism was the biggest threat to Jewish life, but one out of three saw it to be intermarriage.

Why does intermarriage emerge as a social issue rather than a personal dilemma? Intermarriage makes a decrease in the size of the Jewish community in the United States more likely. In marriages that occurred in the 1970s, more than 70 percent of Jews married Jews or people who converted to Judaism. In marriages since 1996, that proportion has dropped to 53 percent. This trend means that American Jews today are just as likely to marry a Gentile as a Jew. For many, religion is a nonissue—neither parent practices religious rituals. Two-thirds of the children of these Jewish–Gentile marriages are not raised as Jews.

Many Jewish Americans respond that intermarriage is inevitable and the Jewish community must build on whatever links the intermarried couple may still have with a Jewish ethnic culture. There are many programs throughout the United States to help Gentile spouses of Jews feel welcome so that the faith will not lose them both. Yet other Jews feel that such efforts may be sending a dangerous signal that intermarriage is inevitable. Therefore, it is not surprising to see that probably more than any other ethnic or religious group, organizations within the Jewish community commission research on the trends in intermarriage.

Source: American Jewish Committee 2005; Chertok, Phillips, and Saxe 2008; Freedman 2003; Sanua 2007; Schwartz 2006; United Jewish Communities 2003.

Added to these developments is the continuing rise in Jewish out-marriages previously noted. Many Jewish religious rituals are centered in the home rather than in the synagogue, from lighting Sabbath candles to observing dietary laws. Therefore, Jews are far more likely to feel that children cannot be brought up in the faith without that family support.

The religious question facing Jews is not so much one of ideology as of observing the commandments of traditional Jewish law. The religious variations among the nearly 6 million Jewish Americans are a product of attempts to accommodate traditional rituals and precepts to life in the dominant society. It is in adhering to such rituals that Jews are most likely to be at odds with the Christian theme advanced in public schools, even if it appears only in holiday parties. In Chapter 1, we introduced the term **marginality** to describe the status of living in two distinct cultures simultaneously. Jews who give some credence to the secular aspects of Christmas celebrations exemplify individuals' accommodating themselves to two cultures. For all but the most Orthodox, this acceptance means disobeying commandments or even accepting non-Jewish traditions by singing Christmas carols or exchanging greeting cards.

marginality
The status of being between two cultures at the same time, such as the status of Jewish immigrants in the United States.

FIGURE 14.4
Generational Patterns by Denomination

Note: Figure assumes each denomination begins with the same number of people.

Source: Gordon and Horowitz 1997. Based on the 1990 National Population Survey and the 1991 New York Jewish Population Study.

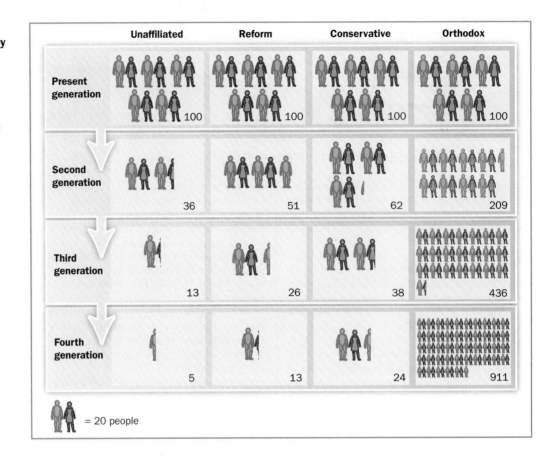

Is there a widespread pattern among Jewish Americans of reviving the old ways? Some Jews, especially those secure in their position, have taken up renewed orthodoxy. It is difficult to say whether the sporadic rise of traditionalism among Jews is a significant force or a fringe movement. Novelist Tom Ross at age 67 retook his birth name, Tom Rosenberg. Shortly after coming to the United States, his parents voluntarily anglicized their name. Now Tom wanted to take another step in reclaiming his roots. Still, at the beginning of the twenty-first century, Jewish leaders in North America and Europe are much more likely to express concern about the increase in the number of secularized Jews than to find reasons to applaud an increase in Yiddishkait (Rosenberg 2000).

Role of Cultural Heritage

For many Jews, religious observance is a very small aspect of their Jewishness. They express their identity instead in a variety of political, cultural, and social activities. For them, acts of worship, fasting, eating permitted foods, and the study of the Torah and the Talmud are irrelevant to being Jewish. Of course, religious Jews find such a position impossible to accept (Liebman 1973).

Many Gentiles mistakenly suppose that a measure of Jewishness is the ability to speak Yiddish. Few people have spoken as many languages as the Jews have through their long history. Yiddish is only one, and it developed in Jewish communities in eastern Europe between the tenth and twelfth centuries. Fluency in Yiddish in the United States has been associated with the immigrant generation and the Orthodox. Sidney Goldstein and Calvin Goldscheider (1968) reported that evidence overwhelmingly supports the conclusion that linguistic assimilation among Jews is almost complete by the third generation. However, in the last generation or two there has been a slight increase in the use of Hebrew. This change probably resulted from increased pride in Israel and a greater interaction between that nation and the United States. Other contributing factors are the increase in the use of Hebrew texts in Jewish day schools and in college Jewish studies programs.

Overall, the differences between Jews and Gentiles have declined in the United States. To a large extent, this reduction is a product of generational changes typical of all ethnic groups. The first-generation Mexican American in Los Angeles contrasts sharply with the middle-class White living in suburban Boston. The convergence in culture and identity is much greater between the fourth-generation Mexican American and his or her White counterpart. A similar convergence is occurring among Jews. This change does not signal the eventual demise of the Jewish identity. Moreover, Jewish identity is not a single identity, as we can see from the heterogeneity in religious observance, dedication to Jewish and Israeli causes, and participation in Jewish organizations.

Being Jewish comes from the family, the faith, and the culture, but it does not require any one criterion. Jewishness transcends nation, religion, or culture. A sense of peoplehood is present that neither anti-Semitic bigotry nor even an ideal state of fellowship among all religions would destroy. American life may have drastically modified Jewish life in the direction of dominant society values, but it has not eliminated it. Milton Gordon (1964) refers to **peoplehood** as a group with a shared feeling. For Jews, this sense of identity originates from a variety of sources, past and present, both within and without (Goldscheider 2003).

peoplehood
Milton Gordon's term for a group with a shared feeling.

Conclusion

Jewish Americans are the product of three waves of immigration originating from three different Jewish communities: the Sephardic, the western European, and the eastern European. They brought different languages and, to some extent, different levels of religious orthodoxy. Today, they have assimilated to form an ethnic group that transcends the initial differences in nationality.

Jews are not a homogeneous group. Among them are the Reform, Conservative, and Orthodox denominations, listed in ascending order of adherence to traditional rituals. Nonreligious Jews make up another group, probably as large as any one segment, and they still see themselves as Jewish.

Jewish identity is reaffirmed from within and outside the Jewish community; however, both sources of affirmation are weaker today. Identity is strengthened by the family, religion, and the vast network of national and community-based organizations. Anti-Semitism outside the Jewish community strengthens the in-group feeling and the perception that survival as a people is threatened.

Today, American Jews face a new challenge: they must maintain their identity in an overwhelmingly Christian society in which discrimination is fading and outbreaks of prejudice are sporadic. Yiddishkait may not so much have decreased as changed. Elements of the Jewish tradition have been shed in part because of modernization and social change. Some of this social change—a decline in anti-Semitic violence and restrictions—is certainly welcome. Although kashrut observance has declined, most Jews care deeply about Israel, and many engage in pro-Israel activities. Commitment has changed with the times, but it has not disappeared (S. Cohen 1988).

Some members of the Jewish community view the apparent assimilation with alarm and warn against the grave likelihood of the total disappearance of a sizable and identifiable Jewish community in the United States. Others see the changes not as erosion but as an accommodation to a pluralistic, multicultural environment. We are witness to a progressive change in the substance and style of Jewish life. According to this view, Jewish identity, the Orthodox and Conservative traditions notwithstanding, has shed some of its traditional characteristics and has acquired others. The strength of this view comes with the knowledge that doomsayers have been present in the American Jewish community for at least two generations. Only the passage of time will reveal the future of Jewish life in the United States (Finestein 1988; Glazer 1990).

Although discrimination against Jews has gone on for centuries, far more ancient than anti-Semitism and the experience of the Diaspora is the subordinate role of women. Women were perhaps the first to be relegated to an inferior role and may be the last to work collectively to struggle for equal rights. Studying women as a subordinate group in Chapter 15 will reaffirm the themes in our study of racial and ethnic groups.

SPECTRUM OF INTERGROUP RELATIONS

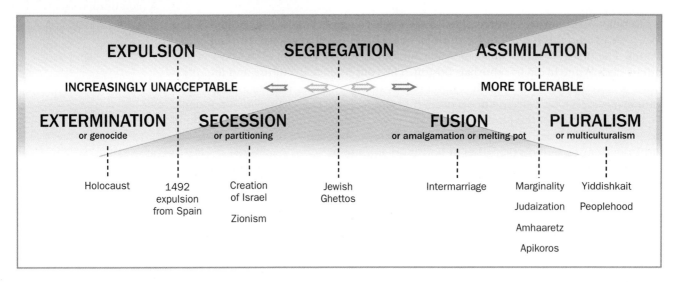

Summary

1. Although Israel hosts the largest Jewish population, the Diaspora has led to significant Jewish populations, especially in the United States, where most live in the urban areas of New York City, Los Angeles, and Miami.

2. Jewish immigration began in the earliest colonial times and has reflected the ebb and flow of immigration from Europe.

3. Anti-Semitism has a long history worldwide, having been institutionalized in many European countries. Although not absent in the United States, it has never been endorsed by government action.

4. The Holocaust is a turning point in modern history and was followed by an influx of Jewish immigrants to the Untied States.

5. Contemporary anti-Semitism in the United States is frequently documented but is as likely to be punctuated by spirited discussions about U.S.–Israeli relations.

6. Jewish Americans demonstrate high levels of occupational success built on extensive formal schooling.

7. Religious life is varied among Jews in the United States and split between nonobservant and observant; among the latter, a variety of expressions range from very conservative to very liberal expression of ritual.

8. The very acceptance of Jews in the United States has led to high levels of intermarriage, leading many in the Jewish community to lament that Jews are assimilating too quickly and losing their identity.

Key Terms

anti-Semitism 330
Diaspora 341
fringe-of-values theory 335
halakha 347
Holocaust 336

Holocaust revisionists 337
in-group virtues 336
Judaization 333
kashrut 345
marginality 349

out-group vices 336
peoplehood 351
Yiddishkait 347
Zionism 341

Review Questions

1. Why are the Jewish people most accurately characterized as an ethnic group?

2. How have the patterns of anti-Semitism changed or remained the same?

3. Why do African American–Jewish American relationships receive special scrutiny?

4. Why is maintaining Jewish identity so difficult in the United States?

5. Why does the family play such a critical role in Jewish identity?

Critical Thinking

1. Most minority groups regard acceptance as a positive outcome. Why do some Jewish Americans seem threatened by being accepted in contemporary Gentile society?

2. Using the Jewish experience as a basis for comparison, how has fusion functioned or not functioned for any other subordinate group when compared with Jews in the United States?

3. In Chapter 5, we presented Marcus Hansen's principle of third-generation interest. How does that apply or not apply to the generational differences displayed by denomination in Figure 14.4?

4. How different and similar have the experiences of women in organized religion been compared with those of women in the Jewish faith?

Women: The Oppressed Majority

SUBORDINATE STATUS **MEANS CONFINEMENT TO SUBORDINATE** roles not justified by a person's abilities. Society is increasingly aware that women are a subordinate group. There are biological differences between males and females; however, one must separate differences of gender from those produced by sexism, distinctions that result from socialization. The feminist movement did not begin with the women's movement of the 1960s but has a long history and, like protest efforts by other subordinate groups, has not been warmly received by society. A comparison of the socioeconomic position of men and women leaves little doubt that they have unequal opportunities in employment and political power. Although men are taking on greater responsibilities with child care and housework, these are still disproportionately the responsibilities of women. Minority women occupy an especially difficult position in that they experience subordinate status by virtue of their race or ethnicity as well as their gender. Minority women are also more likely to be poor, which creates what sociologists have termed the *matrix of domination.*

Women are an oppressed group even though they form the numerical majority. They are a social minority in the United States and throughout Western society. Men dominate in influence, prestige, and wealth. Women do occupy positions of power, but those who do are the exceptions, as evidenced by newspaper accounts that declare "She is the first woman" or "the only woman" to be in a particular position.

Many people, men and women, find it difficult to conceptualize women as a subordinate group. After all, not all women live in ghettos. They no longer have to attend inferior schools. They freely interact and live with their alleged oppressors, men. How, then, are they a subordinate group? Let us reexamine the five properties of a subordinate or minority group introduced in Chapter 1:

1. Women do experience unequal treatment. Although they are not segregated by residence, they are victims of prejudice and discrimination.

2. Women have physical and cultural characteristics that distinguish them from the dominant group (men).

3. Membership in the subordinate group is involuntary.

4. Through the rise of contemporary feminism, women have become increasingly aware of their subordinate status and have developed a greater sense of group solidarity.

5. Women are not forced to marry, yet many women feel that their subordinate status is most irrevocably defined within marriage.

In this chapter, the similarities between women and racial and ethnic groups will become apparent.

The most common analogy about minorities used in the social sciences is the similarity between the status of African Americans and that of women. Blacks are considered a minority group, but, one asks, how can women of all groups be so similar in condition? We recognize some similarities in recent history; for example, an entire generation has observed and participated in both the civil rights movement and the women's movement. A background of suffrage campaigns, demonstrations, sit-ins, lengthy court battles, and self-help groups is common to the movements for equal rights for both women and African Americans. But similarities were recognized long before the recent protests against inequality. In *An American Dilemma* (1944), the famous study of race described in Chapter 1, Gunnar Myrdal observed that a parallel to the Blacks' role in society was found among women. Other observers, such as Helen Mayer Hacker (1951, 1974), later elaborated on the similarities.

What do these groups have in common besides recent protest movements? The negative stereotypes directed at the two groups are quite similar: both groups have been considered emotional, irresponsible, weak, or inferior. Both are thought to fight subtly against the system: women allegedly try to outwit men by feminine wiles, as historically Blacks allegedly outwitted Whites by pretending to be deferential or respectful. To these stereotypes must be added another similarity: neither women nor African Americans are accepting a subordinate role in society any longer.

Nearly all Whites give lip service, even if they do not wholeheartedly believe it, to the contention that African Americans are innately equal to Whites. They are inherently the same. But men and women are not the same, and they vary most dramatically in their roles in reproduction. Biological differences have contributed to sexism. **Sexism** is the ideology that one sex is superior to the other. Quite different is the view that

sexism
The ideology that one sex is superior to the other.

356

there are few differences between the sexes. Such an idea is expressed in the concept of **androgyny**. An androgynous model of behavior permits people to see that humans can be both aggressive and expressive, depending on the requirements of the situation. People do not have to be locked into the behavior that accompanies the labels *masculine* and *feminine*. In the United States, people disagree widely as to what implications, if any, the biological differences between the sexes have for social roles. We will begin our discussion of women as a subordinate group with this topic.

Gender Roles

A college man, done with afternoon classes, heads off to get a pedicure and, while the nail polish is drying, sits on a nearby park bench finishing some needlepoint he started. Meanwhile, a college woman walks through the park chewing tobacco and spitting along the path. What is wrong with this picture? We are witnessing the open violation of how men and women are expected to act. So unlikely are these episodes that I have taken them from sociology teachers who specifically ask their students to go out, violate gender expectations, and record how they feel and how people react to their behavior (Nielsen et al. 2000, 287).

Gender roles are society's expectations of the proper behavior, attitudes, and activities of males and females. Toughness has traditionally been seen in the United States as masculine, desirable only in men, whereas tenderness has been viewed as feminine. A society may require that one sex or the other take the primary responsibility for the socialization of the children, economic support of the family, or religious leadership.

Without question, socialization has a powerful impact on the development of females and males in the United States. Indeed, the gender roles first encountered in early childhood often are a factor in defining a child's popularity. Sociologists Patricia Adler and her colleagues (1992, 1998) observed elementary school children and found that boys typically achieved high status on the basis of their athletic ability, coolness, toughness, social skills, and success in relationships with girls. By contrast, girls gained popularity based on their parents' economic background and their own physical appearance, social skills, and academic success.

It may be obvious that males and females are conditioned to assume certain roles, but the origin of gender roles as we know them is less clear. Many studies have been done on laboratory animals, such as injecting monkeys and rats with male and female hormones. Primates in their natural surroundings have been closely observed for the presence and nature of gender roles. Animal studies do not point to instinctual gender differences similar to what humans are familiar with as masculinity and femininity. Historically, women's work came to be defined as a consequence of the birth process. Men, free of child care responsibilities, generally became the hunters and foragers for food. Even though women must bear children, men could have cared for the young. Exactly why women were assigned that role in societies is not known.

Women's role varies across different cultures. Furthermore, we know that acceptable behavior for men and women changes over time in a society. For example, the men in the royal courts of Europe in the late 1700s fulfilled present-day stereotypes of feminine

The very visible success of women such as Alaska Governor Sarah Palin, who was nominated in 2008 to be vice president of the United States, may lead some people to conclude that gender equality has been accomplished. Yet as even cursory analysis shows in politics and business, women remain underrepresented.

androgyny
The state of being both masculine and feminine, aggressive and passive.

gender roles
Expectations regarding the proper behavior, attitudes, and activities of males and females.

appearance in their display of ornamental dress and personal vanity rather than resembling the men of a century later, although they still engaged in duels and other forms of aggression. The social roles of the sexes have no constants in time or space (Lorber 2005; Taylor et al. 2007).

Sociological Perspectives

Gender differences are maintained in our culture through the systematic socialization of babies and infants, children, adolescents, and adults. Even though different subcultures and even different families vary in child rearing, we teach our children to be boys and girls, even though men and women are more alike than they are different.

We are bombarded with expectations for behavior as men and women from many sources simultaneously. Many individual women hold positions involving high levels of responsibility and competence but may not be accorded the same respect as men. Similarly, individual men find the time to get involved with their children's lives only to meet with disbelief and occasional surprise from health care and educational systems accustomed to dealing only with mothers. Even when individuals are motivated to stretch the social boundaries of gender, social structure and institutions often impede them. Gender differentiation in our culture is embedded in social institutions: the family, of course, but also education, religion, politics, the economy, medicine, and the mass media.

Functionalists maintain that sex differentiation has contributed to overall social stability. Sociologists Talcott Parsons and Robert Bales (1955) argued that to function most efficiently, the family needs adults who will specialize in particular roles. They believed that the arrangement of gender roles with which they were familiar had arisen because marital partners needed a division of labor.

The functionalist view is initially persuasive in explaining the way in which women and men are typically brought up in U.S. society. However, it would lead us to expect even girls and women with no interest in children to still become babysitters and mothers. Similarly, males with a caring feeling for children may be "programmed" into careers in the business world. Clearly, such a differentiation between the sexes can have harmful consequences for the person who does not fit into specific roles, while depriving society of the optimal use of many talented people who are confined by sexual labeling. Consequently, the conflict perspective is increasingly convincing in its analysis of the development of gender roles (Taylor et al. 2007, 38–39).

Conflict theorists do not deny the presence of a differentiation by sex. In fact, they contend that the relationship between females and males has been one of unequal power, with men being dominant over women. Men may have become powerful in preindustrial times because their size, physical strength, and freedom from childbearing duties allowed them to dominate women physically. In contemporary societies, such considerations are not as important, yet cultural beliefs about the sexes are now long established.

Both functionalists and conflict theorists acknowledge that it is not possible to change gender roles drastically without dramatic revisions in a culture's social structure. Functionalists see potential social disorder, or at least unknown social consequences, if all aspects of traditional sex differentiation are disturbed. Yet for conflict theorists, no social structure is ultimately desirable if it has to be maintained through the oppression of its citizens.

Suffragists struggled for many years to convince Congress and the states to pass the Nineteenth Amendment to the Constitution, which they finally did, extending to women the right to vote beginning in 1920.

The Feminist Movement

Women's struggle for equality, like the struggles of other subordinate groups, has been long and multifaceted. From the very beginning, women activists and sympathetic men who spoke of equal rights were ridiculed and scorned.

In a formal sense, the American feminist movement was born in upstate New York in a town called Seneca Falls in the summer of 1848. On July 19, the first women's rights convention began, attended by Elizabeth Cady Stanton, Lucretia Mott, and other pioneers in the struggle for women's rights. This first wave of feminists, as they are currently known, battled ridicule and scorn as they fought for legal and political equality for women, but they were not afraid to risk controversy on behalf of their cause. In 1872, for example, Susan B. Anthony was arrested for attempting to vote in that year's presidential election.

The Suffrage Movement

The **suffragists** worked for years to get women the right to vote. From the beginning, this reform was judged to be crucial. If women voted, it was felt, other reforms would quickly follow. The struggle took so long that many of the initial advocates of women's suffrage died before victory was reached. In 1879, an amendment to the Constitution was introduced that would have given women the right to vote. Not until 1919 was it finally passed, and not until the next year was it ratified as the Nineteenth Amendment to the Constitution.

The opposition to giving women the vote came from all directions. Liquor interests and brewers correctly feared that women would assist in passing laws restricting or prohibiting the sale of their products. The South feared the influence that more Black voters (i.e., Black women) might have. Southerners had also not forgotten the pivotal role women had played in the abolitionist movement. Despite the opposition, the suffrage movement succeeded in gaining women the right to vote, a truly remarkable achievement because it had to rely on male legislators to do so.

The Nineteenth Amendment did not automatically lead to other feminist reforms. Women did not vote as a bloc and have not been elected to office in proportion to their numbers. The feminist movement as an organized effort that gained national attention faded, regaining prominence only in the 1960s. Nevertheless, the women's movement did not die out completely in the first half of the century. Many women carried on the struggle in new areas, such as the effort to lift restrictions on birth control devices (Freeman 1975; O'Neill 1969; Rossi 1964).

The Women's Liberation Movement

Ideologically, the women's movement of the 1960s had its roots in the continuing informal feminist movement that began with the first subordination of women in Western society. Psychologically, it grew in America's kitchens, as women felt unfulfilled and did not know why, and in the labor force, as women were made to feel guilty because they were not at home with families. Demographically, by the 1960s, women had attained greater control about when and whether to become pregnant if they used contraception and, hence, had greater control over the size of the population (Heer and Grossbard-Shectman 1981).

Sociologically, several events delayed progress in the mid-1960s. The civil rights movement and the antiwar movement were slow to embrace women's rights. The New Left seemed as sexist as the rest of society in practice, despite its talk of equality. Groups protesting the draft and demonstrating on college campuses generally rejected women as leaders and assigned them traditional duties such as preparing refreshments and publishing organization newsletters. The core of early feminists often knew each other from participating in other protest or reform groups that had initially been unwilling to accept women's rights as a legitimate goal. Beginning in about 1967, as Chapter 7 showed, the movement for Black equality was no longer as willing to accept help from sympathetic Whites. White men moved on to protest the draft, a cause not as crucial to women's lives. Although somewhat involved in the antiwar movement, many White women began to

suffragists
Women and men who worked successfully to gain women the right to vote.

feminine mystique
Society's view of a woman as only her children's mother and her husband's wife.

struggle for their own rights, although at first they had to fight alone. Eventually, civil rights groups, the New Left, and most established women's groups endorsed the feminist movement with the zeal of new converts, but initially they resisted the concerns of feminists (Freeman 1973, 1983).

The movement has also brought about a reexamination of men's roles. Supporters of "male liberation" wanted to free men from the constraints of the masculine value system. The masculine mystique is as real as the feminine one. Boys are socialized to think that they should be invulnerable, fearless, decisive, and even emotionless in some situations. Men are expected to achieve physically and occupationally at some risk to their own values, not to mention those of others. Failure to take up these roles and attitudes can mean that a man will be considered less than a man. Male liberation is the logical counterpart of female liberation. If women are to redefine their gender role successfully, men must redefine theirs as workers, husbands, and fathers (Messner 1997; National Organization for Men Against Sexism 2008).

Amid the many changing concerns since the mid-1960s, the feminist movement too has undergone significant change. Betty Friedan, a founder of the National Organization for Women (NOW), argued in the early 1960s that women had to understand the **feminine mystique**, recognizing that society saw them only as their children's mother and their husband's wife. Later, in the 1980s, though not denying that women deserved to have the same options in life as men, she called for restructuring the "institution of home and wife." Friedan and others now recognize that many young women are frustrated when time does not permit them to do it all: career, marriage, and motherhood. Difficult issues remain, and feminists continue to discuss and debate concerns such as the limits businesses put on careers of women with children, domestic violence, and male bias in medical research (Friedan 1963, 1981, 1991).

The Economic Picture

He works. She works. They are both physicians—a high-status occupation with financial rewards. He makes $140,000. She makes $88,000. Those are the results of a detailed study of occupations by the U.S. Bureau of the Census in 2004. It looked at the earnings of 821

TABLE 15.1
Women as a Percentage of All Workers in Selected Occupations, 1950, 1980, and 2006

Occupation	1950	1980	2006
PROFESSIONAL WORKERS (%)			
Accountants	14.9	36.2	60.2
Engineers	1.2	4.0	14.5
Lawyers and judges	4.1	12.8	32.6
Physicians	6.5	12.9	32.2
Registered nurses	97.8	96.5	91.3
College professors	22.8	33.9	46.3
OTHER OCCUPATIONS (%)			
Carpenters	0.4	1.5	2.4
Protective services (firefighters, police officers, guards)	2.0	9.5	22.3
Sales clerks, retail	48.9	71.1	49.1
Cashiers	81.7	86.6	74.8
Bookkeepers	77.7	90.5	90.3
Food preparation workers	61.6	66.9	56.6
Private household workers	94.9	97.5	90.3

Sources: Bureau of the Census 1981, 2007a, 388–391.

occupations ranging from chief executives to dishwashers, considering individuals' age, education, and work experience. The unmistakable conclusion was there is a substantial gap in median earnings between full-time male and female workers in the same occupation. He's an air traffic controller and makes $67,000. She earns $56,000. He's a housekeeper and makes $19,000. She earns $15,000. He's a teacher's assistant and makes $20,000. She earns $15,000.

occupational segregation by gender
The tendency for men and women to be employed in different occupations from each other.

Men do not always earn more. The census bureau found two occupations out of 821 in which women typically earn about 1 percent more: hazardous materials recovery workers and telecommunications line installers (Weinberg 2004).

Another aspect of women's subordinate status is that more than any other group, they are confined to certain occupations. **Occupational segregation by gender** is the tendency for men and women to be employed in different occupations from each other. Some sex-typed jobs for women pay well above the minimum wage and carry moderate prestige, such as nursing and teaching. Nevertheless, they are far lower in pay and prestige than such stereotyped male positions as physician, college president, and university professor. When they do enter nontraditional positions, as we have seen, women as a group receive lower wages or salary.

The data in Table 15.1 present an overall view of the male dominance of high-paying occupations. Among the representative occupations chosen, men unquestionably dominate in those that pay well. Women dominate as receptionists, seamstresses, health care workers, and domestic workers. Trends show the proportions of women increasing slightly in the professions, indicating that some women have advanced into better-paying positions, but these gains have not significantly changed the overall picture.

How pervasive is segregation by gender in the workforce? To what degree are women and men concentrated in different occupations? Bureau of Labor Statistics researchers have compiled a segregation index to estimate the percentage of women who would have to change their jobs to make the distribution of men and women in each occupation mirror the relative percentage of each sex in the adult working population. This study showed that 54 percent of women and men workers would need to switch jobs to create a labor force without sex segregation. There has been a steady decline in such segregation, but the decrease was not as great in the 1990s as in earlier decades (Wooton 1997).

Women's earnings have increased significantly over the last quarter century. However, so have the earnings of men. As shown in Figure 15.1, the female–male wage gap has narrowed from women's weekly earnings being just over 62 cents on the dollar earned by men as a group to about 81 cents in 2006. One cannot assume that the trend will continue at the same rate, because much of the narrowing of the gap actually has to do with men's wages leveling off so that women's very modest increases have come closer to matching their male counterparts, while still remaining 20 percent behind (Leicht 2008).

Sources of Discrimination

If we return to the definition of discrimination cited earlier, are not men better able to perform some tasks than women, and vice versa? If ability means performance, there certainly are differences. The typical woman can sew better than the typical man, but the latter can toss a ball farther than the former. These are group differences. Certainly, many women out throw many men, and many men out sew many women, but society expects women to excel at sewing and men to excel at throwing. The differences in those abilities result from cultural conditioning. Women usually

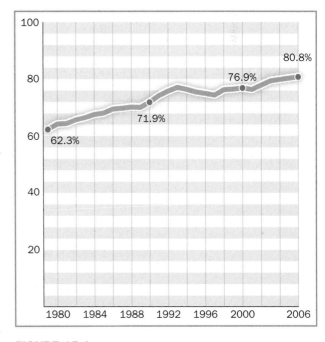

FIGURE 15.1

The Female–Male Earnings Gap: Closing but Still Massive

The gap has narrowed to women earning 80 cents on the men's dollar. However, this gap amounts to trillions of dollars a year because that means millions of working women every year typically receive 80 cents rather than a full dollar.

Source: Department of Labor 2007, 46.

are taught to sew, and men are less likely to learn such a skill. Men are encouraged to participate in sports that require the ability to throw a ball much more than are women. True, as a group, males have greater potential for the muscular development needed to throw a ball, but U.S. society encourages men to realize their potential in this area more than it encourages women to pursue athletic skills.

Today's labor market involves much more than throwing a ball and using a needle and thread, but the analogy to these two skills is repeated time and again. Such examples are used to support sexist practices in all aspects of the workplace. Just as African Americans can suffer from both individual acts of racism and institutional discrimination, women are vulnerable to both sexism and institutional discrimination. Women are subject to direct sexism, such as sexist remarks, and also to differential treatment because of institutional policies.

Removing barriers to equal opportunity would eventually eliminate institutional discrimination. Theoretically, men and women would sew and throw a ball equally well. We say "theoretically" because cultural conditioning would take generations to change. In some formerly male jobs, such as gas station clerk and attendant, society seems quite willing to accept women. In other occupations, such as president, it will take longer; many years may pass before full acceptance can be expected in other fields such as professional contact sports.

Many efforts have been made to eliminate institutional discrimination as it applies to women. The 1964 Civil Rights Act and its enforcement arm, the Equal Employment Opportunity Commission, address cases of sex discrimination. As we saw in Chapter 3, the inclusion of sex bias along with prejudice based on race, color, creed, and national origin was an unexpected last-minute change in the provisions of the landmark 1964 act. Federal legislation has not removed all discrimination against women in employment. The same explanations presented in Chapter 3 for the lag between the laws and reality in race discrimination apply to sex discrimination: lack of money, weak enforcement powers, occasionally weak commitment to using the laws available, and, most important, institutional and structural forces that perpetuate inequality.

What should be done to close the gap between the earnings of women and men? As shown in Figure 15.2, women earn more annually with more formal schooling, just like their male counterparts. However, as women continue their education, the wage gap does not narrow and even shows signs of growing.

In the 1980s, **pay equity**, or comparable worth, was a controversial solution presented to alleviate the second-class status of working women. It directly attempted to secure equal pay when occupational segregation by gender was particularly pervasive. Pay equity calls for equal pay for different types of work that are judged to be comparable by measuring such factors as employee knowledge, skills, effort, responsibility, and working conditions (American Association of University Women 2007; Dey and Hill 2007).

A primary goal of many feminists is to eliminate sex discrimination in the labor force and to equalize job opportunities for women. Without question, women earn less than men. As we noted earlier in both Table 3.1 and Figure 3.3, women earn less than men even when race and education are held constant; that is, college-educated women working

pay equity
The same wages for different types of work that are judged to be comparable by such measures as employee knowledge, skills, effort, responsibility, and working conditions; also called *comparable worth.*

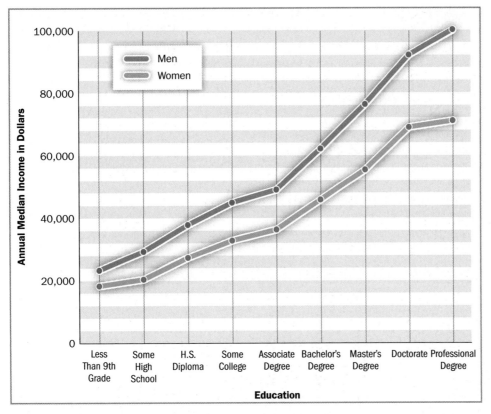

FIGURE 15.2
Financial Return on Education for Women and Men, 2007
Note: See Table 3.1.
Source: DeNavas-Walt et al. 2008, PINC-03.

full-time make less than comparably educated men. Even when additional controls are introduced, such as previous work experience, a substantial earnings gap remains. A detailed analysis of the wage gap that considered schooling, employment history, time with the current employer, and medical leaves of absence found that all these factors can explain less than 42 percent of the wage differences between men and women (Wellington 1994).

This doctrine sounds straightforward, but it is not so simple to put into operation. How exactly does one determine the comparability of jobs to identify comparable worth? Should a zookeeper be paid more than a child care worker? Does our society pay zookeepers more because we value care giving for children less than for animals? Or do zookeepers earn more than child care workers because the former tend to be male and the latter are generally female?

Despite some local initiatives, pay equity has not received much support in the United States except from the feminist movement. From a policy perspective, pay equity would have to broaden the 30-year-old Equal Pay Act and be initiated at the federal level. Proposed legislation such as the Paycheck Fairness Act and the Fair Pay Act has failed to mobilize much support. With the government backing away from affirmative action, it is unlikely to launch an initiative on pay equity (Business and Professional Women 2002; Sorensen 1994).

What about women aspiring to crack the glass ceiling? The phrase **glass ceiling**, as noted in Chapter 3 and illustrated in Figure 3.3, refers to the invisible barrier blocking the promotion of a qualified worker because of gender or minority membership. Despite continuing debate over affirmative action, the consensus is that there is little room at the top for women and minorities. The glass ceiling operates so that all applicants may be welcomed by a firm, but when it comes to the powerful or more visible positions, there

glass ceiling
The barrier that blocks the promotion of a qualified worker because of gender or minority membership.

TABLE 15.2
Major Barriers to Women's Executive Advancement

- Initial placement and clustering in dead-end staff jobs or highly technical professional jobs
- Lack of mentoring
- Lack of management training
- Lack of opportunities for career development
- Lack of opportunities for training tailored to the individual
- Lack of rotation to line positions or job assignments that produce revenue
- Little or no access to critical developmental assignments, including service on highly visible task forces and committees
- Different standards for performance evaluation
- Biased rating and testing systems
- Little or no access to informal communication networks
- Counterproductive behavior and harassment by colleagues

Source: Glass Ceiling Commission, cited in Department of Labor 1995, 7–8.

are limits—generally unstated—on the number of women and non-Whites welcomed or even tolerated (Table 15.2).

Women are doing better in top-management positions than minorities, but they still lag well behind men, according to a study that showed that only 15 percent of the director seats of *Fortune* 500's largest corporations were held by women. As for CEOs of the *Fortune* 500, there are so few—12 as of 2008—that the corporations can be named: Archer Daniels Midland, Avon, Kraft Foods, PepsiCo, Reynolds American, Rite Aid, Safeco, Sara Lee, TJX, WellPoint, Western Union, and Xerox. The other 488 corporations are led by men (Catalyst 2008; CNN Money 2008).

Women are still viewed differently in the world of management. Although studies of top male executives show some improvement over their attitudes about executive women in the last 40 years, stereotypes still abound that block women's ascent up the corporate ladder. In making hiring decisions, executives may assume that women are not serious about their commitment to the job and will be "distracted" by family and home. They assume that women are on a **mommy track**, an unofficial career track that firms use for women who want to divide their attention between work and family. This assumption would be false if applied to all women. It also implies that corporate men are not interested in maintaining a balance between work and family. Even competitive, upwardly mobile women are not always taken seriously in the workplace (Carlson et al. 2006; Heilman 2001; F. Schwartz and Zimmerman 1992).

Family and work continue to present challenges to women and men in the twenty-first century. Sociologist Kathleen Gerson contends in Listen to Our Voices that the workplace is still not adequately meeting the needs of parents.

mommy track
An unofficial corporate career track for women who want to divide their attention between work and family.

sexual harassment
Any unwanted and unwelcome sexual advances that interfere with a person's ability to perform a job and enjoy the benefits of a job.

Sexual Harassment

Under evolving legal standards, **sexual harassment** is recognized as any unwanted and unwelcome sexual advances that interfere with a person's ability to perform a job and enjoy the benefits of a job. Increased national attention was given to harassment in the 1990s and into the present through allegations made against elected officials and high-ranking military officers.

The most obvious example of sexual harassment is the boss who tells an employee, "Put out or get out!" However, the unwelcome advances that constitute sexual harassment may take the form of subtle pressures regarding sexual activity, inappropriate touching, attempted kissing, or sexual assault. Indeed, in the computer age, there is growing

Listen to Our Voices

WHAT DO WOMEN AND MEN WANT?

Young workers today grew up in rapidly changing times: They watched women march into the workplace and adults develop a wide range of alternatives to traditional marriage. Now making their own passage to adulthood, these "children of the gender revolution" have inherited a far different world from that of their parents or grandparents. They may enjoy an expanded set of options, but they also face rising uncertainty about whether and how to craft a marriage, rear children, and build a career. . . .

If the realities of time-demanding workplaces and missing supports for caregiving make it difficult for young adults to achieve the sharing, flexible, and more egalitarian relationships most want, then how can we get past this impasse? Clearly, most young women are not likely to answer this question by returning to patterns that fail to speak to either their highest ideals or their greatest fears. To the contrary, they are forming fallback strategies that stress personal autonomy, including the possibility of single parenthood. Men's most common responses to economic pressures and time-demanding jobs stress a different strategy—one that allows for two incomes but preserves men's claim on the most rewarding careers. Women and men are leaning in different directions, and their conflicting responses are fueling a new gender divide. But this schism stems from the intensification of long-simmering work/family dilemmas, not from a decline of laudable values.

Kathleen Gerson

We need to worry less about the family values of a new generation and more about the institutional barriers that make them so difficult to achieve. Most young adults do not wish to turn back the clock, but they do hope to combine the more traditional value of making a lifelong commitment with the more modern value of having a flexible, egalitarian relationship. Rather than trying to change individual values, we need to provide the social supports that will allow young people to overcome work/family conflicts and realize their most cherished aspirations.

Since a mother's earnings and a father's involvement are both integral to the economic and emotional welfare of children (and also desired by most women and men), we can achieve the best family values only by creating flexible workplaces, ensuring equal economic opportunity for women, outlawing discrimination against all parents, and building child-friendly communities with plentiful, affordable, and high-quality child care. These long-overdue policies will help new generations create the more egalitarian partnerships they desire. Failure to build institutional supports for new social realities will not produce a return to traditional marriage. Instead, following the law of unintended consequences, it will undermine marriage itself.

Source: Gerson 2007, A8, A11.

concern that sexually harassing messages are being sent anonymously over computer networks through e-mail and picture phones.

In 1986, in a unanimous decision (*Meritor Savings Bank v. Vinson*), the Supreme Court declared that sexual harassment by a supervisor violates the federal law against sex discrimination in the workplace as outlined in the 1964 Civil Rights Act. If sufficiently severe, harassment is a violation even if the unwelcome sexual demands are not linked to concrete employment benefits such as a raise or promotion. Women's groups hailed the

feminization of poverty
The trend since 1970 in which women account for a growing proportion of those who live below the poverty line.

displaced homemakers
Women whose primary occupation had been homemaking but who did not find full-time employment after being divorced, separated, or widowed.

court's decisiveness in identifying harassment as a form of discrimination. A federal judge subsequently ruled that the public display of photographs of nude and partly nude women at a workplace constitutes sexual harassment. Despite these rulings, it is very difficult legally and emotionally for a person to bring forward a case of sexual harassment (Domino 1995; Roscigno and Schmidt 2007).

Feminization of Poverty

Since World War II, an increasing proportion of the poor in the United States has been female; many of these poor Americans are divorced or never-married mothers. This alarming trend has come to be known as the **feminization of poverty**. In 2007, 12.5 percent of all families in the United States lived in poverty, but 28.3 percent of families headed by single mothers did so. Not only are female-headed families much more likely to be poor but also their income deficit relative to being nonpoor is much greater than other types of poor families (DeNavas-Walt et al. 2008, 13).

Poor women share many social characteristics with poor men: low educational attainment, lack of market-relevant job skills, and residence in economically deteriorating areas. However, conflict theorists believe that the higher rates of poverty among women can be traced to two distinct causes: sex discrimination and sexual harassment on the job place women at a clear disadvantage when seeking vertical social mobility.

The burden of supporting a family is especially difficult for single mothers, not only because of low salaries but also because of inadequate child support. The average child-support payment reported in 2008 (for money collected in 2003) for the 45 percent who received the *full* award was a mere $120 per week. This level of support is clearly insufficient for rearing a child in the early twenty-first century. In light of these data, federal and state officials have intensified efforts to track down delinquent spouses and ensure the payment of child support: nearly 16 million cases were under investigation in 2006 (Bureau of the Census 2007a, 360).

According to a study based on census data by the advocacy group Women Work, families headed by single mothers and displaced homemakers are four times as likely to live in poverty as other households in the United States. **Displaced homemakers** are defined as women whose primary occupation had been homemaking but who did not find full-time employment after being divorced, separated, or widowed. Single mothers and displaced homemakers tend to work in service jobs, which offer low wages, few benefits, part-time work, and little job security. Moreover, single mothers and displaced homemakers are also more likely to have an unstable housing situation, including frequent changes of residence (Women Work 2007).

Many feminists feel that the continuing dominance of the political system by men contributes to government indifference to the problem of poor women. As more and more women fall below the official poverty line, policy makers will face growing pressure to combat the feminization of poverty.

Education

The experience of women in education has been similar to their experience in the labor force: a long history of contribution but in traditionally defined terms. In 1833, Oberlin College became the first institution of higher learning to admit women, two centuries after the first men's college began in this country. In 1837, Wellesley became the first women's college. But it would be a mistake to believe that these early experiments brought about equality for women in education: at Oberlin, the women were forbidden to speak in public. Furthermore,

> *Washing the men's clothes, caring for their rooms, serving them at table, listening to their orations, but themselves remaining respectfully silent in public assemblages, the Oberlin "coeds" were being prepared for intelligent motherhood and a properly subservient wifehood. (Flexner 1959, 30)*

The early graduates of these schools, despite the emphasis in the curriculum on traditional roles, became the founders of the feminist movement.

Today, research confirms that boys and girls are treated differently in school: teachers give boys more attention. In teaching students the values and customs of the larger society, schools in the United States have treated children as if men's education were more important than that of women. Professors of education Myra and David Sadker (2003) documented this persistence of classroom sexism: the researchers noted that boys receive more teacher attention than girls, mainly because they call out in class eight times more often. Teachers praise boys more than girls and offer boys more academic assistance. Interestingly, they found that this differential treatment was present with both male and female teachers.

Despite these challenges, in many communities across the nation, girls seem to outdo boys in high school, grabbing a disproportionate share of the leadership positions, from valedictorian to class president to yearbook editor—everything, in short, except captain of the boys' athletic teams. Their advantage numerically seems to be continuing after high school. In the 1980s, girls in the United States became more likely than boys to go to college. By 2005, women accounted for more than 57 percent of college students nationwide. And in 2002, for the first time, more women than men in the United States earned doctoral degrees (Bureau of the Census 2007a, 143).

At all levels of schooling, significant changes also occurred with congressional amendments to the Education Act of 1972 and the Department of Health, Education, and Welfare guidelines developed in 1974 and 1975. Collectively called Title IX provisions, the regulations are designed to eliminate sexist practices from almost all school systems. Schools must make these changes or risk the loss of all federal assistance:

1. Schools must eliminate all sex-segregated classes and extracurricular activities. This means an end to all-girl home economics and all-boy shop classes, although single-sex hygiene and physical education classes are permitted.

2. Schools cannot discriminate by sex in admissions or financial aid and cannot inquire into whether an applicant is married, pregnant, or a parent. Single-sex schools are exempted.

3. Schools must end sexist hiring and promotion practices among faculty members.

4. Although women do not have to be permitted to play on all-men's athletic teams, schools must provide more opportunities for women's sports, intramural and extramural (*Federal Register,* June 4, 1975).

Title IX became one of the more controversial steps ever taken by the federal government to promote and ensure equality.

Efforts to bring gender equity to sports have been attacked as excessive. The consequences have not fully been intended: for example, colleges have often cut men's sports rather than build up women's sports. Also, most of the sports with generous college scholarships added for women over the last 30 years are in athletic fields that have not been traditionally attractive to minority women (Suggs 2002).

The impact of Title IX over the last 30 years has been particularly apparent as more opportunities have emerged for women to participate in sports in both high school and college.

Research Focus

CHILD CARE AND THE GENDER DIVIDE

It is a commonly held notion that in dual-income households men and women equally share the housework, but this is not supported by the research. Study after study leads to the same conclusion: men are gradually doing more housework, but women do far more even when they work full time.

The latest study, released in 2008 by the Bureau of Labor Statistics, drew on 70,000 interviews conducted from 2003 to 2006 about couples' activities during a typical 24-hour period (Figure 15.3) the age group of 25–54 is used because it generally includes people who have completed going to school full time but excludes retired people.

We have seen that almost as many women as men hold jobs. Yet the time-use study showed that every hour of the day, the working woman is more likely to be engaged in child care than her husband. This gap is greatest during the early morning hours and the evening period. On the positive note, fathers are indeed engaged in caring for children, but it is still more likely to be cared out by mothers.

The same data shows that as the number of children increases, the mother's time spent on child care on a daily basis increases on the average while for fathers it remains unchanged. Interestingly, college-educated mothers and fathers spend more time engaged in child care than less-educated parents, but the amount of time increases more for the college-educated mothers than the college-educated fathers.

Source: Allard and Janes 2008; Bureau of Labor Statistics 2008.

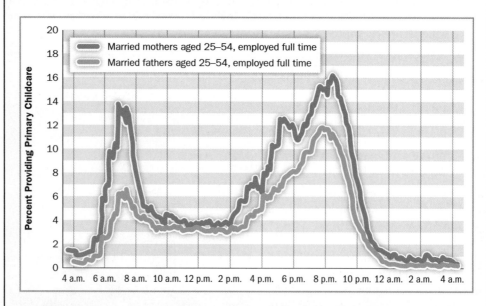

FIGURE 15.3
Hours Spent Providing Child Care

Family Life

Our society generally equates work with wages and holds unpaid work in low esteem. Women who do household chores and volunteer work are given little status in our society. Typically, this unrecognized labor is done on top of wage labor in the formal economy. These demands traditionally placed on a mother and homemaker are so extensive that simultaneously pursuing a career is extremely difficult. For women, the family is, according to sociologists Lewis Coser and Rose Laub Coser (1974) a "greedy institution." More recently, other social scientists have also observed the overwhelming burden of the multiple social roles associated with being a mother and working outside the home.

second shift
The double burden—work outside the home followed by child care and housework—that is faced by many women and that few men share equitably.

Child Care and Housework

A man can act as a homemaker and caregiver for children, but in the United States, women customarily perform these roles. Studies indicate that men do not even think about their children as much as women do. Sociologist Susan Walzer (1996) was interested in whether there are gender differences in the amount of time that parents spend thinking about the care of their children. Drawing on interviews, Walzer found that mothers are much more involved than fathers in the invisible mental labor associated with taking care of a baby. For example, while involved in work outside the home, mothers are more likely to think about their babies and to feel guilty later if they become so consumed with the demands of their jobs that they fail to think about their babies.

Is the gender gap closing in child care? In Research Focus, we consider the latest scientific evidence in answer to this question.

Sociologist Arlie Hochschild has used the term **second shift** to describe the double burden—work outside the home followed by child care and housework—that many women face and that few men share equitably. As shown in Figure 15.4, this issue has become increasingly important as greater proportions of mothers work outside the home. On the basis of interviews with and observations of 52 couples over an eight-year period, Hochschild reports that the wives (and not their husbands) planned domestic schedules and play dates for children while driving home from the office and then began their second shift (Hochschild 1990; Hochschild and Machung 1989).

Hochschild found that the married couples she studied were fraying at the edges psychologically and so were their careers and their marriages. The women she spoke with hardly resembled the beautiful young businesswomen pictured in magazine advertisements, dressed in power suits but with frilled blouses, holding briefcases in one hand and happy young children in the other. Instead, many of Hochschild's female subjects talked about being overtired and emotionally drained by the demands of their multiple roles. They were much more intensely torn by the conflicting demands of work outside the home and family life than were their husbands. Hochschild (1990, 73) concludes that "if we as a culture come to see the urgent need of meeting the new problems posed by the second shift, and if society and government begin to shape new policies that allow working parents more flexibility, then we will be making some progress toward happier times at home and at work." Many feminists share this view.

There is an economic cost to this second shift. Households do benefit from the free labor of women, but

FIGURE 15.4
Labor Force Participation Rates among Mothers
Sources: Department of Labor 2001, 2007, 15.

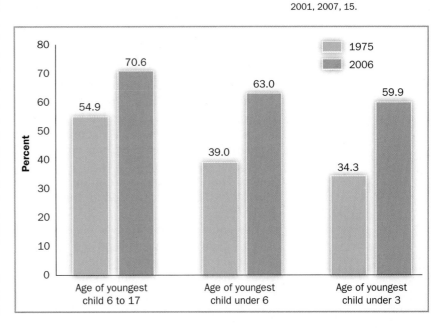

Source: Kirk Anderson, www.kirktoons.com.

women pay what has been called the **mommy tax**: the lower salaries women receive over their lifetime because they have children. Mothers earn less than men and other women over their lifetime because having children causes them to lose job experience, trade higher wages for following the mommy track, and be discriminated against by employers. How high is this mommy tax? Estimates range from 5 percent to 13 percent of lifetime wages for the first child alone. Having two children lowers earnings 10 percent to 19 percent. There is no denying that motherhood and the labor market are intertwined (Budig and England 2001; Szegedy-Maszak 2001).

Abortion

A particularly controversial subject affecting family life in the United States has been the call for women to have greater control over their bodies, especially their reproductive lives, through contraceptive devices and the increased availability of abortions. Abortion law reform was one of the demands NOW made in 1967, and the controversy continues despite many court rulings and the passage of laws at every level of government.

On January 22, 1973, the feminist movement received unexpected assistance from the U.S. Supreme Court in its *Roe v. Wade* decision. By a 7–2 margin, the justices held that the "right to privacy . . . founded in the Fourteenth Amendment's concept of personal liberty . . . is broad enough to encompass a woman's decision whether or not to terminate a pregnancy." However, the Court did set certain limits on a woman's right to abortion. During the last three months of pregnancy, the fetus was ruled capable of life outside the womb. Therefore, states were granted the right to prohibit all abortions in the third trimester except those needed to preserve the life, physical health, or mental health of the mother.

The Court's decision in *Roe v. Wade,* though generally applauded by pro-choice groups, which support the right to legal abortions, was bitterly condemned by those opposed to abortion. For people who call themselves "pro-life," abortion is a moral and often a religious issue. In their view, human life actually begins at the moment of conception rather than when the fetus could stay alive outside the womb. On the basis of this belief, the fetus is a human, not merely a potential life. Termination of this human's life, even

mommy tax
Lower salaries women receive over their lifetime because they have children.

before it has left the womb, is viewed as an act of murder. Consequently, antiabortion activists are alarmed by the more than 1 million legal abortions carried out each year in the United States (Luker 1984).

The early 1990s brought an escalation of violent antiabortion protests. Finally, a 1994 federal law made it a crime to use force or threats or to obstruct, injure, or interfere with anyone providing or receiving abortions and other reproductive health services. In a 6–3 decision, the Supreme Court's majority upheld the constitutionality of a 36-foot buffer zone that keeps antiabortion protesters away from a clinic's entrance and parking lot. Abortion remains a disputed issue both in society and in the courts. The law has apparently had some impact, but acts of violence, including deaths of clinic workers and physicians, continue.

In terms of social class, the first major restriction on the legal right to terminate a pregnancy affected poor people. In 1976, Congress passed the Hyde Amendment, which banned the use of Medicaid and other federal funds for abortions. The Supreme Court upheld this legislation in 1980. State laws also restrict the use of public funds for abortions. Another obstacle facing the poor is access to abortion providers: in the face of vocal prolife public sentiment, fewer and fewer hospitals throughout the world are allowing their physicians to perform abortions, except in extreme cases. Only about 13 percent of counties in the United States have even one provider who is able and willing to perform abortions (R. Jones et al. 2008).

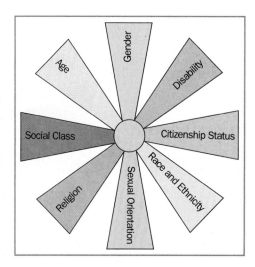

FIGURE 15.5
Matrix of Domination

The matrix of domination illustrates how several social factors—including gender, social class, and race and ethnicity—can converge to create a cumulative impact on a person's social standing.

Political Activity

Women in the United States constitute 53 percent of the voting population and 49 percent of the labor force but only 8 percent of those who hold high government positions. As of the beginning of 2009, Congress included only 74 women (out of 435 members) in the House of Representatives and only 17 women (out of 100 members) in the Senate. The number of women serving in Congress has steadily increased. Only nine states— Alaska, Arizona, Connecticut, Delaware, Hawai'i, Kansas, Michigan, North Carolina, and Washington—had a woman governor at the beginning of 2009. In national elections women tend to vote less Republican than men. In 2008, 56 percent of women backed Barack Obama, the largest swing toward the Democrat presidential nominee during the last 10 elections (Connelly 2008).

The low number of women officeholders until recently has not resulted from women's inactivity in politics. About the same proportion of eligible women and men vote in presidential elections. The League of Women Voters, founded in 1920, performs a valuable function in educating the electorate of both sexes, publishing newsletters describing candidates' positions, and holding debates among candidates. Perhaps women's most visible role in politics until recently has been as unpaid campaign workers for male candidates: doorbell ringers, telephone callers, newsletter printers, and petition carriers.

Runs for elective office in the 1990s showed women overcoming one of their last barriers to electoral office: attracting campaign funds. Running for office is very expensive, and women candidates have begun to convince backers to invest in their political future. Their success as fund-raisers will also contribute to women's acceptance as serious candidates in the future.

Women's political representation is not an issue in just the United States. In A Global View, we look at the different levels of success women have received who seek elected office and some efforts to increase that representation.

Matrix of Domination: Minority Women

Many women experience differential treatment not only because of their gender but also because of race and ethnicity. These citizens face a subordinate status twice defined. A disproportionate share of this low-status group also is poor. The African American feminist Patricia Hill Collins (2000) has termed this the **matrix of domination** (Figure 15.5).

matrix of domination
Cumulative impact of oppression because of race, gender, and class as well as sexual orientation, religion, disability status, and age.

WOMEN ELECTED OFFICIALS: RWANDA AND BEYOND

Chile in 2006 became yet another country to accomplish what the United States has not come close to doing—electing Michelle Bachelet, a woman to head the country. While Hillary Clinton came close to capturing her party's nomination and Sarah Palin became the vice presidential candidate for the Republicans, no woman has been nominated by a major political party in the United States. By contrast, women led 12 countries in 2008 (Argentina, Germany, Ireland, Finland, Chile, New Zealand, Philippines, Liberia, Mozambique, India, Ukraine, and Moldova). A total of 45 countries have had women to serve as prime minister, president, or chancellor.

Although these women rose to power through social circumstances unique to each election and country, their success demonstrates the willingness of many nations to look to women to represent their nation.

As shown in the accompanying table, there is a range of success of women being

Women in National Legislatures (Selected Countries)

More than 25%		10–25%		Less than 10%	
Rwanda	48.8	Singapore	24.5	Japan	9.4
Sweden	47.0	Mexico	23.2	India	9.1
Cuba	43.2	Canada	21.3	Brazil	9.0
Finland	41.5	China	21.3	Kenya	8.9
Argentina	40.0	Poland	20.2	Ukraine	8.2
Netherlands	39.3	Great Britain	19.5	Jordan	6.4
Spain	36.3	France	18.2	Haiti	4.1
South Africa	33.0	United States	16.8	Kuwait	3.8
Afghanistan	27.7	Greece	14.7	Iran	2.8
Australia	26.7	Israel	14.2	Yemen	0.3
Vietnam	25.8	Russia	14.0	Saudi Arabia	0.0
Iraq	25.5	Syria	12.4	Cambodia	0.0

Source: Inter-Parliamentary Union 2008.

Whites dominate non-Whites, men dominate women, and the affluent dominate the poor.

Gender, race, and social class are not the only systems of oppression, but they do profoundly affect women and people of color in the United States. Other forms of categorization and stigmatization can also be included in this matrix, such as sexual orientation, religion, disability status, and age. If we turn to a global stage, we can add citizenship status and being perceived as a "colonial subject" even after colonialism has ended (Winant 2006).

A Global View

elected to national legislatures and parliaments. Worldwide, women represent 18.2 percent of those in national legislatures, with the United States ranking in the middle among 188 countries, with slightly less than 17 percent.

Although only Saudi Arabia allows men but bars women from voting, many countries have taken the step to establish quotas for the purpose of increasing women's representation. In about 40 countries, the government sets aside a certain percentage of seats for women, usually 10 to 30 percent. In about 50 nations, political parties have decided that 20 percent to 40 percent of their candidates should be women. That places a minimum proportion of seats in national legislatures that must be held by women. Canada has the political party quota, Mexico has both types, and the United States has never seriously considered either.

Consider the case of the central African country of Rwanda, where nearly half of the legislators are women and where a woman recently served as prime minister. The genocide in Rwanda was a driving force in women wanting to ensure they would be more involved politically as the country recovered. Since 2003, its constitution mandates that at least 30 percent of seats in the congress (called the Chamber of Deputies) must be female. This also applies to all elected councils throughout the country. These minimum gender quotas are achieved through elections in which only women can stand for election and only women can vote.

Obviously this is a form of affirmative action—a type of policy that has been very controversial in the United States.

What has been the initial impact in the large increase in women in policy-making positions? Rwanda is a very troubled country still recovering from the civil war and genocide of the early 1990s. In response, women created a cross-party alliance called Forum of Women Parliamentarians, focused on advocating on behalf of Rwandan women. Issues on their agenda include recognizing children legally born of unwed mothers, preventing hospitals from holding new mothers and their babies if they are unable to pay for treatment, and cracking down on gender-based violence.

Yet the impact is also limited. Even where the proportion of women elected to office increases, the proportion of top-appointed positions and party leadership roles remain firmly in the hands of men worldwide.

Source: Equal Representation in Government and Democracy 2008; Institute for Democracy and Electoral Assistance 2008; Paxton et al. 2007; Powley 2006; Tripp and Kang 2008; UNIFEM 2008.

Feminists have addressed themselves to the needs of minority women, but the oppression of these women because of their sex is overshadowed by the subordinate status that both White men and White women impose on them because of their race or ethnicity. The question for the Latina (Hispanic woman), African American woman, Asian American woman, Native American woman, and so on appears to be whether she should unify with her brothers against racism or challenge them for their sexism. The answer is that society cannot afford to let up on the effort to eradicate sexism and racism as well as other forces that stigmatize and oppress (Beisel and Kay 2004; Epstein 1999; MacLean and Williams 2008).

The discussion of gender roles among African Americans has always provoked controversy. Advocates of Black nationalism contend that feminism only distracts women from full participation in the African American struggle. The existence of feminist groups among Blacks, in their view, simply divides the Black community and thereby serves the dominant White society. By contrast, Black feminists such as bell hooks (2000) argue that little is to be gained by accepting the gender-role divisions of the dominant society that place women in a separate, subservient position. African American journalist Patricia Raybon (1989) has noted that the media commonly portray Black women in a negative light: as illiterates, as welfare mothers, as prostitutes, and so forth. Black feminists emphasize that it is not solely Whites and White-dominated media that focus on these negative images; Black men (most recently, Black male rap artists) have also been criticized for the way they portray African American women (Threadcraft 2008).

Native Americans stand out as a historical exception to the North American patriarchal tradition. At the time of the arrival of the European settlers, gender roles varied greatly from tribe to tribe. Southern tribes, for reasons unclear to today's scholars, usually were matriarchal and traced descent through the mother. European missionaries sought to make the native peoples more like the Europeans, and this aim included transforming women's role. Some Native American women, like members of other groups, have resisted gender stereotypes (Marubbio 2006).

The plight of Latinas usually is considered part of either the Hispanic or feminist movements, and the distinctive experience of Latinas is ignored. In the past, they have been excluded from decision making in the two social institutions that most affect their daily lives: the family and the Church. The Hispanic family, especially in the lower class, feels the pervasive tradition of male domination. The Catholic Church relegates women to supportive roles while reserving for men the leadership positions (Browne 2001; De Anda 2004).

By considering the matrix of domination, we recognize how much of our discussion has focused on race and ethnicity coupled with data on poverty, low incomes, and meager wealth. Now we recognize that issues of gender domination must be included to fully understand what women of color experience.

Conclusion

Women and men are expected to perform, or at least to prefer to perform, specific tasks in society. The appropriateness to one gender of all but a very few of these tasks cannot be justified by the biological differences between females and males any more than differential treatment based on race can be justified. Psychologists Sandra Bem and Daryl Bem (1970, 99) made the following analogy a generation ago that still may have applicability today.

Suppose that a White male college student decided to room with a Black male friend. The typical White student would not blithely assume that his roommate was better suited to handle all domestic chores. Nor should his conscience allow him to do so even in the unlikely event that his roommate said, "No, that's okay. I like doing housework. I'd be happy to do it." We would suspect that the White student would still feel uncomfortable about taking advantage of the fact that his roommate has simply been socialized to be "happy with

such an arrangement." But change this hypothetical Black roommate to a female marriage partner, and the student's conscience goes to sleep.

The feminist movement has awakened women and men to assumptions based on sex and gender. New opportunities for the sexes require the same commitment from individuals and the government as those made to achieve equality between racial and ethnic groups.

Women are systematically disadvantaged in both employment and the family. Gender inequality is a serious problem, just as racial inequality continues to be a significant social challenge. Separate, socially defined roles for men and women are not limited to the United States. Chapter 16 concentrates on the inequality of racial and ethnic groups in societies other than the United States. Just as sexism is not unique to this nation, neither is racism nor religious intolerance.

Summary

1. Sociologists consider gender roles to be the expectations of behavior. Functionalists see role differences as contributing to carrying out family roles whereas conflict theorists argue they contribute to inequality between men and women.

2. The feminist movement has deep roots in the nineteenth century, and although many younger people today may avoid the label of feminist, the movement continues to work for parity between men and women.

3. The labor force is characterized by occupation segregation by gender and significant differential in earnings for men and women working in the same occupations.

4. The Civil Rights Act of 1964 has played a significant role in reducing sex discrimination, but further measures to achieve pay equity have not been enacted.

5. A pattern of increasing poverty among single women has led to the feminization of poverty.

6. Women have encountered great success in formal schooling. Title IX is helping to eliminate inequities, especially in school athletic programs.

7. Men have increasingly accepted responsibilities for housework and child care, but women continue to assume more responsibility, leading to a phenomenon referred to as a *second shift*.

8. Despite highly public women politicians, the vast majority of elected officials in the United States, especially at the national level, are women. Gender is only one basis for the unequal treatment that women experience; this leads to a formulation called the *matrix of domination* that considers a variety of social dimensions.

Key Terms

androgyny 357
displaced homemakers 366
feminine mystique 360
feminization of poverty 366
gender roles 357
glass ceiling 363

matrix of domination 371
mommy tax 370
mommy track 364
occupational segregation
  by gender 361
pay equity 362

second shift 369
sexism 356
sexual harassment 364
suffragists 359

Review Questions

1. How is women's subordinate position different from that of oppressed racial and ethnic groups? How is it similar?

2. How has the focus of the feminist movement changed from the suffragist movement to the present?

3. How do the patterns of women in the workplace differ from those of men?

4. How has the changing role of women in the United States affected the family?

5. What are the special challenges facing women of subordinate racial and ethnic groups?

Critical Thinking

1. Women have many characteristics similar to those of minority groups, but what are some differences? For example, they are not segregated from men residentially.

2. Earlier in the 1990s, the phrase *angry white men* was used by some men who viewed themselves as victims. In what respect may men see themselves as victims of reverse discrimination? Do you think these views are justified?

3. How are men's and women's roles defined differently when it comes to such concepts as the mommy track, the second shift, and the displaced homemaker?

16

Beyond the United States: The Comparative Perspective

SUBORDINATING PEOPLE BECAUSE OF RACE, NATIONALITY, or religion is not a social phenomenon unique to the United States; it occurs throughout the world. In Mexico, women and the descendants of the Mayans are given second-class status. Despite its being viewed as a homogeneous nation by some, Canada faces racial, linguistic, and tribal issues. Brazil is a large South American nation with a long history of racial inequality. In Israel, Jews and Palestinians struggle over territory and the definition of each other's autonomy. In the Republic of South Africa, the legacy of apartheid dominates the present and the future.

Confrontations along racial or ethnic or religious lines, as Chapter 1 showed, can lead to extermination, expulsion, secession, segregation, fusion, assimilation, or pluralism. At the conclusion of this chapter, we will review how these processes have been illustrated in this chapter as we look beyond the United States.

377

Confrontations between racial and ethnic groups have escalated in frequency and intensity in the twentieth century. In surveying these conflicts, we can see two themes emerge: the previously considered world systems theory and ethnonational conflict. **World systems theory** considers the global economic system as divided between nations that control wealth and those that provide natural resources and labor. Historically, the nations we will be considering reflect this competition between "haves" and "have-nots." Whether the laborers are poor Catholics in Ireland or Black Africans, their contribution to the prosperity of the dominant group created the social inequality that people are trying to address today (Wallerstein 1974; 2004).

Ethnonational conflict refers to conflicts among ethnic, racial, religious, and linguistic groups within nations. In some areas of the world, ethnonational conflicts are more significant than tension between nations as the source of refugees and even death. As we can see in Figure 16.1, countries in all parts of the world, including the most populous nations, have significant diversity within their borders. These conflicts remind us that the processes operating in the United States to deny racial and ethnic groups rights and opportunities are also at work throughout the world (Connor 1994; Olzak 1998).

The sociological perspective on relations between dominant and subordinate groups treats race and ethnicity as social categories. As social concepts, they can be understood only in the context of the shared meanings attached to them by societies and their members. Although relationships between dominant and subordinate groups vary greatly, there are similarities across societies. Racial and ethnic hostilities arise out of economic needs and demands. These needs and demands may not always be realistic; that is, a group may seek out enemies where none exist or where victory will yield no rewards. Racial and ethnic conflicts are both the results and the precipitators of change in the economic and political sectors (Barclay et al. 1976; Coser 1956).

Relations between dominant and subordinate groups differ from society to society, as this chapter will show. Intergroup relations in Mexico, Canada, Brazil, Israel, and South Africa are striking in their similarities and contrasts.

Mexico: Diversity South of the Border

Usually in the discussions of racial and ethnic relations, Mexico is considered only as a source of immigrants to the United States. In questions of economic development, Mexico again typically enters the discussion only as it affects our own economy. However, Mexico, a nation of 108 million people (in the Western hemisphere, only Brazil and the United States are larger) is an exceedingly complex nation (see Table 16.1 on the page 380). It is therefore appropriate that we understand Mexico and its issues of inequality better. This understanding will also shed light on the relationship of its people to the United States.

In the 1520s, Spain overthrew the Aztec Indian tribe that ruled Mexico. Mexico remained a Spanish colony until the 1820s. In 1836, Texas declared its independence from Mexico, and by 1846 Mexico was at war with the United States. As we described in Chapter 9, the Mexican–American War forced Mexico to surrender more than half of its territory. In the 1860s, France sought to turn Mexico into an empire under Austrian prince Maximilian but ultimately withdrew after bitter resistance led by a Mexican Indian, Benito Juárez, who later served as the nation's president.

world systems theory
A view of the global economic system as divided between nations that control wealth and those that provide natural resources and labor.

ethnonational conflicts
Conflicts between ethnic, racial, religious, and linguistic groups within nations. These conflicts replace conflicts between nations.

378

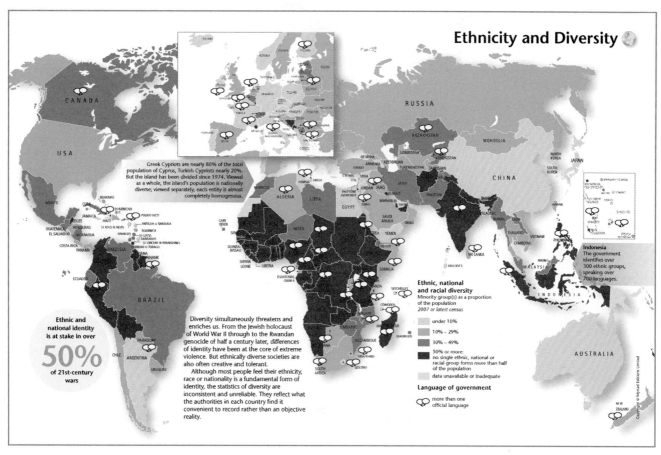

FIGURE 16.1
Ethnic Diversity Worldwide
Source: D. Smith 2008: 22–23.

The Mexican Indian People and the Color Gradient

In contemporary Mexico, a major need has been to reassess the relations between the indigenous peoples—the Mexican Indians, many descended from the Mayas, and the government of Mexico. In 1900, the majority of the Mexican population still spoke Indian languages and lived in closed, semi-isolated villages or tribal communities according to ancestral customs. Many of these people were not a part of the growing industrialization in Mexico and were not truly represented in the national legislature. Perhaps the major change for them in the twentieth century was that many intermarried with the descendants of the Europeans, forming a **mestizo** class of people of mixed ancestry. The term *mestizo* is used throughout the Americas to refer to people of mixed European (usually Spanish) and local indigenous ancestry. Mestizos have become increasingly identified with Mexico's growing middle class. They have developed their own distinct culture and, as the descendants of the European settlers are reduced in number and influence, have become the true bearers of the national Mexican sentiment.

Meanwhile, however, these social changes have left the Mexican Indian people even further behind the rest of the population economically. Indian cultures have been stereotyped as backward and resistant to progress and modern ways of living. Indeed, the existence of the many (at least 56) Indian cultures was seen in much of the twentieth century as an impediment to the development of a national culture in Mexico.

mestizo
People in the Americas of mixed European (usually Spanish) and local indigenous ancestry

TABLE 16.1
Five-Nation Comparison, 2008

Country	Population (in millions)	GNI per capita ($) (USA = $45,8500)	Groups Represented	Current Nation's Formation
Mexico	107.7	12,580	Mexican Indians, 9%	1823: Republic of Mexico declared independence from Spain
Canada	33.3	35,310	French speaking, 24% Aboriginal peoples, 4% "Visible" minorities, 16%	1867: Unified as a colony of England 1948: Independence
Brazil	195.1	9,3700	White, 53% Brown (moreno, mulatto), 39% Afro-Brazilians, 6% Asian and indigenous Indians, 1%	1889: Became independent of Portugal
Israel	7.5	25,930	Jews, 80%	1948: Independence from British mandate under United Nations
Palestinian Territories	4.2	4,247	Others (citizens), 1% Muslims, Christians, Palestinians (noncitizens), 19%	
South Africa	8.3	9,560	Black Africans, 76% Whites, 13% Coloureds, 9% Asians, 3%	1948: Independence from Great Britain

Sources: Author estimates, based on Canak and Swanson 1998; Dahlburg 1998; Haub 2008; South African Institute of Race Relations 2007; Statistics Canada 2007a, 2008a, 2008b.

As noted in Chapter 9, a **color gradient** is the placement of people on a continuum from light to dark skin color rather than in distinct racial groupings by skin color. This is another example of the social construction of race, in which social class is linked to the social reality (or at least the appearance) of racial purity. At the top of this gradient or hierarchy are the *criollos*, the 10 percent of the population who are typically White, well-educated members of the business and intellectual elites with familial roots in Spain. In the middle is the large impoverished mestizo majority, most of whom have brown skin and a mixed racial lineage as a result of intermarriage. At the bottom of the color gradient are the destitute Mexican Indians and a small number of Blacks, some of them the descendants of 200,000 African slaves brought to Mexico. The relatively small Black Mexican community received national attention in 2005 and 2006 following a series of racist events that received media attention. Ironically, although this color gradient is an important part of day-to-day life—enough so that some Mexicans use hair dyes, skin lighteners, and blue or green contact lenses to appear more European—nearly all Mexicans are considered part Mexican Indian because of centuries of intermarriage (Castañeda 1995; Escárcega 2008; Thompson 2005).

On January 1, 1994, rebels from an armed insurgent group called the Zapatista National Liberation Army seized four towns in the state of Chiapas in southern Mexico. Two thousand lightly armed Mayan Indians and peasants backed the rebels—who had named their organization after Emiliano Zapata, a farmer and leader of the 1910 revolution against a corrupt dictatorship. Zapatista leaders declared that they had turned to armed insurrection to protest economic injustices and discrimination against the region's Indian population. The Mexican government mobilized the army to crush the revolt but was forced to retreat as news organizations broadcast pictures of the confrontation around the world. A cease-fire was declared after only 12 days of

color gradient
The placement of people on a continuum from light to dark skin color rather than in distinct racial groupings by skin color.

fighting, but 196 people had already died. Negotiations collapsed between the Mexican government and the Zapatista National Liberation Army, and there has been sporadic violence ever since.

In response to the crisis, the Mexican legislature enacted the Law on Indian Rights and Culture, which went into effect in 2001. The act allows 62 recognized Indian groups to apply their own customs in resolving conflicts and electing leaders. Unfortunately, state legislatures must give final approval to these arrangements, a requirement that severely limits the rights of large Indian groups whose territories span several states. Tired of waiting for state approval, many indigenous communities in Chiapas have declared self-rule without obtaining official recognition.

Although many factors contributed to the Zapatista revolt, the subordinate status of Mexico's Indian citizens, who account for an estimated 14 percent of the nation's population, was surely important. More than 90 percent of the indigenous population lives in houses without access to sewers, compared with 21 percent of the population as a whole. And whereas just 10 percent of Mexican adults are illiterate, the proportion for Mexican Indians is 44 percent (Boudreaux 2002; *Economist* 2004c; J. Smith 2001; Stahler-Sholk 2008; Thompson 2001).

The Status of Women

Often in the United States we consider our own problems to be so significant that we fail to recognize that many of these social issues exist elsewhere. Gender stratification is an example of an issue we share with almost all other countries, and Mexico is no exception.

The poverty of Mexican Indians is well documented and in some instances has led to violent protests for social change.

In 1975, Mexico City was the site of the first United Nations conference on the status of women. Much of the focus was on the situation of women in developing countries; in that regard, Mexico remains typical.

Women in Mexico did not receive the right to vote until 1953. They have made significant progress in that short period in being elected into office, but they have a long way to go. As of 2008, women accounted for 23 percent of Mexico's national assembly (Inter-Parliamentary Union 2008).

Even when Mexican women work outside the home, they are often denied recognition as active and productive household members, and men are typically viewed as heads of the household in every respect. As one consequence, women find it difficult to obtain credit and technical assistance in many parts of Mexico and to inherit land in rural areas.

In the larger economy in Mexico, women often are viewed as the "ideal workers." This appears to be particularly true of the foreign-owned factories, or maquiladoras, of the borderlands (discussed in Chapter 9) that rely heavily on women. For example, in a Tijuana electronics plant, women receive elementary training and work in the least-skilled and least-automated jobs because there is little expectation of advancement, organizing for better working conditions, or developing unions.

Men are preferred over women in the more skilled jobs, and women lose out entirely as factories, even in developing nations such as Mexico, require more complex skills. In 2005, only 45 percent of women were in the paid labor force, compared with about 73 percent in Canada and 70 percent in the United States (Bureau of the Census 2007a, 884).

In recent decades, Mexican women have begun to address an array of economic, political, and health issues. Often this organizing occurs at the grassroots level and outside traditional government forums. Because women continue to serve as household managers for their families, even when they work outside the home, they have been aware of the consequences of the inadequate public services in low-income urban neighborhoods. As far back as 1973, women in Monterrey, the nation's sixth-largest city, began protesting the continuing disruptions of the city's water supply. At first, individual women made complaints to city officials and the water authority, but subsequently, groups of female activists emerged. They sent delegations to confront politicians, organized protest rallies, and blocked traffic as a means of getting media attention. As a result of their efforts, there have been improvements in Monterrey's water service, although the issue of reliable and safe water remains a concern in Mexico and many developing countries (V. Bennett 1995, 2005).

Mexico is beginning to recognize that the issue of social inequality extends beyond poverty. A 2005 survey found that eight out of 10 Mexicans felt it was as important to eliminate discrimination as poverty, yet 40 percent said that they did not want to live next to an Indian community, and one-third considered it "normal" for women not to earn as much as men (Thompson 2005).

Canada: Multiculturalism Up North

Multiculturalism is a fairly recent term in the United States; it is used to refer to diversity. In Canada, it has been adopted as a state policy for more than two decades. Still, many people in the United States, when they think of Canada, see it as a homogeneous nation with a smattering of Arctic-type people—merely a cross between the northern mainland United States and Alaska. This is not the social reality.

One of the continuing discussions among Canadians is the need for a cohesive national identity or a sense of common peoplehood. The immense size of the country, much of which is sparsely populated, and the diversity of its people have complicated this need.

In 1971, Canadian Prime Minister Pierre Trudeau presented to the House of Commons a policy of multiculturalism that sought to permit cultural groups to retain and foster their identity. Specifically, he declared that there should continue to be two official languages, French and English, but no official culture, no single ethnic group with power over any other, just Canadians all. Yet it is not always possible to legislate a pluralistic society, as the case of Canada demonstrates (Schertzer 2008).

The First Nation

Canada, like the United States, has had an adversarial relationship with its native peoples. However, the Canadian experience has not been as violent. During all three stages of Canadian history—French colonialism, British colonialism, and Canadian nationhood—there has been, compared with the United States, little warfare between Canadian Whites and Canadian Native Americans. Yet the legacy today is similar. Prodded by settlers, colonial governments (and later Canadian governments) drove the Native Americans from their lands. Already by the 1830s, Indian reserves were being established that were similar to the reservations in the United States. Tribal members were encouraged to renounce their status and become Canadian citizens. Assimilation was the explicit policy until recently (Champagne 1994; Waldman 1985).

The 1.2 million native peoples of Canada are collectively referred to by the government as the *First Nation* or *Aboriginal Peoples* and represent about 4 percent of the population. This population is classified into the following groups:

> *status Indians*—The more than 600 tribes or bands officially recognized by the government, numbering about 680,000 in 2006, of whom 40 percent live on Indian reserves (or reservations);
>
> *Inuit*—The 50,485 people living in the northern part of the country, who in the past were called Eskimos; and

Métis (pronounced "may-TEE")—Canadians of mixed Aboriginal ancestry, officially numbering 390,000 and many of whom still speak French Métis, a mixed language combining Aboriginal and European words.

Another 35,000 Canadians of mixed native ancestry are counted by the government as First Nation people, but there are perhaps another 600,000 non–status Indians who self-identify themselves as having some Aboriginal ancestry but who are not so considered by the Canadian government (Huteson 2008; Statistics Canada 2008a).

The Métis and non–status Indians have historically enjoyed no separate legal recognition, but efforts continue to secure them special rights under the law, such as designated health, education, and welfare programs. The general public does not understand these legal distinctions, so if a Métis or non–status Indian "looks like an Indian," she or he is subjected to the same treatment, discriminatory or otherwise (Indian and Northern Affairs Canada and Canadian Polar Commission 2000, 4).

The new Canadian federal constitution of 1982 included a charter of rights that "recognized and affirmed . . . the existing aboriginal and treaty rights" of the Canadian Native American, Inuit, and Métis peoples. This recognition received the most visibility through the efforts of the Mohawk, one of the tribes of status Indians. At issue were land rights involving some property areas in Quebec that had spiritual significance for the Mohawk. Their protests and militant confrontations reawakened the Canadian people to the concerns of their diverse native peoples (Amnesty International 1993).

Some of the contemporary issues facing the First Nation of Canada are very similar to those faced by Native Americans in the United States. Contemporary Canadians are shocked to learn of past mistreatment leading to belated remedies. Exposure of past sexual and physical abuse of tens of thousands in boarding schools led to compensation to former students. Tribal people document that environmental justice must be addressed because of the disproportionate pollution they experience. Seeking better opportunities, First Nation people move to urban areas in Canada where social services are slowly meeting the needs.

The social and economic fate of contemporary Aboriginal Peoples reflects many challenges. Only 40 percent even graduate from high school compared to more than 70 percent for the country as a whole. The native peoples of Canada have unemployment rates twice as high and an average income one-third lower (Birchard 2006; Crenson 2005; Silver 2006; Statistics Canada 2001, 2008a).

In a positive step, in 1999 Canada created a new territory in response to a native land claim in which the resident Inuit (formerly called *Eskimos*) dominated. Nunavut ("NOO-nah-voot"), meaning "our land," recognizes the territorial rights of the Inuit. Admirable as this event is, observers noted it was easier to grant such economic rights and autonomy to 29,000 people in the isolated expanse of northern Canada than to the Aboriginal Peoples of the more populated southern provinces of Canada (Krauss 2006b).

A lingering embarrassment in Canadian history was finally acknowledged in 2008. The Canadian government formally apologized to the First Nation people for having forced 150,000 native children to attend government residential schools from 1920s through the early 1970s. Many suffered physical and sexual abuse. Long sought for by First Nation people, the apology seemed long overdue. Earlier in 2006, as a part of a legal settlement, the government set aside $2 billion for payments to surviving students and to document their experiences (M. Farley 2008).

The Québécois

Assimilation and domination have been the plight of most minority groups. The French-speaking people of the province of Quebec—the **Québécois**, as they are known—represent a contrasting case. Since the mid-1960s, they have reasserted their identity and captured the attention of the entire nation.

Quebec accounts for about one-fourth of the nation's population and wealth. Reflecting its early settlement by the French, fully 80 percent of the province's population claims French as its first language, compared with only 24 percent in the nation as a whole (Statistics Canada 2002).

Québécois
The French-speaking people of the province of Quebec in Canada.

Supporters of a Quebec separatist movement participate in a rally. In 1995, a referendum calling for separation from the rest of Canada was narrowly defeated; today support for such a drastic step appears to have declined.

The Québécois have sought to put French Canadian culture on an equal footing with English Canadian culture in the country as a whole and to dominate in the province. At the very least, this effort has been seen as an irritant outside Quebec and has been viewed with great concern by the English-speaking minority in Quebec.

In the 1960s, the Québécois expressed the feeling that bilingual status was not enough. Even to have French recognized as one of two official languages in a nation dominated by the English-speaking population gave the Québécois second-class status in their view. With some leaders threatening to break completely with Canada and make Quebec an independent nation, Canada made French the official language of the province and the only acceptable language for commercial signs and public transactions. New residents are now required to send their children to French schools. The English-speaking residents felt as if they had been made aliens, even though many of them had roots extending back to the 1700s. These changes spurred residents to migrate from Quebec and some corporate headquarters to relocate to the neighboring English-speaking province of Ontario (Salée 1994).

In 1995, the people of Quebec were given a referendum that they would vote on alone: whether they wanted to separate from Canada and form a new nation. In a very close vote, 50.5 percent of the voters indicated a preference to remain united with Canada. The vote was particularly striking, given the confusion over how separation would be accomplished and its significance economically. Separatists vowed to keep working for secession and called for another referendum in the future, although surveys show the support for independence had dropped to 40 percent of the province by 2002. Independence for Quebec would not be easy, because the Supreme Court of Canada ruled in 1998 that Quebec cannot secede without seeking the consent of the central government. Canadians opposed to separation spoke of reconciliation after the bitter election debate, but it was unclear what further concessions they were prepared to make to the separatists. Many French-speaking residents now seem to accept the steps that have been taken, but a minority still seeks full control of financial and political policies (C. Mason 2007).

Canada is characterized by the presence of two linguistic communities: the Anglophone and the Francophone, with the latter occurring largely in the one province of Quebec. Outside Quebec, Canadians are opposed to separatism; within Quebec, they are divided. Language and cultural issues, therefore, both unify and divide a nation of 33 million people.

Immigration and Race

Immigration has also been a significant social force contributing to Canadian multiculturalism. Toronto and Vancouver both have a higher proportion of foreign-born residents than either Los Angeles or New York City. Canada, proportionately to its population, receives consistently the most immigrants of any nation. About 20 percent of its population is foreign-born, with an increasing proportion being of Asian background rather than European (Statistics Canada 2007b).

visible minorities
In Canada, persons other than Aboriginal or First Nation people who are non-White in racial background.

Canada also speaks of its **visible minorities**—persons other than Aboriginal or First Nation people who are non-White in racial background. This would include much of the immigrant population as well as the Black population. In the 2006 census, the visible minority population accounted for 16 percent of the population, compared to less than 5 percent 25 years earlier. The largest visible minority are the Chinese, followed by South Asians collectively, Black Canadians, and Filipinos (Statistics Canada 2008b).

People in the United States tend to view Canada's race relations in favorable terms. In part, this view reflects Canada's role as the "promised land" for slaves escaping the U.S. South and crossing the free North to Canada, where they were unlikely to be recaptured. The view of Canada as a land of positive intergroup relations is also fostered by Canadians' comparing themselves with the United States. They have long been willing to compare their best social institutions to the worst examples of racism in the United States and to pride themselves on being more virtuous and high-minded (McClain 1979).

The social reality, past and present, is quite different. Africans came in 1689 as involuntary immigrants to be enslaved by French colonists. Slavery officially continued until 1833. It never flourished because the Canadian economy did not need a large labor force, so most slaves worked as domestic servants. Blacks from the United States did flee to Canada before slavery ended, but some fugitive slaves returned after Lincoln's issuance of the Emancipation Proclamation in 1863. The early Black arrivals in Canada were greeted in a variety of ways. Often they were warmly received as fugitives from slavery, but as their numbers grew in some areas, Canadians became concerned that they would overwhelm the White population (Winks 1971).

The contemporary Black Canadian population, about 2.5 percent of the nation's population, consists of indigenous Afro-Canadians with several generations of roots in Canada, West Indian immigrants and their descendants, and a number of post–World War II immigrants from the United States. Slightly more than half of Canada's Blacks are foreign born. Racial issues are barely below the surface, as evidenced by rioting in 2008 in a Montreal neighborhood that is predominantly Black and Hispanic. Rioting was precipitated by the police shooting of a Honduran teenager. After a weekend of looting, peace was restored amid promises to improve police–community relations (Gosselin 2008; Statistics Canada 2007b; 2008b).

Before 1966, Canada's immigration policy alternated between restrictive and more open to assist the economy as needed. As in the United States, there were some very exclusionary phases based on race. From 1884 to 1923, Canada levied a Chinese "head tax" that virtually brought Chinese immigration to a halt, although earlier it had been encouraged. Subsequent policies through 1947 were not much better. Current immigration policy favors those with specific skills that make an economic contribution to the country. Yet immigrants as a group are more likely to experience persistent poverty than their Canadian-born counterparts (Picot, Hou, and Cooke 2008).

In 1541, Frenchman Jacques Cartier established the first European settlement along the St. Lawrence River, but within a year he withdrew because of confrontations with the Iroquois. Almost 500 years later, the descendants of the Europeans and Aboriginal Peoples are still trying to resolve Canada's identity as it is shaped by issues of ethnicity, race, and language.

Brazil: Not a Racial Paradise

To someone who is knowledgeable about race and ethnic relations in the United States, Brazil seems familiar in several respects. Like the United States, Brazil was colonized by Europeans who overwhelmed the native people. Like the United States, Brazil imported Black Africans as slaves to meet the demand for laborers. Even today, Brazil is second only to the United States in the number of people of African descent, excluding nations on the African continent. Another similarity is the treatment of indigenous people. Although the focus here is on Black and White people in Brazil, another continuing concern is the treatment of Brazil's native peoples as this developing nation continues to industrialize.

Legacy of Slavery

The current nature of Brazilian race relations is influenced by the legacy of slavery, as is true of Black–White relations in the United States. It is not necessary to repeat here a discussion of the brutality of the slave trade and slavery itself or of the influence of

Increasingly, people of Brazil are coming to terms with the significant social inequality evident along color lines.

slavery on the survival of African cultures and family life. Scholars agree that slavery was not the same in Brazil as it was in the United States, but they disagree on how different it was and how significant these differences were (Elkins 1959; Tannenbaum 1946).

Brazil depended much more than the United States on the slave trade. Estimates place the total number of slaves imported to Brazil at 4 million, eight times the number brought to the United States. At the height of slavery, however, both nations had approximately the same slave population: 4 million to 4.5 million. Brazil's reliance on African-born slaves meant that typical Brazilian slaves had closer ties to Africa than did their U.S. counterparts. Revolts and escapes were more common among slaves in Brazil. The most dramatic example was the slave **quilombo** (or hideaway) of Palmores, whose 20,000 inhabitants repeatedly fought off Portuguese assaults until 1698. Interestingly, these quilombos have reappeared in the news as Black Brazilians have sought to recognize their claims related to these settlements.

The most significant difference between slavery in the southern United States and in Brazil was the amount of *manumission*—the freeing of slaves. For every 1,000 slaves, 100 were freed annually in Brazil, compared to four per year in the U.S. South. It would be hasty to assume, however, as some people have, that Brazilian masters were more benevolent. Quite the contrary. Brazil's slave economy was poorer than that of the U.S. South, and so slave owners in Brazil freed slaves into poverty whenever they became crippled, sick, or old. But this custom does not completely explain the presence of the many freed slaves in Brazil. Again unlike in the United States, the majority of Brazil's population was composed of Africans and their descendants throughout the nineteenth century. Africans were needed as craft workers, shopkeepers, and boatmen, not just as agricultural workers. Freed slaves filled these needs.

In Brazil, race was not seen as a measure of innate inferiority, as it was in the United States. Rather, even during the period of slavery, Brazilians saw free Blacks as contributing to society, which was not the view of White U.S. Southerners. In Brazil, you were inferior if you were a slave. In the United States, you were inferior if you were Black. Not that Brazilians were more enlightened than Americans. Quite the contrary, Brazil belonged to the European tradition of a hierarchical society that did not conceive of all people as equal. Unlike the English, who emphasized individual freedom, however, the Brazilian slave owner had no need to develop a racist defense of slavery. These distinctions help explain why Whites in the United States felt compelled to dominate and simultaneously fear both the slave and the Black man and woman. Brazilians did not have these fears of

quilombo
Slave hideaways in Brazil.

free Blacks and, thus, felt it unnecessary to restrict manumission (Davis 1966; Degler 1971; Harris 1964; Patterson 1982; Skidmore 1972; Sundiata 1987).

mulatto escape hatch Notion that Brazilians of mixed ancestry can move into high-status positions.

The "Racial Democracy" Illusion

For some time in the twentieth century, Brazil was seen by some as a "racial democracy" and even a "racial paradise." Indeed, historically the term *race* is rare in Brazil; the term *côr* or *color* is far more common. Historian Carl Degler (1971) identified the **mulatto escape hatch** as the key to the differences in Brazilian and American race relations. In Brazil, the mulatto or *moreno* (brown) is recognized as a group separate from either *brancos* (Whites) or *prêtos* (Blacks), whereas in the United States, mulattos are classed with Blacks. Yet this escape hatch is an illusion because mulattoes fare only marginally better economically than Black Brazilians or *Afro Brazilians* or *Afro-descendant*, the term used there to refer to the dark end of the Brazilian color gradient and increasingly used by college-educated persons and activists in Brazil. In addition, mulattoes do not escape through mobility into the income and status enjoyed by White Brazilians. Labor market analyses demonstrate that Blacks with the highest levels of education and occupation experience the most discrimination in terms of jobs, mobility, and income. In addition, they face a *glass ceiling* that limits their upward mobility (Fiola 2008; Daniel 2006; Schwartzman 2007).

Today, the use of dozens of terms to describe oneself along the color gradient (see Chapter 12) is obvious in Brazil because, unlike in the United States, people of mixed ancestry are viewed as an identifiable social group. The 2000 census in Brazil classified 53 percent White, 39 percent brown or mulatto, 6 percent Afro-Brazilian, and 1 percent Asian and indigenous Brazilian Indian. Over the past 50 years, the mulatto group has grown, and the proportions of both Whites and Blacks have declined.

In Brazil, today as in the past, light skin color enhances status, but the impact is often exaggerated. When Degler advanced the idea of the mulatto escape hatch, he implied that it was a means to success. The most recent income data controlling for gender, education, and age indicate that people of mixed ancestry earn 12 percent more than Blacks. Yet Whites earn another 26 percent more than the moreno. Clearly, the major distinction is between Whites and all "people of color" rather than between people of mixed ancestry and Afro-Brazilians (Brazil 1981; Dzidzienyo 1987; Silva 1985; Telles, 1992, 2004).

Brazilian Dilemma

Gradually in Brazil there has been the recognition that racial prejudice and discrimination do exist. A 2000 survey in Rio de Janeiro found that 93 percent of those surveyed believe that racism exists in Brazil and 74 percent said there was a lot of bias. Yet 87 percent of the respondents said they themselves were not racist (Buckley 2000).

During the twentieth century, Brazil changed from a nation that prided itself on its freedom from racial intolerance to a country legally attacking discrimination against people of color. One of the first measures was in 1951 when the Afonso Arinos law was unanimously adopted, prohibiting racial discrimination in public places. Opinion is divided over the effectiveness of the law, which has been of no use in overturning subtle forms of discrimination. Even from the start, certain civilian careers, such as the diplomatic and military officer ranks, were virtually closed to Blacks. Curiously, the push for the law came from the United States, after a Black American dancer, Katherine Dunham, was denied a room at a São Paulo luxury hotel.

Today, the income disparity is significant in Brazil. As shown in Figure 16.2, people of color are disproportionately clustered in the lowest income levels of society. Although not as disadvantaged as Blacks in South Africa, which we will take up later in this chapter, the degree of inequality between Whites and people of color is much greater in Brazil than in the United States.

As in other multiracial societies, women of color fare particularly poorly in Brazil. White men, of course, have the highest income, whereas Black men have earning levels comparable to those of White women, and Afro-Brazilian women are the furthest behind (Fiola 2008; Telles 2004).

FIGURE 16.2
Income Distribution by Race
Note: Monthly income for Brazil and United States in 1996; for South Africa, 1998.
Source: Government agencies as reported in Telles 2004, 108.

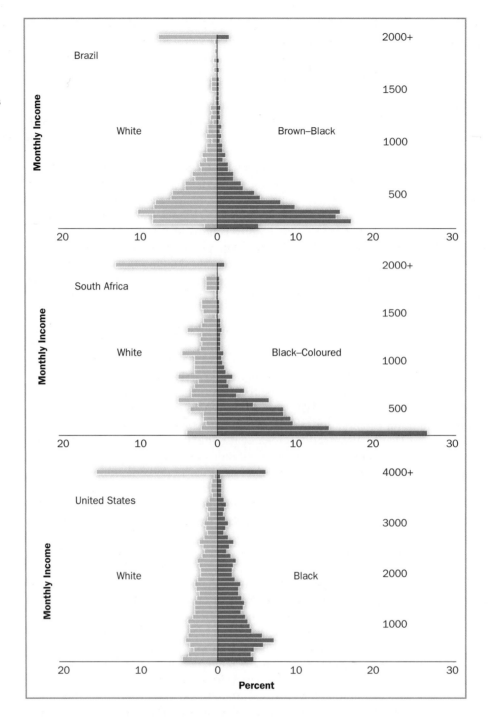

There is a long history of activism among Afro-Americans overcoming the challenge of a society that thinks distinctions are based on social class. After all, if problems are based on poverty, they are easier to overcome than if problems are based on color. However, activism is also understandable because societal wealth is so unequal—the concentration of income and assets in the hands of a few is much greater than even in the United States. For Afro-Brazilians, even professional status can achieve only so much in one's social standing. An individual's blackness does not suddenly become invisible simply because he or she has acquired some social standing. The fame achieved by the Black Brazilian soccer player Pelé is a token exception and does not mean that Blacks have it easy or even have a readily available "escape hatch" through professional sports.

A dramatic step was taken to explicitly acknowledge the role of race when affirmative action measures were introduced. Quotas were begun in 2007, by which students could indicate their race with their college-entrance applications. Reflecting the color gradient and the lack of clear-cut racial categories, committees were actually created to examine photographs of prospective students for the purpose of determining race. In its initial implementation, charges of reverse racism and specific cases of inexplicable classifications being made were common. Coming up with solutions in Brazil will be just as intractable as the problems themselves (Ash 2007; Daniel 2006; Dzidzienyo 1987; Fiola 2008).

Israel and the Palestinians

In 1991, when the Gulf War ended, hopes were high in many parts of the world that a comprehensive Middle East peace plan could be hammered out. Just a decade later, after the terrorist attacks of September 11, 2001, the expectations for a lasting peace were much dimmer. The key elements in any peace plan were to resolve the conflict between Israel and its Arab neighbors and to resolve the challenge of the Palestinian refugees. Although the issues are debated in the political arena, the origins of the conflict can be found in race, ethnicity, and religion.

Nearly 2,000 years ago, the Jews were exiled from Palestine in the **Diaspora**. The exiled Jews settled throughout Europe and elsewhere in the Middle East, where they often encountered hostility and the anti-Semitism described in Chapter 14. With the conversion of the Roman Empire to Christianity, Palestine became the site of many Christian pilgrimages. Beginning in the seventh century, Palestine gradually fell under the Muslim influence of the Arabs. By the beginning of the twentieth century, tourism had become established. In addition, some Jews had migrated from Russia and established settlements that were tolerated by the Ottoman Empire, which then controlled Palestine.

Great Britain expanded its colonial control from Egypt into Palestine during World War I, driving out the Turks. Britain ruled the land but endorsed the eventual establishment of a Jewish national homeland in Palestine. The spirit of **Zionism**, the yearning to establish a Jewish state in the biblical homeland, was well under way. From the Arab perspective, Zionism meant the subjugation, if not the elimination, of the Palestinians.

Thousands of Jews came to settle from throughout the world; even so, in the 1920s, Palestine was only about 15 percent Jewish. Ethnic tension grew as the Arabs of Palestine were threatened by the Zionist fervor. Rioting grew to such a point that in 1939, Britain yielded to Palestinian demands that Jewish immigration be stopped. This occurred at the same time as large numbers of Jews were fleeing Nazism in Europe. After World War II, Jews resumed their demand for a homeland, despite Arab objections. Britain turned to the newly formed United Nations to settle the dispute. In May 1948, the British mandate over Palestine ended, and the state of Israel was founded (Masci 2001).

The Palestinian people define themselves as the people who lived in this former British mandate, along with their descendants on their fathers' side. They are viewed as an ethnic group within the larger group of Arabs. They generally speak Arabic, and most of them (97 percent) are Muslim (mostly Sunni). With a rapid rate of natural increase, the Palestinians have grown in number from 1.4 million at the end of World War II to about 7 million worldwide: 700,000 in Israel, 1.5 million in the West Bank, and 800,000 in the Gaza Strip (Third World Institute 2007, 419).

Arab–Israeli Conflicts

No sooner had Israel been created than the Arab nations—particularly Egypt, Jordan, Iraq, Syria, and Lebanon—announced their intention to restore control to the Palestinian Arabs, by force if necessary. As hostilities broke out, the Israeli military stepped in to preserve the borders, which no Arab nation agreed to recognize. Some 60 percent of the 1.4 million Arabs fled or were expelled from Israeli territory, becoming refugees in neighboring countries. An uneasy peace followed as Israel attempted to encourage new Jewish immigration. Israel also extended the same services that were available to the Jews, such as education and health care, to the non-Jewish Israelis. The new Jewish population continued to grow under the country's Law of Return, which gave every Jew in

Diaspora
The exile of Jews from Palestine.

Zionism
Traditional Jewish religious yearning to return to the biblical homeland, now used to refer to support for the state of Israel.

FIGURE 16.3
Israeli and Palestinian Lands

Sources: Author, based on Masci 2001; *Economist* 2005b, 2005c; Tse 2005, 2006.

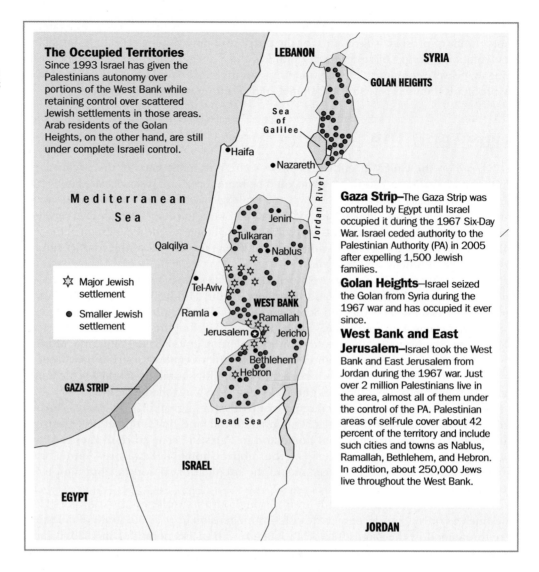

The Occupied Territories
Since 1993 Israel has given the Palestinians autonomy over portions of the West Bank while retaining control over scattered Jewish settlements in those areas. Arab residents of the Golan Heights, on the other hand, are still under complete Israeli control.

Gaza Strip—The Gaza Strip was controlled by Egypt until Israel occupied it during the 1967 Six-Day War. Israel ceded authority to the Palestinian Authority (PA) in 2005 after expelling 1,500 Jewish families.

Golan Heights—Israel seized the Golan from Syria during the 1967 war and has occupied it ever since.

West Bank and East Jerusalem—Israel took the West Bank and East Jerusalem from Jordan during the 1967 war. Just over 2 million Palestinians live in the area, almost all of them under the control of the PA. Palestinian areas of self-rule cover about 42 percent of the territory and include such cities and towns as Nablus, Ramallah, Bethlehem, and Hebron. In addition, about 250,000 Jews live throughout the West Bank.

☆ Major Jewish settlement
● Smaller Jewish settlement

the world the right to settle permanently as a citizen. The question of Jerusalem remained unsettled, and the city was divided into two separate sections—Israeli Jewish and Jordanian Arab—a division both sides refused to regard as permanent.

In 1967, Egypt, followed by Syria, responded to Israel's military actions to take surrounding territory in what came to be called the Six-Day War. In the course of defeating the Arab states' military, Israel occupied the Gaza Strip and the West Bank (Figure 16.3). The defeat was all the more bitter for the Arabs as Israeli-held territory expanded.

Although our primary attention here is on the Palestinians and the Jews, another significant ethnic issue is present in Israel. Among Israel's Jews, about 21 percent are Israeli-born, 32 percent are European or American, 21 percent are African American, and 13 percent are Asian. The Law of Return has brought to Israel Jews of varying cultural backgrounds. European Jews have been the dominant force, but a significant migration of the more religiously observant Jews from North Africa and other parts of the Middle East has created what sociologist Ernest Krausz (1973) called "the two nations." Not only are the various Jewish groups culturally diverse but also there are significant socioeconomic differences: the Europeans generally are more prosperous, better represented in the Knesset (Israel's parliament), and better educated. The secular Jews feel pressure from the more traditional and ultraorthodox Jews, who push for a nation more reflective of Jewish customs and law (Sela-Sheffy 2004; Third World Institute 2007, 291).

The Intifada

The occupied territories were regarded initially by Israel as a security zone between it and its belligerent neighbors. By the 1980s, however, it was clear that the territories were also serving as the location of new settlements for Jews migrating to Israel, especially from Russia. Palestinians, though enjoying some political and monetary support of Arab nations, saw little likelihood of a successful military effort to eliminate Israel. Therefore, in December 1987, they began the first **Intifada**, the uprising against Israel by the Palestinians in the occupied territories through attacks against soldiers, the boycott of Israeli goods, general strikes, resistance, and noncooperation with Israeli authorities. The target of this first Intifada, lasting five years, was the Israelis.

The Intifada was a grassroots, popular movement whose growth in support was as much a surprise to the Palestine Liberation Organization (PLO) and the Arab nations as it was to Israel and its supporters. The broad range of participants in the Intifada—students, workers, union members, professionals, and business leaders—showed the unambiguous Palestinian opposition to occupation. The Intifada began out of the frustration of the Palestinians within Israeli, but the confrontations were later encouraged by the PLO, an umbrella organization for several Palestinian factions of varying militancy.

With television news footage of Israel soldiers appearing to attack defenseless youths, the Intifada transformed world opinion, especially in the United States. Palestinians came to be viewed as people struggling for self-determination rather than as terrorists out to destroy Israel. Instead of Israel being viewed as the "David" and its Arab neighbors "Goliath," Israel came to take on the bully role and the Palestinians the sympathetic underdog role (Hubbard 1993; Third World Institute 2007).

Intifada
The Palestinian uprising against Israeli authorities in the occupied territories.

The Search for Solutions amid Violence

The 1993 Oslo Accords between Israeli Prime Minister Yitzhak Rabin and PLO Chairman Yasser Arafat and subsequent agreements ended the state of war and appeared to set in motion the creation of the first-ever self-governing Palestinian territory in the Gaza Strip and the West Bank. Hard-liners on both sides, however, grew resistant to the move toward separate recognized Palestinian and Israeli states. Rabin was assassinated at a peace rally by an Israeli who felt the government had given up too much. Succeeding governments in Israel took stronger stands against relinquishing control of the occupied territories. Meanwhile, the anti-Israel Hamas party was elected to power following the death of Arafat in 2004.

Despite the assurances at Oslo, Israel did not end its occupation of the Palestinian territories by 1999, justifying its actions as necessary to stop anti-Israel violence originating in Palestinian settlements. Complicating the picture was the continued growth of 125 officially recognized Israeli settlements in the West Bank, bringing the total population to 230,000 by 2007. Palestinians, assisted by Arabs in other countries, mounted a second Intifada from 2000 through 2004, which was precipitated by the Israeli killing of several Palestinians at a Jerusalem mosque. This time, militant Palestinians went outside the occupied territories and bombed civilian sites in Israel through a series of suicide bombings. Each violent episode brought calls for retaliation by the other side and desperate calls for a cease-fire from outside the region. Israel, despite worldwide denunciation, created a "security barrier" of 30-foot-high concrete walls, ditches, and barbed wire to try to protect its Jewish settlers, which served to limit the mobility of peaceful Palestinians trying to access crops, schools, hospitals, and jobs.

Beginning in 2005, Israel started constructing a 30-foot-high barrier for security purposes, but the wall also served to keep Palestinians from schools and jobs.

The immediate problem is to end the violence, but any lasting peace must face a series of difficult issues, including the following:

- the status of Jerusalem, Israel's capital, which is also viewed by Muslims as the third-most-holy city in the world;
- the future of the Jewish settlements in the West Bank of the Palestinian Authority territories;
- the future of Palestinians and other Arabs with Israeli citizenship;
- the creation of a truly independent Palestinian national state with strong leadership;
- Israel–Palestinian Authority relations, with the latter's government under control of Hamas, which is sworn to Israel's destruction; and
- the future of Palestinian refugees elsewhere.

Added worries are the uneasy peace between Israel and its Arab neighbors and the sometimes interrelated events in Lebanon, Iraq, and Iran (Shafir 2007; Bronner 2008; Third World Institute 2007).

The last 60 years have witnessed significant changes: Israel has gone from a land under siege to a nation whose borders are recognized by almost everyone. Israel has come to terms with the various factions of religious and secular Jews trying to coexist. The Palestinian people have gone from disfranchisement to having territory. The current solution is fragile and very temporary, as is any form of secession with a foundation for accommodation amid continuing violence.

Republic of South Africa

In every nation in the world, some racial, ethnic, or religious groups enjoy advantages denied to other groups. Nations differ in the extent of this denial and in whether it is supported by law or by custom. In no other industrial society has the denial been so entrenched in recent law as in the Republic of South Africa.

The Republic of South Africa is different from the rest of Africa because the original African peoples of the area are no longer present. Today, the country is multiracial, as shown in Table 16.2.

The largest group is the Black Africans who migrated from the north in the eighteenth century as well as more recent migrations from neighboring African countries over the last 20 years. The Coloured (or Cape Coloureds), the product of mixed race, and Asians (or Indians) make up the remaining non-Whites. The small White community consists of the English and the Afrikaners, the latter descended from Dutch and other European

TABLE 16.2
Racial Groups in the Republic of South Africa

	Whites (%)	All Non-Whites (%)	Black Africans (%)	Coloureds (%)	Asian Indians (%)
1904	22	78	67	9	2
1936	21	79	69	8	2
1951	21	79	68	9	3
2007	9	91	80	9	2
2021 (projected)	8	90	80	8	2

Note: "All Non-Whites" totals subject to rounding error.

Sources: Author's estimates, based on Statistics South Africa and Bureau of Market Research in MacFarlane 2006a, 8–9; South African Institute of Race Relations 2007, 6, 12; MacFarlane 2008, 2; van den Berghe 1978, 102.

settlers. As in all other multicultural nations we have considered, colonialism and immigration have left their mark.

The Legacy of Colonialism

The permanent settlement of South Africa by Europeans began in 1652, when the Dutch East India Company established a colony in Cape Town as a port of call for shipping vessels bound for India. The area was sparsely populated, and the original inhabitants of the Cape of Good Hope, the Hottentots and Bushmen, were pushed inland like the indigenous peoples of the New World. To fill the need for laborers, the Dutch imported slaves from areas of Africa farther north. Slavery was confined mostly to areas near towns and involved more limited numbers than in the United States. The Boers, seminomads descended from the Dutch, did not remain on the coast but trekked inland to establish vast sheep and cattle ranches. The *trekkers*, as they were known, regularly fought off the Black inhabitants of the interior regions. Sexual relations between Dutch men and slave and Hottentot women were quite common, giving rise to a mulatto group referred to today as Cape Coloureds.

The British entered the scene by acquiring part of South Africa in 1814, at the end of the Napoleonic Wars. The British introduced workers from India as indentured servants on sugar plantations. They had also freed the slaves by 1834, with little compensation to the Dutch slave owners, and had given Blacks almost all political and civil rights. The Boers were not happy with these developments and spent most of the nineteenth century in a violent struggle with the growing number of English colonists. In 1902, the British finally overwhelmed the Boers, leaving bitter memories on both sides. Once in control, however, they recognized that the superior numbers of the non-Whites were a potential threat to their power, as they had been to the power of the Afrikaners.

The growing non-White population consisted of the Coloureds, or mixed population, and the Black tribal groups, collectively called Bantus. The British gave both groups the vote but restricted the franchise to people who met certain property qualifications. **Pass laws** were introduced, placing curfews on the Bantus and limiting their geographic movement. These laws, enforced through "reference books" until 1986, were intended to prevent urban areas from becoming overcrowded with job-seeking Black Africans, a familiar occurrence in colonial Africa (van den Berghe 1965; A. Marx 1998).

Apartheid

In 1948, South Africa was granted its independence from the United Kingdom, and the National Party, dominated by the Afrikaners, assumed control of the government. Under

pass laws
Laws that controlled internal movement by non-Whites in South Africa.

South Africa employed an explicit system of de jure segregation under apartheid that included spatial separation on trains as shown in these separate entry points in Johannesburg. Whites waited at the front of trains, while Black South Africans waited at the rear.

apartheid
The policy of the South African government intended to maintain separation of Blacks, Coloureds, and Asians from the dominant Whites.

the leadership of this party, the rule of White supremacy, already well under way in the colonial period as custom, became more and more formalized into law. To deal with the multiracial population, the Whites devised a policy called apartheid to ensure their dominance. **Apartheid** (in Afrikaans, the language of the Afrikaners, it means "separation" or "apartness") came to mean a policy of separate development, euphemistically called *multinational development* by the government. At the time, these changes were regarded as cosmetic outside South Africa and by most Black South Africans.

The White ruling class was not homogeneous. The English and Afrikaners belonged to different political parties, lived apart, spoke different languages, and worshipped separately, but they shared the belief that some form of apartheid was necessary. Apartheid can perhaps be best understood as a twentieth-century effort to reestablish the master–slave relationship. Blacks could not vote. They could not move throughout the country freely. They were unable to hold jobs unless the government approved. To work at approved jobs, they were forced to live in temporary quarters at great distances from their real homes. Their access to education, health care, and social services was severely limited (W. Wilson 1973).

Events took a significant turn in 1990, when South African Prime Minister F. W. De Klerk legalized 60 banned Black organizations and freed Nelson Mandela, leader of the African National Congress (ANC), after 27 years of imprisonment. Mandela's triumphant remarks after his release appear in Listen to Our Voices.

The next year, De Klerk and Black leaders signed a National Peace Accord, pledging themselves to the establishment of a multiparty democracy and an end to violence. After a series of political defeats, De Klerk called for a referendum in 1992 to allow Whites to vote on ending apartheid. If he failed to receive popular support, he vowed to resign. A record high turnout gave a solid 68.6 percent vote that favored the continued dismantling of legal apartheid and the creation of a new constitution through negotiation. The process toward power sharing ended symbolically when De Klerk and Mandela were jointly awarded the 1993 Nobel Peace Prize (A. Marx 1998; Ottaway and Taylor 1992; Winant 2001).

The Era of Reconciliation and Moving On

In April 1994, South Africa held its first universal election. Apartheid had ended. Nelson Mandela's ANC received 62 percent of the vote, giving him a five-year term as president. Mandela enjoyed the advantage of wide personal support throughout the nation. He retired in 1999 when his second term ended. His successors have faced a daunting agenda because of the legacy of apartheid.

A significant step to help South Africa move past apartheid was the creation of the Truth and Reconciliation Commission (TRC). People were allowed to come forward and confess to horrors they had committed under apartheid from 1961 through 1993. If they were judged by the TRC to be truly remorseful, and most were, they were not subject to prosecution. If they failed to confess to all crimes they had committed, they were prosecuted. The stories gripped the country as people learned that actions taken in the name of the Afrikaner government were often worse than anyone had anticipated (Gobodo-Madikizela 2003).

The immediate relief that came with the end of apartheid has given way to greater concerns about the future of all South Africans. In Research Focus, we consider the views expressed by contemporary South Africans.

With the emergence of the new multiracial government in South Africa, we see a country with enormous promise but many challenges that are similar to those of our own multiracial society. Some of the controversial issues facing the ANC-led government are very familiar to citizens in the United States.

Desperate poverty: Despite the growth of a small but conspicuous middle class among Black South Africans, poverty rates stand at 60.6 percent, compared to 4.0 percent of White South Africans.

Affirmative action: Race-based employment goals and other preference programs have been proposed, yet critics insist that such efforts constitute reverse apartheid.

Listen to Our Voices

AFRICA, IT IS OURS!

Nelson Mandela

Amandla! Amandla! i-Afrika, mayibuye! [Power! Power! Africa, it is ours!]

My friends, comrades and fellow South Africans, I greet you all in the name of peace, democracy and freedom for all. I stand here before you not as a prophet but as a humble servant of you, the people.

Your tireless and heroic sacrifices have made it possible for me to be here today. I therefore place the remaining years of my life in your hands.

On this day of my release, I extend my sincere and warmest gratitude to the millions of my compatriots and those in every corner of the globe who have campaigned tirelessly for my release.

Negotiations on the dismantling of apartheid will have to address the overwhelming demand of our people for a democratic nonracial and unitary South Africa. There must be an end to white monopoly on political power.

And [there must be] a fundamental restructuring of our political and economic systems to ensure that the inequalities of apartheid are addressed and our society thoroughly democratized. . . .

Our struggle has reached a decisive moment. We call on our people to seize this moment so that the process toward democracy is rapid and uninterrupted. We have waited too long for our freedom. We can no longer wait. Now is the time to intensify the struggle on all fronts.

To relax our efforts now would be a mistake which generations to come will not be able to forgive. The sight of freedom looming on the horizon should encourage us to redouble our efforts. It is only through disciplined mass action that our victory can be assured.

We call on our white compatriots to join us in the shaping of a new South Africa. The freedom movement is the political home for you, too. We call on the international community to continue the campaign to isolate the apartheid regime.

To lift sanctions now would be to run the risk of aborting the process toward the complete eradication of apartheid. Our march to freedom is irreversible. We must not allow fear to stand in our way.

Universal suffrage of a common voters' role in a united democratic and nonracial South Africa is the only way to peace and racial harmony.

In conclusion, I wish to go to my own words during my trial in 1964. They are as true today as they were then. I wrote: I have fought against white domination, and I have fought against black domination. I have cherished the idea of a democratic and free society in which all persons live together in harmony and with equal opportunities.

It is an ideal which I hope to live for and to achieve. But if needs be, it is an ideal for which I am prepared to die.

Source: Mandela 1990. Copyright © 1990 by the New York Times Company. Reprinted by permission of the *New York Times.*

Medical care: The nation is trying to confront the duality of private care for the affluent (usually Whites) and government-subsidized care (usually for people of color). AIDS has reached devastating levels, with 12 percent of the population having HIV or AIDS as of 2008. Half of all deaths result from AIDS.

Crime: Although the government-initiated violence under apartheid has ended, the generations of conflict and years of intertribal attacks have created a climate for crime, illegal gun ownership, and disrespect for law enforcement.

Research Focus

LISTENING TO THE PEOPLE

In the United States, we take for granted the regular release of opinion or survey data about what people think about the sensitive issues in their country. However, public opinion surveying does not typically occur in totalitarian countries such as South Africa under apartheid. Today, surveying is now a regular part of South African life and, not too surprisingly, the subject sometimes turns to race relations.

We can examine national surveys of opinions conducted from 2001 through 2006 to find out what adults from all racial groups thought about racism in everyday life. The data from these studies reveal a racial divide on many issues.

Nearly two-thirds of Black Africans (65 percent) indicated that they felt the country was headed in the right direction, whereas only about one-third (36 percent) of Whites felt the same way.

Black South Africans overwhelmingly see unemployment as the major problem facing the nation, whereas Whites place crime and security as the top problem, with government corruption as number two. Blacks, meanwhile, do not see the government as a problem but give priority to both housing and water supply—two issues not ranked highly by their fellow White citizens. More than 60 percent of Blacks but less than half of Whites feel that relations between groups are improving.

All South Africans—whether Black, Coloured, Indian, or White—agree that democracy is preferable to any other kind of government and that South Africa will remain democratic. Blacks are much more likely to see the gap between the rich and poor as a threat to democracy. Blacks are more likely to see education and health care as improving over the 10 years of post-apartheid South Africa, whereas Whites see it as actually getting worse. Just 19 percent of White respondents, however, said they would consider a return to apartheid.

In summary, the survey revealed deep concerns among all South Africans about a number of social and economic issues, but the specific factor of race is not viewed as the dominant problem. Yet the consciousness of racism has not vanished. The majority still see racism as a serious concern. Yet when asked, they generally see their own group as the victim of racism with little recognition of the problems of prejudice and discrimination facing the other groups.

There seemed little doubt from this survey that, as during the apartheid era, South Africa still has a racial problem to solve.

Sources: Economist 2005a; Kaiser Family Foundation 2004; McGreal 2008; Schlemmer 2001a, 2001b.

School integration: Multiracial schools are replacing the apartheid system, but for some, the change is occurring too fast or not fast enough. Although 15 percent of Whites hold a college degree, only 1.8 percent of Black South Africans are so advantaged.

These issues must be addressed with minimal increases in government spending as the government seeks to reverse deficit spending without an increase in taxes that would frighten away needed foreign investment. As difficult as all these challenges are, perhaps the most difficult is land reform (Kane-Berman 2006; South African Institute of Race Relations 2007; Kaiser Family Foundation 2008).

The government has pledged to address the issue of land ownership. Between 1960 and 1990, the government forced Black South Africans from their land and often allowed Whites to settle on it. Beginning in 1994, the government took steps to transfer 30 percent of agricultural land to Black South Africans. Where feasible, the government plans to restore the original inhabitants to their land; where this is not feasible, the government is to make "just and equitable compensation." By 2007, less than 4 percent of the farmland had been transferred. Overall, White South Africans, who make up less than 9 percent of the population, receive 45 percent of the income. There have been some positive signs. Black South Africans have been able to legally own their own homes since the 1980s; by 2008, almost two-thirds owned their homes. To continue to move past apartheid, many South Africans feel redistribution of wealth needs to occur.

The magnitude of this land reform issue cannot be minimized. Originally, the goal was to achieve the land transfer by 2004, but this has now been deferred to 2015. Certain critics say at the current rate it will take until 2060 to reach the 2004 objective. With its other economic problems and now the decision to invest hundreds of millions of dollars in hosting the 2010 football (soccer) World Cup, more new land is likely to be occupied by Black South Africans through squatter arrangements than through government-approved transfer (Kane-Berman 2008; McGreal 2008).

Conclusion

As shown in the figure below, each society, in its own way, illustrates the processes in the Spectrum of Intergroup Relations first introduced in Chapter 1. The examples range from the Holocaust, which precipitated the emergence of Israel, to the efforts to create a multiracial government in South Africa. A study of these five societies, coupled with knowledge of subordinate groups in the United States, will provide the background from which to draw some conclusions about patterns of race and ethnic relations in the world today.

By looking beyond our borders, we gather new insights into the social processes that frame and define intergroup relationships.

The colonial experience has played a role in all cases under consideration in this chapter but particularly in South Africa. In Mexico and South Africa, which have long histories of multiethnic societies, intergroup sexual relations have been widespread but with different results. Mestizos in Mexico occupy a middle racial group and experience less tension, whereas in South Africa, the Cape Coloureds had freedoms under apartheid almost as limited as those of the Black Africans. South Africa enforced de jure segregation, whereas Israeli communities seem to have de facto segregation. Israel's and South Africa's intergroup conflicts have involved the world community. Indigenous people figure in the

SPECTRUM OF INTERGROUP RELATIONS

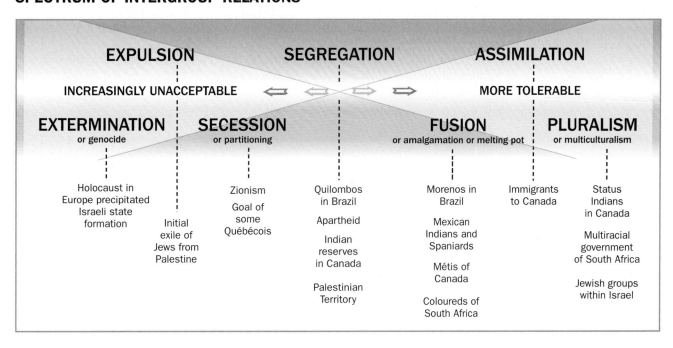

social landscape of Canada, Brazil, and Mexico. Policies giving preference to previously devalued racial groups are in place in both Brazil and South Africa. Complete assimilation is absent in all five societies considered in this chapter and is unlikely to occur in the near future; the legal and informal barriers to assimilation and pluralism vary for subordinate people choosing either option. Looking at the status of women in Mexico reminds us of the worldwide nature of gender stratification and also offers insight into the patterns present in developing nations.

If we add the United States to these societies, the similarities become even more striking. The problems of racial and ethnic adjustment in the United States have dominated our attention, but they parallel past and present experiences in other societies with racial, ethnic, or religious heterogeneity. The U.S. government has been involved in providing educational, financial, and legal support for programs intended to help particular racial or ethnic groups, and it continues to avoid interfering with religious freedom. Bilingual, bicultural programs in schools, autonomy for Native Americans on reservations, and increased participation in decision making by residents of ghettoes and barrios are all viewed as acceptable goals, although they are not pursued to the extent that many subordinate-group people would like.

The analysis of this chapter has reminded us of the global nature of dominant–subordinate relations along dimensions of race, ethnicity, religion, and gender. In the next chapter, we will take an overview of racial and ethnic relations as well as explore social inequality along the dimensions of age, disability status, and sexual orientation.

Summary

1. Mexico's mosaic of mestizos and native indigenous people creates a diversified society with segments of the population that definitely feel disadvantaged and ignored.

2. Canada, with one of the largest proportions of indigenous peoples, continues to develop strategies to promote economic development while preserving cultural traditions. A similar pattern has emerged among the growing immigrant community.

3. The sizable French-speaking population within Canada has asked and receives consideration for its special cultural heritage, which is not fully endorsed by others in the nation.

4. Brazil is not a racial paradise, as has sometimes been suggested, but continues to deal with significant disparity among people of color.

5. Israel has both a significant Arab population and a diverse Jewish community among whom there are sharp political and religious differences.

6. Palestinians in the occupied territories are in a desperate economic situation that has been aggravated by violent divisions within their ranks and by reprisals from Israel in response to attacks from those to within the territories.

7. The apartheid era in South Africa underscores how race can be a tool for total subjugation of millions of people.

8. The South Africa of the post-apartheid era is marked by reconciliation of the different racial groups, which are facing significant issues involving land, education, health, and public safety.

Key Terms

apartheid 394
color gradient 380
Diaspora 389
ethnonational conflict 378
Intifada 391

mestizo 379
mulatto escape hatch 387
pass laws 393
Québécois 383
quilombo 386

visible minorities 384
world systems theory 378
Zionism 389

Review Questions

1. Identify who the native peoples are and what their role has been in each of the societies discussed in this chapter.
2. On what levels can one speak of an identity issue facing Canada as a nation?
3. What role has secession played in Canada and Israel?
4. How have civil uprisings affected intergroup tensions in Mexico and Israel?
5. To what extent are the problems facing Brazil and South Africa today part of the legacy of racial divisions?

Critical Thinking

1. Social construction of race emphasizes how we create arbitrary definitions of skin color that then have social consequences. Drawing on the societies discussed, select one nation and identify how social definitions work in other ways to define group boundaries.
2. Apply the functionalist and conflict approaches of sociology first introduced in Chapter 1 to each of the societies under study in this chapter.
3. The conflicts outlined in this chapter are examples of ethnonational conflicts, but how have the actions or inactions of the United States contributed to these problems?

17

Overcoming Exclusion

THE EXPERIENCE OF SOCIAL DISADVANTAGE IS NOT LIMITED to groups defined by race, ethnicity, gender, or religion. Despite an improving medical and financial situation, the elderly are still as a group at a disadvantage, given the ageism in our society. People with disabilities also have sought to achieve both respect and opportunities. Although the Americans with Disabilities Act (ADA) is a significant step forward, serious advocacy efforts continue. Long-term homophobia has made it a challenge for gays and lesbians to go about their lives. Progress has been mixed; some civil rights legislation has been passed at the local level, but the federal government took positions against avowed homosexuals in the military and sought to prevent legal recognition of gay and lesbian marriage. For each of these groups, as well as the racial and ethnic minorities discussed earlier, it is easy to applaud the progress already made. However, given the level of inequality that still persists, a full agenda for further progress remains.

What metaphor do we use to describe a nation whose racial, ethnic, and religious minorities are on the way to becoming numerical majorities in many cities and, now in the twenty-first century, in several states? For several generations, the image of the melting pot has been used as a convenient description of our culturally diverse nation. The analogy of an alchemist's cauldron was clever, even if a bit ethnocentric. It originated in the Middle Ages, when alchemists used a melting pot to attempt to change less-costly metals into gold and silver.

The Melting Pot was the title of a 1908 play by Israel Zangwill. In this play, a young Russian immigrant to the United States composes a symphony that portrays a nation that serves as a crucible (or pot) where all ethnic and racial groups melt together into a new, superior stock.

The vision of the United States as a melting pot became popular in the first part of the twentieth century, particularly because it suggested that the United States had an almost divinely inspired mission to destroy artificial divisions and create a single humankind. However, the image did not mesh with reality, as the dominant group indicated its unwillingness to welcome Native Americans, African Americans, Hispanics or Latinos, Jews, and Asians, among many others, into the melting pot.

The image of the melting pot is not invoked as much today. Instead, people speak of a salad bowl to describe a country that is ethnically diverse. As we can distinguish the lettuce from the tomatoes from the peppers in a tossed salad, we can see ethnic restaurants and the persistence of foreign languages in conversations on street corners. The dressing over the ingredients is akin to the shared value system and culture, covering but not hiding the different ingredients of the salad.

Yet even the notion of a salad is wilting. Like the melting pot that came before, the image of a salad is static, certainly not indicative of the dynamic changes we see in the United States. It also fails to conjure up the myriad cultural pieces that make up the fabric or mosaic of our diverse nation.

The kaleidoscope offers another familiar and more useful analogy. Patented in 1817 by Scottish scientist Sir David Brewster, the kaleidoscope was a toy and then became a table ornament in the parlors of the rich. Users of this optical device turn a set of mirrors and observe the seemingly endless colors and patterns that are reflected off pieces of glass, tinsel, or beads. The growing popularity of the phrase "people of color" fits well with the idea of the United States as a kaleidoscope. The changing images correspond to the often bewildering array of groups found in our country (Schaefer 1992).

The images created by a kaleidoscope are hard to describe because they change dramatically with little effort. Similarly, in the kaleidoscope of the United States, we find it a challenge to describe the dynamic multiracial nature of this republic. Yet even as we begin to understand the past, present, and future of all the many racial and ethnic groups, we recognize that there are still other people other than racial and ethnic minorities who are stigmatized in society. There are many such groups, such as cancer survivors, ex-convicts, many marginalized religious groups, people with obesity, and transgendered individuals to name a few. We will now consider the cases of the aged, people with disabilities, and the gay and lesbian community.

The Aged: A Social Minority

Older people in the United States are subject to a paradox. They are a significant segment of the population who, as we shall see, often are viewed with negative stereotypes and are subject to discrimination. Yet they also have successfully organized into a potent collective force that wields significant political clout on certain social issues. Unlike other social groups subjected to differential treatment, this social category will include most of us someday. So, in this one case, the notion of the elderly as "them" will eventually give way to "us."

The elderly share the characteristics of subordinate or minority groups that we introduced in Chapter 1. Specifically,

1. the elderly experience unequal treatment in employment and may face prejudice and discrimination;

2. the elderly share physical characteristics that distinguish them from younger people, and their cultural preferences and leisure-time activities often differ from those of the rest of society;

3. membership in this disadvantaged group is involuntary;

4. older people have a strong sense of group solidarity, as reflected in senior citizen centers, retirement communities, and advocacy organizations; and

5. older people generally are married to others of comparable age.

There is one crucial difference between older people and other subordinate groups, such as racial and ethnic minorities or women: all of us who live long will eventually assume the ascribed status of being an older person (Barron 1953; Wagley and Harris 1958).

Who Are the Elderly?

As shown in Figure 17.1, an increasing proportion of the population will be composed of older people. This trend is expected to continue well through the twenty-first century as mortality declines and the postwar baby boomers age. While the elderly population continues to increase, the "oldest old" segment of the population (i.e., people 85 years old and over) is growing at an even faster rate.

Compared with the rest of the population, the elderly are more likely to be female, White, and living in certain states. Men generally have higher death rates than women at every age. As a result, elderly women outnumber men by a ratio of 3 to 2. The difference grows with advancing age, so that among the oldest old group, women outnumber men 5 to 2. About 80 percent of the elderly are White and non-Hispanic. Although the aged population is growing more racially and ethnically diverse, the higher death rates of members of racial and ethnic minorities, coupled with immigration to the United States of younger Latinos and Asians, are likely to keep the older population more White than the nation as a whole. Yet the overall pattern of a more diversified population will also be present among our oldest Americans. As seen in projections in Figure 17.2, the population aged 65 and over will become increasingly non-White and Latino.

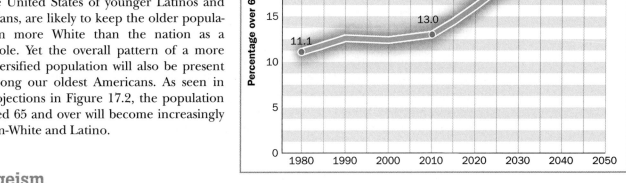

FIGURE 17.1

Actual and Projected Growth of the Elderly Population of the United States, 1980–2050

Sources: Bureau of the Census 2007a, 10; 2008d; Meyer 2001; Sutch and Carter 2006.

Ageism

Respected gerontologist Bernice Neugarten (1996) observed that negative stereotypes of old age are strongly entrenched in a society

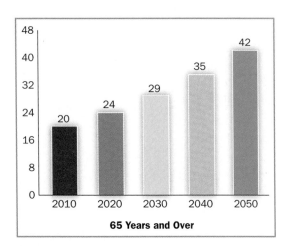

FIGURE 17.2
Minority Population Aged 65 and Older Projected
Source: Bureau of the Census 2008d.

that prides itself on being oriented toward youth and the future. In 1968, physician Robert Butler, the founding director of the National Institute on Aging, coined the term **ageism** to refer to prejudice and discrimination against the elderly. Ageism reflects a deep uneasiness among young and middle-aged people about growing old. For many, old age symbolizes disease and death; seeing the elderly serves as a reminder that they too may someday become old and infirm. By contrast, society glorifies youth, seeing it as interchangeable with beauty and the future. Ageism is so common that Robert Butler (1990, 178) notes that it "knows no one century, nor culture, and is not likely to go away any time soon."

How widespread is ageism? One study showed that based on a photograph alone, college students readily saw a 25-year-old-male potential job holder as active and powerful but a 73-year-old man as sickly, slow, and unreliable. In the 2008 presidential election, the age of 72-year-old John McCain served as a factor in some people's minds about his competency. Criticisms of him as "confused" and "losing his bearings" were used, according to some observers, as code words for him being "just too old" (Levin 1988; Nagourney 2008).

The federal Age Discrimination in Employment Act (ADEA), which went into effect in 1968, was passed to protect workers 40 years of age or older from being fired because of their age and replaced with younger workers who presumably would receive lower salaries. The Supreme Court strengthened federal protection against age discrimination in 1996, ruling unanimously that such lawsuits can be successful even if an older worker is replaced by someone older than 40. Consequently, if a firm unfairly fires a 65-year-old employee to make way for a 45-year-old, this still can constitute age discrimination.

Research shows that before the enactment of the ADEA, there was evidence of hiring discrimination against older workers as well as discrimination in promotions and training. Even with the ADEA, age continues to work against many older people as evidenced by how long it takes them to find employment, the wage loss they experience when they do become reemployed, and the size of court awards to victims of age discrimination (He et al. 2005).

Although firing workers simply because they are old violates federal law, courts have upheld the right to lay off older workers for economic reasons. Critics contend that later the same firms hire younger, cheaper workers to replace experienced older workers. When economic growth began to slow in 2001 and companies cut back on their workforces, complaints of age bias grew sharply as older workers began to suspect they were bearing a disproportionate share of the layoffs. According to the Equal Employment Opportunity Commission, between 1999 and 2004, complaints of age discrimination rose more than 41 percent. However, evidence of a countertrend has emerged. Some firms have been giving larger raises to older workers to encourage their retirement at the higher salary—a tactic that prompts younger workers to complain of age discrimination (Novelli 2004; Uchitelle 2003).

Yet in contradiction to these negative stereotypes present in an ageist society, researchers have found that an older worker can be an asset for employers. One study concluded that older workers can be retrained in new technologies, have lower rates of absenteeism than younger employees, and often are more effective salespeople. The study focused on two corporations based in the United States (the hotel chain Days Inns of America and the holding company Travelers Corporation of Hartford) and a British retail chain, all of which have long-term experience in hiring workers age 50 and over. Clearly, the findings pointed to older workers as good investments. Yet despite such studies, complaints of age bias grew during the economic slowdown beginning in 2001, when companies cut back on their workforces (Equal Employment Opportunity Commission 2001; Telsch 1991, A16).

The courts have made some significant decisions favoring older workers. In 2008, the Supreme Court ruled 7–1 in *Meachan v. Knolls Atomic Power Laboratory* that employers under ADEA had the burden to prove laying off older workers was based not on age but

ageism
Prejudice and discrimination against the elderly.

Research Focus

PASSING ON THE OLD JOB APPLICANT

People continue to worry about the stability of the Social Security system. Indeed the chairman of the Federal Reserve Board suggested that encouraging older workers to work could reduce the problem. Is it easy for older people to find work?

Economist Johanna Lahey tried to assess labor market opportunities for women at different ages. Similar resumes were sent to employers seeking entry-level workers (such as clerical positions) in Boston and St. Petersburg, Florida, seeking interviews. The results were striking. A younger worker was 42 percent more likely to be offered an interview in Massachusetts and 46 percent more so in Florida.

Speculating on why the older applicant had difficulty getting an interview, Lahey decided to make the older applicant look more desirable. For example, the older person's application included the following additions:

- a statement that the applicant is willing to embrace change,
- an attendance award,
- a certificate of recent completion of a computer course, and
- an indication that the applicant already has health insurance.

Although these "extras" might be seen as heading off any appearance that a 62-year-old would be inflexible, undependable, out of touch, or an insurance risk, the call-back rate was still unaffected.

Future research is desirable, but the study mirrored the results of one two decades earlier that shows younger applicants are significantly more welcomed in the job market than are older job seekers.

Source: Bendick et al. 1993; Lahey 2006; Lohr 2008.

"some reasonable factor." In this instance, the employer had stated that the older workers were less "flexible" or "retrainable" but failed to present any convincing basis for their layoffs, which affected 31 employees—30 of whom were old enough to be covered by ADEA (Greenhouse 2008).

So, given these legislative and legal advances, has the climate changed significantly for treating older workers without bias? In Research Focus, we consider an effort to assess ageism in hiring.

A degree of conflict is emerging along generational lines that resembles other types of intergroup tension. Although the conflict involves neither violence nor the degree of subjugation found with other dominant–subordinate relations in the United States, a feeling still prevails that jobs and benefits for the elderly are at the expense of younger generations. Younger people are increasingly unhappy about paying Social Security taxes and underwriting the Medicare program, especially because they speculate that they themselves will never receive benefits from these fiscally insecure programs.

The Economic Picture

The elderly, like the other groups we have considered, do not form a single economic profile. The perception of "elderly" and "poor" as practically synonymous has changed in recent years to a view that the noninstitutionalized elderly are economically better off than the population as a whole. Both views are too simplistic; income varies widely among the aged.

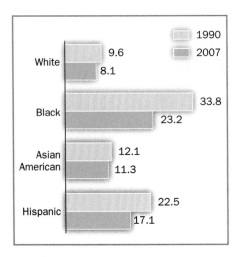

FIGURE 17.3
Poverty Rate among the Elderly, 2007
Note: Data for Whites are for White non-Hispanics.
Source: DeNavas-Walt et al. 2008, 53–57.

There is significant variation in wealth and poverty among the nation's older people. Some individuals and couples find themselves poor in part because of fixed pensions and skyrocketing health care costs. As shown in Figure 17.3, poverty has declined among the elderly of all racial groups.

As a group, older people in the United States are neither homogeneous nor poor. The typical elderly person enjoys a standard of living that is much higher than at any point in the nation's past. Class differences among the elderly tend to narrow somewhat: retirees who had middle-class incomes while younger tend to remain better off after retirement than those who had lower incomes, but the financial gap is declining (He et al. 2005).

The decline in poverty rates is welcome. However, advocates of the position that the elderly are receiving too much at the expense of the younger generations point to the rising affluence of the aged as evidence of an unfair economic burden placed on the young and future generations of workers.

As we can see in the previously mentioned data, the aged who are most likely to experience poverty are the same people more likely to be poor earlier in their lives: female-headed households and racial and ethnic minorities. Although overall the aged are doing well economically, poverty remains a particularly difficult problem for the thousands of elderly who are impoverished annually by paying for long-term medical care (Quadagno 2008).

Advocacy Efforts by the Elderly

As we have seen with racial, ethnic, and gender groups, efforts to bring about desired change often require the formation of political organizations and advocacy groups. This is true with the elderly and, as we will see later, is also true for people with disabilities, gay men, and lesbian women. One such group working on behalf of the elderly is the Gray Panthers. As of 2004, this organization had 40,000 members in 32 states and five foreign countries working to combat prejudice and discrimination against older people. In early 1995, Maggie Kuhn, the best known of the Gray Panthers' founders, died at age 89. Kuhn had spent the last 25 years of her life as a leader in the battle against ageism and other forms of injustice. Her desire to create an advocacy group of the elderly began when she was forced to retire at age 65 from her position on a church staff. Only two weeks before her death, she joined striking transit workers on a picket line (Folkart 1995; Gale 2004; R. Thomas 1995).

The growing collective consciousness among older people also contributed to the establishment of the Older Women's League (OWL) in 1980. OWL focuses on access to health insurance, Social Security benefits, and pension reform. OWL leaders and the group's 15,000 members hope that the organization will serve as a critical link between the feminist movement described in Chapter 15 and activists for "gray power" (Kening 2004).

The largest organization representing the nation's elderly is the American Association of Retired Persons (AARP), which was founded in 1958 by a retired school principal who was having difficulty obtaining insurance because of age prejudice. Many of AARP's services involve discounts and insurance for its 35 million members (44 percent of Americans aged 50 or older). After recognizing that many elderly are still gainfully employed, the full name was dropped and the organization is now simply AARP.

The potential power of AARP is enormous; it represents one out of every four registered voters in the United States. AARP has endorsed voter-registration campaigns, nursing home reforms, and pension reforms. Acknowledging its difficulties in recruiting members of racial and ethnic minority groups, AARP began a Minority Affairs Initiative. The spokeswoman for this initiative, Margaret Dixon, became AARP's first African American president in 1996 (AARP 2003).

People grow old in many different ways. Not all the elderly face the same challenges or enjoy the same resources. Whereas AARP lobbies to protect the elderly in general, other groups work in more specific ways. For example, the National Committee to Preserve Social Security and Medicare, founded in 1982, unsuccessfully lobbied Congress to keep Medicare benefits for the ailing poor elderly. Other large special-interest groups represent retired federal employees, retired teachers, and retired union workers (Quadagno 2008).

The elderly in the United States are better off today financially and physically than ever before. Many of them have strong financial assets and medical care packages that will take care of almost any need. But, as we have seen, a significant segment is impoverished and faces the prospect of declining health and mounting medical bills. Older people of color may have to add being aged to a lifetime of discrimination. As in all other stages of the life course, the aged constitute a diverse group in the United States and around the world.

Although organizations such as the Gray Panthers, OWL, and AARP are undoubtedly valuable, the diversity of the nation's older population necessitates many different responses to the problems of the elderly. For example, older African Americans and Hispanics tend to rely more on family members, friends, and informal social networks than on organizational support systems. Because of their lower incomes and greater incapacity resulting from poor health, older Blacks and Hispanics are more likely to need substantial assistance from family members than are older Whites. In recent years, older people of color have emerged as a distinct political force, independent of the larger elderly population, in some urban centers and in the Southwest. Advocacy groups for the aged are still in their early stages, and low-income elderly often are the least represented (Achenbaumm 1993; Neugarten 1996; Schaefer 2007).

People with Disabilities: Moving On

George Lane was scheduled to appear in court in September 1997 because of a reckless driving misdemeanor charge after an accident that left him unable to walk. Arriving at the Polk County, Tennessee, courthouse, he found that the courtroom was on the second floor in a building without an elevator. The court refused to make any allowance, so he dragged himself up the steps only to learn the case had been postponed. Refusing to repeat the experience at the next hearing date, Lane was forced to have his attorney shuttle information back and forth from the courtroom. The court felt it was not obligated to make any accommodation to his disability; seven years later, the Supreme Court disagreed, ruling 5–4 that Lane's rights had been denied (Greenhouse 2004).

Throughout history, people have been socially disadvantaged, not because of the limits of their own skills and abilities but because assumptions are made about them based on some group characteristics. People with disabilities are such a group. The very term *disabilities* suggests lack of ability in some area, but as we shall see, society often assumes

People with disabilities are no longer willing to keep out of sight and are prepared to become fully functioning members of society as reflected in this young woman doing the club scene in Los Angeles.

disability
Reduced ability to perform tasks one would normally do at a given stage in life.

that a person with a disability is far less capable than she or he is. Furthermore, society limits the life chances of people with disabilities in ways that are unnecessary and unrelated to any physical infirmity.

Disability in Contemporary Society

Societies have always had members with disabilities. Historically, they have dealt differently with people who had physical or mental limitations, but rarely have they been treated as equals. According to the Bureau of the Census, an estimated 41.4 million people had a disability in 2006, or more than one in eight in the population. **Disability** is considered a reduced ability to perform tasks one would normally do at a given stage in life. This includes everyone from those who have difficulty carrying 10 pounds to people who use wheelchairs, crutches, or walkers (Bureau of the Census 2007b, Table C18001).

We often marginalize people with disabilities, but many individuals have accomplished much in their lives. As we can see in Table 17.1, some people's disabilities are well known, while others' go largely unnoticed.

TABLE 17.1

Can you match the person with the disability? All the famous people listed in this table have at least one disability. Match each person with one or more disabilities, then check your answers below.

Match the letters in Column A with the names in Column B.

Column A	Column B
A. Blind	_____ Stevie Wonder
B. Learning disability	_____ Michael J. Fox
C. Polio	_____ Beethoven
D. Epilepsy	_____ Tom Cruise
E. Dwarfism	_____ Patrick Dempsey
F. Parkinson's disease	_____ Napoleon
G. Quadriplegic	_____ Sting
H. Deaf	_____ Franklin Delano Roosevelt
I. Stuttering	_____ John Mellencamp
J. HIV–AIDS	_____ Christopher Reeve
K. Multiple sclerosis	_____ "Mini-me" Verne Troyer
L. Attention deficit disorder	_____ Homer
M. Cancer	_____ James Earl Jones
N. Spina bifida	_____ Frida Kahlo
O. Bipolar disorder	_____ Montel Williams
	_____ Steven Speilberg
	_____ John Lennon
	_____ Jay Leno
	_____ Axl Rose
	_____ Charles Schwab
	_____ Robin Williams
	_____ Lance Armstrong
	_____ Magic Johnson
	_____ Bruce Willis

Source: Author, based on Meyer 2007.
Answers: Wonder A, Fox F, Beethoven H, Cruise B, Dempsey B, Napoleon N, Sting BL, Roosevelt C, Mellencamp B, Reeves G, Mini-me E, Homer A, Jones I, Kahlo CN, Montel Williams K, Spielberg B, Lennon L, Leno I, Rose BL, Schwab B, Williams LO, Armstrong M, Johnson J, Willis L

Disabilities are found in all segments of the population, but racial and ethnic minorities are disproportionately more likely to experience them and also to have less access to assistance. Fewer African Americans and Hispanic people with disabilities are graduating from college compared with White people with disabilities. They also have incomes consistently lower than their White counterparts (Steinmetz 2006).

Although disability knows no social class, about two-thirds of working-age people with a disability in the United States are unemployed. African Americans and Hispanics with disabilities are even more likely to be jobless. Most of them believe that they would be able to work if they were offered the opportunity or if some reasonable accommodation could be made to address the disability (Kirkpatrick 1994; Noble 1995; Shapiro 1993).

Labeling the Disabled

Labeling theorists, drawing on the work of sociologist Erving Goffman (1963), suggest that society attaches a stigma to many forms of disability and that this stigma leads to prejudicial treatment. Indeed, people with disabilities often observe that people without disabilities see them only as blind, deaf, wheelchair users, and so forth, rather than as complex human beings with individual strengths and weaknesses whose blindness or deafness is merely one aspect of their lives.

In Listen to Our Voices, poet Lynn Manning discusses both the subtle and the more overt ways society assigns labels to people with disabilities and the special input it has on an African American male.

In this regard, a review of studies of women with disabilities disclosed that most academic research on people with disabilities does not even differentiate by gender, thereby perpetuating the view that when a disability is present, no other personal characteristic can matter. When gender differences are recognized, such recognition may deny a person's dignity. One study found that women with disabilities were more likely to be discouraged from having children and much more likely to be advised to have hysterectomies than women without disabilities but with similar medical conditions (Fine and Asch 1981, 1988a, 1988b; Gove 1980; Karkabi 1993).

A significant stigma is attached to having a major visible disability. Not wishing to present an image of a "disabled" president, Franklin Roosevelt enlisted the cooperation of the press corps to avoid being shown in a wheelchair or using crutches. This picture shows the president leaving a New York City townhouse in 1933, with a rare view of the president's leg braces.
Source: © New York Daily News, L. P. Reprinted with permission.

As with other subordinate statuses, the mass media have contributed to the stereotyping of people with disabilities. Too often, they are treated with a mixture of pity and fear. Nationwide charity telethons promote a negative image of people with disabilities as being childlike and nonproductive, suggesting that until they are "cured," they cannot contribute to society like other people. At the very least, the poster-child image proclaims that it is not okay to have a disability. By contrast, in literature and film, evil characters with disabilities—from Captain Hook to Dr. Strangelove to Freddy Krueger—reinforce the view that disability is a punishment for evil. Efforts to encourage sober driving or safety in the workplace use images of people with disabilities to frighten people into the appropriate behavior.

Negative attitudes are not the only challenge facing people with disabilities. Among men and women with any kind of disability, 60 percent are employed, compared to 81 percent without a disability. Even for those employed, research shows that people with disabilities are often marginalized, devalued, and even harassed (Robert and Harlan 2006; Steinmetz 2006, 25).

Through institutional discrimination, society is sometimes organized in a way that limits people with disabilities. Architectural barriers and transportation difficulties often add to the problems of people with disabilities when they seek and obtain employment.

Listen to Our Voices

THE MAGIC WAND

Quick-change artist extraordinaire,
I whip out my folded cane
and change from black man
to blind man
    With a flick of my wrist.
    It is a profound
metamorphosis—
    From God-gifted wizard of
roundball
    dominating backboards
across America
    To God-gifted idiot savant
    Pounding out chart-busters on a cock-
eyed whim;
    From sociopathic gangbanger with
death for eyes
    to all-seeing soul with saintly spirit;

Lynn Manning

From rape driven misogynist
to poor motherless child;
From welfare-rich pimp
to disability-rich gimp;
And from "white man's burden"
to every man's burden.
    It is always a profound meta-
morphosis.
    Whether from cursed by man
to cursed by God;
    or from a scripture-condemned
to God-ordained,
    my final form is never of my
choosing;
    I only wield the wand;
    You are the magicians.

Source: Manning 1997.

Simply getting around city streets can be quite difficult for people with mobility challenges. Many streets are not properly equipped with curb cuts for wheelchair users. A genuinely barrier-free building needs more than a ramp; it should also include automatic doors, raised letters and Braille on signs, and toilets that are accessible to people with disabilities. Even if a person with disabilities finds a job, and even if the job is in a barrier-free building, he or she still faces the problem of getting to work in a society in which many rail stations and most buses remain inaccessible to wheelchair users and others with disabilities.

For so many people with disabilities, it is not just a glass ceiling they face; they are even refused entrance through the door. They face challenges to being taken seriously as job applicants, and research shows that the problems intensify further for members with disabilities of racial and ethnic minorities. The Glass Ceiling Commission took a special look at employment opportunities for people with disabilities who are also members of racial and ethnic minorities. The analysis revealed that White people with disabilities are twice as likely to be employed full-time as African American or Hispanic people with disabilities. The primary reason for this is that minorities with disabilities experience dual sources of discrimination: subordinate-group status as a member of a minority race and having a disability. The negative stereotype of having disabilities is added on top of the stereotypes associated with racial and ethnic minorities (Braddock and Bachelder 1994).

Advocacy for Disability Rights

Until recently, people with disabilities as a group have scarcely been thought of in any terms except perhaps pity. Often history has forgotten how deep the mistreatment has been. There has been a steadily growing effort to ensure not only the survival of people with disabilities but also the same rights enjoyed by others. In the early 1960s, Ed Roberts and some other young adults with disabilities wanted to attend the University of California at Berkeley. Reluctant at first, the university was eventually persuaded to admit them and agreed to reserve space in the university infirmary as living quarters for students with disabilities. These students and others established their own student center and became known as the Rolling Quads. They eventually turned their attention to the surrounding community and established the Berkeley Center for Independent Living, which became a model for hundreds of independent living centers (Brannon 1995).

By the early 1970s, following the example of the Rolling Quads, a strong social movement for disability rights had emerged across the United States, which drew on the experiences of the Black civil rights movement and the feminist movement. This movement now includes a variety of organizations; some work on behalf of people with a single disability (such as the National Federation of the Blind), and others represent people with any of many disabilities (such as New York City's Disabled in Action). The large number of Vietnam veterans with disabilities who joined the effort gave a boost to advocacy efforts and a growing legitimacy in larger society.

Many of these organizations worked for the 1990 passage of the Americans with Disabilities Act (ADA). In many respects, this law is the most sweeping antidiscrimination legislation since the 1964 Civil Rights Act. The ADA went into effect in 1992, covering people with a disability, defined as a condition that "substantially limits" a "major life activity" such as walking or seeing. It prohibits bias in employment, transportation, public accommodations, and telecommunication against people with disabilities. Businesses with more than 15 employees cannot refuse to hire a qualified applicant with a disability; these companies are expected to make a "reasonable accommodation" to permit such a worker to do the job. Commercial establishments such as office buildings, hotels, theaters, supermarkets, and dry cleaners are barred from denying service to people with disabilities (Burgdorf, Jr. 2005).

The ADA represents a significant framing of the issues of people with disabilities. Basically, we can see it taking a civil rights view of disabilities that seeks to humanize the way society sees and treats people with disabilities. The ADA does not take the perspective adopted in other nations, such as Great Britain, of seeing disability as totally an entitlement issue; that is, because you have a disability, you automatically receive certain benefits. Rather, its perspective is that people with disabilities are being denied certain rights. As disability rights activist Mark Johnson said, "Black people fought for the right to ride in the front of the bus. We're fighting for the right to get on the bus" (Shapiro 1993, 128; also see Albrecht 2005; Burgdorf 2005).

A more specific concern relevant to people with disabilities has arose at Gallaudet University, the school founded in 1864 to serve deaf students. This institution located in the

visitability
Building private homes to be accessible for visitors with disabilities.

District of Columbia has been the scene of unrest during the last 20 years concerning the selection of its president. For many students and sympathetic supporters, the president of this institution must not only be deaf but also embrace the primacy of American Sign Language (ASL). First in 1988 and then again 2006, students mounted "Deaf President Now" campaigns after presidents were proposed who were not "deaf enough" because they relied too much on reading lips or spoke without using ASL. The disability rights movement has caused people both with and without disabilities to rethink what constitutes fairness and equity (Basken 2007).

Rethinking the rights of people with disabilities began with the ADA but has now come with the call for visitability. **Visitability** refers to making private homes built so that they are accessible for visitors with disabilities. In the mid-1990s, cities such as Atlanta and Austin, Texas, as well as Great Britain passed ordinances encouraging new homes to have at least one no-step entrance, wider doorways, grab bars in bathrooms, and other accommodations. This new idea suggests that all environments should be accessible—not just public places, such as courtrooms or token handicapped-accessible accommodations in hotels, but all living spaces. Many people oppose such a move as unnecessary government interference; others see it as a long-overdue recognition that people with disabilities should be able to move freely throughout the country (Buchholz 2003; Visitability 2008).

Activists remain encouraged since the passage of the ADA. Long-time activists have been joined in their continuing efforts for disability rights by those working on behalf of the veterans of the Iraq and Afghanistan wars who have returned with significant disabilities. Although the ADA has been in effect for less than two decades, studies reveal that people with disabilities feel empowered and perceive increased access to employment opportunities. However, one must remember that civil rights activists felt a measure of optimism after passage of the major civil rights legislation more than 40 years ago (Albrecht 2005; Meyer 2008).

Gays and Lesbians: Coming Out for Equality

When and how did you first realize you were a heterosexual?

What do you think caused your heterosexuality?

Is it possible that your heterosexuality is just a phase you may grow out of?

Why are heterosexuals so promiscuous?

These are not questions heterosexuals are likely to hear being asked because these queries assume something is wrong with being attracted to members of the opposite sex. On the other hand, we are all accustomed to hearing homosexuals questioned about their orientation.

Homosexuality has been forbidden in most periods of Western history, but it has not always been a social issue. For example, at certain times in many societies, it was possible to acknowledge same-sex love and act on it without necessarily encountering open hostility. Yet in general, societies have barely tolerated people who have sexual intimacy in any manner other than heterosexual.

The focus in this chapter is on differential treatment because one is a homosexual—that is, gay or lesbian—but human sexuality is very diverse. Yet typically in the United States, sexual orientation is constructed as either homosexual or heterosexual and ignores people who are *bisexuals*—that is, individuals sexually attracted to both sexes. Sometimes included in discussions about gays, lesbians, and bisexuals are *transgendered persons*—people whose gender identity does not match their physical identity at birth; transgender individuals, for example, may see themselves as both male and female. *Transexuals* are people who see themselves as the sex opposite of their birth identity and may take surgical measures to bring their physical being closer to their gender identity. Sometimes confused with these issues of gender identity and sexual orientation are *transvestites*, which today usually refers to cross-dressers who wear clothing of the opposite sex. These are typically men choosing to wear women's clothing, who may be either gay or heterosexual in their orientation.

Being Gay and Lesbian in the United States

There are anecdotal accounts of public recognition of homosexuality throughout U.S. history, but it was not until the 1920s and 1930s that it became visible. By that time, clubs for gays and lesbians were growing in number, typically in urban areas. Plays, books, and organizations were created to meet the social needs of gays and lesbians. As homosexuality has become more visible, efforts to suppress it have been institutionalized. At about the same time, the U.S. Army hired psychiatrists to screen recruits for evidence of homosexuality and dismissed volunteers who were gay (P. Schwartz 1992).

The studies published by Alfred Kinsey and his research group (1948, 1953) shocked the general public when they documented that almost half of all men had had same-sex fantasies and that about one-third had experienced a homosexual encounter after childhood. Although women reported less homosexual activity, the very fact that lesbian behavior was even raised in a national discussion was unprecedented. The Kinsey reports also launched a public debate about the number of homosexuals in the United States.

Given that gay men and lesbians are severely stigmatized, accurate data are hard to obtain. Researchers for the National Health and Life Survey and the Voter News Service in their election exit polls estimate that 2 percent to 5 percent of U.S. adults identify themselves as gay or lesbian. An analysis of the 2005 American Community Survey of the Bureau of the Census estimates at least 777,000 gay households and a gay and lesbian population around 8.8 million. Although these numbers are estimates, virtually all

All students wish to take advantage of what college life offers. Sigma Phi Beta was organized in 2001 for gay college students. Here are members of the chapter at Arizona State University.

researchers agree that the numbers are rising or, at the very least, the number of people who are reporting they are gay is rising (Dang and Frazer 2004; Gates 2006; Laumann et al. 1994; Romero et al. 2007).

Discussion and growing recognition of a sizable gay population did not lead to a consistent effort to promote understanding over the last 60 years. The general focus was to explore ways to prevent and control homosexuality as a disease, which is what psychiatrists thought it was. Well into the 1960s, discrimination against gays and lesbians was common and legal. Bars frequented by people seeking same-sex partners were raided by police and people were jailed, their names often published in local newspapers. Although not surprising, it was disappointing to hear that the county board in Rhea County, Tennessee, passed unanimously a measure in 2004 that allowed the county to prosecute someone for being gay or lesbian as a "crime against nature." A few days later, after recognizing the losing court battle they would face, the county commissioners rescinded the antigay motion, but clearly they did not take back their view of gays and lesbians (Barry 2004).

Prejudice and Discrimination

Homophobia, the fear of and prejudice toward homosexuality, is present in every facet of life: the family, organized religion, the workplace, official policies, and the mass media. Like the myths and stereotypes of race and gender, those about homosexuality keep gay men and lesbian women oppressed as a group and may also keep sympathetic members of the dominant group, the heterosexual community, from joining in support.

Homophobia is considered a much more respectable form of bigotry than voicing negative feelings and ideas against any other oppressed groups. People still openly avoid homosexuals, and group members are stereotyped on television and in motion pictures. Although homophobia has decreased, many people still feel at ease in expressing their homophobic feelings that a homosexual lifestyle is unacceptable.

homophobia
The fear of and prejudice toward homosexuality.

As we will see later, gays and lesbians have made extensive efforts to make their feelings known, to ask for respect and a variety of rights, and to have their sexual orientation accepted. Their efforts seem to have had some impact on public opinion. In 2008, 55 percent of the public felt that homosexual relations should be legal—a modest increase since 1977, when it was 43 percent. Yet there is a recognition that homosexual men and women should have equal rights in terms of job opportunities. This support has increased to 89 percent in 2008, compared with 56 percent in 1977 (Saad 2008).

The entertainment business is often seen as being welcoming to openly gay and lesbian performers. The reality appears to be different. Although openly gay actors and actresses find employment, starring roles are few and far between. Furthermore, highly visible roles of gay individuals are generally played by heterosexual actors, such as Sean Penn playing the title role in the 2008 motion picture *Milk*, which chronicles the life of Harvey Milk, the first openly gay man to be elected to office in California (Navarro 2008).

The stigmatization of gays and lesbians was seen as a major factor in the slow initial response to the presence of AIDS (acquired immunodeficiency syndrome), which, when it first appeared in the United States, overwhelmingly claimed gay men as its victims. The inattention and the reluctance to develop a national policy forced gay communities in major cities to establish self-help groups to care for the sick, educate the healthy, and lobby for more responsive public policies. The most outspoken AIDS activist group has been the AIDS Coalition to Unleash Power (ACT-UP), which has conducted controversial protests and sit-ins in the halls of government and at scientific conferences. Although initially such efforts may have siphoned away participants from the broader gay rights effort, ultimately, new constituencies of gay men and lesbians were created, along with alliances with sympathetic supporters from the heterosexual community (Adam 1995; Shilts 1982).

In 1998, the nation was shocked by the unprovoked, brutal murder of Matthew Shepard, a University of Wyoming student, by two men. Subsequent investigation showed that Shepard's being gay was the reason his attackers murdered him rather than leaving him alone after robbing the young man. This tragic event galvanized a move to include sexual orientation as a basis of hate crimes in many states. Gays and lesbians themselves began to actively resist their mistreatment, sometimes working with local law enforcement agencies and prosecutors to end antigay violence. Many activists bemoaned the fact that in 2008, the tenth anniversary of Matthew's slaying, there was still no memorial and no antigay violence law in Wyoming (Healy 2008).

Advocacy for Gay and Lesbian Rights

The first homosexual organization in the United States was founded in Chicago in 1924. Such groups grew steadily over the next 50 years, but they were primarily local and were more likely to be self-help and social rather than confrontational. The social movements of the 1950s and 1960s on behalf of African Americans and women caused lesbians and gay men also to reflect more directly on the oppression their sexual orientation caused.

The contemporary gay and lesbian movement marks its beginning in New York City on June 28, 1969. Police raided the Stonewall Inn, an after-hours gay bar, and forced patrons into the street. Instead of meekly dispersing and accepting the disruption, the patrons locked police inside the bar and rioted until police reinforcements arrived. For the next three nights, lesbians and gay men marched through the streets of New York, protesting police raids and other forms of discrimination. Within months, gay liberation groups appeared in cities and campuses throughout the United States (Armstrong and Crage 2006).

Despite the efforts of the lesbian and gay rights movement, in 1986 the Supreme Court in *Bowers v. Hardwick* ruled by a 5–4 vote that the Constitution does not protect homosexual relations between consenting adults, even in the privacy of their own homes. This position held until the Court reversed itself in 2003 by a 6–3 vote in *Lawrence v. Texas*.

The divisiveness of the issue nationally was reflected among the justices. Justice Anthony Kennedy declared that gays are "entitled to respect for their private lives" while Justice Antonio Scalia complained that the decision indicated that the Court had "largely signed on to the so-called homosexual agenda" (Duberman 1993; Humphreys 1972; Moser 2005).

In 2000, the Supreme Court hurt the gay rights movement when it ruled 5–4 that the Boy Scouts organization had a constitutional right to exclude gay members because opposition to homosexuality was part of the organization's message. The Court clearly stated in its ruling that it was not endorsing this view but supporting the right of the organization to hold this position and to limit participation based on it. Despite this and earlier Supreme Court decisions, gays and lesbians worked to establish the principle that sexual orientation should not be the basis for discrimination.

Issues involving gays and lesbians have always been present, but because of advocacy efforts, the concerns are being advanced by political leaders and the courts. In 1993, President Bill Clinton, under pressure from the gay community, reviewed the prohibition of homosexuals from the military. However, he encountered even greater pressure from opponents and eventually compromised in 1994 with the "Don't ask, don't tell" policy. The policy allows lesbians and gay men to continue to serve in the military as long as they keep their homosexuality secret, but commanders can still investigate and dismiss military personnel if they find any evidence that they have committed homosexual acts. Indeed, according to a 2008 report, the military discharged two service members every day (Stone 2008).

For many gay and lesbian couples, the inability to have their relationships recognized legally is the most personal restriction they have to face. Several dozen cities have begun to recognize **domestic partnerships**, defined as two unrelated adults who have chosen to share one another's lives in a relationship of mutual caring, who reside together and agree to be jointly responsible for their dependents, basic living expenses, and other common necessities. Domestic partnership benefits can apply to inheritance, parenting, pensions, taxation, housing, immigration, workplace fringe benefits, and health care. Although the advocacy efforts for legally recognizing domestic partnerships have come from the lesbian and gay community, the majority of the relationships that would benefit would be cohabiting heterosexual couples.

The most vocal debate is over whether gay and lesbian couples should be able to legally get married. Congress enacted the Defense of Marriage Act in 1996, which

domestic partnership
Two unrelated adults who have chosen to share one another's lives in a relationship of mutual caring, who reside together, and who agree to be jointly responsible for their dependents, basic living expenses, and other common necessities.

SEPARATE BUT EQUAL

A continuing social issue at the local, state, and national levels is whether same-sex couples should be recognized. And if recognized, should they be as civil unions or with the same privileges of married men and women?

would deny federal recognition of same-sex marriages. Despite criticism from the gay community and those who are supportive of legal recognition of same-sex marriage, the measure was immensely popular with the public. Despite this action, some states have extended same-sex couples the legal benefits of marriage through civil union and even of marriage. In response, the majority of states passed amendments to their own constitutions to prevent same-sex marriages and civil unions from receiving any recognition within their borders. A 2008 national survey shows the nation very split on this issue, with 56 percent favoring the concept of marriage for same-sex couples (Saad 2008; Surdin 2008).

We have used assimilation throughout this book to describe the process by which individuals forsake their own heritage to become a part of a different culture. Assimilation has emerged as a hot issue in the gay community. Some argue that promoting gay marriage is merely trying to assimilate or to become like the oppressor, adopting their social conventions. Efforts to downplay overt expression of homosexuality are yet another example of assimilation. Critics of assimilation argue that equal treatment is the real issue and should not be the result of conforming to the ways of the heterosexual-dominant society. The debate is unlikely to be resolved soon because full acceptance of gays and lesbians is far removed from today's social and political agenda. But this discussion repeats a pattern found with every subordinate group—how to maintain one's unique identity and become part of a multicultural society (Hartocollis 2006; Hequembourg and Arditi 1999).

The Glass Half Empty

A common expression makes reference to a glass half full or half empty of water. If one is thirsty, it is half empty and in need of being replenished. If one is attempting to clear dirty dishes, it is half full. For many people, especially Whites, the progress of subordinate groups or minorities makes it difficult to understand calls for more programs and new reforms and impossible to understand when minority neighborhoods erupt in violence.

In absolute terms, the glass of water has been filling up, but people in the early twenty-first century do not compare themselves with people in the 1960s. For example, Latinos and African Americans regard the appropriate reference group to be Whites today; compared with them, the glass is half empty at best.

In Figure 17.4, we have shown the current picture and recent changes by comparing African Americans and Hispanics with Whites as well as contemporary data for Native Americans (American Indians). We see that the nation's largest minority groups—African Americans and Hispanics—have higher household income, complete more schooling, and enjoy longer life expectancy today than in 1975. White Americans have made similar strides in all three areas. The gap remains and, if one analyzes it closely, has actually increased in some instances. Both Blacks and Latinos in 2007 had just edged out the income level that Whites had exceeded back in 1975. Three decades behind! Also, Black Americans today have barely matched the life expectancy that Whites had a generation earlier. Similarly, many minority Americans remain entrenched in poverty: nearly one out of four Hispanics and African Americans.

Little has changed since 1975. We have chosen 1975 because that was a year for which we have comparable data for Latinos, Whites, and African Americans. However, the patterns would be no different if we considered 1950, 1960, or 1970.

These data provide only the broadest overview. Detailed analyses do not yield a brighter picture. For example, about one in nine Whites were without health insurance in 2007 compared to one of five African Americans and one of three Latinos. Similarly, 3.9 percent of all doctorates were awarded to African Americans in 1981. By 2002, the proportion had increased only to 5.4 percent. The United States continues to rely on overseas students to fill the places on the educational ladder. The number of doctorates awarded to nonresident aliens (that is, immigrants who gained entry for schooling with no other ties to U.S. citizens) was three times that of Blacks, Asian Americans, Latinos, and American Indians *combined* (Bureau of the Census 2007a; DeNavas-Walt et al. 2008; Hoffer et al. 2001).

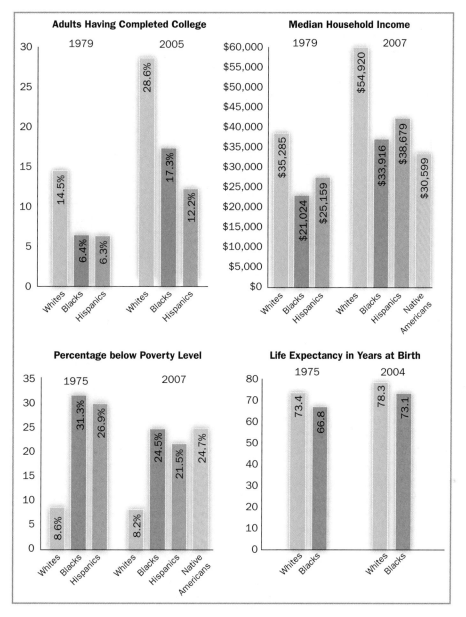

FIGURE 17.4
Changes in Schooling, Income, and Life Expectancy

Note: Native American data are for 2000. Education data include people age 25 and older. Hispanic education 1975 data estimated by author from data for 1970 and 1980. White data are for non-Hispanic (except in education).

Sources: Bureau of the Census 1988, 167; 2005a, 44; DeNavas-Walt et al. 2008, 6, 15; Ogunwole 2006.

Conclusion

As the United States promotes racial, ethnic, and religious diversity, it strives also to impose universal criteria on employers, educators, and realtors so that subordinate racial and ethnic groups can participate fully in the larger society. In some instances, to bring about equality of results—not just equality of opportunity—programs have been developed to give competitive advantages to women and minority men. Only more recently have similar strides been made on behalf of people with disabilities. These latest answers to social inequality have provoked much controversy over how to achieve the admirable goal of a multiracial, multiethnic society, undifferentiated in opportunity and rewards.

The huge outpouring of information for the census documents the racial and ethnic diversity of the entire nation. And as we see in Figure 17.5, although the proportion of specific minorities present may be different in different regions and different communities, the tapestry of racial and ethnic groups is always close at hand wherever one is in the United States.

Relations between racial, ethnic, or religious groups take two broad forms, as situations characterized by either consensus or conflict. Consensus prevails where assimilation or fusion of groups has been completed. Consensus also prevails in a pluralistic society in the sense that members have agreed to respect differences between groups. By eliminating the contending group,

FIGURE 17.5
The Image of Diversity from the Census

Source: 2000 census data reported in Brewer and Suchan 2001, 20.

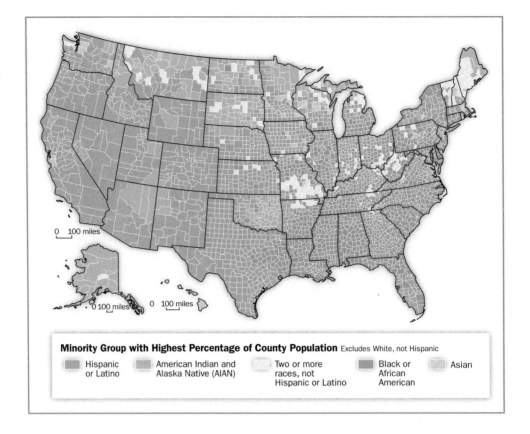

Minority Group with Highest Percentage of County Population Excludes White, not Hispanic

Hispanic or Latino | American Indian and Alaska Native (AIAN) | Two or more races, not Hispanic or Latino | Black or African American | Asian

extermination and expulsion also lead to a consensus society. In the study of intergroup relations, it is often easy to ignore conflict where there is a high degree of consensus because it is assumed that an orderly society has no problems. In some instances, however, this assumption is misleading. Through long periods of history, misery inflicted on a racial, ethnic, or religious group was judged to be appropriate, if not actually divinely inspired.

In recent history, harmonious relations between all racial, ethnic, and religious groups have been widely accepted as a worthy goal. The struggle against oppression and inequality is not new. It dates back at least to the revolutions in England, France, and the American colonies in the seventeenth and eighteenth centuries. The twentieth century was unique in the extension of equality to the less-privileged classes, many of whose members are racial and ethnic minorities. Conflict along racial and ethnic lines is especially bitter now because it evokes memories of slavery, colonial oppression, and overt discrimination. Today's African Americans are much more aware of slavery than contemporary poor people are of seventeenth-century debtors' prison.

Unquestionably, the struggle for justice among racial and ethnic groups has not completely met its goals. While the election of Barack Obama as president was historic and worthy of the global celebration it received, it does not reflect the broad movement of members of racial and ethnic groups into positions of power in the private and public sectors. Many people

are still committed to repression, although they may see it only as the benign neglect of those less privileged. Such repression leads to the dehumanization of both the subordinated individual and the oppressor. Growth in equal rights movements and self-determination for third world countries largely populated by non-White people has moved the world onto a course that seems irreversible. The old ethnic battle lines now renewed in Iran, Sudan, Kenya, the Georgia Republic, and Chechnya in Russia have only added to the tensions.

Self-determination, whether for groups or individuals, often is impossible in societies as they are currently structured. Bringing about social equality, therefore, will entail significant changes in existing institutions. Because such changes are not likely to come about with everyone's willing cooperation, the social costs will be high. However, if there is a trend in racial and ethnic relations in the world today, it is the growing belief that the social costs, however high, must be paid to achieve self-determination.

It is naive to foresee a world of societies in which one person equals one vote and all are accepted without regard to race, ethnicity, religion, gender, age, disability status, or sexual orientation. It is equally unlikely to expect to see a society, let alone a world, that is without a privileged class or prestigious jobholders. Contact between different peoples, as we have seen numerous times, precedes conflict. Contact also may initiate mutual understanding and appreciation.

Summary

1. Many of the same issues of stigmatization, prejudice, discrimination, as well as the mobilization of efforts to bring about positive change are shared by many groups who are not necessarily racial and ethnic minorities.
2. The elderly in the United States are growing in numbers and proportions, with a growing proportion being people of color.
3. Although many gains have been made in ensuring the health and safety of older Americans, those who choose to continue to work often face ageism.
4. Another growing group in the United States is people with disabilities, who in recent years have had their ranks added to by veterans of the wars in Iraq and Afghanistan.
5. Advocacy efforts by people with disabilities and others on their behalf have a long history. A major milestone was achieved in 1990 with the passage of the Americans with Disabilities Act.
6. Like the aged and disabled, people who are gay and lesbian have been working to achieve equality but have yet to achieve the same kind of national recognition through either legislation or legal precedence.
7. Issues such as domestic partnerships and gay marriage dominate newspaper coverage, but day-to-day concerns such as discrimination in employment often remain unaddressed.
8. There is an agreement that racial and ethnic minority groups have made great strides during the last two generations in the United States, but typically the gap between them and White men and women has remained the same.

Key Terms

ageism 404
disability 408

domestic partnership 415
homophobia 413

visitability 412

Review Questions

1. What contributes to the changing image of diversity in the United States?
2. In what ways are the aged, people with disabilities, and gays and lesbians stereotyped?
3. What are common and differing aspects of the effort to mobilize the elderly, people with disabilities, and gay men and lesbians to achieve equality?
4. What has been the role of the federal government in the effort to achieve equality by the aged, people with disabilities, and the gay and lesbian community?
5. What does it mean to overcome "exclusion"?

Critical Thinking

1. Sociologists use the term *master status* to describe a status that dominates others and thereby determines a person's general position in society. To what degree can that term be applied to the three groups considered in this chapter?
2. The media—in advertisements, humor, dramas, and situation comedies—portray life in society. What are some examples, both positive and negative, of how the elderly, people with disabilities, and gays and lesbians are presented in the media that you have seen? In what ways are these groups stereotyped?
3. How might advances in technology, including innovations for the home and computer chat rooms, have a unique effect on each of the groups trying to overcome exclusion discussed in this chapter?
4. How do policy makers trying to bring about change use the model of "half full" and "half empty" either to argue for change on behalf of minorities or to use the same concepts to maintain that the status quo is adequate for addressing issues of social inequality?

Internet Resource Directory

The following is a sample of the thousands of Web sites that offer information on race, ethnicity, religion, and other related topics. They have been grouped by broad areas because most sites touch on a number of areas and subjects. Web sites have been selected that have stable URLs and are in English (or are multilingual and include English). Most of these Web sites, in turn, have links to other useful information.

General

All of Us Are Related, Each of Us Is Unique (Syracuse University)
allrelated.syr.edu

Death Penalty Information Center
www.deathpenaltyinfo.org

Equal Employment Opportunity Commission
www.eeoc.gov

Ethnic Media: New America Media
news.newamericamedia.org/news

FBI Uniform Crime Reports (data on hate crimes)
www.fbi.gov/ucr/ucr.htm#hate

Hate Crimes Laws
www.adl.org/99hatecrime/intro.asp

Hurricane Katrina: U.S. Department of Health and Human Services
www.hhs.gov/disasters/emergency/naturaldisasters/hurricanes/katrina/index.html

Lutheran Immigration and Refugee Service
www.lirs.org

Minorities in Medical School (Association of American Medical Colleges)
www.aamc.org/students/minorities

Minorities in Medicine (Association of American Medical Colleges)
www.aamc.org/students/minorities

The Prejudice Institute
www.prejudiceinstitute.org

Race Traitor (constructing Whiteness)
www.racetraitor.org

Refugees and Immigrants: Lutheran Immigration and Refugee Service
www.lirs.org

Refugees and Immigrants: U.S. Committee for Refugees and Immigrants
www.refugeesusa.org

Southern Poverty Law Center (tolerance education)
splccenter.org and www.tolerance.org

U.S. Census Bureau
www.census.gov

U.S. Census Bureau Revisions to the Standards for the Classification of Federal Data on Race and Ethnicity (Office of Management and Budget)
www.census.gov/population/www/socdemo/race/Ombdir15.html

U.S. Citizenship and Immigration Services
www.uscis.gov

U.S. Commission on Civil Rights
www.usccr.gov

U.S. Commission on Immigration Reform
www.utexas.edu/lbj/uscir

African Americans

African American search engines
blackseek.com and rushmoredrive.com

African American History and Culture (The Smithsonian)
www.si.edu/resource/faq/nmah/afroam.htm

African American Research (National Archives)
www.archives.gov/genealogy/african-american/index.html

Black Collegian Online
www.black-collegian.com

MelaNET (The UnCut Black Experience)
www.melanet.com

Official Kwanzaa Web Site
www.officialkwanzaawebsite.org

Rainbow/PUSH Coalition
www.rainbowpush.org

Southern Christian Leadership Conference (SCLC)
www.sclcnational.org

Asian Americans and Pacific Islanders

Asian American Net
www.asianamerican.net

Asian American Studies, Yale University Guide to
www.library.yale.edu/rsc/asian-american

Asians and Pacific Islanders
www.nea.org/mco/asians.html

Chinese Immigration Records
www.archives.gov/genealogy/heritage/chinese-immigration.html

Densho: The Japanese American Legacy Project
www.densho.org

The Fred Korematsu Story "Of Civil Wrongs and Rights" (by Eric Paul Fornier)
www.pbs.org/pov/pov2001/ofcivilwrongsandrights/index.html

Hmong Home Page
www.stolaf.edu/people/cdr/hmong

Internment Archives
www.internmentarchives.com

Japanese American Citizens League
www.jacl.org

Japanese American Historical Society
www.njahs.org

Japanese American National Museum
www.janm.org

Japanese American Records (National Archives)
www.archives.gov/genealogy/heritage/japanese-americans.html

Little India (magazine)
www.littleindia.com

Little Saigon Net
www.littlesaigon.com

Nation of Hawai'i
hawaii-nation.org

National Japanese American Memorial Foundation
www.njamf.com

Southeast Asia Resource Action Center
www.searac.org

U.S. Census Bureau: Public Information Office
www.census.gov/pubinfo/www/NEWapiML1.html

Hispanics and Latinos

Afro Cubans as well as Cuba and the Caribbean
www.afrocubaweb.com

Hispanic American Records
www.archives.gov/genealogy/heritage/hispanic-americans.html

International Boundaries Research Unit
www.dur.ac.uk/ibru

Julian Samora Research Institute (Michigan State University)
www.jsri.msu.edu

Latin American National Information Center
lanic.utexas.edu

Mexican American Studies and Research Center (University of Arizona)
masrc.arizona.edu

Mexican Migration Project
mmp.opr.princeton.edu

Mexico–U.S. Binational Migration Study Report
www.utexas.edu/lbj/uscir/binational.html

National Council of La Raza
www.nclr.org

Nijmegen Centre for Border Research
www.ru.nl/ncbr

Pew Hispanic Center
pewhispanic.org

Puerto Ricans and the American Dream
prdream.com

Puerto Rican Legal Defense and Education Fund
www.prldef.org

Jews and Judaism

American Jewish Committee
www.ajc.org

Anti-Defamation League
www.adl.org

Hebrew Immigrant Aid Society (HIAS)
www.hias.org

Jewish American History Research
www.archives.gov/genealogy/heritage/jewish-american.html

Jewish Culture
myjewishlearning.com

Judaism and Jewish Resources
shamash.org

Muslims and Arab Americans

American–Arab Anti-Discrimination Committee
www.adc.org

American Muslim Perspective
ampolitics.ghazali.net

Arab American Institute
www.aaiusa.org

Muslim Students' Association
msa-natl.org

Native Americans

Bureau of Indian Affairs
www.doi.gov/bureau-indian-affairs.html

Native American Higher Education Consortium (AIHEC) Virtual Library
www.aihecvl.org

National Congress of American Indians
www.ncai.org

National Indian Youth Council
www.niyc-alb.org

Native American Records
www.archives.gov/genealogy/heritage/native-american/index.html

Native Web
www.nativeweb.org

Smithsonian National Museum of the American Indian
www.nmai.si.edu

Ethnic Groups and Other Subordinate Groups

Administration on Aging
www.aoa.dhhs.gov

Polish Americans: American Institute of Polish Culture
www.ampolinstitute.org

Catholics for a Free Choice
www.cath4choice.org

Disability Social History Project
www.disabilityhistory.org

Ellis Island Immigration Museum
www.ellisisland.com

Ethnicity in Twentieth-Century America (Thomas J. Archdeacon at University of Wisconsin)
history.wisc.edu/archdeacon/404tja

German Americans (German Embassy site)
www.germany-info.org

Human Rights
www.hrweb.org

Interracial Voice (People of Mixed Racial Background)
www.webcom.com/~intvoice

Irish Americans: American Irish Historical Society
www.aihs.org

Internet Resource Directory

Norwegian American Historical Association
www.stolaf.edu/naha

Norwegian Americans: Sons of Norway
www.sofn.com

Norwegian Americans: Vesterheim Norwegian American Museum
www.vesterheim.org

Polish American Association
www.polish.org

Polish Americans: American Institute of Polish Culture
www.ampolinstitute.org

SeniorLink
www.seniorlink.com

Swedish American Museum
www.samac.org

Society and Culture: Disabilities (Yahoo)
www.yahoo.com/Society_and_Culture/Disabilities

Women and Men

National Organization for Women
www.now.org

National Women's History Project
www.nwhp.org

Womensnet (South Africa)
www.womensnet.org.za

Outside the United States

Abya Yala Net (South and Meso American Indian Rights Center)
abyayala.nativeweb.org

African National Congress (South Africa)
www.anc.org.za

Information (general) on countries (CIA World Factbook)
www.odci.gov/cia/publications/factbook

Peace People (Northern Ireland)
www.peacepeople.com

The Author

Richard T. Schaefer
(for e-mail correspondence)
schaeferrt@aol.com

Glossary

Parenthetical numbers refer to the pages on which the term is introduced.

abolitionists Whites and free Blacks who favored the end of slavery. (178)

absolute deprivation The minimum level of subsistence below which families or individuals should not be expected to exist. (61)

acting White Taking school seriously and accepting the authority of teachers and administrators. (200)

affirmative action Positive efforts to recruit subordinate group members, including women, for jobs, promotions, and educational opportunities. (75)

Afrocentric perspective An emphasis on the customs of African cultures and how they have pervaded the history, culture, and behavior of Blacks in the United States and around the world. (30, 177)

ageism Prejudice and discrimination against the elderly. (404)

amalgamation The process by which a dominant group and a subordinate group combine through intermarriage to form a new group. (23)

androgyny The state of being both masculine and feminine, aggressive and passive. (357)

anti-Semitism Anti-Jewish prejudice or discrimination. (330)

apartheid The policy of the South African government intended to maintain separation of Blacks, Coloureds, and Asians from the dominant Whites. (394)

apartheid schools All-Black schools. (200)

arranged marriage When one's marital partner is chosen by others and the relationship is not based on any preexisting mutual attraction. (295)

assimilation The process by which a subordinate individual or group takes on the characteristics of the dominant group. (24)

asylees Foreigners who have already entered the United States and now seek protection because of persecution or a well-founded fear of persecution. (108)

authoritarian personality A psychological construct of a personality type likely to be prejudiced and to use others as scapegoats. (39)

bilingual education A program designed to allow students to learn academic concepts in their native language while they learn a second language. (97)

bilingualism The use of two or more languages in places of work or education and the treatment of each language as legitimate. (97)

biological race The mistaken notion of a genetically isolated human group. (11)

blaming the victim Portraying the problems of racial and ethnic minorities as their fault rather than recognizing society's responsibilities. (16, 287)

blended identity Self-image and worldview that is a combination of religious faith, cultural background based on nationality, and current residency. (267)

Bogardus scale Technique to measure social distance toward different racial and ethnic groups. (50)

borderlands The area of a common culture along the border between Mexico and the United States. (224)

braceros Contracted Mexican laborers brought to the United States during World War II. (240)

brain drain Immigration to the United States of skilled workers, professionals, and technicians who are desperately needed in their home countries. (95, 232)

chain immigration Immigrants sponsor several other immigrants who, on their arrival, may sponsor still more. (87)

Chicanismo An ideology emphasizing pride and positive identity among Mexican Americans. (244)

civil disobedience A tactic promoted by Martin Luther King, Jr., based on the belief that people have the right to disobey unjust laws under certain circumstances. (187)

civil religion The religious dimension in American life that merges the state with sacred beliefs. (131)

class As defined by Max Weber, people who share similar levels of wealth. (14, 208)

colonialism A foreign power's maintenance of political, social, economic, and cultural dominance over people for an extended period. (19)

color-blind racism Use of race-neutral principles to defend the racially unequal status quo. (43)

color gradient The placement of people on a continuum from light to dark skin color rather than in distinct racial groupings by skin color. (222, 249, 380)

conflict perspective A sociological approach that assumes that the social structure is best understood in terms of conflict or tension between competing groups. (16)

contact hypothesis An interactionist perspective stating that intergroup contact between people of equal status in noncompetitive circumstances will reduce prejudice. (51)

creationists People who support a literal interpretation of the biblical book of Genesis on the origins of the universe and argue that evolution should not be presented as established scientific thought. (136)

crossover effect An effect that appears when Native American children who previously scored high on tests now score below average in intelligence when tests are given in English rather than their native languages. (163)

cultural capital Noneconomic forces such as family background and past investments in education that are then reflected in knowledge about the arts and language. (314)

culture of poverty A way of life that involves no future planning, no enduring commitment to marriage, and no work ethic; this culture follows the poor even when they move out of slums or barrios. (242)

curanderismo Hispanic folk medicine. (255)

de facto segregation Segregation that is the result of residential patterns. (200)

deficit model of ethnic identity One's ethnicity is viewed by others as a factor of subtracting away the characteristics corresponding to some ideal ethnic type. (265)

de jure segregation Children assigned to schools specifically to maintain racially separated schools. (185)

denomination A large, organized religion not officially linked with the state or government. (130)

desi Colloquial name for people who trace their ancestry to South Asia, especially India and Pakistan. (294)

Diaspora The exile of Jews from Palestine. (341, 389)

differential justice Whites being dealt with more leniently than Blacks, whether at the time of arrest, indictment, conviction, sentencing, or parole. (211)

disability Reduced ability to perform tasks one would normally do at a given stage in life. (408)

discrimination The denial of opportunities and equal rights to individuals and groups because of prejudice or for other arbitrary reasons. (36, 60)

displaced homemakers Women whose primary occupation had been homemaking but who did not find full-time employment after being divorced, separated, or widowed. (366)

domestic partnership Two unrelated adults who have chosen to share one another's lives in a relationship of mutual caring, who reside together, and who agree to be jointly responsible for their dependents, basic living expenses, and other common necessities. (415)

dry foot, wet foot Policy toward Cuban immigrants that allows those who manage to reach the United States (dry foot) to remain but sends those who are picked up at sea (wet foot) back to Cuba. (229)

dual or split labor market Division of the economy into two areas of employment, the secondary one of which is populated primarily by minorities working at menial jobs. (68)

dysfunction An element of society that may disrupt a social system or decrease its stability. (15)

Ebonics Distinctive dialect with a complex language structure found among many Black Americans. (177)

emigration Leaving a country to settle in another. (18)

environmental justice Efforts to ensure that hazardous substances are controlled so that all communities receive protection regardless of race or socioeconomic circumstances. (74, 168)

ethnic cleansing Policy of ethnic Serbs to eliminate Muslims from parts of Bosnia. (21)

ethnic group A group set apart from others because of its national origin or distinctive cultural patterns. (8)

ethnicity paradox The maintenance of one's ethnic ties in a way that can assist with assimilation in larger society. (139)

ethnocentrism The tendency to assume that one's culture and way of life are superior to all others. (34)

ethnonational conflicts Conflicts between ethnic, racial, religious, and linguistic groups within nations, which replace conflicts between nations. (378)

ethnophaulism Ethnic or racial slurs, including derisive nicknames. (36)

evacuees Japanese Americans interned in camps for the duration of World War II. (317)

exploitation theory A Marxist theory that views racial subordination in the United States as a manifestation of the class system inherent in capitalism. (39)

familism Pride and closeness in the family that result in placing family obligation and loyalty before individual needs. (253)

feminine mystique Society's view of a woman as only her children's mother and her husband's wife. (360)

feminization of poverty The trend since 1970 in which women account for a growing proportion of those who live below the poverty line. (366)

fish-ins Native American tribes' protests over government interference with their traditional rights to fish as they like. (154)

fringe-of-values theory Behavior that is on the border of conduct that a society regards as proper and is often carried out by subordinate groups, subjecting those groups to negative sanctions. (335)

functionalist perspective A sociological approach emphasizing how parts of a society are structured to maintain its stability. (15)

fusion A minority and a majority group combining to form a new group. (23)

gender roles Expectations regarding the proper behavior, attitudes, and activities of males and females. (357)

genocide The deliberate, systematic killing of an entire people or nation. (20)

gerrymandering Redrawing districts bizarrely to create politically advantageous outcomes. (214)

glass ceiling The barrier that blocks the promotion of a qualified worker because of gender or minority membership. (79, 363)

glass escalator The male advantage experienced in occupations dominated by women. (81)

glass wall A barrier to moving laterally in a business to positions that are more likely to lead to upward mobility. (81)

globalization Worldwide integration of government policies, cultures, social movements, and financial markets through trade, movements of people, and the exchange of ideas. (18, 106)

gook syndrome David Riesman's phrase describing Americans' tendency to stereotype Asians and to regard them as all alike and undesirable. (297)

hajj Pilgrimage to Mecca to be completed at least once in a Muslim's lifetime. (265)

halakha Jewish laws covering obligations and duties. (347)

Haoles Native Hawaiians' term for Caucasians. (302)

hate crime Criminal offense committed because of the offender's bias against a race, religion, ethnic or national origin group, or sexual orientation group. (35)

hijab A variety of garments that allow women to follow the guidelines of modest dress. (271)

Holocaust The state-sponsored systematic persecution and annihilation of European Jewry by Nazi Germany and its collaborators. (336)

Holocaust revisionists People who deny the Nazi effort to exterminate the Jews or who minimize the numbers killed. (337)

hometown clubs Nonprofit organizations that maintain close ties to immigrants' hometowns in Mexico and other Latin American countries. (225)

homophobia The fear of and prejudice toward homosexuality. (413)

hui kuan Chinese American benevolent associations organized on the basis of the district of the immigrant's origin in China. (311)

ilchomose The 1.5 generation of Korean Americans—those who immigrated into the United States as children. (300)

immigration Coming into a new country as a permanent resident. (18)

income Salaries, wages, and other money received. (74, 203)

informal economy Transfers of money, goods, or services that are not reported to the government. Common in inner-city neighborhoods and poverty-stricken rural areas. (67)

in-group virtues Proper behavior by one's own group; become unacceptable when practiced by outsiders (out-group vices). (336)

institutional discrimination A denial of opportunities and equal rights to individuals or groups resulting from the normal operations of a society. (63)

intelligence quotient (IQ) The ratio of a person's mental age (as computed by an IQ test) to his or her chronological age, multiplied by 100. (12)

intelligent design View that life is so complex that it must have been created by a higher intelligence. (136)

internal colonialism The treatment of subordinate peoples as colonial subjects by those in power. (20, 146)

Intifada The Palestinian uprising against Israeli authorities in the occupied territories. (391)

irregular or underground economy *See* informal economy. (67)

Islamophobia A range of negative feelings toward Muslims and their religion that ranges from generalized intolerance to hatred. (277)

Issei First-generation immigrants from Japan to the United States. (315)

jihad Struggle against the enemies of Allah, usually taken to mean one's own internal struggle. (266)

Jim Crow Southern laws passed in the late nineteenth century that kept Blacks in their subordinate position. (180)

Judaization The lessening importance of Judaism as a religion and the substitution of cultural traditions as the tie that binds Jews. (333)

kashrut Laws pertaining to permissible (kosher) and forbidden foods and their preparation. (345)

Kibei Japanese Americans of the Nisei generation sent back to Japan for schooling and to have marriages arranged. (316)

kickouts or pushouts Native American school dropouts who leave behind an unproductive academic environment. (163)

kye Rotating credit system used by Korean Americans to subsidize the start-up costs of businesses. (301)

labeling theory A sociological approach introduced by Howard Becker that attempts to explain why certain people are viewed as deviants and others engaging in the same behavior are not. (16)

La Raza Literally meaning "the people," the term refers to the rich heritage of Mexican Americans; it is therefore used to denote a sense of pride among Mexican Americans today. (241)

life chances People's opportunities to provide themselves with material goods, positive living conditions, and favorable life experiences. (253)

maquiladoras Foreign-owned companies on the Mexican side of the border with the United States. (27, 224)

marginality The status of being between two cultures at the same time, such as the status of Jewish immigrants in the United States. (27, 349)

Marielitos People who arrived from Cuba in the third wave of Cuban immigration, most specifically those forcibly deported by way of Mariel Harbor. The term is generally reserved for refugees seen as especially undesirable. (228)

matrix of domination Cumulative impact of oppression because of race, gender, and class as well as sexual orientation, religion, disability status, and age. (371)

melting pot Diverse racial or ethnic groups or both, forming a new creation, a new cultural entity. (23)

mestizo People in the Americas of mixed European (usually Spanish) and local indigenous ancestry. (379)

migration A general term that describes any transfer of population. (18)

millenarian movements Movements, such as the Ghost Dance, that prophesy a cataclysm in the immediate future, to be followed by collective salvation. (147)

minority group A subordinate group whose members have significantly less control or power over their own lives than do the members of a dominant or majority group. (5)

mixed status Families in which one or more members are citizens and one or more are noncitizens. (96, 254)

model or ideal minority A group that, despite past prejudice and discrimination, succeeds economically, socially, and educationally without resorting to political or violent confrontations with Whites. (285)

mojados "Wetbacks"; derisive slang for Mexicans who enter illegally, supposedly by swimming the Rio Grande. (240)

mommy tax Lower salaries women receive over their lifetime because they have children. (370)

mommy track An unofficial corporate career track for women who want to divide their attention between work and family. (364)

mulatto escape hatch Notion that Brazilians of mixed ancestry can move into high-status positions. (387)

nativism Beliefs and policies favoring native-born citizens over immigrants. (90)

naturalization Conferring of citizenship on a person after birth. (100)

neocolonialism Continuing dependence of former colonies on foreign countries. (247)

Neoricans Puerto Ricans who return to the island to settle after living on the U.S. mainland (also called *Nuyoricans*). (246)

Nisei Children born of immigrants from Japan. (315)

normative approach The view that prejudice is influenced by societal norms and situations that encourage or discourage the tolerance of minorities. (39)

occupational segregation by gender The tendency for men and women to be employed in different occupations from each other. (361)

orientalism The simplistic view of the people and history of the Orient, with no recognition of change over time or the diversity within its many cultures. (262)

out-group vices In-group virtues that become unacceptable when practiced by outsiders. (336)

panethnicity The development of solidarity between ethnic subgroups as reflected in the terms *Hispanic* and *Asian American*. (27, 221, 290)

pan-Indianism Intertribal social movements in which several tribes, joined by political goals but not by kinship, unite in a common identity. (154)

pass laws Laws that controlled internal movement by non-Whites in South Africa. (393)

pay equity The same wages for different types of work that are judged to be comparable by such measures as employee knowledge, skills, effort, responsibility, and working conditions; also called *comparable worth*. (362)

peoplehood Milton Gordon's term for a group with a shared feeling. (351)

Pentecostalism A religion similar in many respects to evangelical faiths that believes in the infusion of the Holy Spirit into services and in religious experiences such as faith healing. (256)

pluralism Mutual respect for one another's culture, a respect that allows minorities to express their own culture without suffering prejudice or discrimination. (25)

powwows Native American gatherings of dancing, singing, music playing, and visiting, accompanied by competitions. (156)

prejudice A negative attitude toward an entire category of people such as a racial or ethnic minority. (36)

principle of third-generation interest Marcus Hansen's contention that ethnic interest and awareness increase in the third generation, among the grandchildren of immigrants. (117)

Québécois The French-speaking people of the province of Quebec in Canada. (383)

quilombo Slave hideaways in Brazil. (386)

racial formation A sociohistorical process by which racial categories are created, inhibited, transformed, and destroyed. (13)

racial group A group that is socially set apart because of obvious physical differences. (7)

racial profiling Any arbitrary police-initiated action based on race, ethnicity, or natural origin rather than a person's behavior. (42, 276, 289)

racism A doctrine that one race is superior. (13)

redlining The pattern of discrimination against people trying to buy homes in minority and racially changing neighborhoods. (72, 210)

refugees People living outside their country of citizenship for fear of political or religious persecution. (108)

relative deprivation The conscious experience of a negative discrepancy between legitimate expectations and present actualities. (61, 189)

remittances The monies that immigrants return to their countries of origin. (103, 225)

repatriation The 1930s' program of deporting Mexicans. (240)

resegregation The physical separation of racial and ethnic groups reappearing after a period of relative integration. (23)

restrictive covenants Private contracts or agreements that discourage or prevent minority-group members from purchasing housing in a neighborhood. (184)

reverse discrimination Actions that cause better-qualified White men to be passed over for women and minority men. (78)

riff-raff theory Also called the *rotten-apple theory*; the belief that the riots of the 1960s were caused by discontented youths rather than by social and economic problems facing all African Americans. (189)

rising expectations The increasing sense of frustration that legitimate needs are being blocked. (189)

Sansei The children of the Nisei—that is, the grandchildren of the original immigrants from Japan. (316)

scapegoating theory A person or group blamed irrationally for another person's or group's problems or difficulties. (38)

secessionist minority Groups, such as the Amish, that reject both assimilation and coexistence. (137)

second shift The double burden—work outside the home followed by child care and housework—that is faced by many women and that few men share equitably. (369)

segregation The physical separation of two groups, often imposed on a subordinate group by the dominant group. (22)

self-fulfilling prophecy The tendency to respond to and act on the basis of stereotypes, a predisposition that can lead one to validate false definitions. (17)

sexism The ideology that one sex is superior to the other. (356)

sexual harassment Any unwanted and unwelcome sexual advances that interfere with a person's ability to perform a job and enjoy the benefits of a job. (364)

sinophobes People with a fear of anything associated with China. (91)

slave codes Laws that defined the low position held by slaves in the United States. (175)

slavery reparations Act of making amends for the injustices of slavery. (180)

social capital Collective benefits of durable social networks and their patterns of reciprocal trust. (314)

social distance Tendency to approach or withdraw from a racial group. (50)

sociology The systematic study of social behavior and human groups. (14)

sovereignty Tribal self-rule. (157)

sovereignty movement Effort by the indigenous peoples of Hawai'i to secure a measure of self-government and restoration of their lands. (303)

stereotypes Unreliable, exaggerated generalizations about all members of a group that do not take individual differences into account. (17, 40)

stratification A structured ranking of entire groups of people that perpetuates unequal rewards and power in a society. (14)

suffragists Women and men who worked successfully to gain women the right to vote. (359)

sundown towns Communities in which non-Whites were systematically excluded from living. (184)

symbolic ethnicity Herbert Gans's term that describes emphasis on ethnic food and ethnically associated political issues rather than deeper ties to one's heritage. (118)

tongs Chinese American secret associations. (311)

total discrimination The combination of current discrimination with past discrimination created by poor schools and menial jobs. (62)

tracking The practice of placing students in specific curriculum groups on the basis of test scores and other criteria. (200, 252)

transnationals Immigrants who sustain multiple social relationships that link their societies of origin and settlement. (106)

tsu Clans established along family lines and forming a basis for social organization by Chinese Americans. (311)

underemployment Working at a job for which the worker is overqualified, involuntary working part-time instead of full-time, or being intermittently employed. (205)

victim discounting Tendency to view crime as less socially significant if the victim is viewed as less worthy. (211)

victimization surveys Annual attempts to measure crime rates by interviewing ordinary citizens who may or may not have been crime victims. (211)

Viet Kieu Vietnamese living abroad, such as in the United States. (298)

visible minorities In Canada, persons other than Aboriginal or First Nation people who are non-White in racial background. (384)

visitability Building private homes to be accessible for visitors with disabilities. (412)

wealth An inclusive term encompassing all of a person's material assets, including land and other types of property. (74, 203)

White primary Legal provisions forbidding Black voting in election primaries; in one-party areas of the South, these laws effectively denied Blacks their right to select elected officials. (180)

White privilege Rights or immunities granted as a particular benefit or favor for being White. (116)

world systems theory A view of the global economic system as divided between nations that control wealth and those that provide natural resources and labor. (19, 145, 251, 378)

xenophobia The fear or hatred of strangers or foreigners. (90)

yellow peril A term denoting a generalized prejudice toward Asian people and their customs. (288)

Yiddishkait Jewishness. (347)

Yonsei The fourth generation of Japanese Americans in the United States; the children of the Sansei. (316)

Zionism Traditional Jewish religious yearning to return to the biblical homeland, now used to refer to support for the state of Israel. (341, 389)

zoning laws Legal provisions stipulating land use and the architectural design of housing, often used to keep racial minorities and low-income people out of suburban areas. (211)

References

AARP. 2003. *AARP Home*. Accessed May 12, 2003, at www.aarp.org.

ABC News. 1992. *Primetime Live*. True Colors. Transcript of November 26 episode.

Abdo, Geneive. 2004a. A Muslim Rap Finds Voice. *Chicago Tribune* (June 30): 1, 19.

———. 2004b. New Generation Lifting Muslims. *Chicago Tribune* (September 3): 1, 8.

Abraham, Nabeel, and Andrew Shyrock. 2000. *Arab Detroit: From Margin to Mainstream*. Detroit, MI: Wayne State University Press.

Abrahamson, Alan, and Judy Pasternak. 1998. For U.S. Jews, Era of Plenty Takes Many Far from Roots. *Los Angeles Times* (April 20): A1, A10–11.

Abrahamson, Mark. 1996. *Urban Enclaves: Identity and Place in America*. New York: St. Martin's Press.

Achenbaumm, W. A. 1993. Old Age. Pp. 2051–2062 in Mary Kupeic Coyton, Elliot J. Gorn, and Peter W. Williams, eds., *Encyclopedia of American Social History*. New York: Scribner's.

ACLU. 1996. *Racial Justice*. New York: American Civil Liberties Union.

Adam, Barry D. 1995. *The Rise of a Gay and Lesbian Movement*, rev. ed. New York: Twayne.

Adams, Jane Meredith. 2006. Mystery Shrouds Slaying of Chinatown Businessman. *Washington Post* (March 31): 5.

Adelman, Robert M., and James Clarke Gocker. 2007. Racial Residential Segregation in Urban America. *Sociology Compass* 1(1): 402–423.

Adler, Patricia A., and Peter Adler. 1998. *Peer Power: Preadolescent Culture and Identity*. New Brunswick, NJ: Rutgers University Press.

Adler, Patricia A., Steven J. Kess, and Peter Adler. 1992. Socialization to Gender Role: Popularity among Elementary School Boys and Girls. *Sociology of Education* (July), 65: 169–187.

——— and ———. 2004. Paradise Laborers: Hotel Work in the Global Economy. Ithaca NY: Cornell University.

Adorno, T. W., Else Frenkel-Brunswik, Daniel J. Levinson, and R. Nevitt Sanford. 1950. *The Authoritarian Personality*. New York: Wiley.

Aguilera, Michael Bernabé. 2008. Ethnic, Enclave Economic Impact of. Pp. 453–457 in vol. 1, *Encyclopedia of Race, Ethnicity, and Society*, Richard T. Schaefer, ed. Thousand Oaks, CA: Sage.

Airola, Jim. 2007. The Use of Remittance Income in Mexico. *International Migration Review*, 41 (Winter): 850–859.

Akaka, Daniel. 2008. Akaka Bill. Accessed November 20, 2008, at http://akaka.senate.gov/public/index.cfm?FuseAction=Issues.Home&issue=Akaka%20Bill&content_id=24#Akaka%20Bill.

Albrecht, Gary L. (ed.). 2005. *Encyclopedia of Disability*. Thousand Oaks, CA: Sage Publications.

Allard, Mary Dorinda, and Marianne James. 2008. Time Use of Working Parents: A Visual Essay. *Monthly Labor Review* (June): 3–14.

Allport, Gordon W. 1979. *The Nature of Prejudice*. 25th anniversary ed. Reading, MA: Addison-Wesley.

Alonso-Zaldivar, Ricardo, and Jennifer Oldhan. 2002. New Airport Screener Jobs Going Mostly to Whites. *Los Angeles Times* (September 24): A18.

Alvarez, Sandy. 2008. Haitian and Cuban Immigration: A Comparison. Pp. 576–578 in vol. 1, *Encyclopedia of Race, Ethnicity, and Society*, Richard T. Schaefer, ed. Thousand Oaks, CA: Sage.

Alvarez-Smith, Alma. 2008. Mexican American Legal Defense and Educational Fund. Pp. 892–894 in vol. 2, *Encyclopedia of Race, Ethnicity, and Society*, Richard T. Schaefer, ed. Thousand Oaks, CA: Sage.

Alvord, Valerie. 2000. Refugees' Success Breeds Pressure, Discrimination. *USA Today* (May 1): 74.

American Association of University Women. 2007. *AAUW Pay Equity Resource Kit Equal Pay Day 2007 and Beyond*. Washington, DC: AAUW.

American Community Survey. 2006. *American Community Survey 2005*. Released August 2006 from www.census.gov.

———. 2007. *American Community Survey 2006*. Released August 2007 from www.census.gov.

———. 2008. *American Community Survey 2007*. Released August 2008 from www.census.gov.

American Indian Higher Education Commission. 2008. *The Tribal College Journal*. Accessed August 12, 2008, at www.tribalcollegejournal.org/aihec/aihec.html.

American Jewish Committee. 1965. *Mutual Savings Banks of New York City*. New York: American Jewish Committee.

———. 1966a. *Mutual Savings Banks: A Follow-Up Report*. New York: American Jewish Committee.

———. 1966b. *Patterns of Exclusion from the Executive Suite: Corporate Banking*. New York: American Jewish Committee.

———. 2005. *2005 Annual Survey of American-Jewish Opinion*. New York: AJC.

———. 2007. *2007 Annual Survey of American Jewish Opinion*. New York: AJC.

Amnesty International. 1993. *Amnesty International Report 1993*. New York: Amnesty International.

Anderson, Warwick. 2003. *The Cultivation of Whiteness: Science, Health and Racial Destiny in Australia*. New York: Perseus Books.

Angier, Natalie. 1993. U.S. Opens the Door Just a Crack to Alternative Forms of Medicine. *New York Times* (January 10): 1, 13.

Ansell, Amy E. 2008. Color Blindness. Pp. 320–322 in vol. 1, *Encyclopedia of Race, Ethnicity, and Society*, Richard T. Schaefer, ed. Thousand Oaks, CA: Sage.

Anti-Defamation League (ADL). 2008. *Audit of Anti-Semitic Incidents 2007*. New York: ADL.

Aponte, Robert. 1991. Urban Hispanic Poverty: Disaggregations and Explanations. *Social Problems* (November), 38: 516–528.

Applebome, Peter. 1996. 70 Years after Scopes Trial, Creation Debate Lives. *New York Times* (March 10): 1, 22.

———. 1997. Dispute over Ebonics Reflects a Volatile Mix That Roils Urban Education. *New York Times* (March 1): 8.

Aran, Kenneth, Herman Arthur, Ramon Colon, and Harvey Goldenberg. 1973. *Puerto Rican History and Culture: A Study Guide and Curriculum Outline*. New York: United Federation of Teachers.

Archibold, Randal C. 2007. A City's Violence Feeds on Black-Hispanic Rivalry. *New York Times* (January 17): A1, A15.

———, and Julia Preston. 2008. Homeland Security Stands by Its Fence. *New York Times* (May 21): A1, A19.

Archuleta, Glenda. 1998. Interview with Archuleta (Council for Energy Resource Tribes) by Richard T. Schaefer (September 18).

Armstrong, Elizabeth A., and Suzanna M. Crage. 2006. Movements and Memory: The Making of the Stonewall Myth. *American Sociological Review* (October), 71: 724–751.

Asahina, Robert. 2006. *Just Americans: How Japanese Americans Won a War at Home and Abroad: The Story of the 100th Battalion/442d Regimental Combat Team in World War II*. New York: Gotham.

Asante, Molefi Kete. 2007. *An Afrocentric Manifesto: Toward an African Renaissance*. Cambridge, UK: Polity.

———. 2008. Afrocentricity. Pp. 41–42 in vol. 1, *Encyclopedia of Race, Ethnicity, and Society*, Richard T. Schaefer, ed. Thousand Oaks, CA: Sage.

Ash, Timothy Garton. 2007. Welcome to a Mixed-Up World. *The Global Mail* (Toronto) (July 14): A19.

Asian American Journalists Association. 2000. *All-American: How to Cover Asian America*. San Francisco: AAJA.

AsianWeek. 2008. Days of Valor Culminates with Capitol Hearing on FilAm Vets. *AsianWeek* (April 13): 7.

Attwood, Bain. 2003. *Rights for Aborigines*. Crows Nest, Australia: Allen and Unwin.

Australia. 1997. *Bringing Them Home: Report of the National Inquiry into the Separation of Aboriginal and Torres Strait Islander Children from Their Families*. Accessed at www.humanrights.gov.au.

———. 2008. Apology to Australia's Indigenous Peoples House of Representatives Parliament House, Canberra (February 13). Accessed at www.pm.gov.au/media/speech/2008/speech_0073.cfm.

Avila, Oscar. 2003. Muslim Holiday Testing Schools. *Chicago Tribune* (November 24): 1, 16.

Ayala, César J., and Viviana Carro-Figueroa. 2006. Expropriation and Displacement of Civilians in Vieques, 1940–1950. Pp. 172–205 in *Puerto Rico Under Colonial Rule*, Ramón Bosque-Pérez and José Javier Colón Morera, eds. Albany: State University of New York Press.

Badgett, M. V. Lee, and Heidi I. Hartmann. 1995. The Effectiveness of Equal Employment Opportunity Policies. In *Economic Perspectives in Affirmative Action*, ed. Margaret C. Simms, 55–83. Washington, DC: Joint Center for Political and Economic Studies.

Bagby, Ishan. 2004. *A Portrait of Detroit Mosques: Muslim Views on Policy, Politics and Religion*. Clinton Township, MI: Institute for Social Policy and Understanding.

Balderrama, Francisco E., and Raymond Rodriguez. 2006. *Decade of Betrayal: Mexican Repatriation in the 1930s*. Revised. Albuquerque: University of New Mexico Press.

Baldwin, James. 1967. Negroes Are Anti-Semitic Because They're Anti-White. *New York Times* (May 21): 114.

Baldwin, Neil. 2001. *Henry Ford and the Jews: The Mass Production of Hate*. New York: Public Affairs.

Baltzell, E. Digby. 1964. *The Protestant Establishment: Aristocracy and Caste in America*. New York: Vintage Books.

Bamshad, Michael J., and Steve E. Olson. 2003. Does Race Exist? *Scientific American* (December): 78–85.

Banerjee, Neela. 2000. Fighting Back against Domestic Violence: Asian American Women Organize to Break the Silence. *AsianWeek* (November 30), 22: 13–15.

Banton, Michael. 2007. Max Weber on "Ethnic Communities": A Critique. *Nations and Nationalism*, 13(1): 19–35.

Barclay, William, Krishna Kumar, and Ruth P. Simms. 1976. *Racial Conflict, Discrimination, and Power: Historical and Contemporary Studies*. New York: AMS Press.

Barnes, Jessica S., and Claudette L. Bennett. 2002. *The Asian Population: 2000*. Census Brief C2KBR/01-16. Washington, DC: U.S. Government Printing Office.

Barnes, Patricia M., Patricia F. Adams, and Eric Powell-Grener. 2005. Health Characteristics of the American Indian and Alaska Native Adult Population: United States, 1999–2003. *Advance Data* (April 27).

Barringer, Felicity. 2004. Bitter Division for Sierra Club on Immigration. *New York Times* (March 14): A1, A16.

Barron, Milton L. 1953. Minority Group Characteristics of the Aged in American Society. *Journal of Gerontology* (October), 8: 477–482.

Barry, Ellen. 2004. County Rescinds Vote. *Los Angeles Times* (March 19): A16.

Bartlett, Donald L., and James B. Steele. 2002. Casinos: Wheel of Misfortune. *Time* (December 10), 160: 44–53, 56–58.

Bascara, Victor. 2008. Model Minority. Pp. 910–912 in vol. 2, *Encyclopedia of Race, Ethnicity, and Society*, Richard T. Schaefer, ed. Thousand Oaks, CA: Sage.

Bash, Harry M. 2001. If I'm So White, Why Ain't I Right? Some Methodological Misgivings on Taking Identity Ascriptions at Face Value. Paper presented at the annual meeting of the Midwest Sociological Society, St. Louis.

Basken, Paul. 2007. A Year after Turmoil, Gallaudet Sees Progress and Problems. *Chronicle of Higher Education* (October 20), 54: A27.

Basu, Moni. 2004. In Troubled Times, U.S. Muslims Get Political. *Atlanta Journal-Constitution* (July 24): 1.

Bauder, Harald. 2003. Brain Abuse, or the Devaluation of Immigrant Labour in Canada. *Antipode* (September), 35: 699–717.

Baum, Geraldine. 1998. New Power of Women Recasts Judaism. *Los Angeles Times* (April 21): A1, A14, A15.

Ba-Yunus, Ilyas, and Kassim Kone. 2004. Muslim Americans: A Demographic Report. In *Muslims' Place in the American Public Square*, eds. Zahid H. Bukhari et al., 299–322. Walnut Creek, CA: Atamira Press.

Bean, Frank D., Jennifer Lee, Jeanne Batalova, and Mark Leach. 2004. *Immigration and Fading Color Lines in America*. New York: Russell Sage Foundation.

Bean, Frank D., and G. Stevens. 2003. *America's Newcomers and the Dynamics of Diversity*. New York: Russell Sage Foundation.

Becerra, Hector. 2008. Latino Yes, but with New Tastes. *Los Angeles Times* (May 28): A1, A16.

Beisel, Nicola, and Tamara Kay. 2004. Abortion: Race and Gender in Nineteenth Century America. *American Sociological Review* (August), 69: 498–518.

Bell, Derrick. 1994. The Freedom of Employment Act. *The Nation* 258 (May 23): 708, 710–714.

———. 2004. *Silent Covenants: Brown v. Board of Education and the Unfulfilled Hopes for Racial Reform*. Cambridge, MA: Oxford University Press.

———. 2007. Desegregation's Demise. *Chronicles of Higher Education* (July 13), 53: B11.

Bell, Wendell. 1991. Colonialism and Internal Colonialism. Pp. 52–53 in *The Encyclopedic Dictionary of Sociology*, 4th ed., ed. Richard Lachmann. Guilford, CT: Dushkin Publishing Group.

Bellafante, Ginia. 2005. Young South Asians in America Embrace "Assisted" Marriages. *New York Times* (August 23): A1, A15.

Bellah, Robert. 1967. Civil Religion in America. *Daedalus* 96 (Winter): 1–21.

Belliard, Juan Carlos, and Johnny Ramirez-Johnson. 2005. Medical Pluralism in the Life of a Mexican Immigrant Woman. *Hispanic Journal of Behavioral Sciences* (August), 27: 267–285.

Belluck, Pam. 1997. A New Window to Run Welfare Is a Tight Squeeze for Many Tribes. *New York Times* (September 9): A1, A15.

Belt, Don. 2002. The World of Islam. *National Geographic* (January): 76–85.

Bem, Sandra L. and Daryl J. Bem. 1970. Case Study of a Nonconscious Ideology: Training the Woman to Know Her Place. Pp. 89–99 in *Beliefs, Attitudes, and Human Affairs*, Daryl J. Bem, ed. Belmont, CA: Brooks/Cole.

Bendick, Marc, Jr., Charles W. Jackson, and J. Horacio Romero. 1993. *Employment Discrimination against Older Workers: An Experimental Study of Hiring Practices*. Binghamton, NY: Haworth Press.

Bennett, Brian. 2008. Coming to America. *Time* 171 (February 4).

Bennett, Natalie. 2008. Caribbean Americans. Pp. 241–244 in vol. 1, *Encyclopedia of Race, Ethnicity, and Society*, Richard T. Schaefer, ed. Thousand Oaks, CA: Sage.

Bennett, Phillip. 1993. Ethnic Labels Fail to Keep Up with Reality. *The Cincinnati Enquirer* (November 18): A10.

Bennett, Vivienne S. 1995. Gender, Class, and Water: Women and the Politics of Water Service in Monterrey, Mexico. *Latin American Perspective* (September), 22: 76–99.

———, S. Dávila-Poblete, and M. N. Rico, eds. 2005. *Opposing Currents: The Politics of Water and Gender in Latin America*. Pittsburg: University of Pittsburg Press.

Bennhold, Katrin. 2008. Spurring Secularism, Many French Muslims Find Haven in Catholic Schools. *New York Times* (September 30): A6.

Berger, Joseph. 2008. Salvadorans, Building Their Own Cultural Bridge. *New York Times* (May 4).

Bernstein, Nina. 2007. Some Complain of Class Divide in Chinese-Americans' Charity. *New York Times* (January 20): A1, A13.

Best, Joel. 2001. Social Progress and Social Problems: Toward a Sociology of Gloom. *Sociological Quarterly* 42 (1): 1–12.

Bigelow, Rebecca. 1992. Certain Inalienable Rights. *Friends Journal* (November), 38: 6–8.

Billson, Janet Mancini. 1988. No Owner of Soil: The Concept of Marginality Revisited on Its Sixtieth Birthday. *International Review of Modern Sociology* 18 (Autumn): 183–204.

Birchard, Karen. 2006. Native Suspicion. *Chronicle of Higher Education* (January 13), 52: A46–A49.

Blackfeet Preservation Development Fund. 2006. *The Facts v. the Brochure*. Blackfeet Restoration.

Blackstock, Nelson. 1976. *COINTELPRO: The FBI's Secret War on Political Freedom*. New York: Vintage Press.

Blauner, Robert. 1969. Internal Colonialism and Ghetto Revolt. *Social Problems* 16 (Spring): 393–408.

———. 1972. *Racial Oppression in America*. New York: Harper & Row.

Blood, Michael R. 2006. Schwarzenegger's Hot-Blooded Ethnic Remarks Draw Mixed Reaction. *San Jose Mercury News* (September 9).

Bloom, Leonard. 1971. *The Social Psychology of Race Relations*. Cambridge, MA: Schenkman Publishing.

Bloom, Stephen G. 2000. *Postville: A Clash of Cultures in Heartland America*. New York: Harcourt.

———. 2008. Some Historic Perspective on Postville Raid. *Iowa City Press-Citizen* (May 17): 14A.

Bobo, Lawrence, and Mia Tuan. 2006. *Prejudices in Politics: Group Position, Public Opinion, and the Wisconsin Treaty Rights Dispute*. Cambridge, MA: Harvard University Press.

Bocian, Debbie Gruenstein, Keith S. Ernst, and Wei Li. 2006. *Unfair Lending: The Effect of Race and Ethnicity on the Price of Subprime Mortgages*. Oakland, CA: Center for Responsible Lending.

Boehm, Mike. 2004. Repeating the History. Los Angeles Times. February 20, E2.

Bogardus, Emory. 1968. Comparing Racial Distance in Ethiopia, South Africa, and the United States. *Sociology and Social Research* 52 (January): 149–156.

Bohmer, Susanne, and Kayleen V. Oka. 2007. Teaching Affirmative Action: An Opportunity to Apply, Segregate, and Reinforce Sociological Concepts. *Teaching Sociology* (October), 35: 334–349.

———. 2008. Will Change Happen in Obamerica? Posted July 15, 2008, at contexts.org (American Sociological Association). Accessed at http://contexts.org/obama/author/bonilla-silva.

Bonacich, Edna. 1972. A Theory of Ethnic Antagonism: The Split Labor Market. *American Sociological Review* (October), 37: 547–559.

———. 1976. Advanced Capitalism and Black/White Race Relations in the United States: A Split Labor Market Interpretation. *American Sociological Review* (February), 41: 34–51.

Bonilla-Silva, Eduardo. 1996. Rethinking Racism: Toward a Structural Interpretation. *American Sociological Review* (June), 62: 465–480.

———. 2002. The Linguistics of Color Blind Racism: How to Talk Nasty about Blacks without Sounding Racist. *Critical Sociology* 28 (1–2): 41–64.

———. 2004. From Bi-Racial to Tri-Racial: Towards a New System of Racial Stratification in the USA. *Ethnic and Racial Studies* (November), 27: 931–950.

———. 2006. *Racism without Racists*. 2nd ed. Lanham, MD: Rowman & Littlefield.

———, and Gianpaolo Baiocchi. 2001. Anything but Racism: How Sociologists Limit the Significance of Racism. *Race and Society* 4: 117–131.

———, and David G. Embrick. 2007. "Every Place Has a Ghetto . . .": The Significance of Whites' Social and Residential Segregation. *Symbolic Interaction* 30 (3): 323–345.

Bonus, Rick. 2000. *Locating Filipino Americans: Ethnicity and the Cultural Politics of Space*. Philadelphia, PA: Temple University Press.

Bordt, Rebecca L. 2005. Using a Research Article to Facilitate a Deep Structure Understanding of Discrimination. *Teaching Sociology* (October), 33: 403–410.

Borjas, George J., Jeffery Grogger, and Gordon H. Hanson. 2006. *Immigration and African-American Employment Opportunities: The Response of Wages, Employment, and Incarceration to Labor Supply Shocks.* Working Paper 12518. Cambridge, MA: National Bureau of Economic Research.

Bork, Robert H. 1995. What to Do About the First Amendment. *Commentary* (February), 99: 23–29.

Bositis, David A. 1996. The Farrakhan Factor. *Washington Post National Weekly Edition* (December 16), 14: 24.

Bosman, Julie. 2007. Plan for Arabic School in Brooklyn Arouses Protests. *New York Times* (May 4): A22.

Boudreaux, Ruhid. 2002. Indian Rights Law Is Upheld in Mexico. *Los Angeles Times* (September 7): A3.

Bourdieu, Pierre. 1983. The Forms of Capital. Pp. 241–258 in *Handbook of Theory and Research for the Sociology of Education*, ed. J. G. Richardson. Westport, CT: Greenwood.

———, and Jean-Claude Passeron. 1990. *Reproduction in Education, Society and Culture.* 2nd ed. London: Sage. (Originally published as *La Reproduction* 1970.)

Bowles, Scott. 2000. Bans on Racial Profiling Gain Steam. *USA Today* (June), 2: 3A.

Bowman, Tom. 1998. Evangelicals Allege Bias in U.S. Navy, Marine Chaplain Corps. *Baltimore Sun* 23 (August): A12.

Bowser, Benjamin, and Raymond G. Hunt, eds. 1996. *Impacts of Racism on White Americans.* Beverly Hills, CA: Sage Publications.

Braddock, D., and L. Bachelder 1994. *The Glass Ceiling and Persons with Disabilities.* Washington, DC: The Glass Ceiling Commission.

Brands, H. W., T. H. Breen, R. Hal Williams, and Ariela J. Gross. 2009. *American Stories: A History of the United States.* New York: Pearson Longman.

Brannon, Ruth. 1995. The Use of the Concept of Disability Culture: A Historian's View. *Disability Studies Quarterly* (Fall), 15: 3–15.

Brazil. 1981. *IX Recenseamento Geral do Brasil—1980, 1, P + 1.* Rio de Janeiro: Secretaria de Planejamento da Presidencia da República, Fundacão Instituto Brasilerio de Geografia e Estatistica.

Breines, Winifred. 2007. Struggling to Connect: White and Black Feminism in the Movement Years. *Contexts* 6 (1): 18–24.

Brewer, Cynthia A., and Trudy A. Suchan. 2001. *Mapping Census 2000: The Geography of U.S. Diversity.* Washington, DC: U.S. Government Printing Office.

Brewington, Kelly. 2008. Broken Families. *Baltimore Sun* 26 (January).

Briggs, Xavier de Souza. 2007. "Some of My Best Friends Are . . .": Interracial Friendships, Class, and Segregation in America. *City and Community* 6(4): 263–290.

Brimmer, Andrew. 1995. The Economic Cost of Discrimination against Black Americans. Pp. 9–29 in *Economic Perspectives in Affirmative Action*, ed. Margaret C. Simms. Washington, DC: Joint Center for Political and Economic Studies.

Brittingham, Angela, and G. Patricia de la Cruz. 2005. We the People of Arab Ancestry in the United States. CENSR-21. Washington, DC: U.S. Government Printing Office.

Brodie, Mollyann, Annie Steffenson, Jamie Valdez, Rebecca Levin, and Roberto Suro. 2002. *2002 National Survey of Latinos.* Menlo Park, CA: Henry J. Kaiser Foundation and Pew Hispanic Center.

Bronner, Ethan. 2008. Settlers Who Long to Leave West Bank. *New York Times* (November 14): A6.

Brooks-Gunn, Jeanne, Pamela K. Klebanov, and Greg J. Duncan. 1996. Ethnic Differences in Children's Intelligence Test Scores: Role of Economic Deprivation, Home Environment, and Maternal Characteristics. *Child Development* (April), 67: 396–408.

Brown, Dee. 1971. *Bury My Heart at Wounded Knee.* New York: Holt, Rinehart & Winston.

Brown, Patricia Leigh. 2003. For the Muslim Prom Queen, There Are No Kings Allowed. *New York Times* (June), 9: A1, A24.

Browne, Irene, ed. 2001. *Latinas and African American Women at Work: Race, Gender, and Economic Inequality.* New York: Russell Sage Foundation.

Brulliard, Karin. 2006. A Proper Goodbye: Funeral Homes Learn Immigrants' Traditions. *Washington Post National Weekly Edition* (May 7): 31.

Brunsma, David L., ed. 2006. *Mixed Messages: Multiracial Identities in the "Color-Blind" Era.* Boulder, CO: Lynn Rienner.

Bryan, Susan Montoya. 2006. Navajo Power Plant Lease Approved, Opponents Vow to Fight. *News from Indian Country* (May 29): 6.

Bryson, Ken, and Lynne M. Casper. 1999. Co-Resident Grandparents and Grandchildren. *Current Population Reports* Ser. 823, No. 198. Washington, DC: U.S. Government Printing Office.

Buchannan, Susy. 2006. Indian Blood. *Intelligence Report* (Winter): 34–43.

Buchholz, Barbara Ballinger. 2003. Expanded Access. *Chicago Tribune* (January 26): sect. 16, 1R, 5R.

Buckley, Stephen. 2000. Brazil's Racial Awakening. *Washington Post* (June 12): A12.

Budig, Michelle J. 2002. Male Advantage and the Gender Composition of Jobs: Who Rides the Glass Escalator? *Social Problems* 49 (2): 258–277.

———, and Paula England. 2001. The Wage Penalty for Motherhood. *American Sociological Review* (April), 66: 204–225.

Bukowcyk, John J. 1996. *Polish Americans and Their History: Community, Culture and Politics.* Pittsburgh: University of Pittsburgh Press.

Bureau of the Census. 1975. *Historical Statistics of the United States, Colonial Times to 1970.* Washington, DC: U.S. Government Printing Office.

———. 1981. *Statistical Abstract of the United States, 1981.* Washington, DC: U.S. Government Printing Office.

———. 1988. *Statistical Abstract of the United States, 1988.* Washington, DC: U.S. Government Printing Office.

———. 1996. *Statistical Abstract of the United States, 1996.* Washington, DC: U.S. Government Printing Office.

———. 2002. *Table 1. United States—Race and Hispanic Origin: 1790–1990.* Internet release date: September 13, 2002.

———. 2003. *Statistical Abstract of the United States, 2003.* Washington, DC: U.S. Government Printing Office.

———. 2004. *U.S. Interim Projections by Age, Sex, Race, and Hispanic Origin.* Released March 18, 2004, at www.census.gov/ipc/www/usinterimproj.

———. 2005a. *Statistical Abstract of the United States, 2004–2005.* Washington, DC: U.S. Government Printing Office.

———. 2005b. *Texas Becomes Nation's Newest "Majority-Minority" States, Census Bureau Announces. CB05-118.* Washington, DC: U.S. Government Printing Office.

———. 2007a. *Statistical Abstract of the United States, 2006.* Washington, DC: U.S. Government Printing Office.

———. 2007b. American Community Survey 2006, factfinder.census.gov.

———. 2007c. *The American Community—Asians: 2004.* Report ACS-05. Washington, DC: U.S. Government Printing Office.

———. 2007d. *Educational Attainment in the United States: 2007.* Accessed at www.census.gov/population/www/socdemo/educcation/cps2007.html.

———. 2007e. *Housing Vacancies and Homeownership.* Accessed at www.census.gov/hhes/www/housing/hvs/annual07/ann07t20.html.

———. 2007f. *The American Community—Hispanics 2004.* ACS-03. Washington, DC: U.S. Government Printing Office.

———. 2007g. *2006 American Community Survey. S0201. Selected Population Profile in the United States: Salvadoran.* Accessed August 16, 2008, at www.census.gov.

———. 2007h. *2006 American Community Survey. Selected Economic Characteristics: Puerto Rico and the United States.* Accessed August 16, 2008, at www.census.gov.

———. 2007i. *2006 American Community Survey. Hispanic Population, Metropolitan Areas.* Table B03001. Accessed at www.census.gov.

———. 2007j. *The American Community-Pacific Islanders: 2004.* ACS-06. Washington, DC: U.S. Government Printing Office.

———. 2008a. *Statistical Abstract of the United States, 2007.* Washington, DC: U.S. Government Printing Office.

———. 2008b. American Community Survey 2007. Available at www.census.gov.

———. 2008c. *Families and Living Arrangements: 2007.* Accessed at www.census.gov/population/www/socdemo/hh-fam/cps2007.html.

———. 2008d. *An Older and More Diverse Nation by Midcentury.* Accessed August 14, 2008, at www.census.gov/Press-Release/www/releases/archives/population/012496.html.

———. 2008e. *New Census Bureau Data Provide a Portrait of the Puerto Rico Population: September 23.* Accessed at www.census.gov.

Bureau of Indian Affairs. 1970. *Answers to Your Questions about Indians.* Washington, DC: U.S. Government Printing Office.

———. 1986. *American Indians Today: Answers to Your Questions.* Washington, DC: U.S. Government Printing Office.

———. 1988. *Report of BIA Education: Excellence in Indian Education through the Effective School Process.* Washington, DC: U.S. Government Printing Office.

Bureau of Justice Statistics. 2004. *First Release from State Prisons 2001.* Washington, DC: Bureau of Justice Statistics.

Bureau of Labor Statistics. 2008. American Time Use Survey. Accessed September 14, 2008, at www.bls.gov/tus/overview.htm#1.

Burgdorf, Robert L., Jr. 2005. Americans with Disabilities Act of 1990 (United States). Pp. 93–101 in Gary Albrecht, ed., *Encyclopedia of Disability.* Thousand Oaks, CA: Sage.

Burgess, Mike. 1992. American Indian Religious Freedom Act Hearings. *News from Indian Country* (December): 8–9.

Bush, George W. 2001. *Islam Is Peace.* Accessed October 16, 2004, at www.whitehouse.gov/news/releases.

———. 2005. *President, Lieutenant General Honere Discuss Hurricane Relief in Louisiana.* September 12. Accessed January 31, 2006, at www.whitehouse.gov.

Business and Professional Women. 2002. *Equal Pay Day 2002 Legislative Bankguard.* Accessed April 14, 2002, at www.bpwusa.org/Content/FairPay/Docy/NCPE.

Butler, Robert N. 1990. A Disease Called Ageism. *Journal of the American Geriatrics Society* (February), 38: 178–180.

Byng, Michelle D. 2008. Complex Inequities: The Case of Muslim Americans after 9/11. *American Behavioral Scientist* 51 (January): 659–674.

Cainkar, Louise. 2006. Immigrants from the Arab World. Pp. 182–196 in *The New Chicago*, John P. Koval et al., eds. Philadelphia: Temple University Press.

Calavita, Kitty. 2007. Immigration Law, Race, and Identity. *Annual Reviews of Law and Social Sciences* 3: 1–20.

Camarillo, Albert. 1993. Latin Americans: Mexican Americans and Central Americans. Pp. 855–872 in *Encyclopedia of American Social History*, Mary Koplec Coyton, Elliot J. Gorn, and Peter W. Williams, eds. New York: Charles Scribner.

Camarota, Steven A. 2002. Immigrants from the Middle East. Washington DC: Center for Immigration Statistics. 2007a. *Immigrants in the United States, 2007: A Profile of America's Foreign-Born Population*. Washington, DC: Center for Immigrant Statistics.

———. 2007b. *100 Million More. Projecting the Impact of Immigration on the U.S. Population, 2007 to 2060*. Washington, DC: Center for Immigrant Statistics.

Campbell, Gregory R. 2008b. Native American Health Care. Pp. 949–954 in vol. 2, *Encyclopedia of Race, Ethnicity, and Society*, Richard T. Schaefer, ed. Thousand Oaks, CA: Sage.

———. 2008c. Native American Graves Protection and Repatriation Act of 1990. Pp. 947–949 in vol. 2, *Encyclopedia of Race, Ethnicity, and Society*, Richard T. Schaefer, ed. Thousand Oaks, CA: Sage.

———. 2008d. Sacred Sites, Native American. Pp. 1179–1182 in vol. 3, *Encyclopedia of Race, Ethnicity, and Society*, Richard T. Schaefer, ed. Thousand Oaks, CA: Sage.

Campbell, Gregory R. 2008a. Blood Quantum. Pp. 181–184 in vol. 1, *Encyclopedia of Race, Ethnicity, and Society*, Richard T. Schaefer, ed. Thousand Oaks, CA: Sage.

Canak, William, and Laura Swanson. 1998. *Modern Mexico*. New York: McGraw-Hill.

Cañas, Jesus, Roberto Coronado, and Robert W. Gilman. 2007. Southwest Economy (March/April). Accessed April 18, 2007, at dallasfed.org/research/swe/ 2007/ swe0702b.cfm.

Capps, Randy, Ku Leighton, and Michael Fix. 2002. *How Are Immigrants Faring after Welfare Reform? Preliminary Evidence from Los Angeles and New York City*. Washington, DC: Urban Institute.

Carlson, Allan C. 2003. The Peculiar Legacy of German-Americans. *Society* (January/ February): 77–88.

Carlson, Dawn S., K. Michele Kacmar, and Dwayne Whitten. 2006. What Men Think They Knew About Executive Women. *Harvard Business Review* (September), 84: 28.

Carmichael, Stokely, with Ekwueme Michael Thelwell. 2003. *The Life and Struggles of Stokely Carmichael (Kwame Ture)*. New York: Scribner.

Carnegie Foundation for the Advancement of Teaching. 1990. Native Americans and Higher Education: New Mood of Optimism. *Change* (January–February): 27–30.

Carroll, Joseph. 2006. Public National Anthem Should Be Sung in English. *The Gallup Poll* (May): 3.

———. 2007. Hispanics Support Requiring English Proficiency for Immigrants. Accessed July 5, 2007, at www.gallup.com.

Cart, Julie. 2006. Painful Past, Iffy Future. *Los Angeles Times* (July 23): B1, B6.

Castañeda, Jorge G. 1995. Ferocious Differences. *Atlantic Monthly* (July), 276: 68–69, 71–76.

Catalano, Shannan M. 2006. *Criminal Victimization, 2005*. Bureau of Justice Statistics Bulletin (September): 1–12.

Catalyst. 2001. Women Satisfied with Current Job in Financial Industry but Barriers Still Exist. Press release July 25, 2001; accessed January 31, 2002, at www. catalystwomen.org.

———. 2008. U.S. Women in Business (August 8). Accessed September 13, 2008, at www.catalyst.org.

Centers for Disease Control and Prevention. 2007. U.S. Public Health Service Syphilis Study at Tuskegee. Accessed April 25, 2007, at www.cdc.gov.

Chambers Book of Facts. 2005. Edinburgh: Chambers Harrap Publishers.

Champagne, Duane. 1994. *Native America. Portrait of the Peoples*. Detroit: Visible Ink.

Chan, Sucheng. 1991. *Asian Americans: An Interpretive History*. Boston: Twayne Publishers.

Chanes, Jerome A. 2007. Anti-Semitism. Pp. 90–110 in *American Jewish Yearbook 2007*, David Singer and Lawrence Grossman, eds. New York: American Jewish Committee.

———. 2008. *A Primer in the American Jewish Community*. 3rd ed. New York: American Jewish Committee.

Chang, Cindy. 2007. Asians Flex Muscles in California Politics. *New York Times* (February 27): A11.

Chang, Doris F., and Amy Demyan. 2007. Teachers' Stereotypes of Asian, Black and White Students. *School Psychology Quarterly*, 22 (2): 91–114.

Chase-Dunn, Christopher, and Thomas D. Hall. 1998. World-Systems in North America: Networks, Rise and Fall and Pulsations of Trade in Stateless Systems. *American Indian Culture and Research Journal*, 22(1): 23–72.

Cheng, Lucie, and Philip Q. Yang. 2000. The "Model Minority" Deconstructed. Pp. 459–482 in Min Zhou and James V. Gatewood, eds., *Contemporary Asian American: A Multidisciplinary Reader*. New York: New York University Press.

Cheng, Shu-Ju Ada. 2008. Jim Crow. P. 795 in vol. 2, *Encyclopedia of Race, Ethnicity, and Society*, Richard T. Schaefer, ed. Thousand Oaks, CA: Sage.

Chertok, Fern, Benjamin Phillips, and Leonard Saxe. 2008. *It's Not Just Who Stands Under the Chuppah: Intermarriage and Engagement*. Waltham, MA: Marilyn Cohen Center for Modern Jewish Studies, Brandies University.

Chicago Tribune. 2006. Newark is No. 1 in U.S. Ordinations (May 26): 12.

Chin, Ko-lin. 1996. *Chinatown Gangs: Extortion, Enterprise, and Ethnicity*. New York: Oxford University Press.

Chirot, Daniel, and Jennifer Edwards. 2003. Making Sense of the Senseless: Understanding Genocide. *Contexts* 2 (Spring): 12–19.

Choi, Yoonsun, and Benjamin B. Lahey. 2006. Testing the Model Minority Stereotype: Youth Behaviors across Racial and Ethnic Groups. *Social Science Review* (September): 419–452.

Christopulos, Diana. 1974. Puerto Rico in the Twentieth Century: A Historical Survey. Pp. 123–163 in Adalberto Lopez and James Petras, eds., *Puerto Rico and Puerto Ricans: Studies in History and Society*. New York: Wiley.

Chu, Jeff, and Nadia Mustafa. 2006. Between Two Worlds. *Time* (January 16).

Citizenship and Immigration Services (CIS). 2008. Typical Questions. Accessed February 13, 2008, at www.uscis.gov/files/nativedocuments/Flashcard_questions.pdf.

Citrin, Jack, Amy Lerman, Michael Murakami, and Kathryn Pearson. 2007. Testing Huntington: Is Hispanic Immigration a Threat to American Identity? *Perspectives on Politics* (March), 5: 31–48.

Clark, Kenneth B., and Mamie P. Clark. 1947. Racial Identification and Preferences in Negro Children. Pp. 169–178 in *Readings in Social Psychology*, Theodore M. Newcomb and Eugene L. Hartley, eds. New York: Holt, Rinehart & Winston.

Cleaver, Kathleen. 1982. How TV Wrecked the Black Panthers. *Channels* (November–December): 98–99.

Clemmitt, Marcia. 2005. Intelligent Design. *CQ Researcher* (July 29), 95: 637–660.

CNN Money. 2008. Women CEOs for Fortune 500 Companies. Accessed September 12, 2008, at money.cnn.com.

Cockburn, Andrew. 2003. True Colors: Divided Loyalty in Puerto Rico. *National Geographic Magazine* (March), 203: 34–55.

Cognard-Black, Andrew J. 2004. Will They Stay, or Will They Go? Sex—Atypical among Token Men Who Teach. *Sociological Quarterly*, 45 (1): 113–139.

Cohen, Roger. 2008. Why Obama Should Visit a Mosque. *New York Times* (June 26).

Cohen, Sandy. 2006. Gibson: "I Am Not an Anti-Semite." *Chicago Tribune* (August 2): 2.

Cohen, Steven M. 1991. *Content or Continuity? Alternative Bases for Commitment*. New York: American Jewish Committee.

Cohon, Samuel M. 1995. Not in Our Town. The Courage to Resist Hatred. *The Chronicle*, 6–9, 36, 38, 44, 48–50.

Colburn, David R., Charles E. Young, and Victor M. Yellen. 2008. Admissions and Public Higher Education in California, Texas, and Florida: The Post-Affirmative Action Era. *InterActions: UCLA Journal of Education and Information Studies* 4 (No. 1): 2. Accessed April 20, 2008, at repositories.cdib.org/gseis/interactions/ vol4/issl/art2.

Coleman, James S. 1988. Social Capital in the Creation of Human Capital. *American Journal of Sociology*, 94 (supplement): S95–S120.

Collins, Patricia Hill. 2000. *Black Feminist Thought: Knowledge, Consciousness, and the Politics of Empowerment*, 2nd ed. New York: Routledge.

Collins, Susan M., Barry P. Bosworth, and Miguel A. Soto-Class, eds. 2006. *The Economy of Puerto Rico: Restoring Growth*. Washington, DC: Brookings Institution.

Collura, Heather. 2007. Roommate Concerns Fed by Facebook. *USA Today* (August 8): 6D.

Colón Morera, José Javier, and José E. Rivera Santana. 2006. New Dimensions in Civil Society Mobilization: The Struggle for Peace in Vieques. Pp. 207–236 in *Puerto Rico Under Colonial Rule*, Ramón Bosque-Pérez and José Javier Colón Morera, eds. Albany: State University of New York Press.

Commission on Civil Rights. 1976. *Fulfilling the Letter and Spirit of the Law: Desegregation of the Nation's Public Schools*. Washington, DC: U.S. Government Printing Office.

———. 1981. *Affirmative Action in the 1980s: Dismantling the Process of Discrimination*. Washington, DC: U.S. Government Printing Office.

Commission on Wartime Relocation and Internment of Civilians. 1982a. *Recommendations*. Washington, DC: U.S. Government Printing Office.

———. 1982b. *Report*. Washington, DC: U.S. Government Printing Office.

Committee of 100. 2001. *American Attitudes Towards Chinese Americans and Asian Immigrants*. New York: Committee of 100.

Connelly, Marjorie. 2008. Dissecting the Changing Electorate. *New York Times* (November 8): sect. WK.

Connor, Walter. 1994. *Ethnonationalism: The Quest for Understanding*. Princeton, NJ: Princeton University Press.

Conver, Bill. 1976. Group Chairman Lists Problems Endangering Jewish Family. *Peoria Journal Star* (December 4): A2.

Conyers, James L., Jr. 1996. A Case Study of Social Stratification: An Afrocentric Edification. *Western Journal of Black Studies* (Spring), 20: 9–15.

———. 2004. The Evolution of Africology: An Afrocentric Appraisal. *Journal of Black Studies* (May), 34: 640–652.

Coogan, Michael D. 2003. *The Illustrated Guide to World Religions*. Oxford University Press.

Cooper, Abraham, and Harold Brackman. 2001. Holocaust Deniers Spread Their Lies in the Middle East. *USA Today* (March 8): 15A.

Cooper, Mary H. 2004. Voting Rights. *CQ Researcher* (October 29), 14: 901–924.

Cooper, Richard S., Charles N. Rotimi, and Ryk Ward. 1999. The Puzzle of Hypertension in African Americans. *Scientific American* (February): 56–63.

Cooperman, Alan. 2005. One Way to Pray? *Washington Post National Weekly Edition* (September 5), 22: 10–11.

Cordova, Carlos. 2005. *The Salvadoran Americans.* Westport, CT: Greenwood Press.

Cornacchia, Eugene J., and Dale C. Nelson. 1992. Historical Differences in the Political Experiences of American Blacks and White Ethnics: Revisiting an Unresolved Controversy. *Ethnic and Racial Studies* (January 15): 102–124.

Cornell, Stephen. 1984. Crisis and Response in Indian–White Relations: 1960–1984. *Social Problems* (October), 32: 44–59.

———. 1996. The Variable Ties that Bind: Content and Circumstance in Ethnic Processes. *Ethnic and Racial Studies* (April), 19: 265–289.

———. 2003. *Alaska Native Self-Government and Service Delivery: What Works?* Tucson, AZ: Native Nations Institute for Leadership, Management, and Policy.

———, and Joseph P. Kalt. 1990. Pathways from Poverty: Economic Development and Institution-Building on American Indian Reservations. *American Indian Culture and Research Journal,* 14 (1): 89–125.

Correll, Joshua, Bernadette Park, Charles M. Judd, Bernd Wittenbrink, Melody S. Sadler, and Tracie Keesee. 2007. Across the Thin Blue Line: Police Officers and Racial Bias in the Decision to Shoot. *Journal of Personality and Social Psychology,* 92 (6): 1006–1023.

Cose, Ellis. 1993. *The Rage of a Privileged Class.* New York: HarperCollins.

Coser, Lewis A. 1956. *The Functions of Social Conflict.* New York: Free Press.

———, and Rose Laub Coser. 1974. *Greedy Institutions.* New York: Free Press.

Council on American–Islamic Relations. 2004. Poll: 1-in-4 Americans Holds Anti-Muslim Views. Accessed October 7, 2004, at www.cair-net.org.

Cox, James. 2002. Activists Challenge Corporations That They Say Are Tied to Slavery. *USA Today* (February 21): 1A, 8A, 9A.

Cox, Oliver C. 1942. The Modern Caste School of Social Relations. *Social Forces* (December), 21: 218–226.

Crenson, Matt. 2005. Polluted Town Alarmed by Shortage of Sons. Associated Press. Accessed December 18, 2005, at aol.com.

Crosnoe, Robert. 2005. The Diverse Experiences of Hispanic Students in the American Educational System. Sociological Forum 20: 561–588.

Cumming-Bruce, Nick. 2008. Worlds Refugee Count in 2007, Exceeded 11 Million, U.N. Says. *New York Times* (June 18): A8.

Dahlburg, John-Thor. 1998. Deal Ok'd to End 30 Years of "Trouble" in Northern Ireland. *Los Angeles Times* (April 11): A1, A8–A9.

———. 2001. A New World for Haitians. *Los Angeles Times* (September 4): A1, A9.

Daitz, Ben. 2003. Navajo Miners Battle a Deadly Legacy of Yellow Dust. *New York Times* (May 13): D5, D8.

Dallo, Florence J., Kristine J. Ajrouch, and Soham Al-Snih. 2008. The Ancestry Question and Ethnic Heterogeneity: The Case of Arab Americans. *International Migration Review* (Summer): 505–517.

Dang, Alain, and Somjem Frnzer. 2004. *Black Same-Sex Households in the United States.* Washington, DC: National Gay and Lesbian Task Force Policy Institutes.

Daniel, G. Reginald. 2006. *Race Multiraciality in Brazil and the United States: Converging Paths?* University Park: Pennsylvania State University Press.

Daniels, Roger. 1972. *Concentration Camps, USA.* New York: Holt, Rinehart & Winston.

Dansie, Roberto. 2004. Curanderismo. *Indian Country Today* (December 8): C5.

Dart, Bob. 1998. Preserving America: Lancaster County, PA. *Atlanta Journal and Constitution* (June 28).

David, Gary C. 2003. Rethinking Who's an Arab American: Arab-American Studies in the New Millennium. *Al-Jadid* (Fall): 9.

———. 2004. Scholarship on Arab Americans Distorted Past 9/11. *Al-Jadid* (Winter/Spring): 26–27.

———. 2007. The Creation of "Arab American": Political Activism and Ethnic (Dis)Unity. *Critical Sociology,* 32: 833–862.

———. 2008. Arab Americans. Pp. 84–87 in vol. 2, *Encyclopedia of Race, Ethnicity, and Society,* Richard T. Schaefer, ed. Thousand Oaks, CA: Sage.

———, and Kenneth Kahtan Ayouby. 2004. Perpetual Suspects and Permanent Others: Arab Americans and the War and Terrorism. Pp. 30–71 in *Guerras e Imigracioes,* Marco Aurélio Machado de Oliveira, eds. Campo Grande, Brazil: Universidade Federal de Mato Grosso do Sul.

Davis, David Brion. 1966. *The Problem of Slavery in Western Culture.* Ithaca, NY: Cornell University Press.

Davis, James A., Tom W. Smith, and Peter V. Marsden. 2007. *General Social Surveys, 1972–2006: Cumulative Codebook.* Chicago: NORC.

Davis, Michelle R. 2008. Checking Sources: Evaluating Web Sites Requires Careful Eye. (Released by *Education Week,* March 6.) Accessed June 20, 2008, at www.edweek.org.

Dawson, Michael C., and Rovana Popoff. 2004. Reparations: Justice and Greed in Black and White. *DuBois Review,* 1 (1): 47–91.

De Anda, Roberto M. 2004. *Chicanas and Chicanos in Contemporary Society,* 2nd ed. Lanham, MD: Rowman & Littlefield & Bacon.

Degler, Carl N. 1971. *Neither Black nor White: Slavery and Race Relations in Brazil and the United States.* New York: Macmillan.

de la Garza, Rodolfo O., Louis DeSipio, F. Chris Garcia, John Garcia, and Angelo Falcon. 1992. *Latino Voices: Mexican, Puerto Rican, and Cuban Perspectives on American Politics.* Boulder, CO: Westview Press.

Delgado, Héctor L. 2008a. La Raza. Pp. 830–831 in vol. 2, *Encyclopedia of Race, Ethnicity, and Society,* Richard T. Schaefer, ed. Thousand Oaks, CA: Sage.

———. 2008b. Chicano Movement. Pp. 272–274 in vol. 1, *Encyclopedia of Race, Ethnicity, and Society,* Richard T. Schaefer, ed. Thousand Oaks, CA: Sage.

Dell'Angela, Tracy. 2005. Dakota Indians Say Kids Trapped in "School-to-Prison" Pipeline. *Chicago Tribune* (November 29): 1, 12.

DellaPergola, Sergio. 2007. World Jewish Population, 2007. Pp. 551–600 in *American Jewish Yearbook 2007,* David Singer and Lawrence Grossman, eds. New York: American Jewish Committee.

Del Olmo, Frank. 2003. Slow Motion Carnage at the Border. *Los Angeles Times* (May 18): M5.

Deloria, Vine, Jr. 1969. *Custer Died for Your Sins: An Indian Manifesto.* New York: Avon.

———. 1971. *Of Utmost Good Faith.* New York: Bantam.

———. 1992. Secularism, Civil Religion, and the Religious Freedom of American Indians. *American Indian Culture and Research Journal,* 16 (2): 9–20.

———. 1995. *Red Earth, White Lies.* New York: Scribner's.

———. 2004. Promises Made, Promises Broken. Pp. 143–159 in *Native Universe: Voices of Indian America,* Gerald McMaster and Clifford E. Trofzer, eds. Washington, DC: National Geographic.

———, and Clifford M. Lytle. 1983. *American Indians, American Justice.* Austin: University of Texas Press.

DeNavas-Walt, Carmen, Bernadette D. Proctor, and Jessica Smith. 2008. Income, Poverty, and Health Insurance Coverage in the United States: 2007. *Current Population Reports,* 60–235. Washington, DC: U.S. Government Printing Office.

Dennis, Rutledge M. 2008. Jewry, Black American. Pp. 792–795 in vol. 2, *Encyclopedia of Race, Ethnicity, and Society,* Richard T. Schaefer, ed. Thousand Oaks, CA: Sage.

Denton, Nancy A., and Jacqueline Villarrubia. 2007. Residential Segregation on the Island: The Role of Race and Class in Puerto Rican Neighborhoods. *Sociological Forum* (March), 22: 1573–1586.

DePalma, Anthony. 1995. Racism? Mexico's in Denial. *New York Times* (June 11): E4.

DeParle, Jason. 2007. A Good Provider Is One Who. *New York Times* (April 22): 50–57, 72, 122–123.

Department of Energy. 2000. *Final Report: Task Force against Racial Profiling.* Washington, DC: U.S. Government Printing Office.

Department of Interior. 2005. *Historical Accounting for Individual Indian Monies: A Progress Report.* Washington, DC: U.S. Government Printing Office.

Department of Justice. 2000. *The Civil Liberties Act of 1988: Redress for Japanese Americans.* Accessed June 29, 2000, at www.usdoj.gov/crt/ora/main.html.

———. 2001. *Report to the Congress of the United States: A Review of Restrictions on Persons of Italian Ancestry During World War II.* Accessed February 1, 2002, at www.house.gov/judiciary/Italians.pdf.

———. 2007. Hate Crime Statistics, 2006. Online at www.fbi.gov/ucr/ucr.htm.

———. 2008. Hate Crime Statistics, 2007. Accessed November 21, 2008, at www.fbi.gov.

Department of Labor. 1965. *The Negro Family: The Case for National Action.* Washington, DC: U.S. Government Printing Office.

———. 1995. *Good for Business: Making Full Use of the Nation's Capital.* Washington, DC: U.S. Government Printing Office.

———. 2001. *Working in the 21st Century.* Washington, DC: U.S. Government Printing Office.

———. 2007. *Women in the Labor Force: A Databook.* Washington, DC: U.S. Government Printing Office.

Department of State. 2008a. Dual Nationality. Accessed February 6, 2008, at travel.state.gov/travel/cis_pa_tw/cis/cis_1753.html#.

———. 2008b. Immigrant Visas Issued to Orphans Coming to U.S. Accessed September 3, 2008, at www.travel.state.gov/family/adoption/stats/stats_451.html.

Deutscher, Irwin, Fred P. Pestello, and H. Frances Pestello. 1993. *Sentiments and Acts.* New York: Aldine de Gruyter.

Dey, Judy Goldberg, and Catherine Hill. 2007. *Behind the Pay Gap.* Washington, DC: American Association of University Women.

Diamond, Jared. 2003. Globalization, Then. *Los Angeles Times* (September 14): M1, M3.

Dickson, Lisa M. 2006. Book Review: Italians Then, Mexicans Now. *Industrial and Labor Relations Review,* 60 (2): 293–295.

DiMaggio, Paul. 2005. Cultural Capital. Pp. 167–170 in *Encyclopedia of Social Theory,* George Ritzer, ed. Thousand Oaks, CA: Sage Publications.

Dinnerstein, Leonard. 1994. *Anti-Semitism in America.* New York: Oxford University Press.

DiTomaso, Nancy, Corinne Post, and Rochelle Parks-Yancy. 2007. Workforce Diversity and Inequality: Power, Status, and Numbers. *Annual Review of Sociology,* 33: 473–501.

Dixon, Robyn. 2007. Running for Their Lives. *Los Angeles Times* (September 9): A1, A10.

Dobbin, Frank, Alexandra Kaler, and Erin Kelly. 2007. Diversity Management in Corporate America. *Contexts,* 6 (4): 21–27.

Dolan, Maura. 2000. State Justices Deal New Set Back to Affirmative Action. *Los Angeles Times* (December 1).

Dolan, Sean, and Sandra Stotsky. 1997. *The Polish Americans.* New York: Chelsea House.

Domino, John C. 1995. *Sexual Harassment and the Courts.* New York: HarperCollins.

Dorris, Michael. 1988. For the Indians, No Thanksgiving. *New York Times* (November 24): A23.

Dovidio, John F. 2001. On the Nature of Contemporary Prejudice: The Third Wave. *Journal of Social Issues* (4), 57: 829–849.

Downey, Douglas B. 2008. Black/White Differences in School Performance: The Oppositional Culture Explanation. *Annual Review of Sociology*, 34: 107–126.

Drinkard, Jim. 2006a. Tribes' Special Status a Product of Law and History. *USA Today* (January 31): 6A.

———. 2006b. Tribes' Political Giving Targeted. *USA Today* (January 31): A1.

Duberman, Martin. 1993. *Stonewall*. New York: Dutton.

DuBois, W. E. B. 1903. *The Souls of Black Folks: Essays and Sketches* (reprint). New York: Facade Publications, 1961.

———. 1935. Does the Negro Need Separate Schools? *Journal of Negro Education* (July), 1: 328–335.

———. 1939. *Black Folk: Then and Now*. New York: Holt, Rinehart & Winston.

———. 1952. *Battle for Peace: The Story of My 83rd Birthday*. New York: Masses and Mainstream.

———. 1968. *Dusk of Dawn*. New York: Schocken.

———. 1969a. *An ABC of Color* [1900]. New York: International Publications.

———. 1969b. *The Suppression of the African Slave-Trade to the United States of America, 1638–1870*. New York: Schocken.

———. 1970. *The Negro American Family*. Cambridge, MA: MIT Press.

———. 1996. *The Philadelphia Negro: A Social Study*. Philadelphia: University of Pennsylvania Press (originally published in 1899).

———. 2003. *The Negro Church* [1903]. Walnut Creek: Alta Mira Press.

Dudley, Carl S., and David A. Roozen. 2001. *Faith Communities Today*. Hartford, CT: Hartford Seminary.

Dunn, Ashley. 1994. Southeast Asians Highly Dependent on Welfare in U.S. *New York Times* (May 19): A1, A20.

Durkheim, Émile. 2001. *The Elementary Forms of Religious Life* [1912]. New translation by Carol Cosman. New York: Oxford University Press.

Duszak, Thomas. 1997. Lattimer Massacre Centennial Commemoration. *Polish American Journal* (August). Accessed June 4, 2008, at www.polamjournal.com/Library/APHistory/Lattimer/lattimer.html.

Duthu, N. Bruce. 2008. Broken Justice in Indian Country. *New York Times* (August 11): A21.

Dyson, Michael Eric. 1995. *Making Malcolm: The Myth and Meaning of Malcolm X*. New York: Oxford University Press.

———. 2005. *Is Bill Cosby Right?* New York: Basic Civitas, Perseus Books.

Dzidzienyo, Anani. 1987. Brazil. In *International Handbook on Race and Race Relations*, Jay A. Sigler, ed. New York: Greenwood Press.

Echaveste, Maria. 2005. Target Employees. *American Prospect* (November): A10–A11.

Eckholm, Erik. 2006. Plight Deepens for Black Men, Studies Warn. *New York Times* (March 20): A1, A18.

Eckstrom, Kevin. 2001. New, Diverse Take Spot on Catholic Altars. *Chicago Tribune* (August 31): 8.

Economic Mobility Project. 2007a. *Economic Mobility of Black and White Families*. Washington, DC: Pew Charitable Trust.

Economist. 2004a. An Amish Exception (February 7): 33.

———. 2004b. Who's Winning the Fight? (July 30): 38.

———. 2004c. Indigenous People in South America: A Political Awakening (February 21): 35–37.

———. 2005a. South African Race Relations: If Only the Adults Would Behave Like the Children (April 23): 25–27.

———. 2005b. The Status of Gaza: Now Who Takes the Blame? (August 27): 39.

———. 2005c. Israel and Palestine: Even More Separate (October 22): 47–48.

———. 2006. Gaza: Death and Disintegration All Round (September 9): 48–49.

———. 2008. The Graveyard Shift (May 31): 55–56.

Edmo-Suppah, Lori. 2008. Sho-Ban Holds Summer Graduation Ceremony—Three Earn Diplomas. *Sho-Ban News* (August 6). Accessed August 12, 2008, at www.shobannews.com/education.htm.

Elkins, Stanley. 1959. *Slavery: A Problem in American Institutional and Intellectual Life*. Chicago: University of Chicago Press.

Elliott, Andrea. 2008. Muslim Voters Detect a Snub from Obama. *New York Times* (June 24): A1, A20.

Ellis, Mark R. 2004. Denver's Anti-Chinese Riot. Pp. 142–143 in *Encyclopedia of the Great Plains*, David J. Wishart, ed. Lincoln: University of Nebraska Press.

Ellison, Brandy J. 2008. Tracking. Pp. 1316–1318 in vol. 3, *Encyclopedia of Race, Ethnicity, and Society*, Richard T. Schaefer, ed. Thousand Oaks, CA: Sage.

El Nasser, Haya. 1997. Varied Heritage Claimed and Extolled by Millions. *USA Today* (May 8): 1A, 2A.

Epstein, Cynthia Fuchs. 1999. The Major Myth of the Women's Movement. *Dissent* (Fall): 83–111.

Equal Employment Opportunity Commission. 2001. Age Discrimination in Employment Act (ADEA), Changes FY 1992–FY 2000. Accessed December 10, 2001, at www.eeoc.gov/stats/adea.html.

Equal Representation in Government and Democracy. 2008. Women Prime Ministers and Presidents. Accessed September 12, 2008, at www.ergd.org/Premiers.htm.

Erdmans, Mary Patrice. 1998. *Opposite Poles: Immigrants and Ethnics in Polish Chicago, 1976–1990*. University Park: Pennsylvania State University.

———. 2006. New Chicago Polonia: Urban and Suburban. Pp. 115–127 in *The New Chicago*, John Koval et al., eds. Philadelphia: Temple University Press

Escárcega, Sylvia. 2008. Mexico. Pp. 898–902 in vol. 2, *Encyclopedia of Race, Ethnicity, and Society*, Richard T. Schaefer, ed. Thousand Oaks, CA: Sage.

Eschbach, Karl, and Kalman Applebaum. 2000. Who Goes to Powwows? Evidence from the Survey of American Indians and Alaskan Natives. *American Indian Culture and Research Journal*, 24(2): 65–83.

Espiritu, Yen Le. 1992. *Asian American Panethnicity: Bridging Institutions and Identities*. Philadelphia: Temple University Press.

———, and Diane L. Wolf. 2001. The Paradox of Assimilation: Children of Filipino Immigrants in San Diego. Pp. 157–186 in *Ethnicities: Children of Immigrants in America*, Ruben G. Rumbaut and Alejandro Portes, eds. Berkeley: University of California Press.

European Roma Rights Centre. 2008. Ostravis Case: D. H. and Others v. The Czech Republic. Accessed June 29, 2008, at www.errc.org.

Fallows, Marjorie R. 1979. *Irish Americans: Identity and Assimilation*. Englewood Cliffs, NJ: Prentice Hall.

Farley, Maggie. 2008. Canada to Apologize for Abuse of Native Students. *Los Angeles Times* (June 10): A4.

Fathi, Nazila. 2006. Iran Opens Conference on Holocaust. *New York Times* (December 12).

Favreault, Melissa. 2008. *Discrimination and Economic Mobility*. Washington, DC: Economic Mobility Project, Pew Charitable Trusts.

Feagin, Joe R., and José A. Cobas. 2008. Latinos/as and White Racial Frame: The Procrustean Bed of Assimilation. *Sociological Inquiry* (February), 78: 39–53.

———, and Karyn D. McKinney. 2003. *The Many Costs of Racism*. Lanham, MD: Rowan and Littlefield.

———, and Eileen O'Brien. 2003. *White Men on Race, Power, Privilege, and the Shaping of Cultural Consciousness*. Boston: Beacon Press.

———, Hernán Vera, and Pinar Batur. 2000. *White Racism*, 2nd ed. New York: Routledge.

Ferber, Abby L. 2007. Whiteness Studies and the Erasure of Gender. *Sociology Compass* 1 (1): 256–282.

———. 2008. Privilege. Pp. 1073–1074 in vol. 3, *Encyclopedia of Race, Ethnicity, and Society*, Richard T. Schaefer, ed. Thousand Oaks, CA: Sage.

Ferguson, Ronald. 2007. Parenting Practices, Teenage Lifestyles, and Academic Achievement among African-American Children. *Focus* 25 (Spring–Summer): 18–26.

Fernandez, Manny, and Kareem Fahim. 2006. Five on Plane Are Detained at Newark but Later Freed. *New York Times* (May 5): 29.

Fernandez-Armesto, Felope. 2007. *The World: A History*. Upper Saddle River, NJ: Prentice Hall.

File, Thom. 2008. Voting and Registration in the Election of November 2006. Pp. 20–557 in *Current Population Reports*. Washington, DC: U.S. Government Printing Office.

Finder, Alan. 1994. Muslim Gave Racist Speech, Jackson Says. *New York Times* (January 23): 21.

Fine, Gary. 2008. *Robber's Cave*. Pp. 1163–1164 in vol. 3, *Encyclopedia of Race, Ethnicity, and Society*, Richard T. Schaefer, ed. Thousand Oaks, CA: Sage.

Fine, Michelle, and Adrienne Asch. 1981. Disabled Women: Sexism Without the Pedestal. *Journal of Sociology and Social Welfare* (July), 8: 233–248.

———. 1988a. Disability beyond Stigma: Social Interaction, Discrimination, and Activism. *Journal of Social Issues*, 44(1): 3–21.

———. 1988b. *Women with Disabilities: Essays in Psychology, Culture, and Politics*. Philadelphia: Temple University Press.

Fing, Jing, Shantha Madhavan, and Michael H. Alderman. 1996. The Association between Birthplace and Mortality from Cardiovascular Causes among Black and White Residents of New York City. *New England Journal of Medicine* (November 21), 335: 1545–1551.

Fiola, Jan. 2008. Brazil. Pp. 200–204 in vol. 2, *Encyclopedia of Race, Ethnicity, and Society*, Richard T. Schaefer, ed. Thousand Oaks, CA: Sage.

Fishman, Sylvia Barack, and Daniel Parmer. 2008. *Matrilineal Ascent/Patrilineal Descent: The Gender Imbalance in American Jewish Life*. Waltham, MA: Maurice and Marilyn Cohen Center for Modern Jewish Studies, Brandeis University.

Fitzgerald, Kathleen J. 2008. Native American Identity. Pp. 954–956 in vol. 2, *Encyclopedia of Race, Ethnicity, and Society*, Richard T. Schaefer, ed. Thousand Oaks, CA: Sage.

Fix, Michael E., and Wendy Zimmerman. 1999. *All under One Roof: Mixed Status Families in an Era of Reform*. Washington, DC: Urban Institute.

Fixico, Donald L. 1988. The Federal Policy of Termination and Relocation, 1945–1960. Pp. 260–277 in *The American Indian Experience*, Phillip Weeks, ed. Arlington Heights, IL: Forum Press.

Fleishman, Jeffrey. 2004. "New Anti-Semitism Stirs Old Anxieties." Los Angeles Times, March 27, A1, A6.

Flexner, Eleanor. 1959. *Century of Struggle: The Women's Rights Movement in the United States*. Cambridge, MA: Harvard University Press.

Foerstrer, Amy. 2004. Race, Identity, and Belonging: "Blackness" and the Struggle for Solidarity in a Multiethnic Labor Union. *Social Problems*, 51 (3): 386–409.

Folkhart, Bart A. 1995. Maggie Kuhn, 89; Iconoclastic Founder of Gray Panthers. *Los Angeles Times* (April 23): A34.

Foner, Eric. 2006. *Forever Free: The Story of Emancipation and Reconstruction.* New York: Knopf.

Fong, Stanley L. M. 1965. Assimilation of Chinese in America: Changes in Orientation and Perception. *American Journal of Sociology* (November), 71: 265–273.

———. 1973. Assimilation and Changing Social Roles of Chinese Americans. *Journal of Social Issues*, 29 (2): 115–127.

———. 2002. *The Contemporary Asian American Experience: Beyond the Model Minority,* 2nd ed. Upper Saddle River, NJ: Prentice Hall.

Fordham, Signithia, and John U. Ogbu. 1986. Black Students' School Success: Coping with the Burden of "Acting White." *Urban Review*, 18 (3): 176–206.

Fox, Elaine. 1992. Crossing the Bridge: Adaptive Strategies Among Navajo Health Care Workers. *Free Inquiry in Creative Sociology* (May), 20: 25–34.

Fox, Stephen. 1990. *The Unknown Internment.* Boston: Twayne.

Fox, Susannah, and Gretchen Livingston. 2007. *Hispanics with Lower Levels of Education and English Proficiency Remain Largely Disconnected from the Internet.* Washington, DC: Pew Hispanic Center.

Foy, Paul. 2006. Interior Rejects Goshute Nuclear Waste Stockpile. *Indian Country Today* (September 18), 20: 1.

Frankel, Bruce. 1995. N.Y.'s "Jewish Rosa Parks" Wins Bus Battle. *USA Today* (March 17): 4A.

Frankenberg, Erica, Chungmei Lee, and Gary Orfield. 2003. *A Multiracial Society with Segregated Schools: Are We Losing the Dream?* Cambridge, MA: Civil Rights Project, Harvard University.

Franklin, John Hope, and Alfred A. Moss, Jr. 2000. *From Slavery to Freedom: A History of African Americans,* 8th ed. New York: McGraw-Hill.

Franklin, Stephen. 2007. Farm Workforce Shrivels. *Chicago Tribune* (August 5), section 5: 1, 2.

Frazier, E. Franklin. 1957. *Black Bourgeois: The Rise of a New Middle Class.* New York: Free Press.

———. 1964. *The Negro Church in America.* New York: Schocken.

Freedman, Samuel G. 2003. *Sex and the City* Celebrates Judaism. *USA Today* (July 17): 13A.

———. 2004. Latino Parents Decry Bilingual Programs. *New York Times* (July 14): A21.

Freeman, Jo. 1973. The Origins of the Women's Liberation Movement. *American Journal of Sociology* (January), 78: 792–811.

———. 1975. *The Politics of Women's Liberation.* New York: David McKay.

———. 1983. On the Origins of Social Movements. Pp. 1–30 in *Social Movements of the Sixties and Seventies,* Jo Freeman, ed. New York: Longman.

Freidman, Georges. 1967. *The End of the Jewish People?* Garden City New York: Doubleday.

Friedan, Betty. 1963. *The Feminine Mystique.* New York: Dell.

———. 1981. *The Second Stage.* New York: Summit Books.

———. 1991. Back to *The Feminine Mystique? The Humanist* (January–February), 51: 26–27.

Friends Committee on National Legislation. 1993. American Indian Religious Freedom. *News from Indian Country* (mid-February): 8.

Friess, Steve. 2007. Nevada: English Mandate Repealed. *New York Times* (February 15).

———. 2008. Stars and Strife: Flag Rule Splits Town. *New York Times* (December 18): A20.

Fryer, Ronald G. 2006. Acting White. *Education Next* (Winter): 53–59.

Fuchs, Estelle, and Robert J. Havighurst. 1972. *To Live on This Earth: American Indian Education.* Garden City, NY: Doubleday.

Fuller, Chevon. 1998. Service Redlining. *Civil Rights Journal*, 3 (Fall): 33–36.

Furstenberg, Frank F. 2007. The Making of the Black Family: Race and Class in Qualitative Studies in the Twentieth Century. *Annual Review of Sociology*, 33: 429–448.

Gaines, Patrice. 2005. Political Report: Black Women, White Men Face Similar Confinement Rates. *Focus* (January/February), 33: 7.

Gale. 2004. Gray Panthers. In *Encyclopedia of Associations: National Organizations of the U.S.* Belmont, CA: Gale Cengage.

Gallagher, Mari. 2005. *Chain Reaction: Income, Race, and Access to Chicago's Major Player Grocers.* Chicago: Metro Chicago Information Center.

Gallup. 2008. *Immigration.* Accessed February 6, 2008, at www.gallup.com.

Gallup, George H. 1972. *The Gallup Poll, Public Opinion, 1935–1971.* New York: Random House.

Gans, Herbert J. 1956. American Jewry: Present and Future. *Commentary* (May), 21: 424–425.

———. 1979. Symbolic Ethnicity: The Future of Ethnic Groups and Cultures in America. *Ethnic and Racial Studies* 2 (January): 1–20.

———. 1995. *The War against the Poor: The Underclass and Antipoverty Policy.* New York: Basic Books.

Garfinkel, Herbert. 1959. *When Negroes March.* New York: Atheneum.

Garner, Roberta. 1996. *Contemporary Movements and Ideologies.* New York: McGraw-Hill.

Gates, Gary J. 2006. *Same-Sex Couples and the Gay, Lesbian, Bisexual Population: New Estimates from the American Community Survey.* Los Angeles: Williams Institute.

Gerson, Kathleen. 2007. What Do Women and Men Want? *The American Prospect* (March): A8–A11.

Gerth, H. H., and C. Wright Mills. 1958. *From Max Weber: Essays in Sociology.* New York: Galaxy Books.

Getlin, Josh. 1998. Leaving an Impact on American Culture. *Los Angeles Times* (April 22): A1, A26, A27.

Giago, Tim. 2001. National Media Should Stop Using Obscene Words. *The Denver Post* (January 21).

Gibbs, Nancy. 2001. A Whole New World. *Time* (June 11): 36–45.

Gibson, Campbell, and Kay Jung. 2006. *Historical Census Statistics on the Foreign-Born Population of the United States: 1850 to 2000.* Working Paper No. 81. Washington, DC: Bureau of the Census.

Girardelli, Davide. 2004. Commodified Identities: The Myth of Italian Food in the United States. *Journal of Communication Inquiry* (October), 28: 307–324.

Giroux, Henry A. 1997. Rewriting the Discourse of Racial Identity: Towards a Pedagogy and Politics of Whiteness. *Harvard Educational Review* (Summer) 67: 285–320.

Gittell, Marilyn, and Bill McKinney. 2007. *The Economic Status of Working Women in New York.* New York: Howard Samuels Center.

Gittler, Joseph B., ed. 1981. *Jewish Life in the United States: Perspectives from the Social Sciences.* New York: New York University Press.

Glascock, Stuart. 2008. A Town Confronts the Language Barrier. *Los Angeles Times* (May 25): A20.

Gleason, Philip. 1980. American Identity and Americanization. Pp. 31–58 in *Harvard Encyclopedia of American Ethnic Groups,* Stephen Therstromm, ed. Cambridge, MA: Belknap Press of Harvard University Press.

Glionna, John M. 2004. Finding a Voice in Politics. *Los Angeles Times* (May 22): A1, A22.

Gobodo-Madikizela, Pumla. 2003. *A Human Being Died That Night.* New York: Houghton Mifflin.

Goering, John M. 1971. The Emergence of Ethnic Interests: A Case of Serendipity. *Social Forces* (March), 48: 379–384.

Goffman, Erving. 1963. *Stigma: Notes on Management of Spoiled Identity.* Englewood Cliffs NJ: Prentice Hall.

Gold, Michael. 1965. *Jews Without Money.* New York: Avon.

Gold, Steven J. 2001. *Arab Americans in Detroit.* Accessed October 15, 2004, at www.commurb. org/features/sgold/detroit.html.

Goldscheider, Calvin. 2003. Are American Jews Vanishing Again? *Contexts* (Winter): 18–24.

Goldstein, Sidney, and Calvin Goldscheider. 1968. *Jewish Americans: Three Generations in a Jewish Community.* Englewood Cliffs, NJ: Prentice Hall.

Gomez, David F. 1971. Chicanos: Strangers in Their Own Land. *America* 124 (June 26), pp. 649–652.

Goodnough, Abby. 2004. Honor for Dr. King Splits Florida City, and Faces Reversal. *New York Times* (May 10): A1, A20.

Goodstein, Laurie. 2004. Muslim Women Seeking a Place in the Mosque. *New York Times* (July 22): A1, A16.

———. 2005. Issuing Rebuke: Judge Rejects Teaching of Intelligent Design. *New York Times* (December 21): A1, A21.

Gordon, Anthony, and Richard M. Horowitz. 1997. *Will Your Grandchildren Be Jewish?* Unpublished research based on a 1990 National Jewish Population Survey and the 1991 New York Jewish Population Study.

Gordon, Milton M. 1964. *Assimilation in American Life: The Role of Race, Religion, and National Origins.* New York: Oxford University Press.

Gosselin, Janie. 2008. Montreal looks into riot's spark. *Chicago Tribune* (August 12).

Gouldner, Alvin. 1970. *The Coming Crisis in Western Sociology.* New York: Basic Books.

Gove, Walter R. 1980. *The Labeling of Deviance,* 2nd ed. Beverly Hills, CA: Sage Publications.

Gray-Little, Bernadette, and Hafdahl, Adam R. 2000. Factors Influencing Racial Comparisons of Self-Esteem: A Qualitative Review. *Psychological Bulletin*, 126 (1): 26–54.

Greater New Orleans Fair Housing Action Center. 2007. *For Rent, Unless You're Black.* New Orleans: Greater New Orleans Fair Housing Action Center.

Greeley, Andrew M. 1981. *The Irish Americans: The Rise to Money and Power.* New York: Harper & Row.

Green, Alexander R., et al. 2007. Implicit Bias among Physicians and Its Prediction of Thrombolysis Decisions for Black and White Patients. *Journal of General Internal Medicine* (September), 22: 1231–1238.

Greenhouse, Linda. 1996. Case on Government Interface in Religion Tied to Separation of Powers. *New York Times* (October 16): C23.

———. 2004. Justices Find States Can Be Liable for Not Making Townhouses Accessible to Disabled. *New York Times* (May 18).

———. 2008. Justices, in Beas Case, Rule for Older Workers. *New York Times* (June 20): A15.

Greenhouse, Steven. 2001. Fear and Poverty Sicken Many Migrant Workers in the U.S. *New York Times* (May 13): 14.

Grieco, Elizabeth M. 2001. *The Native Hawaiian and Other Pacific Islander Population 2000.* Brief C2KBR/01-14. Washington, DC: U.S. Government Printing Office.

———, and Rachel C. Cassidy. 2001. Overview of Race and Hispanic Origin. *Current Population Reports.* Ser. CENBR/01-1. Washington, DC: U.S. Government Printing Office.

Grimshaw, Allen D. 1969. *Racial Violence in the United States.* Chicago: Aldine.

Grodsky, Eric, and Devah Pager. 2001. The Structure of Disadvantage: Individual and Occupational Determinants of the Black–White Wage Gap. *American Sociological Review* (August), 66: 542–567.

Grossman, Cathy Lynn. 2008. Muslim Census a Difficult Court. *USA Today* (August 6): 5D.

Guerin-Gonzales, Camille. 1994. *Mexican Workers and American Dreams.* New Brunswick, NJ: Rutgers University Press.

Guest, Kenneth J. 2003. *God in Chinatown: Religion and Survival in New York's Evolving Immigrant Community.* New York: University Press.

Guglielmo, Jennifer, and Salerno Salvatore, eds. 2003. *Are Italians White?* New York: Routledge.

Guzmán, Betsy. 2001. *The Hispanic Population.* Census 2000 Brief Series C2kBR/01-3. Washington, DC: U.S. Government Printing Office.

Haak, Gerald O. 1970. Co-Opting the Oppressors: The Case of the Japanese-Americans. *Society* (October), 7: 23–31.

Hacek, Miro. 2008. Roma. Pp. 1168–1170 in vol. 3, *Encyclopedia of Race, Ethnicity, and Society*, Richard T. Schaefer, ed. Thousand Oaks, CA: Sage.

Hacker, Andrew. 1995. *Two Nations: Black and White, Separate, Hostile, and Unequal*, expanded and updated ed. New York: Ballantine.

Hacker, Helen Mayer. 1951. Women as a Minority Group. *Social Forces* (October), 30: 60–69.

———. 1974. Women as a Minority Group: Twenty Years Later. Pp. 124–134 in *Who Discriminates against Women*, Florence Denmark, ed., Beverly Hills, CA: Sage Publications.

Haeri, Shaykh Fadhilalla. 2004. *The Thoughtful Guide to Islam.* Alresford, UK: O Books.

Hakimzadeh, Shirin, and D'Vera Cohn. 2007. *English Usage among Hispanics in the United States.* Washington, DC: Pew Hispanic Center.

Hallinan, Maureen T. 2003. Ability Grouping and Student Learning. Pp. 95–140 in *Brookings Papers on Education Policy*, Diane Ravitch, ed. Washington, DC: Brookings Institution Press.

Halstead, Mark L. 2008. Islamophobia. Pp. 762–764 in vol. 2, *Encyclopedia of Race, Ethnicity, and Society*, Richard T. Schaefer, ed. Thousand Oaks, CA: Sage.

Halualani, Rona Tamiko. 2002. *In the Name of Hawaiians: Native Identities and Cultural Politics.* Minneapolis: University of Minnesota Press.

Hamm, Jill V., B. Bradford Brown, and Daniel J. Heck. 2005. Bridging the Ethnic Divide: Student and School Characteristics in African American, Latino, and White Adolescents' Cross-Ethnic Friend Nominations. *Journal of Research on Adolescence*, 15 (1): 21–46.

Han, Jean. 2008. Asian America Still Discovering Elusive Identity. (May 16): 19.

Handlin, Oscar. 1951. *The Uprooted: The Epic Story of the Great Migrations That Made the American People.* New York: Grossett and Dunlap.

Hansen, Marcus Lee. 1952. The Third Generation in America. *Commentary* (November 14): 493–500.

Harlan, Louis R. 1972. *Booker T. Washington: The Making of a Black Leader.* New York: Oxford University Press.

Harlow, Caroline Wolf. 2005. *Hate Crime Reported by Victims and Police.* Bureau of Justice Statistics Special Report (November). Accessed May 8, 2008, at www.ojp.usdoj.gov/bjs/pub/pdf/hcrvp.pdf.

Harris, Marvin. 1964. *Patterns of Race in the Americas.* New York: Norton.

Hartocullis, Anemona. 2006. For Some Gays, a Right They Can Forsake. *New York Times* (July 30): sect. ST, 2.

Harzig, Christine. 2008. German Americans. Pp. 540–544 in vol. 1, *Encyclopedia of Race, Ethnicity, and Society*, Richard T. Schaefer, ed. Thousand Oaks, CA: Sage.

Hassrick, Elizabeth McGhee. 2007. *The Transnational Production of White Ethnic Symbolic Identities.* Paper presented at the Annual Meeting of the American Sociological Association.

Haub, Carl. 2008 World Population Data Sheet 2008. Washington DC: Population Reference Bureau.

Hawaii Department of Health. 2001. *Annual Statistics 2000*, A46–A55. Accessed March 20, 2002, at www.hawaii.gov.

Hawkins, Hugh. 1962. *Booker T. Washington and His Critics: The Problem of Negro Leadership.* Boston: Heath.

Hays, Kristen L. 1994. Topeka Comes Full Circle. *Modern Maturity* (April–May): 34.

He, Wan, Manisha Sengupta, Victoria A. Velkoff, and Kimberly A. DeBarros. 2005. 65+ in the United States: 2005. *Current Population Reports.* Ser. P23. No. 209. Washington, DC: U.S. Government Printing Office.

Head, John F. 2007. Why, Even Today, Many Banks Are Wary about American Medicine. *Crisis* (January): 48–49.

Healy, Patrick. 2008. Laramie Killing Given Epilogue a Decade Later. *New York Times* (September 16): A1, A19.

Heer, David M., and Amgra Grossbard-Shectman. 1981. The Impact of the Female Marriage Squeeze and the Contraceptive Revolution on Sex Roles and the Women's Liberation Movement in the United States, 1960 to 1975. *Journal of Marriage and the Family* (February), 43: 49–76.

Heilman, Madeline E. 2001. Description and Prescription: How Gender Stereotypes Present Women's Ascent Up the Organizational Ladder. *Journal of Social Issues*, 57 (4): 657–674.

Hein, Jeremy. 2000. Interpersonal Discrimination against Hmong Americans: Parallels and Variation in Microlevel Racial Inequality. *Sociological Quarterly*, 41 (3): 413–429.

Henig, Samantha. 2006. Colleges Reach Out to American Indians. *Chronicle of Higher Education* (September 15), 53: A39–A41.

Hennessy-Fiske, Molly. 2006. The Town That Didn't Look Away. *Los Angeles Times* (July 23).

Henry, William A., III. 1994. Pride and Prejudice. *Time* (February 28), 143: 21–27.

Hentoff, Nicholas. 1984. Dennis Banks and the Road Block to Indian Ground. *Village Voice* (October), 29: 19–23.

Hequembourg, Amy and Jorge Arditi. 1999. Fractured Resistances: The Debate over Assimilationism among Gays and Lesbians in the United States. *Sociological Quarterly*, 40 (4): 663–680.

Herberg, Will. 1983. *Protestant—Catholic—Jew: An Essay in American Religious Sociology*, rev. ed. Chicago: University of Chicago Press.

Hernández-Arias, P. Rafael. 2008. Salvadoran Americans. Pp. 1185–1187 in vol. 3, *Encyclopedia of Race, Ethnicity, and Society*, Richard T. Schaefer, ed. Thousand Oaks, CA: Sage.

Herrnstein, Richard J., and Charles Murray. 1994. *The Bell Curve: Intelligence and Class Structure in American Life.* New York: Free Press.

Hero, Rodney. 1995. *Latinos and U.S. Politics.* New York: HarperCollins.

Herschthal, Eric. 2004. Indian Students Discuss Pros, Cons of Arranged Marriages. *Daily Princetonian* (October 20).

Herskovits, Melville J. 1941. The Myth of the Negro Past. New York: Harper.

Higham, John. 1966. American Anti-Semitism Historically Reconsidered. Pp. 237–258 in *Jews in the Mind of America*, Charles Herbert Stember, ed. New York: Basic Books.

Hilberg, Soleste, and Ronald G. Tharp. 2002. *Theoretical Perspectives, Research Findings, and Classroom Implications of the Learning Styles of American Indian and Alaska Native Students.* Washington, DC: Eric Digest.

Hill, Robert B. 1999. *The Strengths of African American Families: Twenty-Five Years Later.* Lanham, MD: University Press of America.

Himmelfarb, Harold S. 1982. Research on American Jewish Identity and Identification: Progress, Pitfalls, and Prospects. Pp. 56–95 in *Understanding American Jewry*, Marshall Sklare, ed. New Brunswick, NJ: Transaction Books.

Hirsley, Michael. 1991. Religious Display Needs Firm Count. *Chicago Tribune* (December 20), section 2: 10.

Hochschild, Arlie Russell. 1990. The Second Shift: Employed Women Are Putting in Another Day of Work at Home. *Utne Reader* (March–April), 38: 66–73.

———, and Anne Machung. 1989. *The Second Shift.* New York: Viking.

Hoffer, Thomas B., et al. 2001. *Doctorate Recipients from United States Universities: Summary Report 2000.* Chicago: National Opinion Research Center.

Holzer, Harry J. 2008. The Effects of Immigration on the Employment Outcomes of Black Americans. Testimony before the U.S. Commission on Civil Rights.

Hondagneu-Sotelo, Pierette, ed. 2003. *Gender and U.S. Immigration: Contemporary Trends.* Berkeley: University of California Press.

hooks, bell. 1984. *Feminist Theory: From Margin to Center.* Boston: South End Press.

Horan, Deborah. 2008. Theme Park Tailors Day to Muslims. *Chicago Tribune* (July 25): 1, 5.

Horton, Lynn. 2008. Central Americans in the United States. Pp. 251–256 in vol. 2, *Encyclopedia of Race, Ethnicity, and Society*, Richard T. Schaefer, ed. Thousand Oaks, CA: Sage.

Hosokawa, Bill. 1969. *Nisei: The Quiet Americans.* New York: Morrow.

Hsu, Spencer S. 2008. Pressuring Employers. *Washington Post National Weekly Edition* (August 3), 25: 33.

Hubbard, Amy S. 1993. *U.S. Jewish Community Responses to the Changing Strategy of the Palestinian Nationalist Movement: A Pilot Study.* Paper presented at annual meeting of the Eastern Sociological Society, Boston.

Hudgins, John L. 1992. The Strengths of Black Families Revisited. *The Urban League Review* (Winter), 15: 9–20.

Hughlett, Mike. 2006. Judge: Craigslist Not Liable for Ad Content. *Chicago Tribune* (November 16), section 3: 1.

Hull, Anne. 2003. Translating "Don't Ask, Don't Tell." *Washington Post National Weekly Edition* (December 21): 30–31.

Hulse, Carl. 2008. Republican Senators Block Pay Discrimination Measure. *New York Times* (April 24): A22.

Human Rights Campaign. 2006. *Marriage, Relationship Recognition.* Accessed December 11, 2006, at www.hrc.org.

Human Rights Watch. 1998. *Losing the Vote: The Impact of Felony Disenfranchisement Laws in the United States.* Washington, DC: Human Rights Watch.

———. 2002. Florida Ex-Offenders Barred from Vote Decisive in Election. Accessed February 1, 2002, at www.hrw.org/campaign/elections/results.htm.

Humphreys, Laud. 1972. *Out of the Closets.* Englewood Cliffs, NJ: Prentice Hall.

Hunt, Larry L. 1999. Hispanic Protestantism in the United States: Trends by Decade and Generation. *Social Forces*, 77 (4): 1601–1624.

Hurh, Won Moo. 1994. Majority Americans' Perception of Koreans in the United States: Implications of Ethnic Images and Stereotypes. Pp. 3–21 in *Korean Americans: Conflict and Harmony*, H. Kwon, ed. Chicago: Center for Korean Studies.

———. 1998. *The Korean Americans.* Westport, CT: Greenwood Press.

———, and Kwang Chung Kim. 1982. Race Relations Paradigms and Korean American Research: A Sociology of Knowledge Perspective. Pp. 219–255 in *Koreans in Los Angeles*, E. Yu, E. Phillips, and E. Yang, eds. Los Angeles: Center for Korean American and Korean Studies, California State University.

———. 1984. *Korean Immigrants in America: A Structural Analysis of Ethnic Confinement and Adhesive Adaptation*. Cranbury, NJ: Farleigh Dickinson University Press.

———. 1989. The "Success" Image of Asian Americans: Its Validity, and Its Practical and Theoretical Implications. *Ethnic and Racial Studies* (October 12): 512–538.

Huteson, Pamela Rae. 2008. Canada, First Nations. Pp. 230–233 in vol. 1, *Encyclopedia of Race, Ethnicity, and Society*, Richard T. Schaefer, ed. Thousand Oaks, CA: Sage.

Ignatiev, Noel. 1994. Treason to Whiteness Is Loyalty to Humanity. Interview with Noel Ignatiev. *Utne Reader* (November–December): 83–86.

———. 1995. *How the Irish Became White*. New York: Routledge.

Indian and Northern Affairs Canada and Canadian Polar Commission. 2000. *2000–2001 Estimates*. Ottawa: Canadian Government Publishing.

Indian Country Today. 1999. Parents Ask for Both Traditional and Modern Medical Treatments (May 24): B2.

Indian Trust. 2008. Corbell v. Kempthorne. Accessed August 12 at www.indiantrust.com.

Indianz.com. 2004. Tribal Authority over the Indians Still Unsettled Question. Accessed August 9, 2004, at www.indianz.com.

Inoue, Miyako. 1989. Japanese Americans in St. Louis: From Internees to Professionals. *City and Society* (December), 3: 142–152.

Institute for Democracy and Electoral Assistance. 2008. Electoral Quotas for Women. Accessed September 13, 2008, at www.idea.int/gender/quotas.cfm.

Institute for Jewish and Community Research. 2008. How Many Jews Are in World Today. Accessed September 7, 2008, at bechollashon.org/population/today.php.

Intelligence Report. 2004. Wal-Mart Drops Protocols, but Controversy Lives On (Winter): 3.

International Fund for Agricultural Development. 2007. *Sending Money Home: Worldwide Remittance Flows to Developing and Transition Countries*. Rome, Italy: IFAD.

Inter-Parliamentary Union. 2008. *Women in National Parliaments. Situation as of 31 July 2008*. Accessed September 10, 2008, at www.ipu.org/wmn-e/classif.htm.

Institute for Social and Economic Research and Policy (ISERP). 2008. *ABC News/ USA Today/Columbia University Poll; Blacks, Politics and Society*. New York: ISERP.

Issacson, Jason, and Richard Foltin. 2001. *Election 2000: Post Election*. New York: American Jewish Committee.

Ishii, Miku. 2006. *Multicultural Autobiography*. Unpublished Paper. Chicago: DePaul University.

Iwamasa, Gayle Y. 2008a. Internment Camps. Pp. 745–747 in vol. 2, *Encyclopedia of Race, Ethnicity, and Society*, Richard T. Schaefer, ed. Thousand Oaks, CA: Sage.

———. 2008b. Japanese American Citizens League. Pp. 781–782 in vol. 2, *Encyclopedia of Race, Ethnicity, and Society*, Richard T. Schaefer, ed. Thousand Oaks, CA: Sage.

Jacobs, Tom. 2008. Patriarchy and Paychecks. *Miller-McCune*, 1 (2): 18–19.

Jacobson, Cardell, J. Lynn England, and Robyn J. Barrus. 2008. Familism. Pp. 477–478 in vol. 1, *Encyclopedia of Race, Ethnicity, and Society*, Richard T. Schaefer, ed. Thousand Oaks, CA: Sage.

Jaher, Frederic Caple. 1994. *A Scapegoat in the New Wilderness*. Cambridge, MA: Harvard University Press.

James, Keith, et al. 1995. School Achievement and Dropout among Anglo and Indian Females and Males: A Comparative Examination. *American Indian Culture and Research Journal*, 19 (3): 181–206.

Janisch, Roy F. 2008. Wounded Knee 1890 and 1973. Pp. 1415–1417 in vol. 3, *Encyclopedia of Race, Ethnicity, and Society*, Richard T. Schaefer, ed. Thousand Oaks, CA: Sage.

Jaroszyńska-Kirchmann. 2004. *The Exile Mission: The Polish Political Diaspora and Polish Americans, 1939–1956*. Athens: Ohio University Press.

Jecker, Nancy. 2000. Review of Medical Apartheid. *New England Journal of Medicine* (November 23).

Jefferys, Kelly. 2007. *Refugees of Asylees: 2006*. Washington, DC: Office of Immigration Statistics.

Jenness, Valerie, David A. Smith, and Judith Stepan-Norris. 2008. The Politics of Immigration. *Contemporary Encyclopedia*, 37 (4): vii–viii.

Jimenez, Alfredo. 2005. *Leaving Cuba*. Unpublished paper. DePaul University, Chicago.

Jiménez, Tomás R. 2007. The Next Americans. *Los Angeles Times* (May 27): M1, M7.

Johnson, David. 2005. Uncertain Progress 25 Years After Defying State. *News from Indian County* (June 27), 19: 1, 5.

Johnson, Greg 2005. Narrative Remains: Articulating Indian Identities in the Repatriation Context. *Society for Comparative Study of Society and History* (July), 47: 480–506.

Johnson, Kevin. 1992. German Ancestry Is Strong Beneath Milwaukee Surface. *USA Today* (August 4), 9A.

———. 2004. *Immigration and Civil Rights*. Philadelphia: Temple University Press

———. 2006. MS-13 Gang Growing Extremely Dangerous, FBI Says. *USA Today* (January 6): 2A.

Johnston, Tim. 2008. Australia to Apologize to Aborigines for Past Mistreatment. *New York Times* (January 31).

Joint Center for Political and Economic Studies. 2002. *Black Elected Officials: A Statistical Summary 2002*. Washington, DC: JCPES.

Jolivette, Andrew. 2008. Pan-Indianism. Pp. 1022–1028 in vol. 2, *Encyclopedia of Race, Ethnicity, and Society*, Richard T. Schaefer, ed. Thousand Oaks, CA: Sage.

Jones, Jeffrey M. 2006. Whites, Blacks, Hispanics Disagree About Way Minority Groups Treated. *The Gallup Poll* (July 11). Accessed October 6, 2006, at www.galluppoll.com.

Jones, Nicholas, and Amy Symens Smith. 2001. *The Two or More Races Population: 2000*. Series C2KBR/01-6. Washington, DC: U.S. Government Printing Office.

Jones, Rachel K., Mia R. S. Zolna, Stanley K. Henshaw, and Laurence B. Finer. 2008. Abortion in the United States: Incidence and Access to Services, 2005. *Perspectives on Sexual and Reproductive Health* (March), 40: 6–16.

Jones, Tim. 2003. In Wausau, Hmong at Another Crossroads. *Chicago Tribune* (June 16): 8.

Jonsson, Patrik. 2008. More Blacks Explore Judaism. *Christian Science Monitor* (July 17).

Joseph, Peniel E. 2006. *Waiting 'til the Midnight Hour: A Narrative History of Black Power in America*. New York: Henry Holt & Company.

Jost, Kenneth. 2008. Women in Politics. *CQ Researcher* (March 21), 18.

Kagan, Jerome. 1971. The Magical Aura of the IQ. *Saturday Review of Literature* (December 4), 4: 92–93.

Kaiser Family Foundation. 2004. *South Africa at Ten Years of Democracy*. Washington, DC: Washington Post/Kaiser Family Foundation/Harvard University. Online at www.kff.org/kaiserpolls/southafrica.cfm.

———. 2008. HIV/AIDS Policy Fact Sheet. Menlo Park, CA: Henry J Kaiser Family Foundation.

Kalita, S. Mitra. 2003. *Suburban Sahibs: Three Immigrant Families and Their Passage from India to America*. New Brunswick, NJ: Rutgers University Press.

Kana'iaupuni, Shawn Malia. 2008. Hawaiians. Pp. 599–602 in vol. 1, *Encyclopedia of Race, Ethnicity, and Society*, Richard T. Schaefer, ed. Thousand Oaks, CA: Sage.

Kanamine, Linda. 1992. Amid Crushing Poverty, Glimmers of Hope. *USA Today* (November 30): 7A.

Kane-Berman, John. 2006. "A Call to Redesign Affirmative Action." *Fast Facts* (December): 1.

———. 2008. The Ownership Revolution. *Fast Facts* (September): 1.

Kang, K. Connie. 1996. Filipinos Happy with Life in U.S. but Lack United Voice. *Los Angeles Times* (January 26): A1, A20.

Kao, Grace. 2006. Where Are the Asian and Hispanic Victims of Katrina? *DuBois Review*, 3 (1): 223–231.

———, and Kara Joyner. 2004. Do Race and Ethnicity Matter among Friends? *Sociological Quarterly*, 45 (3): 557–573.

———, and Elizabeth Vaquera. 2006. The Salience of Racial and Ethnic Identification in Friendship Choice among Hispanic Adolescents. *Hispanic Journal of Behavioral Sciences* (February), 28: 23–47.

Karkabi, Barbara. 1993. Researcher in Houston Surveys Disabled Women about Sexuality. *Austin American–Statesman* (May 26): E8.

Kashima, Tetsuden. 2003. *Judgment Without Trial: Japanese Americans Imprisonment During World War II*. Seattle: University of Washington Press.

Katel, Peter. 2006. American Indians. *CQ Researcher* (April 28): 16.

Katz, Michael B., Mark J. Stern, and Jamie J. Fader. 2007. The Mexican Immigration Debate. *Social Science History*, 3 (Summer): 157–189.

Kazal, Russell A. 2004. The Interwar Origins of the White Ethnic: Race, Residence, and German Philadelphia, 1917–1939. *Journal of American Ethnic History* (Summer): 78–131.

Kening, Dan. 2004. OWL Keeps an Eye Out for Issues Affecting Women. *Chicago Tribune* (March 12), sec. 9: 1, 12.

Kent, Mary Mederios. 2007. Immigration and America's Black Population. *Population Bulletin* (December), 62.

Khadaroo, Stacy Teicher. 2008. New Drive to Ban Race Preferences. *Christian Science Monitor* (July 3).

Kibria, Nazli. 2002. *Becoming Asian American: Second-Generation Chinese and Korean American Identities*. Baltimore: Johns Hopkins Press.

Kieh, George Klay, Jr. 1995. Malcolm X and Pan-Africanism. *Western Journal of Black Studies*, 19 (4): 293–299.

Kiely, Kathy. 2008. Latino Vote "Up for Grabs," Could Swing Election. *USA Today* (June 27): 8A.

Killian, Caitlin. 2003. The Other Side of the Veil: North Africa Women in France Respond to the Headscarf Affair. *Gender and Society* (August), 17: 567–590.

Killian, Lewis M. 1975. *The Impossible Revolution, Phase 2: Black Power and the American Dream*. New York: Random House.

Kilson, Martin. 1995. Affirmative Action. *Dissent*, 42 (Fall): 469–470.

Kim, Barbara, and Grace J. Yoo. 2008. Korean Americans. Pp. 811–814 in vol. 2, *Encyclopedia of Race, Ethnicity, and Society*, Richard T. Schaefer, ed. Thousand Oaks, CA: Sage.

Kim, Henry H., and Ralph E. Pyle. 2004. An Exception to the Exception: Second-Generation Korean American Church Participation. *Social Compass*, 3: 321–333.

Kim, Joon K. 2008. Wetbacks. Pp. 1393–1395 in vol. 3, *Encyclopedia of Race, Ethnicity, and Society*, Richard T. Schaefer, ed. Thousand Oaks, CA: Sage.

Kim, Kiljoong. 2006. The Korean Presence in Chicago. In *The New Chicago*, John Koval et al., eds. Philadelphia: Temple University Press.

Kimmons, Leslie C. Baker. 2008. Abolitionism: The People. Pp. 3–5 in vol. 1, *Encyclopedia of Race, Ethnicity, and Society*, Richard T. Schaefer, ed. Thousand Oaks, CA: Sage.

Kimura, Yukiko. 1988. *Issei: Japanese Immigrants in Hawaii*. Honolulu: University of Hawaii Press.

King, Martin Luther, Jr. 1958. *Stride Towards Freedom: The Montgomery Story*. New York: Harper.

———. 1963. *Why We Can't Wait*. New York: Mentor.

———. 1967. *Where Do We Go from Here: Chaos or Community?* New York: Harper & Row.

———. 1971. I Have a Dream. Pp. 346–351 in *Black Protest Thought in the Twentieth Century*, August Meier, Elliott Rudwick, and Francis L. Broderick, eds. Indianapolis, IN: Bobbs-Merrill.

King, Meredith L. 2007. *Immigrants in the U.S. Health Care System*. Washington, DC: Center for American Progress.

King, Peter. 2004c. Private Moments in the Public Eye. *Los Angeles Times* (August 5): A1, A16, A17.

Kinloch, Graham C. 1974. *The Dynamics of Race Relations: A Sociological Analysis*. New York: McGraw-Hill.

Kinsey, Alfred G., Wardell B. Pomeroy, and Paul H. Gebhard. 1953. *Sexual Behavior in the Human Female*. Philadelphia: Saunders.

Kinsey, Alfred G., Wardell B. Pomeroy, and Clyde E. Martin. 1948. *Sexual Behavior in the Human Male*. Philadelphia: Saunders.

Kinzer, Stephen. 2000. Museums and Tribes: A Tricky Truce. *New York Times* (December 24), sec. 2: 1, 39.

Kirkpatrick, P. 1994. Triple Jeopardy: Disability, Race and Poverty in America. *Poverty and Race*, 3: 1–8.

Kitagawa, Evelyn. 1972. Socioeconomic Differences in the United States and Some Implications for Population Policy. Pp. 87–110 in *Demographic and Social Aspects of Population Growth*, Charles F. Westoff and Robert Parke, Jr., eds. Washington, DC: U.S. Government Printing Office.

Kitano, Harry H. L. 1976. *Japanese Americans: The Evolution of a Subculture*, 2nd ed. Englewood Cliffs, NJ: Prentice Hall.

———. 1980. Japanese. In *Harvard Encyclopedia of American Ethnic Groups*, Stephen Thernstrom, ed. Cambridge, MA: Belknap Press of Harvard University Press.

Kitsuse, John I., and Leonard Broom. 1956. *The Managed Casualty: The Japanese American Family in World War II*. Berkeley: University of California Press.

Kivisto, Peter. 2008. *Third Generation Principle*. Pp. 1302–1304 in vol. 3, *Encyclopedia of Race, Ethnicity, and Society*, Richard T. Schaefer, ed. Thousand Oaks, CA: Sage.

Klausner, Samuel Z. 1988. Anti-Semitism in the Executive Suite: Yesterday, Today, and Tomorrow. *Moment* (September), 13: 32–39, 55.

Klein, Jennifer. 2008. Iraqi Americans. Pp. 754–755 in vol. 2, *Encyclopedia of Race, Ethnicity, and Society*, Richard T. Schaefer, ed. Thousand Oaks, CA: Sage.

Knudson, Thomas J. 1987. Zoning the Reservations for Enterprise. *New York Times* (January 25): E4.

Koch, Wendy. 2006b. Push for "Official" English Heats Up. *USA Today* (October 9): 1A.

Kochhar, Rakesh. 2004. *The Wealth of Hispanic Households: 1966 to 2002*. Washington, DC: Pew Hispanic Center.

———. 2006. *Growth in the Foreign-Born Workforce and Employment of the Native Born*. Washington, DC: Pew Hispanic Center.

Koreatown Immigrant Workers Alliance. 2007. *Towards a Community Agenda: A Survey of Workers and Residents in Koreatown, Los Angeles*. Los Angeles: KIWA.

Korecki, Natasha. 2003. Rebuilding Mexico from the Suburbs. *Daily Herald* (Arlington Heights, IL) (November 20).

Koser, Khalid. 2008. *Protecting Displaced Migrants in South Africa*. Brookings Institution (June 23). Accessed at www.brookings.edu.

Krammer, Arnold. 1997. *Undue Process: The Untold Story of America's German Alien Internees*. Lanham, MD: Rowman & Littlefield.

Krauss, Clifford. 2006b. Seven Years into Self-Rule, Inuit Are Struggling. *New York Times* (June 18): 4.

Krausz, Ernest. 1973. Israel's New Citizens. Pp. 385–387 in *1973 Britannica Book of the Year*. Chicago: Encyclopedia Britannica.

Kraybill, Donald B. 2001. *The Riddle of Amish Culture*, rev. ed. Baltimore: Johns Hopkins University Press.

———, ed. 2003. *The Amish and the State*, 2nd ed. Baltimore: John Hopkins University Press.

———. 2008. Amish. Pp. 68–71 in vol. 1, *Encyclopedia of Race, Ethnicity, and Society*, Richard T. Schaefer, ed. Thousand Oaks, CA: Sage.

———, and Steven M. Nolt. 1995. *Amish Enterprises: From Plows to Profits*. Baltimore: Johns Hopkins University Press.

Krueger, Brooke. 2004. When a Dissertation Makes a Difference. Accessed January 15, 2005, at www.racematters.org/devahpager.htm.

Krysan, Maria. 1998. Privacy and the Expression of White Racial Attitudes: A Comparison across Three Contexts. *Public Opinion Quarterly*, 62: 506–544.

Kupper, William P., Jr. 2008. We're Sorry. Accessed January 21, 2008, at www.golfweek.com.

Kwon, Ho-Youn, Kwag Chung Kem, and R. Stephen Warner, eds. 2001. *Korean Americans and Their Religions: Pilgrims and Missionaries from a Different Shore*. Philadelphia: Pennsylvania State University Press.

Kwong, Peter. 1994. The Wages of Fear. *Village Voice* (April 26), 39: 25–29.

Kurien, Prema. 2004. Multiculturalism, Immigrant Religion, and Diasporic Nationalism: The Development of an American Hinduism. *Social Problems*, 51 (3): 362–385.

Lacy, Dan. 1972. *The White Use of Blacks in America*. New York: McGraw-Hill.

LaDuke, Winona. 2006. Hui Na Iwa—The Bones Lives: Hawaiians and NAGPRA. News from Indian Country, April 3, 17.

Lahey, Joanna. 2006. *Age, Women, and Hiring: An Experimental Study*. Boston: Boston College, Center for Retirement Research. Online at escholarship.bc.edu/retirement_papers/134.

Lahiri, Jhumpa. 2006. My Two Lives. *Newsweek* (March 6): 43.

Lal, Barbara Ballis. 1995. Symbolic Interaction Theories. *American Behavioral Scientist* (January), 38: 421–441.

Lamb, David. 1997. Viet Kieu: A Bridge between Two Worlds. *Los Angeles Times* (November 4): A1, A8.

Landale, Nancy S., Nimfa B. Ogena, and Bridget K. Gorman. 2000. Migration and Infant Death: Assimilation or Selective Migration among Puerto Ricans? *American Sociological Review* (December), 65: 888–909.

Landale, Nancy S., and R. S. Oropesa. 2002. White, Black, or Puerto Rican? Racial Self-Identification among Mainland and Island Puerto Ricans. *Social Forces*, 81 (1): 231–254.

———. 2007. Hispanic Families: Stability and Change. *Annual Review of Sociology*, 33: 381–405.

———, and C. Bradatan. 2006. Hispanic Families in the United States: Family Structure and Process in an Era of Family Change. Pp. 138–178, in *Multiple Origins, Uncertain Destinies: Hispanics and the American Future*. Washington, DC: National Academic Press.

LaPiere, Richard T. 1934. Attitudes vs. Actions. *Social Forces* (October 13): 230–237.

———. 1969. Comment of Irwin Deutscher's Looking Backward. *American Sociologist* (February), 4: 41–42.

Lara, Marielena, Cristina Gramboa, M. Iya Kahramanian, Leo S. Morales, and David E. Hayes Bautista. 2005. Acculturation and Latino Health in the United States: A Review of the Literature and Its Sociopolitical Context. Pp. 367–397 in *Annual Review of Public Health 2005*. Palo Alto, CA: Annual Reviews.

Lareau, Annette. 2002. Juvenile Inequality: Social Class and Childrearing in Black Families and White Families. *American Sociological Review* (October), 67: 747–776.

Latino Coalition. 2006. *2005 National Latino Survey Topline*. Washington, DC: Latino Coalition.

Lau, Yvonne M. 2006. Re-Envisioning Filipino American Communities: Evolving Identities, Issues, and Organizations. Pp. 141–153 in *The New Chicago*, John Koval et al., eds. Philadelphia: Temple University Press.

———. 2008. Chinatowns. Pp. 201–205 in vol. 1, *Encyclopedia of Race, Ethnicity, and Society*, Richard T. Schaefer, ed. Thousand Oaks, CA: Sage.

Leavitt, Paul. 2002. Bush Calls Agent Kicked Off Flight "Honorable Fellow." *USA Today* (January 8).

Lauerman, Connie. 1993. Tribal Wave. *Chicago Tribune* (April 5): sec. 2, 1–2.

Laumann, Edward O., John H. Gagnon, Robert T. Michael, and Stuart Michaels. 1994. *The Social Organization of Sexuality: Sexual Practices in the United States*. Chicago: University of Chicago Press.

Lavender, Abraham D., ed. 1977. *A Coat of Many Colors: Jewish Subcommunities in the United States*. Westport, CT: Greenwood Press.

Laxson, Joan D. 1991. "We" See "Them": Tourism and Native Americans. *Annals of Tourism Research*, 18(3): 365–391.

Ledward, Brandon C. 2008. Haole. Pp. 579–581 in vol. 2, *Encyclopedia of Race, Ethnicity, and Society*, Richard T. Schaefer, ed. Thousand Oaks, CA: Sage.

Lee, Jennifer. 2001. Manhattan's Chinatown Reeling from the Effects of September 11. *New York Times* (November 21): B1, B9.

———, and Frank D. Bean. 2007. Redrawing the Color Line. *City and Community* (March), 6: 49–62.

Lee, J. J., and Marion R. Casey. 2006. *Making the Irish American*. New York: New York University Press.

Lee, Sharon M. 1998. Asian Americans: Diverse and Growing. *Population Bulletin* (June): 53.

Lee, Wen Ho, with Helen Zia. 2006. *My Country Versus Me: The First-Hand Account by the Los Alamos Scientist Who Was Falsely Accused of Being a Spy*. New York: Hyperion.

Lee, Yueh-Ting, Sandy Vue, Richard Seklecki, and Yue Ma. 2007. How Did Asian Americans Respond to Negative Stereotypes and Hate Crimes? *American Behavioral Scientist* (October), 51: 271–293.

Leehotz, Robert. 1995. Is Concept of Race a Relic? *Los Angeles Times* (April 15): A1, A14.

LeinWand, Donna. 2004. Muslims See New Opposition to Building Mosques Since 9/11. *USA Today* (March 9): A1, A2.

Leland, John. 2008. In "Sweetie" and "Dear," a Hurt beyond Insult for the Elderly. *New York Times* (October 7): A1, A22.

Lem, Kim. 1976. Asian American Employment. *Civil Rights Digest* (Fall), 9: 12–21.

Leonard, Karen Isaksen. 2003. *Muslims in the United States: The State of Research*. New York: Russell Sage Foundation.

Let Puerto Rico Decide. 2005. *Status Choices.* Accessed October 7, 2006, at www.letpuertoricodecide.com (Citizens' Educated Foundation 2005).

Levin, William C. 1988. Age Stereotyping: College Student Evaluations. *Research on Aging* (March 10): 134–148.

Levine, Naomi, and Martin Hochbaum, eds. 1974. *Poor Jews: An American Awakening.* New Brunswick, NJ: Transaction Books.

Levitt, Peggy. 2004. Salsa and Ketchup: Transnational Migrants Struggle Two Worlds. *Contexts* (Spring): 20–26.

———, and B. Nadya Jaworsky. 2007. Transnational Migration Studies: Past Developments and Future Trends. *Annual Review of Sociology*, 33: 129–156.

Lewin, Tamar. 2006. Campaign to End Race Preferences Splits Michigan. *New York Times* (October 31): A1, A19.

Lewinson, Paul. 1965. *Race, Class, and Party: A History of Negro Suffrage and White Politics in the South.* New York: Universal Library.

Lewis, Amanda E. 2004. "What Group?" Studying Whites and Whiteness in the Era of "Color-Blindness." *Sociological Theory* (December), 22: 623–646.

Lewis, Gregory. 2007. Love Sees No Color. *Sun Sentinel* (June 16): 1A, 17A.

Lewis Mumford Center. 2001. *Ethnic Diversity Grows, Neighborhood Integration Is at a Standstill.* Albany, NY: Lewis Mumford Center.

Lewis, Neil A. 2003. Secrecy Is Barked on 9/11 Detainees. *New York Times* (June 18): A1, A16.

Lewis, Oscar. 1959. *Five Families: Mexican Case Studies in the Culture of Poverty.* New York: Basic Books.

———. 1966. The Culture of Poverty. *Scientific American* (October): 19–25.

Lewis, Shawn D. 2008. Pressuring Culture: Japanese-Style Private School Thrives with U.S. Transplants. *Detroit News* (July 17).

Lewontin, Richard. 2005. The Fallacy of Racial Medicine. *Genewatch* 18 (July–August): 5–7, 17.

Li, Wen Lang. 1976. Chinese Americans: Exclusion from the Melting Pot. Pp. 297–324 in *Minority Report*, Anthony Dworkin and Rosalind Dworkin, eds., New York: Praeger.

Lichtblau, Eric. 2005. Profiling Report Leads to a Clash and a Demotion. *New York Times* (August 24): A1, A9.

Lichter, Daniel T., J. Brian Brown, Zhenchao Qian, and Julie H. Carmalt. 2007. Marital Assimilation among Hispanics: Evidence of Declining Cultural and Economic Incorporation? *Social Science Quarterly*, 88 (3): 745–765.

Liebman, Charles S. 1973. *The Ambivalent American Jew.* Philadelphia: Jewish Publication Society of America.

Light, Ivan H. 1973. *Ethnic Enterprise in America: Business and Welfare among Chinese, Japanese, and Blacks.* Berkeley: University of California Press.

———, Georges Sabagh, Mendi Bozorgmehr, and Claudia Der-Martirosian. 1994. Beyond the Ethnic Enclave Economy. *Social Problems* (February), 41: 65–80.

Lin, Sam Chu. 1996. Painful Memories. *AsianWeek* (July 12), 17: 10.

Lincoln, C. Eric. 1994. *The Black Muslims in America*, 3rd ed. Grand Rapids, MI: William B. Eerdmans.

Lind, Andrew W. 1946. *Hawaii's Japanese: An Experiment in Democracy.* Princeton, NJ: Princeton University Press.

Linn, Mike. 2006. Ferry Carries Symbolic Weight. *USA Today* (August 21): 3A.

Linthicum, Leslie. 1993. Navajo School Working to Revive Language. *News from Indian Country* (late June): 5.

Loewen, James. 2005. *Sundown Towns: A Hidden Dimension of American Racism.* New York: Free Press.

———, and Richard Schaefer. 2008. Sundown Towns. Pp. 301–304 in vol. 2, *Encyclopedia of Race, Ethnicity, and Society*, Richard T. Schaefer, ed. Thousand Oaks, CA: Sage.

Logan, John R. 2001a. *The New Latinos: Who They Are, Where They Are.* Albany: State University of New York, Lewis Mumford Center for Comparative Urban and Regional Research.

———, Richard D. Alba, and Werquan Zhang. 2002. Immigrant Enclaves and Ethnic Communities in New York and Los Angeles. *American Sociological Review* (April), 67: 299–322.

———, Brian J. Stults, and Reynolds Farley. 2004. Segregation of Minorities in the Metropolis: Two Decades of Change. *Demography* (February), 41: 1–22.

Lohr, Steve. 2008. For a Good Retirement, Find Work. Good Luck. *New York Times* (June 22): 3.

Lomax, Louis E. 1971. *The Negro Revolt*, rev. ed. New York: Harper & Row.

Lopata, Helena Znaniecki. 1994. *Polish Americans*, 2nd ed. New Brunswick, NJ: Transaction Books.

Lopez, Ana Alicia Peña López. 2004. Central American Labor Migration, 1980–2000. *Diálgo* (Spring): 3–14.

Lopez, David, and Yen Espiritu. 1990. Panethnicity in the United States: A Theoretical Framework. *Ethnic and Racial Studies* (April 13): 198–224.

Lopez, Julie Amparano. 1992. Women Face Glass Walls as Well as Ceilings. *Wall Street Journal* (March 3).

Lopez, Mark Hugo, and Susan Minushkin. 2008. *2008 National Survey of Latinos: Hispanic Voter Attitudes.* Washington, DC: Pew Hispanic Center.

Lorber, Judith. 2005. *Breaking the Bounds: Degendering and Feminist Change.* New York: W. W. Norton.

Los Angeles Times Poll. 1998. American and Israeli Jews. Los Angeles: Los Angeles Times and Yedioth Ahronoth.

Louie, Andrea. 2004. *Chineseness across Borders: Renegotiation Chinese Identities in China and the United States.* Durham, NC: Duke University Press.

Loury, Glenn C. 1996. Joy and Doubt on the Mall. *Utne Reader* (January–February), 73: 70–73.

Loveman, Mora, and Jeronimo O. Muniz. 2007. How Puerto Rico Became White: Boundary Dynamics and Intercensus Racial Reclassification. *American Sociological Review* (December), 72: 915–939.

Lowenstein, Roger. 2006. What Is She Really Doing to American Jobs and Wages? *New York Times Magazine* (July 9): 36–43ff.

Luce, Clare Boothe. 1975. Refugees and Guilt. *New York Times* (May 11): E19.

Luconi, Stefano. 2001. *From Peasant to White Ethnics: The Italian Experience in Philadelphia.* Albany: State University Press of New York.

Ludwig, Jack. 2004. *Has the Civil Rights Movement Overcome?* Accessed July 15, 2004, at www.gallup.com.

Luker, Kristin. 1984. *Abortion and the Politics of Motherhood.* Berkeley: University of California Press.

Luo, Michael. 2006a. Reform Jews Hope to Unmix Mixed Marriages. *New York Times* (February 12): 1, 30.

———. 2006b. An Orthodox Jewish Woman and Soon, a Spiritual Leader. *New York Times* (August 21): B1, B4.

Lyman, Stanford M. 1974. *Chinese Americans.* New York: Random House.

———. 1986. *Chinatown and Little Tokyo.* Milwood, NY: Associated Faculty Press.

MacFarlane, Marco. 2006a. Demographics. Pp. 1–50 in *South African Survey 2004/2005.* Johannesburg: South African Institute of Race Relations.

———. 2006b. Health and Welfare. Pp. 335–381 in *South African Survey 2004/2005.* Johannesburg: South African Institute of Race Relations.

———. 2008. South Africa in Brief, *Fast Facts*, 10 (October): 1–15.

MacFarquhar, Neil. 2008. Resolute or Fearful, Many Muslims Turn to Home Schooling. *New York Times* (March 26).

Mack, Raymond W. 1996. Whose Affirmative Action? *Society* (March–April), 33: 41–43.

MacLean, Vicky M., and Joyce E. Williams. 2008. Shifting Paradigms: Sociological Presentations of Race. *American Behavioral Scientist* (January), 51: 599–624.

Maddux, William W., Adam D. Galinsky, Amy J. C. Cuddy, and Mark Polifroni. 2008. When Being a Model Minority Is Good . . . and Bad: Realistic Threat Explains Negativity Toward Asian Americans. *Personality and Social Psychology Bulletin* (January) 34: 74–89.

Magin, Janis L. 2008. Occupation of Royal Palace Invigorates Native Hawaiian Movement. *New York Times* (May 3): A14.

Malkin, Michelle. 2004. *In Defense of the Internment: The Case for Racial Profiling in World War II and the War on Terror.* Regency Books.

Mandela, Nelson. 1990. Africa, It Is Ours. *New York Times* (February 12): A10.

Mandelbaum, Robb. 2006. Sour Grapes. *New York Times* (December 10): 62.

Maning, Anita. 1997. Troubled Waters: Environmental Racism Suit Makes Waves. *USA Today* (July 31): A1.

Mann, Keith A. 2008. France. Pp. 506–508 in vol. 1, *Encyclopedia of Race, Ethnicity, and Society*, Richard T. Schaefer, ed. Thousand Oaks, CA: Sage.

Manning, Lynn 1997 "The Magic Wand." Pp.165 in Kenny Fries (ed.) Staring Back: The Disability Experience from the Inside Out. New York: A Plume Book.

Manning, Robert D. 1995. Multiculturalism in the United States: Clashing Concepts, Changing Demographics, and Competing Cultures. *International Journal of Group Tensions* (Summer): 117–168.

Marosi, Richard. 2007. The Nation: A Once-Porous Border Is a Turning-Back Point. *Los Angeles Times* (March 21): A1, A20.

Marshall, Patrick. 2001. Religion in Schools. *CQ Research* (July 12), 11: 1–24.

Marshall, Susan E., and Jen'nan Ghazal Read. 2003. Identity Politics among Arab-American Women. *Social Science Quarterly* (December), 84: 875–891.

Martin, Joel W. 2001. *The Land Looks After Us: A History of Native American Religion.* New York: Oxford University Press.

Marubbio, M. Elise. 2006. *Killing the Indian Maiden: Images of Native American Women in Film.* Lexington: University Press of Kentucky.

Marvasti, Amir. 2005. Being Middle Eastern American: Identity Negotiation in the Context of the War on Terror. *Symbolic Interaction*, 28 (4): 525–547.

———, and Karyn McKinney. 2004. *Middle Eastern Lives in America.* New York: Rowman & Littlefield.

Marx, Anthony. 1998. *Making Race and Nation: A Companion of the United States, South Africa, and Brazil.* Cambridge, UK: Cambridge University Press.

Marx, Karl, and Frederick Engels. 1955. *Selected Works in Two Volumes.* Moscow: Foreign Languages Publishing House.

Masci, David. 2001. Middle East Conflict. *CQ Researcher* (April 6), 11: 273–296.

Mason, Christopher. 2007. Immigrants Reject Quebec's Separatists. *New York Times* (May 20): 6.

Massey, Douglas. 2004. Segregation and Stratification: A Biosocial Perspective. *Dubois Review*, 1 (1): 7–25.

———. 2008. American Apartheid. Pp. 55–57 in vol. 1, *Encyclopedia of Race, Ethnicity, and Society*, Richard T. Schaefer, ed. Thousand Oaks, CA: Sage.

———, and Nancy A. Denton. 1993. *American Apartheid: Segregation and the Making of the Underclass.* Cambridge, MA: Harvard University Press.

———, and Margarita Mooney. 2007. The Effects of America's Three Affirmative Action Programs on Academic Performance. *Social Problems* 54 (1): 99–117.

Masud-Piloto, Felix. 2008a. Cuban Americans. Pp. 357–359 in vol. 1, *Encyclopedia of Race, Ethnicity, and Society*, Richard T. Schaefer, ed. Thousand Oaks, CA: Sage.

———. 2008b. Marielitos. Pp. 872–874 in vol. 2, *Encyclopedia of Race, Ethnicity, and Society*, Richard T. Schaefer, ed. Thousand Oaks, CA: Sage.

Masuoka, Natalie. 2006. Together They Become One: Examining the Predictors of Panethnic Group Consciousness Among Asian Americans and Latinos. *Social Science Quarterly* (December), 87: 993–1011.

Matthiessen, Peter. 1991. *In the Spirit of Crazy Horse*. New York: Peking.

Mauro, Tony. 1995. Ruling Helps Communities Set Guidelines. *USA Today* (December 21): A1, A2.

Maykovich, Minako Kurokawa. 1972a. *Japanese American Identity Dilemma*. Tokyo: Waseda University Press.

———. 1972b. Reciprocity in Racial Stereotypes: White, Black and Yellow. *American Journal of Sociology* (March), 77: 876–877.

McClain, Paula Denice. 1979. *Alienation and Resistance: The Political Behavior of Afro-Canadians*. Palo Alto, CA: R&E Research Associates.

McCloud, Aminah Beverly. 1995. *African American Islam*. New York: Routledge.

———. 2004. Conceptual Discourse: Living as a Muslim in a Pluralistic Society. Pp. 73–83 in *Muslims Place in the American Public Square*, Zahid H. Bukhari et al., eds. Walnut Creek, CA: Altamira Press.

McCoy, Ron. 2004. Truth-in-Marketing. Law Indian Arts and Crafts Act Regulations Published. *American Indian Art Magazine* (Spring), 29: 84.

McGhee, Bernard. 2006. Young Resigns from Wal-Mart Committee amid Criticism of Remarks. *Chicago Tribune* (August 19): 3.

McGreal, Chris. 2008. There's Racism but Not in Public. *The Guardian Weekly* (March 21): 28–29.

McIntosh, Peggy. 1988. *White Privilege: Unpacking the Invisible Knapsack*. Wellesley, MA: Wellesley College Center for Research on Women.

McKinley, James C., Jr. 2005. Mexican Pride and Death in U.S. Service. *New York Times* (March 22): A6.

McKinney, Karyn D. 2003. I Feel "Whiteness" When I Hear People Blaming Whites: Whiteness as Cultural Victimization. *Race and Society* 6: 39–55.

———. 2008. Confronting Young People's Perceptions of Whiteness: Privilege or Liability? *Social Compass* 2. Accessed at www.blackwell-compass.com/subject/sociology.

McNamara, Mary. 2006. Friends Tell of Complicated Man. *Chicago Tribune* (August 4): 8.

McNickle, D'Arcy. 1973. *Native American Tribalism: Indian Survivals and Renewals*. New York: Oxford University Press.

Meagher, Timothy J. 2005. *The Columbia Guide to Irish American History*. New York: Columbia University Press.

Meier, August, and Elliott Rudwick. 1966. *From Plantation to Ghetto: An Interpretive History of American Negroes*. New York: Hill & Wang.

Meier, Matt S., and Feliciano Rivera. 1972. *The Chicanos: A History of Mexican Americans*. New York: Hill & Wang.

Meléndez, Edwin. 1994. Puerto Rico Migration and Occupational Selectivity, 1982–1981. *International Migration Review* (Spring), 28: 49–67.

Menchaca, Charles. 2008. Scholars Learn Hmong Basics. *Wausau Daily Herald* (August 14).

Merenstein, Beth Frankel. 2008. Jewish-Black Relations: A Historical Perspective. Pp. 788–791 in vol. 2, *Encyclopedia of Race, Ethnicity, and Society*, Richard T. Schaefer, ed. Thousand Oaks, CA: Sage.

Merton, Robert K. 1949. Discrimination and the American Creed. Pp. 99–126 in *Discrimination and National Welfare*, Robert M. MacIver, ed. New York: Harper & Row.

———. 1968. *Social Theory and Social Structure*. New York: Free Press.

———. 1976. *Sociological Ambivalence and Other Essays*. New York: Free Press.

Messner, Michael A. 1997. *Politics of Masculinities: Men in Movements*. Thousand Oaks, CA: Sage.

Meyer, Julie. 2001. *Age: 2000*. Census 2000 Brief. Washington, DC: U.S. Government Printing Office.

Meyer, Karen. 2007. *Match the Disability*. Unpublished paper (April 31). Chicago: DePaul University.

———. 2008. Americans with Disabilities Act. In *Encyclopedia of Race, Ethnicity, and Society*, Richard T. Schaefer, ed. Thousand Oaks, CA: Sage.

Meyers, Dowell. *Immigrants and Boomers: Forging a New Social Contract for the Future of America*. New York: Russell Sage.

Meyers, Gustavus. 1943. *History of Bigotry in the United States* (rev. by Henry M. Christman, 1960). New York: Capricorn Books.

Migration News. 1998. Mexico, Dual Nationality, 5 (April). Accessed at migration.ucdavis.edu.

———. 2000. Hometown Clubs, 7 (July). Accessed at migrationnews.ucdavis.edu.

———. 2002. Income, Education, Politics (October). Accessed at migrationnews.ucdavis.edu.

———. 2008. Mexico Remittances, NAFTA, Taxes. Accessed January 2008 at migration.ucdavis.edu.mn.

Mihesuah, Devon A., ed. 2000. *Reparation Reader: Who Owns American Indian Remains?* Lincoln: University of Nebraska Press.

Miller, Norman. 2002. Personalization and the Promise of Contact Theory. *Journal of Social Issues*, 58 (Summer): 387–410.

Min, Pyong Gap. 2006. *Asian Americans: Contemporary Trends and Issues*, 2nd ed. Thousand Oaks, CA: Sage.

Mitra, Diditi. 2008. Pan-Asian Identity. Pp. 1016–1019 in vol. 2, *Encyclopedia of Race, Ethnicity, and Society*, Richard T. Schaefer, ed. Thousand Oaks, CA: Sage.

Miyamoto, S. Frank. 1973. The Forced Evacuation of the Japanese Minority During World War II. *Journal of Social Issues*, 29 (2): 11–31.

Mocha, Frank, ed. 1998. *American "Polonia" and Poland*. New York: Columbia University Press.

Monkman, Karen, Margaret Ronald, and Florence Délimon Théraméne. 2005. Social and Cultural Capital in an Urban Latino School Community. *Urban Education* (January), 40: 4–33.

Montagu, Ashley. 1972. *Statement on Race*. New York: Oxford University Press.

Moore, Joan W. 1970. Colonialism: The Case of the Mexican Americans. *Social Problems* (Spring), 17: 463–472.

———, and Raquel Pinderhughes, eds. 1993. *In the Barrios: Latinos and the Underclass Debate*. New York: Sage.

Moore, Molly. 2008. Inside France's Prisons. *Washington Post National Weekly Edition* (May 5): 22.

Morris, Milton D., and Gary E. Rubin. 1993. The Turbulent Friendship: Black–Jewish Relations in the 1990s. *Annals* (November): 42–60.

Moser, Bob. 2005. The Religious Crusade Against Gays Has Been Building for 30 Years. *Intelligence Report* (Spring): 8–28.

Mosisa, Abraham T. 2006. Foreign-Born Workforce, 2004: A Visual Essay. *Monthly Labor Review* (July), 129: 48–56.

Moskos, Charles C., and John Sibley Butler, eds. 1996. *All That We Can Be: Black Leadership and Racial Integration the Army Way*. New York: Basic Books.

Mostofi, Nilou. 2003. Who We Are: The Perplexity of Iranian-American Identity. *Sociological Quarterly* (Fall), 44: 681–703.

Moulder, Frances V. 1996. *Teaching about Race and Ethnicity: A Message of Despair or a Message of Hope?* Paper presented at annual meeting of the American Sociological Association, New York.

Mouw, Ted, and Barbara Entwisle. 2006. Residential Segregation and Interracial Friendship in Schools. *American Journal of Sociology* (September), 112: 394–441.

Mueller, Jennifer C., Danielle Dirks, and Leslie Houts Picca. 2007. Unmasking Racism: Halloween Costuming and Engagement of the Racial Other. *Qualitative Sociology*, 30: 315–335.

Mullen, Fitzhugh. 2005. The Metrics of the Physician Brain Drain. *New England Journal of Medicine* (October 27), 353: 1810–1818.

Muller, Eli. 2001. Orthodox Jews Relieved by "Yale 5" Loss. *Yale Daily News* (January 12).

Murphy, Dean, and Neela Banerjee. 2005. Catholics in U.S. Keep Faith but Live with Contradictions. *New York Times* (April 11): A1, A16.

Musabji, Heena, and Christina Abraham. 2007. The Threat to Civil Liberties and Its Effect on Muslims in America. *DePaul Journal for Social Justice* (Fall), 1: 83–112.

Muslim American Society. 2008. *Center for Electoral Empowerment: Voting Is Power*. Accessed August 25, 2008, at www.masuip.org.

Myers, Dowell. 2007. *Immigrants and Boomers: Forging a New Social Contract for the Future of America*. New York: Russell Sage Foundation.

———, John Pitkin, and Julie Park. 2004. *California's Immigrants Turn the Corner*. *Urban Initiative Policy Relief*. Los Angeles: University of Southern California.

Myrdal, Gunnar. 1944. *An American Dilemma: The Negro Problem and Modern Democracy*. New York: Harper & Row.

Nabokov, Peter. 1970. *Tijerina and the Courthouse Raid*, 2nd ed. Berkeley, CA: Ramparts Press.

Nagel, Joane. 1988. *The Roots of Red Power: Demographic and Organizational Bases of American Indian Activism 1950–1990*. Paper presented at annual meeting of the American Sociological Association, Atlanta, GA.

———. 1996. *American Indian Ethnic Renewal: Red Power and the Resurgence of Identity and Culture*. New York: Oxford University Press.

Nagourney, Adam. 2008. Age Becomes the New Race and Gender. *New York Times* (June 15): 1, 8.

Naimark, Norman M. 2004. Ethnic Cleaning, History of. Pp. 4799–4802 in *International Encyclopedia of Social and Behavioral Sciences*, N. J. Smelser and P. B. Baltes, eds. New York: Elsevier.

Nash, Manning. 1962. Race and the Ideology of Race. *Current Anthropology* (June), 3: 285–288.

National Advisory Commission on Civil Disorders. 1968. *Report*. New York: Bantam.

National Asian Pacific American Legal Consortium. 2002. Backlash: When America Turned on its Own. Washington DC: NAPALC.

National Center for Health Statistics. 2007. *Health, United States 2007*. Washington, DC: NCHS.

National Conference of Christians and Jews (NCCJ). 1994. *Taking America's Pulse*. New York: NCCJ.

National Indian Gaming Association. 2006. Indian Gaming Facts. Accessed September 27, 2006, at www.indiangaming.org.

———. 2008. *Proceeds of Indian Gaming*. Washington, DC: NIGA.

National Italian American Foundation. 2006. Stop Ethnic Bashing. *New York Times* (January). Accessed June 4, 2008, at www.niaf.org/news/index.asp?id=422.

National Organization for Men Against Sexism. 2008. NOMAS home. Accessed September 12, 2008, at www.nomas.org.

Navarro, Mireya. 1998. With a Vote for "None of the Above," Puerto Ricans Endorse Island's Status Quo. *New York Times* (December 14): A12.

———. 2004. Young Japanese-Americans Honor Ethnic Roots. *New York Times* (August 2): A1, A15.

———. 2008. Out in Hollywood. *New York Times* (September 28): 1, 10.

NCAA (National Collegiate Athletic Association). 2003a. Executive Committee Reviews American Indian Mascot Input. Press release (April 25).

———. 2003b. NCAA Executive Committee Passes Recommendations Regarding American Indian Mascots, Confederate Flag and NCAA Budget. Press release (August 11).

Nelsen, Frank C. 1973. The German-American Immigrants Struggle. *International Review of History and Political Science*, 10 (2): 37–49.

Neugarten, Bernice L. 1996. *The Meanings of Age. Selected Papers of Bernice L. Neugarten.* Ed. with a forward by Dail A. Neugarten. Chicago: University of Chicago Press.

Nevin, Tom. 2008. S Africa's "Open Door" Initiative Under Fire. *African Business* (July): 54.

New America Media. 2007a. *Deep Decisions, Shared Destiny.* San Francisco: New America Media.

———. 2007b. *Deep Divisions, Shared Destiny.* San Francisco: New America Media.

Newman, William M. 1973. *American Pluralism: A Study of Minority Groups and Social Theory.* New York: Harper & Row.

Newport, Frank. 2007. Questions and Answers "About Americans' Religion." Accessed February 7, 2008, at www.gallup.com.

Newsweek, 1971. Success Story: Outwhiting the White. 77 (June 121), pp. 24–25.

New York Times. 1991. For Two, an Answer to Years of Doubt on Use of Peyote in Religious Rite (July 9): A14.

———. 2005a. U.S. Panel Backs Nuclear Dump on Indian Reservation in Utah (September 10): A10.

———. 2005b. Warnings Raised About Exodus of Philippine Doctors and Nurses (November 27): 13.

Niebuhr, Gustav. 1998. Southern Baptists Declare Wife Should "Submit" to Her Husband. *New York Times.*

Nielsen, Joyce McCarl, Glenda Walden, and Charlotte A. Kunkel. 2000. Gendered Heteronormality: Empirical Illusions in Everyday Life. *Sociological Quarterly,* 41 (2): 283–296.

Nishi, Setsuko Matsunga. 1995. Japanese Americans. Pp. 95–133 in *Asian Americans: Contemporary Trends and Issues,* Pyong Gap Min, ed. Thousand Oaks, CA: Sage Publications.

Noble, Barbara Presley. 1995. A Level Playing Field, for Just $121. *New York Times* (March 5): F21.

Noel, Donald L. 1972. *The Origins of American Slavery and Racism.* Columbus, OH: Charles Merrill.

Novelli, William D. 2004. Common Sense: The Case for Age Discrimination Law. Pp. 4, 7 in *Global Report on Aging.* Washington, DC: AARP.

Obama, Barack. 2006. *The Audacity of Hope: Thoughts on Reclaiming the American Dream.* New York: Crown Publishers.

———. 2008. We the People, in Order to Form a More Perfect Union. Philadelphia speech, March 18, 2008. Accessed at www.msnbc.msn.com/id/23690567/print/1/displaymode/1098.

Oberschall, Anthony. 1968. The Los Angeles Riot of August 1965. *Social Problems* (Winter), 15: 322–341.

O'Connor, Anne-Marie. 1998. Church's New Wave of Change. *Los Angeles Times* (March 25): A1, A16.

Office of Immigration Statistics. 2006. *2004 Yearbook of Immigration Statistics.* Washington, DC: U.S. Government Printing Office.

———. 2007. *2006 Yearbook of Immigration Statistics.* Washington, DC: U.S. Department of Homeland Security.

Ogbu, John U. 2004. Collective Identity and the Burden of "Acting White" in Black History, Community, and Education. *Urban Review* (March), 36: 1–35.

———, with Astrid Davis. 2003. *Black American Students in an Affluent Suburb: A Study of Academic Disengagement.* Mahwah, NJ: Lawrence Erlbaum Associates.

Ogunwole, Stella V. 2002. *The American Indian and Alaskan Native Population.* Census 2000 Brief C2KBR/01:15. Washington, DC: U.S. Government Printing Office.

———. 2006. *We the People: American Indians and Alaska Natives in the United States.* Censr-28. Washington, DC: U.S. Government Printing Office.

Ohnuma, Keiko. 1991. Study Finds Asians Unhappy at CSU. *AsianWeek* (August 8), 12: 5.

Olemetson, Lynette. 2005. Adopted in China, Seeking Identity in America. *New York Times* (March 23): A1.

Oliver, Melvin L., and Thomas M. Shapiro. 1996. *Black Wealth/White Wealth: New Perspective on Racial Inequality.* New York: Routledge.

———. 2006. *Black Wealth/White Wealth.* 10th anniversary ed. New York: Routledge.

Olivo, Antonio. 2007. We're No Longer Refugees. *Chicago Tribune* (July 15): sect. 4, pp. 1, 2.

———. 2008. After 6-Year Fight, Citizenship. *Chicago Tribune* (June 19): 5.

Olzak, Susan. 1998. Ethnic Protest in Core and Periphery States. *Ethnic and Racial Studies* (March), 21: 187–217.

Omi, Michael. 2008. Asian-Americans: The Unbearable Whiteness of Being? *Chronicle of Higher Education* (September 25), 55: B56, B58.

———, and Howard Winant. 1994. *Racial Formation in the United States,* 2nd ed. New York: Routledge.

O'Neill, Maggie. 2008. Authoritarian Personality. Pp. 119–121 in vol. 1, *Encyclopedia of Race, Ethnicity, and Society,* Richard T. Schaefer, ed. Thousand Oaks, CA: Sage.

O'Neill, William. 1969. *Everyone Was Brave: The Rise and Fall of Feminism in America.* Chicago: Quadrangle.

Onishi, Norimitsu. 1995. Japanese in America Looking beyond Past to Shape Future. *New York Times* (December 25): 1.

Orfield, Gary. 2002. *Schools More Separate: Consequences of a Decade of Resegregation.* Cambridge, MA: Civil Rights Project, Harvard University.

———. 2007. The Supreme Court and the Resegregation of America's Schools. *Focus* (September–October): 1, 15–16.

———. Susan E. Eaton, and the Harvard Project on School Segregation. 1996. *Dismantling Desegregation: The Quiet Reversal of Brown v. Board of Education.* New York: The New Press.

———, and Chungmei Lee. 2005. *Why Segregation Matters: Poverty and Educational Inequality.* Cambridge, MA: Civil Rights Project.

———. 2007. *Historic Reversals, Accelerating Resegregation, and the Need for New Integration Strategies.* Los Angeles: Civil Rights Project, UCLA.

———, and Holly J. Liebowitz, eds. 1999. *Religion, Race, and Justice in a Changing America.* New York: The Twentieth Century Fund.

Orlov, Ann, and Reed Ueda. 1980. Central and South Americans. Pp. 210–217 in *Harvard Encyclopedia of American Ethnic Groups,* Stephan Thernstrom, ed. Cambridge, MA: Belknap Press of Harvard University Press.

Ortega, Alexander N., Hai Fang, Victor H. Perez, John A. Rizzo, Olivia Carter-Pokras, Steven P. Wallace, and Lillian Gelberg. 2007. Health Care Access, Use of Services, and Experiences among Undocumented Mexican and Other Latinos. *Archives of Internal Medicine* (November 26), 167: 2354–2360.

Ottaway, David S., and Paul Taylor. 1992. A Minority Decides to Stand Aside for Majority Rule. *Washington Post National Weekly Edition* (April 5), 9: 17.

Padget, Martin. 2004. *Indian Country: Travels in the American Southwest, 1840–1935.* Albuquerque: University of New Mexico Press.

Padgett, Tim. 2008. Big Trouble in Little Havana. *Time* (August 25): 31–32.

Padilla, Efren N. 2008a. Filipino Americans. Pp. 493–497 in vol. 1, *Encyclopedia of Race, Ethnicity, and Society,* Richard T. Schaefer, ed. Thousand Oaks, CA: Sage.

———. 2008b. Vietnamese Americans. Pp. 1365–1368 in vol. 3, *Encyclopedia of Race, Ethnicity, and Society,* Richard T. Schaefer, ed. Thousand Oaks, CA: Sage.

Page, Joseph A. 1983. *Perón, a Biography.* New York: Random House.

Page, Scott E. 2007. *The Difference: How the Power of Diversity Creates Better Groups, Firms, Schools, and Societies.* Princeton, NJ: Princeton University Press.

Pager, Devah. 2003. The Mark of a Criminal. *American Journal of Sociology,* 108: 937–975.

———. 2007a. *Marked: Race, Crime, and Finding Work in an Era of Mass Incarceration.* Chicago: University of Chicago Press.

———. 2007b. The Use of Field Experiments for Studies of Employment Discrimination: Contributions, Critiques, and Directions for the Future. *Annals* (January), 609: 104–133.

———, and Lincoln Quillian. 2005. Walking the Talk? What Employers Say versus What They Do. *American Sociological Review* 70 (3): 355–380.

———, and Hana Shepherd. 2008. The Sociology of Discrimination: Racial Discrimination in Employment, Housing, Credit, and Consumer Markets. *Annual Review of Sociology,* 34: 181–209.

———, and Bruce Western. 2006. *Race at Work: Realities of Race and Criminal Record in the NYC Job Market.* Report prepared for 50th anniversary of the New York City Museum on Human Rights. Accessed June 3, 2008, at www.princeton.edu/~pager/race_at_work.pdf.

Park, Robert E. 1928. Human Migration and the Marginal Man. *American Journal of Sociology* (May), 33: 881–893.

———. 1950. Race and Culture: Essays in the Sociology of Contemporary Man. New York: Free Press.

———, and Ernest W. Burgess. 1921. *Introduction to the Science of Sociology.* Chicago: University of Chicago Press.

Parrillo, Vincent. 2008. Italian Americans. Pp. 766–771 in vol. 2, *Encyclopedia of Race, Ethnicity, and Society,* Richard T. Schaefer, ed. Thousand Oaks, CA: Sage.

Parrish, Michael. 1995. Betting on Hard Labour and a Plot of Land. *Los Angeles Times* (July 7): A1, A20.

Parsons, Talcott, and Robert Bales. 1955. Family, Socialization and Interaction Process. Glencoe, IL: Free Press.

Passel, Jeffery S. 2005. *Unauthorized Migrants: Numbers and Characteristics.* Washington, DC: Pew Hispanic Center.

Pastor, Jr., Manuel, Rachel Morello-Frosch, and James L. Saad. 2005. The Air Is Always Cleaner on the Other Side: Race, Space, and Ambient Air Toxics Exposure in California. *Journal of Urban Affairs,* 27 (2): 127–148.

Patterson, Orlando. 1982. *Slavery and Social Death.* Cambridge: Harvard University Press.

Pawel, Miriam. 2006. Farmworkers Reap Little as Union Strays from Its Roots. *Los Angeles Times* (January 8): A1, A28–A30.

Paxton, Pamela, Sheri Kunovich, and Melanie M. Hughes. 2007. Gender in Politics. *Annual Review of Sociology,* 33: 263–284.

Payne, Charles M. 1995. *I've Got the Light of Freedom.* Berkeley: University of California Press.

Pearson, Bryan. 2006. Brain Drain Human Resource Crisis. *The Africa Report* (October): 95–98.

Pease, John, and Lee Martin. 1997. Want Ads and Jobs for the Poor: A Glaring Mismatch. *Sociological Forum,* 12 (4): 545–564.

Peckham, Pat. 2002. Hmong's Resettlement Changes Agency's Focus. *Wausau Daily Herald* (February 10): 1A, 2A.

Pedder, Sophie. 1991. Social Isolation and the Labour Market: Black Americans in Chicago. Paper presented at the Chicago Urban Poverty and Family Life Conference, Chicago.

Pellow, David Naguib, and Robert J. Brulle. 2007. Poisoning the Planet: The Struggle for Environmental Justice. *Contexts,* 6 (Winter): 37–41.

Peréz, Linsandro. 2001. Growing Up in Cuban Miami: Immigrants, the Enclave, and New Generations. Pp. 91–125 in *Ethnicities,* Ruben G. Rumbaut and Alejandro Portes, eds. Berkeley: University of California Press.

Perlmann, Joel. 2005. *Italians Then, Mexicans Now: Immigrant Origins and Second-Generation Progress, 1890–2000.* New York: Russell Sage Foundation.

Perry, Barbara, ed. 2003. *Hate and Bias Crime: A Reader.* New York: Routledge.

Pessar, Patricia R. 1995. *A Visa for a Dream: Dominicans in the United States.* Boston: Allyn & Bacon.

Peterson, William. 1971. *Japanese Americans: Oppression and Success.* New York: Random House.

Pew Charitable Trust. 2000. *Jews and the American Public Square Data.* Accessed May 23, 2001, at www.pewtrusts.org.

Pewewardy, Cornel. 1998. Our Children Can't Wait: Recapturing the Essence of Indigenous Schools in the United States. *Cultural Survival Quarterly* (Spring), 29–34.

Pew Forum on Religion and Public Life. 2008a. *U.S. Religious Landscape Survey.* Washington, DC: Pew Forum. Online at religions.pewforum.org/pdf/report2-religious-landscape-study-full.pdf.

———. 2008b. U.S. Religious Landscape Survey: Religious Beliefs and Practices: Diverse and Political Relevant. Washington DC: Pew Forum on Religion and Public Life.

Pew Hispanic Center. 2006a. *Hispanics at Mid-Decade.* Washington, DC: Pew Hispanic Center.

———. 2006b. *The Size and Characteristics of the Unauthorized Migrant Population in the U.S.: Estimates Based on the March 2005 Current Population Survey.* Washington, DC: Pew Hispanic Center.

———. 2006c. *Hispanics and the 2006 Election.* Washington, DC: Pew Hispanic Center.

———. 2007. *2007 National Survey of Latinos: As Illegal Immigration Issue Heats Up, Hispanics Feel a Chill.* Washington, DC: Pew Hispanic Center.

Pew Research Center. 2004. *Beliefs That Jews Were Responsible for Christ's Death Increase.* Washington, DC: Pew Research Center.

———. 2007. *Muslim Americans: Middle Class and Mostly Mainstream.* Washington, DC: Pew Research Center.

Pfaelzer, Jean. 2007. *Driven Out: The Forgotten War Against Chinese Americans.* New York: Random House.

Pfeifer, Mark. 2008a. Hmong Americans. Pp. 633–636 in vol. 2, *Encyclopedia of Race, Ethnicity, and Society,* Richard T. Schaefer, ed. Thousand Oaks, CA: Sage.

———. 2008b. Vietnamese Americans. Pp. 1365–1368 in vol. 3, *Encyclopedia of Race, Ethnicity, and Society,* Richard T. Schaefer, ed. Thousand Oaks, CA: Sage.

Picot, Garnett, Feng Hou, and Simon Coulombe. 2008. Poverty Dynamics among Recent Immigrants to Canada. *International Migration Review* 42 (Summer): 393–424.

Pido, Antonio J. A. 1986. *The Filipinos in America.* New York: Center for Migration Studies.

Pierotti, Ray, and Larry Erickson. 2004. *Annual Report: NSF Undergraduate Minorities in Environmental Biology Program.* Lawrence: University of Kansas.

Pincus, Fred L. 2003. *Reverse Discrimination: Dismantling the Myth.* Boulder, CO: Lynne Rienner.

———. 2008. *Reverse Discrimination.* Pp. 1159–1161 in vol. 3, *Encyclopedia of Race, Ethnicity, and Society,* Richard T. Schaefer, ed. Thousand Oaks, CA: Sage.

Pinkney, Alphonso. 1975. *Black Americans,* 2nd ed. Englewood Cliffs, NJ: Prentice Hall.

———. 1984. *The Myth of Black Progress.* New York: Cambridge University Press.

Polzin, Theresita. 1973. *The Polish Americans: Whence and Whither.* Pulaski, WI: Franciscan Publishers.

Porter, Eduardo. 2005. Illegal Immigrants Are Bolstering Social Security with Billions. *New York Times* (April 5): A1, C6.

Porter, Jack Nusan. 2008. Holocaust Deniers and Revisionists. Pp. 640–641 in vol. 2, *Encyclopedia of Race, Ethnicity, and Society,* Richard T. Schaefer, ed. Thousand Oaks, CA: Sage.

Portes, Alejandro. 1998. Social Capital: Its Origins and Applications in Modern Society. Pp. 1–24 in *Annual Review of Sociology 1998.* Palo Alto, CA: Annual Review.

———. 2006. Paths of Assimilation in the Second Generation. *Sociological Forum* (September), 21: 499–503.

———, and Rubén G. Rumbaut. 2006. *Immigrant America,* 3rd ed. Berkeley: University of California Press.

Potok, Mark, Luke Visconti, Barbara Frankel, and Nigel Holmes. 2007. The Geography of Hate. *New York Times* (November 23): 11.

Powell-Hopson, Darlene, and Derek Hopson. 1988. Implications of Doll Color Preferences Among Black Preschool Children and White Preschool Children. *Journal of Black Psychology* (February), 14: 57–63.

Powley, Elizabeth. 2006. *Rwanda: The Impact of Women Legislators on Policy Outcomes Affecting Children and Families.* Geneva, Switzerland: UNICEF.

President's Task Force on Puerto Rico's Status. 2005. *Report by the President's Task Force on Puerto Rico's Status.* Washington, DC: U.S. Government Printing Office.

Preston, Julia. 2007a. Judge Voids Ordinance on Illegal Immigrants. *New York Times* (July 27).

———. 2007b. Polls Surveys Ethnic Views among Chief Minorities. *New York Times* (December 13).

———. 2008. U.S. to Speed Deportation of Criminal behind Bars. *New York Times* (January 15): A12.

Public Broadcasting System. 1998. Weekend Edition: National Public Radio with Eric Westervelt and Scott Simon (May 30).

Purdy, Matthew. 2001. Ignoring and Then Embracing the Truth about Racial Profiling. *New York Times* (March 11).

Quadagno, Jill. 2008. *Aging and the Life Course: An Introduction to Social Gerontology,* 4th ed. New York: McGraw-Hill.

Quillian, Lincoln. 2006. New Approaches to Understanding Racial Prejudice and Discrimination. Pp. 299–328 in *Annual Reviews of Sociology 2006,* Karen S. Cook, ed. Palo Alto, CA: Annual Reviews.

Quintanilla, Ray. 2006. Islanders Ask: Where's the Cleanup? *Chicago Tribune* (March 27): 3.

Quirk, Matthew. 2008. How to Grow a Gang. *The Atlantic* (May), 301: 24–25.

Rachlin, Carol. 1970. Tight Shoe Night: Oklahoma Indians Today. Pp. 160–183 in *The American Indian Today,* Stuart Levine and Nancy Oestreich Lurie, eds. Baltimore: Penguin.

Rainey, James. 2000. Farm Workers Union Ends 16-Year Boycott of Grapes. *Los Angeles Times* (November 22): A3, A36, A37.

Ramirez, Margaret. 2000. Study Finds Segregation of Latinos in Catholic Church. *Los Angeles Times* (March 1): A1, A24.

Ramirez, Roberto R., and Patricia de la Cruz. 2003. The Hispanic Population in the United States: March 2003. *Current Population Reports.* Ser. P20, No. 545. Washington, DC: U.S. Government Printing Office.

Rangaswamy, Padma. 2005. Asian Indians in Chicago. In *The New Chicago,* John Koval et al., eds. Philadelphia: Temple University Press.

Rawick, George P. 1972. *From Sundown to Sunup: The Making of the Black Community.* Westport, CT: Greenwood Press.

Raybon, Patricia. 1989. A Case for "Severe Bias." *Newsweek* (October 2), 114: 11.

Read, Jen'nan Ghazal. 2003. The Source of Gender Role Attitudes among Christian and Muslim Arab-American Women. *Sociology of Religion* (Summer), 64: 207–222.

———. 2004. Family, Religion, and Work among Arab American Women. *Journal of Marriage and Family* (November), 66: 1042–1050.

———. 2007. More of a Bridge Than a Gap: Gender Differences in Arab-American Political Engagement. *Social Science Quarterly* (December), 88: 1072–1091.

———, and Michael O. Emerson. 2005. Racial Context, Black Immigration and the U.S. Black/White Health Disparity. *Social Forces* (September): 181–199.

Reckard, E. Scott. 2007. A Power Shift in Koreatown. *Los Angeles Times* (May 25): C1, C4.

Reese, Debbie. 1996. Teaching Young Children about Native Americans. *ERIC Digest* (May), ED0-PS-96-3.

Reeves, Terrance, and Claudette Bennett. 2003. The Asian and Pacific Islander Population in the United States: March 2002. *Current Population Reports.* Ser. P20. No. 540. Washington, DC: U.S. Government Printing Office.

Religion Watch. 1995b. Reform Synagogues Increasingly Adopting Orthodox Practices (March), 10: 7.

Religious Diversity News. 2004. The Oklahoma Headscarf Case. Accessed October 16, 2004, at www.pluralism.org.

Renzulli, Linda, and Lorraine Evans. 2005. School Choice, Charter Schools, and White Flight. *Social Problems,* 52 (2): 398–418.

Reskin, Barbara F. 1998. *The Realities of Affirmative Action in Employment.* Washington, DC: American Sociological Association.

Reverby, Susan M., ed. 2000. *Tuskegee's Truths: Rethinking the Tuskegee Syphilis Study.* Chapel Hill: University of North Carolina Press.

Reyhner, Jon. 2001. *Family, Community, and School Impacts on American Indian and Alaskan Native Students Success.* Paper presented at annual meeting of the National Indian Education Association (October 29).

Reynolds, Jerry. 2006. Drug Trafficking Measure Amended for Tribal Study. *Indian County Today* (December 20), 26: A1.

Rich, Meghan Ashlin. 2008. Resegregation. Pp. 1152–1153 in vol. 3, *Encyclopedia of Race, Ethnicity, and Society,* Richard T. Schaefer, ed. Thousand Oaks, CA: Sage.

Richmond, Anthony H. 2002. Globalization: Implications for Immigrants and Refugees. *Ethnic and Racial Studies* (September), 25: 707–727.

Ridgeway, Greg. 2007. *Analysis of Racial Disparities in the New York Police Department's Stop, Question, and Frisk Pictures.* Santa Monica, CA: RAND.

Ritter, John, and Tom Squitieri. 2002. Afghan-Americans Hear Call to Return. *USA Today* (January 21): 6A.

Rivera-Batiz, Francisco, and Carlos E. Santiago. 1996. *Island Paradox: Puerto Rico in the 1990s.* New York: Russell Sage Foundation.

Robelen, Erik W. 2007. "Moment-of-Silence" Generates Loud Debate in Illinois. *Education Week* (October 24).

Robert, Pamela M. and Sharon L. Harlan. 2006. Mechanisms of Disability Discrimination in Large Bureaucratic Organizations: Ascriptive Inequalities in the Workplace. *The Sociological Quarterly,* 47: 599–630.

Rodríguez, Clara E. 1989. *Puerto Ricans: Born in the USA.* Boston: Unwin Hyman.

Rodríquez, Robert. 1994. Immigrant Bashing: Latinos Besieged by Public Policy Bias. *Black Issues in Higher Education* (February 24), 10: 31–34.

Roediger, David R. 1994. *Towards the Abolition of Whiteness: Essays on Race, Politics, and Working Class History (Haymarket).* New York: Verso Books.

———. 2006. Whiteness and Its Complications. *Chronicle of Higher Education* (July 14), 52: B6–B8.

Rohter, Larry. 1993. Trade Pact Threatens Puerto Rico's Economic Rise. *New York Times* (January 3): 1, 14.

Romero, Adam P., Amanda K. Baumle, M. V. Lee Badgett, and Gary J. Gates. 2007. *Census Snapshot: United States.* Los Angeles: Williams Institute, UCLA School of Law.

Roodt, Marius. 2008. Xenophobic Violence: Simmering Volcano or Nasty Surprise? *Fast Facts* (August): 4–7.

Roof, Wade Clark. 2007. Introduction. *The Annals* (July), 612: 6–12.

Rosales, F. Arturo. 1996. *Chicano! The History of the Mexican American Civil Rights Movement.* Houston: Arte Público Press.

Roscigno, Vincent J., and Theresa Schmidt. 2007. How Sexual Harassment Happens. Pp. 73–88 in Vincent J. Roscigno, *The Face of Discrimination.* Lanham, MD: Rowman & Littlefield.

Rose, Arnold. 1951. *The Roots of Prejudice.* Paris: UNESCO.

Rosenberg, Tom. 2000. Changing My Name After 60 Years. *Newsweek* (July 17), 136: 10.

Rosenblatt, Gary. 2008. What Do We Want from Hebrew Schools? *The Jewish Week* (August 13).

Rosenfeld, Alvin H. 2007. *"Progressive" Jewish Thought and the New Anti-Semitism.* New York: American Jewish Committee.

Rosich, Katherine J. 2007. *Race, Ethnicity, and the Original Justice System.* Washington, DC: American Sociological Association. Online at asanet.org.

Rossi, Alice S. 1964. Equality between the Sexes: An Immodest Proposal. *Daedalus* (Spring), 93: 607–652.

Rothstein, Edward. 2006. The Anti-Semitic Hoax that Refuses to Die. *New York Times* (April 21): B27, B37.

Rudwick, Elliott. 1957. The Niagara Movement. *Journal of Negro History* (July), 42: 177–200.

Rumbaut, Ruben G., Douglas S. Massey, and Frank D. Bean. 2006. Linguistic Life Expectancies: Immigrant Language Retention in Southern California. *Population and Development Review* (September), 32: 447–460.

Rusk, David. 2001. *The "Segregation Tax": The Cost of Racial Segregation to Black Homeowners.* Washington, DC: Brookings Institution.

Ryan, William. 1976. *Blaming the Victim,* rev. ed. New York: Random House.

Ryo, Emily. 2008. Culture of Poverty. Pp. 363–365 in vol. 1, *Encyclopedia of Race, Ethnicity, and Society,* Richard T. Schaefer, ed. Thousand Oaks, CA: Sage.

Saad, Lydia. 1998. America Divided over Status of Puerto Rico. *Gallup Poll Monthly* (March), 390: 278.

———. 2006a. Anti-Muslim Sentiments Fairly Commonplace. *The Gallup Poll* (August 10).

———. 2006b. "Grin and Bear It" Is Motto for Most Air Travelers. Accessed January 28, 2008, at www.gallup.com/poll.

———. 2008. Americans Evenly Divided on Morality of Homosexuality. Accessed September 22, 2008, at www.gallup.com.

Sachs, Susan. 2001. For Newcomers, a Homey New Chinatown. *New York Times* (July 22): A1, A44.

Sadker, Myra Pollack, and David Miller Sadker. 2003. *Teachers, Schools, and Sociology,* 6th ed. New York: McGraw-Hill.

Sahagun, Louis. 2004. Tribes Fear Backlash to Prosperity. *Los Angeles Times* (May 3): B1, B6.

Said, Edward. 1978. *Orientalism.* New York: Viking.

St. Espada, Martín. 2000. ¡Viva Vieques! *The Progressive* (July), 64: 27–29.

Salée, Daniel. 1994. Identity Politics and Multiculturalism in Quebec. *Cultural Survival Quarterly* (Summer–Fall), 89–94.

Salzberger, Ronald P., and Mary G. Turck. 2004. *Reparations for Slavery: A Reader.* London: Rowman & Littlefield.

Sánchez, José Ramón. 2007. *Boricua Power: A Political History of Puerto Ricans in the United States.* New York: New York University Press.

Sanchez, Rene. 1998. The Winter of Their Discontent. *Washington Post National Weekly Edition* (December), 16: 20.

Sandage, Diane. 2008. Peltier, Leonard. Pp. 1033–1035 in vol. 2, *Encyclopedia of Race, Ethnicity, and Society,* Richard T. Schaefer, ed. Thousand Oaks, CA: Sage.

Sandefur, Rebecca L. 2008. Access to Civil Justice and Race, Class, and Gender Inequality. *Annual Review of Sociology,* 34: 339–358.

Santos-Hernández, Jenniffer M. 2008. Puerto Rican Armed Forces of National Liberation. Pp. 1084–1085 in vol. 2, *Encyclopedia of Race, Ethnicity, and Society,* Richard T. Schaefer, ed. Thousand Oaks, CA: Sage.

Sanua, Marianne R. 2007. AJC and Intermarriage: The Complexities and Jewish Continuity, 1960–2006. Pp. 3–32 in *American Jewish Yearbook 2007,* David Singer and Lawrence Grossman, eds. New York: American Jewish Committee.

Sarkisian, Natalia, Mariana Gerena, and Naomi Gerstel. 2007. Extended Family Integration among Euro and Mexican Americans: Ethnicity, Gender, and Class. *Journal of Marriage and Family* (February), 69: 40–54.

Sassler, Sharon L. 2006. School Participation among Immigrant Youths: The Case of Segmented Assimilation in the Early 20th Century. *Sociology of Education* 79 (January): 1–24.

Saulny, Susan. 2007. After Darfur, Starting Anew in the Midwest. *New York Times* (April 2): A1, A20.

Saunders, Rhys. 2007. Third Hate Crime Suspected Sentenced to Prison. *Daily Times* [Farmington, NM] (July 17).

Schaefer, Richard T. 1971. The Ku Klux Klan: Continuity and Change. *Phylon* (Summer), 32: 143–157.

———. 1976. *The Extent and Content of Racial Prejudice in Great Britain.* San Francisco: R&E Research Associates.

———. 1980. The Management of Secrecy: The Ku Klux Klan's Successful Secret. Pp. 161–177 in *Secrecy: A Cross-Cultural Perspective,* Stanton K. Tefft, ed. New York: Human Sciences Press.

———. 1986. Racial Prejudice in a Capitalist State: What Has Happened to the American Creed? *Phylon* 47 (September): 192–198.

———. 1992. People of Color: The "Kaleidoscope" May Be a Better Way to Describe America than "the Melting Pot." *Peoria Journal Star* (January 19): A7.

———. 1996. Education and Prejudice: Unraveling the Relationship. *Sociological Quarterly* (January), 37: 1–16.

———. 2008a. Australia, Indigenous People. Pp. 115–119 in vol. 1, *Encyclopedia of Race, Ethnicity, and Society,* Richard T. Schaefer, ed. Thousand Oaks, CA: Sage.

———. 2008b. Nativism. Pp. 611–612 in vol. 1, *Encyclopedia of Social Problems,* Vincent N. Parrillo, ed. Thousand Oaks, CA: Sage.

———. 2009. *Sociology,* 12th ed. New York: McGraw-Hill.

———, and Sandra L. Schaefer. 1975. Reluctant Welcome: U.S. Responses to the South Vietnamese Refugees. *New Community* (Autumn), 4: 366–370.

———, and William Zellner. 2008. *Extraordinary Groups,* 8th ed. New York: Worth.

Schertzer, Robert. 2008. Recognition or imposition? Federalism, National Minorities, and the Supreme Court of Canada. *Nations and Nationalism,* 14 (1): 105–126.

Schlemmer, Laurence. 2001a. Between a Rainbow and a Hard Place. *Fast Facts* (December): 2–12.

———. 2001b. Race Relations and Racism in Everyday Life. *Fast Facts* (September): 2–12.

Schmidt, Peter. 2007. 5 More States May Curtail Affirmative Action. *Chronicle of Higher Education* (October 19), 54: A1, A19–A20.

Schnittker, Jason, Jeremy Freese, and Brian Powell. 2003. Who Are Feminists and What Do They Believe? The Role of Generations. *American Sociologist Review* (August), 68: 607–622.

Schulz, Amy J. 1998. Navajo Women and the Politics of Identity. *Social Problems* (August), 45: 336–352.

Schwartz, Alex. 2001. *The State of Minority Access to Home Mortgage Lending: A Profile of the New York Metropolitan Area.* Washington, DC: Brooking Institution Center on Urban and Metropolitan Policy.

Schwartz, Felice, and Jean Zimmerman. 1992. *Breaking with Tradition: Women and Work, The New Facts of Life.* New York: Warner Books.

Schwartz, John. 1994. Preserving Endangered Speeches. *Washington Post National Weekly Edition* (March 21), 11: 38.

Schwartz, Margaret. 2006. A Question in the Shape of Your Body. Pp. 9–14 in *Half/Life: Jewish Tales from Interfaith Homes,* Laurel Synder, ed. Brooklyn, NY: Soft Skull Press.

———. 2008. Argentina. Pp. 87–89 in vol. 1, *Encyclopedia of Race, Ethnicity, and Society,* Richard T. Schaefer, ed. Thousand Oaks, CA: Sage.

Schwartz, Pepper. 1992. Sex as a Social Problem. Pp. 794–819 in *Social Problems,* Craig Calhoun and George Ritzer, eds. New York: McGraw-Hill.

Schwartzman, Luisa Farah. 2007. Does Money Whiten? Intergenerational Changes in Racial Classification in Brazil. *American Sociological Review* (December), 72: 940–963.

Schweimler, Daniel. 2007. Argentina's Last Jewish Cowboys (February 12). Accessed September 5, 2008, at www.bbc.com.

Scott, Janny. 2003. Debating Which Private Clubs Are Acceptable and Private. *New York Times* (December 8), sec. 7: 5.

Sears, David O., and J. B. McConahay. 1969. Participation in the Los Angeles Riot. *Social Problems* (Summer), 17: 3–20.

———. 1970. Racial Socialization, Comparison Levels, and the Watts Riot. *Journal of Social Issues* (Winter), 26: 121–140.

———. 1973. *The Politics of Violence: The New Urban Blacks and the Watts Riots.* Boston: Houghton-Mifflin.

Seibert, Deborah. 2002. Interview with Author. *Wausau Daily Herald,* Staff Member (March 27).

Sela-Sheffy, Rakefet. 2004. "What Makes One an Israeli" Negotiating Identities in Everyday Representations of "Israeliness." *Nations and Nationalism*, 10 (40): 479–497.

Selzer, Michael. 1972. *"Kike": Anti-Semitism in America*. New York: Meridian.

Sengupta, Somini. 1997. Asians' Advances Academically Are Found to Obscure a Need. *New York Times* (November 9): 17.

Sentencing Project. 2008. Felony Disenfranchisement. Accessed January 30, 2008, at www.sentencingproject.org/IssueAreaHome.aspx?IssueID=4.

Shaffer, Amanda, and Robert Gottlieb. 2007. Filling in "Food Deserts." *Los Angeles Times* (November 5): A17.

Shafir, Gershon. 2007. Israeli-Palestinian Peacemaking and Its Discontents. *Contexts*, 6 (4): 46–51.

Shaheen, Jack. 2003. Reel Bad Arabs: How Hollywood Vilifies a People. *Annals* (July), 558: 171–193.

Shanklin, Eugenia. 1994. *Anthropology and Race*. Belmont, CA: Wadsworth.

Shapiro, Joseph P. 1993. *No Pity: People with Disabilities Forging a New Civil Rights Movement*. New York: Times Books.

Shapiro, Thomas M. 2004. *The Hidden Cost of Being African American: How Wealth Perpetuates Inequality*. New York: Oxford University Press.

Sherif, Musafer, and Carolyn Sherif. 1969. *Social Psychology*. New York: Harper & Row.

Sherman, C. Bezalel. 1974. Immigration and Emigration: The Jewish Case. Pp. 51–55 in *The Jew in American Society*, Marshall Sklare, ed. New York: Behrman House.

Sheskin, Ira M., and Arnold Dashefsky. 2006. Jewish Population of the United States, 2006. Pp. 131–200 in *American Jewish Year Book 2006*, David Singer and Lawrence Grossman, eds. New York: American Jewish Committee.

———. 2007. Jewish Population in the United States, 2007. Pp. 133–205 in *American Jewish Yearbook 2007*, David Singer and Lawrence Grossman, eds. New York: American Jewish Committee.

Shilts, Randy. 1982. *The Mayor of Castro Street: The Life and Times of Harvey Milk*. New York: St. Martin's.

Shin, Hyon S., and Rosalind Bruno. 2003. *Language Use and English-Speaking Ability: 2000*. C2KBR-29. Washington, DC: U.S. Government Printing Office.

Sigelman, Lee, and Steven A. Tuch. 1997. Metastereotypes: Blacks' Perception of Whites' Stereotypes of Blacks. *Public Opinion Quarterly*, 61 (Spring): 87–101.

Silberman, Charles E. 1971. *Crisis in the Classroom: The Remaking of American Education*. New York: Random House.

Silva, Helga. 1985. *The Children of Mariel*. Miami, FL: Cuban American National Foundation.

Silver, Jim, ed. 2006. *In Their Own Voices: Building Urban Aboriginal Communities*. Halifax, NS: Fernwood Publishing.

Simanski, John. 2007. *Naturalizations in the United States: 2006*. Washington, DC: Office of Immigration Statistics.

Simmons, Ann M. 2007. New Orleans' Blacks See Rental Block. *Los Angeles Times* (April 25): A16.

Simon, Stephanie. 2004. Muslim Call to Prayer Stirs a Midwest Town. *Los Angeles Times* (May 8): A17.

Simon Wisenthal Center. 2008. *iReport: Online Terror + Hate: The First Decade*. Los Angeles: Simon Wisenthal Center.

Simpson, Jacqueline C. 1995. Pluralism: The Evolution of a Nebulous Concept. *American Behavioral Scientist* (January), 38: 459–477.

Skidmore, Thomas E. 1972. Toward a Comparative Analysis of Race Relations Since Abolition in Brazil and the United States. *Journal of Latin American Studies* (May), 4: 1–28.

Sklare, Marshall. 1971. *America's Jews*. New York: Random House.

Skull Valley Goshutes. 2006. Home Page at www.skullvalleygoshutes.org.

Slavin, Robert E., and Alan Cheung. 2003. *Effective Reading Programs for English Language Learners*. Baltimore: Johns Hopkins University, Center for Research on the Education of Students Placed at Risk.

Slavin, Steven, and Mary Pradt. 1979. Anti-Semitism in Banking. *The Bankers Magazine* (July–August), 162: 19–21.

———. 1982. *The Einstein Syndrome: Corporate Anti-Semitism in America Today*. Washington, DC: University Press of America.

Smith, Craig S. 2005. Rioting by Immigrants Embroils Paris Suburbs. *New York Times* (November 5): A1, A6.

Smith, James F. 2001. Mexico's Forgotten Find Cause for New Hope. *Los Angeles Times* (February 23): A1, A12, A13.

Smith, Tom W. 1999. *Measuring Inter-Racial Friendships: Experimental Comparisons*. GSS Methodological Report No. 91. Chicago: NORC.

———. 2006. *Taking America's Pulse III. Intergroup Relations in Contemporary America*. Chicago: National Opinion Research Center, University of Chicago.

Snipp, C. Matthew. 1989. *American Indians: The First of This Land*. New York: Sage.

Snyder, Karrie Ann, and Adam Isaiah Green. 2008. Revisiting the Glass Escalator: The Case of Gender Segregation in a Female Dominated Occupation. *Social Problems*, 55 (2): 271–299.

Society for Human Resource Management. 2008. *2007 State of Workplace Diversity Management*. Alexandria, VA: SHRM.

Soltero, Sonia White. 2004. *Dual Language: Teaching and Learning in Two Languages*. Boston: Allyn & Bacon.

———. 2008. *Bilingual Education*. Pp. 142–146 in vol. 1, *Encyclopedia of Race, Ethnicity, and Society*, Richard T. Schaefer, ed.. Thousand Oaks, CA: Sage.

Song, Tae-Hyon. 1991. *Social Contact and Ethnic Distance between Koreans and the U.S. Whites in the United States*. M.A. thesis, Western Illinois University, Macomb.

Soo, Julie D. 1999. Strained Relations: Why Chinatown's Venerable Associations Are Ending Up in Court. *AsianWeek* (January 14): 15–18.

Sorensen, Elaine. 1994. *Comparable Worth. Is It a Worthy Policy?* Princeton, NJ: Princeton University Press.

South African Institute of Race Relations. 2007. *South Africa Survey 2006/2007*. Johannesburg: SAIRR.

Stahler-Sholk, Richard. 2008. Zapatista Rebellion. Pp. 301–304 in vol. 2, *Encyclopedia of Race, Ethnicity, and Society*, Richard T. Schaefer, ed. Thousand Oaks, CA: Sage.

Stampp, Kenneth M. 1956. *The Peculiar Institution: Slavery in the Ante-Bellum South*. New York: Random House.

Stark, Rodney, and Charles Glock. 1968. *American Piety: The Nature of Religious Commitment*. Berkeley: University of California Press.

Starks, Carolyn. 2002. Sitting Here in Limbo. *Chicago Tribune* (March 26).

Statistics Canada. 2001. *Aboriginal Peoples in Canada*. Ottawa: Canadian Centre for Justice.

———. 2002. *Population*. Accessed May 13, 2002, at www.statcan.ca/english.

———. 2007a. Population by Mother Tongue, 2006 Counts (December 3). Accessed September, 1, 2008, at www.statcan.ca.

———. 2007b. Immigration in Canada: A Portrait of the Foreign-born Population, 2006 Census. Ottawa: Statistics Canada.

———. 2008a. Aboriginal Peoples in Canada in 2006: Inuit, Métis and First Nations, 2006 Census. Ottawa: Statistics Canada.

———. 2008b. Canada's Ethocultural Mosaic, 2006 Census. Ottawa: Statistics Canada.

Staton, Ron. 2004a. Still Fighting for National Hawaiian Recognition. *AsianWeek* (January 22): 8.

Steinhauer, Jennifer. 2006. An Unwelcome Light on Club Where Legends Teed Off. *New York Times* (September 23): A8.

Steinmetz, Erica. 2006. Americans with Disabilities: 2002. *Current Population Reports*. Ser. P70, No. 107. Washington, DC: U.S. Government Printing Office.

Stern, Kenneth S. 2001. Lying about the Holocaust. *Intelligence Report* (Fall), 50–55.

Stone, Andrea. 2008a. From Baghdad to Boise, a Renewal for Iraqi Refugees. *USA Today* (April 22): A1, A2.

———. 2008b. Many Troops Openly Gay, Group Says. *USA Today* (January 8): 3A.

Stone, Emily. 2006. Hearing the Call—In Polish. *Chicago Tribune* (October 13): 15.

Stonequist, Everett V. 1937. *The Marginal Man: A Study in Personality and Culture Conflict*. New York: Scribner's.

Stout, David. 2000. At Indian Bureau, a Milestone and an Apology. *New York Times* (September 9): A47.

Strauss, Gary. 2002. Good Old Boys' Network Still Rules Corporate Boards. *USA Today* (November 1): B1, B2.

Stretesky, Paul, and Michael Lynch. 2002. Environmental Hazards and School Segregation in Hillsborough County, Florida, 1987–1999. *Sociological Quarterly*, 43: 553–573.

Suggs, Welch. 2002. Title IX at 30. *Chronicle of Higher Education* (June 21), 48: A38–A42.

Sullivan, Cheryl. 1986. Seeking Self-Sufficiency. *Christian Science Monitor* (June 25): 16–17.

Sullivan, Keith. 2005. Desperate Moves. *Washington Post National Weekly Edition* (March 14): 9–10.

Sundiata, Ibrahim K. 1987. Late Twentieth Century Patterns of Race Relations in Brazil and the United States. *Phylon* (March), 48: 62–76.

Sung, Betty Lee. 1967. *Mountains of Gold: The Story of the Chinese in America*. New York: Macmillan.

Surdin, Ashley. 2008. Making Waves on Gay Marriage. *Washington Post National Weekly Edition* (June 1): 34.

Suro, Roberto. 1998. *Strangers among Us: Latino Lives in a Changing America*. New York: Vintage Books.

———, and Gabriel Escobar. 2006. *2006 National Survey of Latinos: The Immigration Debate*. Washington, DC: Pew Hispanic Center.

Sutch, Richard, and Susan B. Carter. 2006. *Historical Statistics of US: Earliest Times to the Present*. Cambridge MA: Cambridge University Press.

Swagerty, William R. 1983. Native Peoples and Early European Contacts. Pp. 15–16 in *Encyclopedia of American Social History*, Mary Kupiec Clayton, Elliot J. Gorn, and Peter W. Williams, eds. New York: Scribner's.

Swanson, Stevenson. 2004. Chinatown: Hopes for a Mini-Boom. *Chicago Tribune* (August 1): 1, 5.

Sze, Julie, and Jonathan K. London. 2008. Environmental Justice at the Cross-roads. *Sociology Compass*, 2.

Szegedy-Maszak, Marianne. 2001. Guess Who's Footing the "Mommy Tax?" *U.S. News and World Report* (March 19), 130: 48.

Tafoya, Sonya M., Hans Johnson, and Laura E. Hill. 2004. *Who Chooses to Choose Two?* New York: Russell Sage Foundation and Population Reference Bureau.

Takaki, Ronald. 1989. *Strangers from a Different Shore: A History of Asian Americans*. Boston: Little, Brown.

Takezawa, Yasuko I. 1991. Children of Inmates: The Effects of the Redress Movement among Third Generation Japanese Americans. *Qualitative Sociology* (Spring), 14: 39–56.

Talbani, Aziz, and Parveen Hasanali. 2000. Adolescent Females between Tradition and Modernity: Gender Role Socialization in South Asian Immigrant Culture. *Journal of Adolescence*, 23: 615–627.

Tannenbaum, Frank. 1946. *Slave and Citizen*. New York: Random House.

Taylor, Jonathan B. and Joseph P. Kalt. 2005. *American Indians on Reservations: A Databook of Socioeconomic Change between the 1990 and 2000 Censuses*. Cambridge, MA: The Harvard Project on American Indian Development.

Taylor, Stuart, Jr. 1987. High Court Backs Basing Promotion on a Racial Quota. *New York Times* (February 26): 1, 14.

———. 1988. Justices Back New York Law Ending Sex Bias by Big Clubs. *New York Times* (June 21): A1, A18.

Taylor, Verta, Nancy Whittier, and Leila J. Rupp. 2007. *Feminist Frontiers*, 7th ed. New York: McGraw-Hill.

Tehranian, John. 2008. Middle Easterners: Sometimes White, Sometimes Not. *Chronicle of Higher Education* (September 26), 55: B50, B54.

Telles, Edward E. 1992. Residential Segregation by Skin Color in Brazil. *American Sociological Review* (April), 57: 186–197.

———. 2004. *Race in Another America: The Significance of Skin Color in Brazil*. Princeton, NJ: Princeton University Press.

Telsch, Kathleen. 1991. New Study of Older Workers Finds They Can Become Good Investments. *New York Times* (May 21): A16.

ten Brock, Jacobus, Edward N. Barnhart, and Floyd W. Matson. 1954. *Prejudice, War and the Constitution*. Berkeley: University of California Press.

Terba, Harallamb. 2004. My Name Is Harallamb Terba. Pp. 184–195 in *An Immigrant Class: Oral Histories from Chicago's Newest Immigrants*, Jeff Libman, ed. Chicago: Flying Kite.

Third World Institute. 2007. *The World Guide*, 11th ed. Oxford: New Internationalist.

Thomas, Curlew O., and Barbara Boston Thomas. 1984. Blacks' Socioeconomic Status and the Civil Rights Movement's Decline, 1970–1979: An Examination of Some Hypotheses. *Phylon* (March), 45: 40–51.

Thomas, Dorothy S., and Richard S. Nishimoto. 1946. *The Spoilage: Japanese-American Evacuation and Resettlement*. Berkeley: University of California Press.

Thomas, Robert M., Jr. 1995. Maggie Kuhn, 89, the Founder of the Gray Panthers, Is Dead. *New York Times* (April 23): 47.

Thomas, William Isaac. 1923. *The Unadjusted Girl*. Boston: Little, Brown.

———, and Florian Znaniecki. 1996. *The Polish Peasant in Europe and America* (5 vols.), Eli Zaretsky, ed. Urbana: University of Illinois Press.

Thompson, Ginger. 2001. Fallout of U.S. Recession Drifts South into Mexico. *New York Times* (December 26): C1, C2.

———. 2005. Uneasily, a Latin Land Looks at Its Own Complexion. *New York Times* (May 19): A5.

Thornhill, Esmeralda M. A., ed. 2008. Blacks in Canada: Retrospects, Introspects, Prospects. *Journal of Black Studies* (January), 38: 317–521.

Thornton, Russell. 1981. Demographic Antecedents of the 1890 Ghost Dance. *American Sociological Review* (February), 46: 88–96.

———. 1991. *North American Indians and the Demography of Contact*. Paper presented at annual meeting of the American Sociological Association, Cincinnati, OH.

Threadcraft, Shatema A. 2008. Welfare Queen. Pp. 1384–1386 in vol. 3, *Encyclopedia of Race, Ethnicity, and Society*, Richard T. Schaefer, ed. Thousand Oaks, CA: Sage.

Thrupkaew, Noy. 2002. The Myth of the Model Minority. *American Prospect* (April 8), 13: 38–47.

Time. 1974. Are You a Jew? (September 2), 104: 56, 59.

Timerman, Jacob. 2002. *Prisoner Without a Name, Cell Without a Number*. Madison: University of Wisconsin Press.

Tizon, Thomas Alex. 2004. Internment Lesson Plan Is Under Attack. *Los Angeles Times* (September 12): A21.

Tolzmann, Don Heinrich. 2000. *The German-American Experience*. Amherst, NY: Humanity Books.

Tomlinson, T. M. 1969. The Development of a Riot Ideology among Urban Negroes. Pp. 226–235 in *Racial Violence in the United States*, Allen D. Grimshaw, ed. Chicago: Aldine.

Tong, Benson. 2000. *The Chinese Americans*. Westport, CT: Greenwood Press.

Torres, Lourdes. 2008. Puerto Rico. Pp. 1086–1090 in vol. 2, *Encyclopedia of Race, Ethnicity, and Society*, Richard T. Schaefer, ed. Thousand Oaks, CA: Sage.

Torriero, E. A. 2004a. Political Strife Hits Hmong in St. Paul. *Chicago Tribune* (June 14): 12.

Tough, Paul. 2004. The "Acting White" Myth. *New York Times* (December 12).

Tran, My-Thuan. 2008. Their Nation Lives On. *Los Angeles Times* (April 30): B1, B8–B9.

Tran, Quynh-Giang. 2001. Black Men's Pay in Top Jobs Lags. *Chicago Tribune* (August 15): 1, 13.

Traoré, Rosemary. 2008. Africans in the United States. Pp. 38–40 in vol. 1, *Encyclopedia of Race, Ethnicity, and Society*, Richard T. Schaefer, ed. Thousand Oaks, CA: Sage.

Trimble, Charles E. 2008. Iyeska: Notes from Mixed-Blood Country. *Indian County Today* (May 7): 5.

Triplett, William. 2004. Migrant Farmworkers. *CQ Researcher* (October 8): 14.

Tripp, Aili Mari, and Alice Kang. 2008. The Global Impact of Quotas: On the Fast Track to Increased Female Legislative Representation. *Comparative Political Studies* (March), 41: 338–361.

Trujillo-Pagan, Nicole. 2006. *Hazardous Constructions of Latino Immigrants in the Construction Industry: The Case of a Post-Katrina New Orleans*. Paper presented at annual meeting of the American Sociological Association, Montreal, Quebec, August 10.

Tse, Archie. 2005. Gaza Pullout: Cooperation or Resistance. *New York Times* (August 7): 14.

Tucker, M. Belinda, and Claudia Mitchell-Kernan, eds. 1995. *The Decline in Marriage among African Americans*. New York: Russell Sage.

Ture, Kwame, and Charles Hamilton. 1992. *Black Power: The Politics of Liberation*. New York: Vintage Books.

Turner, Margery Austin, Fred Freiburg, Erin Godfrey, Clark Herbig, Diane K. Levy, and Robin R. Smith. 2002. *All Other Things Being Equal: A Paired Testing Study of Mortgage Lending Institutions*. Washington, DC: Urban Institute.

Turner, Ralph H. 1994. Race Riots Past and Present: A Cultural-Collective Approach. *Symbolic Interaction*, 17(3): 309–324.

Turner, Richard Brent. 2003. *Islam in the African-American Experience*, 2nd ed. Bloomington: Indiana University Press.

Twohey, Megan. 2007. Outside, It's Suburban; Inside, It's Japan." *Chicago Tribune* (December 29): 1, 2.

Tyler, S. Lyman. 1973. *A History of Indian Policy*. Washington, DC: U.S. Government Printing Office.

Tyson, Karolyn, William Darity, Jr., and Domini R. Castellino. 2005. It's Not "a Black Thing": Understanding the Burden of Acting White and Other Dilemmas of High Achievement. *American Sociological Review* (August), 70: 582–605.

Uchitelle, L. 2003. Older Workers Are Thriving Despite Recent Hard Times. *New York Times* (September 8): A1, A15.

Umberger, Mary. 2006. Mortgage Law Under Fire. *Chicago Tribune* (August 18): 1, 8.

UNIFEM. 2008. *Progress of the World's Women 2008/2009; Who Answers to Women? Gender and Accountability*. New York: UNIFEM (United Nations Development Fund for Women).

United Jewish Communities. 2003. *The National Jewish Population Survey 2000–01*. New York: United Jewish Community.

University of North Dakota. 2008. *B.R.I.D.G.E.S.* Accessed July 8, 2008, at www.und.edu/org/bridges/index2.html.

U.S. Committee for Refugees. 2003. *World Refugee Survey 2003*. Washington, DC: U.S. Committee for Refugees.

Usdansky, Margaret L. 1992. Old Ethnic Influences Still Play in Cities. *USA Today* (August 4): 9A.

U.S. English. 2008. *Welcome to U.S. English, Inc.* Accessed February 9, 2008, at www.us-english.org/inc.

Valentine, Charles A. 1968. *Culture and Poverty: Critique and Counter-Proposals*. Chicago: University of Chicago Press.

Van Den Berghe, Pierre L. 1965. *South Africa: A Study in Conflict*. Middletown, CT: Wesleyan University.

———. 1978. *Race and Racism: A Comparative Perspective*, 2nd ed. New York: Wiley.

Varadarajan, Tunko. 1999. A Patel Motel Cartel? *New York Times Magazine* (July 4): 36–39.

Visitability. 2008. *Visitability*. Accessed June 10, 2008, at www.visitability.org.

Vitello, Paul. 2007. Call Him Harry: Village Mayor Symbolizes Indian-Americans' Political Rise. *New York Times* (September 1): A20.

Võ, Linda Trinh. 2004. *Mobilizing an Asian American Community*. Philadelphia: Temple University Press.

Vuong, Vu-Duc. 2006. In the Year of the Hen, Viet-Am Women Rock, What Went Right in San Jose Election. *AsianWeek* (June 16).

Wagley, Charles, and Marvin Harris. 1958. *Minorities in the New World: Six Case Studies*. New York: Columbia University Press.

Waitzkin, Howard. 1986. *The Second Sickness: Contradictions of Capitalistic Health Care*, rev. ed. New York: Free Press.

Wald, Kenneth D. 2008. Homeland Interests, Hostland Politics: Politicized Ethnic Identity among Middle Eastern Heritage Groups in the United States. *International Migration Review* (Summer): 273–301.

Wallerstein, Immanuel. 1974. *The Modern World System*. New York: Academic Press.

Warner, W. Lloyd, and Leo Srole. 1945. *The Social Systems of American Ethnic Groups*. New Haven, CT: Yale University Press.

Waldinger, Roger. 2007. *Between Here and There: How Attached Are Latino Immigrants to Their Native Country?* Washington, DC: Pew Hispanic Center.

Waldman, Carl. 1985. *Atlas of North American Indians*. New York: Facts on File.

Waller, David. 1996. Friendly Fire: When Environmentalists Dehumanize American Indians. *American Indian Culture and Research Journal*, 20 (2): 107–126.

Wallerstein, Immanuel. 2004. *World-Systems Analysis: An Introduction*. Durham, NC: Duke University Press.

Walzer, Susan. 1996. Thinking About the Baby: Gender and Divisions of Infant Care. *Social Problems* (May), 43: 219–234.

Wang, L. Ling-Chi. 1991. Roots and Changing Identity of the Chinese in the United States. *Daedalus* (Spring), 120: 181–206.

Washburn, Wilcomb E. 1984. A Fifty-Year Perspective on the Indian Reorganization Act. *American Anthropologist* (June), 86: 279–289.

Washington, Booker T. 1900. *Up from Slavery: An Autobiography.* New York: A. L. Burt.

Washington, Harriet. 2007. *Medical Apartheid: The Dark History of Medical Experimentation on Black Americans from Colonial Times to Present.* New York: Doubleday.

Watanabe, Teresa. 2007. Reclaiming Cultural Ties. *Los Angeles Times* (May 13): B1, B13.

———, and Susana Enriquez. 2005. Church Redefined. *Los Angeles Times* (April 24): 54.

Waters, Mary. 1990. *Ethnic Options. Choosing Identities in America.* Berkeley: University of California Press.

Watson, Jamal E. 2004. Going Extra Mile to Worship. *Chicago Tribune* (August 8), sect. 4: 1, 4.

Wausau School District. 2006. *Enrollment Reports 2005–2006.* Wausau, WI: Wausau School District.

Wax, Murray L. 1971. *Indian Americans: Unity and Diversity.* Englewood Cliffs, NJ: Prentice Hall.

———, and Robert W. Buchanan. 1975. *Solving "the Indian Problem": The White Man's Burdensome Business.* New York: New York Times Book Company.

Wax, Rosalie. 1967. The Warrior Drop-Outs. *Trans-Action* (May), 4: 40–46.

Weber, Max. 1947. *The Theory of Social and Economic Organization* [1913–1922], trans. by Henderson and T. Parsons. New York: Free Press.

Weglyn, Michi. 1976. *Years of Infamy: The Untold Story of America's Concentration Camps.* New York: Quill Paperbacks.

Wei, William. 1993. *The Asian American Movement.* Philadelphia: Temple University Press.

Weinberg, Daniel H. 2004. Evidence from Census 2000 About Earnings by Detailed Occupation for Men and Women. *CENSR-15.* Washington, DC: U.S. Government Printing Office.

———. 2007. Earnings by Gender: Evidence from Census 2000. *Monthly Labor Review* (July–August): 26–34.

Weiner, Melissa F. 2008. Jewish–Black Relations: The Contemporary Period. Pp. 791–792 in vol. 2, *Encyclopedia of Race, Ethnicity, and Society,* Richard T. Schaefer, ed. Thousand Oaks, CA: Sage.

Weiner, Rebecca. 2008. *The Virtual Jewish History Tour.* Accessed September 8, 2008, at www.jewishvirtuallibrary.org/jsource/vjw/Argentina.html.

Weiner, Tim. 2004. Of Gringos and Old Grudges: This Land Is Their Land. *New York Times* (January 9): A4.

Wellington, Alison J. 1994. Accounting for the Male/Female Wage Gap among Whites: 1976 and 1985. *American Sociological Review* (December), 59: 839–848.

Wells, Robert N., Jr. 1989. *Native Americans' Needs Overlooked by Colleges* (Paper). Canton, NY: St. Lawrence University.

———. 1991. *Indian Education from the Tribal Perspective: A Survey of American Indian Tribal Leaders* (Paper). Canton, NY: St. Lawrence University.

Werner, Erica. 2008. Tribal Casinos and Revenue Continue Growth in 2007. *Notes from Indian Country* (July 21): 26.

Wertheimer, Jack. 1996. *Conservative Synagogues and Their Members.* New York: Jewish Theological Seminary of America.

Wessel, David. 2001. Hidden Costs of Brain Drain. *Wall Street Journal* (March 1): 1.

White, Jack E. 1997. I'm Just Who I Am. *Time* (May 5), 149: 32–34, 36.

White House Initiative. 2006. *White House Initiative on Historically Black Colleges and Universities.* Accessed October 1, 2006, at www.ed.gov/about/inits/list/whhbcu/edlite-index.html.

Whitman, David. 1987. For Latinos, a Growing Divide. *U.S. News and World Report* (August 10), 103: 47–49.

Wickham, DeWayne. 1993. Subtle Racism Thrives. *USA Today* (October 25): 2A. 15, A1, A26.

Wiesel, Elie. 2006. *Night* (trans. from French by Marion Wiesel). New York: Hill and Wang.

Wilkes, Rima, and John Iceland. 2004. Hypersegregation in the Twenty-First Century. *Demography* (February), 41: 23–36.

Willeto, Angela A. 1999. Navajo Culture and Female Influences on Academic Success: Traditional Is Not a Significant Predictor of Achievement among Young Navajos. *Journal of American Indian Education* (Winter), 38: 1–24.

———. 2007. Native American Kids: American Indian Children's Well-Being Indicators for the Nation and Two States. *Social Indicators Research* (August), 83: 149–176.

Williams, Carol J. 2006a. Puerto Rico Could Soon Get Real Vote on Status. *Los Angeles Times* (February 17): A15.

———. 2007. Emotions Run High in Puerto Rican Debate. *Los Angeles Times* (April 26): A27.

Williams, Kim M. 2005. Multiculturalism and the Civil Rights Future. *Daedalus,* 134 (1): 53–60.

Williams, Patricia J. 1997. *Of Race and Risk. The Nation Digital Edition.* Accessed December 12, 1997, at www.thenation.com.

Williams, Vernon J., Jr. 2008. Abolitionism: The Movement. Pp. 1–2 in vol. 1, *Encyclopedia of Race, Ethnicity, and Society,* Richard T. Schaefer, ed. Thousand Oaks, CA: Sage.

Willie, Charles V. 1978. The Inclining Significance of Race. *Society* (July–August), 15: 10, 12–13.

———. 1979. *The Caste and Class Controversy.* Bayside, NY: General Hall.

Willoughby, Brian. 2004. *10 Ways to Fight Hate on Campus.* Montgomery, AL: Southern Poverty Law Center.

Wilson, Duff, and Andrew W. Lehren. 2008. Swapping Passports in Pursuit of Olympic Medals. *New York Times* (June 15): 1, 4.

Wilson, George. 2007. Racialized Life-Chance Opportunities Across the Class Structure: The Case of African Americans. *Annals* 609 (January): 215–272.

Wilson, William Julius. 1973. *Power, Racism and Privilege: Race Relations in Theoretical and Sociohistorical Perspectives.* New York: Macmillan.

———. 1980. *The Declining Significance of Race: Blacks and Changing American Institutions,* 2nd ed. Chicago: University of Chicago Press.

———. 1988. The Ghetto Underclass and the Social Transformation of the Inner City. *The Black Scholar* (May–June), 19: 10–17.

———. 1996. *When Work Disappears: The World of the New Urban Poor.* New York: Knopf.

Winant, Howard. 1994. *Racial Conditions: Politics, Theory, Comparisons.* Minneapolis: University of Minnesota Press.

———. 2001. *The World Is a Ghetto: Race and Democracy Since World War II.* New York: Basic Books.

———. 2004. *The New Politics of Race: Globalism, Difference, Justice.* Minneapolis: University of Minnesota Press.

———. 2006. Race and Racism: Towards a Global Future. *Ethnic and Racial Studies* (September), 29: 986–1003.

Winks, Robin W. 1971. *The Blacks in Canada: A History.* Montreal: McGill-Queen's University Press.

Winseman, Albert L. 2004. *U.S. Churches Looking for a Few White Men.* Accessed July 27, 2004, at www.gallup.com.

Winter, Richard, and Teresa Watanabe. 2007. LAPD Drops Its Plan to Map Muslim Community. *Los Angeles Times* (November 15): A1, A21.

Winter, S. Alan. 2008. *Symbolic Ethnicity.* Pp. 1288–1290 in vol. 3, *Encyclopedia of Race, Ethnicity, and Society,* Richard T. Schaefer, ed. Thousand Oaks, CA: Sage.

Withrow, Brian L. 2006. *Racial Profiling: From Rhetoric to Reason.* Upper Saddle River, NJ: Prentice Hall.

Witt, Bernard. 2007. What Is a Hate Crime? *Chicago Tribune* (June 10): 1, 18.

Woesthoff, Julia M. 2008. Muslims in Europe. Pp. 925–928 in vol. 2, *Encyclopedia of Race, Ethnicity, and Society,* Richard T. Schaefer, ed. Thousand Oaks, CA: Sage.

Wolfe, Ann G. 1972. The Invisible Jewish Poor. Journal of Jewish Communal Services. 48 (3), pp. 259–265.

Women Work. 2007. Women Re-Entering the Workforce Face Substantial Barriers (October 2007). Accessed September 14, 2008, at www.womenwork.org.

Wong, Morrison G. 2006. Chinese Americans. Pp. 110–145 in *Asian Americans: Contemporary Trends and Issues,* 2nd. ed., Pyong Gap Min, ed. Thousand Oaks, CA: Sage Publications.

Woo, Elaine. 1996. Immigrants, U.S. Peers Differ Starkly on Schools. Los Angeles Times (February 22), A1, A19.

Woodson, Carter G. 1968. *The African Background Outlined.* Washington, DC: Association Press (1936). New York: Negro Universities Press.

Woodward, C. Vann. 1974. *The Strange Career of Jim Crow,* 3rd ed. New York: Oxford University Press.

Wooton, Barbara H. 1997. Gender Differences in Occupational Employment. *Monthly Labor Review* (April), 120: 15–24.

Working, Russell. 2007. Illegal Abroad, Hate Web Sites Thrive Here. *Chicago Tribune* (November 13): A1, A15.

Wortham, Robert A. 2008. Du Bois, William Edward Burghardt. Pp. 423–427 in vol. 1, *Encyclopedia of Race, Ethnicity, and Society,* Richard T. Schaefer, ed. Thousand Oaks, CA: Sage.

Wright II, Earl. 2006. W. E. B. Du Bois and the Atlantic University Studies on the Negro Revisited. *Journal of African American Studies,* 9 (4): 3–17.

Wrong, Dennis H. 1972. How Important Is Social Class? *Dissent* (Winter), 19: 278–285.

Wu, Frank M. 2002. *Yellow: Race in America beyond Black and White.* New York: Basic Books.

Wyman, Mark. 1993. *Round-Trip to America. The Immigrants Return to Europe, 1830–1930.* Ithaca, NY: Cornell University Press.

Yamashiro, Jane H. 2008. Nisei. Pp. 985–988 in vol. 2, *Encyclopedia of Race, Ethnicity, and Society,* Richard T. Schaefer, ed. Thousand Oaks, CA: Sage.

Yancey, George. 2003. *Who Is White? Latinos, Asians, and the New Black–Nonblack Divide.* Boulder, CO: Lynne Rienner.

Yee, Albert H. 1973. Myopic Perceptions and Textbooks: Chinese Americans' Search for Identity. *Journal of Social Issues,* 29 (2): 99–113.

Yinger, John. 1995. *Closed Doors, Opportunities Lost: The Continuing Costs of Housing Discrimination.* New York: Russell Sage Foundation.

Yosso, Tara J. 2005. Whose Culture Has Capital? A Critical Race Theory Discussion of Community Cultural Wealth. *Race Ethnicity and Education* (March), 8: 69–91.

Young, Jeffrey R. 2003. Researchers Change Racial Bias on the SAT. *Chronicle of Higher Education* (October 10): A34–A35.

Zaidi, Arisha U. and Muhammad Shuraydi. 2002. Perceptions of arranged marriages by young Pakistani Muslim women living in a western society. Journal of Comparative Family Studies, 33 (Autumn), 495–515.

Zarembro, Alan. 2004. Physician, Remake Thyself: Lured by Higher Pay and Heavy Recruiting, Philippine Doctors Are Getting Additional Degrees and Starting Over in the U.S. as Nurses. *Los Angeles Times* (January 10): A1, A10.

Zell, Sarah, and Emily Skop. 2008. South Americans in the United States. Pp. 1262–1268 in vol. 3, *Encyclopedia of Race, Ethnicity, and Society*, Richard T. Schaefer, ed. Thousand Oaks, CA: Sage.

Zeng, Zhen, and Yu Xie. 2004. Asian-Americans' Earnings Disadvantage Reexamined: The Role of Place of Education. *American Journal of Sociology* (March), 109: 1075–1108.

Zhao, Yilu. 2002. Chinatown Gentrifies, and Evicts. *New York Times* (August 23): A13.

Zhou, Min. 2000. Social Capital in Chinatown: The Role of Community-Based Organizations and Families in the Adaptation of the Younger Generation. Pp. 315–335 in *Contemporary Asian America*, Min Zhou and James V. Gatewood, eds. New York: New York University Press.

———. 2004. Are Asian Americans Becoming "White?" *Contexts* 3 (Winter): 29–37.

———, and Carl L. Bankston, III. 1998. *Growing Up American: How Vietnamese Children Adapt to Life in the United States.* New York: Russell Sage Foundation.

———, and Yoshinori Kamo. 1994. An Analysis of Earnings Patterns for Chinese, Japanese, and Non-Hispanic White Males in the United States. *Sociological Quarterly*, 35 (4): 581–602.

———, and John R. Logan. 1989. Returns on Human Capital in Ethnic Enclaves: New York City's Chinatown. *American Sociological Review* (October), 54: 809–820.

Zia, Helen. 2000. *Asian American Dreams: The Emergence of an American People.* New York: Farrar, Straus & Giroux.

Zimmerman, Seth. 2008. *Immigration and Economic Mobility*. Washington, DC: Economic Mobility Project.

Zogby, James. 2001a. *National Survey: American Teen-Agers and Stereotyping.* Submitted to the National Italian American Foundation by Zogby International. Accessed June 3, 2008, at www.niaf.org/research/report_zogby.asp?print=1&.

———. 2001b. *Arab American Attitudes and the September 11 Attacks*. Washington, DC: Arab American Institute Foundation.

———. 2008. Hate Crime Punished. *Washington Watch* (July 21). Accessed August 24, 2008, at www.aaiusa.org/washington-watch-3620/hate-crime-punished.

Photo Credits

Index

Sidney Silverman Library
and Learning Resource Center
Bergen Community College
400 Paramus Road
Paramus, NJ 07652-1595

www.bergen.edu

Return Postage Guaranteed